THE ROUTLEDGE RESEARCH COMPANION TO EARLY MODERN SPANISH WOMEN WRITERS

In Spain, the two hundred years that elapsed between the beginning of the early modern period and the final years of the Habsburg Empire saw a profusion of works written by women. Whether secular or religious, noble or middle class, early modern Spanish women actively composed creative works such as poetry, prose narratives, and plays. *The Routledge Research Companion to Early Modern Spanish Women Writers* covers the broad array of different kinds of writings – literary as well as extra-literary – that these women wrote, taking into consideration their subject positions and the cultural and historical contexts that influenced and were influenced by them. Beyond merely recognizing the individual women authors who had influence in literary, religious, and intellectual circles, this Research Companion investigates their participation in these circles through their writings, as well as the ways in which their texts informed Spain's cultural production during the early modern period. In order to contextualize women's writings across the historical and cultural spectrum of early modern Spain, the Research Companion is divided into six sections of general thematic interest: Women's Worlds; Conventual Spaces; Secular Literature; Women in the Public Sphere; Private Circles; Women Travelers. Each section is subdivided into chapters that focus on specific issues or topics.

Nieves Baranda is Professor of Spanish Literature at the Universidad Nacional de Educación a Distancia (UNED), Spain.

Anne J. Cruz is Professor of Spanish and Cooper Fellow Emerita at the University of Miami, USA.

THE ROUTLEDGE RESEARCH COMPANION TO EARLY MODERN SPANISH WOMEN WRITERS

Edited by
Nieves Baranda
and Anne J. Cruz

LONDON AND NEW YORK

First published 2018
by Routledge
2 Park Square, Milton Park, Abingdon, Oxon OX14 4RN

and by Routledge
711 Third Avenue, New York, NY 10017

Routledge is an imprint of the Taylor & Francis Group, an informa business

© 2018 Nieves Baranda and Anne J. Cruz

The right of the editors to be identified as the authors of the editorial material, and of the authors for their individual chapters, has been asserted in accordance with sections 77 and 78 of the Copyright, Designs and Patents Act 1988.

All rights reserved. No part of this book may be reprinted or reproduced or utilised in any form or by any electronic, mechanical, or other means, now known or hereafter invented, including photocopying and recording, or in any information storage or retrieval system, without permission in writing from the publishers.

Trademark notice: Product or corporate names may be trademarks or registered trademarks, and are used only for identification and explanation without intent to infringe.

Library of Congress Cataloging in Publication Data
A catalog record for this book has been requested

ISBN: 978-1-4724-3828-7 (hbk)
ISBN: 978-1-315-61290-4 (ebk)

Typeset in Bembo and Minion Pro
by Florence Production Ltd., Stoodleigh, Devon, UK

Printed in the United Kingdom
by Henry Ling Limited

CONTENTS

Contributors ix
Acknowledgments xv

    Introduction 1
    Nieves Baranda Leturio and Anne J. Cruz

SECTION I
Women's worlds 13

1 Aristocracy and the urban elite 15
   Grace E. Coolidge

2 Women's education in early modern Spain 27
   Anne J. Cruz

3 The early modern foundations of the *querella de las mujeres* 41
   Emily C. Francomano

SECTION II
Conventual spaces 61

4 Autobiographies 63
   Isabelle Poutrin

5 Chronicles, biographies, hagiographies 75
   Mercedes Marcos Sánchez

6 Conventual correspondence 87
   María Leticia Sánchez Hernández and Nieves Baranda Leturio

7 Convent theater 103
   María del Carmen Alarcón Román

8 Body, spirit, and verse: reading early modern women's
   religious poetry   115
   Stacey Schlau

SECTION III
Secular literature   133

9 The poetic voice   135
   María Dolores Martos Pérez

10 Literary academies and poetic tournaments   153
    Inmaculada Osuna Rodríguez

11 Novels and narratives   169
    Shifra Armon

12 Women playwrights   187
    Amy R. Williamsen

SECTION IV
Women in the public sphere   203

13 Public poetry   205
    María Carmen Marín Pina

14 Spain's women humanists   219
    Emilie L. Bergmann

15 Women and power   237
    Nieves Romero-Díaz

SECTION V
Private circles   253

16 Didactic treatises   255
    Rosilie Hernández

17 The familial lyric   271
    Gwyn Fox

18 Private correspondence   285
    Vanessa de Cruz Medina

SECTION VI
Women travelers   **297**

19 Foundation narratives   299
    Darcy Donahue

20 Transoceanic religious   315
    Sarah E. Owens

21 Secular women writers in the New World   329
    Rocío Quispe-Agnoli

22 Transnational exchanges   347
    Nieves Baranda Leturio

Index   *363*

CONTRIBUTORS

María del Carmen Alarcón Román received her Ph.D. in Hispanic Studies from the Universidad de Sevilla with a dissertation on the complete works of Sor Francisca de Santa Teresa. Among her publications are Sor Francisca's *Colloquies* (Arcibel, 2007) and "The Poetic Production of Sor Francisca de Santa Teresa, Nun of the Convent of Trinitarians in Madrid: between Daily Life and Spirituality" (Iberoamericana, 2014). Her research includes conventual theater of early modern Seville and Toledo. She is currently working on a collection of plays staged in early modern Seville.

Shifra Armon is Associate Professor of Spanish at the University of Florida. She is the author, most recently, of *Masculine Virtue in Early Modern Spain* (Ashgate, 2015). In 2015 she also contributed an essay entitled "Twisting the Trope: Refiguring the Work of Wedlock in Baroque Spanish Women's Writing." to *Perspectives on Early Modern Women in Iberia and the Americas: Studies in Law, Society, Art and Literature in Honor of Anne J. Cruz*, edited by María Cristina Quintero and Adrienne Martín (Escribana Books). In 2014 *Edad de Oro* published her article entitled "Compromiso y distancia en 'La Venus de Ferrara' de Mariana de Carvajal Saavedra." In 2016, *Comedia Performance* published her theater review of *Las dos bandoleras* by Lope de Vega, directed by Marc Rosich and Carmé Portaceli, performed in 2014 at the Teatro Pavón in Madrid.

Nieves Baranda Leturio is Professor of Spanish Literature at the Universidad Nacional de Educación a Distancia (UNED). She founded the BIESES (Bibliography of Spanish Women Writers, www.bieses.net) research project, which she has directed since 2004. Her publications cover women writers' education, readings, poetic networks, historical writings, and letters, among other topics. She has published *Cortejo a lo prohibido* (Arco, 2006); and edited, with María Carmen Marín Pina, *Letras en la celda. Cultura escrita de los conventos femeninos en la España moderna* (Iberoamericana, 2011). Some recent essays are: "*Feminae poeticae*. Una generación de mujeres poetas a mediados del siglo XVI" (Madrid, 2016); and "Words for Sale: Early Modern Spanish Women's Literary Economy" (Brill, 2016).

Emilie L. Bergmann is Professor of Spanish at the University of California, Berkeley. She is co-editor of the Routledge (2017) *Research Companion to the Works of Sor Juana Inés de la Cruz*. Current research projects and recent publications address questions of gender, sexuality, and childhood in early modern Spain and colonial Spanish America; the visual and the aural in the poetry of Sor Juana Inés de la Cruz; Cervantes and the poetics of madness; representations of the nurturing body in early modern Spain; and cross-dressing, gender transgression, and violence in early modern Spanish theater.

Grace E. Coolidge is Professor of History at Grand Valley State University in Grand Rapids, Michigan. She is the author of *Guardianship, Gender, and the Nobility in Early Modern Spain* (Ashgate, 2011) and has recently edited a volume of essays titled *The Formation of the Child in Early Modern Spain* (Ashgate, 2014). Her current work focuses on illegitimacy and its impact on the early modern nobility.

Anne J. Cruz is Professor of Spanish and Cooper Fellow Emerita, University of Miami. After receiving her Ph.D. from Stanford University, she taught at the University of California, Irvine, and the University of Illinois, Chicago. Her extensive publications include books and articles on early modern Spanish literature and culture, including Petrarchism in Spain, the picaresque novel, Cervantes, and women's writings. Her most recent publications include *The Life and Writings of Luisa de Carvajal y Mendoza* (Toronto: Iter-Centre for Renaissance and Reformation Studies, 2014); and, with María Cristina Quintero, *Beyond Spain's Borders: Women Players in Early Modern National Theaters* (Routledge, 2016). She is an elected member of the Instituto Universitario de la Corte en Europa [University Institute of European Court Studies] Universidad Autónoma de Madrid; and corresponding member of Spain's Royal Academy of History.

Vanessa de Cruz Medina is an independent scholar specializing in cultural and social history. She focuses on the correspondence of Spanish royal and noblewomen and the political and artistic relations between the court of Madrid, the Holy Roman Empire, and Italy in the sixteenth and seventeenth centuries. She has published numerous articles and chapters of books, including "'In Service to my Lady, the Empress, as I have done every other day of my life': Margarita de Cardona, Baroness of Dietrichstein and Lady-in-Waiting of María of Austria" in *The Politics of Female Households: Ladies-in-Waiting across Europe* (Brill, 2014); and "An Illegitimate Habsburg: Ana Dorotea de la Concepción, Marquise of Austria (1611–1694)" in *Early Modern Habsburg Women: Transnational Contexts, Cultural Conflicts, Dynastic Continuities* (Ashgate, 2013). She has been awarded a Beatriu de Pinòs postdoctoral fellowship at the University Pompeu Fabra, Barcelona.

Darcy Donahue is Professor of Spanish and Women's Studies at Miami University of Ohio. Her research interests include the intersection of gender and religion, women writers and early modern conduct literature. She has edited and translated *Ana de San Bartolomé: Autobiography and Other Writings* for the series "The Other Voice" (University of Chicago, 2008). Recent publications include articles in *The Formation of the Child in Early Modern Spain* (Ashgate, 2014), *Perspectives on Early Modern Women in Iberia and the Americas* (Escribana, 2015), and *Nuns' Literacies in Medieval Europe* (BREPOLS, 2015).

Born in New Zealand, **Gwyn Fox** earned her B.A. and M.A. in English and Spanish, and her Ph.D. in Spanish literature at the University of Auckland. She taught at the University of Auckland as honorary research fellow until her recent retirement, and currently assists students at the Universidad de Salamanca with English studies. She has published *Subtle Subversions: Reading Golden Age Sonnets by Iberian Women* (Catholic University of America Press, 2008).

Contributors

Emily C. Francomano is Associate Professor in the Department of Spanish and Portuguese at Georgetown University, where she is also a core faculty member of the Comparative Literature and Medieval Studies Programs. Her scholarly interests revolve around the intersections of medieval and early modern literature, translation, and gender studies. Her recent scholarship includes *Three Spanish Querelle Texts*: Grisel and Mirabella, The Slander against Women, and The Defense of Ladies against Slanderers *by Pere Torrellas and Juan de Flores. A Bilingual Edition and Study* (ITER, 2013); " 'Taking the Gold out of Egypt': Prostitution and the Economy of Salvation in the *Vida de María Egipciaca*" (*Hispanic Review*, 2014), and "Re-reading Woodcut Illustration in *Cárcel de amor* 1493–1496" (*Titivillus*, 2015).

Rosilie Hernández is Associate Professor in the Department of Hispanic and Italian Studies at the University of Illinois, Chicago. Her areas of specialization are the literatures and visual cultures of early modern Spain. She is the author of *Bucolic Metaphors: History, Subjectivity, and Gender in the Early Modern Spanish Pastoral* (University of North Carolina Press, 2006), as well as articles focusing on Cervantes, women writers, and political, economic, and religious treatises. She has co-edited several volumes, including *Women's Literacy in Early Modern Spain and the New World* with Anne J. Cruz (Ashgate, 2011), winner of the Collaborative Project Award for the Society for the Study of Early Modern Women. Her present research focuses on the intersections between political, theological, philosophical, and aesthetic discourses in early modern Spain, presently being developed in a book manuscript tentatively titled "Immaculate Conceptions: The Power of the Religious Imagination in Counter-Reformation Spain."

Mercedes Marcos Sánchez is Associate Professor of General Linguistics at the University of Salamanca, Spain, where she completed her Ph.D. with a dissertation on the poetic language of Leopoldo Panero (Ediciones Universidad Salamanca, 1987). She has published extensively on discourse analysis, linguistic history, and women's conventual writing, which are her usual research topics. She is a member of the database research team BIESES. She has recently published an edition of *Interrogatorio en la causa de la venerable virgen sor Ana María de San José* (Istituto Storico dei Cappuccini, 2015).

María Carmen Marín Pina is Associate Professor of Spanish at the University of Zaragoza, Spain. Her work centers mainly on Spanish chivalric novels and women's writings. She is the author, with Daniel Eisenberg, of *Bibliografía de los libros de caballerías castellanos* (Universidad de Zaragoza, 2000). Her most recent book is *Páginas de sueños. Estudios sobre libros de caballerías castellanos* (2011). Professor Marín Pina has published on Spanish women writers Beatriz Bernal, Feliciana Enríquez de Guzmán, Valentina Pinela, María Nieto, Eugenia Buesso, Luisa Manrique de Lara, and Sor María do Ceu, among others. She is a member of the database research team BIESES.

María Dolores Martos Pérez is Assistant Professor in the Department of Spanish Literature at the Universidad Nacional de Educación a Distancia (UNED, Madrid). A specialist on Baroque poetry, she has published a monograph on the poetry of Agustín de Tejada Páez (2011); editions of Antonio Enríquez Gómez (2012 and 2015); and articles on Góngora. Her articles on female poetry in early modern Spain have appeared in *Criticón* and *Studia Aurea*. She is a member of the database research team BIESES.

Inmaculada Osuna Rodríguez teaches at the Universidad Complutense de Madrid. She is a member of BIESES, as well as of other research teams dedicated to early modern Spanish literature. She specializes in Golden Age Spanish poetry, with research mainly on occasional poetry, Andalusian, and later Baroque poetic production. Her publications include *Poesía y academia en Granada en torno a 1600: la "Poética silva"* (2003) and numerous articles on poetic academies and contests.

Sarah E. Owens is Professor of Spanish at the College of Charleston. She is editor of two award-winning books: *Journey of Five Capuchin Nuns* (2009) and *Women of the Iberian Atlantic* (2012). Her most recent book, *Nuns Navigating the Spanish Empire* (2017), was funded by a fellowship from the National Endowment for the Humanities.

Isabelle Poutrin is Associate Professor of History at Université Paris-Est Créteil (Centre de Recherche en Histoire Européenne Comparée). She is the author of *Le voile et la plume. Autobiographie et sainteté féminine dans l'Espagne moderne* (1995) and numerous articles on female mysticism and sanctity in early modern Spain. She has co-authored, with Marie-Karine Schaub, *Femmes et pouvoir politique. Les princesses d'Europe, XVe–XVIIIe siècle* (2007). Her latest publication focuses on religious coercion and conversion, *Convertir les musulmans. Espagne 1491–1609* (2012).

Rocío Quispe-Agnoli is Professor of Colonial Latin American Studies at Michigan State University. She is affiliated faculty in the American Indian Studies Program and core faculty of the Center for Gender Studies in a Global Context. She has authored *La fe indígena en la escritura: resistencia e identidad en la obra de Guamán Poma de Ayala* (Universidad Nacional Mayor de San Marcos Press, 2006), and *Nobles de papel: identidades oscilantes y genealogías borrosas de María Joaquina Inca y su familia* (Iberoamericana, 2016). Her editions include two special issues of *Cuaderno Internacional de Estudios Humanísticos y Literatura*, "Beyond the Convent: Colonial Women's Voices and Daily Challenges in Spanish America" (2005) and "Mirrors and Mirages: Women's Gaze in Hispanic Literature and Visual Arts" (2015); and a monographic issue of *Letras Femeninas*: "Mirada de mujer: narrativas femeninas de lo visual y narrativas visuales de lo femenino" (2014). She has written over 50 articles on race, ethnicity and identity, women's and gender studies, and visual studies in colonial Spanish America.

Nieves Romero-Díaz is Professor of Spanish at Mount Holyoke College. Her publications include articles on *Celestina*, Cervantes, women poets and playwrights of early modern Spain, and Baroque prose. She has published *Nueva nobleza, nueva novela* (2002); the bilingual edition of María de Guevara's political treatises for "The Other Voice" series (2007); and, among other articles, "Autoridad y genealogías femeninas alrededor de la Infanta María Teresa de Austria" (2009); and "Del sarao zayesco a la carta agrediana. La sociabilidad cortesana femenina en la España de Felipe IV" (2013). Her current research focuses on the intersections of gender and politics during the realm of Philip IV.

María Leticia Sánchez Hernández is a historian of early modern Spain and museum curator for the Spanish National Patrimony in Madrid. She has published *Patronato regio y órdenes religiosas femeninas en el Madrid de los Austrias* (Fundación Universitaria, 1997); and, among other essays, "Capilla de Guadalupe en Las Descalzas Reales de Madrid" (2014) and "Algunos apuntes sobre enfermedades y remedios de Teresa de Jesús" (2015). She has been a member of the BIESES research team, and participated in the "Vida cotidiana en la Edad Moderna" research project led by Gloria Franco Rubio. She was visiting professor at the Universidad Pontificia Comillas and Universidad Pontificia Salamanca.

Contributors

Stacey Schlau is Professor of Spanish and Women's and Gender Studies at West Chester University of Pennsylvania. Her areas of research include early modern Spanish and colonial Latin American women's texts, as well as the cultural history of the Inquisition (*Gendered Crime and Punishment: Women And/In the Hispanic Inquisitions*, Brill, 2012). Essays recently published include "Flying in Formation: Subjectivity and Collectivity in Luisa Melgarejo de Soto's Mystical Practices," in *Devout Laywomen in the Early Modern World* (Ashgate, 2016); and "Solitude: A Gendered Discalced Carmelite Poetic Trope" in *Scripta: Revista internacional de literatura i cultura medieval i moderna* (https://ojs.uv.es/index.php/scripta, 2016). The *Routledge Research Guide to Sor Juana Inés de la Cruz*, co-edited with Emilie Bergmann was published in 2017.

Amy R. Williamsen is Professor of Spanish at the University of North Carolina-Greensboro where she serves as Head of the Department of Languages, Literatures, and Cultures. Her specializations include early modern Spanish literature, Hispanic women writers, theater and performance, contemporary literary theory, and cognitive science. A co-founder of *GEMELA*, she has most recently published an article in *Cervantes*. In addition to her book *Co(s)mic Chaos: Exploring Los trabajos de Persiles y Sigismunda*, her co-edited volumes include *Critical Reflections: Essays on Spanish Golden Age Literature in Honor of James A. Parr*; *Engendering the Early Modern Stage: Women Playwrights in the Spanish Empire*; *Ingeniosa Invención: Studies in Honor of Professor Geoffrey Stagg*; and *María de Zayas: The Dyamics of Discourse*.

ACKNOWLEDGMENTS

Compiling this research companion has proven both a rewarding and exhilarating lesson to us as feminist editors and scholars. We are immensely grateful to our brilliant, generous, and patient contributors, whose interdisciplinary and transnational work instructs us on the many facets of female life experiences, revealing the similarities that, despite their diversity, bond these women writers together as writers, but first and foremost, as women. Their thoroughly researched and deeply probing chapters, which illuminate women's writings as an essential and weighty component of early modern Spain's cultural production, yet whose communality and coherence have yet to be given their due, stand as strong testimony to the value of collaborative research. We thank Erika Gaffney for her initial support of the project, our families for their understanding and support, and the efficacy of Skype for facilitating our many trans-Atlantic communications.

N.B.L.
A.J.C.

INTRODUCTION

Nieves Baranda Leturio and Anne J. Cruz

This research companion offers a much-needed and up-to-date overview of early modern Spanish women writers and their works. Rather than focus on individual women writers, the inventive approach we have chosen has been to trace their history as writers as a collective endeavor. Whether from the nobility or the emerging middle class, and either as religious or secular writers, women participated together in contributing to the many literary and extra-literary genres that proliferated in early modern Spain. Such an approach has in turn allowed our contributors to address the development of women's writings, not as singular occurrences within a predominantly male-dominated literary canon, but instead as women's collaborative efforts in successfully forging their own discursive space. Our commitment to this pioneering project has resulted as well in a Spanish version that will be published simultaneously with this volume in order to make it accessible to native Spanish speakers.

Writing women into history

The two hundred years that elapsed from the beginning of the early modern period to the end of the Habsburg Empire saw a profusion of works written by Spanish women, whose levels of literacy and education had increasingly expanded from the fifteenth through the seventeenth centuries. Yet in comparison to other early modern European women's writings,[1] their works have been slow to be edited and published, both in their own lifetimes and by modern editors. Despite the publication of their works in the early modern period, women writers, with few exceptions, failed to be noticed in literary histories by the overwhelmingly male academic establishment of nineteenth-century Spain.[2] The bibliographical notes of polygraph Manuel Serrano y Sanz (1903–1905) pioneered the study of women writers in the early twentieth century, yet little research was actually accomplished until after the second wave of feminism in the mid-1900s.[3] In 1986, Isabel Barbeito Carneiro's dissertation on women writers of Madrid enriched Serrano's collection, and this initial exploratory phase produced more women writers than were known when Serrano y Sanz first compiled his list, amending and adding to his historical and biographical data. Not only were previously unremarked women writers newly discovered, but women's works were read in new ways, granting female authors their own socio-historical and literary specificity and visibility.[4]

The inscription of women's writings into literary history thus encouraged gender analyses that emphasized, for the first time, the significance of women's social roles and their contributions to the cultural production of early modern Spain. Studies such as those included in our footnotes and in the bibliographies of the volume's individual chapters reveal that women writers did not merely imitate or follow male authors when selecting genres, themes, and varieties of style, but developed their own parallel history, at times resisting and other times emulating men's literary models, but constantly refocusing, by gendering, the authorial perspective from male to female.[5] Indeed, these authors informed and influenced Spain's cultural production during the early modern period in ways that are still being determined. Whether secular or religious, noble or middle class, early modern Spanish women actively composed creative works such as poetry, prose narratives, and plays. Secular women wrote both in the privacy of their homes and for public gatherings such as literary academies and poetry competitions. Several earned their living by writing professionally, publishing short stories, staging plays, or narrating city chronicles. The diversity of women writers across the Iberian Peninsula offers a wide spectrum that was not limited to literary production, however. Many women maintained constant correspondence with family members or with their patrons. Highly educated humanists devoted time to the writing of medical and pedagogical treatises.[6] And because so many women resided in convents or professed as nuns, they produced a significant body of religious works, including autobiographies, hagiographies, religious treatises, spiritual poetry, and foundational texts. Moreover, many Spanish women left Spain for other countries, and women's writings also influenced the writings of women in other parts of the world.

Literary and extra-literary genres

The contributors to this research companion thus intend to examine the vast array of different kinds of writings contributed by Spanish women to the field of early modern literature and to cultural production in general. For reasons of space and coherence, they focus mainly on women who wrote in Castilian and who either resided in Spain or who traveled to other countries but were born in Spain or Portugal.[7] Regardless of their individual social roles, these women authored an extensive variety of literary and extra-literary genres, and many crossed from one genre to another. In a strategic departure from most source books and encyclopedic studies, the volume's chapters are organized not by individual women writers, but instead by referencing the women authors and their texts according to specific themes. In the frequent cases of authors who wrote in several different genres, therefore, their works are referenced in each genre's respective chapter; as an example, Teresa de Ávila's many writings include an autobiography, religious poetry, correspondence, and a foundational text, each of which is discussed in the corresponding chapter. Such an organization is possible because of the increasingly broad knowledge that the contributors now have of individual women's work and of their socio-historical context. While not negating the importance of the male literary canon, this new knowledge allows them to address female authors specifically, without needing to resort to a comparatist view that obliges women's writings to be weighed always against male-authored works. For American and European perspectives, we have invited literary scholars and historians, all leaders in their field, as contributors from the United States, Europe, and New Zealand, and whose references are equally international. The contributors' methodological approach has been not to isolate women authors biographically, but to position them within different but interrelated thematic paradigms that shed light on the inescapably gendered social condition of early modern Spanish culture.

Introduction

The Research Companion's organization: sections I–VI

In order to contextualize women's writings across the historical and cultural spectrum of early modern Spain, the research companion is divided into six sections of general thematic interest, each subdivided into chapters that address specific issues or topics dealt with by women authors. The chapters introduce and describe the terms by which the writings have been classified; identify the women authors who have played a significant role in developing their formal and contextual aspects; contextualize the writings within their time period; and offer possibilities for future research. The volume will thus not only serve as a resource for scholars and teachers of early modern Spain, but for those interested in gender, literary, and cultural studies, and for those seeking to compare women's writings transnationally.

Section I: Women's worlds examines women as subjects in the early modern world of Spain, and the social, cultural, and historical background that permitted them to assume the role of writer. As **Grace E. Coolidge** observes, social standing gave women access to power and authority; within the groups of the nobility, the aristocracy, and the elite, divisions were due not so much to gender as they were to class, whose privileges often allayed the disadvantages ascribed to gender. At a time when cities were expanding and the urban elite was becoming stronger, women also gained from the growth in economic and political power. Spanish married women wielded more power than their European counterparts because the legal system protected their property rights, and were often their children's executors and guardians. This in turn created the need for more literate skills and education than those of lower-class women in towns and the countryside, as noble and elite women were in charge of large households and managed property, while royal women frequently participated in governing the state. **Anne J. Cruz** discusses the numerous factors that comprised the learning and expanding of knowledge for women in the early modern period. Here again, Spanish women were at an advantage over other European women, since both the Church and the State encouraged basic literacy, whether for religious or social reasons, such as the ability to manage their property. Education itself was carried out by tutors, in the home, in elementary schools for girls, and in convents, according to family and economic status. While there is much to study yet regarding the women's acquisition of knowledge, we know that many women were highly literate, and the literature by women is proof that a number of them were as well educated as some men. Women continued their education through private family libraries, thorough art, and social participation—and, although not as common, by their participation in literary jousts and academies, as Inmaculada Osuna's essay will point out. Indeed, women's education was significantly formed by oral means, such as hearing lectures, and sermons, important venues of learning for all social groups, and especially for those who did not have access to more formal education.

Women's education, however, was also considered threatening to the male order; numerous treatises warned of the dangers of female learning. The controversy stemmed in part from the so-called *querelle des femmes*, the medieval debates concerned with women's place within patriarchal society that extended into the early modern period. **Emily Francomano** traces the tradition in Spain to the *cancionero*, or songbook poets, who exchanged poems on women's nature. From as early as the fifteenth century, women intervened in their almost male exclusivity by defending themselves for creating public opinion and engaging in politics. Through its misogynistic tone, which rehearses the negative classical and biblical views of women, the *querelle*, in its alternating profeminine and misogynist writings, sets men and women as contraries, eliciting an awareness of gender difference, and setting the stage for future sexual and textual controversies.

Social standing, education, and male misogyny were aspects of women's lives that, despite their cloistered status, influenced nuns' experiences as well. Economics was a factor: since families could not often cover the marriage dowries of all daughters, the convent was a convenient choice, either as a family strategy to arrange for daughters' futures, even when there was little vocation on the woman's part, or when women themselves rejected the possibility of marriage. Convent education, moreover, ensured that girls learned the four prayers by heart, learned to write letters and keep accounts, and to read religious tract and treatises to protect themselves from their purportedly evil nature, as the *querelle* texts against women defined them. Not all nuns were literate, however; depending on their social status, some never learned to write and relied on their more educated companions to write to their confessors. Internal divisions between the elite, black-veiled nuns and white-veiled nuns who had no dowry and worked at menial tasks reflected their level of literacy and numeracy.[8] Yet, for the great number who professed, literacy allowed them to document their experiences, whether personal or at the behest of their confessors, as in the case of autobiographies, or the lives of other women, as in biographies and hagiographies, and to express themselves through literature—poetry and theater—for the convent's own consumption or for circulation among the different orders. Indeed, the emphasis on writing in the convents has produced the greatest amount of works by early modern Spanish women, much of it still unedited, little known, and unread.[9]

The chapters under the heading of **Section II: Conventual spaces** address the varied non-literary and literary writings by nuns, categorizing them by genre and purpose. **Isabelle Poutrin** provides a thorough overview of the multiple forms of autobiographical texts; as will be the case in the many works by female religious, those of Teresa of Ávila served as their literary model, and, as in the case with the term "by command" discussed in the following chapter, they were mandated by the nuns' confessors. Poutrin makes the important point—valid for all nuns' mystical writings—that they served as confirmation of divine benefaction and promoted the orders' saintliness. **Mercedes Marcos Sánchez** continues with a synopsis of chronicles, biographies, and hagiographies by nuns, texts that are usually considered historiographical, as they comprise a historical narrative of events. She warns, however, that the genre remains little studied, and is still imprecise: frequently anonymous, biographies of nuns easily blend with hagiographies and were, moreover, often censored by the church. Yet the *Vidas* of their companions revealed the authors' erudition: Juliana de la Purificación, for instance, wrote thirty-three biographies of deceased nuns, with numerous patristic comments. Some nuns even wrote lives of the saints and of the Virgin mother, demonstrating their knowledge of doctrine, thus moving beyond the writing "on command" usually required of them. Indeed, not all conventual writing expressed solely spiritual requirements. The need to communicate beyond convent walls is evident in the abundant production of convent correspondence studies by **María Leticia Sánchez Hernández** and **Nieves Baranda Leturio.** The authors investigate the format in which letters were written, circulated, and archived, acknowledging that preservation of these texts was a difficult if not impossible task given their fragility and their dispersal across convents. One of the particularly valuable aspects of this chapter is the discussion of the complexities of epistolary writing, which the nuns' mastered thoroughly in their highly effective rhetoric, making use of elusive techniques in private correspondence against censorship. The variety of letters that fall mainly into the category of "familial" demonstrates that the nuns communicated not only with their families, but also with their friends and patrons. These letters, as well as those addressed to civil and ecclesiastical authorities, show the interdependence between the outside world and the convent.[10]

María Carmen Alarcón Román and **Stacey Schlau** respectively review theater and poetry, the literary production for which many nuns were known, within and outside their convents. Theater served many purposes in the convent, not least among them, the spiritual education of the novitiates and the formation of solidarity among the nuns. It also allowed them to assume roles that they may not have achieved outside the convent, such as playwrights, actresses, and directors. An important contribution by Alarcón Román is her discussion of the public who attended nuns' plays, as she notes that at least during some celebrations, the convents opened their doors to the outside public, including male attendees. Like theater, poetry aims to fulfill at least two goals: the personal articulation of ascetic-mystical tendencies, and the expression of external events, such as liturgical celebrations, nuns' professions, and canonizations. Schlau offers a synthesis of this diverse field, listing numerous primary sources and critical studies on the most renowned mystical poets, including Teresa of Ávila, the sisters Cecilia del Nacimiento and María de San Alberto, Luisa de Carvajal y Mendoza, and Gregoria Francisca de Santa Teresa. She ends by reminding readers of the need for more studies on the collections of poetry as *cancioneros* or songbooks, themselves an example of the communal work of culture produced by nuns.

While religious writings are a significant part of early modern Spain's cultural production by women, secular writers also distinguished themselves by their breadth of participation in many literary genres. **Section III: Secular literature** addresses the literary forms most prevalent in early modern Spain that were written by non-religious women: poetry, narrative, and theater. **María Dolores Martos Pérez** explains that because poetry was conceived of as a male genre, female poetry challenged men's sphere of poetic action, not only in form but through enunciation of their subjectivity. The history of female poetry is the search for women's legitimate expression in a tradition that rejected their agency. Martos Pérez further analyzes their incursion into the poetic field by means of the tensions created between poetic self-awareness and representing the fictional self. The discursive strategies available to women poets, she tells us, run the gamut from neutralizing their poetry by eliminating gender markers through an undifferentiated voice, to adapting the masculine voice to their register, on to subverting male poetic discourse by such methods as eliminating all traces of male enunciation and creating a fully feminine universe, or "humanizing" the woman against male idealization. Voicing themselves through a poetry that, in the seventeenth century, was fast becoming marketable through the printing press thus becomes a means for women to negotiate their social presence. Yet while women's written voice becomes more visible, their actual participation in literary academies, where their voices would be heard, remains uncertain. **Inmaculada Osuna Rodríguez**'s thorough foray into formal academies and poetic jousts distinguishes between them, demonstrating women's higher level of participation in the latter, mainly in the seventeenth century, due to their more accessible nature. Academies registered few women, whereas tournaments allowed for hundreds of female participants, although their contribution was still irregular, with more activity in Aragón. Osuna Rodríguez gives as examples of exceptional participants in tournaments—the nun, Bernarda Romero, Cristobalina Fernández de Alarcón, and Ana Francisca Abarca de Bolea—yet comments that much more work is needed to clarify social perception of women's participation in these social institutions.

Perhaps the genre that most lends itself to comparison with male writings is that of prose fiction, given the long-standing influence of the Italian novella tradition. **Shifra Armon** points out that the women-centered criticism known as gynocriticism breaks from male influence by allowing a female culture to exist independently, and, as feminist criticism itself expanded, women's cultural history assumed importance through the Anglo-American New Criticism's emphasis on historicity. That a woman wrote the only extant novel of chivalry, and that the first professional women writers were María de Zayas, known for her *novelle* collection, and Ana Caro, the chronicler of Seville, demonstrate how well women appropriated genres that had earlier been attributed solely to male authors. Armon traces the lives and literary successes of other women prose writers such as Mariana de Carvajal, Ana Francisca Abarca de Bolea, and Leonor de Meneses. Ironically, according to Armon, if these women writers have been overshadowed by Cervantes, it is precisely due to their fame and writing style that they are now being compared with him at all. Most importantly, women's prose fiction offer a window on women's differing views of their social and legal concerns, such as courtship and marriage, dependent as these are upon men in a patriarchal society. In much the same way, theater by women sets the stage for different experiences from those typically represented by male playwrights. As **Amy R. Williamsen** states in her chapter on female playwrights, secular plays posed challenges to artistic and social conventions through their interrogation of the categories of race, class, and gender. The latter especially is highlighted in female dramaturgy, such as the plays by María de Zayas and Ángela de Azevedo. Williamsen focuses on the actresses' cross-dressing as acts of transgression, whose complex dynamics facilitate exploration of sexuality and desire. As Williamsen asserts, Spanish female-authored plays ascribe agency to women protagonists, inverting the role of women as objects and of male privilege by manipulating the theater's male-established conventions.

One aspect that secular theater shares with secular literature is its eminently visible social character. Plays by their nature require an audience and are addressed to a cultural community. The contributors in **Section IV: Women in the public sphere** discuss the writing for and circulation in society of several kinds of women's texts. **María Carmen Marín Pina** addresses both religious and secular women who entered the world of marketing by means of the printing press. Their publications were dedicated to occasional and civic poetry, and their authors also published poems within their own novels, such as María de Zayas and Leonor de Meneses, or in other authors' anthologies, such as Cristobalina Fernández de Alarcón. Yet another kind of publication for circulation in the public sphere, were pamphlets. Although there are few extant, what we know about them is highly significant: both men and women wrote them, and the majority celebrated historical events, known as *relaciones* or narratives. Because most of these pamphlets were mandated and licensed by civil or religious authorities, such as those written by Ana Caro and Eugenia Bueso, they shine a different light on women writers, as professional chroniclers of important religious and civic events, and thus well integrated into society.

Emilie L. Bergmann focuses on six learned women, from medieval Spain to the New World—Teresa de Cartagena, Luisa Sigea, Oliva Sabuco, Luisa de Padilla, María de Guevara, and Sor Juana Inés de la Cruz. Despite having written humanist treatises demonstrating their erudition, all were challenged by the male patriarchy, and the authorship of some, like Sabuco, questioned and even obliterated. Yet their writings, demonstrate that they belong in the intellectual history of early modern Spain.

This integration is especially noticeable in women who have, besides, involved themselves in political issues, in what **Nieves Romero-Díaz** explains in her chapter, as their attempt to participate in the exercise of power. This chapter reminds us that not only queens participated in politics; numerous women wrote of their concerns as well, an area sorely needing more research.[11] Asserting that women's roles in politics, while they varied from men's, were equally as active, she comments on the same *relaciones* or pamphlets, as well as the various treatises that women such as María de Guevara wrote to Philip IV, expressing her political and military views, in the same way that the nun, María de Jesús de Ágreda, did when she corresponded with him. This genre in particular served as a means for women to enter public space, as Romero-Díaz opines of the aristocrat, Luisa de Carvajal's letters from England to her correspondents in Spain. Studying women's correspondence from the perspective of politics opens up new vistas as to their agency through their writing. Other genres that also place women firmly in the public sphere are the treatises written by women whose humanist education granted them entry into topics proscribed to them.

If the previous section corroborates women's literary agency beyond the enclosures typically assigned early modern women, **Section V: Private circles** reminds us that even in the privacy

Introduction

of their homes, women authors made use of these closed spaces to write and express themselves. While the treatises written for public consumption showed their authors' humanist tendencies and several were published and circulated in their lifetime, there were others that were meant more specifically for didactic purposes and for private readership. **Rosilie Hernández** reviews this kind of literature, which is produced in two locations: the woman's home and the convent. According to Hernández, their writings position the authors as legitimately capable of erudition and worthy heirs to classical, theological, and humanist traditions. Thus, writings such as those by Luisa Sigea, María de Guevara, and Luisa de Padilla, Countess of Aranda, while following male-authored genres, not only include women's voices, but are solely addressed to women, their treatises witnessing social corruption and vice, and exhorting the female reader to virtuous behavior. This is as evident in religious women, whose exemplars, such as María de San José, Feliciana de San José, and Ana de San Bartolomé, instruct their fellow nuns on how to reach a more perfect self. The act of writing, for both these secular and religious didacts, functions as both a tool for others—they instruct women in how to lead better lives—and for themselves, as they construct themselves as knowledgeable and powerful. Hernández points out that didacticism is not limited to treatises, however, as other genres, such as drama and correspondence, may convey an intention to educate women. Correspondence in particular allows women to move beyond the limits of their private residences, whether homes or convents, to their broader readership, in particular family members.

The interest in communicating both with and about the family is a topic taken up by **Gwyn Fox** and **Vanessa de Cruz Medina**. Fox focuses on poetry written by women to members of her own family, noting that this verse was intended for private consumption by these same family members. She discusses the poetry by, among others, Catalina Clara Ramírez de Guzmán, Leonor de la Cueva, the pseudonymous Marcia Belisarda, and the Portuguese nun Violante do Céu, which allowed them to express their emotions on familial matters such as marriage and motherhood, and, in the case of the religious poets, their devotion to the convent sisterhood as an alternative family, their own "marriage" to Christ, and the spiritual motherhood proffered by the Virgin. Fox stresses that these personal poems on what she terms the poets' "inner lives," offer an ideal means to understand early modern kinship networks from a woman's perspective. While women's lyric poetry often reflects women's thoughts on family and other networks, the fact that it pertains to a literary genre, mediated by tradition and the practice of imitation stemming from its history of male authorship, should always be taken into account. Because letters written by women also respond to rhetorical traditions, in her chapter, Vanessa de Cruz Medina alerts us that they cannot necessarily be construed as personal. Nonetheless, the correspondence she cites by noblewomen such as Magdalena de Bobadilla, Estefanía de Requesens, and the Countesses of Lemos, reveal the importance of communicating information, much of it about court politics, across female networks; through their letters, several of these women instructed their daughters and nieces on the various businesses that they ran. Her chapter reveals the extraordinarily rich—quantitatively as well as qualitatively—collections of elite women's correspondence, much of which has still to be edited and studied from the perspective of the letter writers themselves.

Non-noblewomen also wrote letters, however. De Cruz Medina discusses the letters written by women emigrants to the New World; and although the numbers are fewer than those written by men, women's letters document their attempts to travel to America, as in the case of application letters (*cartas de llamada*), register their complaints, such as those addressed to the Mexican Inquisition denouncing husbands for bigamy, and their experiences in the New World.

The transnational and trans-oceanic journeys of Iberian women writers are the theme of **Section VI: Women travelers**. One issue that this section attempts to investigate is the motivation that compelled women to travel in the first place. Recent research on women's writing has proven that, unlike what was previously surmised, early modern women indeed traveled extensively throughout the globe. One main reason for travel was the founding of convents by religious orders outside Spain, as the Catholic Church moved to counter the advance of Protestantism and to propagate Catholicism in the New World. The foundational narratives discussed by **Darcy Donahue** relate how fraught such ventures were, given the great difficulties nuns faced in adjusting to new cultures, even within Europe. Teresa of Ávila's *Book of Foundations* furnished the model for conventual foundations, as her Discalced Order first traveled to the "heretical" country of France under the guidance of Ana de San Bartolomé and Ana de Jesús. Soon, however, other orders also left Spain to different countries, writing down their experiences, such as the autobiographies and biographies by Capuchin nuns who founded the first Capuchin convent in Sardinia, and, inversely, the Franciscan nun Catalina del Espíritu Santo, whose foundational text narrates their flight through Flanders until they found a convent in Lisbon. Studying the nuns who left Europe altogether, **Sarah E. Owens** illustrates the movements of three orders: Franciscans, Capuchins, and Bridgettines as examples of convents that, spreading as far as the Philippines and China, wrote their histories collaboratively over time. For instance, the biography of Sor Jerónima de la Asunción, the founder of the first Franciscan convent in Manila, was a hybrid text that followed Teresa's model, yet combined the biographer's narrative, Sor Jerónima's writings, and letters and biographies of the convent nuns. Owens' analyses of these and other writings, such as the letters by the Capuchin nuns, and the multiple-authored chronicle of the Bridgettines to Mexico, bring to light the significance of these narratives, which not only told the histories of the convents, but documented the travels and travails of the nuns themselves.

Like their religious sisters, secular women also traveled broadly and in far higher numbers than previously suspected. In her chapter, **Rocío Quispe-Agnoli** informs us of numerous cases of women who arrived in the New World and who participated in its colonization. Because these women not only left legal petitions, journals, and personal letters, but wrote in a variety of literary genres, their texts illuminate how gender affected their lives, as they manipulated the discourses available to them for their own purposes. When investigating the letters written by the two vicereines of Mexico, the Countess of Paredes and the Countess of Galve, Quispe-Agnoli finds that those written in Spain express different sentiments than those from Mexico, where the women had assumed their political roles. Moreover, comparing these two sets of letters allows us to note the women's different responses to their experiences as vicereines. And although the Mexican nun, Sor Juana Inés de la Cruz, is justifiably renowned, Quispe-Agnoli calls our attention to the concerns of other Creole women writers, such as María de Estrada and the pseudonymous Clarinda and Amarilis, whose poetry reflects their celebration of America.

But if women traveled frequently across borders, their works did no less. Indeed, translations of women's literary production, whether in manuscript or in print, appeared in numerous countries, a movement that helped to disseminate their ideas, influence other literatures, and acknowledge the authors transnationally. In the last chapter of this section, **Nieves Baranda Leturio** traces the trajectory of women's writings outside the peninsula that were translated into Spanish, and Spanish and Portuguese texts that were translated into other languages. Some belonging to the first category, like Catherine of Siena's and Angela de Foligno's works, dealt with moral and religious topics and wielded great influence on Iberian spiritual development. Spain reciprocated by exporting its own most popular devotional works written by women. As Baranda Leturio shows, both Teresa of Ávila—whose writings are included in several of this volume's chapters—and María de Jesús de Ágreda wrote what could be considered religious best-sellers, both in Spain and abroad. Yet, while other authors' works were translated, the names of the authors themselves were often left out and assigned to male writers. Not only Luisa de Padilla, but María de Zayas was also adapted into French; in Zayas's case, she was either translated anonymously, or her style and plots were criticized in the paratexts. Yet ironically, Zayas—whose violent plots would have scandalized the nun—is, with Saint Teresa, perhaps the best-known of Spanish women writers outside Spain. Still another form of crossing borders was through women's bilingualism. Writers born in Portugal, such as the poet Violante do Céo and the dramatist Ángela de Azevedo, often wrote in Spanish, participating in two cultural systems and, once well-known, were accepted into Madrid literary circles. Other women who wrote in Spanish, such as Isabel Correa, Isabel Henríquez, and Beatriz de Fonseca, were Sephardic Jews who lived in Amsterdam. Through their writings, Baranda Leturio tells us, these authors serve to reconfigure the literary system as they resist the inherent codes of their adopted language.

For future research

The contributors to this volume have presented an impressive number of women authors, both religious and secular, noble and middle class, renowned and little known, from court to the periphery, who have practiced their craft of writing in all literary genres and through letters, autobiographies, biographies, chronicles, and narratives. These women writers have enriched their culture and language and influenced numerous others. As our contributors have observed, however, although research has continued apace, and excellent work is being carried out, there is still much to discover and accomplish in this field, as far too little is known about most women who lived and wrote in the early modern period. Our purpose in organizing the volume thematically has been to move beyond the discrete analyses of individual women writers and possible comparisons with male authors, although we believe these studies continue to be needed. Yet women writers, as we demonstrate in our volume, also have a history all their own, parallel to that of male writers, and their works should be given the centrality that they deserve in early modern studies. We encourage readers to make use of the information presented in the chapters in order to pursue a broader visualization of the generic interconnections among the writers, and to suggest ways in which their works can be read both up close and distant in order to chart social patterns and delineate differences. We believe that this research companion will serve as a cartographic tool to help map the complex and still unfamiliar terrain of early modern Spanish women writers.

Notes

1 While this volume does not attempt a comparative view of European women's writings, on the anthologizing of English women writers, see Gualtieri, 95. Italian women's writings were initially serialized and translated in Margaret King and Albert Rabil, Jr. in *The Other Voice* series in 1983. For early modern French women writers, see Ford and Jondorf, and Nativel. For women writers in early modern Spain, see Marín Pina and Baranda Leturio.
2 The major exception, whose writings were exploited for political and religious purposes, was Saint Teresa of Ávila.
3 See Armon in this volume. As Diana Robin asserts, individual studies of early modern European women writers did not proliferate until the late 1990s ("Intellectual Women"). As we comment below, although belatedly, studies of Spanish women writers followed a parallel development. Two major Spanish presses began collections of women's writings in the 1990s: the series "Biblioteca de Escritoras" in Castalia; and "Feminismos" in Cátedra.
4 See Barbeito; the text is uploaded in BIESES. It is important to note, however, that three years prior to Barbeito, Deyermond published, in Miller, a ground-breaking article on medieval Spanish women writers. Among the several anthologies that followed Barbeito Carneiro in the 1980s focusing

specifically on Spanish women writers, see Galerstein, Jiménez Faro, Navarro, and Wilson. Anthologies that have appeared in the 1990s to the 2000s include those edited by Triviño, Simón Palmer; Olivares and Boyce; Levine, Engelson Marson, and Feiman Waldman; Kaminsky, Doménech Rico; Soufas; Mujica; Caballé; and Romero López, et al. The database *Bibliografía de Escritoras Españolas* (BIESES), initiated in 2004, continues to collect data on women writers, and is a major source for Spanish women's writings, as the contributors to this volume attest by their citations.

5   Well-known women writers also began to be perceived differently by feminist critics, as in the case, for instance, of Teresa of Ávila and María de Zayas. See, among others, Weber, Greer, and Vollendorf. A major effort to view women's writings from a feminist perspective was Zavala and, more recently, de Ros and Hazbun.

6   As Emilie Bergmann discusses in her chapter, Luisa Sigea and Francisca Lebrija, both daughters of humanists, followed in their fathers' footsteps. Oliva Sabuco de Nantes most probably studied with humanists, as did Juliana Morell and, earlier, Beatriz Galindo, at Isabel of Castille's court. For a defense of Oliva and of women in general in the Enlightenment, see Bolufer.

7   Because Portugal formed part of the Spanish monarchy from 1580 to the 1660s, women writers who were born in Portugal and were bilingual in Portuguese and Castilian have been included; see Baranda Leturio's chapter in the volume. For studies of women born in the New World, see Scott; Lavrín and Loreto; Rodríguez and Szurmuk. See also the data base, "Latin American Women Writers," University of Texas Libraries, www.lib.utexas.edu/indexes/titles.php?id=528

8   See Donahue, and Herrera.

9   Arenal and Schlau's pioneering efforts in 1989 resulted in the first anthology of nuns' literary writings, now in its second and expanded edition. Other examples of recently rediscovered women religious are Rees; and Smith and Sabat-Rivers. On the wide variety of conventual writings, see Baranda and Marín Pina "Introduction."

10 See Lehfeldt for a study of convents' permeability.

11 Indeed, feminist anthologies documenting women's participation in politics in early modern Europe are only recently and tentatively including Spanish women's contributions. See Daybell and Norrhem; Jansen; Munns and Richards; others, like Broad and Green, and Broomhall and Tarbin, leave out Spain altogether.

Works cited

Arenal, Electa, and Stacey Schlau. *Untold Sisters: Hispanic Nuns in Their Own Works*. Trans. Amanda Powell. Albuquerque: U New Mexico P, 2010.

Baranda, Nieves. "Mujeres y escritura en el Siglo de Oro: una relación inestable." *Litterae. Cuadernos sobre Cultura Escrita*, 3–4 (2003–2004): 61–83.

Baranda, Nieves, and María Carmen Marín Pina, "Introduction," *Letras en la celda. Cultura escrita de los conventos femeninos en la España moderna*. Madrid: Ibero-Americana, Vervuert, 2014: 11–45.

Barbeito Carneiro, María Isabel. *Escritoras madrileñas del siglo XVII: estudio bibliográfico-crítico*. Madrid: Departamento de Bibliografía, Universidad Complutense, 1986.

Bolufer Peruga, Mónica. *Mujeres e Ilustración: la construcción de la feminidad en la Ilustración española*. Valencia: Ed. Alfonso el Magnánimo, 1998.

Broad, Jacqueline, and Karen Green. *A History of Women's Political Thought in Europe, 1400–1700*. Cambridge: Cambridge UP, 2009.

Broomhall, Susan, and Stephanie Tarbin, eds. *Women, Identities and Communities in Early Modern Europe*. Aldershot, UK: Ashgate, 2008.

Caballé, Anna, ed. *La vida escrita por las mujeres*, vol. 4, *'Por mi alma os digo': De la Edad Media a la Ilustración*. Barcelona: Lumen, 2004.

Daybell, James, and Svante Norrhem, eds. *Gender and Political Culture in Early Modern Europe, 1400–1800*. New York: Routledge, 2017.

Deyermond, Alan. "Spain's First Women Writers." *Women in Hispanic Literature: Icons and Fallen Idols*. Ed. Beth K. Miller. Berkeley: U California P, 1983: 27–52.

Doménech Rico, Fernando, ed. *Teatro breve de mujeres (Siglos XVII–XX)*. Madrid: Asociación de Directores de Escena de España, 1996.

Donahue, Darcy R. "Wondrous Words: Miraculous Literacy and Real Literacy in the Convents of Early Modern Spain." *Women's Literacy in Early Modern Spain and the New World*. Ed. Anne J. Cruz and Rosilie Hernández. Farnham, UK; Burlington, VT: Ashgate, 2011: 105–122.

Ford, Philip, and Gillian Jondorf, eds. *Women's Writing in the French Renaissance. Proceedings of the Fifth Cambridge French Renaissance Colloquium, 7–9 July 1997.* Cambridge: Cambridge UP, 1999.

Galerstein, Carolyn L. *Women Writers of Spain. An Annotated Bio-Bibliographial Guide.* Westport, CT: Greenwood, 1986.

Greer, Margaret. *María de Zayas Tells Baroque Tales of Love and the Cruelty of Men.* University Park, PA: Penn State UP, 2000.

Gualtieri, Gillian. "Canonized Women and Women Canonizers: Gender Dynamics in the *Norton Anthology of English Literature*'s Eight Editions." *Gender Issues* (2011): 94–109.

Herrera, Clara. "Convent Education in Nueva Granada: Black, White, or Tonalities of Grey?" *Women's Literacy in Early Modern Spain and the New World.* Ed. Anne J. Cruz and Rosilie Hernández. Farnham, UK; Burlington, VT: Ashgate, 2011.

Jansen, Sharon L. *Debating Women, Politics, and Power in Early Modern Europe.* New York: Palgrave MacMillan, 2008.

Jiménez Faro, Luzmaría. *Panorama antológico de poetisas españolas (Siglos XV al XX).* Madrid: Ediciones Torremozas, 1987.

Kaminsky, Amy K., ed. *Water Lilies: Flores del agua; An Anthology of Spanish Women Writers from the Fifteenth through the Nineteenth Century.* Minneapolis: U Minnesota P, 1996.

"Latin American Women Writers." Data base. University of Texas Libraries, www.lib.utexas.edu/indexes/titles.php?id=528.

Lavrin, Asunción, and Rosalva Loreto, eds., *Monjas y beatas. La escritura femenina en la espiritualidad barroca novohispana, siglos XVII y XVIII.* Puebla: Universidad de las Américas, 2002.

———. *Diálogos espirituales. Manuscritos femeninos hispanoamericanos, siglos XVI–XIX.* Puebla: Universidad de las Américas, 2006.

Lehfeldt, Elizabeth. *Religious Women in Golden Age Spain: The Permeable Cloister.* Farnham, UK; Burlington, VT: Ashgate, 2005.

Levine, Linda Gould, Ellen Engelson Marson, and Gloria Feiman Waldman, eds. *Spanish Women Writers: A Bio-Bibliographical Source Book.* Westport, CT: Greenwood, 1993.

Marín Pina, María Carmen, and Nieves Baranda, "Bibliografía de escritoras españolas (edad media-siglo XVIII). Una base de datos." *Edad de Oro Cantabrigense. Actas del VII Congreso de la Asociación Internacional del Siglo de Oro (AISO) (Robinson College, Cambridge, 18–22 julio, 2005).* Ed. Anthony Close. Cambridge: Cambridge UP, 2006: 429–435.

Merrim, Stephanie. *Early Modern Women's Writing and Sor Juana Inés de la Cruz.* Nashville: Vanderbilt UP, 1999.

Miller, Beth K., ed. *Women in Hispanic Literature: Icons and Fallen Idols.* Berkeley: U California P, 1983.

Mujica, Barbara, ed. *Early Modern Women Writers: Sophia's Daughters.* New Haven: Yale UP, 2003.

Munns, Jessica, and Penny Richards, eds. *Gender, Power, and Privilege in Early Modern Europe: 1500–1700.* London; New York: Routledge, 2003.

Muriel, Josefina. *Cultura femenina novohispana.* México: Universidad Nacional Autónoma, 1994.

Myers, Kathleen Ann. "Crossing Boundaries: Defining the Field of Female Religious Writing in Colonial Latin America," *Colonial Latin American Review*, 9.2 (2000): 151–165.

Nativel, Colette, ed. *Femmes savants, savoirs des femmes. Du crepuscule de la Renaissance à l'aube des Lumières. Actes du Colloque de Chantilly (22–24 septembre 1995).* Geneva: Droz, 1999.

Navarro, Ana, ed. *Antologia poética de escritoras de los Siglos XVI y XVII.* Madrid: Castalia, 1989.

Olivares, Julián, and Elizabeth S. Boyce, eds. *Tras el espejo la musa escribe: Lírica femenina de los Siglos de Oro.* Madrid: Siglo Veintiuno de España, 1993; 2nd ed. 2012.

Rees, Margaret. *Doña María Vela y Cueto, Cistercian Mystic of Spain's Golden Age.* Lewiston, NY: Edwin Mellen, 2004.

Robin, Diana. "Intellectual Women in Early Modern Europe." *The Ashgate Research Companion to Women and Gender in Early Modern Europe.* Ed. Allyson M. Poska, Jane Couchman, and Katherine A. McIver. Farnham, UK: Ashgate, 2013: 381–406.

Rodríguez, Ileana, and Mónica Szurmuk, eds., *The Cambridge History of Latin American Women's Literature.* Cambridge: Cambridge UP, 2015.

Romero López, Dolores, et al., eds. *Seis siglos de poesía española escrita por mujeres. Pautas poétias y revisiones críticas.* Bern: Peter Lang, 2007.

Ros, Xon de, and Geraldine Hazbun, eds., *A Companion to Spanish Women's Studies.* London: Boydell and Brewer, 2011.

Scott, Nina. *Madres del Verbo/Mothers of the Word. Early Spanish-American Women Writers. A Bilingual Anthology.* Albuquerque: U New Mexico P, 1999.

Simón Palmer, María del Carmen. *Escritoras españolas 1500–1900. Biblioteca Nacional (España)*. Madrid: Chadwyck Healey, 1992.

Smith, Susan, and Georgina Sabat-Rivers, eds. *Marcela de San Félix, Los coloquios del alma: Cuatro dramas alegóricos de Sor Marcela de San Félix, hija de Lope de Vega*. Newark, DE: Juan de la Cuesta, 2006.

Soufas, Teresa Scott., ed. *Women's Acts: Plays by Women Dramatists of Spain's Golden Age*. Lexington: UP Kentucky, 1997.

Triviño, María Victoria. *Escritoras clarisas españolas. Antología*. Madrid: Biblioteca de Autores Cristianos, 1992.

Vollendorf, Lisa. *Reclaiming the Body: María de Zayas' Early Modern Feminism*. Chapel Hill, NC: U of North Carolina P, 2001.

Walker, Claire. *Gender and Politics in Early Modern Europe. English Convents in France and the Low Countries*. New York: Palgrave Macmillan, 2002.

——. *Women, Identities and Communities in Early Modern Europe*. London: Routledge, 2008.

Weber, Alison. *Teresa of Ávila and the Rhetoric of Femininity*. Princeton: Princeton UP, 1996.

Wilson, Katherine M., and Frank J. Warnke, eds., *Women Writers of the Seventeenth Century*. Athens, GA: U Georgia P, 1989.

Zavala, Iris M., ed. *Breve historia feminista de la literatura española (en lengua castellana). IV. La literatura escrita por mujer (de la Edad Media al siglo XVIII)*. Barcelona: Antropos; Puerto Rico: Universidad, 1997.

SECTION I

Women's worlds

1
ARISTOCRACY AND THE URBAN ELITE

Grace E. Coolidge

The early modern Spanish elite, a social class that ranged from the highest titled aristocrats to wealthy urban merchants, can be defined as a social group who had enough property that they did not support themselves through daily labor. In order to manage their economic assets, they used the law courts, they made contracts, they gave dowries, they created entails (*mayorazgos*), and they wrote wills. Many men and women from this social class were educated and could read and write, but even those who were illiterate can be found in early modern property records. Their economic resources tended to empower elite women, giving them access to power because of their social status and the economic advantages it conveyed. The privileges of wealth and power, therefore, frequently mitigated the disadvantages of being born female in a patriarchal society.

Class divisions in early modern Spain

The early modern Spanish nobility had gained power, wealth, and status partly as a result of the Reconquest, Christian Spain's struggle with the Muslim empire that lasted from the Muslim invasion of the peninsula in 711 to Ferdinand and Isabel's formal conquest of Granada in 1492. As the warrior class, they received land, offices, and other privileges in return for their military service. Over the duration of the early modern period, they gradually spent less time fighting and more time at court and holding important government and church positions. Their economic power was based on land and the wool trade.

At the top of the hierarchy, the seigneurial aristocrats were the heads of powerful noble families who had political and judicial jurisdiction over specific communities (Crawford: 2). The highest seigneurial aristocrats (called the grandees) were a tiny group who controlled almost half the land in Castile and exercised immense power over the people on that land (Lynch: 17). In the early part of the sixteenth century, there were thirteen dukes, thirteen marquises, thirty-four counts, and two viscounts in Castile and an additional five dukes, three marquises, nine counts, and three viscounts in Aragon. Comprising only two or three percent of the population, these aristocrats nevertheless owned ninety-seven percent of the land in Castile (Elliott: 113). The economic power of this small group granted them an ability to intervene in politics that successive monarchs failed to eradicate, and helped make the nobility a crucial part of Spain's Renaissance (Nader, *The Mendoza Family in the Spanish Renaissance*: 6). Below this group were the *caballeros*, a group widely defined to include untitled male members of aristocratic families, cavalrymen in royal or noble service, and urban citizens who were wealthy enough that the crown required them to bear arms if necessary (Crawford: 2).

Below the seigneurial lords and the *caballeros* was a more numerous group known as *hidalgos*. This group was quite diverse, encompassing those who held important government posts, those who were members of the military orders, those who were wealthy or came from a distinguished family, and "poor and simple nobles" (Phillips: 104). Some were urban dwellers and many had connections to trade, but their status of *hidalguía* exempted them from paying taxes to the crown, and they enjoyed a privileged judicial status that meant they could not be tortured, condemned to the galleys, or imprisoned for debt (Elliott: 114–115). This group included many families whose identity and life were based on service to the crown, or whose wealth allowed them to purchase the status of *hidalgo* that was for sale after 1520 (Elliott: 116).

Technically just below the hidalgos were the urban elite, non-nobles who owned property and were invested in political stability (Casey: 119–120). This group included members of the clergy, merchants, guild masters, and other professionals such as notaries, lawyers, or government officials, but they were distinguished from the *hidalgos* because they paid taxes (Crawford: 2; Lynch: 16). Elite men could gain social status by participating in city government as aldermen and *regidores*, and these activities allowed their wives and daughters to advance up the social scale also. This social class did not have titles or honorifics, but they owned real property or other resources that meant they were contributors to local governments, litigators in the courts, and had access to education. Because the urban environment facilitated the mixing of social classes, there was always the possibility that the urban elite could move up the social scale and join the ranks of the nobility.

Was there a middle class?

Early modern Spain did not have a "middle class" or "bourgeoisie" in the modern sense. Marie Kelleher defines this group in the medieval period as the "broad middle range of medieval society," a group that had no titles or honorifics but did have ownership of property or other resources over which to litigate (Kelleher: 36). The terms *burgués* and *burguesía* were used in the Middle Ages to refer to city dwellers, but both terms disappeared from written Spanish during the early modern period. Instead, the terms *mediano* and *medianía* were applied to people (such as the urban elite discussed above) who were situated between the nobility and the commoners (J. Cruz: 8–9). In 1677, Diego Ortiz de Zúñiga, the chronicler of Seville, described the *ciudadanos*, who were midway between the nobility and the plebeians, a group who owned property and were invested in political stability (Casey: 119–120).

The modern Spanish middle class has its roots in this group, which by the eighteenth century included urban bureaucrats and *hidalgos*, but in the early modern period the group remained heterogeneous and difficult to classify (Fernández Pérez: 2). *Hidalgos* were a large, legally privileged group who were entitled to use the honorific titles *don* and *doña*. Economically they fell in the middle, between the majority of the population and the aristocrats. However, they sharply distinguished themselves from *pecheros* who might share their economic and social backgrounds but who were required to pay the taxes from which the *hidalgos* were proudly exempt (Crawford: 2–3). In addition, *hidalguía* was not always clear cut. There were numerous disputes over both who was entitled to it and what privileges it carried, and *hidalgos* did not form a unified socio-economic class (Crawford: 8). This middle group was fluid, and the desire for social mobility kept it from being particularly united as its members fought over privilege, local political power, and economic assets.

The historian Jesús Cruz argues that the idea of the middle class as a more unified political and economic unit, as well as the terms *burgués* and *burguesía* were reintroduced in Spain in the early nineteenth century in the context of resistance to Napoleon (Bahamonde and Martínez: 462; J. Cruz: 8–9). Even in the nineteenth century the Spanish middle class was small, as Spain remained largely rural with limited participation in the Industrial Revolution compared to other European countries. The use of the term "middle class" is therefore problematic in the early modern period, before industrialization caused factory owners, shopkeepers, bureaucrats, and office workers to self-consciously separate their identity from that of the "working class" who labored with their hands. In the largely agricultural society of the early modern period, the middle group is too diverse and too fluid to be accurately described as a coherent class. In this chapter, therefore, I have chosen to use the term urban elite to describe a heterogeneous middle group who were not the landed aristocracy, but who owned property and wielded power and influence within their own towns or cities. Some members of this group were *hidalgos*, some had titles, and others were merely wealthy citizens with influence and power in their own municipalities.[1]

Gender versus class

Royal, noble, and elite women in early modern Spain were a group in which class privilege often trumped gender restrictions. The hierarchical nature of early modern society meant that the elite had substantial privileges based on their economic resources and political power. While elite women faced more constraints than their male counterparts, they still had inheritance rights, ownership of their dowries, and access to important political figures. Furthermore, they shared the goals of preserving wealth, status, and family that motivated their male relatives. Royal women served as advisors to and regents for their husbands and sons and were often trusted to administer portions of the Spanish empire. Noblewomen were useful to their families through marriage, inheritance, and guardianship because they helped accumulate land and moveable goods, managed children and assets, and facilitated the smooth transfer of property between generations. The nobility's goal of preserving and expanding its status and wealth gave noblewomen power and authority within their own social class. In the hierarchical society of early modern Spain, women of elite status who were not noble had a more complex relationship with power and authority. They had fewer privileges than aristocratic women but far more than the 75–80% of early modern Spaniards who were peasants. The active roles of elite women connected them to a larger tradition in which Spanish women were a powerful force in all social classes as they held families together, protected children, and compensated for absent men (Poska; Wessell-Lightfoot, *Women, Dowries*).

Although they lived in a patriarchy that restricted some of their movements and options, noble and elite women derived authority from their social status, family connections, wealth, and access to education.[2] The privileged status of these women allowed their management of large households and gave them access to the world of literature and art. Education gave them the tools with which to express themselves, their social status could give them opportunities to participate in the literary debates and dialogues of their day, and their writings give glimpses of the assurance and authority with which they approached their world (Baranda Leturio: 26). The lives of literate women in early modern Spain were thus shaped by the privileges of elite social class as much (if not more) as by the restrictions of gender.

The rule of royal women

Spain had a strong tradition of female rulers who wielded power under various different titles. Medieval examples of this include María of Castile, who ruled Catalunya as lieutenant general for her husband, the king of Aragon, and Berenguela of Castile, who was heir to the throne, queen consort, regent, and queen regnant at various different parts of her life (Bianchini: 2; Earenfight: 131). Isabel of Castile, of course, dominated the beginning of the early modern period (Liss; Weissberger). These powerful women were not exceptions but part of a system that historically included traditions of co-rule (Bianchini: 8). Male monarchs enlisted the help of their wives, mothers, daughters, and underage or non-inheriting sons in administrating their estates and projecting the image of royalty. Margaret of Austria was Governor of the Habsburg Netherlands for her nephew, Charles V, from 1507 to 1515 and again from 1519 to 1530, and Mary of Hungary, sister of Charles V, served in this position from 1531–55 (Lynch: 68). This tradition continued in the early modern period as Margaret of Parma was regent in the Netherlands for her nephew Philip II; Isabel Clara Eugenia, Philip II's daughter, served as both sovereign and governor of the Netherlands; Isabel of Borbón served as regent for her husband Philip IV; and Mariana of Austria was regent for her son, Carlos II (Dandelet: 157; Mitchell: 191; Oliván Santaliestra: 168; van Wyhe).

Royal women in early modern Spain, therefore, were understood by their contemporaries as having political roles to play even if there was debate about the extent and impact of those roles (Sánchez: 4–5). Diplomats, courtiers, and the nobility alternately worried about the extent of royal female influence or enlisted it in support of their goals. Recognizing the royal court as a gendered space fundamentally changes interpretations of the elite, women's power, and early modern politics (A. Cruz: 2). Through this lens, women become more visible as scholars explore how royal mothers, queen regents, and princesses wielded royal power and influence.

Royal women were educated and trained to perform political roles from a young age. The *Infanta* María Teresa, daughter of Philip IV, demonstrated her progress by publicly donning the farthingale (*guardainfante*) in 1643 at the age of five, a gesture that symbolized majesty and virtuosity (Oliván Santaliestra: 169). Royal marriage alliances supported peace treaties and forged alliances between early modern political powers. When Philip III's daughter Ana was ten years old in 1611, her marriage was arranged to Louis XIII, the King of France. Over the next few years she practiced her new role as a French queen, formally welcoming a French nobleman who came to express condolences on the death of her mother (Hoffman: 136). Princesses represented their birth families and were expected to work for the good of the families and dynasties into which they had married.

Even when they did not marry, royal women remained strongly political; the Spanish court had close ties with royal convents, which housed many royal and aristocratic women. Philip III and Margarita of Austria attended daily masses at the Descalzas Reales Convent in Madrid, where the queen also had permission to speak and pray daily with the cloistered nuns whose number included the king's cousin, Margaret of the Cross (Sánchez: 13). Like many noblewomen, Queen Margarita was active in religious reform, requesting Mariana de San José, an Augustinian nun from Palencia, to come to Madrid to help reform the royal convent of Santa Isabel. Mariana was also the first abbess of the Convent of the Encarnación, founded by Margarita of Austria. Sánchez argues that members of the court were aware of and concerned about the influence that this potentially granted the nuns who could be seen as supporting royal authority or, alternately, as challenging an authority that some courtiers felt should have been exclusively male (Sánchez: 23–24).

Queens of Spain presided over complex royal households that were hotbeds of political intrigue that could provide opportunities for female influence. Isabel of Borbón was a rival of her husband's court favorite, the Count-Duke of Olivares, and after his fall in 1642, she began to dominate the life of the court (Oliván Santaliestra: 168). Royal women managed court politics, asserted power, and molded their own images to negotiate the complex gender roles that emerged from a patriarchy with a tradition of strong female rulers. Royal women also shaped court culture through patronage and participation in the written and visual arts and an emphasis on education. In the late fifteenth century, Isabel of Castile educated herself and sponsored publications that were designed to instruct the ladies at her court. She extended this interest to the education of the following generations, both men and women (Alvar Ezquerra; Howe: 43).

The nobility

Traditional historiographies of the nobility emphasize its decline due to an inability to cope effectively with both the emerging "modern world" and the rising middle class (Romaniello and Lipp: 1). More recent work, however, has recognized noble resilience and adaptability to argue that early modern Europe was not a period of noble decline but one of tumult, confusion, and change where the nobility was a "contested space" (Romaniello and Lipp: 2). This newer approach has also been inclined to place politically powerful noblemen in the context of their families in order to explore the negotiations that enabled them to maintain their power, wealth, and prestige. The result allows scholars to acknowledge the crucially important roles played by noblewomen in the complicated negotiations that maintained and increased noble power. When powerful noblemen are studied in the context of their families, it becomes obvious that wives, mothers, daughters, and even aunts and grandmothers were critical elements of the family networks that supported and promoted them (García Hernán, "Los grandes": 602–609; Pastor Zapata: 166–172; Villalón).

Members of the nobility remained focused on the project of accumulating property, wealth, and status. They aimed to consolidate and preserve their power and wealth or to expand it in the search for upward social mobility. Many noblemen recognized that the active participation of well-trained women made this project much more likely to succeed. While they endorsed and supported traditional gender roles that insisted on women's subservience, they also relied heavily on the women of their own families. Noblewomen demonstrated knowledge and even expertise in a wide range of economic, religious, and political activities (Nader, "Introduction": 3). Noblewomen's authority in these spheres undoubtedly benefited them, but it also assisted their families and was often encouraged by elite men.

Spanish inheritance and marriage laws gave women more access to family property, more control over their own dowries, and more chances to control the futures of their children than they had in many other European countries (Coolidge, *Guardianship*: 8; Sperling: 221). Noblewomen were directly involved in estate management and the other economic activities that supported the power of the nobility. The accounts of Magdalena de Bobadilla (1546–1580), a distant relative of the Mendoza family and a member of the royal court, reveal her role in the management of her own property before her marriage. She signed receipts, accounts, letters of credit, and notes to her steward (*mayordomo*), provided a dowry for her maid, and was involved in several lawsuits (Coolidge, "Choosing Her Own Buttons": 144).[3] Magdalena's active economic role was not unusual. Spanish women left numerous notarial records documenting their involvement in lawsuits, wills, and property agreements (Nader, "Introduction": 15).

After marriage, many noblewomen were involved in estate management, and during the medieval and early modern periods, noble marriages were often joint economic ventures between husbands and wives (Beceiro Pita and Córdoba de la Llave: 265). Mencía de Mendoza, Countess of Haro, was left in charge of her husband's estates while he fought in the conquest of Granada from 1481 to 1492. Mencía built a hunting lodge, a chapel in the cathedral of Burgos, and a new palace during her husband's absence (Layna Serrano: 80). The third Duchess of Arcos was in charge of the estate's payroll in 1577 when her husband was absent; the ducal records reveal the substantial purchases she made while wielding that power (García Hernán, "Los grandes": 608–609). The letters of Ana de Mendoza, the Princess of Éboli, reveal how she helped her husband manage the economic and religious affairs of the town of Pastrana before she was abruptly widowed in 1573 (Reed: 157–158). Some noblemen recognized and relied on the economic help of their wives. In 1716 the tenth Duke of Gandía praised his wife for the "prudence and discretion" with which she had helped him pay off the estate's debts during their twenty-five-year marriage.[4]

In an extension of the economic partnership that characterized many marriages, noblemen routinely appointed their wives as executors of their wills, and over 80% of them named their wives as the guardians of their children (Garcia Fernández: 296).[5] Many of these men specified in their wills that they chose their wives as guardians because these women were the most knowledgeable and trustworthy people available to care for their children and their estates.[6] These choices illuminate the gender relations of the elite since they demonstrate that men chose their wives as guardians for reasons of personal trust as well as confidence in their ability to function in the traditionally male realm of estate and property management. Spanish noblemen actively supported the powerful women within their families because these women used their authority and influence to benefit the family.

On a practical level, assuming the office of guardianship meant that many widowed elite women continued to be actively engaged in a wide range of economic and political activities. Ana de Mendoza y de la Cerda, Princess of Éboli, was the legal guardian for her six children after her husband's death in 1573 and before her imprisonment. She ran the estates of Pastrana single-handedly for six years, educated and raised her children, and arranged their marriages (Dadson: 98). Her role as a guardian made her legally male and invested her with all the seigneurial power that her husband had wielded in his lifetime (Coolidge, *Guardianship*: 78). Likewise, the Countess of Palamós, trustee of her daughter's estate after her husband's death in the early sixteenth century, worked diligently to regain what she saw as the family's rightful inheritance through business deals and extensive litigation. The countess's actions reveal another reason why elite men trusted their wives with the administration of their estates, since her actions aided her husband's family and protected their daughter (Pérez-Toribio: 66).

Their active involvement in managing estates and their role as guardians meant that noble-women also often helped arrange the marriages of their children. For noble families, marriage was usually a way to cement alliances between lineages and dynasties and gain access to political power. Arranging marriage was a way that noblewomen demonstrated their agency and political savvy. The Countess of Palamós arranged her daughter's marriage to the Count of Miranda, deliberately modifying her deceased husband's wishes to choose a spouse with more political than economic power (Pérez-Toribio: 67). Arranging marriages was a moment in which age could overcome the traditional gender hierarchy, as aristocratic widows who held guardianship of their children often arranged the marriages of their sons. In 1546, the widowed Marquise of Berlanga gave her son permission to marry María Girón, and in 1605, the widowed Duchess of Medina de Ríoseco arranged her son's marriage to the daughter of the Duke and Duchess of Cea.[7] The women who arranged these marriages were determining the course of the entire dynasty as it moved into the hands of future generations.

Marriage also had an important economic component in the traditional dowry that the bride brought with her at the time of her marriage. Women of high social status traditionally received their dowries from their families. This meant that noble brides were carriers of wealth between families, though dowries did not give young brides immediate economic power. Older women, however, were often involved in accumulating and administering dowries, since Spanish law allowed women to use their own dowry property to dower their daughters.[8] Mayor Álvarez received half her dowry from her mother and the other half from her aunt (Beceiro Pita: 190–191). Other women used their legal authority as guardians to contribute to their daughters' dowries. María Ponce de León, the Duchess of Gandía and guardian of her nine children after the duke's death in 1670 was given permission by her husband to augment their daughter's dowries when arranging their marriages. One of her daughters entered a convent, but María arranged for her other four daughters to marry a prince, two counts, and a marquis respectively.[9] Noblewomen could also handle the financial arrangements for the marriages of their sons. The Princess of Éboli negotiated a complicated deal in which she sold two houses, bought a town, and settled estates and income on her second son, Diego in order to facilitate his marriage to Luisa de Cárdenas in 1577. The marriage was a disaster, ending in a papal annulment in 1590, but the negotiations reveal the economic power of the groom's mother (Reed: 161–164).

If a noble daughter did not marry, she was likely to enter a convent whose membership tended to be reserved for those who could afford the convent dowry. Noblewomen within convents demonstrated the same ability to manage property and economic resources that characterized their married sisters. Individual nuns insisted that their families fulfill the financial obligations that they depended on, and convents themselves were powerful institutions that managed considerable property and assets (Lehfeldt, "Convents as Litigants": 645; Lehfeldt, *Religious Women*: 47). Even when noblewomen did not formally take religious vows, many of them used their position and wealth to support the religious institutions around them. When Ana de Mendoza, Princess of Éboli, was widowed she took on the patronage of the Church of our Lady in Pastrana (which she had founded jointly with her husband), and the patronage of three local monasteries.[10] In Toledo in her 1604 will, the Countess of Cifuentes used her patronage of the convent of San Pedro Mártir to memorialize her own and her husband's family and to enact the role of spiritual guardian of the orphaned youth of Toledo (Fink De Backer: 188–190). Noblewomen were also active patrons of religious reformers such as Teresa of Ávila, welcoming Teresa into their homes and salons, and founding convents for her new reformed order (Manero Sorolla: 118–119; Weber: 364). Their economic power gave noblewomen roles as abbesses, nuns, and patrons of institutions and people, allowing them to shape religious architecture and culture in early modern Spain.

Often well-married, well-educated, and well-traveled, with experience in the royal court and with local politics, noblewomen were also involved in the literature, art, and culture of the time period both as authors and patrons. Their privileged social status gave them opportunities to make their voices heard, and their economic assets meant that they had the means to support other artists and writers. Nieves Baranda Leturio has found close to 500 Spanish works dedicated to women between 1500 and 1700 (Baranda Leturio: 20). These dedications expressed the bonds of patronage with some of the authors being servants, chaplains, or children's teachers who had connections with the noble patrons. Other works honor women as the wives and partners of powerful men. Some of these dedications, moreover, reveal that women directly financed literary works. The Countess of Castellar financed a biography of Fray Jerónimo Gracián by Andrés del Mármol in 1619, and the Duchess of Feria paid for the printing of Matías de San Francisco's *Relación del viaje espiritual* (Relation of the Spiritual Voyage) in 1643 (Baranda Leturio: 25). Active involvement in the economic activities that supported family wealth and preserved elite status and noble privilege gave elite women a rich life experience.

Elite urbanites

The urban elite in early modern Spain were a small group of propertied citizens who wielded power and influence within their town or city. They were often active in urban government, and as a group they encompassed a mix of social statuses with the possibility of social mobility. In her study of the councilmen (*regidores*) of Madrid during the reign of Philip II, Ana Guerrero Mayllo noted their diverse backgrounds. The majority of councilmen (60%) were *hidalgos*, but another third were non-nobles who had professions such as accountants, notaries, magistrates, judges, and lawyers. On either end of the scale were three titled nobles and a tiny group (5%) of successful merchants and laborers who had become rich (Guerrero Mayllo: 11, 35–41). The fluidity of this group gave women an important role as their dowries, family connections, and economic skills could help their husbands and families advance up the social scale or gain social prestige. Women of this social class shared many of the goals and activities of noblewomen and also displayed awareness of their roles and identities as part of the urban community.

Marriage was a crucial institution for the urban elite who dowered their daughters and pursued carefully constructed marriage strategies to help them advance socially (Kelleher: 36). Marriage facilitated social mobility and transferred power, wealth, and municipal offices between generations. Francisco Martínez was able to join the select ranks of the Madrid councilmen in 1596 thanks to his wife who brought the privilege with her as part of her dowry (Guerrero Mayllo: 37). Merchants in eighteenth-century Cádiz saw marriage as an economic issue which could potentially help them advance their commercial interests (Fernández Pérez: 126–127). As in the nobility, women were active participants in the economic aspects of marriage. When Elinor, daughter of the deceased *honrat* Bernat Borell of Valencia, was married in September of 1423, her mother (also named Elinor) handled the transmission of her 22,000-pound dowry, 8,000 pounds of which came from the elder Elinor's own property (Wessell Lightfoot, "The Projects of Marriage": 344). While the younger Elinor had no active role in this transaction, her widowed mother both administered and helped compile her daughter's dowry.

Marriage itself could be a legally restrictive situation for women whose person and property were subject in many ways to their husbands (Korth and Flusche: 397). Local law codes (*fueros*) varied, but for the most part they dictated that married women should be completely subservient to their husbands. Married women were often legally liable for their husbands' debts while being unable to contract debts of their own, and only women could be prosecuted for committing adultery (Segura Graiño: 128–129). A married woman whose husband had an affair with other women had no legal recourse, and it was not unusual for men to expect their wives to care for and acknowledge their illegitimate children. The first Duke of Infantado (d. 1479) asked his wife to take his illegitimate daughters into her household and "guard, discipline, and honor them" after his death, and other noblemen made similar requests.[11] The practice was common enough that María de Guevara complained about it almost two hundred years later in her treatise offering advice to kings in 1663 (Guevara: 79). In spite of these restrictions and inequalities, however, Castilian law also provided protections for married women and their property that dated back to Visigothic Spain and the seventh-century law code entitled the *Fuero Juzgo* (Korth and Flusche: 397–398). As a result, many married women participated actively in the economic lives of their cities and towns, and even developed public personas and a code of honor that regulated their behavior and ways of thinking (Segura Graiño: 131; Taylor: 157–193).

Married women wielded more power than the law allowed for, in part because the Spanish legal system protected their property rights. The law shielded their dowry and *arras* (the bride gift) from their husbands' creditors, permitted them to inherit from their husbands and their children, and gave them the right to administer their property when widowed (Fink De Backer: 180–182). This gave elite women access to family property, and like their noble counterparts, elite men depended on their wives and widows when managing family property, choosing them as executors of their wills and guardians of their children. In 1619 Joseph Bolero, who had a considerable estate but no title, named his wife María guardian of their children "because I am satisfied that like a good mother she will make the most of, care for, look after, and augment their estate."[12]

Elite women also displayed a strong sense of their identity as urban dwellers with connections to particular cities. Through patronage of urban institutions such as churches and convents, they commemorated loved ones and family members and left traces of their own identities on the fabric of their cities (Fink De Backer: 183). Catalina de la Fuente, wife and then widow of a Toledo councilman, built a church and choir for the Dominican convent Madre de Dios in Toledo in 1594. In her preparations for the new chapel, Catalina stipulated that the arms of her own and her husband's family should be the only ones visible and planned a burial chapel for her illegitimate half-brother Juan de la Fuente (Fink de Backer: 192–193). With commendable daughterly devotion, Francisca de Guzmán of Seville commissioned an altarpiece to honor her parents in 1573. More assertively, Brigida Broche commissioned her own funerary altarpiece in the parish church of San Pedro in Seville in 1584 (King: 105).

Conclusion

Noble and elite women in early modern Spain lived in a world where gender definitions were flexible, responding to social and economic pressure. Women at the upper levels of society had a practical power that challenged patriarchal ideals, as they could act effectively, influence people and actions, and achieve their goals, and because their actions benefited their families, elite men depended on women in times of crisis. In this world, elite women had a decided advantage. The benefits of high social status, a powerful family, judicial privileges, education, and, most of all, access to economic resources placed many elite women in a position to exercise power and authority and to influence society and culture. They had the resources to be leaders. They raised children, managed property, built churches, commissioned art, and wrote. Elite women ranged from the active wives and daughters of urban professionals to the great titled ladies of early modern Spain, but they shared a combination of wealth, expertise, experience, talent, and a strong sense of their own identity which is reflected in the work of Hispanic women writers.

Notes

1. For examples of these, see Guerrero Mayllo.
2. For more on women's education, see Anne J. Cruz in this volume.
3. Magdalena's accounts can be found in the Archivo Histórico de la Real Chancillería de Granada (ARCG), Section 502, cabina 3a, file 404, 1.2.
4. Archivo Histórico Nacional (AHN), Sección Nobleza, Osuna, legajo 540, no. 60.
5. For examples of men choosing their wives as executors, see AHN, Nobleza, Osuna, legajo 1765, no. 1.4; legajo 1762, no. 1.2; legajo 2024, no. 2; legajo 540, no. 2a.
6. AHN, Nobleza, Osuna, legajo 1763, no. 15.2; legajo 2025, no. 13.2; legajo 2025, no. 19.2.
7. AHN, Nobleza, Osuna, legajo 309, no. 16; legajo 497, no. 11b.
8. The *Fuero Juzgo*, the *Leyes de Toro*, and the *Siete Partidas* all permitted women to contribute to their daughters' dowries (Korth and Flusche: 398, 401).
9. AHN, Nobleza, Osuna, legajo 540, no. 73; *Historia genealógica*.
10. AHN, Nobleza, Osuna, legajo 1769, no. 15.1.
11. AHN, Nobleza, legajo 1762, no. 8.1.
12. AHN, Nobleza, legajo 2026, no. 22.

Works cited

Alvar Ezquerra, Alfredo. "Modelos Educativos de Isabel la Católica." *La reina Isabel I y las reinas de España: realidad, modelos e imagen historiográfica. Actas de la VIII Reunión Científica de la Fundación Española de*

Historia Moderna (Madrid, 2–4 de Junio de 2004). Vol. I. Ed. María Victoria López-Cordón Corteza and Gloria Angeles Franco Rubio. Madrid: Gráficas Loureiro, S.L., 2005. 123–136.

Bahamonde Magro, Ángel, and Jesús A. Martínez. *Historia de España, siglo XIX*. Madrid: Cátedra, 1994.

Baranda Leturio, Nieves. "Women's Reading Habits: Book Dedications to Female Patrons in Early Modern Spain." *Women's Literacy in Early Modern Spain and the New World*. Ed. Anne J. Cruz and Rosilie Hernández. Farnham, UK: Burlington, VT: Ashgate, 2011: 19–39.

Beceiro Pita, Isabel and Ricardo Córdoba de la Llave. *Parentesco, poder y mentalidad: La nobleza castellana siglos xii–xv*. Madrid: CSIC, 1990.

Bianchini, Janna. *The Queen's Hand: Power and Authority in the Reign of Berenguela of Castile*. Philadelphia: U Pennsylvania P, 2012.

Casey, James. *Early Modern Spain: A Social History*. London and New York: Routledge, 1999.

Coolidge, Grace E. "Choosing Her Own Buttons: The Guardianship of Magdalena de Bobadilla." *Power and Gender in Renaissance Spain: Eight Women of the Mendoza Family, 1450–1650*. Ed. Helen Nader. Urbana and Chicago: U of Illinois P, 2004: 132–151.

———. *Guardianship, Gender, and the Nobility in Early Modern Spain*. Farnham, UK; Burlington, VT: Ashgate, 2011.

Crawford, Michael J. *The Fight for Status and Privilege in Late Medieval and Early Modern Castile, 1465–1598*. University Park, PA: Pennsylvania State UP, 2014.

Cruz, Anne J. and Maria Galli Stampino, eds. *Early Modern Habsburg Women: Transnational Contexts, Cultural Conflicts, Dynastic Continuities*. Farnham, UK; Burlington, VT: Ashgate, 2013.

Cruz, Jesús. *The Rise of Middle Class Culture in Nineteenth-Century Spain*. Baton Rouge: Louisiana State UP, 2011.

Dadson, Trevor J. "The Education, Books and Reading Habits of Ana de Mendoza y de la Cerda, Princess of Éboli (1540–1592)." *Women's Literacy in Early Modern Spain and the New World*. Ed. Anne J. Cruz and Rosilie Hernández. Farnham, UK: Burlington, VT: Ashgate, 2011: 79–102.

Dandelet, Thomas James. *The Renaissance of Empire in Early Modern Europe*. Cambridge: Cambridge UP, 2014.

Earenfight, Theresa. *The King's Other Body: María of Castile and the Crown of Aragon*. Philadelphia: U Pennsylvania P, 2010.

Elliott, J.H. *Imperial Spain, 1469–1716*. London: Penguin Books, 2002.

Fernández Pérez, Paloma. *El rostro familiar de la metrópoli: Redes de parentesco y lazos mercantiles en Cádiz, 1700–1812*. Madrid: Siglo de Veintiuno de España, 1997.

Fink De Backer, Stephanie. "Constructing Convents in Sixteenth-Century Castile: Toledan Widows and Patterns of Patronage." *Widowhood and Visual Culture in Early Modern Europe*. Ed. Allison Levy. Aldershot, UK; Burlington, VT: Ashgate, 2003: 177–194.

Franganillo, Alejandra. "The Education of an Heir to the Throne: Isabel of Borbón and Her Influence on Prince Baltasar Carlos." *The Formation of the Child in Early Modern Spain*. Ed. Grace E. Coolidge. Farnham, UK; Burlington, VT: Ashgate, 2014: 143–164.

García Fernández, Máximo. *Herencia y patrimonio familiar en la Castilla del antiguo régimen (1650–1834): efectos socioeconómicos de la muerte y la partición de bienes*. Valladolid: Secretariado de Publicaciones Universidad de Valladolid, 1995.

García Hernán, David. *La nobleza en la España moderna*. Madrid: Ediciones Istmo, 1992.

———. "Los grandes de España en época de Felipe II: Los duques de Arcos." Ph.D. dissertation. Universidad Complutense de Madrid, 1992.

———. *La artistocracia en la encrucijada. La alta nobleza y la monarquía de Felipe II*. Córdoba, 2000.

Guerrero Mayllo, Ana. *Familia y vida cotidiana de una elite de poder: los regidores madrileños en tiempos de Felipe II*. Madrid: Siglo Veintiuno de España, 1993.

Guevara, María de. *Warnings to the Kings and Advice on Restoring Spain*. Trans. and ed. Nieves Romero-Díaz. Chicago: U Chicago P, 2007.

Historia genealógica de la illustrissima y nobilissima casa de Borja, con las illustres familias que descendien della, Real Academia de la Historia 9/130, 24 bis. N.d.

Hoffman, Martha K. *Raised to Rule: Educating Royalty at the Court of the Spanish Habsburgs, 1601–1634*. Baton Rouge: Louisiana State UP, 2011.

Howe, Elizabeth Teresa. *Education and Women in the Early Modern Hispanic World*. Farnham, UK: Asghate, 2008.

Kelleher, Marie. "Hers by Right: Gendered Legal Assumptions and Women's Property in the Medieval Crown of Aragon." *Journal of Women's History* 22.2 (2010): 34–55.

King, Catherine E. "Lay Patronage and Religious Art." *Ashgate Companion to Women and Gender*. Ed. Allyson Poska, Jane Couchman, Katherine A. McIver. Farnham, UK; Burlington, VT: Ashgate, 2013: 95–113.

Korth, Eugene H. and Della M. Flusche. "Dowry and Inheritance in Colonial Spanish America: Peninsular Law and Chilean Practice." *The Americas* 43.4 (1987): 395–410.

Ladero Quesada, Miguel Ángel. *Los señores de Andalucía: investigaciones sobre nobles y señoríos en los siglos XIII a XV*. Cádiz: Servicio de Publicaciones de la Universidad de Cádiz, 1998.

Layna Serrano, Francisco. *Historia de Guadalajara y sus Mendoza en los siglos XV y XVI*. Vol. 2. Madrid: Aldus, 1942.

Lehfeldt, Elizabeth. "Convents as Litigants: Dowry and Inheritance Disputes in Early-Modern Spain." *Journal of Social History* 33.3 (Spring 2000): 645–664.

——. *Religious Women in Golden Age Spain: The Permeable Cloister*. Aldershot, VT; Burlington, VT: Ashgate, 2005.

——. "Ruling Sexuality: The Political Legitimacy of Isabel of Castile." *Renaissance Quarterly* 53:1 (2000): 31–56.

Liss, Peggy K. *Isabel the Queen: Life and Times*. 1st ed. Philadelphia: U Pennsylvania P, 1992.

——. *Isabel the Queen: Life and Times*. 2nd ed. Philadelphia: U Pennsylvania P, 2004.

López-Cordón Cortezo, María Victoria. *Reflexiones sobre el proceso de la reina*. Madrid: Abada, 2006.

Lynch, John. *Spain 1516–1598: From Nation State to World Empire*. Oxford: Blackwell, 1991.

Manero Sorolla, María Pilar. "On the Margins of the Mendozas: Luisa de la Cerda and María de San José (Salazar)." In *Power and Gender in Renaissance Spain: Eight Women of the Mendoza Family, 1450–1650*. Ed. Helen Nader. Urbana and Chicago: U Illinois P, 2004: 113–131.

Mitchell, Silvia Z. "Growing Up Carlos II: Political Childhood in the Court of the Spanish Habsburgs." *The Formation of the Child in Early Modern Spain*. Ed. Grace E. Coolidge. Farnham, UK; Burlington, VT: Ashgate, 2014: 189–206.

Nader, Helen. "Introduction." *Power and Gender in Renaissance Spain: Eight Women of the Mendoza Family*. Ed. Helen Nader. Urbana and Chicago: U Illinois P, 2004: 1–26.

——. *The Mendoza Family in the Spanish Renaissance, 1350–1550*. New Jersey: Rutgers UP, 1979.

Oliván Santaliestra, Laura. "'My sister is growing up very healthy and beautiful, she loves me': The Childhood of the *Infantas* María Teresa and Margarita María at Court." *The Formation of the Child in Early Modern Spain*. Ed. Grace E. Coolidge. Farnham, UK; Burlington, VT: Ashgate, 2014: 165–187.

Pastor Zapata, José Luis. *Gandia en la baixa Edat Mitjana: La Vila i el Senyoriu dels Borja*. Gráfiques Colomar, S.A.: Oliva, 1992.

Pérez Samper, María Ángeles. *Isabel la Católica*. Madrid: Plaza & Janés, 2005.

——. *Poder y seducción: grandes damas de 1700*. Madrid: Temas de Hoy, 2003.

Pérez-Toribio, Montserrat. "From Mother to Daughter: Educational Lineage in the Correspondence between the Countess of Palamós and Estefania de Requesens." *Women's Literacy in Early Modern Spain and the New World*. Ed. Anne J. Cruz and Rosilie Hernández. Farnham, UK; Burlington, VT: Ashgate, 2011: 59–77.

Phillips, Carla Rahn. *Ciudad Real, 1500–1750: Growth, Crisis, and Readjustment in the Spanish Economy*. Cambridge: Harvard UP, 1979.

Poska, Allyson M. *Women and Authority in Early Modern Spain: The Peasants of Galicia*. Oxford: Oxford UP, 2005.

Reed, Helen H. "Mother Love in the Renaissance: The Princess of Éboli's Letters to her Favorite Son." *Power and Gender in Renaissance Spain: Eight Women of the Mendoza Family, 1450–1650*. Ed. Helen Nader. Urbana and Chicago: U Illinois P, 2004: 152–176.

Romaniello, Matthew P., and Charles Lipp. "The Spaces of Nobility." In *Contested Spaces of Nobility in Early Modern Europe*. Ed. Matthew P. Romaniello and Charles Lipp. Farnham, UK; Burlington, VT: Ashgate, 2011: 1–10.

Sánchez, Magdalena S. *The Empress, the Queen, and the Nun: Women and Power at the Court of Philip III of Spain*. Baltimore and London: Johns Hopkins UP, 1998.

Segura Graíño, Cristina. "Situación juridica y realidad social de las casadas y viudas en el medieval hispano (Andalucia)." *La condicion de la mujer en la Edad Media; Actas del coloquio celebrado en la Casa de Velázquez del 5–7 de Noviembre de 1984*. Madrid: Casa de Velázquez, 1986: 121–134.

Sperling, Jutta Gisela. "The Economics and Politics of Marriage." *Ashgate Companion to Women and Gender*. Ed. Allyson Poska, Jane Couchman, Katherine A. McIver. Farnham, UK; Burlington, VT: Ashgate, 2013: 213–232.

Taylor, Scott K. *Honor and Violence in Golden Age Spain*. New Haven and London: Yale UP, 2008.

Villalon, L. J. Andrew, "The Law's Delay: The Anatomy of an Aristocratic Property Dispute (1350–1577)." Unpublished Ph.D. dissertation. Yale University, 1984.

———. "St. Teresa's Problematic Patrons." *Journal of Medieval and Early Modern Studies.* 29.2 (1999): 357–379.

Weissberger, Barbara F. *Isabel Rules: Constructing Queenship, Wielding Power.* Minneapolis: U of Minnesota P, 2003.

Wessell Lightfoot, Dana. "The Projects of Marriage: Spousal Choice, Dowries, and Domestic Service in Early Fifteenth-Century Valencia." *Viator* 40.1 (2009): 333–353.

———. *Women, Dowries and Agency: Marriage in Fifteenth Century Valencia.* Manchester and New York: Manchester UP, 2013.

Wyhe, Cordula van, ed. *Isabel Clara Eugenia, Female Sovereignty in the Courts of Madrid and Brussels.* London: Paul Holberton, 2011.

2
WOMEN'S EDUCATION IN EARLY MODERN SPAIN

Anne J. Cruz

Women's education in early modern Spain is a multifaceted topic that must be approached taking into consideration numerous complex factors from the medieval period to the eighteenth century that affected women's learning, such as social, economic, and cultural changes, as well as geographical area, social hierarchy and class status, religion, and ethnicity. Yet another factor that must be considered is the increased circulation of printed works that became available over the two centuries and that encouraged learning (López Vidriero). Even education itself needs to be defined according to its purported purpose, since, while the Spanish educational system for men adhered to identifiable phases—from early schooling to university—for different professions and social levels, women's learning followed no set patterns and, indeed, was often proscribed.[1] Juan Luis Vives, the most well known of the educational theorists of the early modern period, recommended that young girls learn practical household tasks such as sewing and cooking, but that they learn to read for their spiritual benefit only:

> I would not approve nor wish to see an astute, smart woman wastefully reading books that lead the way to evils and away from virtues, chastity, and goodness. But her reading of good books written by holy men who worked diligently to teach others to live good lives like they lived, not only seems to me useful, but even necessary.[2]

Given the breadth of studies on education in general and women's literacy in particular, this chapter attempts only an overview of the various spaces of women's education, from early literacy to cultured and learned forms of knowledge.

In early modern Spain, the process of learning to read—an activity that was considered different from that of writing and thus learned separately—was, for women, oriented mainly toward the consumption of religious texts (Beceiro Pita: 15). Yet middle-class and noble girls who were taught by tutors and prepared for marriage had a higher potential for learning, as they received a more expansive education than young girls who were educated in a convent, some of whom then professed as nuns. Little is known of girls' education whose religious and ethnic background were different from that of Old Christians; as I discuss below, *Judeo-conversas* achieved both literacy and numeracy mainly through home schooling or at the homes of teachers, while Moriscas who had learned Arabic from their mothers, after the War of the Alpujarras (1568–1571), were required to attend schools to learn to read and write Spanish (Esteban: 95).[3] Unless specified otherwise, therefore, this chapter will focus mainly on the educational differences of assimilated and Old Christian women who in turn were distinguished by class status.

Schooling in Spain

Although it varied according to the factors mentioned above, women's education was more widespread in Spain than in other countries.[4] Both religion and the state played a part in expecting a minimal level of literacy: convents taught young girls to read so they could follow religious books such as hours and missals, while secular women were often required to understand and sign their names to legal documents.[5] Although they could not attend universities, once middle-class and aristocratic women learned to read and write, which sometimes included other vernacular languages and even Latin, they had continued opportunities for learning throughout their lives through such means as private libraries, theater, and oral literature. Moreover, the latter two venues, along with literature that was frequently read aloud in households, also contributed to the dissemination of knowledge across social differences, as servants joined in listening to readings.[6] As a concept far more fluid than its Spanish translation of *alfabetización* (alphabetization), which is limited to *primeras letras* or first letters, literacy thus extends beyond primary learning, proving as much a product of cultural appropriation throughout adulthood, as of early schooling.[7] This chapter will discuss educational expectations for young girls and women, and the various methods by which they achieved different levels of literacy in the early modern period.

The basic skills of reading and writing were taught mainly to young girls who had access to schools or tutors, largely those who resided in urban settings. Depending on their social level, they had several options: poor and middle-class girls who lived in towns could attend what were called *escuelas de amigas* (schools run by lay women). There is little information about them, but they were most likely run for taking care of toddlers, as a kind of pre-school for working mothers, and also specifically as schools for young girls. Noting the gendered difference in education, this kind of school is mentioned in "Hermana Marica," a ballad attributed to Góngora, and narrated in the voice of a young boy: "Since tomorrow is a feast day / you won't go to the *amiga* / nor I to my school."[8] These schools for girls functioned as well in New Spain, where the women who operated them needed to be licensed with permission from the parish priest to teach Christian doctrine.[9] In Madrid, while most schools for orphaned and poor girls were founded in the eighteenth century, the Convento de Santa Isabel included a school for girls, called Casa del Recogimiento de Santa Isabel, founded by Philip II's daughter, Isabel Clara Eugenia, in 1595. Another, the Colegio de Nuestra Señora de la Paz, was established for girls who had turned seven years of age at the infamous *Inclusa* orphanage, founded in 1572 (Sherwood: 125). The school was supported by the sales of theater tickets to the corrales de la Cruz and Príncipe (Varey and Davis: 23–24).

Convent schools

Other possibilities for receiving an education were the ubiquitous convent schools, such as those in Salamanca, Zaragoza, Toledo, Valladolid, and Madrid.[10] Besides the Discalced Carmelite convents founded by Saint Teresa that provided for girls' instruction, others concerned themselves with women's education.[11] Under the patronage of Fernando de Silva, Count of Cifuentes, the Franciscan order had, in 1527, established a school for girls at the convent of Belén in Cifuentes (Layna Serrano 135); in 1618, the same order, in their convent of Nuestra Señora de las Misericordias in Oropesa, opened a school under the patronage of the Count of

Oropesa, who donated the dowries of 22 nuns and 13 schoolgirls (Atienza López: 192–193). Called *colegios de doncellas* (schools for young girls), these were supervised by the church and their maintenance and growth depended on the fluctuating economies of patronage, dowries, and conventual interests.[12] Cardinal Juan Martínez Silíceo founded the Colegio de Doncellas Nobles in Toledo in 1551, remaining in operation until the twentieth century (Fink De Backer, *Widowhood*: 272).[13] By contrast, education for boys was offered in public grammar schools called *escuelas de primeras letras* or primary schools, whose teachers in Madrid formed a guild in 1642.[14] Education for both boys and girls began early, usually at five to seven years of age; according to Pilar Pérez Cantó, girls could even attend the *colegios* at the age of three (26). Ironically, given the anxiety that girls' education created among religious, this was the age that the Virgin Mary supposedly left her holy parents to study at the temple, a scene reproduced frequently by early modern painters.[15] Other painters, however, such as Zurbarán, Murillo, Roelas, and Martínez Montañés, depicted her receiving instruction from her mother, another source of education in the home. According to Charlene Villaseñor Black, Zurbarán paints Mary at about eight years old, praying, embroidering, and reading, although she may have learned to read earlier (93).

Given their abundance and numerous locations in urban settings, convent schools were thus the principal sources of literacy and of instruction for most early modern women. In these schools, women from different social classes received religious instruction, learning to read biblical teachings, Catholic doctrine, and saints' lives, among other religious texts. Because reading, whether silent or voiced, also offered a means of prayer to the nuns, it became a necessary function within the convent for both students and professed. The difference between oral and silent prayer was established by means of the separation of words in the late medieval period, after centuries of oral reading (Saenger). Mental prayer, which was promoted by Saint Teresa of Ávila in her convents, encouraged reading in silence. Nuns were allowed specific times for silent reading, both individually and in groups. Convent schools imposed the same kind of daily routine on young girls as on the nuns, since their pedagogical purpose was intended to merge with religious instruction. The daily lessons given the girls on embroidery, sewing, and other handicrafts were comparable to the instruction received in reading, writing, and catechism. Although this kind of education prepared young girls for marriage, it did not offer the same level of instruction as that granted to young boys, whose Latin classes at Jesuit and other religious schools prepared them for university. Indeed, María de Zayas would lament the time girls spent on learning to produce handicrafts yet were not allowed a tutor:

> What reason is there for [men] to be wise and assume that we cannot be? In my opinion, there is no answer other than their obstinacy and insistence on our enclosure and keeping us from having teachers. Therefore, the true cause of our being uneducated is not due to any lack of intellectual capital but to the lack of opportunity. For, if during our childhood, just as we are given cloth to embroider on pillows and designs for our hoops, we would be given books and tutors, we would be as qualified for positions and university posts as men are, and probably even more so, as our nature is colder.[16]

One group of young girls did not avail themselves of convent education; most Judeo-conversas (converted Jewish women) were educated in their home or at a tutor's house. In several cases, Sara Nalle tells us, conversas learned by observing their brother's classes. Given that the Moriscos (converted Muslims) were less acculturated into Spanish society, there is less information about the education of Morisca girls than what we are learning now of Judeo-conversas. As part of the long process of Christian evangelization, Moriscos were required to send their male children to parish schools for three years between the ages of five and eight and to pay the teacher's salary.[17] Morisca girls usually remained within the home; their education consisted mainly of learning to carry out domestic tasks, since many Morisca women fulfilled the roles of wives, slaves, and servants.[18] Some, however, were sought out for their knowledge and practice of the medicinal and magic arts, such as midwifery, circumcision, and incantations or spells (Labarta: 225–226). Because women were charged with passing on cultural traditions and rites, from dances and cooking certain foods to burial preparations, as well as of introducing rudimentary Muslim practices and of teaching Arabic to their children, mothers provided most if not all the instruction their daughters would receive (Labarta: 226–227).

Learning to read

Since literacy depended on the written word, learning to recognize letters was the first step toward reading, followed by syllables, and then words. Students began by distinguishing the forms (*figuras*) of vowels and consonants and learning to spell (*deletrear*), then to form syllables (*ayuntamiento de letras*).[19] Although there is mention of *abecedarios* or simple sheets printed with the alphabet and used as the most basic teaching tool, none has survived (Infantes: 17). To the many *cartillas* or alphabet books that were used to teach reading were frequently added *doctrinas* or catechisms containing Catholic doctrine, as the teaching of reading converged with that of religious doctrine. Some of the earliest texts that circulated in the early modern period are the *Cartilla y doctrina en romance del arzobispo de Granada para enseñar niños a leer* (1506) (Alphabet book in Spanish by the Archbishop of Granada to teach children to read) and *Cartilla para mostrar a leer a los mozos. Con la doctrina cristiana que se canta "Amados hermanos"* (1526) (Alphabet book to show boys how to read. With the Christian doctrine to be sung to "Beloved Brethren"). Other textbooks dedicated to elementary instruction included *diálogos de la doctrina cristiana* (Dialogues of Christian Doctrine), *artes de escribir* (arts of writing), and *lecciones de gramárica* (grammar lessons) (Infantes: 16).

Books such as the more advanced *Arte para aprender a leer y escrevir perfectamente en romance y latín* (1532) (Art with which to learn to read and write perfectly in Spanish and Latin), whose introduction comments on what Prince Philip, then 5 or 6 years old, should learn, were usually written for boys' instruction.[20] However, in cases where siblings of both sexes were taught by humanist tutors in their homes, girls would have received a similar education.[21] As more information is gleaned about the education of girls from higher social levels, as in the case of the Mendoza family, the notion that Latin was a language learned only by young boys needs to be corrected accordingly. Among the women who received a humanist education equal to that of a man's, are the classical scholars Beatriz Galindo (1465?–1534); María Pacheco (1496?–1531); Luisa Sigea (1522–1560); Juliana Morell (1594–1653); and Ana Francisca Abarca de Bolea (1602–1686).[22]

Aristocratic and royal education

While convents took in poor girls as well as those who could pay dowries for their instruction, children of wealthy non-nobles and nobles alike could also study in the home with their mothers or with tutors hired for the purpose of serving as the child's teacher and companion. Tutors represented an expensive addition to a household, so the social and economic level of girls taught by them was a distinguishing factor. And since mothers were usually in charge of arranging for children's education and were themselves highly educated, it is not surprising that they would take on that role. In her study of the iconography of the education of the Virgin Mary, for example, Emilie Bergmann comments that the child's "acquisition of literacy through mother-daughter bonding over a book suggests a maternal genealogy of wisdom, as well as acknowledging the role of mothers as teachers" (244). Although the early modern Spanish nobility represented less than ten percent of the population, according to Grace Coolidge, the country had the highest proportion of noble families in Europe (9). Because of their level of education, educated noble and royal women left a disproportionate mark in early modern politics, society, and culture. As Helen Nader states of the eight female members of the Mendoza family about whom she writes, for example, they "managed, bought, and sold family property [. . .] they wrote poetry, letters, and memoirs [. . .] endowed and supervised hospitals, built funerary chapels for themselves and their husbands, [. . .] initiated religious reforms and engaged in political activities at the highest levels of government. In short, Mendoza women displayed competencies and initiative that contradicted both the law and patriarchal assumptions about women's inferiority" (3).[23]

No noblewoman could have carried out such activities without having received an exceptional level of education, yet these women's childhoods remain little known. We learn through a servant's testimony that the motherless María Pacheco, one of the leaders of the Comunero rebellion, was educated by her father, who hired humanists to teach her and her brother Latin, Greek, math, history, poetry, and Scripture (Fink De Backer, "Rebel": 72). Undoubtedly, the Mendoza women's social status and wealth separated them from those who were of lower status, but women of all levels of society contributed to the formation of the family economy and welfare by managing a household, and numerous women contributed to society through their interest in charity and education (Nader: 5–6). Noblewomen took serious interest in the care of young girls and children's education: Brianda de Mendoza y Luna founded a girl's school in 1524 in Guadalajara (Coolidge: 73); and Blanca de la Cerda, together with her husband, Fernando de Silva, cofounded the de Doncellas de Belén in Cifuentes (Fink de Backer, *Widowhood*: 272). Inés de Zúñiga y Velasco, and wife of the Count-Duke of Olivares, asked the Jesuits for instructors to teach the children of Galicia to read and write "as it was the most basic need for other arts and most lacking in that land."[24] One book written by a noblewoman concerned with children's education is that of the Countess of Aranda, Luisa de Padilla's *Nobleza virtuosa* (Virtuous Nobility) whose pseudonymous author presents it as a "Cartilla para instruir niños nobles" (Alphabet book to instruct noble children).[25]

Royal children were educated according to their high station, with no expense spared to contract humanists and clerics as their teachers. Their early childhood was entrusted to the care of noblewomen, called *ayas*, similar to a governess; as they matured, a male *ayo* was assigned to serve administrative or public events, and often were also in charge of their teaching and as surrogate parents.[26] Queen Isabel of Castile (1451–1504) is the most famous example of a mother-educator; to educate her four daughters and one son, she hired two of the most well-known humanists in Italy: Pietro Martire d'Anghiera and Lucio Marineo Siculo (Salvador Miguel: 218–219). Both were in charge also of educating young male nobles, as the former founded an academy by order of the queen.[27] Isabel was also responsible for Antonio de Nebrija's translation of his Latin grammar into Spanish so that, as the grammarian stated, "religious women and young unmarried women could learn some Latin without having to rely on male teachers."[28] She also hired Beatriz Galindo, known as "la Latina" (The Latinist) for her command of the language, to teach her and her daughters. The Infantas were educated by Alessandro Geraldini, who penned a life of Catherine of Alexandria and was later the first bishop of Santo Domingo, as well as the religious Diego de Deza, Pedro de Ampudia, and Andrés de Miránda, all of whom were well remunerated (Aram: 49; Valdivieso: 271–272). The young girls were instructed in reading since their seventh birthday; Juana of Castile, at ten years of age, owned Boethius's *De consolatione* and composed poems in Latin (Aram: 50–51). The interest of the Catholic queen's daughters in education did not abate when they grew up and married into other courts; it was not coincidental that Vives would write his *Education of a Christian Woman* at the request of Catherine of Aragón, intended for her and Henry VIII's daughter, Mary Tudor. Impressed by her knowledge of literature, Erasmus said of Catherine, "she is astonishingly well read, far beyond what would be surprising in a woman."[29] María of Aragón, who herself had been educated by Vives and Beatriz Galindo, also prepared her daughter well: Isabel of Portugal, Charles V's future wife, was highly educated and fluent in four languages. She took the need to educate young girls to heart by promoting and patronizing schools in New Spain for indigenous girls (Vega and Cárdenas de Vega: 24).

Charles and Isabel's younger daughter, Juana of Portugal, was educated along with her brother, Prince Philip; like him, she was well trained in literature, history, and, especially, music (Cruz, "Juana": 105–106). Their older sister, María of Austria, Holy Roman Empress, was the patron of composer Tomás Luis de Victoria, and had great influence over her sons, emperors Rudolf and Matthias. Philip II's two daughters, Isabel Clara Eugenia (1566–1633) and Catalina Micaela (1567–1597), were educated at court under the supervision of the Duchess of Alba, who had been their mother, Isabel de Valois's lady-in-waiting, after her death in 1568. Both sisters learned Latin, French, and Portuguese, the languages of their dynastic inheritance (Albaladejo Martínez: 118). As part of their court upbringing, they also took singing and dancing lessons and learned to play instruments, mainly the harp, viol, and guitar (Albaladejo Martínez: 119). Other entertainments included attending plays and masques, poetical jousts, bullfights, and *juegos de cañas* (horse-riding competitions). Although they received conventional instruction in primary letters, new systems of writing were devised as they grew older. These were designed as "games of letters" and small memory books, which could be written on and erased.[30] One form of learning, however, was not presented as a game, but as a means to expand the Infantas' knowledge of government. When traveling to Simancas, Philip would immerse himself in the archives. He would select the documents copied by the clearest handwriting, and send them to his daughters for their reading practice and so they might grasp a sense of government policies.[31]

Other pastimes, although not strictly pedagogical, also granted certain knowledge and skills to royal daughters: María Teresa of Austria, Philip IV's daughter with Isabel of Borbón, enjoyed plays at court and even assumed various roles. For the arrival of her stepmother and cousin, Mariana of Austria, to the Spanish court, she played the role of Jupiter, god of Olympus, which offered a lesson in Greek mythology.[32] Her half-sister, Margarita María of Austria, also enjoyed theater, composing a play complete with verse and coplas, which she staged in private at the Buen Retiro for the king (Oliván Santaliestra: 182). As Oliván Santaliestra points out, however, although they received instruction in reading and writing, and also learned dancing and playing musical instruments, the infantas' education was directed primarily toward political training, civility, and religious cultivation in preparation for a dynastic marriage at a foreign court (183).

Women's literacy rates

While the overall percentage of women who achieved basic literacy—the ability to read and to sign their names—remained low in comparison with that of men, recent quantification of women's signatures, considered the most common method of gauging rates of alphabetization in the early modern period, has proved that women's literacy levels were higher than what had been thought in the past.[33] One successful method has been to measure literacy rates by assigning women's socio-economic status to that of their husbands. In Madrid and Valladolid, for example, women married to men who held certain occupations such as merchants, secretaries, surgeons, and accountants were more literate than those from working and artisan classes, who could not sign their names, while wives of men in the legal profession had the highest rate (62%) of alphabetization.[34] Geographical location has proved crucial in determining levels of literacy: women outside Madrid and Valladolid were not as well educated. Sara Nalle's research of women's wills in Cuenca demonstrates that while male literacy was similar to those cities, only 12% of women could sign their testaments.[35] Of the few who were literate, 70% were wives of town officials, lawyers, and local nobles.

Inquisition documents and trials from criminal courts, which are also used to quantify literacy, render similar results.[36] When the women were from rural areas and/or assigned lower occupations, their level of literacy dropped considerably. In contrast, levels of education rose markedly for urban women, especially conversas, who were often involved in family businesses. Nalle's studies of Inquisition documents demonstrate that in the seventeenth century, literacy was a high priority for newly arrived Luso-conversas in Cuenca, whose fathers or husbands were merchants, bankers, or of other professions ("Literacy and Education"). Indeed, with a 40% literacy rate, Portuguese Judeo-conversa women were even more highly educated than conversas in Spain.

Expanding knowledge

Learning to read and write opened many worlds to women, enriching their lives and allowing them to contribute to early modern cultural production, from communicating with their families through letters, organizing their households, and writing their own memoirs, to composing literature, plays, and treatises, and participating in cultural, economic, and scientific activities. Some women continued to learn throughout their lives, such as Queen Isabel, who studied Latin as an adult with Beatriz Galindo, and nuns who learned how to read and write after they professed in the convent. Additionally, although not all literate women continued to learn and contribute to written culture beyond their childhood, and it is well known that numerous moral treatises opposed women's education,[37] middle-class and aristocratic women had access to books and other forms of knowledge, such as oral literature, art, and theater from the time they were children. Nieves Baranda Leturio points out that while there were no books written specifically for children's entertainment, as boys and girls were avid spectators and listeners, oral literature, such as stories read aloud, sermons, and plays, facilitated learning beyond their schooling. Young girls could and often did avail themselves of saints' lives, romances of chivalry, and *novelle* as their reading material (Baranda Leturio, "Una literatura": 131–132, 138). As we know, Saint Teresa of Ávila famously rejected her early attraction to novels of chivalry, yet these remained influential in her later writings (Slade). And although children were not allowed in the public corrales, where plays were staged, those who attended convent schools were likely to watch the convent plays put on by the nuns. Moreover, as we have discussed, noble and royal women took part in plays and masks at court. The young Isabel de Valois, for instance, often staged masques with her ladies in waiting that were based on literary episodes.

Noble and royal women were also privileged in holding collections of books and art from a very young age, as girls raised in humanist households enjoyed family libraries that remained at their disposal as adults. Again, Isabel of Castile is exemplary, as she owned one of the most impressive libraries in Europe (Sánchez Cantón, *Libros*; Ruiz García, *Los libros*). Inheriting her father's collection of 400 works, she ordered books for her court in several languages that were clearly intended for her children's reading (Cátedra and Rojo: 77). Her own books included mainly religious treatises, not counting those on governing and state matters (Ruiz García,

"Las prácticas"). Although exceptional cases, the noblewomen Mencía de Mendoza (1508–1554) and Ana de Mendoza y de la Cerda, Princess of Éboli (1540–1592) had access to their great family libraries, and often collected books themselves.[38] Mencía inherited her father's outstanding library of 632 volumes, which were divided into the categories of philosophy, literature, religion, medicine, history, general knowledge, cosmography, law, science and the arts, and "various" (Sánchez Cantón, *Biblioteca*). She read books generally proscribed to women, such as Ovid's *Metamorphoses* and *Art of Love*, and Erasmus's *Adagia*. Also a member of the powerful Mendoza clan, Ana de Mendoza received an excellent education at home, possibly with tutors; moreover, her mother, famous for her learning, possessed a library of 288 books, with which Ana may very well have been familiar. Trevor Dadson states that, from the inventory's first page on, the books listed threw down "the gauntlet to the authorities who tried, with little success, to limit what females could and should read," given the number of novels of chivalry included (Dadson: 87). Classics were well represented, with Homer, Thucydides, Ovid, Cicero, Vergil, Seneca, Juvenal, Catullus, Martial, Palautus, and Terence, as well as the Italian authors Petrarch and Castiglione. Other works included historical and political treatises, legal texts, books of devotion, and educational works (Dadson: 90–91). Another noblewoman, María de Guevara, Countess of Escalante, demonstrates her preference for historical narratives, distinguishing between primary and secondary sources as she reads documents from her family archives: "This is the truth of what I have been able to acquire and know, both from the histories I have read as from the original documents that I have in my archives, which go back over three hundred years."[39]

Non-noble wives also benefited from their husbands' book collections; Pedro Cátedra and Anastasio Rojo have combed the inventories of 278 women in the Valladolid archives between 1529 and 1599 whose husbands held government, medical, legal, banking, merchant, or artisanal occupations, to show that their libraries, similarly to those of noblewomen's, included a wide variety of books, from the bible and spiritual treatises and hagiographies, to prose fiction, including Boccaccio's *Decameron*, Rojas's *Celestina*, Montemayor's *Diana*, and Cervantes's *Galatea*. Although far fewer than religious books, these and others of poetry by such renowned Italian poets as Petrarch, Dante, and Sannazaro, and Spanish poets Mena, Encina, Boscán, Garcilaso, and Ercilla could also be found among the collections (Cátedra and Rojo: 160–161). Miscellanous texts, from classical authors Homer, Aristotle, Seneca, Cicero, Juvenal, and Ovid, to Renaissance writers Erasmus, Alciato, Castiglione, Mexía, Luján and Pérez de Moya, as well as books on music, mathematics, navigation, architecture, history, and painting, give proof of the wide variety of readings available. While, as Carmen Álvarez Márquez writes, it is difficult to know for sure whether the books were read by women, the fact alone that they bought, sold, inventoried, and inherited as part of the household confirms that books were considered essential belongings to all members of the family.

Carmen Álvarez Márquez writes that in Seville, non-noblewomen's main reading material tended to be religious, yet there was also interest in books of entertainment. The following is a brief list of non-aristocratic women who nevertheless had numerous books in their possession. Ana de Deza receives in 1576 from her brother, Diego de Deza, the Bishop of Coria, a donation including a total of 120 books, along with her own, making her the second-largest female owner of books, after the widow María de los Reyes, who possesses 250 books in Latin and Spanish (23). However, other women owned books of chivalry, such as María de Sedano and the conversa Inés de Jerez, who owned both the *Guarino Mesquino* and Aesop's *Fables*, while Inés de Alfaro, the printer Jacobo Cromberger's widow, possessed the *History of Captain Hernando d'Avalos* and the *Celestina* (Álvarez Márquez: 26). The eight books belonging to Juana Jiménez Ponce were almost equally divided between religious and secular, among them, the *Flos sanctorum*, Torquemada's *Jardín de flores curiosas*, and Kempis's *Contemptus mundi*, but also Boscán and Garcilaso's poetry, Montemayor's *Diana*, and the *Celestina*.

Future research

While much knowledge has been gained about women's education, there is still more to investigate regarding the methods applied toward learning by religious and secular, and non-noble and aristocratic young girls. Did most girls learn from the same books as boys? Were there special texts for young women? What kind of political instruction did noble and royal daughters receive? We know of women's reading practices and book collecting by the research done of post-mortem inventories of secular women. However, more studies still need to be made regarding the kinds of collections archived in convents. And although women were the dedicatees of many books and patrons of writers, as Nieves Baranda Leturio has pointed out, what was the author's main purpose in dedicating books to them?[40]

Perhaps the area least studied with regard to women's education is their knowledge of early modern scientific methods. The work of Cristina Borderías, Montserrat Cabré, Isabel Morant, and Teresa Ortiz Gómez, among others, has contributed richly to the historiography of medieval and early modern women and science.[41] Research has also been done on Oliva Sabuco de Nantes, whose extraordinary book on a new medical philosophy was dedicated to Philip II, yet who is still under suspicion as its legitimate author (Buxó; Pomata). Very little has been written about her and other women's introduction to early modern scientific knowledge. And although we know that women minorities such as Gypsies and Moriscas in early modern Spain were persecuted for their practice of magic, the crossover between this knowledge and that of the medical arts is one that would be of great interest, since both were passed on from mothers to daughters. And as a final possibility for future research, the correspondence between mothers and daughters and that between women friends is a significant source of information not only on women's education and pedagogy, but on early modern family and gender relations.[42] As family archives are made available to scholars, more letters will surely surface.

Notes

1 For general education in Spain, see Negrín Fajardo, Kagan, and Nalle, "Literary and Culture."
2 "Yo por mi parte no aprobaría ni querría ver a la mujer astuta y sagaz en mal leer en aquellos libros que abren camino a las maldades y desencaminan a las virtudes y a la honestidad y bondad. Pero que lea buenos libros compuestos por santos varones, los cuales pusieron tanta diligencia en enseñar a los otros bien vivir como ellos vivieron, esto me parece no solo útil, más aún necesario" (Vives fol. 5v). All translations are mine unless otherwise noted.
3 "Reading and writing Arabic be removed from them, and orders given so they will learn the reign's vulgar tongue and abandon Arabic, and for this there should be schools to teach boys and girls" (se les quite el leer y escrivir en arábigo y se de orden como aprendan la lengua vulgar del Reyno porque dexen la arábiga, y para esto aya escuelas para abezalles a los niños y a las niñas) (AGS, leg. 3291, qtd. in Esteban 94). From 1525, schools for Morisco boys were founded in an effort to integrate them into Catholic practices (Lea 142–148; Medina). Although Charles V had decreed in 1538 that the Morisco boy's school in Valencia be expanded to open one for Morisca girls, it will not be until 1606 that Moriscas enroll in the convent of Santa Úrsula (Esteban 102). Morisco children under seven years of age (and at times, 12) were assimilated into Old Christian families and not expelled with their parents during the Morisco expulsion, 1609–1614 (Esteban 87–89).
4 See Luna 105, who cites Francesco Agostino della Chiesa's *Theatro delle donne letterate* (1620); and Garrett Mattingly: "the fuller participation of women was one of the chief differences of the Spanish Renaissance" (qtd. in Howe 44).

5 Earlier studies of early modern education in Spain focused mainly on that of males. According to Kagan, no more than 10–15% of the Spanish population could read and write, based on the percentage of the nobility and clerks at the beginning of the sixteenth century, to whom these skills became essential (xxix); Nalle's classic study, "Literacy and Culture in Early Modern Castile," greatly modified these numbers according to area, years, social standing, and gender: in 1510, only one man out of eleven tried by the Inquisition could read; the next generation jumped from one out of four, and literacy in Cuenca increased to 54% for males born between 1571 and 1590 (70). In women's case, "The most literate Castilian women came from Madrid, where in 1650 one quarter of female testators could sign their wills" ("Literacy and Culture" 69). Signing was considered proof of writing ability, but not necessarily of knowledge of cultured or literary forms.
6 See Frenk, *Entre la voz*; and "La ortografía."
7 For the English application of the term, see Ferguson and Suzuki; the authors suggest "literacies" as a better term by which to discuss its various definitions (575).
8 "Mañana que es fiesta, / no irás tu a la amiga / ni yo iré a la escuela" (cited in Revuelta Guerrero and Rufino Caro, 160). For a view of *amiga* schools from the sixteenth through the nineteenth century in Spain, see Revuelta Guerrero and Cano González, and Cano González. The curriculum did not vary much through the years: "in the cities, [the girls] learn to read, write, embroider, and draw" (En las ciudades aprenden a leer, escribir, el bordado y el dibujo) (Revuelta Guerrero and Cano González, 176).
9 The women also required permission in writing to operate the schools. The priest's license ensured that they "led a good life and customs, and their baptismal certificate corroborated their cleanliness of blood" (Larroyo: 121). See also Gonzalbo Aizpuru.
10 Baranda Leturio ("L'éducation") lists, among others, the Colegio de las Once Mil Vírgenes in Salamanca (1518); convent of Franciscan tertiaries in Guadalajara (1524); Colegio de las Vírgenes, Zaragoza (1531); Colegio de doncellas vírgenes de Nuestra Señora de los Remedios, Toledo (1551); Colegio de doncellas nobles de Nuestra Señora de la Asunción, Valladolid (1589); Colegio de Nuestra Señora de las Vírgenes, Guadalajara (1591); Colegio de huérfanas in Santiago de Compostela (1600); Colegio de la Presentación de Leganés, Madrid (1603); Colegio de la Inmaculada Concepción, Granada (1607); and Colegio del Corpus Christi, Murcia (1610).
11 For an extensive study of the more than 2,000 convents founded in early modern Spain that, however, does not specify which included schools for girls, see Atienza López. Knox's study on convents founded by Irish nuns in Spain is sorely lacking in documentation and its conclusions remain entirely speculative.
12 For more information, see my "Introduction" in *Women's Literacy*.
13 For more information on *colegios de doncellas*, see Graña Cid.
14 The guild was named "Hermandad de San Casiano;" see Cotarelo y Mori, vol. I, 218–228. For contracts signed in early modern Seville between male teachers and their pupils, see Álvarez Márquez. For *escuelas de primeras letras* in Pamplona, see Laspalas Pérez, who gives a breakdown of the numbers of teachers and their students in numerous cities of early modern Spain (185–186).
15 Villaseñor Black quotes Francisco Pacheco's *El arte de la pintura*, in which he describes Mary as "three years old, some saying even younger" (585). She studies the "Presentation at the Temple" at three and Mary's betrothal to Joseph at twelve as reflecting the ages of real girls from noble families who were sent to the convent and married (96).
16 "Qué razon hay para que ellos sean sabios y presuman que nosotras no podemos serlo? Esto no tiene, a mi parecer, más respuesta, que su impiedad o tiranía en encerrarnos y no darnos maestros. Y así, la verdadera causa de no ser las mujeres doctas no es defecto del caudal, sino falta de la aplicación. Porque si en nuestra crianza, como nos ponen el cambray en las almohadillas y los dibujos en el bastidor, nos dieran libros y preceptores, fuéramos tan aptas para los puestos y para las cátedras, como los hombres, y quizá más agudas, por ser de natural más frío." Zayas, "Al que leyere," *Novelas amorosas y ejemplares* (159–160). Galenic humoral theory stated that women were cold and moist (Aughterson: 42).
17 Besides official schools, since 1502, Catholic diooceses and Franciscan and Dominican orders assumed the role of evangelizing Morisco children by teaching Catholic doctrine (Fernández Chaves and Pérez García: 359).
18 Many Moriscas worked outside the home as well in the silk industry, picking olives, and as washer-women and bakers (Labarta: 230).
19 This method was employed across early modern Europe; see Saez: 170.
20 The *Arte* was written by the Erasmian humanist Bernabé Bustos, tutor to the pages at Charles V's court (Redondo: 77).
21 For examples of these books, see Infantes, especially 19–23.

22 On Galindo and Pacheco, see Márquez de la Plata; on Sigea, see Baranda Leturio ("Luisa Sigea"); and on Abarca de Bolea, see Campo Guiral. Morell was unusual in that she was the first woman to have received a university degree in Avignon; she later professed in the Dominican convent of Avignon (Lamy: 23; Séguin: 48–50, 125–126).
23 For a broader view of their family relations and social networks, see the encyclopedic tome on twenty-eight Mendoza women by Alegre Carvajal.
24 "Pide la Condesa de Monterrey a los jesuitas para un colegio personas que enseñen a los niños de dicho Condado y Estado a leer y escribir por ser como es el fundamento más necesario para las otras artes y de que hay más falta en aquella tierra" (cited by Martínez 34). No doubt this instruction was meant for young boys as instruction was to be given by the Jesuits.
25 Despite writing for children's education, Padilla herself was childless. See Bergmann's chapter in this volume.
26 Hoffman (29–30). See her excellent book on the rearing of Philip III's children.
27 According to d'Anghiera, the queen was very pleased with the academy (see his epistle 113, cited in Cro).
28 "Para que las mugeres religiosas y vírgenes dedicadas a Dios sin participación de varones pudiessen conocer algo de la lengua latina" (*Introducciones Latinas—contrapuesto el romance al latin* [Salamanca: 1486]). Cited in Fantazzi: 24.
29 Cited by Starkey, who nevertheless reproaches Catherine's education for having taught her courtly love poetry (17).
30 The book by Pedro de Guevara was titled *Nueva y sutil invención en seys instrumentos intitulado juego y exercicio de letras de las seren ísimas Infantas doña Ysabel y doña Catalina de Austria* (New and subtle invention in six instruments entitled game and exercise of letters of the Most Serene Infantas Doña Isabel and Doña Catalina of Austria). See Martínez Hernández: 29.
31 In a letter to Philip II's secretary Juan Vázquez de Molina, the Simancas archivist Diego de Ayala writes that "y aunque está su Majestad en Valladolid pide papeles a mi hijo y se los lleva para que los lea la serenísima Infanta, que huelga ponerla en negocios" (And although His Majesty is in Valladolid, he asks my son for documents and he takes them so the most serene Infanta may read them, as he enjoys involving her in [government] business). Information generously sent me by Julia Teresa Rodríguez Diego, Director of the Archivo General de Simancas, July 10, 2014.
32 Oliván Santaliestra: 173.
33 For the significance of methods of quantification, see Viñao Frago, and Nalle "Literacy and Education."
34 See Rojo Vega. Nalle's most recent work shows that these occupations were held mainly by conversos, demonstrating the high literacy level of conversa women ("Literacy and Education"). This section is considerably indebted to Nalle's research.
35 Nalle, "Literacy and Education."
36 According to Nalle, the low rates for women who appeared in inquisitorial courts, which varied from a high of 22% in Andalucía to a low of 0% in Toledo, were due to their lower socio-economic stratum ("Literacy and Education").
37 See, for instance, Pedro Sánchez's *Árbol de consideración y varia doctrina*, which argues that men should not marry a woman who can write and not reject one who cannot read (qtd. in Cátedra and Rojo: 54).
38 See Cruz, "Reading" and Dadson, respectively.
39 "Esto es la verdad de lo que he podido adquirir y saber, así por las historias que he leído como por los papeles originales que tengo en mi archivo, que son de más de trescientos años a esta parte" (Baranda Leturio, *Cortejo a lo prohibido*: 52).
40 On dedications to women patrons, see Baranda Leturio, "Women's Reading Habits."
41 See studies by these critics listed in the works cited.
42 See Pérez-Toribio for correspondence between the Countess of Palamós and her daughter. See also Vanessa de Cruz in this volume.

Works cited

Aguilera y Arjona, A. "La caridad en Madrid. Guía de los establecimientos benéficos oficiales y privados." *Por Esos Mundos* 7. 2 (julio 1906): 51–60.
Albaladejo Martínez, María. "Las infantas Isabel Clara Eugenia y Catalina Micaela: modelos de la perfecta princesa educada e instruida." *Anales de Historia del Arte* 24, No. Esp. (Diciembre 2014): 115–127.

Álvarez Márquez, Ma. Carmen. "Mujeres lectoras en el siglo XVI en Sevilla." *Historia. Instituciones. Documentos* 31 (2004): 19–40.

———. "La enseñanza de las primeras letras y el aprendizaje de las artes del libro en el siglo XVI en Sevilla." *Historia. Instituciones. Documentos* 22 (1995): 39–85.

Apoyo al Desarrollo de Archivos y Bibliotecas de México. www.adabi.org.mx/content/Notas.jsfx?id=781

Aram, Bethany. *La reina Juana. Gobierno, piedad y dinastía*. Madrid: Marcial Pons, 2001.

Arroyo, Francisco. *Historia comparada de la educación en México*. Porrúa: México, 1962.

Atienza López, Ángela. *Tiempos de conventos: una historia social de las fundaciones en la España moderna*. Madrid: Marcial Pons, 2008.

Aughterson, Kate, ed. *Renaissance Woman: A Sourcebook: Constructions of Femininity in England*. New York: Routledge, 1995.

Baranda Leturio, Nieves. "Women's Reading Habits: Book Dedications to Female Patrons in Early Modern Spain." *Women's Literacy in Early Modern Spain and the New World*. Ed. Anne J. Cruz and Rosilie Hernández. Farnham, UK; Burlington, VT: Ashgate, 2011: 19–39.

———. "L'éducation des femmes dans l'Espagne post-tridentine." *Genre et identités aux Pays-Bas Méridionaux. L'éducation religieuse des femmes après le concile de Trente*. Louvain-la-Neuve: Bruylant-Academia, 2010: 29–63.

———. "Luisa Sigea, la brillante excepción femenina." *Melchor Cano y Luisa Sigea: dos figuras del renacimiento español*. Ed. Miguel Ángel Pérez Prieto. Tarancón: Seminario de Estudios Renacentistas Conquenses, 2008: 131–151.

———. *Cortejo a lo prohibido: lectoras y escritoras en la España moderna*. Madrid: Arco, 2005.

———. "¿Una literatura para la infancia en el siglo XVII?" *La formation de l'enfant en Espagne aux XVIE et XVIIe siècles*. Ed. Augustin Redondo. Paris: Presses de la Sorbonne Nouvelle, 1996: 125–139.

Beceiro Pita, Isabel. "La relación de las mujeres castellanas con la cultura escrita (siglo XIII–inicios del XVI)." *Libro y lectura en la Península Ibérica y América: siglos XIII a XVIII*. Ed. Antonio Castillo Gómez. Salamanca: Junta de Castilla y León, 2003: 15–52.

Bergmann, Emilie L. "Learning at her Mother's Knee? Saint Anne, the Virgin Mary, and the Iconography of Women's Literacy." *Women's Literacy in Early Modern Spain and the New World*. Ed. Anne J. Cruz and Rosilie Hernández. Farnham, UK; Burlington, VT: Ashgate, 2011: 243–261.

Bernabé Martínez, Bartolomé "Valores pedagógicos de las *Artes de leer* y *Doctrinas* hispanas de los XVII y XVIII." *De las primeras letras. Cartillas españolas para enseñar a leer del siglo XVII*. Ed. Víctor Infantes and Ana Martínez Pereira. Vol. 1. Salamanca: Ediciones Universidad de Salamanca, 2003: 31–48.

Buxó, José Pascual. "Oliva Sabuco de Nantes (siglo XVI): sabiduría femenina y condena social." *Destiempos* 19 (marzo-abril 2009): 93–110.

Cabré, Montserrat. "Women or Healers?: Household Practices and the Categories of Health Care in Late Medieval Iberia." *Bulletin of the History of Medicine* 82.1 (January 2008): 18–51.

Campo Guiral, María de los Ángeles. *Doña Ana Francisca Abarca de Bolea*. Zaragoza: Gobierno de Aragón, Departamento de Cultura y Educación, 1993.

Capel Martínez, Rosa María. "Mujer y educación en el Antiguo Régimen." *Historia de la Educación* 26 (2007): 85–110.

Cátedra, Pedro M., and Anastasio Rojo. *Bibliotecas y lecturas de mujeres, siglo XVI*. Salamanca: Instituto de Historia del Libro y de la Lectura, 2004.

Ciscar Pallarés, Eugenio. "Cruz o firma en la práctica procesal (Contribución a la medición de la alfabetización en el Reino de Valencia, siglos XVI–XVIII)," *Estudis: revista de historia moderna*, 24 (1998): 37–62.

Coolidge, Grace. *Guardianship, Gender, and the Nobility in Early Modern Spain*. Farnham, UK; Burlington, VT: Ashgate, 2011.

Cotarelo y Mori, Emilio. *Diccionario biográfico y bibliográfico de calígrafos españoles*. Madrid: Imp. de Revista de Archivos, Bibliotecas y Museos. 2 vols., 1913–1916.

Cro, Stelio. "Pedro Mártir de Anglería's *De Orbe Novo*." *Topos y Tropos* 3 (2005): 1–17.

Cruz, Anne J., "Introduction." *Women's Literacy in Early Modern Spain and the New World*. Ed. Anne J. Cruz and Rosilie Hernández. Farnham, UK; Burlington, VT: Ashgate, 2011: 1–16.

———. "Reading over Men's Shoulders: Noblewomen's Libraries and Reading Practices." *Women's Literacy in Early Modern Spain and the New World*. Ed. Anne J. Cruz and Rosilie Hernández. Farnham, UK; Burlington, VT: Ashgate, 2011: 41–58.

———. "Juana of Austria, Patron of the Arts and Regent of Spain, 1554–59." *The Rule of Women in Early Modern Europe*. Ed. Anne J. Cruz and Mihoko Suzuki. Urbana-Champaign: U Illinois P, 2009: 103–122.

Dadson, Trevor J. "The Education, Books and Reading Habits of Ana de Mendoza y de la Cerda, Princess of Éboli (1540–1592)." *Women's Literacy in Early Modern Spain and the New World*. Ed. Anne J. Cruz and Rosilie Hernández. Farnham, UK; Burlington, VT: Ashgate, 2011: 79–102.
Fantazzi, Charles. "Introduction: Prelude to the Other Voice in Vives." *Juan Luis Vives. The Education of a Christian Woman: A Sixteenth-Century Manual*. Ed. And trans. Charles Fantazzi. Chicago: U of Chicago P, 2000: 1–42.
Ferguson, Margaret, and Mihoko Suzuki. "Women's Literacies and Social Hierarchy in Early Modern England." *Literature Compass* 12/11 (2015): 575–590.
Fernández Cháves, Manuel, and Rafael M. Pérez García. *En los márgenes de la ciudad de Dios: Moriscos en Sevilla*. Valencia: Universitat de València, 2009.
Fink De Baker, Stephanie. *Widowhood in Early Modern Spain: Protectors, Proprietors, and Patrons*. Leiden: Brill, 2010.
———. "Rebel with a Cause: The Marriage of María Pacheco and the Formation of Mendoza Identity." *Power and Gender in Renaissance Spain: Eight Women of the Mendoza Family, 1450–1650*. Ed. Helen Nader. Urbana-Champaign: U Illinois P, 2: 71–92.
Frenk, Margit. *Entre la voz y el silencio*. Alcalá de Henares: Centro de Estudios Cervantinos, 1997.
———. "La ortografía elocuente (testimonios de lectura oral en el Siglo de Oro)." *Actas del VIII Congreso de la Asociación Internacional de Hispanistas: 22–27 agosto 1983*. Ed. A. David Kossoff et al. Vol. 2. Providence: Asociación Internacional de Hispanistas Congreso, 1983: 549–556.
Gonzalbo Aizpuru, Pilar. "La escuela de primeras letras." *Historia de la educación en la época colonial: la educación de los criollos y la vida urbana*. México: El Colegio de México, Centro de Estudios Históricos, 1990: 25–41.
Graña Cid, María del Mar. "Mujeres y educación en la prerreforma castellana: los colegios de doncellas." *Las sabias mujeres. Educación, saber y autoría (siglos III–XVII)*. Ed. María del Mar Graña Cid. Madrid: Asociación Cultural Al-Mudayna, 1994: 117–146.
Hoffman, Martha. *Raised to Rule: Educating Royalty at the Court of the Spanish Habsburgs, 1601–1634*. Baton Rouge: Louisiana State UP, 2011.
Howe, Elizabeth Teresa. *Education and Women in the Early Modern Hispanic World*. Aldershot, UK; Burlington, VT: Ashgate, 2008.
Infantes, Víctor. "La memoria impresa de la enseñanza." *De las primeras letras: cartillas españolas para enseñar a leer del siglo XVII*. Ed. Víctor Infantes and Ana Martínez Pereira. Vol. 1. Salamanca: Ediciones Universidad de Salamanca, 2003: 13–29.
Kagan, Richard L. *Students and Society in Early Modern Spain*. Baltimore: Johns Hopkins UP, 1974.
Knox, Andrea. "The Convent as Cultural Conduit: Irish Matronage in Early Modern Spain." *Quidditas* 30 (2009): 128–139.
Labarta Gómez, Ana. "La mujer morisca: sus actividades." *La mujer en Al-Andalus. Reflejos históricos de su actividad y categorías sociales*. Ed. María J. Viguera. Madrid: Seminario de Estudios de la Mujer; Ediciones de la Universidad Autónoma de Madrid, 1985: 219–231.
Lamy, Theresa M. *Juliana Morell: Child Prodigy, Religious Reformer, Spiritual Writer*. New York: ProQuestNYU, 1991.
Larroyo, Francisco. *Historia comparada de la educación en México*. México: Porrúa, 1962.
Laspalas Pérez, Francisco Javier. "Aspectos socio-económicos de la enseñanza de primeras letras en Pamplona (1551–1650)." *Historia de la educación: Revista interuniversitaria* 8 (1989): 181–198.
Layna Serrano, Francisco. *Historia de la villa condal de Cifuentes*. Guadalajara: AACHE, 1997.
Luna, Lola. *Leyendo como mujer la imagen de una mujer*. Barcelona: Anthropos, 2006.
Márquez de la Plata, Vicenta María. *Mujeres renacentistas en la corte de Isabel la Católica*. Madrid: Castalia, 2005.
Martínez Hernández, Santiago. "'Enlightened Queen, clear Cynthia, beauteous moon': The Political and Courtly Apprenticeship of the Infanta Isabel Clara Eugenia." *Isabel Clara Eugenia: Female Sovereignty in the Courts of Madrid and Brussels*. Ed. Cordula Van Wyhe. Madrid: CEEH/Paul Holberton, 2011: 21–59.
Nader, Helen. "Introduction: The World of the Mendozas." *Power and Gender in Renaissance Spain: Eight Women of the Mendoza Family, 1450–1650*. Ed. Helen Nader. Urbana-Champaign: U Illinois P, 2004: 1–26.
Nalle, Sara T. "Literacy and Education among Judeo-*conversa* Women in Castile, Portugal, and Amsterdam, 1560–1700." *Early Modern Women: An Interdisciplinary Journal* 11.1 (2016): 69–89.
———. "Literacy and Culture in Early Modern Castile." *Past and Present* 125 (1989): 65–96.
Negrín Fajardo, Olegario, ed., *Historia de la educación española*. Madrid: UNED, 2006.
Oliván Santaliestra, Laura. "'My sister is growing up very healthy and beautiful, she loves me.' The Childhood of the Infantas María Teresa and Margarita María at Court." *The Formation of the Child in Early Modern Spain*. Ed. Grace E. Coolidge. Farnham, UK; Burlington, VT: Ashgate, 2014: 165–187.

Ortiz Gómez, Teresa. "Entre la salud y la enfermedad: mujeres, ciencia y medicina en la historiografía española actual." *La historia de las mujeres: perspectivas actuales.* Ed. Cristina Borderías. Barcelona: Icaria, 2009: 163–196.

Pacheco, Francisco. *El arte de la pintura.* Ed. Bonaventura Bassegoda i Hugas. Madrid: Cátedra, 1990.

Pérez-Toribio, Montserrat. "From Mother to Daughter: Educational Lineage in the Correspondence between the Countess of Palamós and Estefania de Requesens." *Women's Literacy in Early Modern Spain and the New World.* Ed. Anne J. Cruz and Rosilie Hernández. Farnham, UK; Burlington, VT: Ashgate, 2011: 59–77.

Pomata, Gianna, ed. and transl. *Oliva Sabuco de Nantes. The True Medicine.* Series "The Other Voice." Toronto: Centre for Reformation and Renaissance Studies; Iter, 2010.

Redondo, Augustin. "Les livrets de lecture (*cartillas para enseñar a leer*) au XVIe siècle: lecture et message doctrinal." *La formation de l'enfant en Espagne aux XVIe et XVIIe siècles.* Ed. Augustin Redondo. Paris: Presses de la Sorbonne Nouvelle, 1996: 71–91.

Revuelta Guerrero, Clara, and Rufino Cano González. "Las escuelas de amiga: espacios femeninos de trabajo y educación de párvulos y de niñas." *Aula* 16 (2010): 155–185.

Río Barredo, María José del. "Enfance et education d'Anne d'Autriche à la cour d'Espagne (1601–1615)." *Anne d'Autriche. Infante d'Espagne et reine de France.* Ed. Chantal Grell. Paris: CEEH-Perrin, 2009: 11–39.

Rivera Vázquez, Evaristo. *Galicia y los jesuitas. Sus colegios y enseñanza en los siglos XVI al XVIII.* La Coruña: Fundación Pedro Barrié de la Maza, 1989.

Rojo Vega, Anastasio. "Un sondeo acerca de la capacidad de lectura y escritura en Valladolid. 1550–1575," *Signo: revista de historia de la cultura escrita* 3 (1996): 25–40.

Ruiz García, Elisa. *Las prácticas de lectura de una reina: Isabel I de Castilla.* Alicante: Biblioteca Virtual Miguel de Cervantes, 2006. www.cervantesvirtual.com/nd/ark:/59851/bmcv98j8}./s

———. *Los libros de Isabel la Catolica: arqueologia de un patrimonio escrito.* Madrid: Fund. German Sanchez Ruipérez, 2004.

Saenger, Paul. *Space between Words: The Origins of Silent Reading.* Stanford: Stanford UP, 1997.

Saez, Ricardo. "Enseignement et petites écoles au tournent du XVIe siècle à Toledo: des textes aux pratiques." *La formation de l'enfant en Espagne aux XVIe et XVIIe siècles.* Ed. Augustin Redondo. Paris: Presses de la Sorbonne Nouvelle, 1996: 161–173.

Salvador Miguel, Nicasio. *Isabel la Católica. Educación, mecenazgo y entorno literario.* Alcalá de Henares: Centro de Estudios Cervantinos, 2008.

Sánchez Cantón, Francisco Javier. *Libros, tapices y cuadros que coleccionó Isabel la Católica.* Madrid: Consejo Superior de Investigaciones Científicas, 1950.

———. *La biblioteca del marqués del Cenete, iniciada por el cardinal Mendoza (1470–1523).* Madrid: Aguirre, 1942.

Séguin, Pierre. *Ligueur, reclus & écrivain, 1558–1636.* Senlis: Eugéne Dufresne, 1896.

Sherwood, Joan. *Poverty in Eighteenth-Century Spain: The Women and Children of the Inclusa.* Toronto: U Toronto P, 1988.

Slade, Carole A. "'Este Gran Dios de las Cavallerías' [This Great God of Chivalric Deeds]: St. Teresa's Performances of the Novels of Chivalry." *The Vernacular Spirit: Essays on Medieval Religious Literature.* Ed. R. Blumenfeld-Kosinski, et al. New York: Palgrave Macmillan, 2002: 297–316.

Starkey, David. *Six Wives: The Queens of Henry VIII.* New York: Perennial, 2004.

Valdivieso, María Isabel. "La educación en la corte de la Reina Católica." *Miscelánea Comillas* 69.134 (2011): 255–273.

Varey, J. E., and Charles Davis. *Los corrales de comedias y los hospitales de Madrid: 1615–1849. Estudio y documentos.* Woodbridge, UK: Tamesis, 1997.

Vega, José de Jesús, and María Luisa Cárdenas de Vega. *América virreinal: la educación de la mujer, 1503–1821.* México: Editorial Jus, 1989.

Villaseñor Black, Charlene. "Paintings of the Education of the Virgin Mary and the Lives of Girls in Early Modern Spain." *The Formation of the Child in Early Modern Spain.* Ed. Grace Coolidge. Farnham, UK; Burlington, VT: Ashgate, 2014: 93–119.

Viñao Frago, Antonio. "Alfabetización y primeras letras (siglos XVI–XVII)," *Escribir y leer en el siglo de Cervantes,* ed. Antonio Castillo. Barcelona: Gedisa, 1999: 39–84.

Vives, Juan Luis. *Instrucción de la mujer cristiana.* Trad. Juan Justinianio. Ed. Elizabeth Teresa Howe. Madrid: Salamanca Fundación Universitaria Española; Universidad Pontificia, 1995.

Zayas, María de. *Novelas amorosas y ejemplares.* Ed. Julián Olivares. Madrid: Cátedra, 2000.

3
THE EARLY MODERN FOUNDATIONS OF THE *QUERELLA DE LAS MUJERES*

Emily C. Francomano

The *Querelle des femmes*, often called the *Querella de las mujeres* in Hispanic studies, is difficult to define.[1] Consisting of a vast multilingual and intertextual network of texts produced from the Middle Ages onwards, by both male and female authors, the *querelle* refers both to women as the subject of debate and to women as disputants in works that seek to define their moral, physical, and intellectual qualities, generally in contrast to those of men. Many *querelle* texts also seek to prescribe and proscribe relationships between the sexes, and to question the institutional and customary subjugation of women to men. Engaging in the *querelle*, therefore, is both a political and a rhetorical practice, at once a reflection of perceived gender norms and of desires to (re)shape them. Constance Jordan, writing of the extensive reach of the *querelle*, remarks that not only was it concerned with the place of women within patriarchal society, but also with the very "nature of authority" (308).

The roots of the *querelle* stretch far back into the past, while its central arguments and conceits have maintained their currency well into modernity. Indeed, the ubiquity and persistence of "the question of woman" obscures any notion of a single origin and consequently, "anyone wondering where to begin to understand [it] [...] must recognize that it is possible to begin almost anywhere" (Bloch, *Medieval Misogyny*: 13).[2] This chapter will consider representative foundational texts of the *querella*, which emerged in Spanish letters as a distinct and highly influential literary mode in the middle of the fifteenth century, when a series of texts defaming and championing women appeared within the cultural ambience of the court of Juan II of Castile and his queen consort, María of Aragon. At the same time, *cancionero* poets active in various courts in Castile, Aragon, and Navarre also composed and exchanged verses on the nature of women. A generation later, in the milieu of the court of the Catholic Monarchs, Isabel I of Castile and Fernando of Aragon, writers familiar with the first waves of the literary polemic, wove the debate into prose fictions.[3]

As María Jesús Lacarra notes, the *querella* embraces three separate but complementary orientations: women writers, women readers, and women as a literary theme (339). By and large, the fifteenth-century *querella* belongs to the second and third of these categories. Nevertheless, it is in this period as well that Teresa de Cartagena added her voice to the *querella*, providing an early demonstration of how the debate on the nature of women formed part of many women writers' authorial self-fashioning from the fifteenth century onwards. Greater numbers of women writers entered into the *querella* in the sixteenth and seventeenth centuries, as was the case for the European *querelle* more generally. Further, and despite the almost exclusively male authorship of the *querella*, historical women played important roles in their creation, as dedicatees, patronesses, and intended readers, including María of Aragon, Isabel I, and other aristocratic women in their courts. Women's *matrocinio*, or "matronage," to use Ana Vargas Martínez's coinage, constituted "a form of intervening in the *querella*, of creating public opinions, of engaging in politics" (265).[4] The foundational *querella* texts, like those of the pan-European *querelle*, such as Christine de Pizan's *La cité des dames*, Boccaccio's *Corbaccio*, and Agrippa's *De nobilitate et praecellentia foeminei sexus*, had a lasting influence.

The arguments presented throughout the *querelle* are remarkably consistent. Christine de Pizan, writing as a resistant reader of Le Fèvre's *Lamentations of Matheolus* in the early fifteenth century, remarked that it seemed as if, "philosophers, and poets and [. . .] orators all speak from one and the same mouth," when speaking of women's faults (3). Works championing women also tend to follow set patterns. Indeed, the repetitiveness of the *querelle* texts has led some readers to consider them parts of a literary game of little moment. However, much recent scholarship on the *querelle*, and the Iberian *querella* more specifically, has focused on the need for the historicized study of works that have frequently been evaluated from anachronistic perspectives or read as inconsequential rhetorical exercises and light entertainment.[5] As Julie Campbell notes, scholarship on the *querelle* has evolved from considerations of its relation to twentieth-century feminism to its "function as a barometer of social and cultural tensions" (361). The commonplaces of the debate served varied ideological agendas specific to the time and place of their enunciation. If the content of the *querelle* depended upon "a splendid little store of off-the-peg items, ready for embellishment and rearrangement in new contexts," (Blamires, *The Case for Women*: 11), those contexts, literary, historical, geographical, political, and social, gave the debate its significance.

Antecedents and authorities of the *querella*

The antecedents of the *querella* can be found in the medieval literature of misogyny. A series of quips attributed to Diogenes and Socrates in the thirteenth-century *Bocados de oro* exemplify the central rhetorical strategy of the misogynist tradition: "There is no greater evil than Woman [. . .] [Socrates] saw a sick woman, unable to leave her bed, and he said, 'evil stays with evil' [. . .] He saw a young woman learning to write and he said, 'do not heap evil upon evil'" (43, 63–64).[6] This repeated equation of *la muger* with *el mal*, like other pronouncements "in which *woman* is the subject of the sentence and the predicate a more general term" and "the use of the substantive *woman* or *women* with a capital *W*," have the effect of reducing Woman and women to an undifferentiated category (Bloch, *Medieval Misogyny*: 5). In such medieval definitions of *woman*, as Susan Mosher Stuard similarly observes, the authors "speak and think of a category rather than of women as they knew them" (144). In *Bocados*, Socrates' students ask if their mothers and sisters are exempt from the universalizing equation of women with evil. The answer they receive is a resounding, yet unsatisfactory "no." This tension between the category "Woman," and women in lived experience pervades the *querella*.

Late medieval and early modern writers on the inferiority, instability, sexual depravity, garrulousness, and shrewdness of women, and the consequent danger they posed to men, had many authorities at their disposal. Misogynist texts turned repeatedly to biblical wisdom literature, the second account of the generation of man and woman in Genesis, and to the sayings of the Fathers of the Church. They also turned with frequency to Aristotelian and Galenic physiology, which taught that females were "defective" or "deformed" males, and associated women with the body and materiality. This view was echoed in the humoral theory that judged men to be generally hot and dry, and women cold and moist, a difference which accounted for menstruation.[7] Sources of imitation and citation were also to be found in popular proverbs, classical satire, and school texts, such as Juvenal's *Satires* and Ovid's *Ars Amoris* and *Remedia Amoris*. Medieval writers who developed the canon, such as Boccaccio, Walter Map, and Jehan Le Fèvre, had also become renowned experts on the subject by the fifteenth century. Many misogynistic works were aimed at inspiring clerical celibacy, while others offered advice regarding sexual hygiene, remedies for lovesickness, and palliatives for amorous rejection. Listing examples of the "power of women" over the men who become sexually involved with them is yet another abiding rhetorical strategy used in antifeminine works. Solomon, the primordial authority on women, also serves as a negative exemplar, one in a long line of wise and powerful men so blinded by lust that they fall victim to the wiles of non-submissive women, become idolaters, and cede their dominance to women.[8]

The authorities available to writers wishing to write in praise of women, though fewer than the cornucopia on offer to antifeminine writers, were also plentiful. In fact, in many cases, profeminine arguments drew upon the same texts as the misogynist proofs.[9] Genesis, used as the indisputable evidence of Eve's inferiority to men in misogynist writing, was countered by a series of arguments for her superiority to Adam due to her creation in a nobler place and from nobler materials than the first human. Eve's alleged guilt for the Fall was contested by profeminine writers who argued for Adam's greater responsibility and gullibility. The writings of the Church Fathers in praise of virginity and of the historical women they knew also provided models. Even Aristotle could be turned to the service of exalting rather than denigrating women. Above all, the case for women in medieval and early modern literature relied upon stories of exemplary women whose actions belied the litanies of misogynist's reasons for their *horror feminae*. Catalogues of biblical heroines, heroic women of classical antiquity, and female saints abound in the profeminine tradition. Boccaccio's *De mulieribus claris* (*Famous Women*) served many later writers as a reference, making him an authority for a range of positions in the debate.

Medieval and early modern profeminine texts rarely offer new definitions of femininity, nor do they question women's frailty and physical inferiority to men. Rather, they present an alternate interpretation of shared definitions and alternate conclusions to theological exegeses. Both profeminine and misogynist writings present men and women, masculinity and femininity, as contraries, reflecting the Aristotelian and Scholastic polarities of categories of thought.[10] Following humoral theory, many writings on women equate physiological sex with character. However, some authors suggest that gender performance may not always be a reflection of biology. For example, it is repeatedly averred that many women, though naturally prone to vice, have managed to overcome the inherent barriers of femininity in order either to act like men or to demonstrate those virtues most valued in women, such as chastity, piety, and obedience. The possibility of overcoming one's sex, celebrated by profeminine authors, implies some awareness on their part that the supposedly universal and transhistorical definitions of *woman* do not always adequately describe individual women. As Archer argues, Hispanic texts that address issues of sexuality and gender identity reveal "a real concern with the viability of the authoritative view of women" which is "essentially contradictory," resulting in a "strong sense of indeterminacy" (*The Problem of Woman* 204).

A recurrent trope in medieval and early modern writings about women neatly encapsulates the "woman question" itself: *Mulierem fortem quis inveniet?* (Who shall find a valiant woman?) (*Vulgate Bible*, Proverbs 31:10; trans. *Douay-Rheims*). In the Bible, King Solomon's rhetorical question introduces a peon to the model wife who is industrious, wise, and a credit to her husband, in contrast to the querulous and dangerously seductive women whom Proverbs urges men to avoid: "Who shall find a valiant woman? Far and from the uttermost coasts is the price of her. / The heart of her husband trusteth in her, and he shall have no need of spoils. / She will render him good, and not evil, all the days of her life." In many late medieval and early modern works that address the nature of women, the question not only sparks discussions of ideal feminine behavior, but also serves as an authoritative proof that good women are non-existent. While many profeminine texts echo Solomon's praise for the good wife, the *Lamentations of Matheolus* (c.1371–1372) typifies the misogynist interpretation: "Solomon, in his works, makes an amazing comment, which supports my case, for he exclaims, 'Who could find a virtuous woman?' The implication here is, of course, that this would be impossible" (Le Fèvre: 194).[11]

Historical contexts

The *querella* emerged in Spanish letters in a period marked by many struggles for dominance between powerful factions in the nobility, and by related cultural shifts concerning nobility, courtliness, and religious orthodoxy. The importance of gender politics and gender *in* politics was highlighted by the reigns of three Trastámaran sovereigns, Juan II (1405–1454), Enrique IV (1425–1474), and Isabel I (1451–1504). Juan II's long reign began under the antagonistic co-regency of his uncle Fernando of Antequera (d. 1416) and his mother Catherine of Lancaster (1373–1418). After reaching his majority, Juan's rule was troubled, in large part due to the enormous power he gave to his favorite, Álvaro de Luna (1388–1453), who was rumored to hold complete control over the king, through witchcraft and sexual enthrallment. Royal courts had long been the locales for oral and written expressions of misogyny, but their vehemence and the responses they provoked intensified in the ambience of the court of Juan II and María of Aragon, where the polemic between the defenders and defamers of women formed part of the rivalries between the Castilian and Aragonese nobility.[12]

When Enrique IV succeeded to the throne, he earned the moniker of "The Impotent," despite the birth of a recognized heir, Juana of Castile (c. 1462–1530), whom Enrique's enemies alleged was in truth the daughter of the royal favorite, Beltrán de la Cueva (c. 1443–1492). Enrique's rivals among the nobility deposed him in effigy in 1465, reputedly shouting "¡A tierra puto!" (Down with the faggot/male prostitute!) as they did so. The anecdote shows how closely sexual activity and royal power were associated in the political imagination of the time. After Enrique's death, Isabel eventually ascended the throne after a civil war pitting her supporters against those of her niece, Juana of Castile. Isabel retained her rights and status as sovereign queen following her marriage to Fernando of Aragon, and both Juan II and Enrique IV were portrayed as weak, effeminate, heterodox, and sexually deviant by chroniclers wishing to celebrate Isabel I as the savior of her kingdom who at last achieved the goal of defeating territories under Muslim rule.

Margarete Zimmerman observes that the "fundamental historicity" of the *querelle* "is particularly visible in phases where the speed picks up and the arguments become more intense [. . .] [and] new foci of the discussion are developed" (35). Throughout the period, the texts of the *querella* were in continual intertextual dialogue with works addressing other subjects that were heatedly debated at the time, such as the status of *conversos*, Marian theology, and the debate between arms and letters.[13] Further, as Barbara Weissberger has observed, during Isabel's reign, issues of "queenship, gender, power, sexuality, ethnicity, and religion" intersected in the *querella*. Isabel herself embodied "a threat to the patriarchal status quo," even though her political and cultural agendas were design to reconfirm it ("Deceitful Sects": 225).

Foundations of the querella de las mujeres

The first wave of the *querella*: 1430s–1460s

Numerous poems and treatises on the "woman question," authored by men who held important positions in the courts of Castile and the Crown of Aragon, appeared in quick succession from the 1430s on. Two works served as textual instigators of the debate in the middle of the fifteenth century: Alfonso Martínez de Toledo's treatise, the *Arcipreste de Talavera* o *Corbacho* (1438), so titled in homage to Boccaccio's *Corbaccio* (c. 1355); and Pere Torrellas's *Maldezir de mugeres* (*Slander against Women*) (ca. 1445). Both widely-read works came to represent misogyny as a whole. They are gynophobic and anxiety-ridden, painting women as frightening creatures that deprive men of power. Ironically, by envisioning the vulnerability of men to women, these texts put the supposedly natural and unquestionable order of male superiority into question.

Martínez de Toledo (1398–1470), who served as chaplain to Juan II and later to his son, Enrique IV, offers the *Arcipreste* as a guide for young men that will teach them how to avoid and protect themselves from sin in the form of "loco amor" (crazed love), which he describes as a kind of sexual enthrallment by "las viçiosas mujeres" (depraved women). Throughout, the *Arcipreste* warns against the spiritual and physical dangers of earthly love and particularly against the apotheosis of female objects of desire in the courtly "religion of love."[14] Divided into four parts, the *Arcipreste* first invites readers to fear "loco amor" in thirty-eight chapters delineating how love for women causes destruction and sacrilege. Loving women poses a danger to men because it inverts the natural order of the sexes, bringing misfortune on any man who makes himself subject to women's capricious authority (60). Martínez de Toledo does not deny the rare existence of good women and alludes to Proverbs by likening them to precious rubies (97).

Women are a source of continual horrified wonder, mockery, and rhetorical invention in the second part of the *Arcipreste*, which encourages readers to laugh at the maddening women depicted in its exemplary tales and parodic dialogues mimicking hysterical female voices. Indeed, Martínez de Toledo gives the lie to his own affirmation that the "faults, vices, and blemishes" of wicked women "are numberless and cannot be described," since much of the book is devoted to providing a detailed inventory of such vices and the ways that they lead men to sin (14).[15]

While the preface states that the *Arcipreste* will describe the evils of *viçiosas mugeres* (wicked women), the following chapters frequently speak of *la muger* (Woman) as a single category and attribute negative characteristics to *toda muger* (every woman), for example, "To doubt that the wicked woman is envious would be to sin against the Holy Ghost, for every woman, when she sees another more comely than she, is like to die of envy" (116).[16] Parts three and four, which are much briefer than the first two, are dedicated to an explanation of the humors and their effects on sexual conduct, followed by warnings against attributing sin to the power of those same astral signs and humors and the necessity of accepting the will of God.

The *Arcipreste* was successful in the context of its first historical audiences and later gained its own canonical status among generations of readers. First printed in 1498, five more editions followed between 1499 and 1547. There is some evidence that the *Arcipreste* was received by its late medieval audiences as something less than a serious and didactic work. The printed editions, some of which only reproduce the second part of the treatise, and whose titles advertise that the book is about "the vices of wicked women," also contain an epilogue in which the author-figure dreams of "over one thousand famous ladies, well-known and renowned," who attack the writer and demand that he burn the book.[17] The book is saved when the author begs their forgiveness (305–306). The epilogue ends with an interjection that echoes yet undercuts the book's earlier warnings, "Woe to the man who sleeps alone with his pains and in whose house the distaff never enters the whole year through!" (306).[18] Martínez de Toledo was long dead when the first printed edition of his *Arcipreste de Talavera* appeared, and scholars disagree about his possible authorship of the epilogue, yet its presence serves as an ironic commentary on the text, suggesting that the book itself is in many ways subject to women, just like the woebegone men brought under their sway that Martínez de Toledo describes in the early chapters of the *Arcipreste*.

Pere Torrellas (c. 1420–c. 1492) was a Catalonian courtier in the service of Juan II of Navarre and Aragon (1398–1479). The exact date, circumstances, and intentions of his composition of the *Maldezir* are unknown; however, by the 1450s it had become infamous in the courts of Castile and the Crown of Aragon. The *Maldezir* begins with the admonition, "the man in love who courts / a woman, destroys himself," and goes on to detail women's indiscriminate lust, hypocrisy, love of flattery, capriciousness, cunning, greed, and mendacity (53–54).[19] Although Torrellas cites no authorities on the nature of women, he alludes to the Aristotelian notion that women are "defective men," born due to gestational damage or privation: "Woman is that animal / we call an imperfect man, / procreated by defect / of nature's good heat" (60–61).[20]

The majority of Torrellas's poetic proofs of women's iniquity in the *Maldezir* concern men's vulnerability. One stanza, however, alleges that women behave badly because they fully understand their actual political and social subordination: "Feeling that they are subjugated / and lacking any power / in order to take control / women form shady sects" (58–59).[21] These verses "tacitly acknowledge the inequities inherent in the traditional gender hierarchy" (Weissberger, "Deceitful Sects": 213). While Torrellas is not objecting to patriarchy, the poem here does seem to recognize that the subjugation of women not only leads to women's dissatisfaction, but also may negatively affect men. The *Maldezir* concludes with an about-face; the final stanza praises an unknown beloved lady whose singular virtues are an exception to the rule (60–63).[22]

Despite the *Maldezir*'s palinode, Torrellas's contemporaries interpreted the poem as an unmitigated attack on women requiring either a chivalrous response in their defense or a vigorous affirmation of misogyny.[23] Suero de Ribera (c. 1410–1475), the poet known only as Carvajal (fl. 1450s–1460s), and Anton de Montoro (c. 1404–c. 1477), all wrote verses berating Torrellas and other *maldizientes* for their lack of nobility and courtliness. Montoro also wrote verses in agreement with the *Maldezir*. The humanist and statesman Gómez Manrique (c. 1412–1490) composed a rebuttal to the *Maldezir*, refuting each of its assertions and praising women in stanzas imitating Torrellas' rhyme and meter.[24] The *Maldezir* and its responses circulated in fifteenth-century *cancionero* manuscripts and also in the *Cancionero General*, printed throughout the sixteenth century. The *cancionero* context suggests that debating the nature of women in the courts of Castile and Aragon was one way that male courtiers might assert their cultural and symbolic capital. Suero de Ribera's response to Torrellas neatly captures the spirit of this display when he affirms that "noble men must / defend women" (282).[25]

Juan Rodríguez del Padrón's *Triunfo de las donas* (c. 1440) and Diego de Valera's *Defensa de las virtuosas mugeres* (before 1445) were both dedicated to María of Aragon (1403–1445), the first wife of Juan II and an active patron of the court's cultural activities, and were possibly written at her behest. The *Libro de las virtuosas e claras mugeres*, attributed to Álvaro de Luna, the favorite of Juan II, was composed with the same courtly environment in 1446. Pere Torrellas also wrote a *Defensa de las donas* at some point following the composition of his (in)famous poem, yet his *Defensa* did not enjoy the wide and long-lived diffusion of his incendiary *Maldezir*.

These treatises all champion women's merit by first explaining the logical weakness of the misogynists' universalizing disparagement, often repeating the antifeminine arguments in order to turn them into profeminine propositions, and then by providing copious exempla of good women. This last rhetorical strategy functioned as a response to Solomon's famous question, *mulierem fortem quis inveniet?* by showing readers just how many women of worth populate scripture, history, and even the present day. Like the versified challenges to Torrellas's *Maldezir*, the treatises are also acts of self-promotion; each author-figure presents himself as an ideal courtier and a learned man, proffering a service to ladies and to the court.

Rodríguez del Padrón (fl. 1440s), a well-traveled court and ecclesiastical official, takes direct aim at the misogynists in the *Triunfo de las donas* in order to argue for the moral, intellectual, and political capabilities of women. Following his dedication to "the most learned" Queen María, Rodríguez del Padrón opens the *Triunfo* with a courtly scene in which young men discuss questions of honor, virtue, and nobility, and ask the author to write a treatise containing his opinions on the subject (211–213). Such a treatise should be dedicated only to the most noble and virtuous of readers, so courtiers decide to ask "la questión odiosa" (that hateful question), namely, are men superior to women or women to men? (213). The author then describes his meditation on the conundrum, which begins with a rehearsal of all the misogynist *topoi*. He is overheard by a nymph, Cardiana, who scolds him for blindly following the teaching of the "slanderous and vituperous Corbacho" (Maldiçiente et vituperoso Corbacho) who relies upon fictions rather than trusted authorities for his accusations (216). Cardiana lists fifty-four proofs of the merit of women, citing scriptural and philosophical antecedents, including Aristotle, as well as numerous examples of legendary good women and evil men. She begins with commonplaces regarding Eve's creation in a better place of superior material to Adam, her standing as one of the "delights of paradise," and Adam's greater guilt, since "knowledge was prohibited to man, but not to woman" and Adam sinned knowingly while Eve was tricked (217–221).[26] Cardiana, like other defenders of women, champions the virtues of charity, piety, and obedience. The *Triunfo*, however moves beyond profeminine commonplaces when Cardiana explains that women are more chaste and virtuous than men, because not only are the female "shameful organs" hidden, unlike men's, but also because during a rape the female victim looks up to the skies, while her attacker looks at the ground (222). This last supposed proof no doubt seemed as dubious in the fifteenth century as it does today, and was perhaps intended as a touch of lubricious and dark humor.

The *Triunfo* enters into the realm of satire when Cardiana defends women's use of cosmetics, so frequently decried by misogynist writings. When women paint their faces, she argues, it enhances their natural and God-given beauty, in contrast to all of the beautifying chicanery of men who pad their calves and corset their waists in order to appear more attractive (222). Cardiana offers the story of the biblical judge and heroine Deborah as proof that "women should rule and fight when it is fitting, just like men, who have empowered themselves alone to rule through tyranny" (234).[27] Cardiana's thirty-third affirmation suffices as a general summation of the *Triunfo*: "it is clear that there have been a greater number of evil men than women and a greater number of good women than men" (241).[28] Cardiana concludes by praising Queen María's lineage, an indication of Rodríguez del Padrón's political sympathies. The dreamer awakes and takes the tale of Cardiana and her defense of women back to the court. The *Triunfo* was quite popular in the Castilian court, and in 1460 was translated into French for Philip the Good of Burgundy.

Diego de Valera (1412–1488), a widely traveled courtier and a prolific author, was the son of Juan II of Castile's royal physician. He declares in the proem to the *Defensa de las virtuosas mugeres* that he writes as if to a male friend who wishes to understand the rational for the "horrible material" propagated by a "new sect" of men "who take reckless delight in defaming women (230).[29] Such men, Valera explains via an excursus on mythological founts of wisdom, are ignorant and crude. Further, these blasphemers' hearts are fickle and will "move like leaves on the wind," Valera says, echoing one of the commonplaces of misogynist invectives (231).[30] The *Defensa* proper is a brief text, but it is accompanied by Valera's extensive gloss, allowing for the display of his own humanistic erudition: the defenders of women have traveled to the zenith of Parnassus, drunk from the Pirene fountain, and they have heard Apollo's lyre and the sweet songs of the muses.

Valera's repudiation of misogyny is delivered in the form of a catalogue of good women from the Bible and history, who all, though their cultivation of the cardinal virtues disprove the misogynists' claim that women are naturally weak and inclined to vice. He begins with famous virgins and chaste wives, including the story of Lucretia, a staple in catalogues of good women. A Roman matron who stabs herself in the heart after she has been raped, Lucretia exemplifies the value of feminine honor. Despite her innocence and lack of any adulterous desires, Lucretia does not allow even a suspicion of unchastity to tarnish her and her husband's reputation. The stories of virgin martyrs, which also proliferate in the catalogue, place a similarly high price on the protection of chastity, conveying the idea that "the only good virgin is a dead virgin," since a woman's virginity and chastity are lost once the male gaze or lustful thought lights upon her (Bloch, "Chaucer's Maiden's Head": 120).

The ranks of good women in the Defensa are swelled by thousands of nameless virginal Israelites, nations of chaste and constant women (Germans, Indians, Menians), and the eleven thousand virgin martyrs in St. Ursula's entourage. Valera's overall persuasive strategy is to refute the misogynist claim that all women are wicked with copia, abundance as unassailable proof, shored up even further by the amplificatory gloss providing the legends of each good woman or group of women.[31] Individual examples in the catalogue epitomize how profeminine works often explain the behavior of heroic women by stating that performed with "manly heart" (con viril coraçon) and left aside their "womanish habits" (dexados los femíneos apostamientos) (272).[32]

In order to prove, contrary to misogynist belief, that contemporary women can also overcome their muliebrity, Valera offers readers three examples from the recent past: María Coronel, famous for staving off the sexual advances of Pedro The Cruel (1334–1369), either by disfiguring her face with boiling oil, according to some sources, or for combating her sexual appetites during her husband's absence by mutilating her genitals with a burning brand, according to others; the unnamed "Mother of Alvar Pérez de Osorio," a modern-day Lucretia, who chose death over a ruined reputation; and Doña María García, a *beata* who died a virgin at the age of eighty (243). Of the ill-informed misogynist authors, Valera says women should "Forgive them for they know not what they do," yet he takes both Ovid and Boccaccio to task, criticizing the *De arte amandi* and the *Corbaccio* as rants written by old men who should have known better (247–248).

The conclusion to Valera's legendary catalogue exemplifies how both misogynist and profeminine texts agreed about women's natural physical and mental inferiority by asking, "Lord, what blindness is this that occupies mortal vision? Could there be anything more virtuous than those women, to whom Nature gave weak bodies, tender hearts, and generally sluggish intelligence, yet who are even more virtuous than men, to whom valiant bodies, quick intelligence, and strong hearts are a natural gift?" (240).[33]

Álvaro de Luna, the powerful favorite of Juan II of Castile and political enemy of Valera, outdoes the *Defensa*'s *copia* in the *Libro de las virtuosas e claras mugeres* (*Book of Virtuous and Illustrious Women*), an extensive, tripartite catalogue of over one hundred exemplary women from the Bible, Antiquity, and the Christian calendar of saints. The catalogue is introduced by a preface by Juan de Mena, Luna's political supporter, who praises him as a man worthy of lasting admiration and memory, a subject for others to write about due to his bravery in combat, political skill, and intelligence. Mena claims to be thanking Luna on behalf of all the illustrious and virtuous women of the day for having rendered them the honor of writing a defense of women's honor

(554). In his poems, Luna declares that he will use reason, logic, and authority to refute the commonly held negative views of women, and takes aim at the claim that women's natural inferiority to men necessarily makes them more prone to vice, citing Aristotle's *Ethics* as proof that women can become accustomed to behaving sinfully or virtuously, just as men do (141, 144–145). Citing Solomon's praise of the *mulier fortis*, Luna argues that all of the other negative remarks about women by the wise king found in the Bible apply not to all women but only to the *desordenadas* (unruly women) (154).

The women in Luna's catalogue belong to the same well-known repertoire that his predecessors drew upon, although he includes no contemporary examples. Lucretia's familiar story provides the first chapter of the second section, on pagan women. The catalogue ends on a note of authorial uncertainty. Faced with the decision of which famed woman should conclude the third and final section, Luna says he first thought of Saint Elizabeth, and then of Saints Pelagia and Cassia—two harlot saints, whose stories revolve around repentance for sexual sins—before electing Saint Catherine of Alexandria, famed for sanctity, beauty, and wisdom as his ultimate example, perhaps intending his conclusion to be a posthumous homage to Catherine of Lancaster (536). The legend revolves around the saint's debate with fifty philosophers, leading to their conversion to Christianity, and Luna argues that St. Catherine excels even Aristotle and Plato in wisdom (543). The valedictory argument of the book returns to Genesis and the creation of Woman in the image of and as companion to Man (549). Queen María died in 1445, and it is possible that Luna's reference to marriage at the close of the *Libro* was intended to inspire Juan II to remarry.[34]

These attacks and defenses of women all rely upon a certain gender orthodoxy, based upon the supposedly natural physiological and moral inferiority of women. The biblical account of creation and fall, supported by Aristotelianism and humoral theory, explained the existence of women, as secondary human beings made for, after, and from men, and, further, as marked forever by original sin in physical ways that men are not. The dividing lines of the debate, then, are drawn within a structural and conceptual order in which women are *a priori* as something other and lesser than men. The heroines praised in the profeminine catalogues are cultural ideograms, often corresponding to what Blamires sums up as a fantasy of "meek, compassionate, virtuous women" who are "voluntary domestic and sexual cushion[s]" for men (Blamires, *The Case for Women*: 5–6). The stories of Lucretia and her avatars teach that the female chastity that supports male honor is not only vulnerable and must be guarded from the mere suspicion of its corruption, but also that it is more valuable than a woman's life. As Pamela Benson remarks, in this way, defenses "tame" images of unruly and independent women in order to counter "the threatening notion that women are equal to men," implicit in rebuttals to misogynist invective (*Renaissance Feminism*: 47). Conduct literature written for women, such as Martín de Córdoba's *Jardín de nobles donzellas* (1468–1469) and the anonymous fifteenth-century *Castigos que un savio dava a sus hijas*, appeal to the same catalogues of profeminine exemplarity, encouraging female readers to be living paradigms and placing chastity above all other virtues.

These works attacking or defending women also all concern how men should relate to women, and consequently clearly demonstrate that male comportment and courtliness are just as, and perhaps more, important in this stage of debate literature than notions of feminine behavior. Eloquence, finesse, and the ability to argue successfully on both sides of the divide were often valued over sincerity in this context. Depending upon the position of the writer and his intended audiences, woman and women are discussed either as a problem for or boon to men. As man's "Other," Woman may not be evil incarnate, but she is certainly not "one of us." Nevertheless, and despite their affirmations of woman's natural inferiority, these defenses call the authority of misogyny into question.

Emily C. Francomano

Teresa de Cartagena (ca. 1425–?)

Teresa de Cartagena, the author of two spiritual treatises, is one of a small group of medieval Iberian women writers whose works have come down to us. An educated woman who participated directly in the *querella*, she is an example of the distance between the cultural ideograms constructed by male authors in the debate and the experience of historical women.[35] Teresa wrote from within the convent where she lived, though she mentions having studied at Salamanca in her first treatise, the *Arboleda de los enfermos* (*Grove of the Infirm*) (c. 1450). While the precise nature of her studies there is unknown, it was not uncommon for aristocratic women to be well educated at the time.[36] Teresa was a member of the influential Cartagena and Santa María family, whose members were highly visible in the political and cultural spheres of the Trastámaran courts. Her grandfather, Pablo de Santa María (c. 1350–1435), was one of the most prominent *converso* churchmen of his age and served as Juan II's tutor, while her father, Pedro de Cartagena (1387–1478), was a knight of Juan's court and later served as a counselor to both Enrique IV and the Catholic Monarchs. Her uncle, Alonso de Cartagena, was a prolific writer and influential humanist who, among his other works, translated Boccaccio's *De claris mulieribus* into Spanish.

The *Arboleda de enfermos* is a meditation on the spiritual value of suffering, in which Teresa describes how her own suffering from deafness imposed a beneficial, if painful, isolation upon her. The ailment allowed her to focus inwardly on her spirituality, she wrote, and to "glory" in her suffering (44). The *Arboleda* counsels readers to accept suffering and sickness with patience and to likewise "glory generously and willingly in our sickness" because of the humility and virtuous disavowal of temporal things that they inspire (45).[37] In the *Arboleda*, Teresa asserted the value of the female body as a conduit for theological reflection (Rivera Garretas: 19). Yet it is in her second treatise, the *Admiraçión operum Dei* (*Wonder at the Works of God*) (ca. 1477), that Teresa intervened in the *querella*. Although she wrote from the isolation of the convent and her deafness, the two treatises appear to have circulated among the same audiences that were the intended readership of the anti- and profeminine male-authored works discussed above. Both the *Arboleda* and the *Admiraçión* were dedicated to Juana de Mendoza (d. 1493), who held the important court position of *camarera mayor* to Isabel I and who was married to the poet and politician Gómez Manrique.[38]

In the introduction to the *Admiraçión*, Teresa states that it was written as a response to the "wonder" (*admiraçión*) that the *Arboleda* had caused in readers unable to believe that a woman had written so admirably. Making use of many forms of topical and gendered authorial modesty, Teresa speaks of her "weak womanly understanding" (*flaco mugeril entendimiento*) and the "womanly text of little substance" (*obra mugeril e de poca sustancia*) it produced, in order to reprimand those readers who do not believe that she could have authored the *Arboleda* because to doubt its authorship is to doubt the mercy and divine judgment of God (86–88). Teresa goes on to explain that the gendered customs of society make her authorship seem miraculous because, from time immemorial "men have had the practice of writing books and learning and applying their learning," and therefore it only seems natural that only men should write and unnatural in women (89).[39] Moreover, Teresa gives her own exegesis of the creation story in Genesis, using the very Aristotelian and Scholastic oppositions of male and female to argue for the complementarity of the sexes. God did indeed make men valiant, strong, and of greater intelligence than women, but He created this "marvelous arrangement" (*maravillosa dispusyçión*) for the preservation of humanity (92). Furthermore, Teresa observes, citing Judith's heroism, just as God at times graces women with extraordinary fortitude so he graced her to write (93). Using the theory of gender polarity, Teresa affirms the naturalness of women writing: "For clearly it is more within the reach of a woman to be eloquent than strong, and more modest for her to be skilled than daring, and easier for her to use the pen than the sword" (93).[40] Teresa de Cartagena's *Admiración* is at once a self-defense and a defense of women's equality in receiving God's grace, which can confer intellectual abilities and authority.[41]

The second wave: the *querella* in fiction

In the later fifteenth century, several writers responded to the polemics of the first wave of the *querella* by continuing to pose "the woman question" in fiction, particularly in the tales of frustrated and tragic desire identified with the genre known as the sentimental romance.[42] While many fictional works can be said to engage implicitly in the debate because they feature characters that confirm or counter misogynist claims that all women are reprehensible, several sentimental romances include scenes in which characters engage in formal debates and systematically present arguments from the pro- and antifeminine repertoires.[43] In these works, written for mixed audiences of men and women, and which frame the *querella* within the imagined lives and adventures of the protagonists, the debate itself becomes a subject of analysis. The sentimental romances thus weave the *querella* in to their interrogations of courtly love and explorations of the ideological conflicts inherent in the performance of masculinity and femininity.

In the anonymous *Triste deleytación*, written at some point after 1458, two female characters, La Doncella and La Madrina, review the arguments against and in defense of women during a conversation about vagaries of love and the fragility of female honor. La Doncella reports that she has only vaguely understood Rodríguez del Padrón's defense of women in the *Triunfo* (52). La Madrina reviews the profeminine arguments and their misogynist refutations, referring to Torrellas as "our mortal enemy" (54).[44] The conversation ends on an ambiguous and ironic note, with La Doncella remarking that her friend seems to enjoy arguing from both perspectives, rather than defend women. La Madrina, who has consistently appealed to lived experience over authority, replies in her own defense that self-evident truths must not be denied (55).[45]

The debate takes on even greater weight in two romances that were composed at some point in the 1470s or 1480s in the context of the Isabeline court, and went on to be extremely popular in Spanish and in translation throughout Europe in the sixteenth century, Diego de San Pedro's *Cárcel de amor* (*The Prison of Love*), first printed in 1492, and Juan de Flores's *Grisel y Mirabella* (*Grisel and Mirabella*, known throughout Europe as *Aurelio and Isabel*), first printed in 1495. San Pedro and Flores were both courtiers and *letrados*, San Pedro in the service of the eminent Tellez Girón family, and Flores in the court of the Catholic Monarchs. The *querella* appears in both formal and allusive guises in the two romances, which stage the debates and their consequences in the courts of rulers conflicted by the mutually exclusive terms of love and justice, settings that must have clearly resonated with the political agenda of the Catholic Monarchs.[46] Both romances allude to the political environment in which Isabel I came to power and reigned.

Cárcel de amor tells the story of an unsuccessful courtship. Leriano, a young nobleman is unable to be the recognized love-servant of the princess Laureola, who explains that, while she does not want him to die of lovesickness, cannot risk her honor by accepting his love. The courtship, such as it is, is carried out in a series of letters in which the *querella* is a clear intertextual reference. Laureola responds to Leriano's complaints of lovesickness by writing that she is in an impossible position. She fears that her letters will become public and no matter how she reacts she will be the subject of slander, though she would prefer to be "vilified for her cruelty than maligned for her mercy," that is, for favoring him with letters that can cure his suffering (28).[47] Her words foreshadow the accusations of fornication that follow; her "mercy," supposed to be a virtue, is a vice in the eyes of the law (52–53). Fearing that she will be thought *movible* (fickle), like so many women before her, Laureola writes in her final attempt to dissuade Leriano from dying of love, that his death will cause her to be the object of further criticism (62). In her last letter to Leriano, Laureola also tries to put their relationship into a different courtly context, that of royal patronage. She asks him to wait until her father's death, when she will presumably inherit the throne and be able to compensate him with honors and wealth (62–63).

A friend, Tefeo, drawing upon Ovidian and Boccaccian precedents, tries to cure Leriano of his lovesickness with a strong dose of antifeminine diatribe, by relating the "infinite evils of women."[48] Despite the repeated rejections that he has received from Laureola, Leriano declares that he cannot be convinced. Rather, his last words will be in praise of women and then launches into a long recitation, drawn principally from Diego de Valera's *Tratado en defensa de las virtuosas mugeres*, of fifteen reasons that the *maldicientes* (slanderers) err in speaking ill of women, twenty reasons men are indebted to women, and a catalogue of twenty good women, including María Coronel, Isabel de las Casas, and the *beata* Marí García.[49] Leriano concludes that men who defame women are blasphemers who besmirch their own honor (76).

In *Cárcel*, the discourse of misogyny is ineffective; Leriano has the last word, and thus, it would seem that the defense of women has won the day. Nevertheless, Leriano's profeminine martyrdom seems to suggest that the consequence of defending women may be death. *Cárcel*'s denouement is ambiguous: is Leriano a profeminine and courtly hero to be applauded, or a failed lover whose vulnerability to women leads to his demise? Is Laureola a *belle dame sans merci*, who has cruelly caused the death of a valiant and nobleman, or is she the victim of a courtly code that damns her regardless of whether she unsubmissively protects her honor or acquiesces? Leriano's rather hackneyed contribution to the *querella* does not solve the underlying questions asked by the romance.

In *Cárcel*, the formal defense of women is triggered by Tefeo's attempt to cure Leriano through misogyny; the *querella* is a rhetorical set piece peformed by Leriano, inserted as a parenthesis in the plot. In *Grisel y Mirabella*, dedicated to an unnamed lady assumed to be Isabel I herself, a fictional trial pitting men against women reduces the debate to a single question: do men seduce women, and are they thereby guilty for women's sins, or is it the other way around? The trial is ordered by a king who wishes to set a precedent after his council is unable to determine who to blame when the knight Grisel and the princess Mirabella are discovered *in flagrante*. The king commissions Torrellas, here resuscitated as a fictional character, to argue on the behalf of men, and Braçayda, a character from medieval retellings of the Trojan War to oppose him.

Braçayda bases her defense, like many a combatant in the *querella* before her, on women's relative weakness, to which she adds women's lack of discursive power in a world where men control access to knowledge and the legal system. However, Braçayda is not so much making the case for women as making a case against men and Torrellas. As the weaker, less educated, less discreet, less knowing half of humanity, women cannot be at fault in cases of sexual seduction, Braçayda avers. Consequently, women cannot force men to engage in sexual relations, while men can easily force women (110–113, 120–121). As the powerless subjects of male control, she argues, women cannot be to blame if they are easily led to sin by men. Virtue, Braçayda contends, is no benefit to women, because men will slander even the most virtuous of women, and women would rather sin in secret than be lambasted in public (120–121). Perhaps the most interesting rhetorical move Braçayda makes in the trial occurs when she converts the *topos* of the "power of women" as irresistible seducers into the "power of men," whose attractions and wiles can neither be denied nor resisted. Women, she argues, are unable to resist men's persuasive speech, letters, musical performances, and even their looks (110–113, 118–119). Torrellas responds to each of Braçayda's arguments by restating and amplifying all of the slurs found in his *Maldezir*.

He adds that should women one day be freed from the restraints of shame, they would pursue and seduce men just as avidly as men do women, a vision that Flores develops in another romance that draws upon the *querella*, *Triunfo de amor* (*The Triumph of Love*) (114–115). Torrellas is declared the victor of the trial. Mirabella, and by extension, all women are condemned.

Braçayda's most forceful statements interrogate the very nature of the debate. Echoing the famous question posed by Chaucer's Wife of Bath, "who painted the lion?" (v.692), Braçayda declares, "for, in our ignorance, we have no one to write in our favor, while you men, who hold pen in hand, can say whatever you want" (126–127).[50] After women are found guilty, Braçayda also protests the fundamental futility of trying to defend women when the outcome of the trial, despite all the trappings of a fair hearing, was predetermined, since men wrote the laws to their own advantage. The laws, she proclaims, "condemn the ravished victim to death—and [say] long live the rapist!" (138–139).[51]

Braçayda also takes aim at the rhetoric and posturing of courtly love, chiding men for their hyperbolic complaints of melancholy, torture, and "dying of love," defaming women who reciprocate their love and women who refuse it alike. As in *Cárcel*, in *Grisel y Mirabella*, the figurative term of "dying of love" becomes literal. Both Grisel and Mirabella commit suicide: Grisel throws himself into the bonfire to save Mirabella from the death to which she is condemned, while Mirabella throws herself into a pit of lions, unable to face life without Grisel. Torrellas, having become infatuated with Braçayda, is lured to his death at the hands of all the angry women of the court, who tear the woman-hater apart, recalling the murder of Orpheus by a horde of Bacchae in Ovid's *Metamorphoses*.

Braçayda's speeches in *Grisel y Mirabella*, much like Christine de Pizan's objections to *Matheolus* and Teresa de Cartagena's appeal to theological authority, move beyond the discursive bounds of profeminine defenses to question the structural misogyny at work in patriarchal society. Yet, the accusations leveled at women in Torrellas's *Maldezir* would also seem to be proved by his violent death at the hands of women who are furious in *Grisel y Mirabella* because they know they are *sobjectas* (subjugated) to the established political and social gender hierarchy. In Torrellas's case, women are indeed dangerous to men and he, a man in love, is tricked by their wiles, rendered powerless, and destroyed.

Cárcel and *Grisel* are fictional explorations of the case for and against women and their material consequences. If, in *Cárcel*, Leriano dies convinced by the profeminine arguments of the debate, in *Grisel*, Torrellas dies as a result of his triumph on the misogynist side; in each text, the debaters reach a conclusion, but the debate itself remains inconclusive. While Mirabella is cut from the same cloth as some of the heroines in the profeminine catalogues, and willingly dies as proof of her steadfast love, Laureola, the royal writer, and Braçayda, the vengeful debater, are less easy to place. The debate changes substantially when it is embedded in these late medieval fictions because, unlike the tendentious treatises and verses of the first wave of the *querella*, *Triste deleytación*, *Cárcel de amor*, and *Grisel y Mirabella*, are dialogic, humanist fictions that not only present multiple viewpoints and imagine various lived experiences, but also encourage readers to continue the protagonists' questioning of the status quo and the nature of the *querella* itself.

Fifteenth-century writers enjoyed a veritable rhetorical arsenal of commonplaces for arguing, on the one hand, in the defense of women and, on the other, for proving the superiority of the male sex and the iniquity of women. For the male writers of the first wave of the *querella*, to pose the "woman question" was a form of begging the question, since the answer was a foregone conclusion. Wisdom and conduct literature written for men, such as *Bocados de oro*, or the *Arcipreste de Talavera* present *woman* as category to be mastered and a figure to be avoided in the interests of men's health and honor. *Cancionero* poetry and the profeminine treatises written in the middle decades of the fifteenth-century, in turn, explore the rhetorical possibilities and the courtly posturing available to men arguing in the defense and defamation of women and love. Teresa de Cartagena took the challenge a step further by playing upon the difference between natural, sexually differentiated bodies and the God-given equality of intellectual potential. Fiction, unlike the polemical works, placed the *querella* within dialogic frames that bring the act of debating under scrutiny while also imagining women taking active and authoritative roles as orators and writers, providing contesting images and counter narratives to those excluding women from public speech and from taking up the pen.

Socrates' quip, equating a woman's intellectual pursuits with the compounding of evil, is an apt trope with which to begin a discussion of the discursive background concerning the nature and proper behavior of women from which the writers considered throughout this volume emerged, for it concisely demonstrates how discourses of cultural authority defined women by their exclusion from learning. What is more, the images of women offered by the *querella* provided historical women writers, such as Teresa de Cartagena, material in relation to which they might engage in literary acts of self-fashioning and reflection upon women's roles as authors, and as the agents rather than the objects of discourse. Allusions to the *querella* abound in late medieval and early modern literature. Later authors, María de Zayas and Sor Juana Inés de la Cruz, to name just two notable examples, inherited and extended the *querella* tradition, adding more women's voices to the defense. Their acts of writing were acts "opposing cultural hierarchies, mappings, and orthodoxies of gendered spaces, roles and belief," as Amanda Powell and Stacy Schlau describe the cultural production of early modern and colonial women (48). Within the horizons of expectation of their varied genres, the foundational *querella* texts all respond to the misalignments between gender orthodoxy and experience. This indeterminacy did not end with the fifteenth century. The texts of the *querella* enjoyed a lasting cultural presence, and their influence can be clearly felt throughout the early modern period.

Notes

1 On the history and usage of the term "querelle des femmes," see Zimmerman, "The '*Querelle des Femmes*' as a Cultural Studies Paradigm," which recaps and reflects upon a prior essay, co-authored with Bock, "Die *Querelle des Femmes* in Europa."
2 Some scholars consider the *querelle* a coherent, European tradition lasting from the fourteenth century until the French Revolution, while others define its parameters as spanning from the Middle Ages to the twentieth century, encompassing all texts from Europe and the Americas that comment upon the nature and status of women. Kelly asserted the existence of a coherent tradition in her groundbreaking article "Early Feminist Theory and the *Querelle des Femmes*, 1400–1789." Benson, on the other hand, argues for the consideration of separate medieval and Renaissance *querelles* ("Querelle des femmes"). A broad, transatlantic definition guides the approaches of the series *La Querella de las mujeres*, edited by Segura, and the anthology *La Querella de Mujeres en Europa e Hispanoamérica*, ed. Ramírez Almazán et al.
3 The *querella* in Iberia extended beyond works composed in Spanish such as Eiximenis's *Llibre de les dones* (1396) and Jaume Roig's *Spill* (c. 1460), which lie beyond the scope of this essay. For a descriptive bibliography of the *querella* see Weiss, "Bibliography of Primary Texts." For numerous excerpts, see Archer, ed. *Misoginia y defensa de las mujeres*, which also includes biblical, classical, and sixteenth-century examples. For an anthology of European *querelle* texts, see Blamires, ed. *Woman Defamed*. Campbell's "The *Querelle des femmes*" provides an excellent introduction to the state of scholarship on the *querelle* in the English, French, and Italian contexts.
4 "Una forma de intervenir en la Querella, de crear opinión en el mundo, de hacer política."
5 See, for example, studies by Archer, Francomano, Lacarra, Muñoz-Fernández, Rivera Garretas, Solomon, Vargas Martínez, Vélez-Sainz, Weissberger, Weiss, and Zimmerman listed in the bibliography. For the broader European context see, for example, Kolsky, Stanton, and Warner.
6 "Non ha [...] peor mal que la muger [...] E vió a una muger enferma que se non podíe mover en su lecho, e dixo: El mal queda con el mal [...] E vido una moça que deprendíe escrevir, e dixo:

Non acrescientes el mal con el mal." *Bocados de oro*, a compendium of advice and sayings of philosophers intended to mold the conduct and beliefs of its inscribed male readers, was first compiled in the thirteenth century and circulated throughout the fifteenth. The observation about women learning to read must have been important for the book's compilers, because a few lines later, Socrates repeats the sentiment: "E vio una moça que aprendie escrevir, e dixo: Añades al escurpión veganbre sobre su veganbre" (And he saw a young woman who was learning to write, and he said, 'you are adding poison to the scorpion's poison) (64).

7   On humoral theory and its importance for medieval and early modern ideas of gender classification, see Paster.
8   Aristotle and Virgil figure frequently among the ranks of such enamored sages. On "the power of women," topos see Smith.
9   In order to avoid imposing anachronistic political and philosophical constructs upon pre-modern works, here *feminist* and the related terms *pro-* and *proto-feminist* are not used. Rather, for the sake of conciseness, *misogynist* and *antifeminine* are used as catchalls to refer to those texts and authorial stances that express hatred of women (*misogyny*), fear of women (gynophobia or *horror feminae*), and the rejection of marriage (*misogamy*). The term *profeminine* is used to refer to those texts and authors that defend women in response to misogynist attacks by praising femininity and feminine virtues, as traditionally defined. On the term *profeminine*, see Blamires, *The Case of Women* 11–12.
10 On the formation and institutionalization of Aristotelian sex polarity, see Allen. On the relation between Aristotelian sex polarity and changing legal customs in the later middle ages, see Stuard. On humanistic responses to the Aristotelian revolution and their relation to the *querella,* see Rivera Garretas.
11 Conduct literature for women also frequently cites the biblical verses in praise of the good wife in order to instruct readers how to emulate her. For example, Fray Luis de León's *La perfecta casada* is an extended gloss on the biblical *mujer de valor*.
12 See McGovern, Oñate 39–113, Serrano, and Vélez-Sainz 45–51.
13 See Muñoz Fernández, Weiss, "Qué demandamos" 237–249; Weissberger, "Deceitful Sects" 207–212; and Rivera Garretas.
14 On the connections between the *Arcipreste de Talavera* and other misogynist texts of the fifteenth century and men's health, see Solomon. On the "religion of love" and its relationship to the literature of misogyny, see Gerli, "La 'religión del amor.'" For further study on theories of love in the period, see Cátedra, *Amor y pedagogía* and *Tratados de amor*.
15 "Non han número nin cuento, nin escrevir se podrían, como de cada día el que con las mugeres platicare, verá cosas en ellas incognitas, nuevas e nunca escriptas, vistas nin sabidas" (64). The English translation, titled *Little Sermons on Sin*, is by Lesley Byrd Simpson.
16 "Envidiosa ser la muger mala dubdar en ello sería pecar en el Espíritu Santo: por cuanto toda muger, quandoquier que ve otra de sí más fermosa, de envidia se quiere morir" (160).
17 "Desque adormido comencé de soñar que sobre mí veía señoras meas de mill . . . de nombre e renombre famosas" (305). Translation by the author. *Little Sermons on Sin* does not reproduce the epilogue.
18 "¡Guay del ombre que solo duerme con dolor de axaqueca e en su casa rueca nunca entra todo el año!"
19 "Quien bien amando persigue / dona, a si mesmo destruye."
20 "Mujer es un animal / que se diz' hombre imperfecto, / procreado en el defecto / del buen calor natural."
21 "Sintiendo que son subjectas / e sin nengund poderío, / a fin de aver señorío / tienen engañosas sectas."
22 "Aquesta es la condición / de las mugeres comuna."
23 One reason that the verses were scandalous in the eyes of many of Torrellas's fifteenth-century readers was his importation of the misogynist repertoire of women's faults into context of courtly poetry (Archer, "Las coplas").
24 Dutton and Krogstad provide the texts of all known versions of the *Maldezir* as well as of the poetic responses to Torrellas in *El cancionero del siglo XV, ca. 1360–1520,* 7 vols. The poems are also available on the University of Liverpool, UK, website, "An Electronic Corpus of 15th Century Castilian *Cancionero* Manuscripts," http://cancionerovirtual.liv.ac.uk
25 "Los fidalgos han de ser / defensa de las mujeres."
26 "Uno de los plazeres del paraíso"; "el ombre peccó de cierta sabiduría, e la muger por engaño e por ignorancia."

27 "Las donas deven regir e batallar quando conviene, segund que los onbres, los quales por tiranía el regimiento tienen occupado."
28 "paresçe claro auer seido mayor número el de los malos onbres, et mayor el de las buenas mugeres."
29 "Aquestos començadores de nueva seta, que rotamente les plaze en general de todas las mugeres maldezir. E pues tanto te agrada saberlo, comoquiera triste me sea exerçer la torpe mano en tan orrible materia [. . .] soy cierto que, vistas por ti sus conclusiones, ligeramente anchilarás su opinión."
30 "Los coraçones de los tales así son ligeros como las fojas de los árboles, que todo viento las mueve."
31 As Glenda McLeod observes in her study of catalogues of good and bad women, the concatenation of examples provided historically authorized definitions of women by creating the sense "a general consensus [. . .] based on a culture's written legacy" (3).
32 "Non como hembra los lugares escondidos buscó nin las leyes de paz demandó, mas con viril coraçon dexados los fémineos apostamientos, governadora e regidora en las batallas con gran vigor se mostró."
33 "Ya Dios, ¿pues qué çeguedat es esta, que así ocupa la vista de los mortales? ¿puede ser cosa más virtuosa que aquellas que la natura crio cuerpos flacos, coraçones tiernos, comúnmente ingenio perezoso, ser falladas en muchas virtudes antepuestas a los varones, a quien por don natural fue otorgado cuerpos valientes, diligente ingenio, coraçones duros?"
34 Luna promoted Juan II's second marriage in 1447 to Isabel of Portugal, mother of the future Queen Isabel I. However, Luna and Isabel entered into conflict, leading to Luna's eventual execution. A copy of the *Libro de las virtuosas y claras mugeres* appears in the inventory of Queen Isabel I's books and may have come down to her through her mother. Abby McGovern suggests that the omission of contemporary women from the *Libro* is intended as a veiled criticism of Queen María.
35 On medieval women writers see Deyermond and Surtz, *Writing Women*. For early modern women writers who participated in the *querella* see Ramírez Alamzán et al., and Segura Graiño, ed., *La Querella de las Mujeres I. Análisis de textos*.
36 See Nader: 6, and Howe.
37 "Si liberalmente y de buen grado nos gloriaremos en nuestras enfermedades, porque more en nuestras ánmas la virtut de Cristo" (62). English translations of *Arboleda* and the *Admiraçión* are from Seidenspinner-Núñez, *The Writings of Teresa de Cartagena*.
38 Surtz, "In Search of Juana de Mendoza."
39 "La causa porque los varones se maravillan que muger aya hecho tractado es por no ser acostumbrado en el estado fimíneo, más solamente en el varonil. Ca los varones hazer libros e aprender çiençias, e vsar dellas [. . .] parece ser acudi oir baatural curso" (115).
40 "Que manifiesto es que más a mano viene a la henbra ser eloquente que no ser fuerte, e más onesto la es ser entendida que no osada, e más ligera cosa le será usar de la péñola que de la espada" (120).
41 For further analysis of the works of *Teresa de Cartagena* and ample bibliographic references, see Kim, *Between Desire and Passion* and *El saber femenino*, and Seidenspinner-Núñez, "Introduction" and "Interpretive Essay."
42 Deliberation about the very existence and parameters of the genre is ongoing, but there is a general consensus, at least in practice, among critics that a series of short, formally hybrid stories about unrequited or tragic love, produced between 1440 and 1550, form the genre.
43 Blamires distinguishes between works that make "formal," or systematically presented contributions to the debate on women, and those that make "incidental" contributions by referencing debate commonplaces (*The Case for Women* 9).
44 "Nuestro amigo mortal"; Rodríguez del Padrón is lauded as "aquel más virtuoso de todos los hombres" (52).
45 "Quien la verdad del todo niega, atorga más la mentira, porque cosas hay que no se pueden decir el contrario, por tener los fines y evidencias muy ciertos."
46 See Weissberger 219–21, and Gerli "Conflictive Subjectivity."
47 "Afeada por cruel que amanzillada por piadosa."
48 "Infinidos males de las mugeres."
49 According to *Cárcel de amor*, Isabel de las Casas is exemplary because even though she never married Pedro Girón, the father of her illustrious sons, she refused to marry any other man and died as a chaste widow and signs of sanctity attended her death.
50 "Porque en nuestra simplicidad no ay quién scriva en favor nuestro. Y vosotros que tenéis la pluma en la mano: pintáis como queréis."
51 "Quieren que muera la que es forçada y viva el forçador."

Works cited

Primary works

An Electronic Corpus of 15th Century Castilian Cancionero Manuscripts. http://cancionerovirtual.liv.ac.uk
"Bocados de oro." *Kritische Ausgabe des altspanischen Textes*. Ed. Mechthild Crombach. Bonn: Romanisches Seminar der Universität Bonn, 1971.
Boccaccio, Giovanni. *Famous Women*. Trans. Virginia Brown. Cambridge, MA: Harvard UP, 2001.
——. *The Corbaccio*. Trans. Anthony Cassell. Urbana: U Illinois P, 1975.
Castigos y dotrinas que un sabio dava a sus hijas/Lessons and Teachings that a Wise Man Gave to His Daughters. Trans. Emily C. Francomano. In *Medieval Conduct Literature: An Anthology of Vernacular Guides to Behaviour for Youths, with English Translations*. Ed. Mark D. Johnston. Toronto: U Toronto P, 2009: 250–284.
Chaucer, Geoffrey. "The Wife of Bath's Prologue." *The Riverside Chaucer*. Ed. Larry Dean Benson. 3rd ed. Oxford New York: Oxford UP, 2008: 105–122.
Christine de Pizan. *The Book of the City of Ladies*. Trans. Earl Jeffrey Richards. New York: Persea, 1982.
Eiximenis, Francesc. *Llibre de Les Dones*. Eds. Frank Naccarato, et al. Barcelona: Curial Edicions Catalanes, 1981.
F. A. d. C., *Triste deleytaçión: An Anonymous Fifteenth Century Castilian Romance*. Ed. E. Michael Gerli. Washington, DC: Georgetown UP, 1982.
Flores, Juan de. *Grisel y Mirabella*. In *Three Spanish Querelle Texts*. Ed. and trans. Emily C. Francomano. Toronto: ITER/CRRS, 2013: 85–178.
Le Fèvre, Jehan. *The Lamentations of Matheolus*. In *Woman Defamed and Woman Defended: An Anthology of Medieval Texts*. Ed. Alcuin Blamires. Oxford: Oxford UP, 1992: 177–197.
Luis de León. *La perfecta casada*. Ed. Mercedes Etreros. Madrid: Taurus 1987.
Luna, Álvaro de. *Libro de las virtuosas y claras mugeres*. Ed. Julio Vélez-Sainz. Madrid: Cátedra, 2009.
Martín de Córdoba. *Jardín de nobles donzellas*. Ed. Harriet Goldberg. Chapel Hill: U North Carolina Department of Romance Languages, 1974.
Martínez de Toledo, Alfonso. *Arcipreste de Talavera*. Ed. E. Michael Gerli. Madrid: Cátedra, 1992.
——. *Little Sermons on Sin*. Trans. Lesley Byrd Simpson. Berkeley: U California P, 1959.
Ribera, Suero de. *Respuesta de Suero de Ribera en defensión de las donas*. In *La poesía cancioneril castellana*. Ed. E. Michael Gerli. Madrid: Akal, 1994: 281–282.
Rodríguez del Padrón, Juan. *Triunfo de las donas*. In *Obras completas*. Ed. César Hernández Alonso. Madrid: Editora Nacional, 1982: 211–258.
Roig, Jaume. *Espill: o, Llibre de les dones*. Ed. Marina Gustà. Barcelona: Edicions 62, 1978.
San Pedro, Diego de. *Cárcel de amor. Con la continuación de Nicolás Núñez*. Ed. Carmen Parrilla. Barcelona: Crítica, 1995.
Teresa de Cartagena. *The Writings of Teresa de Cartagena*. Ed. and Trans. Dayle Seidenspinner-Núñez. Woodbridge, UK: Brewer, 1998.
——. *Arboleda de los enfermos. Admiraçión operum dey*. Ed. Lewis Joseph Hutton. Madrid: *Anejos del Boletín de la Real Academia*, 1967.
Torrellas, Pere. *Maldezir de mugeres/The Slander against Women. Three Spanish Querelle Texts*. Ed. and trans. Emily C. Francomano. Toronto: ITER/CRRS, 2013: 55–64.
Valera, Diego de. *Defensa de virtuosas mujeres*. Ed. Federica Accorsi. Biblioteca Studi Ispanici 22. Florence: ETS, 2009.

Secondary works

Allen, Prudence. *The Concept of Woman: The Aristotelian Revolution 750 BC-AD 1250*. 2nd ed. Grand Rapids MI: Eerdmans, 1997 [originally Published, Montreal: Eden Press, 1985].
Archer, Robert. *The Problem of Woman in Late-Medieval Hispanic Literature*. Woodbridge: Tamesis, 2005.
——. "Las Coplas 'de las calidades de las donas' de Pere Torroella y la tradición lírica Catalana." *Boletín de la Real Academia de Buenas Letras de Barcelona* 47 (1999–2000): 405–423.
Archer, Robert. Ed. *Misoginia y defensa de las mujeres: antología de textos medievales*. Madrid: Cátedra, 2001.
Benson, Pamela J. "Querelle des femmes." In *Encyclopedia on Women in the Renaissance*. Ed. Diana Robin, Anne R. Larsen, and Carole Levin. Santa Barbara: ABC Clio, 2007: 307–311.

———. *The Invention of the Renaissance Woman: The Challenge of Female Independence in the Literature and Thought of Italy and England*. University Park, PA: Pennsylvania State UP, 1992.

Blamires, Alcuin. *The Case for Women in Medieval Culture*. Oxford: Clarendon, 1997.

———. "Refiguring the 'Scandalous Excess' of Women: The Wife of Bath and Liberality." *Gender in Debate from the Middle Ages to the Renaissance*. Eds. Thelma S. Fenster and Claire A. Lees. New York: Palgrave, 2002: 57–78.

Blamires, Alcuin. ed. *Woman Defamed and Woman Defended: An Anthology of Medieval Texts*. Oxford: Oxford UP, 1992.

Bloch, R. Howard. *Medieval Misogyny and the Invention of Western Romantic Love*. Chicago: U Chicago P, 1991.

———. "Chaucer's Maiden's head: 'The Physician's Tale' and the Poetics of Virginity," *Representations* 28 (1989): 133–134.

Campbell, Julie D. "The *Querelle des Femmes*." In *The Ashgate Research Companion to Women and Gender in Early Modern Europe*. Ed. Allyson M. Poska, Allyson Jane Couchman, and Katherine A. McIver. Farnham, UK: Ashgate, 2013: 361–379.

Cátedra, Pedro M. *Amor y pedagogía en la España medieval. Estudios de doctrina amorosa y práctica literaria*. Salamanca: Ediciones Universidad de Salamanca, 1989.

Cátedra, Pedro M., ed. *Tratados de amor en torno de* Celestina, *siglos XV–XVI*. Madrid: Sociedad Estatal España Nuevo Milenio, 2001.

Deyermond, Alan D. "Spain's First Women Writers." In *Women in Hispanic Literature: Icons and Fallen Idols*. Ed. Beth Miller. Berkeley: U California P, 1983: 27–62.

Francomano, Emily C. "Introduction." *Three Spanish Querelle Texts:* Grisel and Mirabella, The Slander, *and* The Defense of Ladies Against Slanderers. *A Bilingual Edition and Study*. The Other Voice in Early Modern Europe. Toronto: Centre for Reformation and Renaissance Studies, 2013: 1–51.

Gerli, E. Michael. "Conflictive Subjectivity and The Politics of Truth and Justice in *Cárcel de amor*." *Queen Isabel I of Castile: power, patronage, persona*. Ed. Barbara F. Weissberger. Woodbridge UK: Támesis, 2008: 149–168.

———. "La 'religión del amor' y el antifeminismo en las letras castellanas del siglo XV." *Hispanic Review* 49.1 (1981): 65–86.

Howe, Elizabeth Teresa. *Education and Women in The Early Modern Hispanic World*. Aldershot, UK: Ashgate, 2008.

Jordan, Constance. *Renaissance Feminism*. Ithaca: Cornell UP, 1990.

Kelly, Joan. *Women, History, and Theory*. Chicago: U Chicago P, 1984.

Kim, Yonsoo. *Between Desire and Passion: Teresa de Cartagena*. Leiden: Brill, 2012.

———. *El saber femenino y el sufrimiento corporal de la Temprana Edad Moderna: Arboleda de enfermos y Admiraçión Operum Dey de Teresa de Cartagena*. Córdoba: Universidad de Córdoba, 2008.

Kolsky, Stephen. *The Ghost of Boccaccio: Writings on Famous Women in Renaissance Italy*. Turnhout: Brepols, 2005.

Lacarra, María Jesús. "Algunos datos para la historia de la misoginia en la Edad Media." *Studia in Honorem Prof. M. de Riquer*. Quaderns Crema 1 (1986): 339–361.

McGovern, Abby. "Writing the Antithesis of María of Aragón: Alvaro de Luna's Rendering of Giovanni Boccaccio's *De mulieribus claris*." *Scripta: Revista internacional de literatura i cultura medieval i moderna* 2 (2013): 225–337.

McLeod, Glenda. *Virtue and Venom: Catalogs of Women from Antiquity to the Renaissance*. Ann Arbor: U Michigan P, 1991.

Muñoz Fernández, Ángela. "Las cuestiones de Minerva. *Problemata* en torno a la acción femenina en los debates culturales del siglo XV castellano." *Mujeres de la Edad Media: actividades políticas, socioeconómicas y culturales*. Ed. María del Carmen García Herrero and Cristina Pérez Galán. Zaragoza: Fernando el Católico, 2014: 139–165.

———. "El linaje de Cristo a la luz del 'giro genealógico' del siglo XV: la respuesta de Juana de la Cruz (1481–1534)." *Anuario de Estudios Medievales* 44.1 (2014): 433–473.

———. "María y el marco teológico de la Querella de las Mujeres (Interferencias y transferencias con los debates culturales de la Castilla siglo XV)." *Arenal* 20.2 (2013): 235–262.

Nader, Helen. "Introduction: The World of the Mendozas." *Power and Gender in Renaissance Spain: Eight Women of the Mendoza Family, 1450–1650*. Urbana and Chicago: U Illinois P, 2004: 1–26.

Oñate, María del Pilar. *El feminismo en la literatura española*. Madrid: Espasa Calpe, 1938.

Paster, Gail Kern. "The Unbearable Coldness of Female Being: Women's Imperfection and the Humoral Economy." *English Literary Renaissance* 28.3 (1998): 416–440.

Powell, Amanda and Stacey Schlau. "Framing 'Mujeres alborotadas': Early Modern and Colonial Women's Cultural Production." *Letras Femeninas* 35.1 (2009): 43–60.

Ramírez Almzán, Dolores, et al., eds. *La Querella de Mujeres en Europa e Hispanoamérica*. Sevilla: Junta de Andalucía, 2011.

Rivera Garretas, María-Milagros. "La diferencia sexual en la historia de la Querella de las Mujeres." In *The Querelle des Femmes* in the Romania: Studies in Honour of Friederike Hassauer. Ed. Wolfram Aichinger, Marlen Bidwell-Steiner, Judith Bösch, and Eva Cescutti. Vienna: Turia und Kant, 2003: 13–26.

Ruiz García, Elsa. *Los libros de Isabel la Católica: Arqueología de un patrimonio escrito*. Salamanca: Instituto de Historia del Libro y de la Lectura, 2004.

Segura, Cristina Graíño, ed. *La Querel-la/ya de las Mujeres*. Madrid: Asociación Cultural Almudanya, 2009–2011.

Seidenspinner-Núñez, Dayle. "Introduction." Teresa de Cartagena. *The Writings of Teresa de Cartagena*. Ed. and trans. Dayle Seidenspinner–Núñez. Woodbridge, UK: Brewer, 1998: 1–21.

———. "Interpretive Essay." Teresa de Cartagena. *The Writings of Teresa de Cartagena*. Ed. and trans. Dayle Seidenspinner–Núñez. Woodbridge, UK: Brewer, 1998: 113–138.

Serrano, Florence. "Del debate a la propaganda política mediante la *Querella de las Mujeres* en Juan Rodríguez del Padrón, Diego de Valera y Álvaro de Luna. *Talia dixit* 7 (2012): 97–115.

Smith, Susan L. *The Power of Women: A Topos in Medieval Art and Literature*. Philadelphia: U Pennsylvania P, 1995.

Solomon, Michael R. *The Literature of Misogyny in Medieval Spain: The "Arcipreste de Talavera" and the "Spill."* New York: Cambridge UP, 1997.

Stanton, Domna C. *The Dynamics of Gender in Early Modern France: Women Writ, Women Writing*. Farnham, UK: Ashgate, 2014.

Stuard, Susan Mosher. "The Dominion of Gender or How Women Fared in the Middle Ages." In *Becoming Visible: Women in European History*. Ed. Renate Bridenthal, Susan Mosher Stuard, and Merry E. Wiesner. Boston: Houghton Mifflin, 1998: 129–152.

Surtz, Ronald E. "In Search of Juana de Mendoza." *Power and Gender in Renaissance Spain: Eight Women of the Mendoza Family, 1450–1650*. Ed. Helen Nader. Urbana and Chicago: U Illinois P, 2004: 48–70.

———. *Writing Women in Late Medieval and Early Modern Spain: The Mothers of Saint Teresa of Ávila*. Philadelphia: U Pennsylvania P, 1995.

Vargas Martínez, Ana. "Sobre los discursos políticos a favor de las mujeres (El *Triunfo de las donas* de Juan Rodríguez de la Cámara)." *Arenal* 20.2 (2013): 263–288.

Vélez-Sainz, Julio. "Introducción." Luna, Álvaro de. *Libro de las virtuosas y claras mugeres*. Ed. Julio Vélez-Sainz. Madrid: Cátedra, 2009.

Warner, Lyndan. *The Ideas of Man and Woman in Renaissance France Print, Rhetoric and Law*. Farnham, UK: Ashgate, 2011.

Weiss, Julian. "Bibliography of Primary Texts in Spanish, ca. 1430–1520." *Gender in Debate from the Early Middle Ages to the Renaissance*. Ed. Thelma Fenster and Clare Lees. New York: Palgrave, 2002: 275–281.

———. "¿Qué demandamos de las mugeres?: Forming the Debate on Women in Late Medieval and Early Modern Spain (With A Baroque Response)." *Gender in Debate from the Early Middle Ages to the Renaissance*. Ed. Thelma Fenster and Clare Lees. New York: Palgrave, 2002: 237–274.

Weissberger, Barbara F. "'Deceitful Sects': The Debate about Women in the Age of Isabel the Catholic." *Gender in Debate from the Early Middle Ages to the Renaissance*. Ed. Thelma S. Fenster and Clare A. Lees. New York: Palgrave, 2002: 207–236.

———. "*A Tierra Puto!* Alfonso de Palencia's Discourse of Effeminacy." *Queer Iberia: Sexualities, Cultures, and Crossings from the Middle Ages to the Renaissance*. Ed. Josiah Blackmore and Gregory S. Hutcheson. Durham, NC: Duke UP, 1999: 291–324.

Zimmerman, Margarete. "The Old Quarrel: More than Just Rhetoric?" *The Querelle des Femmes* in the Romania: Studies in Honour of Friederike Hassauer. Ed. Wolfram Aichinger, Marlen Bidwell-Steiner, Juthith Bösch, and Eva Cescutti. Vienna: Turia und Kant, 2003: 27–42.

———. "The '*Querelle des Femmes*' as a Cultural Studies Paradigm." *Time, Space, and Women's Lives in Early Modern Europe*. Ed. Thomas Kuehn and Anne Jacobson Schutte. Kirksville, MO: Truman State UP, 2001: 17–28.

Zimmermann, Margarete and Gisela Bock. "Die *Querelle des femmes* in Europa. Eine begriffs- und forschungsgeschichtliche Einführung." *Die Europäische Querelle Des Femmes: Geschlechterdebatten Seit Dem 15. Jahrhundert*. Stuttgart: Metzler, 1997: 9–38.

SECTION II

Conventual spaces

4
AUTOBIOGRAPHIES

Isabelle Poutrin

The term "autobiography" must be used with care when applying it to women's conventual literature, insofar as the genre varied in its conceptualization of individual identity (Durán López: 31), and progressively established its parameters during the early modern period. The expression "ego-document"[1] is therefore more appropriate, given the diversity of texts narrated in first person that were written in Spanish convents between 1580 and the first half of the eighteenth century. In his pioneering study of Spanish autobiographies, Manuel Serrano y Sanz excluded "the numerous spiritual lives written by our nuns, where external events are totally neglected or hardly mentioned."[2] Serrano y Sanz's rejection in turn relegated to oblivion what today constitutes an abundant body of works that hold great historical and literary value and, furthermore, are without equal in male authors' writings. The growing interest in women's conventual autobiographies since the decades of the 1990s is due to two essential historiographical developments: the emergence and consolidation of genre studies in the academic field, and the renewed critical attention to religion and spirituality from the perspective of social studies and of mentalities. The surge in research dealing with these texts has thus led to a complete reassessment of early modern women's roles, both in the literature of the period and in the history of Catholicism in Spain.

To better understand the different types of autobiographical texts, it is necessary to take into consideration the designations used by authors themselves, despite their lack of precision. Certain texts, designated as "my life" or "the discourse of my life," adopt the form of a narrative. They begin with the author's childhood and follow the stages of her life at key moments of her personal spiritual development, such as her awareness of her religious vocation, the obstacles she faced that prevented her from dedicating herself to the contemplative life, and the means awarded her by God with which to resolve conflictive situations. In such cases, the literary models that made the most impact, and that are sometimes explicitly mentioned, are St. Augustine's *Confessions* and, for those written after the 1590s, the first chapters of Teresa of Ávila's *Book of Her Life*, even though the precise themes of personal conversion or of change of life appear in only a minority of conventual autobiographies. These narratives belong, *stricto sensu*, to the genre of autobiography and are of most interest for studying women's history in its different aspects. Other texts in first-person narration are of interest to the history of spirituality and mysticism; for instance, the "examination of conscience" (*cuenta de conciencia*) designated all the ways by which the authors described their various inner states.

Another autobiographical form is that of "favors" or "graces," that is, the narration of spiritual experiences that exceeded the limits of religious experience regarded as normal at that time. These texts usually recount ecstatic episodes at which time the nun-author envisioned a being belonging to the "Heavenly court" (Christ, the Virgin, saints, or angels); the typical scene would include gestures, discourses, and other sensory signs. The narratives of favors could also constitute a separate text addressed to the confessor and at times, following the life narrative, marking the passage from the autobiographical narration and remembrance of the past, to the account of the author's most recent experiences. In other texts, the narratives of favors are inserted within the narration of events that took place inside the convent. In all cases, these narratives draw the reader's attention by briefly indicating a particular liturgical date ("on Saint Dominic's day") or a specific moment ("while praying"; "after communion"). The category of "favors and graces" also includes "intelligences," that is, the immediate and illuminating comprehension of the arguments of Catholic dogma not understood through reason and that are called "mysteries" by the Church, such as the dogma of the Holy Trinity or of the Eucharist. Another modality of "favors and graces" is that of "revelations," defined by the theologian Leandro de Granada as "a knowledge born from a light superior than the natural one, and therefore supernatural"[3] (4r). The visions of Christ's life and Passion, the sudden understanding of verses from Holy Scripture, and the knowledge of the state of the souls of the deceased, are all part of this category of revelations. The textual typology and terminology utilized by the authors largely reflected the tendency of Spanish mystical theology during the Catholic Reformation to favor the spiritual life's search for the most extraordinary and frequent mystical graces, independently from the normal development of divine grace in the soul (Krynen: 285–323).

The point in common of these conventual ego-documents is that they were written by mandate and in obeisance; that is, in the context of a relationship of spiritual guidance between a clergyman (the confessor or the father superior) and a woman dedicated to the contemplative life (whether a professed nun or a beata). Despite the loss of a great many conventual files, dozens of handwritten autobiographical notebooks, either in copies or originals, have been preserved, while many other texts have left their trace in the form of excerpts found inserted in printed hagiographies. The confessor's mandate, therefore, was essential in the production and dissemination of these texts, as it was his duty to guide her to salvation by helping her escape the innumerable traps of the contemplative life, such as temptations, diabolical illusions, times of discouragement, or the enmity among the convent sisters. Nonetheless, not all nuns received orders to write their life's account; only those who stood out in the eyes of their confessor or of the religious order's superiors due to the distinctive nature of their spiritual experience.

The confessor's mandate served several purposes, since there were multiple possible uses of the autobiographical accounts. At the beginning of the *Book of Her Life*, Teresa of Ávila explains that her confessors wanted to ascertain the authenticity of her mystical experiences through a careful examination of her life's narrative. The autobiographical writing was, on the one hand, a requirement of the "discernment of spirits," by which the confessor or other theologians identified, on the basis of the nun's text, whether her spiritual itinerary followed orthodox Catholic criteria (Bilinkoff: 27–28). Indeed, the abundant production of autobiographical texts in women's convents is due to the cultural, political, and social factors that constituted the historical framework on which the texts' literary interpretation is based. A leading factor was the evolution of the models proposed by the late medieval Church to be imitated by worshippers. For centuries, saints-kings and bishops had been the privileged models, but the canonization of women saints by the papacy granted greater agency to contemplative women as direct channels of communication with God, thus elevating the value of the written expression of their spiritual experiences (Vauchez). From Northern Europe and Italy, the model of the "mystic-nun writer" was transposed to the Iberian Peninsula (Surtz, *Writing Women*). The Dominican tertiary, Catherine of Siena (1347–1380), canonized in 1461 and famous for her stigmata, became the most important model for nuns, thanks to the translation of her writings and their publication in sixteenth-century Spain. Numerous women's autobiographical texts contain episodes inspired by the saint's experiences: extreme ascetic exercises, vows of chastity at seven years of age, the interchange of the women's hearts with that of Jesus, and mystical marriages accompanied by the gift of a wedding ring. Another important figure in the formation of the model of mystic-nun writers was Sister Juana de la Cruz (1481–1534), abbess of the Franciscan tertiaries of Cubas in the diocesis of Toledo. This visionary nun preached publicly during her ecstasies; the *Book of Consolation* (*Libro del conorte*), a collection of her sermons from 1509 written by a nun from her convent, remained in manuscript, but Juana de la Cruz's fame spread thanks to the published hagiographies by Antonio Daza (1610) and Pedro Navarro (1622) (García Andrés; Surtz, *The Guitar of God*). The Franciscan tertiary contributed decisively to the visionary mysticism that was frequently expressed in many first-person accounts of visions and revelations such as the *Light of the Mind* (*Luz del entendimiento*) by the Cistercian nun María Magdalena de la Santísima Trinidad (c.1589–1677), and the *Mystical City of God* (*La mística ciudad de Dios*) by the Franciscan Conceptionist María de Jesús de Ágreda (1602–1665), Philip IV's confidant and author, among other texts, of an unfinished account of her life.

Another reason religious women's autobiographical narratives assumed importance was the advance of the Counter-Reformation, since against the Protestants' refutations, the Catholic Church established itself as the single depository of Christian truth and the single beneficiary of divine grace. Mystical graces received by nuns provided a telling evidence of the fact that God remained present in the Church. Furthermore, religious orders that undertook their internal reform shortly before or after the Council of Trent (1545–1563) intensified their competition in the field of holiness, launching canonization proceedings in Rome that could become long and costly, but whose success was an enormous source of prestige for the Church. The early canonization in 1622 of Teresa of Ávila (1515–1582), founder of the Discalced Carmelites, and the publication of her *Book of Her Life* as part of her *Works* (*Obras*) (1588), elevated her status to that of the main model for many nuns and other religious women. Her canonization also served as a powerful incentive for religious orders to promote the beatification of their own nuns with the Congregation of Rites in Rome, in particular if they had been founders of the order and were also mystics. Although their expectations were frustrated in the vast majority of cases, the cases were supported by the nuns' confessors. The purpose of mandating the autobiographical writings, therefore, was to leave evidence of the nun's ongoing progress in Christian virtues and, in the most promising case, of her special choice by God to elevate her to sainthood. The confessor's mandate was thus intended to present written evidence for an eventual beatification process, following the rules established by Pope Urban VIII in 1634. Although the confessors were not interested in literary classifications, they wanted to gather abundant biographical material, with distinct chronological sequences and anecdotes that would demonstrate the authors' virtues; in turn, the narratives of favors were important to show the extent to which the nun-writer had been chosen by God. The Poor Clare, Jerónima de la Asunción (1555–1630), founder of the first Poor Clare convent in the Philippines and whose portrait was painted by Velázquez shortly before embarking in 1620, began the account of her life after her arrival to Manila. In the informative process, opened in 1631, her "papers" were deemed as a fully credible source of her life and virtues (*Sacra Rituum Congregatio*, 1631).[4] If the cause for canonization was not finally presented in Rome, at the very least, the memory of the divine graces received by the nun was preserved for the order's written history and for the conventual community.

The mandates varied considerably in their instructions as to how to write life accounts. The Capuchin nun María Ángela Astorch (1592–1665) states at the beginning of her text that she was formally mandated to write a complete account of her life, that is, an autobiography: "I am writing the discourse of my life, by dint of obedience, and by Your Grace's express mandate, which I have resisted many times, before I was commanded under strict and holy obedience (Astorch 25)."[5] Here is the typical relational structure between the confessor and the nun, compelled by the Church's double hierarchy of gender and function: the confessor initiates the situation by means of his authority; his formal mandate overcomes the nun's revulsion to reveal in writing her most intimate experiences. The Discalced Carmelite, Ana de San Agustín (1555–1624), Teresa of Ávila's companion, received her mandate from the highest authority, the general of the Discalced Order, Alonso de Jesús María, which was similar to the mandates received by other nuns:

> I hereby command, by virtue of the Holy Spirit and holy obedience, the following precept to mother Ana de San Agustín [. . .] to write and note plainly and truthfully all the extraordinary things of particular favors and gifts she has received from God, as far back as she can remember. That she carefully recall from memory and gather everything she has written and copied, and send it to me, and to any nun who has knowledge of this, I command her to state as much under the same precept.
> *Ana de San Agustín, f. 92bis*[6]

In this case, the command was not intended as spiritual guidance, but for writing the history of a recently founded order, and to gather material on the nun's mystical experiences for her possible cause for beatification. By contrast, the Franciscan beata, Mariana de Jesús Baquero (1606–1683), a widow who lived with her brother, a priest, enjoyed much more freedom in her choice of memories:

> Let the Holy Spirit convey His divine light and give His spirit and grace to me to act according to his divine pleasure and will, as in this, his day I begin to write as my obedience requires, which shall be about the favors that God has bestowed upon me. [. . .] I say, therefore, that Your Grace should note that I write only what God has worked in me, as I will remain silent about my life, so as not to set a bad example to whoever reads it.
> *Baquero: 1*[7]

The confessor's endeavor to control the spiritual and hagiographic project is compatible with the author's wish to focus her account solely on the divine action she receives, as she perceives it guiding her life.

Indeed, the confessor's or father superior's mandate to write was usually intended for women whose spirituality had come under great pressure for many years. This was the case of Mariana de Jesús (1565–1624), a Mercedarian tertiary highly venerated in Madrid, who dictated the account of her life to her confessor (Mariana de Jesús, 1965); and of Mariana de San José (1568–1638), who had already founded several Augustinian convents when she received the order to write the account of her life (Muñoz). The writing of one's life, therefore, was associated with an incipient fame of holiness. Nuns' autobiographies were considered the most valued material for hagiographies, to the extent that a good number of women's autobiographies are known only by the fragments included in biographies written by a deceased nun's confessor or another ecclesiastical author. The biographer would insert excerpts from autobiographical texts in his chapters of the nun's *Life* (*Vida*). Among the numerous examples, the second autobiography of a distant relative of Saint Teresa's, the Augustinian nun Leonor de Ahumada (1613–1661), was preserved by the Sevillian priest Fernando de Ahumada, her cousin, confessor, and the text's addressee before writing her biography.[8]

Several basic elements enter into the writing of conventual autobiographical texts in the seventeenth century: the influence of the mystic-nun writer selected as a model; a strong relationship, whether imitative or emulative, with Saint Teresa, evidenced both in the writing and in the reception of divine favors; and the anticipation of the theologians' judgment (as the first readers of a text destined, perhaps, to a much wider audience). One must add to this the hagiographic convent culture acquired by the nuns (Bilinkoff: 98–109; Poutrin, "La lecture"), as well as the concepts of mystical theology and representations that enriched their vocabulary and conventual imaginary. Consequently, each nun's autobiography, even when studied independently from others, can be seen as forming part of the totality of early modern women mystics' autobiographies, as it shared many of the same features and, if at least partially published, contributed to the genre's evolution (Le Brun: 14).

The confessor's mandate was indispensable in authorizing women's writing at three different levels: personal, conventual, and public. The deeply transgressive nature of first-person writing by women whose vocation theoretically required the annihilation of their personal will could be tolerated by society only by means of strict institutionalization. The mandate was necessary even in the eyes of the nun-writer herself, as she should have internalized the obligatory norms of obedience, humility, and silence demanded of female monastic behavior. Additionally, when pondering the discernment of spirits, many nuns expressed fear that they might be victims of the devil's deception. Writing was thus viewed as a deeply anxiety-provoking activity; this is how the Franciscan tertiary, Catalina de Jesús y San Francisco (1639–1671), describes it to her confessor, after burning the papers of the account of her life, and being mandated to write it again:

> After I had burned it, I felt so much anguish inside me, that although I had experienced this feeling many times before, none seemed so grievous, and I came close to screaming. If I did not, it was because the Lord held me back, as otherwise it would have been impossible not to scream, such was my sorrow and forlornness. I was so punished that when I received Your Grace's mandate, I could do little but obey, and I felt extreme inner joy in doing so; yet somehow my reasoning is always there, thinking that [writing] is not convenient and there is no need or use for it; it will only follow if my judgment and bad reasoning are won over and I obey.
>
> *Bernique: 117–118; Vollendorf: 120–143*[9]

The mandate, moreover, had to overcome the resistance of the nun's own religious community, since writing was not part of the regular observance and at this stage, the nun's reputation for holiness had not yet been consolidated, and thus it could raise the Inquisition's suspicions about the community. Nuns were aware that the Holy Office could ruin the reputation of certain holy women, as had been the case of the Dominican nun of Lisbon, María de la Visitación, in the 1540s, who was condemned despite the approval by distinguished theologians (Granada). The dissemination of the nun-writer's writings, whether due to the confessor's indiscretion or other nuns' spying, called for the Inquisition's intervention. As was evinced in Teresa of Ávila's life, conventual reforms could generate opposition and conflicts. María de la Antigua (1566–1617), a white-veiled nun in the Poor Clare convent of Marchena, wrote as mandated by her confessor, but in secret from her mother superior, having denounced the slackening of the regular observance among the nuns. Some reported her to the mother superior "and told her that Mother María de la Antigua wanted to be considered a saint, and that she was writing many papers to send outside the convent" (*Sacra Rituum Congregatio* 1671, 39r–v). In brief, the confessor's command served as a guarantee to Catholics who read the published book that the nun's subservience as regards her gender and vocation had been maintained. Saint Paul's prohibition against women's education complicated the publication of texts under their authors' name. In order to shield their publication from censorship, books frequently cited the mandate in their titles. The title of the autobiography by the Toledo Carmelite tertiary, Isabel de Jesús (1611–1682), mentions the confessor in his double role of the text's executor and editor: "Treasure of the Carmelo[. . .] Found and Discovered at the Death, and the Life that the Venerable Mother Isabel de Jesús Left Written about Herself, by Order of her Confessor, [. . .] Brought to Light by her Confessor, the Rev. Fr. Manuel de Paredes, Predicant of the Order."[10] In the process of dissemination of the published work, the number of censures and authorizations by theologians that precede women's autobiographies and revelations also ensured that the texts were authorized by experts, situating them alongside a series of prestigious historical precedents, such as the works of the saints Catherine of Siena, Angela de Foligno, Bridget of Sweden, and Teresa of Ávila, the authors most frequently mentioned in the paratexts of the nuns' writings.

Most recently, literary studies have questioned the value of the confessor's mandate and the nun's subservient role as regards her confessor. Indeed, on the one hand, there appears to be a profound contradiction between the annihilation of the *self*, required by the nun's vocation, and, on the other, the degree of individual awareness and agency required by both convent foundations and reform, and the writing of her own life's account (Amelang, "Los usos": 202–203). This contradiction has encouraged a line of study that calls attention to the rhetorical devices deployed by nuns to gain the censors' benevolence and to neutralize criticisms. The discourse's systematic self-deprecation, so much a part of the Teresian style, constituted a deliberate strategy, a "rhetoric of humility" (Weber, *Teresa*) that allowed for subverting gender hierarchy. The tension builds from the devaluation of the *self*, expressed through doubts, protestations, resistance, anxiety, and the subversion of the relationship between the nun and the confessor through which the woman gains agency, until the mandate to write becomes nothing but a formality. Behind the assertions of humility can be observed the nuns' tremendous longing to express their own identity, defying the Church's long-standing tradition of misogyny (Herpoel, *A la zaga*; Velasco, *Demons*; Vollendorf; Weber, *Teresa*). Autobiographical writing served as a means for women to gain spiritual authority, an endeavor fraught with difficulties, since society simultaneously banned and valued the expression of women's mystical experiences, doubly constraining the authors (Velasco, *Demons*).

Another fruitful line of study is that of the writing process as co-authored by the nun and her confessor(s). The confessor's mandate to write enjoined a collaborative effort whose objective it was to produce a text capable of passing the censors' examination and achieve publication status. In order to study conventual autobiographies quantitatively, more data are necessary than can be obtained by exploring conventual archives. Poutrin (*Le voile*) has tracked more than one hundred authors of autobiographies and of narratives of favors; other studies have added to the numbers of texts (Amelang, "Los usos"; Durán López). In any case, textual inventories will always remain incomplete, given the destruction of papers by nuns and confessors, as well as the ravages of time suffered by conventual archives.

The autobiographical writing that took place in women's convents belongs to a distinct type, in the sense that the authors could be considered pertaining to a spiritual elite, although not necessarily exceptional. The authors' basic profile suggests the elitist nature of their practice.

Few authors stand out for their political significance, such as Luisa de Carvajal y Mendoza (1566–1614), a self-proclaimed missionary in England imbued by the Jesuit spirit (Carvajal y Mendoza, Cruz). Most authors were native to Old and New Castile, born between 1535 and 1635, of noble or literate background. They were, in the main, convent founders and mother superiors, and belonged to the Discalced Carmelite and Franciscan orders, although some belonged to other orders, such as Augustinians or Dominicans (Poutrin, *Le voile*: 351–353). There was little probability, at the beginning of the seventeenth century, for a white-veiled nun or a pious woman of humble origin to be mandated to write her life. Exceptions, such as the autobiography by Ana de San Bartolomé (1549–1626), are due to her exceptional nature as a lay sister and daughter of Castilian farmers, yet also one of Teresa of Ávila's closest companions and a privileged witness of the early days of the Discalced Carmelites (Donahue; Urkiza). The formulation of a trend towards democratization at the end of the seventeenth century must therefore be proposed cautiously.

The status of conventual autobiographical writing has attracted the attention of researchers since Arenal and Schlau's ground-breaking study (1989), and recent studies have analyzed the genre as participating closely in women's writing practices (Baranda and Marín Pina: 2014). Since autobiographical writing was mandated in Catalonia and in the New World, as well as in Castile, their comparison should be carried out to further determine the circulation of models and texts. Despite the increasing number of studies of conventual culture, few women authors are acknowledged as writers; nevertheless, although the recognition given to the Teresian *Book of Her Life* as an inimitable model has likely undervalued all others, the literary quality of autobiographies deserves more attention than it has received to date.

Additionally, the theological or spiritual content itself of these autobiographies as well as of accounts of revelations is a subject that has been hardly researched (Haliczer), apart from Teresian studies, and beyond a hagiographic perspective (García Barriuso). Yet first-person women's texts raise fundamental issues to the history of early modern religious culture: taking the author to be the recipient of the teachings of male religious or of the literature available in her environment compels the study of the possible sources of her theological knowledge, such as the circulation of predicants, of ideas and books, of the contents of conventual libraries, and of the various applications of literacy. Investigating the reformulation of theological notions, for example, as a feminine or proto-feminist expression of Christianity, as in the case of Sister Juana de la Cruz (Graña Cid), opens up perspectives on the women's appropriation of learned discourse, as well as on the possibility of an alternative theology at the start of the Catholic Reformation and the censorship mechanisms that thwarted it. Another area of interest is the function of women's books of revelations as part of the Church's means of communication during the critical period of the Counter Reformation. For instance, Marina de Escobar's *Wondrous Life* (*Vida maravillosa de doña Marina de Escobar*), a collection of accounts related to the visions of this famous visionary of Valladolid (1554–1633), conveys a mystical theology in line with the works by her confessor, the Jesuit Luis de la Puente (La Puente; Poutrin, "Una lección"), but offers much more attractive forms of expression for elite readers. In this sense, first-person revelations and visions may be considered as a form of devout literature that developed in the first decades of the seventeenth century, and rivaled literary fiction.

Conventual autobiographies are also a major source of social and cultural history, historical anthropology, and even political history. In his study of autobiographies by craftsmen, James Amelang (1998) made use of the autobiographical manuscript by Lucía de Jesús (c. 1601–1653), a carpenter's daughter from Madrid who worked as a maid, and whose forays into the supernatural world gave meaning to her earthly afflictions. This text, similar to that by the so-called poor Sevillian, Ana de Jesús (c. 1560–1617), a widow who fed her large family by working with her hands, are rare testimonies of the lives of poor women who found shelter and comfort in the Tertiary Orders and in their relationship with their confessor. Other women authors experienced an arduous life, such as the Franciscan from Burgos, Juana de Jesús María (1574–1650), famous for her stigmata (Ameyugo; Poutrin, "Juana Rodríguez"), and the Augustinian nun, Mauricia del Sacramento (v. 1600–1674) (Villerino: 193–274), both of whom professed in the convent after a married life full of violence and disappointments; also, the beata María Quintana (1684–1734), and María del Santísimo Sacramento who, although from a later period, presents comparable features (Sánchez Ortega). At a time when few secular women, in particular from a humble or middle-class background, wrote autobiographical narratives, these texts offer very rich material for the study of social interactions and relationships between women and men, given the typically obligatory depreciation of the married status in the nuns' religious discourse. The systematic study of autobiographies and their insertion in the wider corpus of sources will meaningfully enhance the analysis of social practices and cultural representations (Poutrin, "L'identité sociale").

In conclusion, women's conventual autobiographies pose an exciting challenge to researchers. These texts are strongly encoded in the Church's spiritual and hagiographic tradition, inseparable from the objectives of prestige and power of the religious orders, reflective of the archetypes and commonplaces due to the influence of social and gender hierarchies, and derived as complex literary objects from the intervention of the women authors' confessors and companions, yet they nevertheless offer the broadest space for women's individual expression at the time. The capacity of many of their authors to communicate their experiences and express their subjectivity through the various instruments by which religious women's voices could be heard, undoubtedly results in a key element of attraction for researchers when investigating women's writings.

Notes

1 The term "ego-document," introduced c. 1955 by the Dutch historian Jacob Presser, describes all kind of documents written in first person, such as autobiographies, memories, diaries, etc. (Dekker 7).
2 "las numerosas vidas espirituales que nuestras religiosas escribieron, donde los hechos externos quedan relegados al olvido o mencionados ligeramente."
3 "un conocimiento nacido de luz superior a la natural, y por eso sobrenatural."
4 On her founding activity, see Owens in this volume. Owens is preparing an edition of her autobiography.
5 "Escribo el discurso de mi vida, a fuerza de obediencia, y mandato expreso de Vuestra Señoría, el cual tengo resistido muchas veces antes de mandármelo con el rigor de santa obediencia."
6 "Por la presente mando en virtud de Espíritu Santo, santa obediencia y debajo de precepto a la madre Ana de San Agustín [. . .] que llana y verdaderamente escriba y apunte todas las cosas extraordinarias de particulares mercedes y regalos que hubiere recibido de Dios, desde que se acuerda. Haciendo por eso memoria con cuidado y juntando todo lo que hubiere escrito y escribiere de nuevo, me lo envíe, y a cualquiera religiosa que algo de esto supiere, mando que lo diga debajo del mismo precepto."
7 "El Espíritu Santo me comunique su divina luz y me dé su espíritu y gracia para que en todo haga su divino gusto y voluntad, pues en su día comienzo a escribir lo que la obediencia me manda que serán los favores que de Dios he recibido. [. . .] Digo, pues, que advierta V. M. que solo escribo lo que Dios ha obrado en mí, que mi vida la callaré, por no dar mal ejemplo al que la leyere." Other examples in Poutrin, Le voile, 119–123.
8 Libro de la vida de la venerable Madre Sóror Leonor de Ahumada, religiosa del convento de Nuestra Señora de las Nieves de la ciudad de Córdoba, Córdoba, 1674.
9 "Quedé, después de haberlo quemado, tan apretada interiormente que con haber tenido hartos, no me parece que he tenido ninguno tan penoso, que me faltaba poco para dar gritos, y si no lo hice, fue por tenerme el Señor, que de otra suerte no pudiera, según era mi dolor y desamparo. Quedé tan castigada que, cuando vino el mandato de V. P., no había que hacer mucho en obedecer y sentí harta

alegría interior en ello; pero mi juicio se está siempre de un modo, teniéndole hecho de que no conviene ni hay necesidad ni utilidad alguna, solo se seguiría el quebrantar mi juicio [y] mal entendimiento, y obedecer."

10 Tesoro del Carmelo [. . .] hallado and descubierto en la Muerte, and Vida que de sí dexó escrita, por Orden de su Confesor, la Venerable Madre Isabel de Jesús [. . .] Sacale a luz su Confesor el R. P. Fr. Manuel de Paredes, Predicador de dicho Orden.

Works cited

Ahumada, Fernando de. *Libro de la vida de la venerable Madre Soror Leonor de Ahumada, religiosa del convento de Nuestra Señora de las Nieves de la ciudad de Córdoba*. Sevilla: Juan de Osuna, 1674.

Amelang, James. "Los usos de la autobiografía: Monjas y beatas en la Cataluña moderna." En James Amelang y Mary Nash, eds. *Historia y género. Las mujeres en la Europa moderna y contemporánea*. Valencia: Alfons el Magnanim, 1990: 191–212.

———. *The Flight of Icarus. Artisan Autobiography in Early Modern Europe*. Stanford: Stanford UP, 1998.

Ameyugo, Francisco de. *Nueva Maravilla de la Gracia, descubierta en la vida de la Venerable Madre Sor Juana de Jesús Ma*ría. Madrid: Bernardo de Villadiego, 1673.

Ana de Jesús, *Vida de la venerable Ana de Jesús escrita por ella misma*, ms. autógrafo, ms. 13493. Madrid: Biblioteca Nacional de España: 1610–1617.

Ana de San Agustín, *Autobiografía*. copia s. XVIII, ms. 6472. Madrid: Biblioteca Nacional de España: 1609–1622.

Ana de San Bartolomé. *Autobiography and Other Writings*. Ed. and trans. Darcy Donahue. Chicago: U Chicago P, 2008.

Arenal, Electa, and Georgina Sabat-Rivers, eds. *Literatura conventual femenina: Sor Marcela de San Félix, hija de Lope de Vega. Obra completa*. Barcelona: PPU, 1992.

Arenal, Electa, and Stacey Schlau, eds. *Untold Sisters: Hispanic Nuns in Their Own Words*. Albuquerque: U New Mexico P, 1989; reed. 2010.

Astorch, María Ángela (Beata). *Mi camino interior. Relatos autobiográficos—Cuentas de espíritu—Opúsculos espirituales—Cartas*, ed. Lazaro Iriarte. Madrid: Hermanos Menores Capuchinos de la Provincia de Navarra-Cantabria-Aragón, 1985.

Ayape Moriones, Eugenio. *Historia de dos monjas místicas del siglo XVII. Sor Isabel de Jesús (1586—1684), Sor Isabel de la Madre de Dios (1614–1687)*. Madrid: Ediciones Augustinus, 1989.

Baquero, Pedro. *Vida de la Venerable Mariana de Jesús, por otro nombre dona Mariana Baquero, Tercera del Orden de Nuestra Padre San Francisco, que dexo escrita de su mano, por obediencia de su confesor, sacada a luz por el Lic. Don—su hermano*. Madrid: Francisco Sanz, 1688.

Baranda, Nieves, and María Carmen Marín Pina, eds. *Letras en la celda: Cultura escrita de los conventos femeninos en la España moderna*. Madrid: Vervuet, 2014.

Bernique, Juan. *Idea de perfección y virtudes. Vida de la V. M. Catalina de Jesús y San Francisco, hija de su tercera orden y fundadora del colegio de la Doncellas pobres de S. Clara de la ciudad de Alcalá de Henares*. Universidad Complutense de Madrid: Alcalá, 1693.

Bilinkoff, Jodi. *Related Lives: Confessors and their Female Penitents*. Ithaca: Cornell UP, 2005.

Carvajal y Mendoza, Luisa de. *Escritos autobiográficos de la Venerable Luisa de Carvajal*. Barcelona: Juan Flors, 1966.

Cruz, Anne J., ed. *The Life and Writings of Luisa de Carvajal y Mendoza*. Toronto: Iter/CRRS, 2014.

De la Madre de Dios, Efren, and Otto Steggink. *Tiempo y vida de Santa Teresa*. Madrid: BAC, 1978.

Dekker, Rudolf, ed. *Egodocuments and history: autobiographical writing in its social context since the Middle Ages*. Hilversum: Verloren, 2002.

Duran López, Fernando. *Un cielo abreviado. Introducción crítica a una historia de la autobiografía religiosa en España*. Madrid: Fundación Universitaria Española, 2007.

Esteban Martin, Francisco. *Venerable María Vela, religiosa cisterciense, 1561–1617*. Ávila: Signum Christi, 1986.

Fernández Álvarez, Manuel. *Casadas, monjas, rameras y brujas. La olvidada historia de la mujer española en el Renacimiento*. Madrid: Espasa Fórum, 2002.

García Andrés, Inocente, ed. *El conhorte: Sermones de una mujer: la santa Juana, 1481–1534*. Madrid: Fundación Universitaria Española—Universidad Pontificia de Salamanca, 1999.

García Barriuso, Patrocinio. *La Monja de Carrión, Sor Luisa de la Ascensión Colmenares Cabezón (Aportación documental para una biografía)*. Madrid: Monte Casino, 1986.

Graña Cid, María del Mar. "¿Una memoria femenina de escritura espiritual? La recepción de las místicas medievales en el convento de Santa María de la Cruz de Cubas." *Letras en la celda: Cultura escrita de los conventos femeninos en la España moderna.* Ed. Nieves Baranda and María Carmen Marín Pina. Madrid: Vervuet, 2014: 189–205.

Granada, Leandro de. *Luz de las Maravillas que Dios ha obrado desde el principio del mundo en las almas.* Valladolid: Herederos de Diego Fernández de Cordoba, 1607.

Granada, Luis de. *Historia de Sor María de la Visitación. Sermón de las caídas públicas.* Ed. Álvaro Huerga. Barcelona: Juan Flors, 1962.

Haliczer, Stephen. *Between Exaltation and Infamy: Female Mystics in Golden Age Spain.* Oxford: Oxford UP, 2002.

Herpoel, Sonja. "Transgresión y seducción: textos de monjas hispánicas, 1616." *Anuario de Literatura Comparada,* 3 (2013): 233–248.

——. *A la zaga de Santa Teresa: Autobiografías por mandato,* Amsterdam: Rodolpi, 1999.

Ibsen, Kristine. *Women's Spiritual Autobiography in Colonial Spanish America.* Gainesville: UP Florida, 1999.

Isabel de Jesús, Tesoro del Carmelo escondido en el Campo de la Iglesia, hallado y descubierto en la Muerte, y Vida que de sí dexo escrita, por Orden de su Confesor, la Venerable Madre Isabel de Jesús, Beata Profesa, y Madre que fue de la Tercera Orden de Mugeres, del Orden de Nuestra Señora del Carmen de Antigua Observancia, de la Cuidad de Toledo. Sacale a luz su Confesor el R. P. Fr. Manuel de Paredes, Predicador de dicho Orden. Madrid, Juan de Paredes, 1685.

Krynen, Jean. *Saint Jean de la Croix et l'aventure de la mystique espagnole.* Toulouse: Presses universitaires du Mirail, France-Ibérie recherche, 1990.

Puente, Luis de la. *Vida maravillosa de la venerable virgen Marine de Escobar, natural de Valladolid.* Madrid: Francisco Nieto, 1665.

Lavrin, Asunción, y Rosalva Loreto, eds. *Monjas y beatas: La escritura femenina en la espiritualidad barroca novohispana, siglos XVII y XVIII.* México: Archivo General de la Nación / Universidad de las Américas, 2002.

Le Brun, Jacques. *Sœur et amante. Les biographies spirituelles féminines du XVIIe siècle.* Genève: Droz, 2013.

Mariana de Jesús. [*Autobiografía*]. En Elías Gómez Domínguez, ed. *La Madre Mariana. Aportaciones a la vida de una Madrileña.* Madrid: Editorial Tirso de Molina, 1965.

Muñoz, Luis. *Vida de la venerable Mariana de San Joseph, Fundadora de la Recolección de las Monjas Augustinas. Priora del Real Convento de la Encarnación, hallada en unos papeles escritos de su mano.* Madrid: Imprenta Real, 1645.

Muñoz Fernández, Ángela. *Beatas y santas neo-castellanas: ambivalencia de la religión y políticas correctoras del poder (ss. XIV–XVII).* Madrid: Comunidad de Madrid, 1994.

Muñoz Fernández, Ángela, y María del Mar Graña Cid. *Religiosidad femenina: expectativas y realidades, s. VIII–XVIII.* Madrid: Asociación Cultural Al-Mudayna, 1991.

Perry, Mary Elizabeth. "Magdalens and Jezebels in Counter-Reformation Spain." *Culture and Control in Counter-Reformation Spain.* Ed. Anne J. Cruz and Mary Elizabeth Perry. Minneapolis: U Minnesota P, 1992: 124–144.

Pons Fuster, Francisco. *Místicos, beatas y alumbrados. Ribera y la espiritualidad valenciana del s. XVII.* Valencia: Alfons el Magnanim, 1991.

Poutrin, Isabelle. "Juana Rodríguez, una autora mística olvidada (Burgos, siglo XVII)." *Estudios sobre escritoras hispánicas en honor de Georgina Sabat-Rivers.* Ed. Lou Charnon-Deutsch. Madrid, Castalia, 1992: 268–283.

——. "Para qué servían los libros de revelaciones de mujeres? Deleites místicos, movilización católica y entretenimiento devoto en la España barroca." En Nieves Baranda y María Carmen Marín Pina, eds. *Letras en la celda: Cultura escrita de los conventos femeninos en la España moderna.* Madrid: Vervuet, 2014: 147–158.

——. "L'identité sociale dans les écrits autobiographiques féminins de l'Espagne moderne." *Au plus près du secret des cœurs? Nouvelles lectures historiques des écrits du for privé en Europe du XVIe au XVIIIe siècle.* Ed. Jean-Pierre Bardet y François-Joseph Ruggiu. Paris: PUPS, 2005: 93–110.

——. "La lecture hagiographique comme pratique religieuse féminine (Espagne, XVIe–XVIIe siècles)." Madrid: *Mélanges de la Casa de Velázquez, Nouvelle Série,* 33 (2) "Le temps des saints" (2003): 79–96.

——. "Una lección de teología moderna: la Vida Maravillosa *de doña Marina de Escobar* (1665)" *Historia Social,* 57 (2007): 127–143.

——. *Le voile et la plume. Autobiographie et sainteté féminine dans l'Espagne moderne.* Madrid: Casa de Velázquez, 1995.

Sacra Rituum Congregatio. *Proceso ordinario de la Madre Jerónima de la Asunción*, 1631. Archivio Segreto Vaticano: S. Congr. Rit., processus 1654.

———. *Información, y actos hechos [. . .] en orden a la loable vida, virtudes y milagros de la Venerable Sor María de la Antigua [. . .]*, 1671, Archivio Segreto Vaticano: S. Congr. Rit., processus 1093.

Sánchez Lora, José Luis. *Mujeres, conventos y formas de la religiosidad barroca*. Madrid: Fundación Universitaria Española, 1988.

Sánchez Ortega, María Helena. *Confesión y trayectoria femenina. Vida de la Venerable Quintana*. Madrid: CSIC, 1996.

———. *Pecadoras de verano, arrepentidas en invierno. La trayectoria de la conversión femenina*. Madrid: Alianza, 1995.

Sanmartín Bastida, Rebeca. *La representación de las místicas: Sor María de Santo Domingo en su contexto europeo*. Santander: Real Sociedad Menéndez Pelayo, 2012.

Serrano y Sanz, Manuel. *Autobiografías y memorias coleccionadas e ilustradas*. Madrid: Bailly-Baillère, 1905.

Surtz, Ronald E. *The Guitar of God. Gender, Power and Authority in the Visionary World of Mother Juana de la Cruz (1481–1534)*. Philadelphia: U Philadelphia P, 1990.

———. *Writing Women in Late Medieval and Early Modern Spain. The Mothers of Santa Teresa de Avila*. Philadelphia: U Pennsylvania P, 1995.

Torres, Concha, ed. *Ana de Jesús, Cartas (1590—1621). Religiosidad y vida cotidiana en la clausura femenina del siglo de Oro*. Salamanca: Universidad de Salamanca, 1995.

Urkiza, Julián. *Obras completas de la Beata Ana de San Bartolomé*. Rome: Theresianum, 1981.

Vauchez, André. *La sainteté en Occident au derniers siècles du Moyen Âge d'après les procès de canonisation et les documents hagiographiques*. Rome: École française de Rome, 1981.

Velasco, Sherry. "Visualizing Gender on the Page in Convent Literature." *Women, Texts and Authority in the Early Modern Spanish Word*. Ed. Marta V. Vicente and Luis R. Corteguera. Aldershot: Ashgate, 2003: 127–148.

———. *Demons, Nausea and Resistance in the Autobiography of Isabel de Jesus, 1611—1682*. Albuquerque: U New Mexico P, 1996.

Villerino, Alonso de. *Esclarecido Solar de las Religiosas Recoletas de Nuestro Padre San Agustín, y vidas de las insignas hijas de sus conventos, t. II*. Madrid: Bernardo de Villadiego, 1691.

Vollendorf, Lisa. *The Lives of Women: A New History of Inquisitional S*pain. Nashville: Vanderbilt UP, 2005.

Weber, Alison. "The Three Lives of the *Vida*: The Uses of Convent Autobiography." *Women, Texts and Authority in the Early Modern Spanish Word*. Ed. Marta V. Vicente and Luis R. Corteguera. Burlington, VT: Ashgate, 2003: 107–125.

———. *Teresa of Avila and the Rhetoric of Femininity*. Princeton: Princeton UP, 1990.

5
CHRONICLES, BIOGRAPHIES, HAGIOGRAPHIES

Mercedes Marcos Sánchez

The classification of genres written by religious women that concern us here—chronicles, biographies, and hagiographies—forms part of the so-called historiographical or historical-literary genres. Each has its own characteristics and functions, distinctive features that allow the genre's own separate conceptualization. While a chronicle is the historical narration of events in chronological order, a biography is the narration of the discourse of a life, and a hagiography, that of the life of a saint (from Gr. *hagios*, saint). Nuns in the early modern period practiced all these genres and, consequently, one of their activities *qua* nuns was to function as female historians. This aspect, however, has not been fully studied within what Nieves Baranda Leturio and Maria Carmen Marín Pina call "the world of women's conventual writing" (11). Save for the exceptions indicated by Baranda Leturio of studies of nuns as historians in Germany, Ireland, and Mexico, to which we can add her own, hers with Marín Pina, and Marcos Sánchez's, her statement that "in Spain, there is still not even an inexact demarcation of this genre[1] [chronicles]," remains true today ("Fundación y memoria": 170). The statement can be applied as well to the other two genres addressed in this chapter. Filling in these lacunae is a complex task, in part because of the numbers of anonymous manuscripts that continue to be discovered, both in the private archives of monasteries and in public libraries, since, particularly in the seventeenth century, nuns wrote many brief chronicles of their convent's foundation, as well as lives of deceased nuns. Moreover, on examination, the chronicles reveal significant generic hybridization, to the extent that it is difficult to discern where hagiography begins and where it ends, as it permeates the entire text.[2] Indeed, nuns' chronicles, biographies, and hagiographies are multifaceted religious writings by women that allow multi- and interdisciplinary approaches. The following, therefore, cannot offer more than a partial view of these genres, although it may point to areas of future research.

Chronicles and biographies: historians by command

The term "by command" as applied to nuns' writings is characteristic of conventual genres, as it justifies the nuns' very act of writing. Although the term's rhetorical weight has tended to be exaggerated, it conceals a reality that must not be overlooked, since such a mandate conditions the kind of writing it produces. The model for most female historians writing "on command" was Teresa of Ávila, who wrote history when the profession of historian was reserved to "wise, dispassionate, and authoritative" men (Jerónimo de San Josef: 39), values not commonly acknowledged as corresponding to women. In 1644, the Carmelite historian Francisco de Santa María, when referring to the *Libro de las fundaciones* (*Book of Foundations*), asserted that Teresa was a historian who performed this "profession with such spirit and care that she not only set a model for life, but also for literature" (461). Such a profession was not learned through university studies, which were banned to women, but was granted as a gift from nature: in Teresa, he writes, "we see the three most valued virtues of the historian: brevity, clarity, and truthfulness. [. . .] So that nothing was invented by the art of history that was not planted by nature in her mind, with which God would so be served" (Francisco de Santa María: 463).

In her *Libro de la vida* (*Book of Her Life*), the saint had written, at her confessor's behest, the chronicle of the foundation of the first Discalced Carmelite monastery, San José in Ávila. In 1573, in Salamanca, she receives what she calls the command, perhaps a simple suggestion, to continue the history of foundations that she had written to date. If the difference between memoirs and chronicle is that memoirs imply an autobiographical element, it could be said that Teresa's chronicles are memoirs to which other doctrinal and even biographical elements[3] are added to objective details about events, always from the author's subjective view. Although her writings need not be analyzed here,[4] some of their aspects, in particular those that influenced the development of subsequent foundational and conventual chronicles, should be highlighted.

The saint narrates her initial reluctance to write the history of her foundations, but she seems to realize from the start the usefulness of such a document. Thus, after narrating some anecdotes from the lives of the first Carmelite nuns of San José in Ávila, she acknowledges that there are advantages in relating their history "because sometimes, those who join are encouraged to imitate them. But, if the Lord wished this to be known, the prelates could order [the convents'] prioresses to write about it" (*Fundaciones*: 1.5). It is not possible to know to what extent learned men such as lawyers (*letrados*) influenced the acceptance of history's exemplary function, common to all three genres, since such a concept was recognized at the time.[5] There is no doubt that the Carmelite friars knew how to regain and promote their founders' notion, placing it at the service of an entire historiographical program of the reformed order. Thus, for example, the heirs of Saint Teresa, as Christopher Wilson calls them, Ana de Jesús and Ana de San Bartolomé, were faced with the obligation to write their experiences as founders of the Carmelite order in France.[6] Ana de Jesús, furthermore, had written a foundational chronicle of the convent of San José in Granada,[7] at the behest of Jerónimo Gracián de la Madre de Dios, then Provincial Superior of the Discalced Carmelites. Ana de San Bartolomé, at the behest of the Provincial Superior, Nicolás de Jesús María Doria, recounts Teresa of Ávila's last years in a text described by Julián Urkiza as "a complement to Mother Teresa's *Fundaciones* first of all for the many foundational news it gives, and second, for the frequent references made by Ana to the *Fundaciones*" (44). A few years later, she writes another historical-autobiographical text, *Noticias sobre los orígenes del Carmelo teresiano en Francia* (*News about the Origins of the Teresian Carmelites in France*), because "one of these superiors has ordered me to write about what happened to us in the trip to Spain" (Urkiza: 222). In the case of both writers, it is clear that the foundational chronicle was instituted as a separate genre according to the Carmelites' conventual literature (Manero, "Ana de Jesús cronista": 648). These chronicles followed the model of the *Fundaciones*, as chroniclers narrated their own experiences in a pattern according to the following stages: a) preparations for the foundation; b) difficulties encountered; and c) successful establishment of the convent and achievement of goals (Urkiza: 46).[8] It is also obvious that a relationship is established between the orders' historiographical program and the nuns' involuntary depreciation to mere "silent sources of data," as according to Asunción Lavrin, "[t]hey were quite conscious of their roles as keepers of their own memory" (323). Indeed, except for the chronicle of the foundation of Granada by Ana de Jesús and published along with the first edition of Teresa's *Fundaciones*

(Brussels, 1610),[9] the Carmelite chronicles remained unpublished, although they were consulted as sources by Carmelite historians. This is the general tendency of the chroniclers' historiographical procedure for all religious orders.[10] Carmelite historians have left evidence of their working method: at a very early stage, as a consequence of Teresa's death, for the purpose of promoting her beatification and, simultaneously, of recounting the history of the Discalced Carmelites, the order was given to all convents for nuns to respond to certain questionnaires, and measures were taken to verify the certainty of information therein expressed.[11] Since nuns' writings were tools of documentation, although in many cases they were not submitted for the chronicler's elaboration,[12] he used them in his works, relegating their female authors to anonymity and invisibility. In fact, many informants did not consider themselves authors, and passed on their texts under the name of the convent they were representing, as a product of a collective work of memory. Proof of this is the existence of several manuscripts preserved in the National Library of Spain, from several monasteries and the Discalced Carmelite archives in Madrid. Their analysis reveals that the historians constructed their chronicles from provincial precepts, questionnaires, and their responses by several nuns or convents. Thanks to them, we now know the names of women biographers and chroniclers, and can analyze the existing relationship between manuscripts and published chronicles, and perceive the questionnaires' unifying factor in the drafting of chronicles and biographies. Thus, for example, ms. 7018 includes several foundational chronicles that later became part of volume III of the *Reforma de los Descalzos de Nuestra Señora del Carmen* (Reform of the Discalced of Nuestra Señora del Carmen), prepared by José de Santa Teresa, in 1683; ms. 8693, also reveals the oral or written narration of certain Carmelites of Toledo, among them, Catalina de Cristo; María Evangelista (146r–154v); Inés de San José (184r–195v); and Isabel del Santísimo Sacramento (139r–144v), who recounted the life of the venerable mother María de Jesús. These accounts respond to fifteen typical questions that allowed the historian to assess the veracity of the information: i.e., whether the narrator has witnessed what is being told, or whether the narrator refers to what is known through indirect sources. As to the actual contents, the questions focus on the different stages in which the hagiographical accounts are classified: birth and parents, taking the habit, observance of rules, offices performed, and how the nun practiced her virtues in illnesses, death, and miracles in life and after death. Also expressly asked was whether the body is in an incorrupt state, whether it emanates a sweet odor and "exudes oil," signs almost essential to certify her holiness. The Church interrogations would not have been needed to direct the nuns' biographical account, accustomed as they were to reading about saints' lives, but undoubtedly, the questions guided them on the points of interest on which the nuns were expected to focus, and therefore limited the each nun's freedom to compose her narrative.

One might ask whether the history written by women was manipulated by men.[13] In the absence of an exhaustive study, it would seem to be the case. In one extreme case, María de San José (Salazar), one of Saint Teresa's companions and founder of the Discalced Carmelites of Lisbon, was fully silenced by the Order's sixteenth- and seventeenth-century Spanish historians, whom María Pilar Manero Sorolla holds responsible, "among other things, for baroque misrepresentations evidently perpetrated on the figure of Saint Teresa and her nuns" ("Diálogos": 501). As her autobiographical vindication, María de San José wrote a *Historia de la fundación de los Descalzos y Descalzas Carmelitas* (History of the Foundation of the Male and Female Discalced Carmelitas),[14] in which she addresses present and future Carmelites and communicates the vicissitudes she suffered in both Seville and in Lisbon, where she founded the convent of San Alberto. Her account focuses on the persecutions she suffered from friars and their attempt to manipulate the work and the order's constitutions. She is the author of another singular work, the *Libro de recreaciones* (Book of Recreations), written in dialogue form, similar to Luis de León's

De los nombres de Cristo (On the names of Christ). In this work, besides some autobiographical elements related to her mode of prayer, she contributes biographical details about Teresa of Ávila, such as very precise information on her parents and brothers; an extremely vivid physical description of the saint, a feature that distinguishes her from other biographers, who generally omit physiological details in their biographies. After praising the Carmelites, in the last of the Recreations, she accounts for the foundation of Seville, as she experienced it, in great detail. Although this text, as in the case of the Lisbon foundational history, is more in line with autobiographical memoirs than with conventual chronicles properly speaking, it is undoubtedly a source of important historical data for the history of the Discalced Carmelites.

As commented above, the circumstances surrounding canonization processes and the foundational chronicles entrusted to the religious orders' historians were the direct cause of the many accounts written by early modern nuns that then became historical sources. Aware of their texts' final purpose, the nuns arranged them according to the format that suited each occasion. The conventual chronicle's format was known through the different orders' general or provincial chronicles, which were very much read at the time, both inside and outside the convents.[15] This format was adopted by several nuns, among them, Ana de Jesús, Poor Clare (?–1629); Juliana de la Purificación, Augustinian Recollect (1614–1686); Manuela de la Santísima Trinidad, Discalced Franciscan (1622–1696); Ana Gertrudis Venegas de Carvajal, Capuchin nun (1638–1680); Eufrasia de San José, Discalced Carmelite (?–1634); and Magdalena de Christo, Mercedarian (1629–1706). The chronicle's pattern of composition began with the narration, in general not very extensive, of the convent's foundation, followed by the *vidas* (lives) of the nuns "designated by their virtue" who lived in the convent.

In 1629, a book called *Nacimiento y criança de D. Ysabel de Avalos, y por otro nombre Ysabel de la Cruz* (Birth and Childhood of Ysabel de Avalos, also known as Ysabel de la Cruz) appears in Granada. Despite the female author's attempt to remain unnoticed in a manner typical of religious authors as a sign of their humility, the censorship in the paratext specifies that it was written by Ana de Jesús, abbess of the Encarnación in Granada, and that it is not only a biography, but a foundational narrative. Ana de Jesús addresses her nuns, making her intentions very clear: that she writes the book in order to save her predecessors from oblivion, and to avert introducing lax customs in the saintly rites established by the convent founder, Isabel de la Cruz. These holy rites are reflected in the lives of the other nuns whose biographies she writes, ordered chronologically by their death. Mainly focusing on the nuns' virtues, penances, and deaths, the lives written by Ana de Jesús are not very extensive and resemble letters of edification or necrologies more than *Lives* per se.[16]

Juliana de la Purificación, an Augustinian Recollect nun in the convent of the Encarnación in Valladolid, was given the charge in 1648 to write the lives of deceased nuns "for the comfort and edification of the present nuns who live in this holy house, and as an example for future nuns" (8). From that moment until her death, she carefully wrote the *Libro de las virtudes y muertes de nuestras difuntas* (Book of the Virtues and Deaths of our Deceased).[17] Although the book is dedicated "To all nuns from this convent of Nuestra Señora de la Encarnación in Valladolid," it seems clear that, for the author, the work not only constituted a book of the deceased, but needed to be published, although it should first be revised by someone with "a style more cultured than mine, which is typical of a woman without books, virtue, or talent, and with so little experience that I joined this convent when I was fifteen years old and have barely spoken to any secular persons, except to my parents" (8). Nevertheless, Juliana de la Purificación demonstrates a remarkable prose style, carrying out the duties of a historian with great care by using sources available to her, and citing numerous patristic and erudite comments in her composition of a total of 33 biographies, in addition to her chapter in the Valladolid convent's foundational narrative (52r–60r). There are two criteria for ordering these lives: the first follows the nuns' hierarchy, since the book begins with the deceased prioresses and continues with the choir nuns and non-choir nuns;[18] the second, that of chronology, according to the year of each death. The perspective from which the nuns, who are the subject of the biographies, are viewed includes always the same virtues (prayer, mortification, silence, humility, obedience, prudence, modesty, poverty) and death. The task of sister Juliana, interrupted by her death, was continued by an anonymous nun, who writes a biography of her predecessor and indicates that Alonso de Villerino took the book as source for his well-known chronicle, *Esclarecido solar de las religiosas recoletas de N.P. San Agustín* (Illuminated Site of the Recollect Nuns of Our Father Saint Augustine), published in two parts, in 1690 and 1691 respectively, in which he included most of the lives written by Juliana. The anonymous nun, lacking her predecessor's narrative skills, continues the book of deceased nuns, simply recounting their lives almost as a brief recorded note.

Eufrasia de San José is a Carmelite nun whose existence has been substantiated thanks to the preservation of the materials utilized by her order's historians when composing the numerous volumes of the *Reforma de los Descalços* (The Discalced Reform), currently housed in the National Library of Spain. Mss. 7018 mentions the following nuns whose writings contributed to the volumes: María de San José, who narrates in 1636 the lives of three nuns from the Madrid convent of Santa Ana (2–26); Manuela de la Madre de Dios, who writes a memoir of the foundation, and the elections of prioresses, professions, and deceased nuns of the convent of Cuerva (101–136); Isabel de San José, who in 1639 signs the memoir of the foundation of the convent of San José de Cuenca (137–169);[19] María de la Encarnación, who recounts information about the convent of Consuegra, including the "Vida de la venerable Francisca de las Llagas" (Life of the venerable Francisca de las Llagas), considered "very good" by the historian (180–199); and Eufrasia de San José, who in 1634 signs the "Fundación del Convento de Arenas, de religiosas carmelitas descalzas y traslación dél a la ciudad de Guadalaxara" (Foundation of the Convent of Arenas, of Discalced Carmelite nuns and transfer to the city of Guadalajara) (308–322). Other nuns whose signatures appear in the same manuscript, have connections to the nuns of Ocaña: María de Santa Teresa (363); María de la Trinidad (366v–371); and Brianda de San Joseph, who remits information about the convent of Malagón to Jerónimo de San José (409–415).

In 1696, in Salamanca, another book was welcomed by its contemporaries for its authorship and publication by a female historian, the Discalced Franciscan nun, Manuela de la Santísima Trinidad. The book, called *Fundación del convento de la Puríssima Concepción de Franciscas Descalzas de la ciudad de Salamanca* [Foundation of the Discalced Franciscan convent of the Purísima Concepción in the city of Salamanca],[20] responds to the same exemplary purpose as the other chronicles and, likewise, to the need to obey the command of a Provincial Superior. As Marcos Sánchez suggests, however, other motives are at play. She has studied in detail the book's writing process, revealing that it is the product of a collective task by the convent's nuns. As with the book by Manuela de la Santísima Trinidad, other works, such as *Monte de la myrra y collado del incienso* (Myrrh mountain and Incense Hill), chronicling the Capuchin monastery of Santa Ana in Plasencia,[21] add richly to our knowledge of everyday seventeenth-century conventual life. Their religious devotion and personal affection led some nuns to write, with more details than allowed in a collective chronicle, biographies of other nuns with whom they had had close relationships: whether as prelate and inferior, teacher and novice, or prioress and abbess-secretary. This last case was not infrequent, since many nuns did not acquire the necessary skills to write and, consequently, needed another nun to serve as their secretary, even for personal messages addressed to their confessors. One remarkable text is the *Relación de la vida de la venerable madre*

Catalina de Cristo (Account of the life of the venerable mother Catalina de Cristo), written immediately after the nun's death on January 3, 1594, by Leonor de la Misericordia.[22] The narrative, presented as a collective work by the nuns of Barcelona, recounts the life of Catalina de Cristo in five sections: childhood and youth, reception of the habit and novitiate in the Carmelites of Medina del Campo, foundation of the convent of Soria, foundation of the convent of Barcelona, and disease and death. The author had witnessed much of what she narrates; for other events, she gathered information by asking convents for details of Catalina's life. The result of her work is a text in which the three genres naturally coexist: the chronicle, both foundational and conventual, since Catalina would also receive news about the nuns in Barcelona; the biography, with its objective data, physical description of Catalina de Cristo, very similar to Teresa of Ávila; and the hagiography, with its wonderful component of visions, revelations, prophecies, etc., insistence in the narration of a holy childhood, prayers that were recited, and extreme and extravagant penances. The motivation for writing is clearly hagiographical: to praise moral and religious virtues and to emphasize the nun's holiness at all times.

Hagiographies

Throughout the seventeenth century, female conventual literature included works that were entirely hagiographical. In 1601, there appeared the *Libro de las alabanzas y excelencias de la gloriosa santa Anna* (Book of the Praises and Excellences of the Glorious Saint Anne), authored by Valentina Pinelo, an Augustinian nun from the convent of San Leandro in Seville. And, at mid-century, *Catorce vidas de santas de la Orden del Cister* (Fourteen Holy Lives from the Cistercian Order) (1655) was published in Zaragoza, written by Ana Francisca Abarca de Bolea. Closing the century, the *Vida de Nuestra Seráfica Madre Santa Clara* (Life of Our Seraphic Mother Saint Clare) (1700) was published; it was written by the Poor Clare, Mariana Sallent, in the ballad octosyllabic rhyme. Much earlier, in the late medieval period, another nun, Isabel de Villena, had dared to write, in the Valencian language, *Vita Christi* (Life of Christ), a devotional genre very popular at the time and recommended reading by Saint Teresa for the nuns in her convents. This work, posthumous and unfinished, was edited in Valencia in 1497 by her successor, Aldonza de Montsoriu. Written with a clear educational intention from a woman's perspective, it has attracted the attention of historians, theologians, and literature scholars. In contrast to other *Vitae Christi* of the medieval tradition, Isabel de Villena's book is considered to be unique, since it constitutes a reinterpretation of the different episodes of the life of Christ from his mother's eyes. In the words of Rosanna Cantavella, who believes Isabel de Villena to be the most important writer of the Iberian Peninsula of her time, and an admirable advocate for her gender (97), "[t]his is not so much a *Vita Christi* as a *Vita Mariae*." Save for the works of Mariana Sallent, praised as a poet during her time, but who has been almost forgotten today, these works have received deserved attention by literary scholars.[23]

Unlike the *Vidas* inserted in chronicles, whose literary efforts were voluntarily relegated to the background, the nuns who ventured to write the history of the Virgin Mary, of Saint Anne, her mother, and of several medieval saints, did so contravening the customary prohibition to women to write about these themes. Both Valentina Pinelo and Ana Abarca de Bolea kept contact with the literary and intellectual circles of their times; they were known beyond the walls of their convents, and wrote with the style and erudition of contemporary male historians. Their work was well documented, as they researched inside and outside their convents' archives and libraries. Through their many marginal notes, they demonstrated that, although they applied the usual rhetorical clichés, they were learned authors, and had no intention of pretending otherwise. Valentina Pinelo, who claims to have lived in the convent of San Leandro in Seville since she was four years old, demonstrates in her work a solid knowledge not only of Scripture, but also of the Church Fathers and of philosophers such as Plato and Aristotle, whom she quotes frequently. She also manages with great ease the rhetorical strategies of philosophical treatises, such as etymology, analogy, and examples. Her book, *Las alabanzas de Santa Ana* (Praises to Saint Anne), is not only a hagiography, but a set of doctrinal treatises on prayer, works of mercy, the virtues of the religious life, tribulation, and patience. For her part, Abarca de Bolea's *Catorce vidas de santas* seems at first to be an homage to the order in which she professed, although Bejarano Pellicer considers that, because she chose saints who were writers, the work is a vindication of female intellectual life (5–6). Certainly, Abarca de Bolea's contemporaries never thought that the work by this Aragonese intellectual was one of devotion; instead, they welcomed her as a female chronicler and historian, as is indicated in the text's paratext; she herself acknowledges in the prologue that she always felt drawn to imitating "scientific women." Thus, we are no longer dealing with female historians on command, but with willing historians who, along with the devotional reasons announced strategically at the fore to the reader, also propose a moral doctrine, examples of "reform" for their nuns, and even attempt their own conventual promotion through the prestige that writing brings them (Oltra: 85).

Conclusion

Chronicles, biographies, and hagiographies, therefore, are presented as privileged genres of early modern female conventual writing. In them, women appear as historiographical subjects, sources, and objects. Texts produced at that time are still to be explored; those that have already been analyzed reveal their rich contributions to women's history, religious history, cultural history, social history, literary history, anthropology, etc. The foregoing proves that there is still much work to be done in all areas in order to answer as to why so many nuns wrote so many lives, why they summarized so many foundational moments, but did so anonymously;[24] why their works were not published or not under their name; why, some actually were published; and why chronicles, lives, and hagiographies all follow the same patterns of composition. These answers require significant contextualization and historical research because, as we have seen, it is impossible to decouple conventual writing from the historical moment, from monastic culture, or from the relationships of female authors with the male members of their respective orders, men who had final authority over them. From other perspectives, also, many questions may be asked the texts regarding their primary functions, the symbolic power they wielded, and the image, whether attempted, achieved or allowed, of themselves that the nuns conveyed through their writing. Certainly, more research needs to be carried out in the future.

Notes

1 In her studies, Atienza claims the importance of the chronicle genre for early modern historiography, but focuses mainly on male authors.
2 The hagiographic permeability in nuns' writings has been noted by, among others, Barbeito Carneiro, Arenal and Schlau, and Donahue.
3 The author herself justifies the mix of genres in the *Fundaciones* by the command she received: "I am also ordered, if I have the opportunity, to deal with matters of prayer and of the deception that could occur by those who do not go beyond these matters when they can" ("Prólogo": 5).
4 The bibliography on Teresa of Ávila is immense; see, nevertheless, the magnificent introduction by Egido to the *Fundaciones*. For a general bibliography, see Sánchez. See also Donahue in this volume.
5 The prologues of the religious orders' chronicles include many theories on the historical profession, its methodology, and generic functions. For the features of Baroque religious chronicles, see Atienza.

6. Similar to the chronicles by Saint Teresa's heirs is the *Relación* by Catalina del Espíritu Santo, Poor Clare nun (?–1627). See Baranda Leturio ("Un cuchillo"), and Donahue in this volume.
7. This chronicle was published along with the first editions of Teresa's *Fundaciones*. See Manero Sorolla for a study of the authors and her 1994 edition of the chronicle.
8. This pattern coincides, in general terms, with the prototypical scheme of narration noted by Marcos in her analysis of the Burgos chapter of the *Fundaciones*, where she indicates the following stages: 1) initial situation and presentation of characters; 2) a plethora of complications, actions, and failed resolutions; 3) first partial resolutions/victories; 4) final resolution and situation; and, 5) evaluation and exhortation to the addressee.
9. Promoted, precisely, by Father Gracián and Ana de Jesús herself.
10. On general aspects of religious historiography, see Atienza ("Las crónicas").
11. The collection of historiographical sources was similar in all religious orders (Atienza, "Las crónicas").
12. The literal inclusion of nuns' manuscripts can be seen in collations of even superficial data related to the foundation and nuns of a convent in any of the provincial chronicles of the different religious orders. They are evident as well even in nuns' biographies published by the most seventeenth- and eighteenth-century prestigious biographers. None mentions the source of nuns' manuscripts, save for some honorable exceptions, such as that by Luis Ignacio de Zevallos (1737). Nonetheless, we owe the information about chronicles by some nuns and the publication of their texts to the zeal of some chroniclers. This is the case of Magdalena de Cristo (1629–1706), whose texts were included in the chronicle of Ledesma (1709) immediately after her death. Ledesma offers, furthermore, important information on his order's historiographical procedures.
13. The nuns' manuscripts sent to the historians of the religious orders for their use in constructing their chronicles, along with those that served as a base for the Vidas (Lives) that were profusely published in the seventeenth- and eighteenth centuries, were no doubt subjected to different editorial processes, such as deletions, additions, rewritings, etc., as in the case of, for example, the publication of Teresa of Avila's manuscripts, which show the modifications applied by her editor, Gracián de la Madre de Dios. The reason for such modifications was not always a matter of style. Without a doubt, a careful comparison of the nuns' manuscripts and the texts published in the chronicles will no doubt shed light on the true value of early modern women's writing.
14. María de San José (Salazar) has been studied by Pérez García, Weber, Manero Sorolla ("Diálogos"), and Morujão. There is still no accessible Spanish edition of the nun's works. The most recent edition was published by Simeón de la Sagrada Familia, *Escritos espirituales* (Rome: Postulación General OCD, 1979). The *Historia de la fundación de los Descalzos y Descalzas Carmelitas* is preserved in the ms. 2176 of the National Library of Spain. The title is probably due to Florencio de la Madre de Dios, who states that he found the papers in Lisbon, and confirms that they were written by María de San José.
15. For the format, properties, and functions of chronicles written by nuns, see Lowe, Evangelisti, and Winston-Allen.
16. It was and still is customary for religious orders to send notice to convents of the deaths of community members, with a brief summary of their lives, including their birth, secular name, professing and taking of the habit, all virtues that serve to edify the summary's female readers. These same details were usually recorded in a book, usually called *Libro de Difuntas* [Books of the Deceased]. These and letters of edification are held in convent archives and have always been documentary sources for the writing of convent chronicles and nuns' *Lives*.
17. A copy of this book's manuscript is kept in the Real Monasterio de la Encarnación in Madrid. I thank Leticia Sánchez Hernández for allowing me to access the document.
18. The expression "non-choir nuns" refers to lay nuns dedicated to the most tedious occupations in the convent (cooking, cleaning, etc.). In general, they could not read, and therefore they were not able to recite the Divine Office, and substituted the attendance to the choir by the praying of Our Fathers.
19. The memoire of the convent of San José in Cuenca states that it was commissioned by the Provincial Superior, Pedro de San Marcos to document "its beginnings and why the convent, which started in Huete in 1588, was founded." It includes the "Virtudes y exercicios de las Religiosas que han profesado y muerto en esta case" (Virtues and spiritual exercises of the nuns who professed and died in this house), and another memoire of elections and professions, in which Isabel de San José copies information from the corresponding books of her convent's archives.
20. For a detailed study of Manuela de la Santísima Trinidad, see Prada Camín and Marcos Sánchez, and Marcos Sánchez.

21 Although it was published in 1718 by the licentiate Juan Joseph Sáenz de Lezcano, the book, as evidenced on the cover, was written by Capuchin nuns. As in the case of the book by Juliana de la Purificación, thanks to the anonymous Capuchin nun who continued the work begun by another nun, we know the name of its main author, Ana Gertrudis Venegas de Carvajal.
22 The work remained unpublished until 1995, when Pedro Rodríguez and Ildefonso Adeva published it in the editorial Monte Carmelo. For details on the life of Leonor de la Misericordia, the book's authorship and features, see the editors' introduction.
23 An updated review of Villena's work may be found in Cantavella and Twomey. On Valentina Pinelo, see especially Luna, and Marín Pina; on Ana Abarca de Bolea, see Oltra and Campo Guiral. Other references in BIESES: www.bieses.net
24 For abundant information, see the BIESES database: www.bieses.net

Works cited

Ana de Jesús, OCD. "Fundación del convento de San Joseph de Granada." *Libro de las Fundaciones de las Hermanas Descalças Carmelitas, que escriuió la Madre Fundadora Santa Teresa de Jesús*. Bruselas: Rojas Velpio, 1610.

——. *Nacimiento y criança de D. Ysabel de Avalos, y por otro nombre Ysabel de la Cruz, abadesa y fundadora que fue deste Monasterio de la Encarnacion de Granada. Con algunas vidas de otras religiosas del mismo convento. Compuesto por una religiosa de la misma casa*. Granada: Francisco Heylan, 1629.

Arenal, Electa and Stacey Schlau, eds. *Untold Sisters: Hispanic Nuns in Their Own Works*. Revised ed. Albuquerque: U New Mexico P, 2010.

Atienza López, Ángela. "Estudio introductorio: La Rioja, sus conventos y la cronística religiosa de época barroca." *Conventos de la Rioja. Su historia en las crónicas religiosas de época barroca*. Ed. Ángela Atienza López, Elena Catalán Martínez and Fernando Muñoz Sánchez. Logroño: Instituto de Estudios Riojanos, 2011: 13–60.

——. "Las crónicas de las órdenes religiosas en la España Moderna. Construcciones culturales y militantes de época barroca." *Iglesia memorable. Crónicas, Historias, escritos. . .a mayor gloria. Siglos XVI–XVIII*. Ed. Ángela Atienza López. Madrid: Silex Ediciones, 2012: 25–50.

Baranda Leturio, Nieves. *Cortejo a lo prohibido. Lectoras y escritoras en la España Moderna*. Madrid: Arco Libros, 2005.

——. "Fundación y memoria en las capuchinas españolas de la Edad Moderna." *Memoria e comunità femminili. Spagna e Italia, secc. XV–XVII*. Ed. Gabriella Zarri and Nieves Baranda Leturio. Florence: Firenze UP; UNED, 2011: 169–185.

——. "'Un cuchillo que atraviesa el alma.' Mujeres católicas y propaganda en las contiendas religiosas de la Europa Moderna." *Scritture, carismi e istituzioni: percorsi di vita religiosa in età moderna. Studi per Gabriella Zarri*. Ed. Concetta Bianca, and Anna Scattigno. Roma: Edizioni di Storia e Letteratura, 2017.

Baranda Leturio, Nieves, and Maria Carmen Marín Pina. "El universo de la escritura conventual femenina: deslindes y perspectivas." In *Letras en la celda. Cultura escrita de los conventos femeninos en la España moderna*. Ed. Nieves Baranda Leturio and María Carmen Marín Pina. Madrid y Frankfurt am Main: Iberoamericana-Vervuert, 2014: 11–45.

Barbeito Carneiro, Isabel. "¿Por qué escribieron las mujeres en el Siglo de Oro?" *Cuadernos de Historia Moderna*, 9 (1997): 183–193.

——. *Mujeres y literatura del Siglo de Oro. Espacios profanos y conventuales*. Madrid: Safekat, 2007.

——. *Vidas ejemplares en la Edad Moderna. Provincia franciscana de Castilla*. Guadalajara: Aache Ediciones de Guadalajara, 2012. e-book.

Bejarano Pellicer, Clara. "Santas medievales a los ojos barrocos." *Tiempos modernos: Revista Electrónica de Historia Moderna* 25 (2012): 1–36.

Campo Guiral, María de los Ángeles. *Doña Ana Francisca Abarca de Bolea*. Zaragoza: Departamento de Cultura y Educación, 1993.

Cantavella, Rosanna. "Intellectual, Contemplative, Administrator: Isabel de Villena and the Vindication of Women." *A Companion to Spanish Women's Studies*, Ed. Xon de Ros and Geraldine Hazbun. Woodbridge: Tamesis, 2011: 97–108.

Catalina del Espíritu Santo, OSC. *Relación de como se ha fundado en Alcantara de Portugal, iunto a Lisboa, el muy deuoto Monasterio de N.S. de la Quietación por Phelippe II. de gloriosa memoria para las monjas peregrinas de S. Clara de la primera regla, venidas de la Prouincia de Alemania Baxa: despues de los hereges las auer perseguido, y desterrado de tierras en tierras por quatro vezes*. Lisbon: Pedro Craesbeck, 1627.

Diego Sánchez, Manuel. *Bibliografía sistemática de Santa Teresa de Jesús*. Madrid: Editorial de Espiritualidad, 2008.
Donahue, Darcy R. "Wondrous Words: Miraculous Literacy and Real Literacy in the Convents of Early Modern Spain." In *Women's Literacy in Early Modern Spain and the New World*. Ed. Anne J. Cruz and Rosilie Hernández. Farnham, UK; Burlington, VT: Ashgate, 2011: 105–122.
Egido, Teófanes. "Libro de las Fundaciones." *Introducción a la lectura de Santa Teresa*. Ed. Alberto Barrientos. Madrid: Editorial de Espiritualidad, 2002.
Francisco de Santa María, OCD. *Reforma de los Descalços de Nuestra Señora del Carmen*. Madrid: Diego Díaz de la Carrera, 1644.
Jerónimo de San José, OCD. *Genio de la Historia*. Zaragoza: Imprenta de Diego Dormer, 1651.
Juliana de la Purificación. *Libro de las vidas y dichosas muertes de nuestras religiosas*. Manuscrito. Madrid: Real Monasterio de la Encarnación, 1648–1686.
Lavrin, Asunción. *Brides of Christ*. Stanford: Stanford UP, 2008.
Ledesma, Francisco. *Historia breve de la fundación del convento de la Puríssima Concepción de María Santíssima, llamado comúnmente de Alarcón. Y del convento de San Fernando de Religiosas del Real orden de Nuestra Señora de la Merced, Redención de Cautivos (. . .) y la vida, obras y escritos de la venerable Madre Soror Magdalena de Christo, una de las Fundadoras de su Convento de San Fernando*. Madrid: Francisco Antonio de Villa-Diego, 1709.
Leonor de la Misericordia, OCD. *Vida de la Venerable Catalina de Cristo*. Ed. Pedro Rodríguez and Ildefonso Adeva. Burgos: Monte Carmelo, 1995.
Lowe, K. J. P. *Nun's Chronicles and Convent Culture in Renaissance Counter-Reformation Italy*. Cambridge: Cambridge UP, 2003.
Luna, Lola. "Valentina Pinelo y la genealogía de la Historia." *Leyendo como una mujer la imagen de la mujer*. Barcelona: Anthropos, 1996: 49–68.
——. "Sor Valentina Pinelo, intérprete de las Escrituras." *Cuadernos Hispanoamericanos* 464 (1989): 91–104.
Manero Sorolla, María Pilar. "Diálogos de carmelitas: *Libro de Recreaciones* de María de San José." *Actas del X Congreso de la Asociación Internacional de Hispanistas, Barcelona 21–26 de agosto de 1989*. Vol. 1. Ed. Antonio Vilanova. Barcelona: PPU, 1992: 501–516.
——. "Ana de Jesús cronista de la fundación del primer Carmen descalzo de París." *Bulletin Hispanique* 95/2 (1993): 647–672.
——. "Ana de Jesús: cronista de la fundación del Carmen de Granada." *Actas de XI Congreso de la Asociación Internacional de Hispanistas*. Vol. 2. Ed. Juan Villegas. Irvine, CA: Asociación Internacional de Hispanistas, 1994: 42–57.
Manuela de la Santísima Trinidad. *Fundación del Convento de la Purísima Concepción de Franciscas Descalzas de la ciudad de Salamanca, su regla y modo de vivir, con la relación de las vidas de algunas religiosas señaladas en virtud en dicho convento*. Salamanca: Imprenta de María Estévez, 1696.
Marcos, Juan Antonio. "El arte de narrar en las *Fundaciones* de Teresa de Jesús. 'Vivir para contarlo'." *Revista de Espiritualidad* 71 (2012): 449–474.
Marcos Sánchez, Mercedes. "Sor Manuela de la Santísima Trinidad. Una escritora salmantina del siglo XVII." *Sor María de Jesús de Ágreda y la literatura conventual femenina en el Siglo de Oro*. Ed. Miguel Zugasti. Soria: Diputación de Soria, 2008: 127–150.
María de San José Salazar. *Libro de recreaciones*. Ms. 3508. Madrid: Biblioteca Nacional de España.
——. *Escritos espirituales*. Ed. Simeón de la Sagrada Familia. Rome: Postulación General OCD, 1979.
——. *Book for the Hour of Recreation*. Ed. and introd. Alison Weber. Trans. Amanda Powell. Chicago: U of Chicago P, 2004.
Marín Pina, María Carmen. "Cuantas fueren las cabeças tantos han de ser los pareceres: censura al 'Libro de Santa Ana' de Valentina Pinelo." *Voz y letra* 17/2 (2006): 33–50.
——. "Un emblema de Joannes Sambucus en el prólogo al Libro de Santa Ana (1601) de Valentina Pinelo." *'Aún aprendo': estudios dedicados al profesor Leonardo Romero Tobar*. Ed. Ángeles Ezama et al. Zaragoza: Prensas Universitarias de Zaragoza, 2012: 619–628.
Morujão, Isabel. "María de San José (Salazar) O. C. D., fundadora del primer Carmelo descalzo femenino en Portugal." *Revista de Espiritualidad* 63 (2004): 177–211.
Oltra, José Miguel. "La hagiografía como pretexto autobiográfico en Ana Francisca Abarca de Bolea." *La réception du texte littéraire. Colloque franco-espagnol. Jaca, Abril 1986*. Zaragoza: Casa de Velázquez; Universidad de Zaragoza, 1988: 77–104.
Pérez García, María de la Cruz. *María de San José, Salazar. La humanista colaboradora de Santa Teresa. Perseguida*. Burgos: Monte Carmelo, 2009.

Pinelo, Valentina. *Libro de las alabanzas y excelencias de la gloriosa santa Anna, compuesto por doña Valentina Pinelo, monja profesa en el Monasterio de san Leandro de Sevilla de la Orden de san Agustín.* Seville: En casa de Clemente Hidalgo, 1601.

Prada Camín, María Fernanda and Mercedes Marcos Sánchez. *Historia, vida y palabra del Monasterio de la Purísima Concepción (Franciscas Descalzas) de Salamanca.* Salamanca: Universidad Pontificia de Salamanca, 2001.

Sallent, Mariana. *Vida de nuestra seráfica Madre santa Clara, que escribía sor Mariana Sallent, monja profesa en el religiosísimo convento de santa Clara de la Ciudad de Borja. Dedicado al Santo Cristo del Coro del mismo convento.* Zaragoza: Domingo Gascón, impresor, 1700.

Teresa de Jesús. *Obras Completas.* Madrid: B. A. C., 1997.

Twomey, Lesley K. *The Fabric of Marian Devotion in Isabel de Villena's* Vita Christi. Woodbridge: Tamesis, 2013.

Urniza, Julián. "Introducción a los escritos históricos-biográficos." *Bta. Ana de San Bartolomé. Obras Completas.* Madrid: B. A. C., 1998.

Venegas de Carvajal, Ana Gertrudis. *Monte de la myrra y collado del incienso, trasladados por la imitación al seráfico Monasterio de Señora Santa Ana de las M. Capuchinas de la nobilísima ciudad de Plasencia y chrónica de la fundación dél, y de las venerables religiosas que en él han florecido en todo género de virtudes. Escrita por las mismas madres y publicada por el Licenciado don Juan Joseph Sáenz de Lezcano[. . .].* Madrid: Imprenta de Miguel Gómez, 1718.

Weber, Alison. *Teresa of Avila and the Rhetoric of Feminity.* Princeton: Princeton UP, 1990.

——. "María de San José (Salazar): Saint Teresa's 'Difficult' Daughter." *The Heirs of St. Teresa of Avila.* Ed. Christopher Wilson. Washington, DC; Rome: ICS Publications Edizioni Carmelitane; Institute of Carmelite Studies Institutum Carmelitanum, 2006: 1–20.

Wilson, Christopher, ed. *The Heirs of St. Teresa of Avila.* Washington, DC; Rome: ICS Publications Edizioni Carmelitane/Institute of Carmelite Studies Institutum Carmelitanum, 2006.

Winston-Allen, Anne. *Convent Chronicles. Women Writing About Women and Reform in the Late Middle Ages.* University Park, PA: Penn State UP, 2004.

Zevallos, Luis Ignacio de. *Chronica de el observantissimo convento de Madres Capuchinas de la Exaltacion de el Santisimo Sacramento en la ciudad de Murcia. Tomo segundo.* Madrid: Imprenta de la viuda de Pedro Enguera, 1737.

6
CONVENTUAL CORRESPONDENCE

*María Leticia Sánchez Hernández and
Nieves Baranda Leturio*

Since the late Middle Ages, letters have served as one of the most efficient means of communication in the female conventual world. The epistolary genre has traditionally been associated with women's writing and, in particular, with the monastic life. In light of the Tridentine rules of conventual enclosure, ratified in the *Circa Pastoralis* (Pius V, 1565), epistolary exchange provided nuns with a privileged way to remain in contact and to obviate their perpetual confinement, leading, on the one hand, to the creation of networks among convents and, on the other, to networks between convents and civil, religious, and cultural authorities. Epistolary activity in Spanish female convents achieved an impressive level of production during the sixteenth and seventeenth centuries. Although we know of previous cases, as in many other aspects of nuns' writing, Teresa of Ávila was the first nun who abundantly and systematically produced letters. When, in 1562, she began the founding of Discalced Carmelite convents, Teresa's epistolary activity increasingly became the epicenter of her writing practice, constituting an indispensable mode of communication between the Carmelites and their environment.

Volume and preservation of letters

Letters were one of the most regular means of communication for nuns. For them, letters formed above all a genuine conversation or dialogue between absent writers. One need only to review some figures to get a glimpse of the phenomenon's extension and strength. Although 476 letters by Saint Teresa are currently extant (Álvarez, *Santa Teresa*; Peers), according to the nun herself, this was only a small part of her production, which in total likely included more than 14,600 letters, since during her last twenty years she drafted an average of two letters daily. This figure does not take into account those she wrote before 1562, when letters became an essential means of communication for her (Rodríguez and Egido: 430–434). Ana de San Bartolomé, her secretary and nurse, states that "sometimes she stayed up dispatching and writing letters until two in the morning"[1] and there are numerous testimonies to the heavy burden of maintaining an intense and extensive correspondence (Rodríguez and Egido: 428–430).

However, unlike other forms of writing such as autobiography or poetry, the custom of writing letters in convents was not introduced by the saint. There are earlier testimonies, for example, of Teresa of Ayala, prioress of the monastery of Santo Domingo el Real in Toledo in the late fourteenth century (García Rey), by the Borja family of the Poor Clare monastery of Gandía (Triviño: 21–34), and—perhaps the earliest example—of the Italian Dominican nun, Catalina de Siena, whose letters were translated and printed in Spanish (Alcalá, 1512). Nonetheless, very few letters from the Middle Ages are preserved, whereas from the sixteenth century, when more women became literate, nuns' epistolary activity increased exponentially. For example, among extant letters alone, there are 262 letters at the Capuchin convent in Toledo from their Mexican sisters (Alba González: IV); 665 by Ana de San Bartolomé; 216 by Mariana de San José; 53 by Ana de Jesús; 105 by Isabel de los Ángeles (vii); 377 by Beatriz de la Concepción (Serouet: 17); 361 by Isabel de Santo Domingo (Giménez Alvira: 256); and more than 1,000 by María de Jesús de Ágreda (Morte Acín: 246). These numbers represent a small sample that can be easily expanded with collections that comprise fewer letters.

Despite these figures, since most letters are private documents, once their writers or recipients are deceased, they are usually of no interest and are lost or destroyed. Teresa of Ávila's correspondence proves our point: despite the fact that she was a venerated nun and a model for her own order, the quantity of preserved letters in comparison with those she probably wrote is less than 5%. We must then assume that even more letters were lost for other nuns, not only due to chance or to their physical deterioration, but to the decision to destroy personal correspondence (Rodríguez and Egido: 430–434). Convents did not usually archive their nuns' correspondence unless they represented model of holiness or were prominent community members.[2] This decision did not necessarily depend on the convent; since letters are documents written to be sent, they were destroyed or preserved by the recipients and only very few writers kept copies of their letters. Usually, personal letters were sent directly to the addressee and no record or notes were kept, as happened with the correspondence of noble families. The case of María de Jesús de Ágreda is an exception: although in her correspondence with Philip IV, he orders her to respond in writing on the side he leaves blank of his own letter—and not to disclose the contents to any one—she disobeys and keeps a copy of all letters she receives from and sends to the monarch (Morte Acín: 250). With this exception, the lots of letters kept in conventual archives were either deposited by the recipient, returned to the author, or they were conserved among the nun's papers. As an example, the originals of 32 letters sent by Ángela de Buenaventura from the Discalced Franciscan convent in Salamanca to her protector, Bishop Martín de Ontiveros are kept in the convent archive, suggesting that they were first archived by the bishop and then sent to the convent, although we do not know when or why (Marcos "Writing": 120n.17).

Some correspondence is archived for reasons having nothing to do with holiness, as in the case of letters that form part of trial records of cases initiated for heresy or other crimes, which are presented as evidence during the proceedings. Thus, there is extensive correspondence by Luisa de la Ascensión, largely addressed to her relatives (García Barriuso: 106–109),[3] as well as 105 letters and other documents by Teresa del Valle y de la Cerda, protégée of the Count-Duke of Olivares, in Inquisitorial archives (Barbeito, *Cárceles*: 99–265; Boyle; González de la Peña). An exceptional case from the second half of the sixteenth century, recovered by Francisco J. Lorenzo Pinar, is that of the letters exchanged among Bernardina de Benavides, from the *beata*'s residence of Santa Ana in Toro (Zamora); her lover, Francisco de León, tailor and merchant; and his cousin and the residence's priest, Lázaro León. Although *beatas* or religious lay women were not subject to the same constraints as professed nuns in convents, their community life and vows required that they remain chaste. This correspondence is a rare testimony of an illicit sexual relationship that resulted in jealousy and abandonment.

Some problems related to the preservation of letters are due to their private circulation in manuscript; therefore, they were rarely printed. There are exceptions, starting with Catalina de Siena, whose correspondence was published in Italy at the end of the fifteenth century, first partially in Bologna (1498), followed by the extensive Venetian compilation of 1501. This edition, which became the model for female religious correspondence in Europe, was soon translated into Spanish by Cardinal Cisneros.[4] In Italy, throughout the sixteenth century, there were numerous epistolary collections written by prominent nuns and printed due to their holiness and fame, such as those by Paola Antonia Negri (1563) (Prosperi: 230–231); and by Battistina Vernazza (1587) (Solfaroli). In Spain, however, women's correspondence was never published save for Teresa of Ávila's letters, which, despite her canonization in 1622, were not printed until 1658, although some individual letters were included in previous works (Castillo: 158–160). All in all, the two published volumes of her correspondence present an extremely selective number, as only 65 letters were chosen (less than 15% of what we know she wrote). They were published in an annotated edition by the Bishop of Osma (Soria), Juan de Palafox y Mendoza (Marchetti). This selective limitation has been practiced on the few published letters written by nuns in early modern Spain; fragments or the entire letters are sometimes included in the order or convent's biographies and histories. For example, Antonio de Lorea published seven fragments of letters and eight letters in full by Hipólita de Jesús Rocabertí (Ahumada: 55); Juan de Ellacuriaga includes some of the nun's spiritual letters in the *Vida de la Venerable Madre Ana Phelipa de los Angeles* (Life of the Venerable Mother Ana Phelipa de los Angeles), and Francisco Soto y Marne (278–288) illustrates the virtues of Ana Calderón de Cristo (m. 1680) with some of her epistles. A remarkable case is that of María de San José (Salazar), a direct disciple of Teresa of Ávila. Her few letters, complete and in fragments, as well as poems, have mainly been transmitted through the *Chronica de carmelitas descalços, particular do reyno do Portugal* (Chronicle of the Discalced Carmelites from the Kingdom of Portugal) by Belchior de Santa Anna (1675). He devotes much attention to María de San José in order to write the foundation of the Discalced Carmelites in Lisbon and its first years; his narrative includes several letters, complete and in fragments, as well as poems. María de San José spent the last months of her life forcibly cloistered in the convent of Cuerva (Toledo) after opposing the modification of the constitutions established by Teresa of Ávila, as did Nicolás de Jesús María Doria, when he was appointed vicar general in 1588 (Manero Sorolla). Consequently, her name disappears from the histories of the Carmelites of Castile and there are few copies of her writings. Nevertheless, her defense by the Portuguese chronicler, Belchior de Santa Anna, allowed the preservation of several of her letters, as well as most of the poems we have today (Morujão).

An additional problem that frequently occurs with correspondence and their study is the letters' dispersal. For example, the main collections of original letters by Teresa of Ávila are preserved in the Carmelite convents of Valladolid (40 letters), Alcalá de Henares (11), and Seville (8); in addition, there are the series of letters in manuscript copy by nuns, the most important of which are preserved in the Carmelite convent of Consuegra (Toledo) and in the National Library in Madrid (Álvarez and Pascual). In Teresa's case, the dispersal may have been due in part to her sainthood, as there was interest in collecting letters or their fragments as relics (her signature, for example; Mujica, *Teresa*: 178–181).[5] There are other lots of nuns' dispersed letters in various convents and state archives: for instance, the 216 manuscript letters by Mariana de San José are located in the Augustinian convents of Salamanca, Pamplona, and Madrid; and in the Royal Palace Archive (Madrid); National Historical Archive (Madrid); and the Médici Archive of Florence. Letters by Ana de San Bartolomé are scattered over eight countries and 65 cities (Urkiza: 792–793); and those by Beatriz de la Concepción (1569–1643)—around 300 letters—are archived in the Carmelite convents of Brussels, Paris, Limoges, Madrid, and Salamanca. This dispersal is also due to the nuns' travels, as the most active played important social and political roles in various sites across and outside Spain; in other cases, letters preserved in smaller lots are kept in a single archive, generally in the writer's convent.

These preliminary considerations provide an overview of the genre's vastness and of the scarce and fragmented knowledge we have of it. The lack of data and studies about the many letters written by nuns allows only a general idea, one based on the correspondence that has been edited or is best known. This chapter, therefore, can only offer a partial approach to one of the literary genres that most characterize the writings of early modern nuns.

The epistolary style

Letter writing in the early modern period is a complex issue, since it requires a familiarity with rhetoric, not only the kind deployed for headers (addresses, appropriate dating, introductory phrases), but also the contents' argument and closing (Martín Baños). Nuns who write letters, therefore, must not only be literate, but they also must count with the appropriate training and practice to engage in the epistolary art. Religious letters follow standards established in medieval manuals still in use in the early modern period. They consist of five parts, as in the case of secular letters, although the content accommodates a religious spirit and similar in form to Teresa of Ávila's letters: a header with the anagram *JHS* or *IHS* (the first three letters of Jesus Christ's name in Greek, *IHΣOYΣ*) with the /H/ drawn as a cross; the *salutatio*, with formulas such as "la gracia del Espíritu Santo sea con . . ." (may the grace of the Holy Ghost be with . . .) or "JHS sea con . . ." (may JHS be with . . .); the treatment received by the recipient, as per his/her dignity, using forms of respect, dignity or relation, such as "vuestra paternidad" (your fatherhood), "vuestra merced" (your grace), "vuestra reverencia" (your reverence), "mi padre" (my father), "mi hija" (my daughter), "vuestra ilustrísima" (your illustrious lordship). These are followed by the *narratio* or letter's body, where the writer expounds on the document's purpose; the *petitio*, the message's culmination with a plea for money, materials, orations, and assignments; the date, specifying the day of the week or month, and the religious festivity; and the closing, containing a farewell formula, such as "indigna sierva, su hija" (unworthy servant, your daughter).[6] A postscript is often added to these formal sections, as a result of miscellaneous issues discussed, and uninterrupted or extended writing in time, which often led to several additions (Giménez Alvira: 267–268). On the outside of the signed and folded letter, the sender wrote the *superscript* or recipient's address. The letter was sealed with wax, stamped with *IHS* or with the skull and crossbones.[7] The letters of Teresa of Ávila are the perfect model for the early modern epistle, in which social respect prevailed: large sheets of good paper, broad handwriting, quality ink, and allowance for the header spaces, according to the recipient's dignity, and taking special interest in matters of health. This does not imply that these rules were rigorously applied, since, as Constance Marina states, Teresa rejected what she considered formulaic courtesy, believing it hypocritical (243–244). Thus, she preferred functional simplicity and the use of an opening and closing rhetoric that reflected Christian concepts, as in the case of other religious writers such as Saint John of the Cross or John of Ávila.

In this regard, Teresa of Ávila became a direct model for other Spanish nuns' letter writing. Ana de San Bartolomé (1545–1626) recounts that she learned to write in order to assist Teresa of Ávila with her letter writing, and she did so by imitating her handwriting (Urkiza: 100–101). From 1577, Ana de San Bartolomé functioned as her scribe, due to the saint's ill health and to the abundant correspondence. This important function as copyist-secretary was closely related to the humanist epistolary mode and strongly tied to the development of self-awareness in the early modern period. Initially, she wrote what Teresa dictated, but later, she became the author of her own letters. Writing among Discalced Carmelites owes its significance to the method of diffusion derived from Teresa of Ávila's epistolary practices. These practices extended to other orders, such as the Augustinian Recollect nuns, founded by Mariana de San José, a great admirer of Teresa of Ávila. The Augustinian nun was so impressed by her writing that she took Teresa's letters as her model, yet another of the saint's aspects that Mariana de San José imitated in her own experiences. In turn, throughout her order's convents, she tried to implement the closest uniformity possible, stating that, "all of us should write, sign, and speak in a given manner [. . .] not only being content that this is understood in our convent, but that it is said and understood alike in all of them."[8]

The complexities of letter writing surpassed even the explicit rules of the many epistolary manuals that circulated at the time. The letters' numerous functions often demanded a careful handling of the language of negotiation, persuasion, affection, control, etc., through which the author fashioned her image and achieved her goals. Because few letters written by nuns have been analyzed from this perspective, it is difficult to formulate a new viewpoint that is not based on what has already been studied about Teresa of Ávila, Mariana de San José, Sister María de Jesús de Ágreda, and a few others. Teresa's style has been characterized as colloquial, although critics have repeatedly admonished as illusory the notion that she wrote just as she spoke, given that she is so cautious with her words (García de la Concha; Slade; Weber). The extensive correspondence and the pressure to keep writing did not always permit careful editing and re-writing (Cammarata: 48–49), but in most of the cases this did not affect the ability of these women to deploy highly effective rhetoric. Teresa of Ávila had the capacity to stand up to and argue with some of her noble and powerful correspondents, who were accustomed to having their wishes granted. These relationships, such as the relationship of Sister María de Jesús de Ágreda with Philip IV, were most often marked by inequality, with the nuns occupying an inferior position. In order to be effective, the nuns tended to reinforce this situation. Teresa of Ávila created an image of herself as humble and desiring to please her correspondents, while at the same time presenting herself as an instrument of God, so that her own intentions formed part of a divine plan (Mujica, *Teresa*: 140–142). Clara de Jesús María did the same in order to legitimize and authorize the guidance that she offered to Fray Martín de Ontiveros and to be persuasive (Marcos, "La escritura": 126–127).

Teresa of Ávila's tactics have been observed in numerous letters, for example those she wrote to María de Mendoza (Pérez González) and to Beatriz de Castilla y Mendoza, regarding family resources (Marina, 1676–1682). In the letters, she avoided direct confrontation, deferring to her readers and their good intentions and she attributed negative behaviors to the influence of others, insisting on the good will and desire for agreement of her correspondents. By applying these means of persuasion, Teresa managed to maintain her own unwavering goals. María de Jesús acted similarly, writing declarations of humility and protestations of frailty and ignorance to capture the benevolence of her readers (C. Baranda Leturio, *Cartas*: 61). However, as Consolación Baranda Leturio has noted, this rhetoric was often based on the widespread use of "clichéd expressions and catch phrases that created a sort of rhetorical mesh into which specific issues were then introduced"[9] (C. Baranda Leturio, *Cartas*: 62).

Because early modern correspondence was not protected by any general principle of immunity (Rodríguez: 81), letters were careful to use elusive techniques in varied degrees depending on the confidentiality of the topics covered. María de Jesús de Ágreda used an impersonal voice ("they have told me," "they assure me"),[10] as well as references to "issues," "business," or "matters"[11] with which her readers were familiar (C. Baranda Leturio, *Cartas*: 63). The same can be observed in Teresa's letters (Grané: 9–42). This kind of rhetoric, typically used in letters written by the elite, helped to prevent the possibility of third parties having access to all of the contents, should the correspondence fall into their hands. Marcos coined the phrase "contención expresiva" (expressive restraint) to describe an attenuated form of speaking, which she attributes more to mistrust than to economy of expression ("La escritura": 122). A frequent and clearly effective feature of the letters (Giménez Alvira: 263–264), it served to block their complete comprehension in the past and still today. The following sentence is an example of such private correspondence, written by Isabel de los Ángeles: "one of these days, in service of the Lord, I shall write, if I can, at length to our Father General and to my good companion. So for now, I shall say no more and shall do what my Mother tells me, to write to the Mothers of France who love my beloved companion" (258–259).[12] Here, it may be difficult to achieve a full understanding of all of issues at hand, yet while a detailed reconstruction of the historical context might be necessary, it may not always be successful.

Often the nuns' correspondence was intimate or family-related; therefore, their writing style tended to be colloquial, with more or less colorful and fitting features depending on their level of education. Even so, the letters still contain expressions of humility and are repeatedly respectful towards the recipient (Giménez Alvira: 262). Their emphatic treatment, like their colloquial language, is not only formal, but also includes expressions of both respect ("your reverence" for a clergyman) and affection, as in the case of Isabel de los Ángeles, who frequently refers to her recipients, her Carmelite companions in Spain, as "my mother of my soul," or "my true friend."[13] The letters, when introducing their topics, are surprisingly disorganized to a modern reader, yet this demonstrates another similarity with the spoken language. However, nuns also had their own particular style. A good example is the telegraphic style used by Beatriz de la Concepción, clearly the result of her need to cover many topics in a limited amount of time:

> My mother, Don Juan Básquez has not arrived. They all talk better than they act. I'd like to have my books and for the wool, your reverence, ask Doña Juliana to hurry, since she is very slow. I wish the [holy] image had arrived and that it is pleasing. I have already written the story. [With it] a book of our venerable Mother's hand-written letters was sent. I sent the letter to Fray Ángel. He is very ill with a fever and it is horribly cold.
>
> Beatriz de la Concepción[14]

Correspondence: privacy and circulation

Early modern cloistered nuns had no private life and therefore, their letters were not strictly personal. According to the *Constituciones y ordenaciones de la Madre de Dios de Salamanca* (Constitutions and Orders of the [Convent] of the Mother of God of Salamanca) (1541):

> [T]he letters that arrive at the [convent] door should be sent to the Mother, who is under my strict mandate to read them all regardless of their author, with the exception of those from the Prelate about some particular [monastic] order. And regarding this, I leave it up to her conscience that once she reads them, she deals with them in a manner that is of service to our Lord and to the peace and calm of his house; and likewise, I command that none of her nuns write, or receive a letter without taking it first unopened to the Mother, who shall be obliged to read them all, and that those she deems may be sent, to be sent, and the others, that she tear up.[15]
>
> Marcos, "La escritura": 118–119, n.15

This control of a convent's correspondence was carried out with the help of other convent posts. The 1619 constitution of the Augustinian Recollect order assigned the turnstile nun the task of delivering to the prioress all the letters and notes that arrived from outside, so they would then be read and distributed (Sánchez Hernández, *El monasterio*: 211; *Patronato*: 74–75). The rules of the Poor Clares, which governed the convents of the Poor Clares at Gandia and the Descalzas Reales in Madrid, determined that all correspondence be controlled by the *auscultatriz*, that is, the nun who oversaw the conversations in the convent locutory (Sánchez Hernández, *Patronato*: 75).

Every letter sent to or from a convent, therefore, was duly inspected and could be censored or seized, if deemed necessary. This system was fully accepted and only letters marked as being "of conscience" were officially excluded from it; that is, those dealing with spiritual issues of a very specific nature, most often directed to a nun's confessor or spiritual director. These letters, whether received or sent, were also delivered to the prelate nun, who then closed them without reading, and she did the same with letters addressed to nuns under this rubric (Lavrin: 144; Marcos, "La escritura": 112–113, 119). Also escaping this strict supervision were those letters written by the convents' prelate nuns, who applied the rules according to their criteria. Mariana de San José, for instance, explains in her own correspondence that it is advisable to read, out loud and to the entire community, those parts of letters that deal with common topics, excluding those that addressed issues about specific nuns or convents (Sánchez Hernández, "Vida cotidiana": 98). Correspondence was not only censored, it could also be intercepted or lost, or could fall into the wrong hands. For this reason, in their letters—just as in secular letters—the nuns took certain measures to prevent the unintentional disclosure of possibly damaging information. In some of her letters, Teresa of Ávila repeatedly warned "this is not for letters"[16] when she writes about two main topics: political and spiritual issues (Marina: 206). Ana de Jesús was also very careful about her letters and even included instructions (Torres: 28).

Thus, in the nuns' letters there is always tension between what is stated and what goes unsaid, between what is understood and what must be explained. In this latter case, letters sometimes included encrypted language, as in María de Jesús de Ágreda's political letters to the Borja family. The hazardous nature of some of this correspondence is evidenced by her use of code words to discuss issues related to the king and the monarchy. This was common practice as well in state letters and, in varying degrees, in individual correspondence. Most encryption replaced certain words with others whose meaning was known only by the sender and recipient (C. Baranda Leturio, *Cartas* 33; Galende Díaz). This system was used by Teresa of Ávila in her letters to Father Jerónimo Gracián, especially when she learned that their correspondence was being intercepted. For example, she inserted "águilas" (eagles) for the Discalced Carmelite friars; "aves nocturnas" (nocturnal birds) for the Discalced Carmelite nuns; "cuervos" (crows) for the Jesuits; and "Laurencia" or "Ángela" for herself, among other pseudonyms (Cuevas; Marina: 206–207). This type of code was also used by María de Jesús de Ágreda in her correspondence with Francisco de Borja: here, "el enfermo" (the ill person) is Felipe IV; the "dedo malo" (evil finger) is Luis de Haro; and the "médico" (physician) is the author herself. This system of communication permitted the discussion of many more issues and helped to protect authors in case their letters were intercepted. The coded letters did not follow the usual formalities of letter writing, either in their organization or vocabulary, using instead a colloquial style and lacking the traditional restrictions, although they often contained strange or disturbing vocabulary due to their hidden meaning (Cuevas: 579–580). María de Jesús de Ágreda wrote in code to discuss her fears regarding the possible harassment over having written the life of the Virgin Mary, *Mística ciudad de Dios* (Mystical City of God); and the problems of Francisco de Borja with the nuns at the convent of the Descalzas Reales (C. Baranda Leturio, *Cartas*; Morte Acín: 266–283). The system's effectiveness was due to its simplicity, since, as Marina (208–210) suggests, these letters continue to confuse critics today, who are unable to agree on the identity of "Esperanza" in Teresa's letters. Another method consisted of sending letters through a third party, who acted as an intermediary, in order to avoid raising suspicions. For example, in the letters that Teresa of Ávila wrote to María de San José (Salazar), she included sealed letters addressed to Gracián that María de San José would turn over without reading, so Teresa would not be suspected of writing to Gracián (Mujica, *Teresa*: 46–47).

In the early modern period, the private contents of letters were not only threatened during their sending. In order for a letter not to be shared among several individuals, it had to expressly state this, and that it treated a particularly delicate issue. Mujica speaks of the public nature of personal letters (*Teresa*: 45–47) to explain how Teresa of Ávila's letters circulated among her family, friends, and siblings. It was not only expected that they be shared, but specific instructions were given, for instance, that what was written for one individual be read by a group, whether it was news, spiritual comfort, or instructions. Yet, although letters' circulation among groups was common, it also depended on the type of letter being sent.

Types of letter

Early modern correspondence is characterized, above all, by its versatility. Its rhetorical framework was sufficiently flexible to permit a multitude of issues and uses. Diverse classifications have been proposed and partially accepted by scholars, although some, such as Erasmus's classification, have been quite widely accepted (Martín Baños: 506–531). Despite their differences, nuns' letters tend to fall mainly into the "familial" category, leaving aside the "lettere di governo" (Zarri "La lettera": 265–266), or official letters dealing with civil and ecclesiastical authorities. However, many variations can be found within this familial correspondence, as critics who have attempted to establish their own classifications have observed. Tomás Álvarez (*Santa Teresa*) grouped Teresa of Ávila's letters into six categories according to their topic: purchase-sale of houses for the creation of new communities; family situation of her siblings in America; her own health and that of those around her; the discernment of spirits and the description of contemplative prayer and the mystical states; consolation of the afflicted; and her spiritual state within the framework of everyday life. Marina differentiated the letters on the basis of their purpose; compliance (138–145); congratulations (145–153); consolation (153–159); recommendation (160–168); thanks (168–175); grievance (175–192); business (192–202); and spiritual (202–215). Asunción Lavrin (44) takes a broader view of the letters written by nuns in Spanish America, which were quite similar to those of the peninsula, dividing them into two major categories: letters dealing with material life, and those dealing with spiritual issues. Without specific studies to soundly support a particular classification, however, critics' perspective is based intuitively on their own reading experience, which, except for the spiritual letters, opens up a wide range of blurred possibilities. This chapter prefers to classify the letters according to the relations between the correspondents, the topics covered, and their final purpose, categorizing them as spiritual, business, personal, and political. While these categories serve as valid labels for describing some of their additional characteristics, in no way should they be considered subgroups. In a number of cases, the classification depends on the category in which it is included, for example: is a spiritual letter directed to the king or the Count-Duke of Olivares political or spiritual? Is a letter to a family member with instructions to purchase or build viewed as personal or business related? It is also necessary to consider that the same nun may use quite distinct registers depending upon the recipient or the topic of her letters, thus a letter may not be viewed as falling under only one label.

Spiritual letters

According to Mercedes Marcos ("La textualización": 278), the Italian spiritual letters studied by Adriano Prosperi are "those in which the nun explicitly describes some form of spiritual doctrine, while in the other type of letters, in which she exposes her soul is in search of guidance, we should call [. . .] accounts of conscience."[17] The distinction made by Marcos may be compared to that made by Zarri regarding nuns' spiritual letters and their letters of obedience ("La lettera": 269–272) and essentially responds to whether the nun adopted the attitude of teacher or spiritual disciple. The letters "of obedience" are an extension of confession, which may be considered to have an oral and a written phase, one that is not subject to secrecy but may be consulted with other theologians. Among examples of this are the letters written by Ángela de San Buenaventura to her confessor (Marcos "La textualización"). The nun was obligated to write to her confessor every week, in order to transmit her feelings almost immediately, a far cry from the reflection about their feelings that can be detected in others. This continual obligation was perhaps the cause of her reiterated rejection of writing, which she referred to as "that" (*eso*), although she revealed similar negative feelings with regard to her everyday convent activities.

Although they were also spiritual, the letters from Clara de Jesús María, Ángela's companion, to her protector, Bishop Martín López de Ontiveros, were different. Sister Clara was devoutly religious, following the model of the exemplary religious (Marcos "La escritura": 114), and even before professing, while a widow, she showed signs of holiness. Yet though she spoke of her states of conscience in her correspondence, the relationship between the nun and the bishop was that of a daughter to a father. She tells him of her personal and financial difficulties, as well as some of her visions, and the clergyman confides his problems to her. In this way, they developed a relationship of mutual assistance, with the nun as counselor to the priest, acting as God's delegate voice, communicating the deity's solution to the priest through her prayers (Marcos, "La escritura": 126–127).

Business letters

Business letters comprise a broad category, from the institutional arena, where the nuns are the convent representatives, to material matters in need of attention and management, intertwined with personal and emotional issues. Zarri ("La lettera": 266) refers to the first as "of government," as they reflect the convent's relationships with local authorities, who may at times also be family members. These are reciprocal relationships: the nuns pray for the concerns of powerful individuals and in return, they receive alms. These letters, which also express affection and personal relations, show the convent's influence, revealed by the identity of the letter's recipients. An interesting example is that of Mariana de San José (1568–1638), founder of the Augustinian Recollect order and of the convent of the Encarnación in Madrid in 1611, which was sponsored by Philip III and Margaret of Austria. Although written by a nun, her letters are not restricted to the conventual or spiritual sphere, even though many of their recipients were monks and friars of the Augustinian order. They are letters from a woman of considerable religious power who is not limited solely to her priory, as the convent was founded by the Spanish monarchy. That the convent of the Encarnación was directly connected to the Alcázar, the Madrid palace, allowed the royal family and the court to maintain direct contact and communication with her. These privileged relationships permitted her to correspond with different personalities—civil and ecclesiastic—creating a network of clients from which she could obtain clear benefits for her convents and exchange favors. The religious letters of her earlier days (1605–1610) gave way to writings that were more focused on monastic reforms and collaboration with the monarchy so as to implement the regulations of the Council of Trent. It should be noted that by writing the majority of the letters at court (1611–1637), many of them include instructions for other centers to follow certain procedures.

As was the case with Teresa of Ávila, Mariana's letters offer a view of their times—1600–1640—the reigns of Philip III and Philip IV, along with the personalities of their wives,

Margaret of Austria and Isabel of Borbón, and the influence of the monarchs' favorites, the Duke of Lerma and the Count-Duke of Olivares. They reflect upon the situation of the Catholic Church, thanks to the correspondence maintained with Pope Urban VIII, and the Patriarch of the Indies and the king's chaplain, Alfonso de Guzmán y Silva. Mariana de San José's goal was to defend the religious–political union of the dual Habsburg Spanish and Austrian monarchies. From her convent, she negotiated with the politically powerful, while at the same time expanding her reform of the Augustinian Recollect order, writing to civil and ecclesiastic leaders as well as to prioresses, nuns, male religious, and confessors. Depending on whom she writes to, she discusses church issues, offers opinions on political events, resolves and judges the attitudes of nuns within her jurisdiction and in others, and counsels her family relatives on their behavior in life.

One of the most significant recipients of Mariana de San José's letters was the Barberini family, who lived in Rome and had excellent relations with the Papal court. The most important of these letters are directed to Cardinal Francesco Barberini, whom she had met in person in Madrid during his visit to the convent of the Encarnación in 1626. In her letters, she attempted to gain his support for the canonization of her friend Luisa de Carvajal y Mendoza, who had died in London in 1614, proselytizing for the Catholic cause. One suggestive aspect of this correspondence is that it established a permanent link between the Encarnación and Rome. Other distinguished nuns of the convent (the prioresses Aldonza del Santísimo Sacramento, daughter of the viceroy of Naples, Juan de Zúñiga; Catalina de la Encarnación; and the subprioress, Ana Margarita de San José, Philip IV's illegitimate daughter), continued to write to the Barberini family after Mariana's death in 1638, to try to persuade them on their interests, mainly Carvajal y Mendoza's canonization, but also on recommendations for certain positions. These important relationships for the convent were handled through courtesy letters, as well as the distribution of small gifts on certain occasions, that then allowed for the subsequent petitions of favors when necessary (Sánchez Hernández, "Servidoras": 314–315).

Political letters

Political correspondence may be considered a special subtype of business letters, since they form part of the convent's power networks, although they are addressed directly to the top political leaders. The most well-known case in Spain is that of María de Jesús de Ágreda, who maintained a correspondence with Philip IV for some twenty-two years, from 1653 to 1665. However, we may also consider as "political" the letters written by María de Jesús to the Borja family, or those by Teresa del Valle y de la Cerda to the Count-Duke of Olivares (Boyle; González de la Peña).

María de Jesús de Ágreda (1602–1665), a nun with noble family ties, lived in an isolated convent north of Castile (Ágreda, Soria), far from the Madrid court and from other large cities. Her renowned holiness drew the attention of Philip IV, who visited her July 10, 1643, following the Catalan uprising. They then initiated a long correspondence requested by the king himself, distinguished for its strictly political-religious content. At the beginning, María de Jesús believed that she could influence the monarch's politics, but after 1648 she wrote on solely religious topics in the hope of effecting change in the monarch, a desire that would never bear fruit and that would be the source of deep frustration for her. It is difficult to classify the relationship between María de Jesús de Ágreda and Philip IV, and to know the true reason for their extended correspondence. Clearly, they had mutual interests: María de Jesús needed support to publish her written work and to complete the construction of her convent in Ágreda, while Philip IV felt comfortable and protected by receiving the advice of such a charismatic nun, whom he considered to be a spiritual guide and intermediary before God. There was also a progressive relationship of affection and loyalty, confined to the personal sphere, given that the religious influence on political issues was limited (Hernández). María de Jesús demonstrated unconditional loyalty toward the king by letting him keep in his possession a copy of her *Mística ciudad de Dios*, which she sent to him with one of her letters, requesting that he show it to no one and confirming the suspicion that her superiors wished to destroy the work (C. Baranda Leturio, *María*: 160–161; Morte Acín: 245–266). The correspondence network of María de Jesús was quite extensive and included other members of the royal family (Queen Isabel of Borbón; Prince Baltasar Carlos; Princess María Teresa of Austria, whom she continued to befriend after she was crowned queen of France; and Queen Mariana of Austria); as well as nobles, and others holding high political positions. Among the letters to these, and highlighted for their importance, extensive dedication over time, and the number written,[18] are the letters she wrote to Fernando and Francisco de Borja, from 1628 to 1664. According to Consolación Baranda Leturio (*Cartas*: 65), "these texts reveal the determination and degree of interest with which she intervened in political intrigues; many are the opposite of her correspondence with Philip IV, revealing his intimate thoughts about herself [. . .]. The irritation, weariness, and frustration she could express to Francisco de Borja disclose an inadvertent and very revealing facet of this personality and, ultimately, the awareness of having failed to achieve her objectives of the projected reform."[19]

Personal letters

The letters we call personal make up the majority of nuns' correspondence, addressed to family members, companions, and individuals with whom they maintained a trusting and warm relationship. To this category belong the letters by Isabel de los Ángeles, Beatriz de la Concepción, Isabel de Santo Domingo, and many by Teresa of Ávila and Mariana de San José. These are letters in which emotional links are expressed, frequently to the recipients and their group, but that also include practical issues. Among good examples of these are the letters written by Isabel de Santo Domingo, a Discalced Carmelite in Zaragoza (Giménez Alvira), whose recipients include Feliciana de San José, of the same order, and Batista de Lanuza, the nun's protector and later, her biographer. Although her letters are familiar, they discuss everyday problems, decisions taken regarding major issues or relating to the authorities, issues requiring advice and that are discussed with another convent of the same order. In this group we may also add the letters of Mariana de San José on convent life, which covered three aspects: issues related to the nuns; considerations regarding the prioress as convent leader; and Mariana's self-perception of herself as founder. These issues mainly appear in the letters sent to prioresses and nuns at other convents, especially in the letters written to María del Espíritu Santo,[20] whom she considered to be an excellent nun and prioress. They are letters written to a friend, with no censoring of any kind, and with the knowledge that they would not be read by third parties, they encouraged confidences between them (Sánchez Hernández, "Vida cotidiana": 91–92).

Issues for further study

Nuns' correspondence is, without a doubt, one of the most extensive areas of study still pending in the field of early modern Spanish women's writing. There are numerous testimonies awaiting recovery in archives and convents, which must be identified, edited, and annotated. Without further critical materials of this type and without further investigation, the overall perspective will remain provisional. For the specific letters, it is necessary to determine information about the recipients (education, social status, biographical data, etc.). It is also necessary to examine the motivation behind the letters, as well as their conservation, writing networks, and rhetorical skills. We also need to investigate the volume of lost letters, and the extant letters' material difficulties, topics, and silences, which at times communicate more than what is actually being said. There are many letters extant that require even a partial editing, such as those by the Mexican Capuchins conserved in Toledo; the Poor Clares mentioned by Triviño; Mariana de San José, studied by Sánchez Hernández; Luisa de la Ascensión, referred to by García Barriuso (103–132); the Poor Clare nuns; Margarita de la Cruz de Austria; Ana María de San José; and Ana de la Cruz Ribera (Triviño). Many of the edited letters, almost all of which were written by Carmelite nuns, await further study in order to expand upon diverse aspects. This is the case with those of Isabel de los Ángeles, Beatriz de la Concepción, Leonor de San Bernardo, and Ana de Jesús, who immigrated to France.

Recent historiographical trends have highlighted religious correspondence as one of the main documentary sources to be used in the study of the everyday and spiritual aspects of female conventual life. It also offers information on other topics, some of which have been explored while others have not: conflicts (Ana de Jesús: 22–24); illness and medical attention (Mujica, "Corpus sanus"; Owens; Sánchez Hernández "Algunos apuntes"); cultural exchange (Ana de Jesús: 38–41; Fernández Gracia); economic knowledge (Martín); readings; female teaching; emotional and personal links (Ana de Jesús: 25–26); relationships; self-representation; and material life (Ana de Jesús: 27–29). As Cammarata affirms, "Letters are a valuable resource for critical inquiry because they reveal the complex dimensions of personhood and the experiences that shape social and political theories" (41). These issues should be analyzed with the required critical precautions, given that female writings tend to be based on censorship and silence, demanding that we consider both that which is stated and that which is not—that which falls within the gaps of the text.

Notes

1 "le acaecía estar despachando y escribiendo cartas hasta las dos de la mañana" in Saint Teresa de Ávila's beatification and canonization processes (*Procesos* 286n.71).
2 On the few preserved letters by Cecilia del Nacimiento and on those by Hipólita de Rocaberti, see Freitas Carvalho: 132–134, cited in Ahumada: 53.
3 Four hundred and eight letters by Luisa de la Ascensión to her brother and to other relatives are archived in the Convent of Santa Clara in Carrión, although other letters are elsewhere.
4 Published in Alcalá de Henares by Arnao Guillén de Brocar, 1512 (Salvador y Conde: 215–217).
5 For example, Mariana de San José thanks Lorenzo de Aponte, her confessor, for lending her a letter by Teresa of Ávila and informs him that she will keep it as long as he does not force her to return it. This letter is currently archived in the reliquary of the Convent of the Encarnación in Madrid (Sánchez Hernández "Un manuscrito").
6 For a detailed analysis of other letters and their sections' characteristics, see González de la Peña, and Giménez Alvira.
7 In a letter to her brother, Lorenzo, Teresa asks him to send her a stamp with Jesus Christ's anagram, IHS, instead of the skull and bones: "no puedo sufrir sellar con esta muerte" (I cannot stand to seal with the stamp of death) (Rodríguez and Egido: 443).
8 "que todas escribiéramos, nos firmáramos y habláramos de una manera [. . .] no solo nos habemos de contentar de que en el convento adonde estamos se entienda esto, sino que de todos juntos se diga y se entienda así" (Sánchez, "Vida cotidiana": 97).
9 "fórmulas acuñadas y frases hechas que configuran una especie de mallazo retórico en el que se introducen los asuntos concretos."
10 "me han dicho," "me aseguran."
11 "asuntos," "negocios," "materias."

12 "un día destos, siendo Dios sirbido escribiré, si puedo, largo a Nuestro Padre General y a mi buena conpañera. Que por el presente no diré más y aré lo que mi Madre me manda en escribir a las madres de Francia que aman a mi amada conpañera."
13 "vuestra reverencia," "mi madre de mi alma," "mi verdadera amiga."
14 "Don Juan Básquez, mi Madre, no a llegado. Todos tienen mejores palabras que echos. Yo querría mis libros y por las lanas Vuestra Reberenzia dé priesa a Doña Juliana, que es muy espaziosa. La ymajen querría ubiese llegado y que fuese a gusto. Ya e escrito la istoria. Allí yba un libro de cartas de letra de nuestra benerable Madre. La carta yo la enbié al Padre Fray Angel. Está con cuartanas muy malo y aze terrible frío."
15 "de las cartas que a la puerta vinieren sean llevadas a la Madre, a la cual mando estrechamente todas las lea sin diferencia alguna de personas excepto si no fuesen del Prelado para alguna particular religión. Y sobre esto le encargo la conciencia y así leídas de las que le pareciere o haga de ellas que vea convenir al servicio de nuestro Señor y la paz y sosiego de su casa; y así mismo mando a sus hermanas que ninguna escriba ni reciba carta sin que primero que la abra no las lleve a la Madre, la cual sea obligada a la leer todas y las que les pareciere que se deben ir vayan y las otras rasgue."
16 "no es para carta."
17 "aquellas en que la monja vierte explícitamente alguna forma de doctrina espiritual, mientras que ese otro tipo de cartas en los que se desnuda el alma en busca de dirección debería llamarse [. . .] cuentas de conciencia."
18 There are 220 letters from María de Jesús de Ágreda preserved in the convent of the Descalzas Reales in Madrid, although most likely many more were actually written.
19 "estos textos evidencian la determinación y el grado de interés con que intervino en algunas intrigas políticas; muchos son el reverso de la correspondencia con Felipe IV, nos indican lo que pensaba íntimamente de ella [. . .] Los desahogos de irritación, cansancio y frustración que se puede permitir con Francisco de Borja muestran una faceta inadvertida y muy reveladora de este personaje y, en última instancia, la conciencia de haber fracasado en los objetivos de reforma proyectados."
20 María del Espíritu Santo succeeded Mariana as prioress in the Valladolid convent, and later was prioress in Carmona and Seville.

Works cited

Ahumada Batlle, Eulàlia "La carta privada a l'època moderna: un epistolari conventual femení inèdit." *Manuscrits: Revista d'història moderna*, 29 (2011): 51–64.
Alba González, Emilia. "Presencia de América en Toledo: aportación cultural y social (el establecimiento de las capuchinas toledanas en Nueva España)." Unpublished Ph.D. Dissertation. Madrid: Universidad Complutense, 1998. http://eprints.ucm.es/2484/1/H0036401.pdf 4 Feb. 2015
Álvarez, Tomás. *Santa Teresa de Jesús. Cartas*. Burgos: Monte Carmelo, 2014.
Álvarez, Tomás, and Rafael Pascual. *Estudios Teresianos V. Autógrafos, ubicación y contenido*. Burgos, Monte Carmelo, 2014.
Baranda Leturio, Consolación, ed. *María de Jesús de Ágreda. Correspondencia con Felipe IV. Religión y razón de estado*. Madrid: Castalia, 1991.
———. *Cartas de sor María de Jesús de Ágreda a Fernando de Borja y Francisco de Borja (1628–1664). Estudio y edición*. Valladolid: Universidad de Valladolid, 2013.
Barbeito, Isabel. *Cárceles y mujeres en el siglo XVII*. Madrid: Castalia; Instituto de la Mujer, 1991.
Beatriz de la Concepción, O. C. D. *Lettres choisies de Béatrix de la Conception*. Ed. Pierre Serouet. Paris: Desclée de Brouwer, 1967.
Belchior de Santa Anna, *Chronica de carmelitas descalços, particular do reyno do Portugal e provincia de Sam Felippe*, I. Lisbon: Officina de Henrique Valente de Oliveira, 1675.
Boyle, Margaret. "Inquisition and Epistolary Negotiation: Examining the Correspondence of Teresa de la Valle y Cerda [sic]." *Letras femeninas*, 35/1 (2009): 293–310.
Cammarata, Joan F. "Letters from the Convent: St. Teresa of Ávila's Epistolary Mode." *The Catholic Church and Unruly Women Writers*. Ed. Jeanna DelRosso, Leigh Eicke, and Ana Kothe. New York: Palgrave, 2007: 41–53.
Carvalho, José Adriano Freitas. "Las cartas de la monja Cecilia del Nacimiento, OCD. Un diálogo: dudas y seguridades." *Cinco siglos de cartas. Historia y prácticas epistolares en las épocas moderna y contemporánea*. Ed. Antonio Castillo and Verónica Sierra. Huelva: Universidad de Huelva, 2014: 123–141.

Casas Nadal, Montserrat. "Consideraciones sobre las cartas de Santa Catalina de Siena a las mujeres de su tiempo y su recepción en España." *Anuario de Estudios Medievales*, 28 (1998): 889–910.

Castillo, Antonio. "Cartas desde el convento. Modelos epistolares femeninos en la España de la Contrarreforma." *Cuadernos de Historia Moderna*, Anejo XIII (2014): 141–168.

Concejo, Pilar. "Fórmulas sociales y estrategias retóricas en el epistolario de Teresa de Jesús." *Santa Teresa y la literatura mística hispánica*. Ed. Manuel Criado de Val. Madrid: Edi 6, 1984: 275–295.

Cuevas, Cristóbal. "Los criptónimos en el epistolario teresiano." In *Actas del congreso internacional teresiano. 4–7 octubre, 1982*. Salamanca: Universidad Pontificia/Universidad de Salamanca/Ministerio de Cultura, 1983. II: 557–580.

Ellacuriaga, Juan de. *Vida de la Venerable Madre Ana Phelipa de los Angeles, Recoleta Agustina professa en el Convento de la Villa de Medina de el Campo*. Madrid: Alonso Balvás, 1728.

Fernández Gracia, Ricardo. *Estampa, Contrarreforma y Carmelo teresiano. La colección de grabados de las Carmelitas Descalzas de Pamplona y Leonor de la Misericordia (Ayanz y Beaumont)*. Pamplona: Caja de Ahorros y Monte de Piedad de Navarra, 2004.

Galende Díaz, Juan Carlos. "La correspondencia diplomática: criptografía hispánica durante la Edad Moderna." *La correspondencia en la historia. Modelos y prácticas de la escritura epistolar*. Ed. Carlos Sáez and Antonio Castillo. Madrid: Calambur, 2002: 145–156.

García Barriuso, Patrocinio. *La monja de Carrión, sor Luisa de la Ascensión Colmenares Cabezón (aportación documental para una biografía)*. Madrid: Ediciones Monte Casino, 1986.

García de la Concha, Víctor. *El arte literario de santa Teresa*. Barcelona: Ariel, 1978.

García Rey [Verardo]. "La famosa priora doña Teresa de Ayala (Su correspondencia íntima con los monarcas de su tiempo)." *Boletín de la Real Academia de la Historia*, 96 (1930): 754–755.

Giménez Alvira, Elena. "Cartas al dictado. El epistolario de la madre Isabel de Santo Domingo (Convento de San José de carmelitas descalzas de Zaragoza)." *Letras en la celda. Cultura escrita de los conventos femeninos en la España Moderna*. Ed. Nieves Baranda Leturio and María Carmen Marín Pina. Madrid: Iberoamericana, 2014: 255–271.

González de la Peña, María del Val. "'No sé dejar la pluma': las cartas de Benedicta Teresa al conde-duque de Olivares." *Cartas—Lettres—Lettere. Discursos, prácticas y representaciones epistolares (siglos XIV–XX)*. Ed. Antonio Castillo Gómez and Verónica Sierra Blas. Alcalá de Henares: Universidad de Alcalá, 2014: 307–328.

Grané, Francesc. "Teresa de Jesús o El arte de la comunicación." *Epistolario y escritos breves de santa Teresa de Jesús. Actas del V Congreso Internacional Teresiano en preparación del V Centenario de su nacimiento (1515–2015)*. Ed. Francisco Javier Sancho Fermín, Rómulo H. Cuartas Londoño, and Jerzy Nawojowski. Burgos: Editorial Monte Carmelo; Universidad de la Mística—CITeS, 2015.

Hernández, Rosilie. "Friends in High Places: The Correspondence of Felipe IV and sor María de Ágreda." *Perspectives on Early Modern Women in Iberia and the Americas: Studies in Law, Society, Art and Literature in Honor of Anne J. Cruz*. New York: Escribana Books, 2015: 422–442.

Isabel de los Ángeles. *Cartas de la M. Isabel de los Ángeles, O. C. D. (1565—1644)*. Ed. Pierre Serouet. Burgos: Monte Carmelo, 1963.

Lavrin, Asunción. "De su puño y letra: epístolas conventuales." *II congreso internacional. El monacato femenino en el imperio español. Monasterios, beaterios, recogimientos y colegios. Homenaje a Josefina Muriel*. Ed. Manuel Ramos Medina. Mexico: Condumex, 1995: 43–61.

Lorenzo Pinar, Francisco J. *Beatas y mancebas*. Zamora: Semuret, 1995.

Manero Sorolla, María Pilar. "Exilios y destierros en la vida y en la obra de María de Salazar." *Anuario de la Sociedad Española de Literatura General y Comparada*, 6–7 (1988): 51–59.

Marchetti, Elisabetta. "Le lettere di Teresa di Gesù. Prime traduzioni ed edizioni italiane", *Per lettera. La scrittura epistolare femminile tra archivio e tipografia. Secoli XV–XVII*. Ed. Gabriella Zarri. Rome: Viella, 1999: 263–284.

Marcos Sánchez, Mercedes, "La escritura epistolar en el monasterio de la Purísima Concepción (Franciscas Descalzas) de Salamanca: las cartas privadas de sor Clara de Jesús María (1603–1685)." *Memoria e comunitá femminili, Spagna e Italia secc XV–XVII/Memoria y comunidades femeninas, España e Italia siglos XV–XVII*. Ed. Gabriella Zarri and Nieves Baranda Leturio. Florence and Madrid: Firenze UP and UNED, 2011: 87–130.

——. "La textualización de la conciencia: sobre los papeles de sor Ángela de San Buenaventura (Pérez de Montañés)." *Letras en la celda. Cultura escrita de los conventos femeninos en la España Moderna*. Ed. Nieves Baranda Leturio and María Carmen Marín Pina. Madrid: Iberoamericana, 2014: 273–288.

Marina, Constance. "The Business of Courtesy: An Examination of the Letters of Teresa of Ávila." Unpublished Ph.D. Dissertation. Harvard University, 1993.

Martín, Victoriano. "Gestión, dinero y finanzas en las cartas de santa Teresa." In coord. Francisco Javier Sancho Fermín, Rómulo H. Cuartas Londoño and Jerzy Nawojowski. *Epistolario y escritos breves de santa Teresa de Jesús. Actas del V Congreso Internacional Teresiano en preparación del V Centenario de su nacimiento (1515–2015)*. Burgos, editorial Monte Carmelo: Universidad de la Mística—CITeS, 2015: 313–319.

Martín Baños, Pedro. *El arte epistolar en el Renacimiento europeo, 1400–1600*. Bilbao: Universidad de Deusto, 2005.

Morte Acín, Ana. *Misticismo y conspiración. Sor María de Ágreda en el reinado de Felipe IV*. Zaragoza: Institución Fernando el Católico, 2010.

Morujão, Isabel. "Entre duas memórias: María de San José (Salazar) O. C. D., fundadora do primeiro Carmelo descalço feminino em Portugal." *Península. Revista de Estudos Ibéricos* (2003): 241–260 [trans. *Revista de espiritualidad*, 63 (2004): 177–211.

Mujica, Bárbara. "Letters to Friend and Foe: Ana de Jesús in France and the Low Countries." *Hispanic Studies in Honor of Robert L. Fiore*. Ed. Chad M. Gasta and Julia Domínguez. Newark, DE: Juan de la Cuesta, 2009: 327–345.

———. *Teresa de Avila, Lettered Woman*. Nashville: Vanderbilt UP, 2009.

———. "Corpus sanus, mens sana, spiritus sanus: cuerpo, mente y espíritu en las cartas de Teresa de Jesús." *Los cinco sentidos del convento: Europa y el Nuevo Mundo*. Ed. Josefina C. López. Caracas: Universidad Católica Andrés Bello, 2010: 13–23.

Owens, Sarah E. "The Cloister as Therapeutic Space: Breast Cancer Narratives in the Early Modern World." *Literature and Medicine* 30.2 (Fall 2012): 295–314.

Peers, E. Allison, ed. and trans. *The Letters of St Teresa of Jesus*. London: Sheed and Ward, 1980.

Pérez González, María José. "Aspectos pragmáticos de una carta teresiana." *Teresa de Jesús: V centenario de su nacimiento: historia, literatura y pensamiento*. Ed. Jesús García Rojo. Salamanca: Diputación de Salamanca, 2015: 201–209.

Procesos de beatificación y canonización de Sta. Teresa de Jesús. Ed. Silverio de Santa Teresa. 3 vols. Burgos: Tipografía El Monte Carmelo, 1934–1935.

Prosperi, Adriano. "Lettere spirituali." *Donne e fede*. Ed. Lucetta Scaraffia and Gabriella Zarri. Bari: Llaterza, 1994: 227–251.

Rodríguez, Carmen. "Infraestructura del epistolario de santa Teresa. Los correos del siglo XVI." In *Actas del congreso internacional teresiano. 4–7 octubre, 1982*. Salamanca: Universidad Pontificia/Universidad de Salamanca/Ministerio de Cultura, 1983: I, 65–90.

Rodríguez Martínez, Luis and Egido, Teófanes. "Epistolario." *Introducción a la lectura de Santa Teresa*. Ed. Alberto Barrientos. Madrid: Editorial de Espiritualidad, 1978: 427–472.

Salvador y Conde, José, ed. *Epistolario de Santa Catalina de Siena: espíritu y doctrina*. Salamanca: San Esteban, 1982.

Sánchez Hernández, María Leticia. *El monasterio de la Encarnación de Madrid, un modelo de vida religiosa en el siglo XVII*. Salamanca: Ed. Escurialenses, 1986.

———. "Un manuscrito de Santa Teresa en el Monasterio de la Encarnación de Madrid." *Reales Sitios* 101 (1989): 63–68.

———. *Patronato regio y órdenes femeninas religiosas en el Madrid de Los Austrias: Descalzas Reales, Encarnación y Santa Isabel*. Madrid: Fundación Universitaria Española, 1997.

———. "Vida cotidiana y coordenadas socio-religiosas en el epistolario de Mariana de San José (1603–1638)." In *Memoria e comunitá femminili, Spagna e Italia secc XV–XVII/Memoria y comunidades femeninas, España e Italia siglos XV–XVII*. Ed. Gabriella Zarri and Nieves Baranda Leturio. Florence; Madrid: Florence UP; UNED, 2011: 87–109.

———. "Buscando autenticidad y autonomía: el epistolario de Francisca de San Ambrosio (1604–1608), monja en el monasterio de la Encarnación de Madrid." *Letras en la celda. Cultura escrita de los conventos femeninos en la España Moderna*. Ed. Nieves Baranda Leturio and María Carmen Marín Pina. Madrid: Iberoamericana, 2014: 289–308.

———. "Servidoras de Dios, leales al Papa. Las monjas de los Monasterios Reales." *La doble lealtad: entre el servicio al rey y la obligación a la Iglesia*. Libros de la Corte.es. Monográfico 1 (2014): 293–318.

———. "Algunos apuntes sobre enfermedades y remedios de Teresa de Jesús." *Cuadernos de Historia Moderna* 14 (2015): 235–258.

Seco Serrano, Carlos. *Cartas de Sor María de Jesús de Ágreda y de Felipe IV*. Biblioteca de Autores Españoles 108; 109. 2 vols. Madrid: Atlas, 1958.

Serouet, Pierre, ed. *Cartas de la M. Isabel De Los Angeles, O. C. D. (1565—1644)*. Burgos: Monte Carmelo, 1963.

———. *Lettres choisies: de Béatrix de la Conception*. Brugge-París: Desclée de Brouwer, 1967.

———. *Leonor de San Bernardo. Lettres (1634–1638)*. Brugge-París: Desclée de Brouwer, 1981.

Slade, Carole. *St. Teresa of Avila, Author of a Heroic Life*. Berkeley: U California P, 1995.

Solfaroli Camillocci. "La monaca esemplare. Lettere spirituali di madre Battistina Vernazza (1497–1587)." *Per lettera. La scrittura epistolare femminile tra archivio e tipografia. Secoli XV–XVII*. Ed. Gabriella Zarri. Rome: Viella, 1999: 235–261.

Soto y Marne, Francisco. *Chronica de la Santa Provincia de San Miguel del Orden y Regular Observancia de Nuestro Padre San Francisco*. Parte II, Salamanca: Eugenio Garcia de Honorato y San Miguel, 1743.

Teresa de Jesús. *Cartas de la gloriosa madre Santa Teresa de Jesús con notas del excelentíssimo . . . Juan de Palafox y Mendoza . . . tomo primero*. Zaragoza: Diego Dormer, 1658.

Torres, Concepción. *Ana de Jesús. Cartas (1590–1621). Religiosidad y vida cotidiana en la clausura femenina del Siglo de Oro*. Salamanca: Universidad de Salamanca, 1995.

Triviño, María Victoria. *Escritoras clarisas españolas. Antología*. Madrid: Biblioteca de Autores Cristianos, 1992.

Trueba Lawand, Jamile. *El arte epistolar en el renacimiento español*. Madrid: Tamesis, 1996.

Urkiza, Julen, ed. *Ana de San Bartolomé, discípula y heredera de S. Teresa. Obras completas*. Burgos: Monte Carmelo, 1999.

Weber, Alison. *Teresa of Avila and the Rhetoric of Femininity*. Princeton: Princeton UP, 1996.

Zarri, Gabriella. "La lettera monástica tra uso e abuso: tipologie ed esempi (secoli XV–XVII)." *Cartas-Lettres-Lettere. Discursos, prácticas y representaciones epistolares (Siglos XIV–XX)*. Ed. Antonio Castillo and Verónica Sierra. Alcalá de Henares: Universidad de Alcalá, 2014: 259–272.

7
CONVENT THEATER

María del Carmen Alarcón Román

A retrospective look

Early modern Spanish female convent theater has remained practically ignored by drama historians; it is, in fact, not until 2003 that it appears mentioned in a history of Spanish theater. According to Fernando Doménech, "although marginal compared to the great Baroque theater that was being developed outside convent walls, it is indeed a world of great originality, showing to what extent theater had an influence on even the most unexpected circles of the [Spanish] Golden Age" ("El Teatro": 1258).[1] Most of the texts were forgotten for a long time in convent archives (sometimes due to the difficulties of accessing the cloister) or scattered in different libraries, and were never printed, unlike many other convent writings, such as poetry. In the case of the plays by the nun, Francisca de Santa Teresa (1654–1709), for example, although they were intended to be published, a copyist's temporary illness halted their publication and they were eventually forgotten. Indeed, a significant number of texts have never been retrieved and only their titles have reached us. This is the case of the only colloquy written by Gregoria Francisca de Santa Teresa (1653–1736); the plays of Ignacia de Jesús Nazareno (1719–1792?);[2] the so-called dances of Luisa del Espíritu Santo (1711–1777); and the interlude of Escolástica Teresa Cónsul (eighteenth century).

The authors' names are only to be found in Serrano y Sanz's *Apuntes*, which published some of their works, such as Ignacia's two "Festivities." Expanding on the data and documents provided by Serrano y Sanz, Isabel Barbeito's extensive archival and cataloguing work retrieved the names of the two seventeenth-century playwright nuns from Madrid, Marcela de San Félix. the daughter of Lope de Vega, and Francisca de Santa Teresa (*Escritoras madrileñas*). As the interest in literature written by women in the early modern Spain increased, Lope's daughter soon caught the critics' attention. Her works were published in two editions; the first by José A. Ramírez Nuño and Clara Isabel Delgado Ramírez (1987); and the second by Electa Arenal and Georgina Sabat-Rivers (1989). Numerous works on her texts began to appear shortly, such as those by Arenal (*The Convent, Vida y Teatro*); Sabat de Rivers ("Voces"; "Literatura"); and Arenal and Stacey Schlau (*Untold Sisters*; "Not Only"; "Leyendo"). These scholars provided the first critical views of her poetry and plays, and are responsible for her reputation as one of the main figures of conventual literature and as the most important playwright nun.[3] Schlau edited and studied the brief but groundbreaking works of two Carmelite nuns from Valladolid, María de San Alberto and Cecilia del Nacimiento, who have also been studied by others.[4]

In 1996, Doménech ("Autoras; "Adiciones") included the Carmelite nuns in Juan Antonio Hormigón's catalogue of playwrights, along with significant textual commentary. In his edition of *Teatro breve de mujeres*, he added a eulogy by Sor Marcela and the interlude, *Entremés del estudiante y la sorda*, by Francisca de Santa Teresa. Moreover, Doménech must be credited for defining the concept of nuns' conventual theater, as opposed to non-conventual theater written by nuns, in which he includes the Mexican nun, Sor Juana Inés de la Cruz, and the Portuguese nun, María do Céu. Conventual theater, to Doménech, is "a theater written, directed, and performed by women (the nuns or novices) for an audience of women (the community of nuns). [. . .] Its origins [. . .], as concerns topics and style, lie in the *autos de Navidad* [Christmas one-act plays] and *autos sacramentales* [one-act plays for Corpus Christi]" ("Autoras": 397). This theater's relationship to conventual theater not written by nuns (but most likely performed by them), such as Alonso Martín Brahones and Balzañón, should be established. This matter, which has barely been touched upon, will surely bring out many important facts about stage practice in female cloisters.[5]

In 1999, Alarcón Román investigated the other great writer of the Trinitarian convent in Madrid, Francisca de Santa Teresa, who unquestionably followed in the tradition of Sor Marcela's theater, but with her own literary style. Alarcón Román's publications followed with several studies on the nun's poetic and dramatic works.[6] She published, in 2007, two pieces that constitute a representative sample of Francisca de Santa Teresa's theater, *Coloquio para la profesión de sor Manuela Petronila* (Colloquy for the Professing of Manuela Petronila) and *Coloquio al Nacimiento de Nuestro Redentor* (Colloquy on the Birth of Our Redeemer), a preview of Alarcón Román's forthcoming critical edition of the nun's complete works ("Literatura"). She has also focused on individual plays performed by nuns, especially in Seville, both anonymous and composed by known male authors, such as Alonso Martín Brahones.[7] Valerie Hegstrom ("Theatre", "El Convento") and Anna-Lisa Halling (*Feminine*) have also written on conventual theater and its productions.[8] Current interest in monastic literature and the subsequent need to share knowledge and research have encouraged the participation of scholars of conventual theater in two recent conferences, where some of the latest research in the field was presented: *Letras en la celda. Cultura escrita de los conventos femeninos en la España moderna* (Letters behind the Grille. Written Culture in the Convents in Early Modern Spain) (Madrid, 2012),[9] organized by the BIESES group, and *Trazado caminos: viajes, encrucijadas y direcciones* (Tracing Roads: Voyages, Crossings, and Directions) (Lisbon, 2014), by the GEMELA group.[10]

The colloquy, a subgenre of conventual theater, has been addressed and defined by Arenal and Sabat-Rivers as a term that may have been taken from Jesuit theater. According to them, these allegorical one-act plays have their origin in medieval genres such as the liturgical drama or the debate, and are related to the *auto sacramental*. Their characteristic independence from longer plays sets them apart from other subgenres of brief theatre, such as the interlude (*Literatura conventual*: 32–33, 36–37). Moreover, it is a hybrid model, as it combines secular and religious topics, comedy and gravity, medieval and Renaissance forms, academic and popular sources, real and allegorical characters, and regular and irregular versification.[11] Doménech also referred to the colloquy as "a dramatic genre in its own right" created by Sor Marcela, and defined it as "a play of medium length, few characters (generally allegorical), and with a doctrinal purpose, meant to be performed at solemn occasions, especially a nun's professing ceremony. [. . .] It is a theater of little dramatic action, but generally with great lyrical and sometimes doctrinal value" (*Autoras*: 397).[12] Alarcón expands on this definition and establishes the main features of this private and occasional dramatic category:

> These plays are generally staged for the celebration of liturgical feasts such as Corpus Christi, Epiphany, and especially Christmas. Written in polymetric verse, their length can vary a

great deal [. . .] and dramatic action is often scarce or non-existent, in favor of a prevalence of lyricism and the very important presence of music [. . .]. The play unfolds in one single act through a dialogue between allegorical characters [. . .], although at times what could be called "real" characters appear: [. . .] shepherds, conventional comical figures [. . .], and sometimes the nuns even represent themselves with their own names. We can therefore appreciate different influences in the development of this typically conventual genre: the tradition of the *autos de Navidad*, the baroque *auto sacramental* and the realism of minor commercial comedy pieces. The aim of these "occasional" plays, apart from the celebration of religious events [. . .], is two-fold; they seek to make the strict life of the cloister more enjoyable; and they send the community a doctrinal or theological message defending the virtues and advantages of religious life in contrast to the dangers of the outside world, extolling spiritual rather than vile matter, or simply singing the praises of the Lord. They could therefore easily become a very effective means of preaching. However, the prevailing baroque style affected these pieces as well, and therefore the comic element is always present even alongside their serious content.

"*Tras las huellas*": 262–263

The pieces' characterization is still incomplete and poses some problems, however. One would be that Sor Marcela and Francisca also referred to their plays as colloquies, despite their apparent origins in the *auto pastoral* [one-act shepherd's play]. Indeed, the different denominations that appear at the beginning of the plays ("fiesta," "festejo," "diálogo," "dance," "auto," "sainetillo"), sometimes sharing traits with the colloquy and equally undefined, reflect the vagueness of genre definition. This is coupled, moreover, with the presence of dramatic forms stemming from well-known brief secular drama, such as eulogies or interludes, thus revealing a connection to the outside world.[13]

The convent as an intellectual community: Carmelites and Trinitarians

Drama composed and performed by nuns forms part of the great variety of genres that, with very diverse goals, make up the vast universe of female convent literature.[14] It is not an isolated practice in Spain, and there are well-known examples of conventual theater in Italy and colonial Latin America.[15] Elissa Weaver points out the existence of "an ancient tradition of religious drama in convents throughout Europe" and the fact that the establishment of female monasteries in learned communities played a part in its origin (50). Critics have thus insisted on the convent as a physical and intellectual space, a complex microcosm that promoted women's cultural development and enabled a certain degree of creative autonomy,[16] and the transmission of a female identity, both on an individual level and in a collective sense (Zarri and Baranda Leturio: 1, 7). Although the cloister's population came from diverse backgrounds, convents often lodged women of high social status who had already received a cultured education at home. Upon their arrival at the convent, these women would assume the most important duties in the community, such as that of mother superior (prioress, abbess), vicar, or novice mistress, which allowed them to oversee the appropriate education of the girls and young women aspiring to take their definite vows. Convents thus served as centers of education for women and the focus of women's literacy in early modern Spain (Pérez Baltasar: 142; Zarri: 50).

Convent literature produced a greater number of written texts than those created in a secular context, where women had far fewer opportunities. Setting aside the voluntary or compulsory character of their religious occupation and the duality between mandated writing and writing by personal initiative, it was within the cloister that these women's intelligence and literary inclinations found an adequate means of expression. Sánchez Dueñas has warned about the error of maintaining the traditional idealized image of the convent as a space for a woman's personal and intellectual liberation, as its structure and working system were indeed of great complexity. He calls our attention to the very different motivations that could lead women to taking the habit; the problems, degradation, and misery of convent life, and the strict control and zeal of the ecclesiastical authorities, particularly after the Council of Trent. Not all nuns were interested in writing, and oftentimes this was an obligation imposed by their superiors, who at the same time censored their works and were responsible for the loss of many of them (Sánchez Dueñas: 37–51). However, the same author admits that, despite these limitations, "it is in a conventual context that women came to achieve a certain degree of power and freedom, internal but with outside projections, even if this happened at all times under the strict vigilance of male authorities" (48).[17]

Leaving aside its undeniable effect of confining, silencing, and obscuring the female voice, other researchers have stressed as well how this space acquires, at the same time and quite paradoxically, an added value for the development of a culture with a big share of autonomy and independence.[18] It is true that the ecclesiastical power they were sworn to obey replaced in many ways the authority of a father or a husband, but writing offered them the chance to express a certain degree of rebellion and criticism, which sometimes escaped the restrictions of religious censorship. The cloister thus constitutes a shelter for their creative freedom, a reality that is evidenced in the case of the theatre. Contrary to moralistic conceptions, its practice developed quite naturally and with hardly any restraints in female convents, and not even ecclesiastical restrictions and prohibitions could stop it.[19]

Although there were others, the orders of the Carmelites and Trinitarians are the most prominent examples of creation and development of learning communities for the genres of theater and poetry. Under Teresian encouragement, the convents of the Carmelite order were the center of important literary activity, whose result is the existence of several dramatic pieces and a large body of poetry, many lyrical compositions including dramatic or quasi-dramatic features (Baranda Leturio; Borrego Gutiérrez: 13). At the Discalced Carmelite convent in Valladolid, the nuns María de San Alberto and Cecilia del Nacimiento, the first known playwright nuns, received an excellent education from their mother, Cecilia de Morillas, considered to be one of the most important women of letters of the time. The anonymous author of *Diálogo*, performed by the Carmelite nuns in Toledo, also shows an outstanding breadth of knowledge that suggests the author must have received solid instruction (Alarcón Román, "El Teatro"). Moreover, theater tradition in the Toledo community seems to have survived even to our days, as we have recently found out.[20] At the Discalced Trinitarian convent in Madrid, poetic and theater practice lasted more than a century thanks to the efforts of Marcela de San Félix, Francisca de Santa Teresa, and Ignacia de Jesús Nazareno, members of a real "theater school" according to Doménech, although the plays also took place in other convents of the Order (Doménech Rico, *El teatro*: 1255).[21] These three nuns, along with the biological sisters María and Cecilia, are a perfect example of educated women who, due to their privileged social or family background, had access to an education reserved to a chosen few, and which was then continued, expanded, and shared within the cloister walls.

Functions and purposes of conventual theater

The subversion of the patriarchal structure

Some scholars have tried to establish the diverse functions and aims of theater within the cloister. First of all, it was an effective tool for spiritual and religious education, completing the instruction received during the novitiate. Arenal and Sabat-Rivers have deemed Sor Marcela's colloquies a true "art of creating nuns," and the same could be said of those written by her disciple, Francisca de Santa Teresa (*Literatura*: 42). Vollendorf (101–102) has spoken of a "purgative" function, meaning that the Soul (novice) has to begin a journey full of hardship and temptation in order to achieve spiritual perfection. The theater pieces thus play the role of a guide for the ascetic life (Alarcón Román, "La reescritura"; "El teatro"), as the creation of plays is prompted by convent hierarchy. At least in the case of the spiritual colloquies for nuns' professions, the author generally plays the role of mistress of novices when ordered by the superior to compose a play for the instruction and training of the community.[22] Their theater could therefore be defined as being halfway between writing on command and their own literary will. However, it could also be considered as a "means to subvert the patriarchal structure" and as a vehicle for independent thinking, inaccessible to women outside the convent walls.[23] Last but not least, it was a usual form of entertainment that imitated entertainment from outside the convent and made the monotony of cloister life more bearable.[24]

In the plays of the Trinitarian nuns Sor Marcela and Francisca, we can appreciate some examples of a critical attitude against male authority, specifically against the excessive rigor and observance sometimes shown by confessors, who in the religious sphere personify patriarchal rule. In one of Sor Marcela's colloquies, the allegorical character, Indiscreet Zeal, represents the confessors' obsessive persecution of even the most insignificant offenses on the part of the nuns. Francisca, for her part, would take advantage of these clerics' attendance at her plays to call out to them scornfully and taunt them for their severity at the play's ending. Critics approaching the subject from feminist and gender perspectives have focused their attention on the "specificity of the feminine" (Baranda Leturio: 7) and on the images of women projected by plays authored by nuns, who appear somewhat different from the role reserved to them in a patriarchal society. For example, female characters and allegorical figures (Soul, Obedience, Poverty. . .) are present, assuming roles of power, control, and independence against male power as represented by World, Deceit, Appetite, etc. (Hegstrom, "Theatre": 213).

The experience of the monastic life allowed nuns to develop a strong sense of solidarity among women (Halling: 6), inside the "divine family" that these communities built once they broke their ties with their home and shared responsibility to achieve the expectations of a pious life (Arenal and Schlau, *Untold*: 5; Vollendorf: 103). Moreover, the Soul is an unusual female protagonist, as she contrasts with what was typical in allegorical dramas, where the main figure would be Man or Reason. She shares some common traits with the "manly woman" archetype in secular comedy. Just like a warrior, she must constantly battle her greatest enemies: mundane instincts, vice, and sin (Halling: 27–71). But she is not alone in this, for other female characters (virtues, powers) come to her aid and together with the Soul they form the "female trinity,"reflecting their collaboration and women's proto-feminine solidarity and resistance against male authority.[25]

The mise en scene: *the audience*

The staging of plays provided nuns with the possibility of taking part in activities that, due to their social background or their spiritual inclination, they could hardly perform in the outside world. They not only became playwrights, but also directors (autores de comedias), actresses, and set designers. They were also part of the audience, incorporating the complexity of theater production to the private space of the cloister. Generally, the nun who composed the play created a modest theater "company" with the help of the novices, sometimes working as an actress as well, as was the case of Francisca. The set design aspects of these plays have caught the attention of scholars, who have analyzed the convent as stage space and have made a possible reconstruction of the staging (Alarcón Román, "Nuns"; Borrego Gutiérrez; Hegstrom, "El convento"). Convents offered a wide range of possibilities for physical spaces where staging could take place: yards, gardens, the recreation room in the Carmelite convent, and the Trinitarian meeting hall. The scarcity of stage directions, even more extreme than in commercial theater of the corrales, seems to point to an uncomplicated *mise en scene*, due to the simplicity of the plot and the simple set required for plays that usually took place in an undefined location. Given the moderation in entertainment required of the religious life, the content and message of the plays seems to be given more importance than their theatricality and the technical aspects of the staging.

However, this was not always the case; some texts reflect a greater complexity, as proven by the abundant asides in María de San Alberto's plays. Yet the so-called implicit stage directions inserted in the dialogues must also be taken into account. These indirectly gave the plays a theatrical character that linked them to the stage conventions of the time (Halling: 13–15). A theater-like piece such as *La Máscara* (The Mask) in honor of Carlos II, attributed to Sister Francisca, contributes as well interesting facts about conventual staging. They testify to both the freedom and spontaneity with which nuns often carried out their occasional drama activities (Alarcón Román, "Escritura"). Poverty and lack of resources were no obstacle to women determined to organize their leisure activity, as their imagination and feminine skills in handicrafts and dressmaking often compensated for the lack of materials (Hegstrom, "El Convento": 368–371).

The audience of these plays is of great interest as concerns the plays' diffusion. Hegstrom ("Theatre": 213) believes that an all-female audience allowed for a degree of freedom and complicity that would have been unthinkable in the case of a mixed audience, as it allowed them to avoid male censorship. However, the audience was not always made up exclusively of nuns.[26] Although this might have been the case in Christmas-themed plays, as they took place at a more intimate liturgical moment, on other occasions the doors were open to people outside the community, some of whom were men. Francisca's profession colloquies, for example, reveal the attendance of the novices' families and their confessors, often referred to by name. The playwright took advantage of these circumstances both to thank the young woman's family for their generosity and sing her praises, and to criticize the confessors' rigor. Their severity must nevertheless have been relative, as proven by the fact that theater representations were allowed in the Trinitarian convent for approximately a century and that the confessors were in fact members of the audience. This reality allows for a perception of the cloister quite different from the traditional image, as the convent does not remain an absolutely closed and impenetrable space; its thick walls do not prevent the cultural permeability between the feminine inside world and outside life.[27] The presence of a heterogeneous audience at convent theater enabled the playwrights to become visible to the outside world, if only in small circles.[28]

The future of female convent theater

Currently, we have only a partial, disconnected knowledge of the kind of drama that was staged in women's convents. It is necessary, therefore, to edit the texts that have not been published[29] or have as yet no critical editions, and to conduct overall studies of collected works (following the Italian case model, for example) which, according to the criteria of chronological, thematic, or genre, would gather the results of the main research areas and include new aspects in order to provide a global vision of this kind of literary production. From a historical perspective, the anonymous pieces and those of known authorship must be counted, composition and production dates must be established, as well as their geographical extension. The plays' evolution through time and the orders where they took place need to be determined; all this information could give us an idea of the diffusion of nuns' plays. Similarly, the concept of female conventual theater should be defined more precisely, and the different subgenres should be differentiated according to their particular features.

Given that the nuns demonstrated extensive knowledge about both secular and religious literary tradition (Vollendorf: 96) and that convent theater has clear associations with secular theatre and generally with literature outside the cloister, research should continue to find possible literary influences, intertextual relationships, and coincidences as a means of determining their origin and configuration, of interpreting the deeper meaning of the texts, and of identifying those features that might be considered characteristic of this theater activity. As mentioned above, some sources have already been suggested: the allegorical affinity with the *auto sacramental*; the influence of medieval and Renaissance debates in the dialogue structure of colloquies; the educational purpose taken from Jesuit theater; the important imprint of mystical Carmelite poetry in lyrical passages;[30] the *auto pastoril* as the origin of Christmas-themed plays; and the presence in some of the works of interlude stock characters typical of brief theater. Some scholars have studied possible sources; Arenal and Schlau have commented on some coincidences between Lope de Vega's comedies and his daughter's colloquies, such as the "erotic seduction" of the divine (Arenal and Schlau, "Not Only": 229–230), and Gascón (39 and ff.) compared *Coloquio espiritual intitulado "Muerte del Apetito"* (Spiritual Colloquy titled "Death of Appetite") to the saint's play, *Vida y muerte de Santa Teresa de Jesús* (Life and Death of St. Teresa of Ávila), written by Lope de Vega. For her part, Tigschelaar (*Redemption* and *Marcela*) has contrasted the content of these plays with the mysticism inherent to certain neo-Platonic texts by Saint Augustine and Hildegard of Bingen's *Ordo virtutum*.

An in-depth study on the diversity of registers deployed may reveal the astonishing richness of language of this type of theater (Alarcón Román, "La producción": 77–83), as well as the expression of a possible female rhetoric. These plays encompass a wide variety of styles, from the elaborate language characteristic of spiritual texts and exalted lyricism, to the typical colloquial and popular dialogues, reflecting traditional scenes of everyday life inside the convent. In the latter, the particular and surprising use of humor has already been pointed out as a peculiar feature by early critics, but further analysis of the plays' comic elements will provide a different and suggestive perspective of the genre.[31] The diversity of characters appearing in these plays constitutes a line of research barely touched upon, one that reveals the variety of sources and influences of conventual theater, with the allegorical figures of the *auto sacramental* coexisting with rustic shepherds of Christmas plays, and the interlude's stock characters (ridiculous old man, student, astrologer, pedant, etc.). But the most interesting aspect, without a doubt, is the self-representation of the actress-nuns, with their real discourse superimposed over the plays' fictional dialogue. Finally, comparative studies of female conventual theater traditions in Spain with those in Italy and colonial Latin America need to be carried out; such studies will prove particularly enriching, given the undeniable connections between them.

Notes

1 Palacios includes the section "La musa dramática en el claustro" in his article "Noticia sobre el parnaso", 126–131. Recently, Escabias has devoted a section to conventual theater in her *Guía básica*, 97–138.
2 Doménech Rico, "Autoras" 511.
3 Mesa and Barbeito Carneiro, ("La ingeniosa") published the earliest studies on Sor Marcela. See also Arenal and Sabat Rivers, "Voces," "Una hija"; Arenal, "Vida"; López Estrada; Kaminsky; Smith, "The Female," "Notes," *El convento*; Vollendorf 100–106; Smith and Sabat de Rivers; Barbeito Carneiro, *Mujeres* 393–404; Halling 27–71; Gascón; Tigschelaar, "Redemption," "Marcela" and Vélez Sáinz and

Rodríguez Ibarra. Samson (158–159) notes that Marcela's theater is the best known; while Halling (1) remarks on the researchers' recent efforts to make conventual theater better known, although he admits that most have focused their attention on Marcela and María de San Alberto.

4   See Alonso Cortés (113–155), Cecilia del Nacimiento, Schlau, "The Drama," "Tórnome"; Arenal and Schlau, *Untold Sisters*; María de San Alberto, *Viva*; Barbeito Carneiro, *Mujeres* 335–350; Toft; and Borrego Gutiérrez.

5   Baranda Leturio and Marín state that "whether written by the nuns or by male authors at their request, the texts formed part of the same conventual genre and fulfilled similar functions, so both types must be considered when studying the topic", 32.

6   Alarcón Román, "Tras las huellas," "El convento," "Nuns," "Escritura," "La producción," "La reescritura."

7   Alarcón Román, "El cumpleaños," "El teatro," "Devoción," "El teatro como didáctica."

8   Hegstrom has staged productions by university students of plays such as *La fiestecilla del Nacimiento* by María de San Alberto (Brigham Young University, 1994); and *La muerte del Apetito* (Brigham Young University, Spanish Golden Age Theater, 2008) by Marcela de San Félix.

9   For an anthology based on the conference, see Baranda Leturio and Marín Pina. The conference panel on conventual theater included Borrego Gutiérrez, "Villancicos y fiestas teatrales barrocas en el convento vallisoletano de la Concepción del Carmen"; Hegstrom, "El convento como espacio escénico y la monja como actriz: montajes teatrales en tres conventos en Valladolid, Madrid y Lisboa"; and Idoia Martínez del Mozo, "Más allá del convento: el *Entremés del estudiante y la sorda* de sor Francisca de Santa Teresa." Hegstrom's paper was published in the conference anthology.

10 The conference by GEMELA (Grupo de Estudios sobre la Mujer en España y las Américas, pre-1800) included papers by María A. Sáenz Pérez, "Trazando nuevos caminos en el teatro conven(tual)(cional): los *Coloquios espirituales* teatralizados de Sor Marcela de San Félix"; and Halling "Space and Identitty in Sor Francisca de Santa Teresa's Christmas Plays."

11 Arenal y Schlau, "Not only" 222.

12 See also Gascón, 40. Given the similarity between the colloquy and the *auto sacramental*, Gascón remarks on the wide variety of topics employed in the former in contrast to the inherent, although not exclusive, Eucharistic themes of the *auto sacramental*.

13 Vollendorf (95) notes that the *Entremés del estudiante y la sorda* (Interlude of the Student and the Deaf Woman) by Francisca de Santa Teresa, seems to have been composed for public theaters rather than for convent audiences.

14 Pérez Baltasar 137 and ff.; Arenal and Schlau,"Not only" 1, 13; Vollendorf 94–95; Baranda Leturio y Marín Pina 11–45; and Lavrin 65–66. Lavrin notes that, from the seventeenth century until the mid-eighteenth century, a remarkable increase in religious writing took place, both spontaneous and by request (65–66).

15 See Arellano and Eichmann, Parodi and Barruchi, and Arana for colonial Latin American theater, and Weaver for Italian convent theater.

16 Arenal, "The Convent" 149; Pérez Baltasar; Alarcón Román, "El convento"; Arenal and Schlau, "Leyendo" 129–133.

17 See also Arenal and Schlau, "Leyendo" 133.

18 Arenal, "The Convent" 149; Barbeito Carneiro, *Mujeres* 8; Hegstrom, "Theater" 211; Arenal and Schlau, "Leyendo"133; Francisca de Santa Teresa, 7–11; Halling 13, 15. Some of these critics have referred to the convent as a catalyst for autonomy, a catalyst for intellectual pursuit, sanctuaries for the studious, refuges, female spaces of knowledge, and liberating spaces.

19 In 1671, the performance of *autos* and plays were forbidden in the convent and church of Saint Paula of Seville (Sánchez-Arjona: 454). What especially scandalized the ecclesiastical hierarchy of Mexico and Peru was the excessive use of female convents as public places for the performance of secular plays by public companies (Hegstrom, "Theater": 213–214). Bishops, vicars, and confessors must have proven more understanding and flexible with plays composed by nuns, due to their clearly spiritual and pedagogical nature.

20 I am grateful to Prioress Mother María Rosa for information on the topic: "we continue to produce small theater plays for different festivities, always composed by the nuns, but just for the occasion. Once it passes, the play is abandoned. Or maybe saved for another festivity" (letter, February 26, 2015). This information makes us think of the vast numbers of dramatic texts that may have been destroyed after their performance in this and other convents.

21 Baranda Leturio and Marín Pina refer to the testimony of Ángela María de la Concepción, founder of the Trinitarian convent of El Toboso (32, n.19).
22 Sor Marcela wrote under the command of Mariana de Santa Inés. Years later, when she herself held the position of Mother Minister, she requested that Francisca write plays.
23 Hegstrom ("Theater": 211, 216). With regard to the collective writing memory of the communities, Baranda Leturio asserts that "even if we could not possibly describe it as subversive, it does transmit a particular genealogy that allows women a space of power" (Zarri and Baranda Leturio: 7).
24 For functions and purposes of Sister Marcela's theater, see Vollendorf 106, and Weber 39.
25 Smith, "The Female" 239; Vollendorf 100–101; Weber 39; and Halling 71.
26 "Some authors explicitly mentioned the audience to whom they address themselves: their Sisters, confessors, and church authorities. For some poems, such as those created for the taking of vows, the audience was much larger-the families of the new Brides of Christ and worshippers of the parish in which the convent's church was located" (Arenal y Schlau, "Not only": 13).
27 See Lehfeldt. According to Vollendorf, "the convent wall functioned as both a barrier and a link between those communities and the outside world" (96). Zarri considers that the cloisters were at the same time places of choice or restriction, self-fulfillment or oppression (Zarri and Baranda Leturio: 1; and Zarri: 50).
28 In the case of Sister Francisca, her literary and dramatic work must have been known (and acknowledged) in certain social circles of Madrid, as she was called upon several times to write for other churches and convents.
29 Urzáiz's catalogue includes a great number of them.
30 Francisca de Santa Teresa 77–80; Alarcón Román, "La producción" 58–63; "La reescritura" 351–352; Borrego Gutiérrez 30–33.
31 Barbeito Carneiro "La ingeniosa"; Arenal and Schlau, *Untold Sisters* 237, 244–245; "Not only" 222–223; Doménech Rico, "Autoras" 397; Alarcón Román, "Tras las huellas" 263; Vollendorf 101–102.

Works cited

Alarcón Román, M. Carmen. "Tras las huellas de Sor Marcela: Sor Francisca de Santa Teresa y el teatro conventual femenino del siglo XVII." *Autoras y actrices en la historia del teatro español*. Ed. Luciano García Lorenzo. Murcia: Festival de Almagro/Universidad de Murcia, 2000: 257–266.

——. "El convento como espacio intelectual en el Siglo de Oro: la dramaturga y poetisa Sor Francisca de Santa Teresa (1654–1709)." *Entretejiendo saberes. Actas del IV Seminario de la Asociación Universitaria de Estudios de Mujeres (AUDEM), Sevilla, 17–19 octubre 2002*. Ed. Mercedes Arriaga Flórez, et al. Seville: Secretariado de Recursos Audiovisuales y Nuevas Tecnologías. Vicerrectorado de Calidad y Nuevas Tecnologías de la Universidad de Sevilla [CD-Rom].

——. "El cumpleaños de la abadesa: una loa de Alonso Martín Brahones en el convento de Santa Inés de Sevilla (1671)." *Teatro. Revista de estudios teatrales*, 19 (2003): 107–134.

——. "El teatro en los conventos femeninos de Sevilla durante el Siglo de Oro: un festejo cómico de 1678." *Memoria de la palabra. Actas del VI Congreso de la Asociación Internacional Siglo de Oro*, vol. I. Ed. María Luisa Lobato and Francisco Domínguez. Madrid; Frankfurt am Main: Iberoamericana-Vervuert, 2004: 183–199.

——. "Devoción y ocio en la clausura femenina sevillana durante el siglo XVII: el teatro en honor de los Santos Juanes." *Actas del Congreso "El Siglo de Oro en el nuevo milenio"*, vol. 1. Ed. Carlos Mata and Miguel Zugasti. Barañáin: Ediciones Universidad de Navarra, 2005: 117–128.

——. "Nuns and actresses: the performance of dramatic works in the convent of the Trinitarias Descalzas of Madrid. The plays written by Sister Francisca of Santa Teresa (1654–1709)." *Heroines of the Golden StAge. Women and Drama in Spain and England, 1500–1700*. Ed. Rina Walthaus and Marguerite Corporaal. Kassel: Reichenberger, 2008: 88–110.

——. "Escritura y fiesta en los conventos femeninos del siglo XVII. Relación de una *Máscara* atribuida a Sor Francisca de Santa Teresa." *De lo sagrado y lo profano. Mujeres tras/entre/sin fronteras*. Ed. Mercedes Arriaga Flórez et al. Seville: ArCibel Editores, 2008: 19–30.

——. "La producción poética de sor Francisca de Santa Teresa (1654–1709), religiosa del convento de trinitarias de Madrid: entre la cotidianeidad y la espiritualidad." *Letras en la celda. Cultura escrita en los conventos femeninos en la España moderna*. Ed. Nieves Baranda and María Carmen Marín Pina. Madrid; Frankfurt am Main: Iberoamericana-Vervuert, 2014: 345–361.

——. "La reescritura del discurso místico y visionario en la obra de sor Francisca de Santa Teresa." *Revista de Escritoras Ibéricas*, 2 (2014): 43–65.

——. "El teatro como didáctica del camino de perfección. El *Diálogo* que representaron las carmelitas descalzas de Toledo en la [profesión] de la madre Ana de San José. Año de 1660." *Medievalia* 18.2 (2015): 247–272.

——. "Literatura conventual femenina en el Siglo de Oro. El manuscrito de sor Francisca de Santa Teresa (1654–1709). Estudio y edición." Unpublished Ph.D. dissertation. Universidad de Sevilla, 2015.

Alonso Cortés, Blanca. *Dos monjas vallisoletanas poetisas*. Valladolid: Imprenta Castellana, 1944.

Arellano, Ignacio and Andrés Eichmann, eds. *Entremeses, loas y coloquios de Potosí (Colección del convento de Santa Teresa)*. Madrid; Frankfurt am Main: Iberoamericana-Vervuert, 2005.

Arenal, Electa. "The Convent as Catalyst for Autonomy. Two Hispanic Nuns of the Seventeenth Century." *Women in Hispanic Literature. Icons and Fallen Idols*. Ed. Beth Miller. Berkeley: U California P, 1983: 147–183.

——. "Vida y teatro conventual: Sor Marcela de San Félix." *La creatividad femenina en el barroco hispánico*. Ed. Monika Bosse, Barbara Potthast, and André Stoll. Kassel: Reichenberger, 1999: 209–219.

Arenal, Electa, and Georgina Sabat-Rivers. *Literatura Conventual Femenina: Sor Marcela de San Félix, hija de Lope de Vega. Obra completa*. Madrid: PPU, 1988.

——. "Voces del convento: Sor Marcela, la hija de Lope." *Actas del IX Congreso de la Asociación Internacional de Hispanistas*. Ed. Sebastian Neumeister. Frankfurt am Main: Vervuert Verlag, 1989: 591–600.

——. "Una hija de Lope escritora." *Ínsula*, 42.484 (1990): 5.

Arenal, Electa, and Stacey Schlau, eds. *Untold Sisters. Hispanic Nuns in Their Own Works*. Albuquerque: U New Mexico P, 1989; 2010.

——. "Not Only her Father s Daughter: Sor Marcela de San Félix Stages a Nun's Profession." *Engendering the Early Modern Stage: Women Playwrights in the Spanish Empire*. Ed. Valerie Hegstrom and Amy Williamsen. New Orleans: UP of the South, 1999: 221–238.

——. "'Leyendo yo y escribiendo ella': The Convent as Intellectual Community". *Letras femeninas* 32.1 (2006): 129–147.

Baranda Leturio, Nieves. "Cantos al sacro epitalamio o sea pliegos poéticos para las tomas de velo." *Bulletin Hispanique* 113.1 (2011): 269–296.

Baranda Leturio, Nieves and M. Carmen Marín Pina. "El universo de la escritura conventual femenina: deslindes y perspectivas." In *Letras en la celda. Cultura escrita de los conventos femeninos en la España moderna*. Ed. Nieves Baranda Leturio and M. Carmen Marín Pina. Madrid; Frankfurt am Main: Iberoamericana-Vervuert, 2014: 11–45.

Barbeito Carneiro, María Isabel. "La ingeniosa provisora Sor Marcela de Vega." *Cuadernos bibliográficos*, XLIV (1982): 59–70.

——. *Escritoras madrileñas del siglo XVII. Estudio bibilográfico-crítico, 2 vols*. Madrid: Universidad Complutense, 1986.

——. *Mujeres del Madrid Barroco. Voces testimoniales*. Madrid: Horas y Horas/Dirección General de la Mujer, 1992.

——. *Mujeres y literatura del Siglo de Oro. Espacios profanos y espacios conventuales*. Madrid: Safekat, 2007.

Barruchi y Arana, Joaquín. *Relación del festejo que a los Marqueses de las Amarillas les hicieron las Señoras Religiosas del Convento de San Jerónimo* (México, 1756). Ed. Frederick Luciani. Madrid; Frankfurt am Main: Iberoamericana-Vervuert, 2011.

BIESES (Bibliografía de Escritoras Españolas). www.uned.es/bieses

Borrego Gutiérrez, Esther. "De la lírica a la escena. Tres fiestas teatrales en el convento vallisoletano de la Concepción del Carmen (1600–1643)." *Revista de Escritoras Ibéricas*, 2 (2014): 11–40.

Cecilia del Nacimiento. *Obras completas*. Ed. J. M. Díaz Cerón. Madrid: Editorial de la Espiritualidad, 1971.

Doménech Rico, Fernando. "Autoras en el teatro español. Siglos XVI–XVIII." In *Autoras en la historia del teatro español (1500–1994), vol. I (Siglos XVII–XVIII)*. Dir. Juan Antonio Hormigón. Madrid: Publicaciones de la Asociación de Directores de Escena de España, 1996: 391–604.

——. *Teatro breve de mujeres (siglos XVII–XX)*. Madrid: Publicaciones de la Asociación de Directores de Escena de España, 1996.

——. "Adiciones a las fichas de las autoras (siglos XVII–XIX)." *Autoras en la historia del teatro español (1500–1994), vol. II. Siglo XX (1900–1975)*. Dir. Juan Antonio Hormigón. Madrid: Publicaciones de la Asociación de Directores de Escena de España, 1997: 133–134, 141–143.

——. "El teatro escrito por mujeres." *Historia del teatro español. I. De la Edad Media a los Siglos de Oro*, Madrid: Gredos, 2003: 1243–1259.

Escabias, Juana. *Dramaturgas del Siglo de Oro. Guía básica*. Madrid: Huerga y Fierro Editores, 2013.
Francisca de Santa Teresa. *Coloquios*. Ed. M. Carmen Alarcón Román. Seville: ArCiBel Editores, 2007.
Gascón, Christopher D. *The Women Saint in Spanish Golden Age Drama*. Lewisburg, DE: Bucknell UP, 2006.
Halling, Anna-Lisa. "Feminine Voice and Space in Early Modern Iberian Convent." Unpublished Ph.D. dissertation. Vanderbilt University, 2012.
Hegstrom, Valerie. "Theater in the Convent." *Engendering the Early Modern Stage: Women Playwrights in the Spanish Empire*. Ed. Valerie Hegstrom and Amy Williamsen. New Orleans: UP of the South, 1999: 211–217.
———. "El convento como espacio escénico y la monja como actriz: montajes teatrales en tres conventos de Valladolid, Madrid y Lisboa." *Letras en la celda. Cultura escrita en los conventos femeninos en la España moderna*. Ed. Nieves Baranda Leturio and M. Carmen Marín Pina. Madrid; Frankfurt am Main: Iberoamericana-Vervuert, 2014: 363–376.
Kaminsky, Amy Katz. *Water Lilies. Flores de agua. An Anthology of Spanish Women Writers from the Fifteenth through the Nineteenth Century*. London; Minneapolis: U Minnesota P, 1996.
Lavrin, Asunción. "Erudición, devoción y creatividad tras las rejas conventuales." *Letras en la celda. Cultura escrita de los conventos femeninos en la España moderna*. Ed. Nieves Baranda Leturio and María Carmen Marín Pina. Madrid; Frankfurt am Main: Iberoamericana-Vervuert, 2014: 65–88.
Lehfeldt, Elizabeth. *Religious Women in Golden Age Spain: The Permeable Cloister*. Farnham, UK: Ashgate, 2005.
López Estrada, Francisco. "Vida y obra literaria de Sor Marcela de San Félix, hija de Lope y monja de la Villa y Corte." *Ínsula*, 521 (1990): 5.
María de San Alberto. *Viva al siglo, muerta al mundo. Obras escogidas*. Ed. Stacey Schlau. New Orleans: UP of the South, 1998.
Mesa, Carlos E. "Marcela Lope de Vega (1605–1688)." *Arco*, 205 (1978): 47–57.
Palacios Fernández, Emilio. "Noticia sobre el parnaso dramático femenino en el siglo XVIII." *Autoras y actrices en la historia del teatro español*. Ed. Luciano García Lorenzo. Murcia: Festival de Almagro-Universidad de Murcia, 2000: 81–131.
Parodi, Claudia. "Teatro de monjas en la Nueva España." *De palabras, imágenes y símbolos: homenaje a José Pascual Buxó*. Enrique Ballón Aguirre y Óscar Rivera Rodas (eds.). México: Universidad Nacional Autónoma de México, 2002: 233–251.
Pérez Baltasar, María Dolores. "Saber y creación literaria: los claustros femeninos en la Edad Moderna." *Cuadernos de Historia Moderna*, 20 (1998): 129–143.
Ramírez Nuño, José A., and Clara Isabel Delgado Ramírez. *Sor Marcela de San Félix Lope de Vega y Luján (Hija de Félix Lope de Vega y Carpio, Toledo 1605-Madrid 1688). Obra poética completa*. Córdoba: Publicaciones del Monte de Piedad y Caja de Ahorros de Córdoba, 1987.
Sabat de Rivers, Georgina. "Voces del convento: Sor Marcela, la hija de Lope." *Actas del IX Congreso de la Asociación Internacional de Hispanistas, Berlín, (18–23 agosto 1986)*. Ed. Sebastian Neumeister. Frankfurt am Main: Vervuert Verlag, 1989: 591–600.
———. "Literatura manuscrita de convento: poesía y teatro de la hija de Lope en el Madrid del XVII". *Culturas en la Edad de Oro*. Ed. José María Díez Borque. Madrid: Editorial Complutense, 1995: 223–237.
Samson, Alexander. "Distinct Drama? Female Dramatists in Golden Age Spain." *A Companion to Spanish Women s Studies*. Ed. Xon de Ros and Geraldine Hazbun. Woodbridge: Tamesis, 2011: 157–172.
Sánchez Arjona, José. *Noticias referentes a los Anales del Teatro en Sevilla. Desde Lope de Rueda hasta finales del siglo XVII*. Seville: Ayuntamiento de Sevilla, 1994.
Sánchez Dueñas, Blas. *De la invisibilidad a la creación. Oralidad, concepción teórica y material preceptivo en la producción literaria femenina hasta el siglo XVIII*. Seville: Renacimiento, 2008.
Schlau, Stacey. "The Drama of Religious Life: Early Modern Convent Playwrights María de San Alberto and Cecilia del Nacimiento." *A stage of their own/Un escenario propio. Actas selectas. Tomo I. España*. Ed. Patricia W. O Connor and Kirsten F. Nigro. Ottawa: Girol Books, 1998.
———. "'Tórnome morena.'African Voices, Dark Skin and Gypsy Rythms in María de San Alberto's Plays and Poetry" [forthcoming].
Serrano y Sanz, Manuel. *Apuntes para una biblioteca de escritoras españolas desde el año 1401 al 1833, 4 vols*. Madrid: Rivadeneyra, 1903–1905.
Smith, Susan M. "The Female Trinity of Sor Marcela de San Felix." *Engendering the Early Modern Stage: Women Playwrights of the Spanish Empire*. Ed. Valerie Hegstrom and Amy Williamsen. New Orleans, UP of the South, 1999: 239–256.

———. "Notes on a Newly-discovered Play: Is Marcela de San Félix the Author?" *Bulletin of the Comediantes*, 52.1 (2000): 147–170.

———. *El convento de las Trinitarias Descalzas de Madrid y la vida de sor Marcela*. Madrid: Real Academia Española; Espasa Calpe, 2001.

Smith, Susan M., and Georgina Sabat de Rivers. *Los coloquios del Alma: cuatro dramas alegóricos de sor Marcela de San Félix, hija de Lope de Vega*. Newark, DE: Juan de la Cuesta, 2006.

Tigchelaar, Alisa J. "Redemption Theology in Mystical Convent Drama: 'The Already and the Not Yet' in Hildegard of Bingen's *Ordo Virtutum* and Marcela de San Félix's *Breve festejo*." *Mirabilia: Revista Eletrónica do História Antiga e Medieval*, 15 (2012): 86–127.

———. "Marcela de San Félix's Mystic Theology through Drama: Platonic and Agustinian Influences." *International Studies on Law and Education 17 mai-ago 2014, CEMOrOc-Feusp/IJI- Univ do Porto*, (2014): 19–48.

Toft, Evelyn. "Cecilia del Nacimiento, Second-Generation Mystic of the Convent Reform." *A New Companion to Hispanic Mysticism*. Ed. Hilaire Kallendorf. Leiden: Brill, 2010: 231–252.

Urzáiz Tortajada, Héctor. *Catálogo de autores teatrales del siglo XVII*, 2 vols. Madrid: Fundación Universitaria Española, 2000.

Vélez Sáinz, Julio and Gemma Rodríguez Ibarra (eds.). *Dramaturgas barrocas (Feliciana Enríquez de Guzmán y sor Marcela de San Félix): teatro breve*. Madrid: Ediciones del Orto, 2014.

Vollendorf, Lisa. *The Lives of Women: a New History of Inquisitional Spain*. Nashville: Vanderbilt UP, 2005.

Weaver, Elissa B. *Convent Theater in Early Modern Italy: Spiritual Fun and Learning for Women*. New York: Cambridge UP, 2007.

Weber, Alison. "Literature by Women Religious in Early Modern Catholic Europe and the New World." *The Ashgate Research Companion to Women and Gender in Early Modern Europe*. Ed. Allyson M. Poska, Jane Couchman, and Katherine A. McIver. Farnham, UK: Ashgate, 2013: 33–51.

Zarri, Gabriella. "La scrittura monástica." *Letras en la celda. Cultura escrita de los conventos femeninos en la España moderna*. Ed. Nieves Baranda Leturio and M. Carmen Marín Pina. Madrid; Frankfurt am Main: Iberoamericana-Vervuert, 2014: 50–64.

Zarri, Gabriella, and Nieves Baranda Leturio. "Presentazione-Presentación." *Memoria e comunità femminili. Spagna e Italia, secc. XV–XVII/Memoria y comunidades femeninas. España e Italia, siglos XV–XVII*. Ed. Gabriella Zarri and Nieves Baranda Leturio. Firenze: Firenze UP; UNED, 2011: 1–11.

8
BODY, SPIRIT, AND VERSE
Reading early modern women's religious poetry

Stacey Schlau

Studies of early modern women's religious poetic production in Spain form a substantial, although unevenly distributed corpus of work. Currently, a wide range of critical perspectives generates rich and varied readings of canonical authors, and a trend toward expanding the canon slowly gathers momentum. Historically, the trajectory of scholarship about religious poetry has reflected prevailing ideological currents. Two periods stand out: late nineteenth to early twentieth centuries and late twentieth century. In the earlier period, scholars such as Marcelino Menéndez y Pelayo and Ramón Menéndez Pidal highlighted a few salient female figures, most prominently St. Teresa of Ávila, whom they saw as providing textual support for the goal of affirming Spanish heroism and national pride, buttressed by Catholicism. During that same period, Manuel Serrano y Sanz's landmark two-volume set *Apuntes para una biblioteca de escritoras españolas desde 1401 a 1833* (Notes Toward a Library of Spanish Women Writers from 1401 to 1833), influential to this day, delineates a rich female tradition of writing, although far from flawlessly. Despite its problems, Serrano y Sanz's work became the original source for information about many religious poets whose work is being rediscovered and studied in the twenty-first century. Subsequently, in the latter part of the twentieth century, two disparate tendencies produced the richest outpouring of scholarship: the increasing importance of feminist perspectives in literary history and criticism since the 1970s and the five-hundredth anniversary of Teresa of Ávila's death in 1982. In general, context and ideology have remained more prominently studied features than poetics, although that tendency has not been consistent, and is clearly shifting today to a more holistic view of the work: the opening up of the canon and a less traditional hierarchizing of literary genres has occurred fairly recently.

Naturally, much of the religious poetry written by women was produced in convents, by nuns. In "Producción y consumo poéticos en los conventos femeninos" (Poetic Production and Consumption in Convents), Nieves Baranda asserts that while it is possible that St. Teresa was the first woman to write religious poetry in Spain, we cannot be sure (167, n. 5). A useful overview of poetic production in early modern convents, her article argues that St. Teresa served as a model for many, the recreational period in Carmelite convents encouraged poetic production, and convent *cancioneros* constituted important contributions. Emphasizing that the Discalced Carmelites were not the only religious order that produced poetry, she cites the example of Ana de San Jerónimo, a Discalced Franciscan, who sent Augustinian nuns *coplas* (four-line stanzas, usually octosyllabic), and who also sent poems to another nun in the same package as two holy cards and a book (171). Baranda affirms that, "The nuns participated in all tendencies of religious poetry that appeared during the second half of the sixteenth century: versions of psalms, Petrarchan spiritual poetry, devout songs, the aesthetics of religious Baroque, and spiritual ballads" (171).[1] Indeed, she asserts, the use of traditional meters, language, and the emphasis on orality facilitated widespread poetic competition among nuns, even including illiterate sisters (182–183).

Asceticism, mysticism, and poetry

The conflation of poetry with ascetic-mystical expression represents a dominant tendency in the critical literature. That is, it is commonly asserted that two categories of female religious poetry predominate: ascetic-mystical and occasional (e.g., for professions, Christmas, beatifications, canonizations), with an often-unvoiced hierarchizing of the former over the latter.[2] Much of the scholarship on mystic poetry has focused on St. Teresa of Ávila, Luisa de Carvajal y Mendoza, and Cecilia del Nacimiento's work, with some studies of other poets, such as Gregoria Francisca de Santa Teresa.

Regarding language and mystical experience, many critics have averred that gender plays a significant role, because the female mystic speaks from an already-marginalized position. The male ecstatic (especially St. John of the Cross), on the other hand, borrows the female poetic voice knowing that he can return to masculinity outside of discourse. One manifestation of that gendering is through *imitatio*, often inspired through the Eucharist. In "In Her Image," for instance, Julián Olivares reviews the poetry of Luisa de Carvajal, María de la Antigua, and Marcela de San Félix. Echoing earlier critics, such as Arenal and Schlau, he argues that early modern women religious frequently identify with Christ's flesh and humanity, especially his suffering (112). He further asserts that drinking Christ's blood from the wound is a metaphor for mystical knowledge (116), and that by consuming the deity, the mystic celebrates the female body (117). The primary focus of devotion for these women becomes the Eucharist (121). In sum, he sees these poets as having gendered commonalities, rooted in the state induced by taking communion.

This chapter represents an attempt to synthesize an extremely diverse and wide-ranging field, covering many writers. The majority of the studies of religious poetry discussed here treat nun-poets. While scholars have examined the work of a rather large number of women poets of religious verse, however, most literary-historical studies have concentrated on relatively few: Teresa of Ávila (1515–1582), Cecilia del Nacimiento (1570–1646), and Luisa de Carvajal y Mendoza (1566–1614) (who did not profess), and, to a lesser extent, Marcela de San Félix (1605–1687), Violante do Ceo or Céu (1601 or 1607–1693), María de San Alberto (1568–1640), Gregoria Francisca de Santa Teresa (1653–1736), and Ana de San Jerónimo (1696–1771), in addition to a few studies of poets such as Ana de la Trinidad (1577–1613) and María de la Antigua (1566–1617). Many writers of early modern religious verse have gained critical attention primarily for their prose, while their poetry is little studied. Such is the case, for instance, of Ana de San Bartolomé (1549–1626), Ana de Jesús (1545–1621), María de San José (Salazar) (1548–1603), and Luisa Manrique de Lara (1604–1660).[3] This chapter focuses on research about a few poets to give a sense of the field as it has developed and as it stands now.

Anthologies and bibliographies

When Serrano y Sanz published his anthology of women writers at the turn of the twentieth century, he laid the groundwork of the primary sources for the studies that have followed. The anthology/bibliography was and remains significant for the historical study of women's literary production. Poets are heavily represented in his collection, and in the early modern period religious poetry predominates. A rich catalog of names, fragments of texts, and archival references, the information contained in *Apuntes* has continued to facilitate scholarly work, despite the confusion, conflation, and errors regarding some names, dates, and attributions. Now available online, more about this groundbreaking work can be found in other essays in this volume.

Other bibliographies that contain entries about religious poets have continued to lay the foundation for critical studies. Covering early modern Madrid, Isabel Barbeito Carneiro's doctoral dissertation, *Escritoras madrileñas del siglo XVII: Estudio bibliográfico-crítico* (Universidad Complutense de Madrid, 1986), offers a complete, accurate list of writers and works, with full citations. In this century, Nieves Baranda created and continues to direct the extremely valuable BIESES.net (Biblioteca de Escritoras Españolas) project, a rich and multifaceted electronic resource that nurtures scholars worldwide. BIESES is possible partly because of the work carried out by an international collaboration of scholars and graduate students. Complete versions of Barbeito's bibliography, as well as those of Jesús Rebollo Prieto, *Las escritoras de Castilla y León (1400–1800). Ensayo bibliográfico* (Women Writers of Castile and León (1400–1800): A Bibliographic Essay); Manuel Diego Sánchez's *Bibliografía sistemática de santa Teresa de Jesús* (Systematic Bibliography of St. Teresa of Jesus); and Emilio Palacios Fernández, *Bibliografía del siglo XVIII* (Bibliography of the Eighteenth Century), are available on BIESES. All are eminently useful, though their very comprehensive nature makes perusal a herculean task at times.[4]

The best-known and also most scholarly print anthology of early modern Spanish poetry by women is Julián Olivares and Elizabeth Boyce's *Tras el espejo la musa escribe. Lírica femenina de los Siglos de oro* (The Muse Writes through the Mirror: Female Lyric in the Golden Age), whose second, expanded edition appeared in 2012. A valuable classroom tool, with an excellent introduction and selected works of twelve writers, the volume includes religious poetry by nine: Violante do Céu,[5] Marcia Belisarda (María de Santa Isabel), Cecilia del Nacimiento, María de San Alberto, Ana Francisca Abarca de Bolea, Cristobalina Fernández de Alarcón, Luisa de Carvajal y Mendoza, María de la Antigua, and Marcela de San Félix. *Tras el espejo* reflects the meticulous scholarship of its editors, including accurate transcriptions of texts from manuscripts and well-researched biographical and textual details; at times they correct the errors of other researchers, a practical advantage.

In the volume, Olivares and Boyce offer a comprehensive, cogent introductory study, arranged thematically. They present an overview of the social context in which women wrote, based on previous feminist work (especially by Carolyn Walker Bynum), as well as summarizing approaches to the poetic texts. The segment on religious poetry (54–74) is itself divided into sub-sections: Eucharistic poetry and mysticism, female Christ and somatic mysticism, the male Christ figure, authority and writing, and hagiography and convent life. Overall, they argue, what distinguishes female from male religious poets "was expressing their own positionality as a woman with the object of their desire, God, in a poetic discourse that was already feminized" (24).[6]

Another useful anthology, intended for a more popular audience, is *Antología poética de escritoras de los siglos XVI y XVII* (Poetic Anthology of Women Writers of the Sixteenth and Seventeenth Centuries), edited by Ana Navarro. The volume includes several early modern religious poets: Teresa of Ávila, María de la Antigua, Luisa de la Ascensión (Monja de Carrión), Marcela de San Félix, Gregoria Francisca de Santa Teresa, Violante do Céu, and Isabel de Jesús, as well as the Mexican Juana Inés de la Cruz. Overtly reflecting the ideological orientation of its editor, Navarro's introduction to the volume situates itself in that school of feminist scholarship that argues that socio-cultural restrictions on women led to the production of fewer, lower-quality works than men's (8). Indeed, she offers some conventional judgments, such as when she notes about St. Teresa's "Vivo sin vivir en mí" (I live without living in myself) that "it rises above the general mediocrity of her poetic production" (33)[7] or when she asserts, regarding mystical writing, that it is more difficult to ascertain the authenticity of the experience in the seventeenth century than in the sixteenth. She includes a psychoanalytic interpretation, noting that the later set of visions were a manifestation of neurosis (36).

Another feminist project, whose first edition appeared during the same time period as Navarro's anthology, is *Untold Sisters: Hispanic Nuns in Their Own Works*.[8] A combined anthology and critical study containing bilingual selections (in English and Spanish) of writing by women religious, the book includes poetry by Cecilia del Nacimiento, Marcela de San Félix, and María de San Alberto, as well as long, in-depth studies of each of the writers represented. Arenal and Schlau's volume sprang from a desire to begin the recovery of women's writing; its focus on nuns' works reflects the assumption that in order to understand women's thoughts, feelings, and experiences in the early modern period, it is necessary to examine texts authored by nuns, since they were the majority of women with the time, freedom, and resources for creative work.

Bárbara Mujica's anthology, *Women Writers of Early Modern Spain: Sophia's Daughters* (2004), recapitulates several of the authors included in *Untold Sisters*, including the three previously mentioned. Like *Untold Sisters*, *Sophia's Daughters* lends itself to classroom use.

Two collections of critical essays

Julián Olivares edited *Studies on Women's Poetry of the Golden Age: Tras el espejo la musa escribe* as a companion volume for *Tras el espejo*. The included essays, written in English, are intended for classroom use, to enrich understanding of the anthologized poets. The volume offers useful readings for students and specialists alike, including a section of six essays on religious poetry.

Three chapters are devoted to the Sobrino Morillas sisters, María de San Alberto and Cecilia del Nacimiento. Alison Weber's contribution, "Could Women Write Mystical Poetry?: The Literary Daughters of Juan de la Cruz," analyzes María de San Alberto's "Liras sobre la noche oscura" (*Liras* on the Dark Night) and Cecilia del Nacimiento's "Canciones a la transformación del alma" (Songs on the Soul's Transformation) against the background of San Juan de la Cruz's "Noche oscura" (Dark Night). Weber argues that the two Discalced Carmelite nuns recognized his poem as a "fictive utterance" (190), an allegory (191). Unlike San Juan de la Cruz, they could not however separate tenor and vehicle in separate texts and genres (198), nor could they sever allegory from lyric fiction (201). Elizabeth Rhodes also compares Cecilia del Nacimiento's "Canciones a la transformación del alma" to San Juan's poem, arguing that while the female voice allowed San Juan to express desire in the gender deemed appropriate for such an emotion (211), she notes that Cecilia del Nacimiento's is a poetics of abstraction, not embodied desire (212). Stacey Schlau also writes about María de San Alberto's poems, providing a detailed textual analysis of those of that appear in *Tras el espejo*.

The other three chapters on religious poetry discuss Marcela de San Félix, Luisa de Carvajal, and María de la Antigua respectively. Electa Arenal offers an overview of Sor Marcela's work, focusing on the theme of solitude and using two poems as examples: "Villancico a la profesión de la Hermana Isabel del Santísimo Sacramento" (Carol on the Profession of Sister Isabel del Santísimo Sacramento) and "Jaculatorias disfrazadas en hábito de seguidillas" (Brief Prayers Disguised in the Habit of Seguidillas). Anne Cruz discusses Luisa de Carvajal's Eucharistic poetry, emphasizing the poet's identification with Christ, and his perceived physical presence. Finally, Julián Olivares takes up the *Coloquios* (Colloquies) by María de la Antigua, addressing the nun-poet's status as a white-veiled nun and her illiteracy, which required that others transcribe her words to the written page. His interest in María de la Antigua's work reflects the canon expansion noted earlier.

The recent collection of essays about early modern Spanish women writers, edited by Nieves Baranda Leturio and María Carmen Marín Pina, *Letras en la celda: Cultura escrita de los conventos femeninos en la España moderna* (The Literary Cell: Convent Writing Culture in Modern Spain), points toward new directions in research in the field, and especially previously unstudied writers. Two essays focus on religious poets: Inmaculada Osuna Rodríguez's "Poesía intramuros: Creación y recepción poética en el convento de Santa María de las Dueñas (Sevilla) a principio del siglo XVII" (Poetic Creation and Reception in the Convent of Santa María de las Dueñas [Seville] In the Early Seventeenth Century) and María Carmen Alarcón Román's "La producción poética de sor Francisca de Santa Teresa (1654–1709): Entre la cotidianeidad y la espiritualidad" (The Poetic Production of Sor Francisca de Santa Teresa [1654–1709]: Between Daily Life and Spirituality).[9] The first situates convent poetic production in Seville from 1616–1622 in the context of the lively national advocacy of the Immaculate Conception, primarily discussing the work of Constanza Osorio (1565–1637), whom Osuna describes as the most important literary figure of the convent, and that of María de Sandoval, whose poetry directly addresses the Immaculate Conception. The second essay offers an introduction to the work of a Trinitarian nun-poet, Francisca de Santa Teresa, from the same Madrid convent as Marcela de San Félix. Her approximately fifty-one poems were mostly occasional and meant to be sung, although some also reflected her mystical experiences. In many, the theme of spiritual indifference dominates. Alarcón notes that her poetry may be characterized as depicting "the natural joining of spirituality and daily life, between religious feeling carried to its ultimate consequences and the recounting of daily vicissitudes of community life in the convent" (352).[10]

Saint Teresa of Ávila

No discussion of mystical poetry by Spanish early modern women can omit St. Teresa. For over a century, scholars of historical, literary, and religious studies have written hundreds, perhaps thousands of volumes about her life and writings. At the turn of the nineteenth into the twentieth century, a "Teresa boom" coincided with the years from the anniversary of the saint's death in 1582 to the anniversary of her canonization in 1922. Denise DuPont discusses Ramón Menéndez Pidal, Miguel de Unamuno, Emilia Pardo Bazán, José Martínez Ruiz, and Blanca de los Ríos's appropriation of St. Teresa, as well as their assessment of her literary worth. Thus, although Menéndez Pidal, for instance, asserted in 1899 that St. Teresa had no interest in authorship, he later wrote that, in order to write, she had deployed a "a willful linguistic demotion of social class" (qtd. in García de la Concha, *Estudios* 11, qtd. in DuPont 32).[11] This assessment has persisted: Víctor García de la Concha has later stated that the saint had "a true literary vocation" (*Al aire* 34).[12]

During the first half of the twentieth century, the generation represented by such eminent critics as E. Allison Peers and Helmut Hatzfeld devoted many pages to the saint's writing. She appears, for instance, in Hatzfeld's *Estudios literarios sobre mística española* (Literary Studies on Spanish Mysticism), a classic of the canon. To a large degree, along with Menéndez Pidal, their interpretations shaped readings of St. Teresa for generations. Peers' translation of St. Teresa's complete works remained the most authoritative for decades.[13]

Then, in the late twentieth century, both religious and feminist academics concentrated on the saint. Several Discalced Carmelite scholars, such as Alfredo Barrientos, Teófanes Egido, and Kiernan Kavanaugh, devoted much time and energy to studying (and, in Kavanaugh's case, translating) her work. A great deal of feminist and feminist-influenced scholarship about St.

Teresa has also appeared since the 1970s and 1980s; among the best-known writing from this perspective are Gillian Ahlgren, Mary E. Giles, Josefina López, Mary Luti, Bárbara Mujica, Rosa Rossi, Carol Slade, and Alison Weber. Julia Kristeva has written a novel based on her life and Mujica a novel, on which a play, *God's Gypsy*, was based.

Despite St. Teresa's iconic presence in print—anthologies, monographs, journals, collections of essays, and books—the Discalced Carmelite founder's poetic production has been relatively neglected in the critical literature, when compared to the attention paid to her prose. Partly, the reason lies in an attitude first articulated by Marcelino Menéndez y Pelayo and others of his generation, but which continues to prevail. In 1998, for instance, Juan Serrano and Susan Serrano's introductory study to their translations of San Juan's "Cántico espiritual" (Spiritual Canticle), and "Vivo sin vivir en mí" and "Si el amor que me teneis" (If the Love You Have For Me) respectively, argue that San Juan was the quintessential mystic poet while St. Teresa was "unschooled," "almost naïve" (36). And when Georgina Sabat-Rivers compared Marcela de San Félix's work to St. Teresa's (1993), she noted that both seemed to avail themselves of the Platonic-Christian ideas that defined art as the product of God's eloquence and not of learned rules (21).

In 1984, Lía Noemí Uriarte Rebaudi insisted that St. Teresa's poetry was hardly known and little studied, with two exceptions, Ángel Custodio Vega's *La poesía de Santa Teresa* (St. Teresa's Poetry) and Víctor García de la Concha's "La lírica de Santa Teresa en la poesía carmelitana" (St. Teresa's Lyric in Carmelite Poetry). While Vega's book offers an overview of the kinds of poetry that St. Teresa authored (as opposed to those attributed to her), and then discusses in each of the poems in depth, it reflects the same dichotomy as earlier scholarship in its comparison of her poetry (characterized as "simple") and San Juan's (characterized as "complex") (xv–xvii). Vega does assert that St. Teresa's is better, but he also avers that "[f]eminine tenderness and a delicate temperament in her heart always led her to quintessentially feminine stances of love, reverence, surrender, spiritual caresses" (31).[14] The tendency to attribute poetic characteristics to gender reflects a traditional framework evidenced in earlier scholarship, whether it appears as stereotypically "feminine" or in the version of the "mujer varonil" (masculine woman). The overview section of Víctor García de la Concha's lengthy book chapter, "La lírica de Santa Teresa," covers much of the same ground as Vega's. He asserts that her poetry contains two basic sets of themes: mystical experience and the ascetic, devotional environment of Discalced Carmelite convents.[15] In addition, the chapter thoughtfully engages Helmut Hatzfeld's interpretation of St. Teresa's poetry, devoting the most space to a highly technical, detailed analysis of the poetics in some of St. Teresa's poems.

A solid introduction in English to St. Teresa's poetry, Brian C. Morris's "The Poetry of Santa Teresa" is one of the earliest influenced by late twentieth-century critical frameworks. Morris argues that the Saint of Ávila's enduring doctrine of action makes her poetry affirmative and imperative; love must be channeled toward deeds (246). Marrying sound and meaning, and availing herself of the "lighter, more rhythmic, vein of the cancioneros" (245), St. Teresa composed occasional and mystical poems using the "serviceable and recurrent motifs as the wound, the hunt, the soul as a dwelling, the sayal [sackcloth], and such fundamental themes as the muerte en vida [death in life] and contempt for worldly things" (244).

Other critics confirm Morris's judgments. While María C. Albín focuses on the mystical eroticism evident in the saint's poetry, arguing that her mystical love is based in Christ's corporality (38), Manuel Asensi Pérez undertakes a textual analysis of the theme of death in "Vivo sin vivir en mí." Another book-length study, Elizabeth Teresa Howe's *Mystical Imagery: Santa Teresa de Jesús and San Juan de la Cruz*, organizes a detailed textual analysis of the saint's prose and poetry by focusing on imagery, especially simile. Howe affirms, in concert with most other critics, that St. Teresa's style is "colloquial and elliptical," her language "vivid, direct, and familiar" (322).

Pedro Ruiz Pérez elaborates a similar conceptual framework, focusing on the communicative aspect of St. Teresa's poetry, written for pragmatic reasons: "surge con una intencionalidad primaria de acto de canto y petición exhortativa, que en esencia son los mismos fines que los que la Iglesia establece para la oración: alabar a Dios, darle gracias y pedirle beneficios" (189) [springs from the primary intentionality of the acts of singing and exhortative petitioning, which in essence are the same goals that the Church established for prayer: to praise God, thank him, and ask him for favors.] Further, he repeats that St. Teresa's language was "llano" (plain), that she chose forms and meters that were easy to follow, based in song, and that her intentions were far more utilitarian than literary (191).

Elena Carrera's article on St. Teresa's "Muero porque no muero" emphasizes the poem's connection with the *cancioneros*, particularly regarding a concept of love that goes beyond the Neoplatonic separation of body and soul (730). She develops a lengthy analysis of the paradoxical title, linking the oral quality of the lines to the thematic thread of suffering love. Carrera's focus on St. Teresa's identification with the Passion of Christ leads to her conclusion: "Drawing on *cancionero* formulations of desire, Teresa's 'Muero porque no muero' suggests that the experience of reciprocated love can also be intensified by wilful desire, and that desire can help the lover move towards, and become transformed into, the beloved" (742).

Luis González-Cruz comes to a similar conclusion in his study of the cross as image in St. Teresa's poetry. That is, while he views the cross as having multiple meanings, he argues that it exemplifies the Saint's preferred structure of thesis, antithesis, and synthesis to explicate religious symbolism. The cross unites humanity with the divine, and ultimately comes to represent redemption (189).

Cecilia del Nacimiento and María de San Alberto

Two biological sisters who professed together in the Valladolid Discalced Carmelite convent have been addressed not only as poets, but also as cultural arbiters and leaders of their convent. The younger, Cecilia del Nacimiento, a frequently studied mystic poet of the period, initially drew scholarly attention because some of her poems were, until the mid-twentieth century, attributed to San Juan de la Cruz. José María Díaz Cerón published an edition of her work in 1971, when almost no other early modern religious woman poet was available in print. In the scholarship, her mystical poetry continues to be compared to that of San Juan de la Cruz. Several critics have undertaken a comparative analysis of her "Liras a la transformación del alma en Dios" (Liras to the Transformation of the Soul in God) with his "Noche oscura" (e. g., Rhodes, "Gender"; Toft, "Second-Generation" 239–243 and "Mystic"; and Weber, "Could Women"). Elsewhere, Evelyn Toft, unlike Elizabeth Rhodes, argues that Cecilia del Nacimiento's poetically expressed relationship with the divinity is intimate and all-encompassing ("Joy" 96). Like Rhodes, however, she asserts that Cecilia del Nacimiento's work follows the tradition established by St. Teresa of Ávila and St. John of the Cross ("Joy" 83).

Rather than comparing her poetry to San Juan's, in chapter 2 of *Untold Sisters*, Arenal and Schlau situate Cecilia del Nacimiento's poetry in the context of a female creative tradition, encouraged by both her biological mother, the humanist Cecilia Morillas Sobrino, and the Teresian emphasis on recreation and poetic expressiveness in Discalced Carmelite convents. Along with her biological and religious sister, María de San Alberto, the younger Sobrino produced a poetic *oeuvre* that followed the two tendencies pioneered by St. Teresa, and continued by many: a metaphorical account of her mystical experiences and occasional poems for a variety of occasions, including the celebration of the Saint of Ávila.

María de San Alberto has also been the object of several studies. After *Untold Sisters*, Schlau undertook an edition of her selected works, with a lengthy bilingual introductory study. In addition, aside from the essay that appeared in the Olivares collection, she has published an article analyzing the use of Black language, imagery, and themes in María de San Alberto's poems ("Tórnome morena"). Previously, only Blanca Alonso Cortés had written about the older Sobrino Morillas sister; she had been mostly left in the literary shadows, behind Cecilia del Nacimiento. Subsequently, as discussed above, Weber has written about her "Liras sobre la noche oscura" ("Could Women?"), as have Olivares and Boyce in their introduction to the second edition of *Tras el espejo* and García de la Concha and Álvarez Pellitero in their introductory study to the *Libro de romances y coplas del Carmelo de Valladolid (c. 1590–1609)* (Book of *Romances* and *Coplas* from the Discalced Carmelite Convent of Valladolid). García de la Concha makes the claim that Cecilia del Nacimiento was a much better poet than María de San Alberto (xv), but he criticizes Gerardo de Santa Cruz, an early scholar and cataloguer of the Discalced Carmelite convent archive in Valladolid, for attributing almost all the tercets and *octavas* to María de San Alberto and the *loas* and sonnets to Cecilia del Nacimiento (xv). In her dissertation, cited above, Rubí Ugofsky-Méndez also discusses Cecilia del Nacimiento and María de San Alberto, although she does not refer to much of the previous scholarship regarding the older sister (62). The scholarly pattern of preferring Cecilia del Nacimiento's poetry to María de San Alberto's continues to this day; in his discussion of the female Teresian poetic tradition, for instance, Jesús Fernando Cáseda Teresa lists Cecilia del Nacimiento and Ana de Jesús, but not María de San Alberto (88, n. 9).

Luisa de Carvajal y Mendoza

Many biographies of Luisa de Carvajal y Mendoza have appeared, although there are fewer studies of her poetry. Critics who have written about the poetry often situate the writing in the theological tradition of the Catholic Church. While asserting that the Teresian garden appears in Carvajal's work, Margaret Ann Rees, for instance, focuses on the religious and theological influences evident in Carvajal's poetry and prose: St. Ignatius of Loyola, Fray Luis de León, the *Song of Songs* (and Bernard de Clairvaux's discussion of it), and San Juan de la Cruz. Olivares and Boyce emphasize that Carvajal and María de la Antigua follow San Juan de la Cruz in their use of nature for its spiritual symbolism (77). Olivares also argued that in Carvajal's poetry, the absence of the beloved is an allegory of the quasi-mystic anguish caused by the absent Eucharist ("In Her Image": 125).

Further biographic, religious, and literary contextualization and analysis of seven of Carvajal's sonnets can be found in Gwyn Fox's chapter on the would-be missionary and mystic poet in *Subtle Subversions*. Fox emphasizes that despite Carvajal's yearning to transcend the body, it "remains insistently present, both as a canvas on which to paint Christ-like suffering and as a participant in the pleasure of physical union" (251).

Perhaps the most consistent and prolific scholar of Carvajal's work is Anne J. Cruz, whose work on the missionary-mystic-poet spans decades. Her "Words Made Flesh: Luisa de Carvajal's Eucharistic Poetry" offers first a biography, then an overview of the poems, suggesting that they followed a popular pastoral model, and that the author used the conventions of the Petrarchan love lyric (257). Cruz here emphasizes Carvajal's identification with Christ, while in "Luisa de Carvajal y Mendoza y su conexión jesuita" (Luisa de Carvajal y Mendoza and Her Jesuit Connection) she uses Jessica Benjamin's connection between sexuality and power as theoretical frame for discussing Carvajal. An earlier article, "'Chains of Desire': Luisa de Carvajal y Mendoza's Poetics of Penance," argues for a gendered analysis of Carvajal's poetry. A psychologically based literary analysis of selected poems, the essay contrasts Carvajal's worldview with that of medieval mystics; Cruz suggests that hers is a "poetics of penance" (103).

Reflecting growing scholarly and popular interest in Carvajal, Cruz recently published *The Life and Writings of Luisa de Carvajal y Mendoza* (2014). Her introductory study provides a scholarly yet accessible overview of the writer, affording readers a strong sense of Carvajal's historical context, life trajectory, and literary worth, as well as offering an extensive bibliography. Selected poems are translated, taken from Carvajal's first biographer, Luis Muñoz.[16]

Most recently, Mary Barnard's article on Carvajal's poetry focuses both on recurring themes in early modern mystical poetry, such as Christ as body and Christ at the Column, but also points toward a fruitful new direction: the relationship to material culture and to Carvajal's aristocratic origins. She suggests that, "[h]er poetry is embedded with vestiges of her aristocratic culture, for she remained an aristocrat at heart despite her rejection of its privileges and material trappings [. . .] a central feature of her poetry [is] the intersection of the body and the material," which characterizes how "she portrays Christ and the mystical union, and constructs her identity as penitent, ascetic, and mystic" (456).

Gregoria Francisca de Santa Teresa

Proof that interest in Gregoria Francisca de Santa Teresa's work continues, Belén Molina Huete's 2013 paper, "Preneoclasicismo y mística: La poesía de sor Gregoria Francisca de Santa Teresa" (Pre-Neoclassicism and Mysticism: The Poetry of Sor Gregoria Francisca de Santa Teresa), provides an excellent historical review of the scholarship on Sor Gregoria, especially in the nineteenth and twentieth centuries, as well as an incisive critique of previous lines of investigation (localist and feminist, for instance). Molina Huete ends with a call for a future edition, following several criteria she proposes, regarding the context and stylistics of the Seville nun's poetry.

An often-cited article by Alvin Sherman argues that Sor Gregoria Francisca de Santa Teresa uses a "double-edged rhetoric" that both conforms to social expectations of feminine mystic discourse and reflects despair regarding her position in the Church (192). His framework relies on contrasting the use of the feminine in San Juan's poetry, in which the "amada" (beloved woman) is merely metaphorical, with the same process for women mystics, which results in the denial of the autonomous self (193). In "El pajarillo" (The Little Bird), Sor Gregoria's best-known poem, the contrast between physical and spiritual worlds, in which the former signifies suffering and incarceration, and the latter happiness and freedom, dominates (196). Sherman treats the poetic voice as if it were Sor Gregoria herself, arguing that while she seeks union with God, that union also brings destruction and frustration. The transformation into the butterfly signifies that life is change, but ultimately that metamorphosis requires sacrifice: the denial of the physical persona and the surrender of the soul (198).

Mary Elizabeth Perry has also written about Gregoria de Santa Teresa's poetry; similarly, to Sherman she notes her use of imagery of nature, but also emphasizes that Sor Gregoria wrote longingly and with love of her relationship with Jesus, and her loneliness without him (76). Perry remarks that like her predecessor in the convent, María de San José (Salazar), Gregoria de Santa Teresa uses martial language to describe the soul's struggle against the devil, but contrasts her expression of inner conflict and struggle with María de San José's determination (76). She ends with a textual analysis of "El pajarillo."

Ana de la Trinidad

Much of the scholarship on women's religious poetry in early modern Spain has been carried out in Spain, by Spaniards. Until the past few decades, since the inception of women's studies as an academic discipline, critics from other countries have rarely intervened (except regarding

St. Teresa). Spanish literary historians continue to conduct a great deal of the archival and bibliographic research in this field, aided by government funding of research and publication, and by national and regional interest. One such study is Jesús Fernando Cáseda Teresa's article on Sor Ana de la Trinidad's sonnets, "La poesía mística de Sor Ana de la Trinidad" (Sor Ana de la Trinidad's Mystical Poetry). A professor at the University of La Rioja, Cáseda Teresa argues that Calahorra was a cultural center during the early modern period. Asserting regional pride, he considers that Ana de la Trinidad's work represents a sterling example of excellence in mystical poetry in both form and content, and he offers a useful analysis of the thematic and formal characteristics of the nineteen extant sonnets by the author, who lived a good part of her life (1577–1613) as a Discalced Carmelite nun in Calahorra.[17]

Rejecting the contention by critics such as José Emilio Orozco that rhythm and tone in St. Teresa and St. John's poetry reflects the tradition of "poesía cantada" (sung poetry), Cáseda Teresa argues that Sor Ana de la Trinidad's poetry represents another, Italianate tendency in mystical poetry, inherited from San Juan de la Cruz's study of Boscán and Garcilaso at the University of Salamanca. This tendency, in which Sor Ana participates, "utilizes the lira, poems of eleven-syllable lines, cuartets, liras in stanzas etc." (Cáseda Teresa 88).[18]

The standard tropes of the *portus quietus*, night, wandering soul, resonant solitude, and burning flame appear (92), he notes, in her poetry; her writing encapsulates the quintessential struggle of mystical poetry to express the indescribable, to seek the adjective that reveals that which is difficult to grasp (89). The use of the sonnet distances her work from St. Teresa's more popular meters and genres, but the consistent presence of a poetic first-person voice who continually offers herself to the divinity, recreating the illuminative stage of mystical experience, aligns Sor Ana with her literary and religious sisters (89). Cáseda Teresa asserts that in her sonnets the first quartet expresses the enormity and goodness of heaven; the second reveals the cruel world, human and limited; and the tercets first present an accessible, friendly deity and then express the author's giving in to, merging with that divinity (90). In sum, he offers this poet as an exemplar, in the name of Calahorra.

Violante do Céu (or Ceo)

Violante do Céu's work has long been acknowledged, but little studied. In *Tras el espejo*, Olivares and Boyce note this; they cite primarily from Margarida Vieira Mendes's introduction to her modern edition of Sor Violante's first book, *Rimas várias*. That volume, first privately published in France in 1646, contained poems in both Portuguese and Spanish; only thirty-seven of the ninety-seven included were religious (Olivares and Boyce: 190).[19] Subsequently, Gwyn Fox included a chapter on her (secular) sonnets in her *Subtle Subversions: Reading Golden Age Sonnets by Iberian Women* (2008). Also, as mentioned previously, Olivares and Boyce discuss her religious poetry in *Tras el espejo*. And, in his "Género sexuado, género literario y ansiedad autorial en la poesía sacra de sor Violante del Cielo" (Gender, Literary Genre, and Anxiety of Authorship in Sor Violante del Cielo's Sacred Poetry), Olivares compares her religious poetry with Sor Juana Inés de la Cruz's. Regarding her religious sonnets written in Portuguese, he argues, only those whose theme is devotion escape a sense of anxiety of authorship (331). Recently, after a series of articles on the Portuguese nun-poet (listed in BIESES), Isabel Morujão published a volume in which Sor Violante appears in Spanish, *Por Trás da Grade. Poesia Conventual Feminina em Portugal (Séculos XVI–XVIII)* (Through the Grille: Female Conventual Poetry in Portugal (Sixteenth through Eighteenth Centuries). Indeed, it is to be expected Morujão's volume will foment scholarship on this nun-poet, who occupies a unique place in literary history as a writer in two languages.

Marcela de San Félix

Marcela de San Félix has received a modicum of scholarly attention, at least partly because she was a daughter of Lope de Vega. Her works have been published: after bilingual selections appeared in *Untold Sisters*, Georgina Sabat-Rivers and Electa Arenal undertook a complete edition with a long introductory study, *Literatura conventual femenina* (Female Conventual Literature, 1998), currently available in electronic format. Olivares and Boyce also discuss her work at some length in their introduction. Finally, Arenal and Sabat-Rivers each published an article on her poetry focused on the theme of solitude: Arenal's considers two of Sor Marcela's lesser-known poems, while Sabat-Rivers discusses two of her better-known poems to solitude ("Soledades").

María de San José

María Pilar Manero Sorolla and Mary Elizabeth Perry have written about the poetry of one of St. Teresa's most famous spiritual daughters, María de San José (Salazar). Manero's essay serves as an introduction to María de San José's poetry; she reviews the number, trajectory, forms, and themes, and then asserts the poet's importance in the genre, (mistakenly) characterizing the body of work as "ascético-místico" (196) (ascetic-mystical). She notes that Sor María wrote twenty-three poems, fourteen of them near the end of her life, in Lisbon (1585–1593). Perry, on the other hand, focuses on a single poem, "Ramillete de mirra" (Bouquet of Myrrh), comparing it with Gregoria de Santa Teresa's work.

Cancioneros

Collective compilations of poetry from (mostly Discalced Carmelite) convents have also attracted some scholarly interest, especially in the past twenty-five years. The best known, *Libro de romances y coplas del Carmelo de Valladolid (c. 1590–1609)* (Book of *coplas* and *romances* from the Discalced Carmelite Convent of Valladolid), which the Junta de Castilla y León published during the commemoration year of St. Teresa's death (1982) in a two-volume set that included a facsimile edition, was edited and contained a lengthy introduction by Víctor García de la Concha and Ana Álvarez Pellitero. The edition unites thorough scholarship with careful transcription, as well as a facsimile of the manuscript.[20] García de la Concha and Álvarez Pellitero assert that the *Libro* was compiled before 1614, when St. Teresa was beatified (xxi), but after María de San Alberto and Cecilia del Nacimiento professed in 1588. A description of the compilation reveals that it included about 132 poems, which they divide into several thematic categories: 1) Christmas; 2) Holy Sacrament; 3) Holy Trinity; 4) Virgin Mary; 5) saints; 6) habits and veils; 7) asceticism and religious life; and two other series. In spite of the title, there are only twelve *coplas* and *romances* included. Most critics agree that the *Libro* was possible largely due to the Sobrino sisters' contributions to convent creative production. As mentioned, the editors state that Cecilia del Nacimiento wrote much better poetry than María de San Alberto (xv). The pages about the two sisters are largely based on the first in-depth study of the two writers, Blanca Alonso Cortés's 1944 thesis, *Dos monjas vallisoletanas poetisas* (Two Nun-Poets of Valladolid).

A recent dissertation by Rubí Ugofsky-Méndez, "La voz femenina en libertad: El discurso masculino reconfigurado por mujeres en 'El libro de romances y coplas del Carmelo de Valladolid' (c. 1590–1609)," analyzes the *cancionero* from an implicitly Catholic perspective. Ugofsky-Méndez prefaces the study of the Valladolid *cancionero* with a review of earlier scholarship, especially about St. Teresa's poetry, asserting that both Emilio Orozco Díaz (*Estudios sobre San Juan de la Cruz* [Studies of St. John of the Cross]) and Noemí Uriarte Rebaudi ("Santa Teresa y la poesía" [St. Teresa and Poetry]) affirm that the purpose of Teresian poetry was to stimulate spirituality through verses written to be sung (Ugofsky-Méndez, "Voz": x, 51). Ugofsky-Méndez also notes that her work dovetails with another dissertation, by Matilde del Tránsito Chaves de Tobar, "La vida musical en los conventos femeninos de Alba de Tormes, Salamanca" (Musical Life in The Convents of Alba de Tormes, Salamanca), which studies *cancioneros* as a form of musical activity in convents of several religious orders in seventeenth-century Salamanca ("Voz": 69).[21]

One important trend in recent years, led by younger scholars, is the study of convent *cancioneros* inspired by St. Teresa in languages other than Spanish. To take two examples: Daniel Hanna's dissertation and subsequent articles analyze Discalced Carmelite poetry in French from convents in France, while Verónica Gómez Zaragoza has written extensively about convent *cancioneros* in Catalan, especially the compilation from the Discalced Carmelite convent de la Inmaculada Concepción in Barcelona (1586). Their work opens the way for a rich new vein of research, barely tapped thus far.

Another interesting, relatively untapped area of research on collective poetry writing is evident in Marina Romero Frías's discussion of the poetry in Spanish produced in the Capuchine convent in Sardinia. The four founders from Madrid all wrote poetry and fomented poetry writing among their charges as a fundraising activity, since it created the public perception that the convent gave the island cultural luster, which encouraged public and private donations, thus benefiting the nuns (408).

Future directions

Aside from the work being accomplished on compilations of poetry; studies of poetry in other languages, but related to the Spanish tradition especially through religious orders; and analyses of poets only recently brought into the canon, this field will undoubtedly continue to expand and to develop more in-depth literary and historical research. It is likely that more discoveries and analyses will emerge on the Iberian Peninsula during the coming years. Archives and libraries continue to yield new materials. More editions are needed, such as the one Molina Huete suggests of Gregoria Francisca de Santa Teresa, to pave the way for further critical analysis. More archival research should lead to publishing other early modern poets, even when the author remains anonymous, as is the case of the poems "de una monja concepcionista del siglo XVI" (of a sixteenth-century Conceptionist nun) that Jesús Domínguez Bordona published almost a century ago. More studies relating religious poetry to music of the period are needed. In addition, there is much work to be done extracting poetry from within prose works (*vidas* and other treatises). Expanding the study of themes and techniques used in convent poetry would enrich the field, as would comparisons of female religious poets with their male counterparts. Finally, as noted above, the study of *cancioneros* offers enormous possibilities for future scholarship.

Regarding specific poets, several possibilities seem likely. More, updated examinations of St. Teresa's poetry are needed. In addition, more work should be done on poets such as Beatriz de Aguilar, María de la Antigua, and Eularia Teixidor.[22] Manuela de la Santísima Trinidad's poetry has only recently begun to be acknowledged, as in the study of the Discalced Franciscan convent in Salamanca by María Fernanda Prada Carmín and Mercedes Marcos Santos. Six of her poems, published in an eighteenth-century Order chronicle by Juan Antonio Domínguez, are available on line through BIESES, so more research on this poet should be forthcoming.

Paradoxically, at the same time that electronic technology distances many scholars from on-site archival research, the internet facilitates the recovery and distribution of previously neglected works. Certainly, a great deal remains to be discovered in convent and other archives, and private libraries. Examination of religious poetry by women in particular requires determination, because so much was not formally published and because, until recently, the same few figures have been studied repeatedly. The field is opening up at a rapid rate: we can look forward to many new findings in the future.

Notes

1 "Las monjas participaron en todas las corrientes de poesía religiosa que se desarrollan a partir de la segunda mitad del XVI: versiones de los salmos, poesía petrarquista a lo divino, los cantos devotos, la estética del conceptismo sacro y el romancero espiritual." All translations are the author's.
2 Several critics have written about individual poems for profession. Nieves Baranda's overview, "Cantos al sacro epitalamio" (Songs for the Sacred Wedding), treats several poets' verses celebrating profession.
3 These writers' verses are available to some extent. For instance, poems by Manrique de Lara appear in Serrano y Sanz II, 29–37.
4 Although Palacios Fernández's bibliography of the eighteenth century orders and enriches our understanding of available primary and secondary sources, it includes some odd choices, such as the entry for the edition in English of the *Book of the Hour of Recreation* by the sixteenth-century Carmelite María de San José (Salazar) (1548–1603).
5 An example of increasing interest in another poet, Maria do Céu, is in Valerie Hegstrom's forthcoming edition and translation, "From a Convent in Lisbon: Plays, Poems, Biography, and Letters Selected from Her Spanish and Portuguese Works."
6 "[E]ra el de expresar su propia relación femenina con el objeto de su deseo, Dios, en un discurso poético ya feminizado."
7 "[D]estaca sobre la mediocridad global de su producción poética.
8 A revised second edition appeared in 2012.
9 This author is not to be confused with Gregoria Francisca de Santa Teresa (1653–1736), of the Discalced Carmelite Seville convent.
10 "la natural conviviencia entre espiritualidad y cotidianeidad, entre el sentimiento religioso llevado hasta sus últimas consecuencias y el costumbrismo de los avatares diarios de la vida común en el claustro." See also Alarcón Román, "La reescritura del discurso místico."
11 "positiva voluntad de degradación lingüística de clase." Menéndez Pidal wrote almost exclusively about the saint's prose, however.
12 "una auténtica voluntad literaria."
13 Peers also published the influential *Studies of the Spanish Mystics*.
14 "La ternura femenina y la delicadeza temperamental de su corazón la llevan siempre a posturas de amor netamente femeninas, de reverencia, de entrega, de caricia espiritual."
15 García de la Concha also emphasizes the pedagogical intent of all the saint's writings ("La lírica" 329).
16 Carvajal's poetry is available online through the Biblioteca Virtual Cervantes.
17 Cecilia del Nacimiento plays an ancillary, but important role in his narrative, since she was prioress when the younger woman professed. Sor Ana asked that all her poetry be burned after her death, but Cecilia del Nacimiento rescued some, having taken copies of nineteen sonnets when she returned to the Valladolid convent in 1610.
18 "[I]mpone la lira, los poemas de base endecasilábica, cuartetos y estrofas aliradas, etc."
19 Her *Parnaso Lusitano de Divinos e Humanos Versos*, also in both Portuguese and Spanish contained primarily religious verse; it was not published until 1733, posthumously.
20 Álvarez Pellitero has also written about the Medina del Campo Discalced Carmelite convent *cancionero*: "Cancionero del Carmelo de Medina del Campo (1604–1622)."
21 http://gredos.usal.es/jspui/bitstream/10366/76443/1/DDEMPC_TransitoChavesM_Conventos FemeninosAlbadeTormes.pdf
22 A collection of Aguilar's *romances* in praise of God's favors, published in Córdoba in 1610, is available online through the Biblioteca Virtual Cervantes. And Verónica Gómez Zaragoza has written about Teixidor.

Works cited

Editions and translations

Alarcón, Justo. www.los-poetas.com/h/luisa.htm
Carvajal y Mendoza, Luisa de. bib.cervantesvirtual.com/servlet/SirveObras/01372742000248729755024/index.htm.
Cruz, Anne J., ed. and trans. *The Life and Writings of Luisa de Carvajal y Mendoza: Autobiography, Poetry, Correspondence*. Toronto: Centre for Reformation and Renaissance Studies, 2014.
Díaz Cerón, José M., ed. *Obras completes de Cecilia del Nacimiento*. Intro. J. M. Díaz Cerón. Madrid: Editorial de la Espiritualidad, 1971.
Domínguez Bordona, Jesús. "Poesías de una monja concepcionista del siglo XVI." Separata, *Revista de la Biblioteca, Archivo y Museo del Ayuntamiento de Madrid*. Madrid: Imprenta Municipal, 1927. www.bieses.net
Donnelly, Kevin and Sandra Sider, ed. and trans. *Journeys of a Mystic Soul in Poetry and Prose*. Intro. Kevin Donnelly; prose trans. Kevin Donnelly, poetry trans. Sandra Sider. Toronto: Centre for Reformation and Renaissance Studies, 2012.
García de la Concha and Ana Álvarez Pellitero, ed. and intro. *Libro de romances y coplas del Carmelo de Valladolid (c. 1590–1609)*. 2 Vols. Salamanca: Consejo General de Castilla y León, 1982.
González Marañén, Jesús and Camilo María Abad, ed. *Epistolario y poesías*. Biblioteca de Autores Españoles. Vol. 179. Madrid: Ediciones Atlas, 1965.
Hegstrom Valerie, ed. and trans. "From a Convent in Lisbon: Plays, Poems, Biography, and Letters Selected from Her Spanish and Portuguese Works." Toronto: Centre for Reformation and Renaissance Studies [forthcoming].
Muñoz, Luis. *Vida y virtudes de la venerable virgen Doña Luisa de Carvajal y Mendoca: Su jornada a Inglaterra, y sucesos en aquel Reyno. Van al fin algunas poesías espirituales suyas, parto de su devoción, y ingenio. Al Rey Nuestro Señor*. Madrid: Imprenta Real, 1632.
Sabat-Rivers, Georgina and Electa Arenal, ed. and intro. *Literatura conventual femenina. Sor Marcela de san Felix, hija de Lope de Vega. Obra completa. Coloquios espirituales, loas y otros poemas*. Prologue José María Díez Borque. Barcelona: PPU, 1998. www.intratext.com/IXT/ESL0014/
Schlau, Stacey. *Viva al siglo, muerta al mundo. Obras escogidas de María de san Alberto (1568–1640)*. New Orleans: UP of the South, 1998.
Serrano y Sanz, Manuel. *Apuntes para una biblioteca de escritoras españolas desde el año 1401 al 1833*. 2 Vols. Madrid: Sucesores de Rivadeneyra, 1903–1905. www.bieses.net; http://scans.library.utoronto.ca/pdf/4/2/apuntesparaunabi01serruoft/apuntesparaunabi01serruoft.pdf

Critical studies

Alarcón Román, María del Carmen. "La producción poética de sor Francisca de Santa Teresa (1654–1709): Entre la cotidianeidad y la espiritualidad." Baranda Leturio and Marín Piña: 345–361.
——. "La reescritura del discurso místico y visionario en la obra de sor Francisca de Santa Teresa (1644–1709)," *Revista de Escritoras Ibéricas* 2 (2014): 43–65.
Albin, María C. "El erotismo sagrado en la poesía de Teresa de Ávila." *Crítica Hispánica* 29.1–2 (2007): 31–45.
Alonso Cortés, Blanca. *Dos monjas vallisoletanas poetisas*. Madrid: n. p., 1944.
Álvarez Pellitero, Ana. "Cancionero del Carmelo de Medina del Campo (1604–1622)." *Actas del Congreso Internacional Teresiano, 4–7 octubre 1982*. El Congreso: Salamanca, 1983: 525–543.
Arenal, Electa. "Sex and Class in the Seventeenth-Century Cloister: Sor Marcela de San Félix's Love Poems to God." Olivares, *Studies* 233–254.
Arenal, Electa, and Stacey Schlau. *Untold Sisters: Hispanic Nuns in Their Own Works*. Trans. Amanda Powell, Electa Arenal, and Stacey Schlau. Rev. 2 ed. Albuquerque: U New Mexico P, 2012.
Asensi Pérez, Manuel. "Teresa de Ahumada: Vivo sin vivir en mí." Romero López et al.: 63–73.
Baranda, Nieves. "Producción y consumo poéticos en los conventos femeninos." *Bulletin Hispanique* 115.1 (2013): 165–184.
Baranda Leturio, Nieves, and María Carmen Marín Piña, ed. *Letras en la celda: Cultura escrita de los conventos femeninos en la España moderna*. Madrid and Frankfurt: Iberoamericana Vervuert, 2014.

Barbeito Carneiro, Isabel. *Escritoras madrileñas del siglo XVII: Estudio bibliográfico-crítico*. Madrid: Universidad Complutense, 1986. www.bieses.net

Barnard, Mary E. "Aristocrat and Mystic: Writing the Material in Luisa de Carvajal y Mendoza." *Perspectives on Early Modern Women in Iberia and the Americas*. Ed. Adrienne Martín and María Cristina Quintero. New York: Escribana, 2015: 455–475.

Carrera, Elena. "Lovesickness and the Therapy of Desire: Aquinas, *cancionero* Poetry, and Teresa of Avila's 'Muero porque no muero'." *Bulletin of Hispanic Studies* 86.6 (2009): 729–742.

Cáseda Teresa, Jesús Fernando. "La poesía mística de Sor Ana de la Trinidad." *Kalakorikos* 1 (1996): 85–93. Dialnet.unirioja.es/.../192109

Charnon-Deutsch, Lou, ed. *Studies on Hispanic Women Writers in Honor of Georgina Sabat-Rivers*. Madrid: Castalia, 1992.

Chaves de Tobar, Matilde del Tránsito. "La vida musical en los conventos femeninos de Alba de Tormes, Salamanca." http://gredos.usal.es/jspui/bitstream/10366/76443/1/DDEMPC_TransitoChavesM_ConventosFemeninosAlbadeTormes.pdf

Cruz, Anne J. "'Chains of Desire': Luisa de Carvajal y Mendoza's Poetics of Penance." Charnon-Deutsch: 97–112.

——. "Luisa Carvajal y Mendoza: Soneto espiritual de Silva." Romero López et al.: 115–121.

——. "Luisa de Carvajal y Mendoza y su conexión jesuita." *AIH Actas XI, 2012*. cvc.cervantes.es/.../aih_11_2_012.pdf

——. "Words Made Flesh: Luisa de Carvajal's Eucaristic Poetry." Olivares, *Studies* 255–269.

Domínguez Bordona, Jesús. "Poesías de una monja concepcionista del siglo XVI." Separata, *Revista de la Biblioteca, Archivo y Museo del Ayuntamiento de Madrid*. Madrid: Imprenta Municipal, 1927. www.bieses.net

DuPont, Denise. *Writing Teresa: The Saint from Ávila at the fin-de-siglo*. Lewisburg, PA: Bucknell UP, 2012.

Fox, Gwyn. *Subtle Subversions: Reading Golden Age Sonnets by Iberian Women*. Washington, DC: Catholic U America P, 2008.

García de la Concha, Víctor. *Al aire de su vuelo*. Barcelona: Galaxia Gutenberg/Círculo de Lectores, 2004.

——. "La lírica de Santa Teresa en la poesía carmelitana." *El arte literario de Santa Teresa*. Víctor García de la Concha. Barcelona: Ariel, 1978: 317–376.

González-Cruz, Luis F. "Conciliación de opuestos: La cruz en la poesía de Santa Teresa." *Revista de Estudios Hispánicos* 18.2 (1984): 183–193.

Hanna, Daniel J. "Carmelite Poetry in France and the Low Countries: The Tradition of Teresa of Avila." Unpublished Ph.D. dissertation, Princeton University, 2012.

——. "Translating Teresa: *Muero porque no muero* in 17th-century France." *1611: Revista de la Historia de la Traducción* 8.8 (2014): n.p.

——. "*Un trait théreséien*: French Carmelite Poetry in the Tradition of Teresa of Ávila." *Bulletin of Spanish Studies* [forthcoming].

Hatzfeld, Helmut. *Estudios literarios sobre mística española*. Madrid: Gredos, 1955.

——. *Santa Teresa de Avila*. New York: Twayne, 1969.

Howe, Elizabeth Teresa. *Mystical Imagery: Santa Teresa de Jesús and San Juan de la Cruz*. New York: Peter Lang, 1988.

Manero Sorolla, María Pilar. "La poesía de María de san José (Salazar)." Charnon-Deutsch: 187–222.

Molina Huete, Belén. "Preneoclasicismo y mística: La poesía de Sor Gregoria Francisca de Santa Teresa." http://riuma.uma.es/xmlui/bitstream/handle/10630/6330/Nueva_versi%C3%B3n-Molina_Huete_Gregoria.pdf?sequence=6

Morris, C. Brian. "The Poetry of Santa Teresa." *Hispania* 69.2 (1986): 244–250.

Morujão, Isabel. *Por Trás da Grade. Poesia Conventual Feminina em Portugal (Séculos XVI–XVIII)*. Lisbon: Imprensa Nacional-Casa da Moeda, 2013.

Mujica, Barbara. *Sister Teresa*. New York: Overlook, 2007.

Mújica, Barbara, ed. *Women Writers of Early Modern Spain: Sophia's Daughters*. New Haven and London: Yale UP, 2004.

Navarro, Ana, ed. *Antología poética de escritoras de los siglos XVI y XVII*. Madrid: Editorial Castalia, Instituto de la Mujer, 1989.

Olivares, Julián. "Género sexuado, género literario y ansiedad autorial en la poesía sacra de sor Violante del Cielo." *Eros divino: Estudios sobre la poesía religiosa iberoamericana del siglo XVII*. Ed. Julián Olivares. Zaragoza: Prensas Universitarias de Zaragoza, 2011: 307–344.

———. "In Her Image: Christ and the Female Body in Women's Religious Poetry of the Golden Age." *Calíope* 1.1–2 (1995): 111–133.
———. "Sor María de la Antigua's *Coloquios* with Examiners, Editors, Saints, and Gods." Olivares: 270–280.
Olivares, Julián, ed. *Studies on Women's Poetry of the Golden Age: Tras el espejo la musa escribe*. Woodbridge: Tamesis, 2009.
Olivares, Julián, and Elizabeth Boyce, ed. *Tras el espejo la musa escribe (segunda edición revisada). Lírica femenina en los siglos de oro*. Madrid: Siglo XXI, 2012.
Osuna Rodríguez, Inmaculada. "Poesía intramuros: Creación y recepción poética en el convento de Santa María de las Dueñas (Sevilla) a principio del siglo XVII." Baranda Leturio and Marín Pina: 115–131.
Peers, E. Allison. *Studies of the Spanish Mystics*. 3 Vols. London and New York: Sheldon P. MacMillan, 1927–1930.
Peers, E. Allison, ed. and trans. *The Complete Works of Saint Teresa of Jesus*. 3 Vols. From the critical ed. of Silverio de Santa Teresa. New York: Sheed and Ward, 1946.
Perry, Mary Elizabeth. "María de San José, Ana de Jesús and Gregoria Francisca de Santa Teresa: Subversion and Seduction: Perception of the Body in Writings of Religious Women in Counter Reformational Spain." *Religion, Body and Gender in Early Modern Spain*. ed. Alain Saint-Saens. San Francisco: Mellen Research UP, 1991: 68–78.
Polo, José, ed. *Estudios sobre Santa Teresa*. Málaga: U Málaga P, 1998.
Rebollo Prieto, Jesús. "Las escritoras de Castilla y León (1400–1800). Ensayo bibliográfico." Diss. UNED, 2006. www.bieses.net
Rees, Margaret Ann. "Luisa de Carvajal y Mendoza's Paradisal Garden, lectio divina, and Ignatian Spiritual Exercises." *Bulletin of Hispanic Studies* 86.6 (2009): 763–773.
Rhodes, Elizabeth. "Gender in the Night: Juan de la Cruz and Cecilia del Nacimiento." Olivares, *Studies* 202–217.
———. "Gender in the Night: Juan de la Cruz and Cecilia del Nacimiento." *Calíope* 13.2 (2007): 39–61.
Romero Frías, Marina. "Poesía y clausura en la isla de Cerdeña: Las capuchinas del Convento de san José de Sássari." Baranda Leturio and Marín Pina: 405–421.
Romero López, Dolores, Itzíar López Guil, Rita Catrina Imboden, and Cristina Albizu Yeregui, ed. *Seis siglos de poesía española escrita por mujeres: Pautas poéticas y revisiones críticas*. Bern: Peter Lang, 2007.
Ruiz Pérez, Pedro. "Santa Teresa de Jesús: Pragmática y poética." La espiritualidad [española] del siglo XVI: aspectos literarios y lingüísticos. Ed. *María Jesús Mancho Duque*. Salamanca: Ediciones U de Salamanca, 1997: 185–191.
Sabat-Rivers, Georgina. "Soledades de sor Marcela." *La Torre (NE)* 7.25 (1993): 17–35.
Sánchez, Manuel Diego. *Bibliografía sistemática de santa Teresa de Jesús*. Madrid: Editorial de Espiritualidad, 2008. www.bieses.net
Schlau, Stacey. "María de San Alberto: Bridging Popular and 'High' Spanish Poetic Traditions Through the Sacred." Olivares, *Studies*: 218–232.
———. "'Tornome morena': African Voices, Dark Skin, and Gypsy Rhythms in María de san Alberto's Plays and Poetry." *Cervantes y la cuestión racial*. Ed. Baltasar Fra-Molinero. Spec. issue of *Annals of Scholarship* 19.3 (2010): 33–58.
Serrano, Juan and Susan Serrano. "Of Spiritual Love and the Sublime: Translating Spanish Mystical Poetry." *Translation Review* 56 (1998): 36–43.
Sherman, Jr., Alvin F. "The Lover and the Captive: Sor Gregoria Francisca de Santa Teresa's Mystical Search for the Feminine Self in 'El pajarillo'." *Dieciocho: Hispanic Enlightenment* 19.2 (1996): 191–201.
Toft, Evelyn. "Cecilia del Nacimiento: Mystic in the Tradition of John of the Cross." *The Mystical Gesture: Essays on Medieval and Early Modern Spiritual Culture in Honor of Mary E. Giles*. Ed. Robert Boenig. Aldershot: Ashgate, 2000: 169–184.
———. "Cecilia del Nacimiento: Second-Generation Mystic of the Carmelite Reform." *A New Companion to Hispanic Mysticism*. Ed. Hilaire Kallendorf. Leiden: Brill, 2010: 231–252.
———. "Joy in the Presence of the Bridegroom: The Contemplative Poetry of Cecilia del Nacimiento." *Studia Mystica* 22 (2001): 83–96.
Ugofsky-Méndez, Rubí. "La voz femenina en libertad: El discurso masculino reconfigurado por mujeres en 'El libro de romances y coplas del Carmelo de Valladolid' (c. 1590–1609)." Unpublished Ph.D. dissertation, University of Nebraska-Lincoln, 2011.
———. *Voces femeninas españolas desde dentro: El discurso masculino reconfigurado por mujeres en El libro de romances y coplas del Carmelo de Valladolid, (c. 1590–1609)*. New York: Peter Lang, 2014.

Uriarte Rebaudi, Lía Noemí. "Santa Teresa y la poesía." *Santa Teresa y la literatura mística hispánica: Actas del I Congreso internacional sobre Santa Teresa y la mística hispánica*. Ed. Manuel Criado de Val. Madrid: EDI-6, 1984: 405–411.

Vega, Ángel Custodio. *La poesía de Santa Teresa*. Madrid: Biblioteca de Autores Cristianos, Editorial Católica, 1972.

Vieira Mendes, Margarida. "Apresentação." *Rimas varias*. By Violante do Céu. 7–38. Lisbon: Presença, 1993.

Weber, Alison. "Could Women Write Mystical Poetry?: The Literary Daughters of Juan de la Cruz." Olivares, *Studies* 185–201.

Zaragoza, Verònica. http://castellinterior.wordpress.com/2014/08/25/dos-cents-anys-i-mes-de-poesies-i-cancons-al-convent-de-la-immaculada-concepcio-de-barcelona-1588/

———. "'Pues que tiene libertad por decir alguna cosa.' Noticia del cuaderno poético de Sor Eularia Teixidor (siglo XVIII)." *Ausencias: Escritoras en los márgenes de la cultura*. Ed. Mercedes Arriaga Flórez et al. Seville: ArCiBel Editores, 2013: 1351–1372.

SECTION III
Secular literature

9
THE POETIC VOICE

María Dolores Martos Pérez

In early modern Spain, the writing of poetry was conceived and regulated from the male perspective; literary tradition, therefore, offered very few models that served to encourage female agency. When women assumed the process of literary creation to express their female subjectivity, they challenged male literary and social structures as well as a traditionally masculine language. The female voice thus modified previous modes of poetic communication by necessarily decentering codified literary conventions. Each model of enunciation, from its emission to its reception, entailed a communicative intent that served to articulate the author's subjectivity from a female perspective (Olivares and Boyce: 17).

In addition to the problematized lyrical subject, early modern women writers faced other issues derived from their undefined authorial status that resisted the conventional interpretation of poetic authorship: the poet's initial identity as one who creates discourse is merely formal, and is determined and specified in the enunciating roles acquired throughout this discourse (Luján: 56). However, the search for a "poetic or lyrical" identity that operates within the poem itself, and the authorial impulse that operates in the social sphere, suggest a trajectory that allows us to go from the text to the position that women began to occupy in the literary field during the early modern period (Bourdieu: 64). According to Karlheinz Stierle (56), poets elaborate a discourse to inquire into their own identity, and it is the poem's architecture that shapes this search. For female poets, this identity is inherently related to the literary tradition, which generally excludes them, and to the location of their voice in a literary field ruled by the notion of *imitatio*. In this sense, the different modes of Petrarchist imitation studied by Ignacio Navarrete (218) should also be applied to the female lyric to stress the way in which the transformation of Petrarchan codes (Cruz: 9, 122) often subsumes, both implicitly and explicitly, the author's own poetics. For this purpose, a systematic analysis of self-reflexive or metapoetic texts by women authors would be useful as direct testimony of women's understanding of the creative process and of their own space in literary history.

Women's "anxiety of authorship," in contrast to Harold Bloom's "anxiety of influence," results from their difficulty in forming part of the literary tradition, a tradition created by male authors and based on the dynamics of masculine rivalry (Gilbert and Gubar: 48–49). Women's poetic voice, therefore, must equal or exceed male authority in order to legitimize their writing, since women are left outside the competition that is based on literary history as a male event, and on the poet's affirmation against his precursors (Oedipal rivalry in inter-poetic relations)

(Gilbert and Gubar: 46–53). The male subject is not only culture's sole subject, culture itself has been constructed from the male voice. Thus, female poets go to great lengths in the search for an expression of their subjectivity in order to reverse the dominant masculine voice/female subject binomial... Women's writing not only gives meaning to female experiences, it naturalizes them through cultural practices, a situation that occurred when their poems began to be published at the start of the seventeenth century,[1] at a time when women authors could count with feminine models to undertake their poetic activity.

Therefore, many poetic issues are involved in the female subject's transformation into an agent of articulation, of amorous behavior, and other thematics that activate literary discourse. In order to study the poetic voice in the early modern period, and the manner in which the creative female subject locates herself therein, it is necessary to analyze the intertextual communication within the poem, between the "fictitious self" and her equally fictitious addressee (Smith: 39), along with the information derived from this communication about the implicit author and her communicative intent as substitute for the real female author (Levin). From there, one can establish the base for predominant trends in the feminine poetic discourse of the sixteenth and seventeenth centuries, exemplified in female authors such as Isabel de Vega, María de Santa Isabel, Cristobalina Fernández de Alarcón, Leonor de la Cueva, Bernarda Ferreira de Lacerda, Hipólita de Narváez, Catalina Clara Ramírez de Guzmán, Marcia Belisarda, and Violante do Céu.

Voice and gender: the communicative labyrinth

In order to become part of a literary field that only accepts the masculine, an initial strategy would be to assume the male voice or to disguise one's gender through appearance. Yet, in attempting to insert their voice, Renaissance and Baroque female poets have been relentless in exploring the discursive strategies available to them, following a trajectory that plumbs the many ways to express their feminine subjectivity and distance themselves from the masculinization of poetic discourse. This entails alternating between a gendered and a non-gendered poetics.[2] Degendering the grammatical gender results in the deletion of gender markers in both the poetic subject and object; in contrast, when gender is marked, poetic discourse becomes feminized and the poetic voice asserts both her gender and authorial identity. In any case, what is most important is that in each poem, female authors problematize the poetic voice while at the same time they convert it into an unquestionable reality through the text itself. The text thus becomes the mediating mechanism between the representation of intimate subjectivity and fiction, as well as the mirror of the female poet's self-awareness and image.

As other studies have averred (in particular, Olivares and Boyce), research tends to move in two directions. First, whether female poets write from a conscious, gendered perspective; that is, whether they show self-awareness about themselves as a means to defend the feminine perspective in literature. Second, to what extent and with what communicative intent are conventional premises broken. The texts in which the lyric subject is neutral, with undefined gender, correspond to the first category; at the opposite extreme, there is a direct expression of a female voice and the subversion of regular enunciation schemes. In between the two extremes is a large corpus of poems with intermediate strategies for the code's acceptance or transgression, representing the female voice's different degrees of authorization. Because textual strategies are subject to the particularities of different poetic genres, it is essential to study the enunciating schemes from this gender variability, as Olivares has done with Violante do Céu's poetry ("Género sexuado": 317–324). These general trends are evinced in the following examples that link the enunciating voice and gender awareness from the three aspects of 1) male voice; 2) neutral voice or no gender determination; and 3) female voice.

The male poetic voice

The most important lyrical tradition, love poetry, does not, by itself, reject poems written by women. In the sixteenth and, to a lesser extent, in the seventeenth centuries, the poem is understood as a verbal artifice built on the simultaneous reiteration and variation of an inherited model. Consequently, female authors compose within this code to become part of a previous tradition, demonstrating that they are able to appropriate poetic discourse by accepting the conventions of the medieval courtly love tradition, opting for a male poetic subject, or by neutralizing the gender of both the enunciator and the addressee. These strategies doubly validated the passive role assigned women by accepting the existence of a strongly gendered amatory poetic code that contemplated a male speaker only as agent of desire; and by subjecting the authors to the law of decorum that prevented women from expressing their desire for men.[3]

Almost all female poets followed these tendencies; Nieves Baranda, for example, states that "The most remarkable aspect of Isabel de Vega's love poetry is the lack of a female poetic voice, which would have corresponded to the author."[4] The poet manages two poetic models: on the one hand, she imitates Petrarch by having a male as the speaking subject, consistent with a female "you;" on the other, she utilizes a neutral discourse with no gender marker for the subject. This can be seen in Isabel de Vega's sonnet "Si muero por servirte estando ausente" (If I die from serving you by being absent):

> After I have died and you have repented,
> if you keep wanting to be rational,
> you will suffer for remaining unknown.
> But I, who will live always by loving you,
> when you are saddened by regret and pain,
> will wish to flee from you to comfort you.
>
> *ll:8–14*[5]

And in the following sonnet's quartet:

> My emotion is so engaged
> in contemplating the good dwelling in my soul
> that it does not listen or understand, my lady,
> the transfer of others' torments.
>
> *ll. 1–4*[6]

Additionally, in Isabel de Vega's *Glosa*[7] to the villancico "Nunca más verán mis ojos / cosas que les den placer / hasta tornaros a ver. Glosa" (My eyes will never see / what gives them pleasure / until I see you again. Gloss):

> What now can I see, my lady,
> after having seen you in me?
> For he who has seen and adores you
> cannot live one hour
> longer than the time he lives in you.[8]

In Leonor de la Cueva's "Soneto a Floris" (Sonnet to Floris), the female lover's absence is also mourned by a male lyrical subject:

> I am absent from your delightful eyes;
> in brief, absent and full of concerns;
> if this cruel absence is followed by jealousy,
> I confess, Floris, that it will fill me with anger.
>
> *ll: 1–4*[9]

And yet another poem begins by the male lover pleading with his cruel beloved: "Enough of disdain and enough of harshness, / Clori, no more cruelty, no more anger."[10]

The neutral voice, or without gender markers: a space for negotiation

From the standpoint of poetic enunciation, women's poetry often presents a poetic subject with a suggestive gender ambiguity (Montes: 137). Given that it is very difficult in a Romance language for a speaker or interlocutor to conceal his or her gender, the avoidance of gender markers denotes the female poet's fully conscious intent to insist on gender indetermination, both for the enunciating agent and the interlocutor (Perelmuter: 71–83). The more depersonalized the poem, with no trace of the female self—and the more ungendered the emitter or the receptor—the more neutral the discourse and the less it vindicates the female condition. One among many examples is Cristobalina Fernández de Alarcón's *canción*, "Cansados ojos míos" (My Tired Eyes) (Espinosa, *Flores de poetas ilustres*: 1605), a song to the emotions of amorous suffering, so skillfully managed throughout the text for the purpose of avoiding the lyric subject's determination by gender.

Several poems by María de Santa Isabel also rewrite the Petrarchan love lyric through an undifferentiated voice, for example, as in the "Romance melancólico" (Melancholy Ballad) and "Procurad, memorias tristes" (Try, Sad Memories), in which she addresses inanimate interlocutors, such as thought and memories, to reinforce the discourse's gender neutrality. Similarly, the following sonnet on the absence and disdain of the lover dispenses with the interlocutor and speaks with an undifferentiated poetic voice:

> When dawn embroiders with pearls
> tapestries strewn with beautiful flowers,
> favors are returned as flatteries
> to the flowers she then enriches and endows [. . .].
> Thus, I did likewise when I saw the sun's beautiful dawn
> that banished the dark fog
> of an absence, if no longer the sun nor
> a rational bird, this miraculous beauty I venerate
> with simple and pure truth,
> yet the reward was stern and unyielding disdain.
>
> *ll: 1–11*[11]

Female poets deploy a series of strategies in order to distance or eliminate gender marking. There are many possibilities, ranging from the dissolution of the poetic voice to more nuanced mechanisms, such as a fictive mask projected, for example, in the doubling of the soul or heart.

In Luisa Sigea's octaves, "Un fin, una esperanza, un cómo o cuándo" (An End, a Hope, A How or When), the lyric subject remains undetermined until the poem's ending, in the middle of the last octave, where she employs *praeteritio*, revealing the poetic voice's female identity only at the end:

> I remain behind on this occasion only,
> and the discontent being so near,
> I recount sad nights, and I can never
> count the end of the evil I recount;
> I am *myself* afraid of my own self;
> For what my thought threatens me;
> but let life go by and let it go fast,
> as my account will have no end.
>
> *ll: 25–32*[12]

The same technique is deployed Violante do Céu in her *romance* "¡Oh!, cesen ya los remedios" (Oh! May Remedies Cease!) in her *Rimas varias* (Varied Poetry), in which the female poetic voice appears only in the third line from the end:

> Death to who, while being constant,
> was so wrongly *corresponded*,
> who repaying truths
> received lies only.
>
> *ll: 29–32*[13]

The female voice: from adaptation to subtle subversion

In contrast to the code of medieval courtly lyrics, the spiritual tradition provides a more flexible framework in which to express female subjectivity, since it allows women to assume voice through ungendered discourse. Christ is often the addressee of religious poetry, locating the enunciation of the female subject to the extreme end of the spectrum by following mystical tradition, in which the Bride (the Soul) addresses Christ, the Spouse, as in the model followed by San Juan de la Cruz in his *Noche oscura del alma* (*Dark Night of the Soul*). This is the case, for example, of Luisa de Carvajal's sonnet (1566–1614): "Ay, soledad amarga y enojosa" (Oh, Bitter and Maddening Solitude). Similarly, Jerónima de la Asunción's "Soliloquio" (Soliloquy) begins and ends with an explicit female lyric subject, whereas the poetic voice's gender is undifferentiated in the poem's text: "I am yours, I was born for you: / what do you order me to do?" (ll: 1–2 and 73–74).[14] Luisa de la Ascensión, in turn, creates a mystical poetry nourished by a female poetic voice that speaks in solitude with the "other," as in the *romance* "A la soledad interior con mi dulcísimo Jesús y divino Esposo" (To the inner solitude with my sweet Jesus and divine Spouse):

> Illuminated by this sun,
> I ask for solitude and alone
> I ask for it so I will not be alone,
> but in good company.
>
> *ll: 3–16*[15]

Marcela de San Félix's (1605–1687) poems are equally evocative and include delicately suggestive expressions of love to the Spouse or Beloved.

Another significant reference is the lyric tradition of the *Cantar de los cantares* (*Song of Songs*), in which the poetic and erotic codes of both the courtly and pastoral conventions are incorporated, as the female poetic voice expresses her passionate love for the Beloved. Marcela de San Félix's delicately beautiful "Romance de un alma que temía distraerse al salir de un retiro" (Ballad of a Soul Fearing Distraction Upon Leaving a Retreat) where the female "self" who is "in love" (line 4)[16] appeals to the loving fire to which a male "you" is added who answers to the name of "my sweet beloved":

> If with sweet violence
> your love binds me,
> your caresses oblige me,
> your beauty kills me;
> if you know that you keep me
> captive and bewitched,
> and for the love for your eyes
> burning in glowing flames.
>
> *ll: 53–60*[17]

Despite this naturalized feminine enunciation, the religious poetic discourse is not exempt from problems and contrary to the love poetry (Olivares and Boyce: 24), as they warn, because, far from the rhetorical codification of feminine amorous discourse, sacred poetry implied a new definition of the beloved and of the relationship with the female subject.

In this kind of amatory discourse, the female voice allowed female poets to further approach their subject, although there are significant exceptions, such as that of Luisa de Carvajal, who opts for an opposite dynamics of enunciation: the use of the male voice in this sonnet, in which Silva receives the body of Christ through the Blessed Sacrament (Cruz, *Life and Writings*):

> Receive, Silva, from your sweet Beloved
> this close embrace, with immense love brimming,
> and through my right side's opening
> enter, little dove, within my breast.
> Repose on the sacred flowering bed,
> and inflame yourself with love so passionate,
> that not until the strong knot has fully tied
> will it ever be wholly satisfied.
> See how I relinquish to you, my love,
> all my being and eminence sublime,
> cherish this gift by my love proffered,
> you will find in me such glorious company,
> and in my very own arms held tenderly
> you will enjoy what no one has deserved.[18]

Poems are a space of encounter between the expression of subjectivity and the rewriting of a literary code, locating the writer on their time and inserting them in the cultural tradition. And women are not different: they do not write to express a feeling, but to raise their voice from the margin and to question the reasons that held them on their marginalized situation with regards to an artistic discourse dominated by men. Female poets therefore deploy a series of discursive strategies, creating a space for negotiation, where the code's rules are respected, while they insert their own voice, introducing ornaments, with a different degree, in the conventionality of the discourse.

The poetic voice

All poems represent a space wherein the expression of one kind of subjectivity and the rewriting of a literary code come together, situating the author in his time and inscribing him in the culture of the period. Women poets are no different: they write not to express an emotion but to raise their voice from the margins and question the reasons why there were kept marginalized from a poetic discourse ruled by men (Olivares and Boyce: 25). They therefore exercise a series of discursive strategies in order to create a space for negotiation where the rules of the poetic code are respected, yet where their voices continuously cause large and small fissures in the conventional discourse (Baranda, *Cortejo*: 127; Jones: 4; Olivares and Boyce: 30). For example, in the following sonnet on the vagaries of love, Leonor de la Cueva y Silva leaves to the adjectival rhyme the space where she inserts the female voice:

> I know not whether I die or I have life,
> I am not within myself nor cannot find me outside,
> Nor do I care to look for me among so much forgetfulness,
> in such sorrow and pain am I *dressed*.
> I regret seeing me *abhorred* [. . .]
> everything upsets and leaves me *unbearable*.
>
> *ll: 1–5, 8*[19]

For intimate or familiar themes (Fox: 71), female poets construct their discourse in the female poetic voice, such as for example the sorrowful stanzas with which Leonor de la Cueva mourns her father's death in her poem "Liras en la muerte de mi querido padre y señor" (Stanzas for the Death of my Dear Father and Lord):

> In such terrible sorrow,
> I find no rest, pleasure or joy;
> I am estranged from everything,
> and my sole relief and comfort
> is this misfortune of mine,
> as heaven deprives me from all others.
>
> *ll: 6–12*[20]

Courtly love poetry projected a female image devised by the male imaginary. Women poets either adapted to its formulas or sought other ways in which to represent the female subject (Ibeas). Olivares and Boyce identify two subversive strategies in women's love lyrics: "the de-sublimation or de-idealization of the courtly model," and the "regeneration" of amatory discourse, both defined by the active role given the female poetic subject (38). This subversion resulted from the change in traditional enunciation, which required redefining poetic discourse according to the enunciating female and the addressed subject. Based on this new conceptualization of male discourse, different modes of enunciation were formed responding to different strategies. The first mode corresponds to a female speaker and male addressee, adapting the traditional Petrarchist mode by reversing the enunciative order. However, few poems in the period assumed a female voice addressing their desire to a male lover. One sonnet, in María de Zayas's play, *La traición en la amistad* (*Friendship Betrayed*), has a female speaker who addresses the male interlocutor, Liseo, confessing her loving surrender to (and before) his eyes:

> Let me die, Liseo, for your eyes,
> and let your eyes enjoy killing me;

that I may wish your eyes to cheer me,
and anger me a hundred thousand times. [. . .]
Oh, sweet ungrateful lover! You, whose eyes contain
as much treachery as beauty,
for my eyes, that are wounded by yours.[21]

The second kind of enunciating strategies corresponds to a female speaker who addresses another female, fully redefining the enunciating roles of the Petrarchan love lyric by eliminating all traces of male enunciation. Here, several modes of enunciation overlap, not necessarily mutually exclusive, as all deal with conventional female affective expression—from Sappho to the troubadour lyric tradition—whose purpose is solely to create a feminine discursive universe. The strategy, which grants autonomy to female expression, may well also be interpreted as a lesbian expression of desire; in all cases, it achieves a complete feminization of poetic discourse (Powell: 55–56).

Violante do Céu's *romance*, "Amada prenda del alma" (My Soul's Beloved Token), therefore, applies conventionalized formulas from Petrarchist love poetry to a communicative strategy that includes only women:

Oh, how different we are,
sweet token, you and I!
You are unhappy with me
and I am so happy with you.[22]

This is also the case of *romance* 77, which follows the same communicative activity: here, the female poetic subject addresses Menandra, who is characterized with all the attributes of a homicide lover:

That I live in you transformed,
Menandra, you have well found out.
Since when shooting arrows at me,
you find yourself wounded.
Oh you, my idolized homicide
of my thoughts [. . .][23]

There are numerous examples in which female authors find diverse formulas to subvert poetic discourse, creating an autonomous space for their expression (Fox: 198–245; Olivares and Boyce). For instance, the tradition of satirical-burlesque poetry allows male social roles to be criticized, converting men into risible objects, as in the case of Catalina Clara Ramírez de Guzmán's sonnet, "Respondiendo a un soneto de un hombre ridículo cuyo apellido era Castaño" (In Response to a Sonnet by a Ridiculous Man Named Castaño):

You are the instrument of my joy
and my song throughout the year.
Seeing you, Castaño, clearly, is what I lament;
only your chestnut color [falseness] would be more damaging,
but if you proceed so heedlessly,
you will be more presumptuous than treacherous.[24]

In the same way, in her "Soneto a un hombre pequeño, D. Francisco de Arévalo" (Sonnet to a Short Man, Don Francisco de Arévalo), Ramírez "chooses to ridicule in men that on which they most pride themselves: their assumed natural superiority in intelligence and in action, their attractiveness to women, and their stature and figure" (Fox: 155; Olivares and Boyce: 155–156). Nevertheless, we should note that female self, in both poems, is not made explicit, perhaps to attenuate the ridicule.

Another group of "subtly subversive" poems, as Gwyn Fox calls them, are those that invert the male rhetorical canon when describing women, for example, by humanizing the woman against the idealization of the courtly love tradition. Marcia Belisarda deconstructs Petrarchan aesthetics in her "Romance burlesco para un billete" (Burlesque Ballad for a Love Letter), creating a self-portrayal in un-idealized terms. The different parts of the female body, emblems of ideal beauty, are presented instead as those belonging to real women: the face "is neither wide, nor narrow, / nor frighteningly ugly, / nor murderously beautiful."[25] Similarly, the eyes are embrasures,[26] the nose is snub, the mouth emits noble breath; and her "hands, in winter, / resemble purple carrots / for and when / they are very loving."[27] She ends by stating that,

> In short, I am a perfect woman
> and this truth is quite evident,
> as I neither lack nor have too many
> arms, legs, molars, or other teeth.[28]

The above forms part of the "desublimation" or "de-idealization" of the courtly love tradition that Olivares and Boyce note in Ramírez de Guzmán's self-portrait, "Retrato de la autora habiéndosele pedido un galán suyo" (Portrait of the Author Requested by a Suitor).

It is also possible to trace the change in perspective in the selection of poetic themes when reformulated by women poets. The portrait of the beloved (*descriptio viri*) described by Marcela de San Félix in "El jardín del convento" (The Convent Garden) subverts the usual *descriptio puellae* and turns the male body, in this case the beloved as Christ, into an object of desire gazed upon by the female lover. His hands are jasmine blossoms; his odor, that of "fragrant rosehip"; and, in contrast to the conventional Petrarchist code of female beauty, it is the male beloved's lips that are coral, his neck, the hue of lilies, and his hair, golden like the broom flower:

> Like your beautiful lips,
> Sweet affront to coral,
> violets show me
> their carmine color.
> Always majestic
> the snow-white lily,
> your lovely neck
> resembles fortuitously.
> The prolific broom flower,
> As blond as it is beautiful,
> of your golden hair
> grant me tender memories.[29]

Other poems offer new readings of classical myths from a female perspective. Hipólita de Narváez's sonnet on myth of Hero and Leander rewrites the story by giving voice to the female character of Hero, who mourns her beloved's death:[30]

> And woeful me, an uncertain sea,
> dying in the waters of my lament,
> I do not expect any good after death
>
> *ll: 12–14.*[31]

Eco's *romance*, "Claras fuentecillas" (Clear Fountains), in María de Zayas's novel, *El castigo en la miseria* (*Avarice Punished*), in which the nymph addresses the fountain as an inanimate being, tranasforms Narcissus's usual agency into the portrait of a betraying lover:

> Murmur that I have been
> Sad Eco,
> Although disregarded,
> I have always followed him,
> and that if I ask him
> to hear my complaint,
> he disdainfully leaves
> my eyes crying.[32]

The traditional separation between love poetry and religious poetry continues to expand throughout the Baroque period to include the corpus of occasional poetry, which broadens the enunciating theses and tones, and provides essential information on the configuration of this kind of feminine poetic subject and its pragmatic context. This kind of poetry is particularly interesting for being less fictitious than love poetry and for enunciative voice, which generally does not eliminate the female speaker's markers. In fact, it is a poetry of circumstance that depends on historical anecdotes and real events, which are then poeticized.

According to Baranda, in Isabel de Vega's courtly love poetry, she expressly identifies herself as a female speaker. Indeed, if in love poetry (with some of the subtle subversions noted above) the Petrarchan code remains operative, in occasional poetry, there is a female speaker with a clear authorial awareness:

> If my writing would rise, oh great Hurtado,
> like your own glorious writing, to the third heaven
> from where you descended in swift flight
> with Apollo's muses and stolen knowledge, [. . .]
> Since if I wish to show my gratitude
> for the heroic verse with which you favor
> my muse, unworthy of such renown.
> Allow me to applaud your worth with my silence [. . .].[33]

In the same way, the presence of historical interlocutors compels the poetic voice to identify with the empirical female author, beyond the conventionally immanent and fictitious lyric subject. Although in Violante's occasional poetry the lyric subject does not usually have a gender marker, in some poems of praise and religious worship, the author creates a female self with a clear awareness of the historical subject she is writing about. This is evident in the *canción* "A los condes de Arcos" (To the Counts of Arcos):

> and while I venerate, absorbed,
> the memories of your name,

(so they will remain in everything noteworthy)
allow me, oh great Laurencio,
to applaud your worth with my silence.³⁴

Again, in the second stanza of the canción "Al padre Fray Domingo de Santo Tomás por un sermón que hizo sobre el caso de Santa Engracia" (To Fray Domingo de Santo Tomás for a Sermon He Gave on the Case of Saint Engracia):

I listened absorbed, but crazy, I show off
such vain presumptuousness, audacious arrogance,
that after listening to your understanding
I ask you to listen to my ignorance [. . .].³⁵

And we read in yet another occasional *canción*, "Al Ilustrísimo señor Alexandre Castracani Obispo de Nicastro" (To the Most Illustrious Sir Alexandre Castracani, Bishop of Nicastro):

Let me say, my lord, I who joyfully
Saw your humanized Godly acts,
that I received your favor, Oh, holy Nuncio.
Let me say, my lord, I, who to the ages
I hope to be a wonder thanks to fortune
as I am not worthy of such favor.³⁶

In these three poems, the female author's pragmatic context, owing to her personal closeness to her interlocutors, seems to infer a higher degree of identity between the real speaker and the poetic voice, as is specified by the metapoetic allusions of the titles.

The cultivation of this kind of poetry, in addition to other historical and cultural factors, allowed female poets to participate in public life, while responding to their desire to give voice to their historical present and assume a role in its future. For some female poets, such as Luisa Domonte Ortiz de Zúñiga, there have been preserved a great quantity of texts, mainly of occasional poetry mostly in the form of pamphlets. Although she probably wrote other poetic genres, this author's name is identified from her occasional poetry in academies and jousts. As in the case of Cristobalina Fernández de Alarcón, Ortiz de Zúñiga's poems were written within an urban context, showing that female authors were inscribed within a literary circuit, in an official ideological "program" that authorized their poetry for social purposes, and at the same time, allowed them to participate in local and national poetic academies that situated them on the literary map (Osuna: 146–147).³⁷

The poetic voice and the printing press: from the private petrarchan self to a communicative self

Based on the number of published works and their diffusion by means of the printing press, women writers achieved more authority in the seventeenth century. By mid-century, published works by both men and women formed an essential part of the poetic landscape, not only those of renowned poets but an expanding list by female authors. Works by María de Santa Isabel (1600–1646), better known by the pseudonym of Marcia Belisarda, perfectly illustrate this situation: although the manuscript was ultimately never published, she prepares one with her poems to be printed, compiling and accompanying them with a prologue and preliminary texts praising her poems.

The nun prepared her poetry for wide dissemination through the printing press, despite the fact that the 148 poems she included in the volume were a product of her conventual environment, and marked by its circumstances.

In the prologue to the manuscript, María de Santa Isabel reveals her intent to become known as a writer when she mentions saving her texts from oblivion and distributing them to a wide public. She also shows a clear authorial awareness, for example, when she asserts that "these lines are made known by their legitimate author."[38] And, finally, she also defends equality between women and men, stating that "who gave women a soul also gave one to men, and the women's is no different from the men's, and what [God] gave to many women, he denied to many men."[39] The authors of María de Santa Isabel's preliminaries also reveal that they perceive the collection of her poems as prepared for a volume, in the same format as the *Rimas varias* (Various Rhymes), a book form common in mid-century. One of the preliminaries' titles reads: "A las nunca bien encarecidas, ni bastantemente alabadas varias poesías de este libro" (To the never So Well Praised nor Sufficiently Lauded Several Poems of this Book).

As the seventeenth century progressed, the female poetic voice appeared more often in highly valued poetry genres, demonstrating female poetry's integration and naturalization in the Baroque literary canon. In Bernarda Ferreira Lacerda's epic poem, *Hespaña libertada* (Hispania Liberated), the poetic voice has a full authorial awareness, specified in the feminine gender markers when Ferreira speaks with her own voice in the prologue stanzas: "that, although by a woman, my verse will be / celebrated throughout the universe"; "of our illiterate female wit"; and, at the end, "But let us stop here, daring muse / for the feminine voice makes me falter."[40] The choice of the epic, the most prestigious genre, points to the author's legitimation strategy, and is another proof of the author's creative self-awareness, according to Baranda: "Although this fact may disrupt the conventional poetic system, in that a marginalized speaker is publicly involved, its effect is barely perceptible. This does not mean that the question must be set aside since, while the genre itself is not altered by the work, in the literary system in which it wishes to participate, the female voice has a significant and innovative effect from a social perspective."[41]

This must not lead us to believe that the poetic self-awareness of women writers that had gained ground at the time, and was sometimes clearly evident—was anything new. Instead, the printing press and the market had created a new communication framework whereby authorial assertion was strengthened and reflected in a whole series of textual strategies. Although in the genre of lyric poetry, unlike prose or theater, manuscript circulation coexisted with print (García: 289–336), more and more female authors conceived of writing as combined with the printing press. This resulted in women's important positioning in the literary field, their emergence in the public space and the possibility to of receiving economic gain, to which only a few had access, it is true, but that did occur, as in the case of Ana Caro, who wrote panegyric poems for prominent members of the ruling classes.

Poetic voice and authorial awareness

Gender conditions the role of women as speakers within the cultural system. The strategies that women put in place to overcome this exclusion demonstrate that they gradually achieved entry into the early modern literary world. In this process, as noted by the critics, the construction of female authorial identity has become an area of great interest. Due to the distinctiveness of lyric poetry, in particular its classification as a humble genre and to the lack of precepts, not only female but also male poets move between *recusatio* and affirmation. There is a definite will among poets to represent themselves within their texts, from the "transfer of sentimental introspection to an intellectual—and progressively—to an aesthetic reflection."[42]

Among the strategies of self-represention, that of singular authorial awareness was specified through the poet's name as authorial marker, which is then textualized in the poem itself. This self-referentiality bears a stronger meaning in the case of female writers. Ricoeur located it as the first on the scale of the individualizing mechanisms to identify the "self" within the poem. It corresponds to the "self's" goal to become individualized, and that the reader understand the bond and continuity that exist between the one who writes and signs the printed matter, and the one who lived the experience (physical and mental) referred to in the poem (Lejeune).

Two poets formulate both these cases with different results. One of Violante do Céu's epistles, "La Musa que de vos favorecida" (The Muse Favored by You) ends as follows:

> And while every moment is one century
> may God keep you, my lord, as I wish,
> your already forgotten, Soror Violante,
> but in Heaven, until I see you again.[43]

Her strategy is to displace and at the same time, unfold the intra-poetic "self" in order to create an illusion of a spatio-temporary simultaneity of the act of speaking with that of writing, identifying the lyric subject's voice with the "historical self." Although it is part of the rhetoric of epistolary endings, the author leaves her signature at the end of the text. As in the previous *romance*, Violante also includes herself in her *silva*, "A el Rey nosso Senhor Dom Pedro o II em agradecimiento devido a sua grande liberalidade por huma mercé, que fez a Authora neste dia de seus desposorios" (To the King Our Lord Dom Pedro II, in Gratitude for His Generosity, For a Favor He Gave the Author the Day of Her Profession). She signs the last line, "and live to be the most triumphant / among all Monarchs. Soror Violante."[44]

Nevertheless, the most interesting case is that of Ana Caro de Mallén. She playfully hides her last name in the *humilitas* topos, together with the addressee's name in her dedication to the *Relación en que se da cuenta de las grandiosas fiestas que en el Convento de N. P. S. Francisco de la Ciudad de Sevilla se han hecho a los Santos Mártires de Japón* (Account of the Grand Celebrations Held in the Convent of our Father, St Francis of the City of Seville in Honor of the Holy Martyrs of Japan):

> Receive, Sir Juan de Elosidieta,
> this rude discourse in your protection,
> that from a rough and imperfect hand
> your rare value comes to light;
> you may well say that it has been a trick
> to take advantage of you, that for you, I am *Caro*,
> since I have wanted what is worth nothing
> to equal the highest greatness.[45]

The author includes her name as part of the symbolic exchanges between patron and protégé. Nonetheless, the self-reference seems to have the intent of self-canonization, although clearly sharing the purpose with praise to the addressee, from whom she seeks protection or economic benefit.

The authorial function is deployed by means of other strategies, such as addressing other poets, whose works the female author then praises as a poet in her own right. Thus, for instance,

María de Santa Isabel's (Marcia Belisarda) poems dedicated to contemporary poets and writers reveal her interest in being placed alongside them: "Alabando la fábula de Hércules y Deyanira de don Jerónimo Pantoja, escrita en octavas elegantes" (Praising the fable of Hercules and Deianira by Jerónimo Pantoja, written in elegant octaves); "Alabando las novelas de don Pedro de Paz, vecino de Toledo y de ingenio lucidísimo" (Praising Pedro de Paz's Novels, Toledo Neighbor and Magnificent Wit). María de Santa Isabel's two poems, both titled "Para una novela (For a Novel), are, according to Vinatea, probably refer to the sonnet and the *decima*[46] "For a novel" ("Para una novela") which, according to Vinatea probably refers to the novel *La garduña de Sevilla* (The Marten of Seville) by Alonso de Castillo Solórzano, while her "Décimas estrambotadas para una novela" (Estrambota *décimas* for a Novel) could refer to the novel *La esclava de su amante (Her Lover's Slave)* by María de Zayas.

Other poems by María de Santa Isabel evince her leaving aside an "intimate self" for one that thematizes her condition as a poet, with allusions to contexts that refer to the act of writing, connoting the poem as "real" communication and of an exchange of poetry, as in the case of the following sonnet: "Sonnet to forced consonants about which sonnets had been written [. . .] with different subjects, different persons, given to me as a theme, not fainting in view of a disdain."[47] The Toledo poet's entire book of poetry takes up the writing process as a major theme. Additionally, the collection's organization, as well as the comments in the paratexts leave little doubt of the author's desire to be acknowledged as a writer. María de Santa Isabel's pseudonym of Marcia Belisarda, revealed in the preliminaries where she is praised, was not intended to hide the author; it is, instead, a playful combination of her own name; it could also be in deference to the playwright Lope de Vega, whose own novels were addressed to a "Marcia Leonarda" (*Novelas a Marcia Leonarda*).[48]

In all the various poetic voices she deploys, Marcia Belisarda puts into action almost all of the possible forms of enunciation. She recreates the Petrarchan lyric code in its decline and forges a new poetic voice that expresses conventual occasional poetry and celebratory religious poems. Her poetry thus leaves evidence of the significant reflection that took place over the literary codes and their struggles in the new literary arena of the seventeenth century, when the female poetic voice emerges to take advantage of the fissures of a system unprepared for female authors.

Future areas of study

Female lyric poetry still requires much more study. It is necessary to continue to plumb its many aspects, such as its various sub-genres, which include satirical, religious, and occasional poetry. Other poetry that has much to contribute to the study of the female voice in early modern Spain are meta-poetic and self-referential poems in which the poet refers to her own creative work, as well as her metaphorical allusions to the myths of Phaeton and the Phoenix, which function as referents for their self-representation as female writers, and other images and symbols that may have the same self-referential function but that have remained unstudied. Poetry covers a wide range of modes of expression that are inscribed within women's discourse, extending beyond prose texts and paratextual commentary. The degree of orthodoxy or heterodoxy of women's discourse with respect to the literary tradition need to be weighed according to each female author's poetic trajectory (Sabat de Rivers) and understood in relation to their strategies of self-legitimation. The various expressions of the female voice, therefore, should be analyzed in order to gauge their progression as to their authorial stance. Sixteenth- and seventeenth-century women's poetry challenges the hegemony of masculine poetic discourse by seeking its own voice within this rhetorical and symbolic universe. Tension is thus generated by the female poets' simultaneously attempting to maintain traditional poetic codes and transgressing their framework by eliminating conventional order. Between these two extremes can be seen a gamut of discursive practices that range from the attenuation of the female voice to its frank assertion.

In general, women poets tend to adapt themselves to traditional poetic discourse, although many of their poems place in doubt male symbolic hegemony, since the very existence of female poetry asserts its female authorship. For this reason, the appearance of women's signatures and other identification in poems and paratexts is significant; while the poems themselves may adhere to literary tradition, these paratextual data reveal valuable information, as they function at the level of the historical subject, outside the fictional realm of the poetic self. Not surprisingly, the female poet assumes an inclusive and conciliatory stance that then allows her integration within the male-dominated literary tradition while asserting herself as author, a position defined by Olivares and Boyce as that of "subversive conformism" (53–54). Such tendencies, however, are not uniformly present in all female authors, but become apparent throughout their poetic career, demonstrating that the changes to the literary field carried out by women poets break with the masculine uniformity presented by the traditional literary historiography of early modern Spain.

Notes

1 See this chapter's last subheading.
2 Despite the later chronology, see Medina (162–180).
3 For an outline of the tendencies of love poetry to accept, adapt to, and subvert it, see Olivares and Boyce: 24–37.
4 "El aspecto más llamativo de la poesía amorosa de Vega es la ausencia de una voz poética femenina, como correspondería a la autora" (Baranda, "Isabel de Vega" 99–112, 108–110).
5 "Después de muerto yo y tú arrepentida / si a la razón quisieres sujetarte / ternás dolor por ser desconocida. / Mas yo, que viviré siempre en amarte, / quando el pesar te tenga y entristezida / huyr desearé por consolarte."
6 "Mi sentimiento está tan ocupado / en contemplar el bien que en mi alma mora / que no escucha ni entiende, mi señora, / de los agenos males el traslado."
7 *Glosa* is a poetic composition of differing meters through which, generally, another poem is explained by the construction of a new poem.
8 "¿Qué puedo ya ver, señora, / habiéndote visto en mí? / y el que te vido y te adora / no puede vivir un hora / más de cuanto vive en ti."
9 "Ausente estoy de tus divinos ojos; / en fin, ausente y lleno de desvelos; / si al ausencia cruel siguen los celos, / confieso, Floris, que me dan enojos" (Navarro: 84–85).
10 "Basta el desdén and bastan los rigores, / Clori, no más crueldad, no más enojos" (Fox: 214–215).
11 "Cuando borda de perlas el aurora / tapetes que matizan bellas flores, / en lisonjas retornan los favores / con que las enriquece y enamora. [. . .]. / Así yo cuando vi la aurora hermosa / del sol que desterró la niebla oscura / de una ausencia, si ya no sol ni ave / racional, la belleza milagrosa / venero con verdad sencilla y pura, / y el premio fue un desdén severo y grave" (Olivares and Boyce: 249).
12 Serrano y Sanz: 25–26. The author uses the adjective *propia*, denoting her female gender. "Por sola esta ocasión atrás me quedo, / y estando tan propincuo el descontento / las tristes noches cuento, y nunca puedo / hallar cuento en el mal que en ella cuento; / ya de mí *propia* en esto tengo miedo / por lo que me amenaza el pensamiento; / mas pase así la vida y pase presto, / pues no puede haber fin mi presupuesto."
13 The author uses the adjective *correspondida*, denoting her female gender. "Muera quien, siendo constante, / fue tan mal *correspondida*, / que tributando verdades / adquirió solo mentiras" (Olivares and Boyce: 220).
14 The author uses the adjective *vuestra*, denoting her female gender. "Vuestra soy, para vos nací: / ¿qué mandáis hacer de mí?" (ll: 1–2, 73–74; Serrano y Sanz: 181–183).
15 "De aqueste sol alumbrada / pido soledad y sola / la pido por no estar sola, / sino bien acompañada" (ll: 13–16; Navarro: 110).

16 The author uses the adjective *enamorada*, denoting her female gender.
17 "Si con dulces violencias / tus amores me enlazan, / tus caricias me obligan, / tu hermosura me mata; / si sabes que me tienes / cautiva y hechizada, / y de amor por tus ojos / ardiendo en vivas llamas" (Navarro: 117–131).
18 "De inmenso amor aqueste abrazo estrecho / recibe, Silva, de tu dulce Amado, / y por la puerta deste diestro lado / éntrate, palomilla, acá en mi pecho. / Reposa en el florido y sacro lecho, / y abrásate en amor tan abrasado, / que hasta el fuerte nudo haya apretado, / no sea posible quedé satisfecho. / Mira cómo te entrego, amiga mía, / todo mi ser y alteza sublimada; / estima aqueste don que de amor te ofrece; / tendrás en mí gloriosa compañía, / y entre mis mismos brazos regalada / gozarás lo que nadie no merece" (original and translation in Cruz, *Life and Writings*: 176–177). See Cruz, "Transgendering": 130–135.
19 The author uses adjectives such as *vestida, aborrecida, desabrida*, denoting her female gender: "Ni sé si muero ni si tengo vida, / ni estoy en mí ni fuera puedo hallarme, / ni en tanto olvido cuido de buscarme, / que estoy de pena y de dolor vest*ida*. / Dame pesar el verme aborrec*ida* [. . .] / todo me enfada y deja desabr*ida*" (Olivares and Boyce: 104).
20 "En tan terrible pena, / ni hallo descanso, gusto ni alegría; / de todo estoy ajena, / y solo tengo la desdicha mía / por alivio y consuelo, / que de todo lo más me priva el cielo" (Fox: 61–62; Navarro: 194).
21 "Que muera yo, Liseo, por tus ojos, / y que gusten tus ojos de matarme; / que quiera con tus ojos alegrarme, / y tus ojos me den cien mil enojos. [. . .] / ¡Ay, dulce ingrato! que en los ojos tienes / tan grande deslealtad como belleza, / para unos ojos que a tus ojos hieren" (Navarro: 207).
22 "Oh, ¡qué diversas estamos, / dulce prenda, vos y yo! / Vos infelice conmigo / y yo dichosa con vos" (*Rimas varias*, ll: 20–27).
23 "Si vivo en ti transformada, / Menandra, bien lo averiguas, / pues cuando me tiras flechas / hallas en ti las heridas. / Oh tú, de mis pensamientos / idolatrada homicida" (*Rimas varias*, ll: 1–4, 33–34).
24 "Castaño" signifies both chestnut-colored hair and treacherous or false; the last line puns with the color of the etymon "blond mouth" for an unskilled lover or fop. "De mi alegría sois el instrumento / y mi antífona sois de todo el año. / Veros, Castaño, claro, es lo que siento; / solo el ser zaino fuera mayor daño, / pero si procedéis tan desatento / más seréis boquirrubio que castaño."
25 "ni bien es ancha, ni angosta, / ni espantable por lo fea, / ni matante por lo hermosa."
26 Windows in fortified medieval walls through which guns were aimed at the enemy. Here, the female poet hyperbolizes her sunken eyes.
27 "Las manos, en el invierno, / repiten a zanahorias / moradas porque y por cuando / son ellas muy amorosas." In contrast to the skin's paleness in the Petrarchan canon, the cold weather has turned this lady's hands purple, the original color of carrots in the early modern period, further allowing the poet to pun with the paronomasia of "moradas" (purple) and "enamoradas" (in love), in a clearly ironic game with the aesthetic canon.
28 "En fin, soy mujer cabal / y esta verdad es notoria, / porque miembros, muelas, dientes / ni me faltan ni me sobran."
29 "De tus hermosos labios, / del coral dulce afrenta, / su cárdeno color / me muestran las violetas. / Majestuosa siempre / la cándida azucena, / tu bellísimo cuello / venturoso semeja. / La fecunda retama, / tan rubia como bella, / de tus cabellos de oro / me da memorias tiernas."
30 The inclusion of three female poets (Cristobalina Fernández de Alarcón, and the sisters Luciana and Hipólita de Narváez) in Pedro de Espinosa's anthology confirms both that it was at the vanguard of poetic movements and women's poetry's place in seventeenth-century literature.
31 "Y desdichada yo, quien mar incierto, / muriendo entre las aguas de mi llanto, / aún no espero tal bien después de muerta."
32 "Murmurad que he sido / Eco desdichada, / aunque despreciada, / siempre le he seguido, / y que si le pido / que escuche mi queja, / desdeñoso deja / mis ojos llora" (Navarro: 209–212; Olivares and Boyce: 177).
33 "Si llegara mi pluma, o gran Hurtado, / qual la gloriosa tuya al terçer çielo / de do truxiste con veloçe buelo / de Apolo musas y el saver hurtado, [. . .] / Pues si quiero mostrarme agradesçida / al verso heroyco con que favoreçes / mi musa yndigna de tan gran renombre [. . .]." The author puns on the male poet's name "Hurtado de Mendoza" and "hurtado" (stolen).
34 "y mientras de tu nombre las memorias / absorta reverencio, / (porque queden en todo más notorias) / permite, oh gran Laurencio, / que aplauda tu valor con mi silencio."

35 "Absorta escuché, mas loca ostento / tan vana presunción, audaz jactancia, / que después de escuchar tu entendimiento / solicito que escuches mi ignorancia."
36 "Dígalo yo, señor, que tus Deidades / humanadas miré, cuando dichosa, / conseguí tu favor, oh Nuncio santo. / Dígalo yo, señor, que a las edades / portento espero ser por venturosa / ya que no por capaz de favor tanto."
37 See Osuna's chapter in this volume.
38 "dando a conocer estos versos su legítimo autor" (f. 2r; Vinatea: 109–110).
39 "que quien dio alma a la mujer le dio al hombre y que no es of otra calidad esta, aquella, y que muchas concedió lo que negó a muchos" (f. 2r; Vinatea: 109–110).
40 "que, aunque de muger, será mi verso / celebrado por todo el universo"; "de nuestro inculto ingenio femenino", "Mas paremos aquí, musa atrevida, / pues la femínea boz me desfallece."
41 "Aunque el hecho en sí sea desestabilizador para el sistema,—simplemente por ser un enunciador excluido el que participa públicamente–, su efecto apenas es perceptible. Eso no quiere decir que debamos dejar la cuestión a un lado, puesto que si no existe el género desde la obra misma, en el sistema literario en el que desea participar tiene una proyección relevante e innovadora desde una perspectiva social" (Baranda, "Mujer, escritura y fama": 231).
42 "traslado de la introspección de orden sentimental a la reflexión de carácter intelectual y, progresivamente, estético" (Ruiz: 264).
43 "Y mientras es un siglo cada instante / Dios os guarde, señor, como deseo, / vuestra olvidada ya, soror Violante, / pero del Cielo no mientras no os veo."
44 "e vivey para ser o mais triunfante / de todos os Monarcas. Sor Violante."
45 The author uses her last name "Caro" which also means "expensive": "Recibid, señor Juan de Elosidieta, / este rudo discurso en vuestro amparo, / que de mano tan tosca e imperfeta / sale a lucir en vuestro valor raro; / podréis decir muy bien que ha sido treta / el valerme de vos, que os cuesta Caro, / pues he querido lo que nada vale / que a la mayor grandeza casi iguale" (*Relación* h. 2).
46 Ten octosyllabic-line poem.
47 "Si no impide mi amor el mismo cielo. Soneto a consonantes forçossos sobre que avían escrito [roto] sonetos con asuntos diferentes, diferentes personas, diéronme por asunto no desmayar a vista de un desdén."
48 In decimas by Jacinto Quintero of the minor friars, to these works by María de Santa Isabel (Del Padre Jacinto Quintero de los clérigos menores, a estas obras de María de Santa Isabel), Marcia Belisarda-María de santa Isabel's identification is already evident from the title, and even more explicit in LL. 11–14. And the sonnet To the never well exhorted, or sufficiently praised several poems of this book (A las nunca bien encarecidas, ni bastantemente alabadas varias poesías de este libro) praises the Toledo writer's poetry, playing with her real and poetic names.

Works cited

Baranda, Nieves. "Mujer, escritura y fama: la *Hespaña Libertada* (1618) de doña Bernarda Ferreira de Lacerda." *Península. Revista de Estudos Ibéricos* (2003): 225–239.

———. "Isabel de Vega, poeta con musa (Alcalá, 1558, 1568)." *Epos* 30 (2014): 99–112.

Bloom, Harold. *The Anxiety of Influence*. Oxford; New York: Oxford UP, 1997.

Borrachero Mendíbil, Aránzazu. "El autorretrato en la poesía de Catalina Clara Ramírez de Guzmán." *Studies on Women's Poetry of the Golden Age. Tras el espejo la musa escribe*. Ed. Julián Olivares. Woodbridge: Tamesis, 2009: 81–122.

Bourdieu, Pierre. *Las reglas del arte. Génesis y estructura del campo literario*. Trad. Thomas Kauf. Barcelona: Anagrama, 2002.

Cruz, Anne J. *Imitación y transformación: el petrarquismo en la poesía de Boscán y Garcilaso de la Vega*. Amsterdam; Philadelphia: John Benjamins, 1988.

———. "Transgendering the Mystical Voice: Angela de Foligno, San Juan, Santa Teresa, Luisa de Carvajal y Mendoza." *Echoes and Inscriptions: Comparative Approaches to Early Modem Literatures*. Ed. Barbara Simerka and Christopher Weimer. Lewisburg, PA: Bucknell UP, 2000. 127–141.

———. *The Lives and Writings of Luisa de Carvajal y Mendoza*. Toronto: Iter, 2014.

Fox, Gwyn. *Subtle Subversions. Reading Golden Age Sonnets by Iberian Women*. Washington: Catholic U America P, 2008.

García Aguilar, Ignacio. *Poesía y edición en el Siglo de Oro*. Madrid: Calambur, 2009.

Gilbert, Sandra, and Susan Gubar. *The Madwoman in the Attic: The Woman Writer and the Nineteenth-Century Literary Imagination*. New Haven: Yale UP, 1979.

Ibeas Vuelta, Nieves. "El sujeto poético y la autoridad de la voz femenina en Christine de Pizan." *Aproximaciones diversas al texto literario: [V Coloquio celebrado en la Universidad de Murcia del 20 al 22 de marzo de 1996]*. Murcia: U de Murcia, 1996: 129–136.

Jones, Rosalind Ann. *The Currency of Eros: Women's Love Lyric in Europe, 1540–1620*. Bloomington: Indiana UP, 1990.

Lejeune, Philippe. "Autobographie, roman, et nom prope." *Moi aussi*. Paris: Seuil, 1986: 37–72.

Levin, J. I. "La poesía lirica sotto il profilo della comunicazione." *La semiótica nei Paesi Slavi*. Ed. Carlo Prevignano. Milán: Feltrinelli, 1979: 426–442.

Luján Atienza, Ángel Luis. *Pragmática del discurso lírico*. Madrid: Arco-Libros, 2005.

Martos Pérez, María Dolores. "La enunciación lírica en las *Rimas varias* (1646) de sor Violante do Céu." *Letras en la celda. Cultura escrita de los conventos femeninos en la España moderna*. Ed. Nieves Baranda Leturio and María Carmen Marín Pina. Frankfurt-Madrid: Iberoamericana-Vervuert, 2014: 423–438.

Medina, Raquel, y Bárbara Zecchi. *Sexualidad y escritura (1850–2000)*. Barcelona: Anthropos, 2002.

Montes Doncel, Rosa Eugenia. *Pragmática de la lírica y escritura femenina. Sor Juana Inés de la Cruz*, Cáceres: Universidad de Extremadura; Universidad de la Coruña, 2008.

Navarrete, Ignacio. *Los huérfanos de Petrarca. Poesía y teoría en la España renacentista*. Trad. Antonio Cortijo Ocaña. Madrid: Gredos, 1997.

Navarro, Ana. *Antología poética de escritoras*. Madrid: Castalia, 1989.

Olivares, Julián. "Género sexuado, género literario y ansiedad autorial en la poesía sacra de sor Violante do Céu." *Eros divino. Estudios sobre la poesía religiosa iberoamericana del siglo XVII*. Ed. Julián Olivares. Zaragoza: Prensas Universitarias de Zaragoza, 2010: 307–333.

Olivares, Julián, and Elizabeth S. Boyce, eds. *Tras el espejo la musa escribe. Lírica femenina de los Siglos de Oro*. Madrid: Siglo XXI, 2012.

Osuna, Inmaculada. "Cristobalina Fernández de Alarcón y la poesía de circunstancias." *Studies on Women's Poetry of the Golden Age. Tras el espejo la musa escribe*. Ed. Julián Olivares. Woodbridge: Tamesis, 2009: 123–148.

Perelmulter, Rosa. *Los límites de la femineidad en sor Juana: estrategias retóricas y recepción literaria*. Madrid; Frankfurt: Iberoamericana-Vervuert, 2003.

Powell, Amanda, "'¡Oh qué diversas estamos, / dulce prenda, vos y yo!' Multiple Voicings in Love Poems to Women by Marcia Belisarda, Catalina Clara Ramírez de Guzmán and sor Violante del Cielo." *Studies on Women's Poetry of the Golden Age. Tras el espejo la musa escribe*. Ed. Julián Olivares. Woodbridge: Tamesis, 2009: 51–80.

Ruiz Pérez, Pedro. *La rúbrica del poeta. La expresión de la autoconciencia poética de Boscán a Góngora*. Valladolid: U Valladolid, 2009.

Sabat de Rivers, Georgina. "Veintiún sonetos de sor Juana y su casuística del amor." www.cervantesvirtual.com/nd/ark:/59851/bmcbr936

Serrano y Sanz, Manuel. *Apuntes para una biblioteca de escritoras españolas desde el año 1401 al 1833*, 4 vols. Madrid: Rivadeneyra, 1903–1905.

Smith, B. H. "Poetry as Fiction." *On the Margins of Discourse. The Relation of Literature to Language*. Chicago U Chicago P, 1987: 14–40.

Stierle, Karlheinz. "Lenguaje e identidad del poema. El ejemplo de Hölderlin." *Teorías sobre la Lírica*. Comp. Fernando Cabo Aseguinolaza. Madrid: Arco Libros, 1999: 203–268.

Vinatea Recoba, Rosa Martina. "Estudio, edición y notas de la obra poética de Marcia Belisarda." Ph.D. dissertation. Madrid: UNED, 2013.

10
LITERARY ACADEMIES AND POETIC TOURNAMENTS

Inmaculada Osuna Rodríguez

Literary academies and tournaments held a prominent place in sixteenth- and seventeenth-century society. Academies were private meetings that had the purpose of sharing intellectual concerns, including poetic and otherwise learned production; poetic tournaments consisted of public contests, usually with a final ceremony at which, among several discourses, the winning poems were read. Consequently, both had a strong oral component (Carrasco "Oralidad"; Egido "Literatura"; Lacadena), although they did not fully dispense with written forms, such as the poems' eventual publication for dissemination. All this has had both positive and negative consequences for their study: on the one hand, the poetry's oral nature and circumstantial purpose have led to the loss of most of its production and of essential factors related to the context for which it was conceived. On the other, the social relevance of academies and tournaments generated substantial documentation, although often scarce or fragmented, and literary interest is often superseded by the religious, social, or political causes that sustained these events. Furthermore, as we will see below, the study of women's contribution to these events presents a specific set of issues, due to early modern Spain's averseness to women's participation in public writing.

The demarcation between academies and tournaments is difficult to establish. As summarized by José María Ferri Coll (697), the term "academy" was used with four different meanings: groups governed by bylaws that held regular meetings under a patron's protection; sessions or extraordinary celebrations for a specific commemorative or festive event; social gatherings, not formalized as academies but considered as such by their participants; and some public contests, particularly since the mid-seventeenth century. Currently, the term is usually applied to the first two cases: regulated academies with periodic meetings, and the extraordinary academies, although for lack of information, at times some other social gatherings or literary meetings are included, even if their specific function remains unknown (Egido "Poesía"; Ferri; Robbins: 7–46, etc.).

Academies received no institutional support but were promoted by private individuals, usually from the nobility or other wealthy and learned classes, which hindered their continued existence and the preservation of minutes, transcripts, or literary production. One distinctive feature was their gatherings' exclusive nature, limited to their members and to infrequent invited speakers. The academy characteristically allocated to each participant an "asunto," a subject matter or specific theme that often must adhere to pre-established conditions (language, tone, metrics if in verse, etc.), to be orally recited at the following meeting. However, some gatherings followed the procedures of poetic tournaments, with all the participants writing and competing on the same theme. In these cases, it is possible to speak of an "academic contest," although this term, not used at that time, has not become widespread as a critical concept.

Unlike academies, poetic tournaments were aimed toward the wider public, with open calls to participate, sometimes not solely in the city where they took place, but in other parts of Spain. Poets were not chosen in advance or subject to prior acceptance. At times, women's participation was banned, but, as we will see, this was not frequent, nor was it always possible to judge whether the ban was meant to be interpreted ambiguously or ironically. As with the academies, each tournament selected several obligatory poetic subjects for the participants, with their corresponding themes, meters, tones, etc. Once the poems were submitted, they were publicized in up to three successive stages: copies were exhibited anonymously for public reading on the wall at the site of the tournament for several days; the poems were then recited orally, usually revealing their authorship, at the final ceremony where awards were given; and, if the tournament minutes were published, the poems would be included in a volume destined for the public at large. At all stages, in particular in the first and last, awards were not essential for the poems to be disseminated; indeed, the volumes would include, together with awarded compositions, other poems deemed meritorious, even those submitted with the express intent of not vying for the prize.

The rise in the social importance of tournaments and academies was linked to growing urban development and to the local elites' involvement. The most prominent tournaments proliferated under the protection of the local civil and ecclesiastical institutions wishing to enhance certain celebrations, particularly religious and royal events, such as saints' beatifications and canonizations, church and chapel inaugurations, and royal births and deaths. Additionally, academies served to stimulate local bonds, often assuming representative or preeminent positions in their civic environment, as announced in some ceremonial speeches and their names ("Academy of Granada," or "Academy of Madrid" for instance), although their membership remained selective.

Thousands of participants joined in these activities in the early modern period. A wide range of motives underlay the personal decision of each to take part, from the rare contribution owing to an author's friendship with the promoters, or the mere wish to join the celebration, to a driving desire for intellectual recognition. The extant material from these reunions contains representative, albeit partial, data on participation and authorship. This is in part due to the low quantity of published literary production—which nonetheless must have corresponded mainly to the most socially significant events—as well as to the fragility and dispersal of the manuscripts. Moreover, the tournament transcripts usually did not publish all the compositions, either due to their loss or so as not to raise the volume's price. Poems were, besides, often anonymous or signed with pseudonyms; the practice served to indicate that the author belonged to a select group that shared their knowledge of his hidden identity, and, in religious tournaments, it served to underscore the poet's devotional motivation. Even so, there were many occasional authors whose other works are not known today, although prominent writers did not spurn these forms of social recognition.

Women's participation was quite unequal: in academies, it is scarce and poorly documented; in contests, although also a minority, women seem to have participated more. Their contribution was, in general, late, however. Throughout the sixteenth century, as in subsequent centuries, women's eventual participation in literary circles likely occurred through more private channels than tournaments, and by less formalized means than academies. One such venue was their early and sustained contribution to court practices, such as the poems exchanged by ladies and knights in the form of questions and answers (Baranda, "Notas"). Women's involvement in tournaments and academies did not have an appreciable continuity until the beginning of the seventeenth century, when it was encouraged by the convergence of two processes. Thanks to its increased circulation, female writing reached a significant degree of social visibility during the last quarter of the sixteenth century, coinciding with the public projection of Teresa of Ávila's works. Both nuns in convents and, in the secular sector, women from the lower nobility and the middle class contributed to this surge (Baranda, *Cortejo*: 82). In addition, the literary practices of academies and tournaments expanded across the various social levels in the final decades of the sixteenth century. Academies extended their membership beyond learned circles, in a clear orientation towards a celebratory and recreational literature; in propitious contexts, they were becoming consolidated as genuine structures of power, appealing to writers in pursuit of professional and social acceptance (Cruz). In turn, tournaments had mostly depended on the initiative of individuals or of restricted academic circles (universities, schools, etc.) almost until the last third of the sixteenth century. From then on, they began to aim more broadly at popular celebrations, at the request of municipal authorities and influential religious orders, even though some contests continued to be promoted and organized by educational institutions (Osuna, "Justas siglo XVI": 272–276). In both cases, although in different degrees, the expansion beyond the usual learned and educational spheres probably facilitated women's access. Tournaments and academies, therefore, share several features and methodologies, yet their distinct social nature and their varied acceptance of women's writing suggest that we must deal with them differently.

Women in academies

While academies were known to have met throughout the sixteenth century, their rise as a social phenomenon did not take place until the end of the century or beginning of the seventeenth century, in key cities such as Madrid, Valencia, and Zaragoza (Cañas; Egido, "Academias": 103–107; Mas, *Academias valencianas*; Mas, *Academias y justas*: 47–172; Sánchez: 26–31, 221–227).[1] Regular academies, which held periodic meetings, have barely left documentary traces, for several reasons: their contributions have been lost or only a few are known, and they are dispersed in miscellanies not always identified as academy production. The consistent cataloguing, by way of minutes, of their rules and literary production is rarely preserved, as was done by the Valencia academy, Academia de los Nocturnos (1591–1594) (Academy of the Nocturnals), and the Aragon academy, Pítima contra the ociosidad (1608) (Remedy against Idleness).

Very little is known about women's contributions to academies that met periodically.[2] As we will see, there is strong reason to believe that these were male-dominated, and that their gender exclusivity affected women's active and regular participation, yet perhaps not their attendance, which may have been encouraged when meetings were held in domestic spaces with close family or social bonds. The academy "Remedy against Idleness," promoted by the Count of Guimerá, illustrates the ambiguity of certain situations.[3] The bylaws were signed by his wife, Isabel Inés de Eril, Countess of Guimerá, and her mother, Cecilia de Sentmenat, Countess of Eril; however, their status in the academy is not fully clear. Some incidents seem to equate them with academy members, whereas others reveal discrepancies. While their signatures precede those of the members, they were informed of the bylaws after they had been agreed to; the women merely "praised and approved them,"[4] signing as witnesses (Sánchez: 258). They attended some sessions, as reflected in the minutes, and were sometimes penalized for breaching the rules (Sánchez: 259–260), which again differentiates them from the role of mere silent spectators; nevertheless, their attendance was sporadic and they did not use pseudonyms, unlike academy members. They also garnered attention and respect within the academy, as revealed in an internal poetic contest praising Saint Inés, with signs of homage to the Countess of Guimerá

(Egido, "Academies": 107). But the countesses do not appear in the literary assignments, and no poem of theirs is preserved in the volume, although the minutes of the last days allude to certain letters they should write, without indicating whether these are meant to be literary or if they were actually written.

Some academies in fictional works mention the presence of a female public. Their testimony must nonetheless be weighed carefully, given the sources' literary objectives, which are not subject to historical authenticity and are frequently narrated in a burlesque tone. The *tapada*,[5] a supposedly anonymous female assistant, sometimes appears under the cover of her veil as a standard character in the humorous writings of real academies. The ephemeral and censored attempts by fictional ladies who attend academies in several plays, as Jean-Pierre Étienvre has argued (354–355), seem to respond in particular to the theatrical convention of recreating on stage women's aspirations for literacy, and playwrights resort to the archetypal Italian academies rather than to the Spanish reality of the moment. This is the case, for instance, of Lope de Vega's *La dama boba* (*The Foolish Lady*), where, at an academy meeting, Nise is characterized as *entendida* (learned) and taunted as *bachillera* (university graduate),[6] eager to exhibit her intellectual prowess. Fictional academies with female characters also appeared in novels, either as part of their narrative structure or in episodes intended to include poetry (Étienvre: 362–364; King).[7]

Among fictional academies, we shall highlight, for its verisimilitude, the one recreated by Luis Vélez de Guevara in the ninth chapter of *El diablo cojuelo* (1640) (*The Limping Devil*). It appears as a regular academy in Seville under the Count of Torre's patronage and frequented by writers and an anonymous group of *tapadas*; one of the participants, Ana Caro, reads a poem composed by her. The author may have been inspired by a real academy: the female writer evoked in the novel among male participants is not discordant with the Seville poet and playwright, Ana Caro de Mallén's authorial profile, characterized by her public and professional writing. Indeed, as we will see, there are records of her participation among the literary academics at the Madrid court. However, there is still no evidence of her attendance, and as in all works of fiction, her appearance in *El diablo cojuelo* cannot be considered as proof.

Women's almost total exclusion from academies was due, therefore, to the primary difference between these and the tournaments: their private or semi-private nature, with restricted access (Baranda, "Reflexiones": 310). The reason is likely based on underlying social and ideological factors. The social rise of academies and their foothold in urban culture distanced them from the gendered codes of sociability that had governed courtly customs in the fifteenth and first half of the sixteenth centuries. The court environment was decisive for literary practices that allowed for female authorship, and went hand in hand with humanist patronage (Borreguero) and with courtly entertainment (Baranda "Notas"; Pérez Priego), a few traces of which are still visible in the seventeenth century (Baranda, *Cortejo*: 239). Academies, however, flourished in an urban culture that, while it did not exclude the nobility, neither did it encourage courtliness, save for Madrid, and even there, with nuances that did not correspond to sixteenth-century court life. The academy members were usually part of local oligarchies and of the literate professional world, with interests that noticeably differed from Renaissance humanism (Cruz: 74–76). There are sporadic exceptions but, in general, towards the end of the sixteenth century, the ideological structures that had impelled women's integration in humanist circles had weakened.

Women's exclusion was pertinent to the cultural elitism aimed for by these academies' promoters, although often the academies inclined toward themes of little intellectual importance. In contrast to tournaments, academies held periodically required a continued sociability; their purpose did not lend itself to female authors' systematic integration as they were dedicated to purely literary exercises, no matter if the agreed topic for each meeting was cultured, ludic, meta-literary, religious, or political. In the sessions, an abundance of love lyrics in trivial or anecdotal tones (Robbins) and a prolific burlesque foundation coexisted with more serious subjects (devotional, panegyric, moral). Thus, the excuse of producing exemplary religious and civic poems, fully operative in tournaments, in academies served for only part of the means of production. Such a pretext was important, if not essential, for the relatively limited acceptance of women's public writing, both in tournaments and in other literary works. It is therefore significant that, despite women's scarce contribution to the academies, they do appear in extraordinary academies—those not requiring regular attendance and that emphasized extra-literary motive that gave rise to the extraordinary literary act.

These extraordinary academies are better known, in general, because a large number of them were printed in the second half of the seventeenth century; thanks to this there are abundant data about their participants and development. Some were likely related to periodic academies, but we should not extrapolate from them conclusions that pertain to the former, given their chronological, geographical, and contextual peculiarities. Published transcripts of extraordinary academies appear more often after 1650; their location is limited to Madrid, Granada, Valencia, and, to a lesser extent, Seville and Salamanca; and their special circumstances might have created a different attitude, more disposed to broader social visibility, which would explain both their interest in being disseminated in print, and, hypothetically, their openness toward women's contributions. Even so, not even these extraordinary academies accepted women unreservedly.

Two cases stand out of female writers whose renown went beyond their writing occasional poetry: Ana Caro de Mallén and María de Zayas. Both cases exemplify the difficulties in differentiating between extraordinary academies and poetic tournaments, especially when they are considered academic contests. Ana Caro is mentioned in a *vejamen*[8] of the literary celebration held for Carnival in 1638 at the Buen Retiro Palace, a royal recreational residence; another *vejamen* locates María de Zayas in a contest organized in 1643 by the Academy of Santo Tomás in Barcelona. Despite the undoubted relevance of these two allusions to Caro and Zayas, certain ambiguity prevails because, as often is the case in *vejámenes*, there are many questionable allusions and the burlesque tone makes it difficult to distinguish between truth and exaggeration or irony.

From the literary event held in 1638 (academy, tournament, or contest, as it was indistinctly called by all three names), there are only a few manuscript pieces (Bergman: 551–568; Julio: 283–284), among which there are three *vejámenes*, including the one mentioning Ana Caro (Julio: 295–296). The composition that Caro supposedly contributed is not known, and the reference allows us only to assume her possible participation in the celebration.[9] The event, like the one held a year earlier in *Academia burlesca que se hizo en Buen Retiro* (Burlesque Academy Held at the Buen Retiro) was formalized as a "contest," with predefined subjects for poets' competitive participation, without forcing them to select a specific theme. However, a tournament open to any interested party does not seem plausible within this royal framework. Additionally, we should not forget Caro's contribution to the sumptuous celebrations of 1637, of particular political significance: her *Contexto de las Reales Fiestas que se hicieron en el Palacio del Buen Retiro a la coronación de Rey de Romanos, y entrada en Madrid de la Señora Princesa de Cariñán* (Context of the Royal Celebrations Held in the Buen Retiro Palace for the Coronation of the King of the Romans and Entry in Madrid of the Lady Princess of Cariñán).[10] It would not be surprising, then, if, for the celebrations of 1638, prior personal contacts provided Caro with an invitation to a restricted academy, despite the lack of recurring traces of her involvement in the literary life of Madrid.

Of a different nature is the contest of 1643 prepared by the Academy of Santo Tomás in Barcelona. This academy counted with an institutional base and continued operation. Linked to the Dominican Convent of Santa Catalina, it was composed of the convent's members and secular doctors and students; occasionally, it organized literary activities open to the public (Brown, "Context": 180–183). Zayas participated with a poem, lost today, in a contest that celebrated the donation of a relic to the convent. The fact that only the *vejamen* is preserved makes it difficult to reconstruct the context.[11] Kenneth Brown has analyzed Zayas's burlesque treatment as a "manly woman"[12] by Francesc Fontanella, who was in charge of the *vejamen* ("María de Zayas": 358–359; "Context": 180–183).[13] This familiarity could explain the Madrid writer's presence in this semi-private event. As evidenced by the text, other women took part, but apparently with a different function or reason. These are grouped at the end, under the generic title of *setmaneras* (women who carried out academic duties one week at a time), although they are later individualized with their names; also, their presentation changes to a laudatory tone. Nonetheless, Zayas appears at one point in the discourse—also possibly in the contest—exclusively dominated by men, and is not exempt from the general burlesque treatment.

In short, both *vejámenes* audaciously treat Caro and Zayas with humor, comparable to the tone used with male participants. This leads to consider their integration—relatively normalized, although circumstantial—within the intellectual bases that supported these poetic events. Nevertheless, these testimonies should not lead to generalizations. For the second half of the seventeenth century, the published transcripts of extraordinary academies evince much more precisely the extent of women's absence. The records archived in the National Library of Spain of thirty-three academies, almost all of which are extraordinary, register only four female participants, in Madrid and Granada (Bègue: 64, 101, 215, 265); the abundant documentation from Valencia contributed by Mas i Usó adds only one more woman (*Academias valencianas*: 99–104). All of the cases seem exceptional: either the author is anonymous, unlike all or almost all other participants; the author's contribution is submitted to the academy without her attending the celebration; the author is praised instead of being mocked in the *vejamen*; or the published record suggests that the author was absent from the event's original plan, as when she is not included in the initial distribution of subjects, or when the poem appears in a section added after the final *vejamen*.

As a whole, then, the academies, in particular extraordinary ones, did not fully ban women's participation, but accepted them infrequently, sporadically, and at times in an aloof manner, unlike the characteristic interaction and sociability of their male participants.

Women in tournaments

By contrast, tournaments constitute an opportune environment in which to gauge the extent and significance of women's contributions to public poetry in early modern Spain.[14] Nieves Baranda notes the participation of around two hundred and fifty women in sixty tournaments during the seventeenth century ("Reflexiones": 312). The high number leads us to conclude that the public nature of the invitations to participate in tournaments was decisive, unlike the restricted access to academies and other aspects of their development discussed above. Although quite a few women contributed to tournaments with their poems, they did not assume administrative levels: they do not appear as judges and do not have major organizational duties in public contests, although nuns were probably directly involved in female convents' more modest tournaments. It was also rare for the event's published volume to be dedicated to a woman.[15]

Women's poetic participation did not progressively increase, nor was it uniform throughout the country. Almost nothing is known about women's contribution to tournaments in the sixteenth century. Save for Catalan-speaking areas, tournaments were closely involved with university and scholarly interests until almost the last decades of the century, which made women's participation difficult, although there were exceptions. The sixteenth-century author, Catalina de Paz, is supposed to have written poems in Latin and Spanish, and participated in the contests of Alcalá and Seville, two outstanding focal points of peninsular humanism (Baranda, *Notas*: 9–10). Nonetheless, it was not until the beginning of the seventeenth century, when tournaments' social expansion was consolidated, that women's participation, albeit scattered and in a minority, gained visibility. Despite possible precedents, the contest held in 1601 in Barcelona for the canonization of the saint, Raimundo de Peñafort, proved to be a significant milestone: the published transcript includes two poems written by a woman, but other women whose compositions were not published are also included in the *sentencia*.[16] From the beginning of the century, the increasing participation by women in tournaments reaches its zenith in those dedicated to Saint Teresa in 1614, and is maintained until the 1630s, although concentrated in certain geographic areas (Zaragoza and Madrid), and notably declines after 1650 (Baranda, *Cortejo*: 216–217).

The geographic distribution of women's participation is quite irregular. Its continuity and abundance are remarkable in the Catalonia–Aragon area. In the specific area of Aragon, the situation is exceptional: we have ample and reliable data for the twelve contests held during the first half of the seventeenth century, in which more than 150 women took part (Marín Pina, "Certámenes": 148). Although all of these included female participation, either for religious or civic themes, two stand out in 1619 in Zaragoza, and one in 1650 in Huesca: each contest included twenty to thirty female authors. In general, the women's social levels, as with the other participants in Aragon tournaments, are varied: they include nuns and laywomen, mostly from the urban patrician class and nobility, and, in isolated cases, titled nobility. However, after mid-century, a sudden halt in the printing of tournament transcripts in Aragon apparently stopped this trajectory.

This situation was not widespread in the entire Catalonia-Aragon area. Tournaments in Barcelona included early female participation, held throughout the century, in Spanish, Latin, and Catalan; however, participation was less numerous than in Aragon, with the contest organized by the church of Santa María del Mar (1656), which included sixteen female authors, Barcelonas's most significant contest. In Gerona, seven women participated in the only tournament that has been studied, which was held in 1622.[17] In Valencia figures decrease to similar levels of those in Castile; save for an anonymous *serrana* (mountain woman), we barely glean seven female names clustered in the religious contests held before the first quarter of the seventeenth century, none of which counted with more than three women.[18]

In the area of Castile, women's participation was more dispersed and scarce. The most important tournaments were held in Madrid (Baranda, *Cortejo*: 217–244). Nevertheless, from a total of twelve contests, not all of which included women, only 26 women authors participated; indeed, no women participated in one of the most important tournaments, the one dedicated to the patron of Madrid, San Isidro, in 1620. Their chronological distribution, in turn, expands during the century, although without reaching high numbers: if there were female participants, two or four were usually involved in each tournament, with at most, six. None of the women appears in more than one tournament in Madrid, although two reappear in cities near to each other, Salamanca and Toledo. Moreover, since the court was centered in Madrid, the complete absence of any titled noblewomen among the authors is significant. Toledo, closely related to the Madrid environment, also counted with female participation in tournaments, with analogous ups and downs; the most significant tournament, given its social and literary level, included up to seven women. It was promoted in 1616 by Archbishop Bernardo de Sandoval y Rojas, a relative of the Duke of Lerma, Philip III's favorite.[19]

There was much geographic and temporal dispersion in other cities.[20] During the seventeenth century, female participation in Salamanca is evinced in most of eight printed tournament transcripts, although no more than five women appear in each contest, and only fourteen in total. In Granada, in another eight published contests, barely nine female authors are registered, more than half in one contest only, held in 1650 (Osuna, "Poesía": 245–246). Other isolated cases, some with one single participating woman, appear throughout most of Spain.[21]

This sample gives an idea of the panorama's irregular parameters as regards geography, the concentration of female participation in certain contests, and the disparity of different periods depending on the city. Conclusions are hard to reach if we consider the lack of documentation about tournaments for certain periods and cities. This adds to the particular circumstances that influence women's participation in each case, such as the networks that promoted them and socialization strategies (contests, literary praises, epistolary exchanges, etc.), which has been pointed out by Nieves Romero-Díaz ("Aproximaciones": 103–106, 116–117) as a means of integrating the tournaments with other kinds of female poetic production within their social and cultural community.

More research is needed on why, in the seventeenth century, there are no women participants at all in certain contests held in cities such as Salamanca and Madrid where their participation, while low, remained otherwise constant. Factors such as chance, or having to do with the celebration and the nature and characteristics of the calls, in particular if these were made by brotherhoods or restricted professional groups, could well have caused or affected women's lack of involvement, sometimes with only one or two participants per contest. These factors are in need of the appropriate historical and social analyses, depending on the location of the tournament.

Few women appear in different contests in one single city, and they rarely appear in different cities, especially if these are not close to each other. These women were probably only occasional and even ephemeral writers: In the overwhelming majority of the cases, other works by them are not known. However, three authors from different geographic locations, conditions, and literary interests exemplify the major exceptions: Bernarda Romero, Cristobalina Fernández de Alarcón, and Ana Francisca Abarca de Bolea.

Bernarda Romero, a nun in the Cistercian convent of Gratia Dei (or of Zaydía) in Valencia, participated in tournaments of her city for approximately twenty years. Nothing has been written on her life or literary production beyond these contests, however. Her first two known interventions, prior to 1602, are in two of the three tournament transcripts organized and printed by Bernardo Catalán de Valeriola, the promoter of the Academy of the Nocturnals. Most likely an advocate of the convent, Valeriola celebrated there the first tournament in which Bernarda appeared. However, the nun's other five contributions, which took place afterward until 1621, entailed more extensive, institutionalized celebrations involving various religious orders.

For her part, Cristobalina Fernández de Alarcón (c. 1576–1646) was a secular writer, fully integrated into a very active intellectual environment of learned scholars and professionals with no traceable influence of noble patronage (Osuna, "Cristobalina"). She spent her life in Antequera, close to the Andalusian cities of Granada, Seville, and Córdoba. Of her presumably substantial poetic production, only 17 compositions are known, almost all occasional;[22] of these, eight were published in tournament transcripts. She participated in five contests with religious themes between 1614 and 1636, which took place in several cities (Cordoba, Toledo, Seville, Antequera, and Granada); and some of her other poems were probably written for similar events. Her contributions are unique for their frequency, temporal extent, and geographic diversity. Fernández de Alarcón's participation outside her city of residence seems to have been supported by her immediate circle, since other poets from Antequera coincided with her at some of these tournaments. She could also have had personal contacts in other cities, such as Seville or Granada. Additionally, the contests in Cordoba and Toledo tended to side with the literary movement that favored Luis de Góngora, whose cultured poetic practice was at the center of a controversy over its complexity; her poetic style, like that of other Andalusian authors, has been interpreted as a sign of personal adhesion to Gongorine poetics (Osuna, "Cristobalina": 141–146).

Ana Francisca Abarca de Bolea (1602–c.1686) also took part in an active intellectual circle, although from the distance imposed by her monastic life in the convent of Santa María de Casbas (Huesca). Her contribution to tournaments known to have taken place includes only three poems for two royal events: the funeral rites for Prince Baltasar Carlos (Zaragoza, 1646) and Philip IV's second nuptials (Huesca, 1650). Her biographical data and contemporary references allow us to contextualize her poetry in light of her distinguished family ties, as well as her personal and epistolary contacts with important Aragon intellectuals (Campo); one of them was her nephew, the Marquis of Torres, and Juan Francisco Andrés de Uztarroz, who played a relevant role in these contests. Her participation, therefore, may have been due to her close relationships with this group. In addition, unlike other tournament participants, her literary production was not limited to these compositions. The author published three works and, in one of them, the *Vigilia y octavario de san Juan Baptista* (The Vigil and Octave of St John the Baptist), she inserted more than one hundred poems, including two that she had submitted to the contests.[23] It is also possible that Abarca de Bolea, perhaps like other lesser-known nuns elsewhere, may have served as model or intellectual incentive to her community, since three other nuns from her convent submitted their contributions to tournaments around the same time, one to the Huesca tournament (1650) and two to Salamanca (1658).

These three examples, as well as the many names of women with no known biographical or literary profiles, lead us to reflect on the irregular geographical and chronological landscape of the tournaments mentioned. Apart from the female authors' personal circumstances, we should weigh other social and cultural variables: for instance, which peculiarities of the urban elites may explain the geographical contrasts; to what extent the differences between populous cities and small communities affected women's participation and their social acceptance; which factors, such as the tournament calls for participation, their religious or civic purposes, and the female authors' religious or secular status, might have influenced this panorama; and the convents' attitudes as regards participation in these tournaments.[24]

Much more needs to be studied regarding the social perception of female participation in these events. Some calls expressly state their exclusion, while others are ambiguous. One tournament in Malaga, in 1640, established that "poems will not be accepted from any woman, even nuns, if she does not show a license from the church authorities for such submissions, because tournament participants complain to the jury that these women are favored";[25] another, from 1648, in Madrid, that "papers will not be received past the deadline, or in the name of a lady, or of a pseudonym."[26] Sometimes, the tension generated by the alleged partiality in granting awards is evident. Anonymous submissions were also suspect; their proscription, if any, was equally for men and women, but at times they specifically addressed women. Thus, a tournament dedicated to Saint Teresa (Zaragoza, 1622) pronounced that "if nuns or secular women write, they must understand that, although their family names will be shown respect, the merits of their writing are what will count most. And because some authors who doubt their own abilities often write under these ladies' names to oblige judges to reward them for courtesy's sake, they are warned that, in this case, they will receive perfumed gloves only, as a favor to the pseudonymous authors."[27] In general, however, these kinds of warnings and explicit prohibitions did not seem to be very common.

For the scholar, anonymity and the use of pseudonyms by both male and female writers present serious challenges: in religious tournaments, for instance, male poets often remained anonymous to demonstrate a lack of interest in awards and in literary recognition in favor of exclusively spiritual motives. In other cases, pseudonyms were used to show the male author's disinclination towards poetry's public dissemination, since in certain environments the genre was still perceived as reserved for an immediate circle of readers and circulated in manuscript. Women also availed themselves of these practices, albeit not necessarily for the same reasons. While men holding important positions were concerned over the perceived damage that writing poetry might inflict on their professional image, aristocratic women experienced similar qualms if they felt they should safeguard their dignity.[28] Additionally, prejudice against women writers' social visibility was stronger and affected more social levels.

Several forms of anonymity and pseudonyms explicitly referenced a female gender, such as anonymous attributions identifying female categories (a lady, or a nun); literary attributions solely for women (a *serrana*); pseudonyms attributed by women writers themselves ("Arminda"); and female pseudonyms and false attributions to real women, invented by male writers. All these procedures equally impede the quantification and analysis of women's participation, but each varies according to their motives and implications. For example, using false female identities might suggest that the contemporary public considered women's writing to be prestigious (Baranda, "Reflexiones": 315; Marín Pina, "Certámenes": 149) and this public esteem was not at stake even if some people were aware of the false attribution. Furthermore, there is another positive counterpart when authorial concealment of the woman's name did not reject the author's female gender. The tension between the dominant moral discourse, which objected to women's public projection, and women's sustained contribution to poetic contests seems evident. It was no doubt often resolved, however, for other than literary reasons, such as adherence to the dominant mentality, religious devotion, observance of indisputable social values, and the wish to contribute to the celebration's splendor and to collective civic pride. Nevertheless, in many cases, women's use of anonymity or pseudonyms offered them a middle ground between being publicly exposed and remaining silent.

Within intellectual environments, female authors who challenged male writers' worth against their own did not go unnoticed. The playwright and novelist, Juan Pérez de Montalbán, mentions María de Zayas in his "Índice de los ingenios de Madrid" (Index of Madrid's Literary Talents), not only praising her play and book of short stories, but also stating that "she has contributed to contests with great success."[29] The scholar and poet, Rodrigo Caro, includes Ana Caro among the "illustrious men who flourished"[30] in Seville since the reign of Philip II and, together with her plays' success, he alludes to her participation "in many literary tournaments, in which she almost always wins first prize."[31] As to Cristobalina Fernández de Alarcón, the local historian, Francisco de Cabrera, stressed that Góngora and Lope de Vega, "impressed by such a high and dashing spirit, always awarded her with the first prize in literary contests and tournaments, not for being a woman, but for her erudite and elegant writing"[32] (Osuna, "Cristobalina": 127). These statements give proof that at least some contests may have offered women writers opportunities for prestige analogous to those for other literary works. Even so, Baranda notes the pradoxical general absence of well-known female writers in tournaments, in contrast to their literary contributions in other occasional contexts, such as books' preliminaries. In light of the numerous female poets who took part sporadically in contests, professional women writers may have decided against participating in them for fear of being considered amateurs, and thus jeopardizing their inclusion as authentic writers in the hegemonic literary circles dominated by men (Baranda, *Cortejo*: 235–237).

Future research

As we have seen, literary academies and tournaments offer a wide and complex field of study, although conditioned by the dispersal, scarcity, and variety of the sources. Their poetic production has traditionally received little attention from critics, since as a whole it is considered of low quality, with the poems' presumed faults resulting from the stipulations imposed by the calls and the conservative events celebrated by the contests. Nonetheless, these events have been of interest to bibliographical studies and those focusing on specific local and regional literary milieus given their special civic and, on occasion, editorial relevance.

Certainly, research on women's contributions to these events will encourage new and renewed studies of local and regional contests that will reveal more cases and record useful data for broader studies on tournaments and academies. It will still be difficult, however, to expand our knowledge of female participants, both regarding biographical information and literary production. Even authors such as Ana Caro and María de Zayas suffer from a lack of documentation, despite having been extensively researched. However, these areas of study are open to the possibilities offered by the increasing cataloguing and digitalization of archives and sources, as well as by the growth of databases able to provide a greater amount of bio-bibliographic information, easily recoverable through search systems.[33]

Many literary aspects of these poetic events have yet to be critically evaluated. Reviewing the manuscript circulation allows for both small and significant findings; additionally, there are other fruitful aspects of occasional poetry to be studied, whether in manuscript or printed form, that will supplement information on academies when mapping sociability networks. This is the case, for example, of poetic contributions to book preliminaries, of the transcripts of celebrations and funeral rites outside the usual contests, and of single-themed collective volumes that lie somewhere between spontaneous contributions and extraordinary academies, and are thus often disregarded by critics for lacking strong academic connections. Some examples of these volumes are the tributes to Lope de Vega and Pérez de Montalbán, *Fama póstuma*, 1635 (Posthumous Fame); and *Lágrimas panegíricas*, 1639 (Panegyric Tears), respectively; with contributions by women writers as well as works with fewer participants, such as *Anfiteatro de Felipe el Grande*, 1631 (Philip IV's Amphitheater), compiled by José de Pellicer; and *Elogios al Palacio Real del Buen Retiro*, 1635 (Praises to the Buen Retiro Royal Palace) by Diego de Covarrubias.

Continued research and analyses point to different directions besides increasingly sophisticated searches for data on women's literary production. This fragmented landscape, with its dispersed authors, places, and periods, and delimited by constrictive mechanisms, has tended to favor (even in this essay) a more sociological, rather than an authorial or stylistic approach. Concerns that have only been sketched here may be investigated further and analyzed in detail, such as the chronological and geographical mappings of women's participation, the detection of sociability networks and their contextualized study, the identification of social bases that explain various sorts of fluctuations, the systematization of data, and conclusions about social perceptions of female participation.

In general, aspects of formal poetics, for both men's and women's contributions, have been overlooked. For female poetry, work still outstanding includes researching several areas to observe, for instance, the systematization of formal variables—for example, metric and tonal preferences; the degree of assimilation of contemporary literary trends; the critical commentary in *sentencias* and *vejámenes* regarding women's poetry; and the eventual adoption of a discourse marking the female voice and its constraints within the public space. Moreover, as with other subgenres of poetry, we should not forget the recovery, editing, and literary study of women's contributions that, despite the restrictions imposed on them, are valuable both in themselves and as representative of literary trends in early modern Spain.

Notes

1. Both Sánchez and King (21–84) adhere to less rigorous criteria than the above, and other studies have added to their theses in the following decades; nonetheless, with due caution, the former are still the main starting point for academies. For an updated bibliographic review, see Ferri Coll.
2. See, for example, Sánchez on the Marquise del Valle's continuation of the academy created by her husband, Hernán Cortés (†1547) (198); on the Countess of Ficalho attending the Duke of Alba's academy at the end of the sixteenth century (295); the poetic and musical meetings of Agustina de Torres in Salamanca (c. 1572) (295); and Jacinta Nisa and Ana Vicencia de Mendoza's participation at one "Academy of Huesca" in 1595 (251). Although beyond our time limits, we might add the academy, or perhaps social gathering, promoted in Valencia by María Egual, Marquise of Castellfort, *circa* 1705 (Mas, *Academias valencianas*: 379–386). In general, this information is not very specific and does not detail the literary contribution or regularity of the women's attendance; perhaps they consider a social gathering or meeting as an academy; I prefer not to include them in women's participation in regular academies, despite their hypothetical value.
3. On the "Pítima" academy and its bylaws, see Sánchez (252–261). Sánchez should be complemented with King (65–67) and Egido ("Academias": 107–109).
4. "Loaron y aprobaron."
5. The term referred to women who covered themselves with a veil or mantle. Conduct manuals, such as *Education of a Christian Woman*, by Juan Luis Vives, urged women to veil their face, leaving only one eye visible.
6. Term used in Golden Age literature to ridicule cultured women who conceitedly boasted about their knowledge.
7. For academic episodes in novels and other narratives by women, see María de Zayas, Mariana de Carvajal and Ana Francisca Abarca de Bolea (Romero-Díaz: 108–113).
8. A demeaning composition read in academies against the participants in academic discussions, poetry contests, and examinations for university degrees. The *vejamen* satirized participants, usually with a high degree of conventionalism. Sometimes, it met its genuine function to criticize poems presented to academies, but there were often other humorous reasons, such as authors' physical or moral features, their names and aliases, fictitious extravagant anecdotes (Cara; Brown "Aproximación"; Carrasco "Notas").
9. The author, Alfonso de Batres, begins his *vejamen* to Caro by envisaging her from the distance as a complaining woman, "and not in very bad dirges" ("no en muy malas endechas"). With an ironic exchange of attributes, playing with the categorization of learned women ("entendidas") as ugly, and male poets as untidy, he shows her from afar as "beautiful as two thousand learned women, and from a closer distance she seemed as tidy as a similar number of poets" ("hermosa como dos mil entendidas, y desde más cerca aseada como otros tantos poetas"); he deduces that she must be Ana Caro, who, "among many, many men and with very little urge to marry, complained about her boredom" ("que entre muchísimos hombres y entre poquísima gana de casarse, se quejaba de su hastío"); and Batres compares her attitude to that of the *mondongas* or palace maids of honor eager to find a husband. With both clichés, that of *entendidas* and that of *mondongas*, he alludes to two themes from the contest held in 1637 (Julio: 295–296). Zuese contrasts this burlesque image with the more laudatory and harmonious portrait drawn by authors from Andalusia, such as Vélez de Guevara.
10. See Marín Pina's chapter in this volume.
11. See Brown "Context," and Fontanella, "Introduction": 60–61, 129–164.
12. "Mujer varonil."
13. In the first lines, Zayas is described sarcastically as a manly woman, with a pun also on the author's last name of Zayas (sayas for petticoats or skirts): "of a manly face and mustache, although with petticoat and, save for what is missing underneath, she resembled a knight" ("de rostro y bigote varonil, aunque con sayas, y, salvo por lo que no hay debajo de ellas, semejante a un caballero"); with regards to the presented *glosa*, he reproaches her for having missed the mark in one of her strophes to opt for the award: the poet will be crowned with only the hoop of a farthingale.
14. There is no over-all study on tournaments. For bibliography, see Delgado and Mas (*Academias y justas*: 1–42); for other references, see Osuna, "Justas siglo XVI"; "Justas primera mitad XVII."
15. We highlight the case of Luisa de Padilla, Countess of Aranda, to whom a tournament is addressed in honor of Saint Ramón Nonato (Zaragoza, 1617). The dedication presents her as a learned, devout woman who promotes literature at a time when she and her husband are deploying several strategies to increase the family's prestige (Acquier: 179–184).

16 The *sentencia* was a discourse, usually in verse, that communicated the judges' decision in the contest, mentioning the winning poets and other participants; its use was not generalized, since often its purpose was met by other means, such as epigraphs or brief comments on the prize before each poem. For data on tournament participation, see BIESES (www.bieses.net).
17 Three participants are considered invalid, due to the young age of the supposed authors (Riquer: 563).
18 They are compiled in Mas's indices (*Academias valencianas*: 407, 415, 455, 492, 501, 505); on the corresponding tournaments, see Mas, *Academias y justas*.
19 For information on Madrid and Toledo, see Baranda: 220–222, 227–228.
20 For more details, see the corresponding files in BIESES.
21 Tournaments were even held in medium-sized communities: in a tournament held in Antequera, in 1636, there were up to five female participants (Molina: 132). See Cristobalina Fernández de Alarcón's case below.
22 To those in Osuna ("Cristobalina"), three compositions published by Molina (135–143) should be added. The remaining tournament poems are among those selected by Olivares and Boyce (441–475).
23 See Armon in this volume.
24 Domínguez Guzmán (46–50) emphasized conventual participation. Marín Pina ("Fuera") studies Aragonese cases, taking into consideration the connections with the outside world and events, the texts' pragmatic and editorial differences versus those written in the convent, and their contribution to the religious community's social visibility.
25 "De ninguna fembra se admitan versos, aunque sea monja, cuando no conste que trae licencia del ordinario para despachar semejantes estafetas, porque se quejan los justadores por claustro que la cortesía las prefiere."
26 "No se recibirá papel fuera del término, ni en nombre de dama, ni supuesto."
27 "Si escribieren algunas religiosas o señoras seglares, tengan entendido que, aunque se debe guardar particular decoro a sus nombres, se mirará más a los méritos de sus escritos. Y porque algunos escritores, desconfiados de sí mismos, suelen escribir a nombre de las tales señoras, para obligar con esto a los jueces a que les premien por ley de cortesía, se advierte que, en este caso, solamente se les darán guantes bien aderezados, en gracia de los autores fingidos."
28 On the warnings to titled noblewomen against public writing, see Baranda (*Cortejo*: 86–87).
29 "Ha escrito a los certámenes con grande acierto."
30 "Hombres insignes que florecieron."
31 "En muchas justas literarias, en las cuales casi siempre se le ha dado el primer premio."
32 "Admirados de tan alto y tan gallardo espíritu, le dieron siempre el primer lugar en los concursos y justas literarias, no a título de mujer, sino en consideración de su docta y elegante pluma."
33 For an important example, see BIESES.

Works cited

Academia burlesca que se hizo en Buen Retiro a la majestad de Filipo Cuarto el Grande. Año de 1637. Ed. María Teresa Julio. Madrid: Iberoamericana-Vervuert, 2007.

Acquier, Marie-Laure. "Le concours poétique de Saragosse sous l'égide de la comtesse d'Aranda (1617–1618): une médiatisation littéraire escamotée." *La médiatisation du littéraire dans l'Europe des XVIIe et XVIIIe siècles*. Ed. Florence Boulerie. Tübingen: Gunter Narr Verlag, 2013: 171–184.

Baranda, Nieves. "Notas para un cancionerillo de poetas cortesanas del siglo XVI." *Destiempos* 19 (2009): 8–27.

——. "Reflexiones en torno a una metodología para el estudio de las mujeres escritoras en justas del Siglo de Oro." *Memoria de la palabra. Actas del VI Congreso de la Asociación Internacional Siglo de Oro*. Vol. 1. Ed. María Luisa Lobato y Francisco Domínguez Matito. Madrid: Iberoamericana-Vervuert, 2004: 307–316.

——. *Cortejo a lo prohibido. Lectoras y escritoras en la España Moderna*. Madrid, Arco/Libros, 2005.

Bègue, Alain. *Las academias literarias en la segunda mitad del siglo XVII. Catálogo descriptivo de los impresos de la Biblioteca Nacional de España*. Madrid: Biblioteca Nacional, 2007.

Bergman, Hannah E. "El 'Juicio final de todos los poetas españoles muertos y vivos' (Ms. inédito) y el 'Certamen poético de 1638.'" *Boletín de la Real Academia Española* 55 (1975): 551–610.

Borreguero Beltrán, Cristina. "*Puellae doctae* en las cortes peninsulares." *Dossiers Feministes* 15 (2011): 76–100.

Brown, Kenneth. "Context i text del Vexamen d'Academia de Francesc Fontanella." *Llengua & Literatura* 2 (1987): 173–252.

——. "Aproximación a una teoría del *vejamen* de academia en castellano y catalán en los siglos XVII y XVIII: de las academias españolas a la Enciclopedia francesa." *De las academias a la Enciclopedia: el discurso del saber en la Modernidad*. Ed. Evangelina Rodríguez Cuadros. Valencia: Edicions Alfons el Magnànim, 1993: 225–262.

——. "María de Zayas y Sotomayor: Escribiendo poesía en Barcelona en época de guerra (1643)." *Dicenda* 11 (1993): 355–360.

Campo Guiral, María de los Ángeles. *Doña Ana Francisca Abarca de Bolea*. Zaragoza, Diputación General de Aragón, 1993.

Cañas Murillo, Jesús. "Corte y academias literarias en la España de Felipe IV." *Anuario de Estudios Filológicos* 35 (2012): 5–26.

Cara, Giovanni. *Il "vejamen" in Spagna. Juicio y regocijo letterario nella prima metà del XVII secolo*. Rome, Bulzoni, 2001.

Caro de Mallén, Ana. *Contexto de las reales fiestas que se hizieron en el Palacio del Buen Retiro a la coronación de Rey de romanos, y entrada en Madrid de la Señora Princesa de Cariñan. En tres discursos*. Madrid: Imprenta del Reino, 1637.

Carrasco Urgoiti, Soledad. "La oralidad del vejamen de academia." *Edad de Oro* 7 (1988): 49–57.

——. "Notas sobre el vejamen de academia en la segunda mitad del siglo XVII." *Revista Hispánica Moderna* 31 (1965): 97–111.

Cruz, Anne J. "Art of the State: The *academias literarias* as Sites of Symbolic Economies in Golden Age Spain." *Caliope* 1 (1995): 72–95.

Delgado, Juan. "Bibliografía sobre justas poéticas." *Edad de Oro* 7 (1988): 197–207.

Domínguez Guzmán, Aurora. "De monjas y poesía de ocasión en la España del Seiscientos." *La mujer y la transgresión de códigos en la Literatura Española: Escritura. Lectura. Textos (1001–2000)*. Ed. María José Porro Herrera. Córdoba: Universidad de Córdoba, 2001: 41–50.

Egido, Aurora. "Las academias literarias de Zaragoza en el siglo XVII." *La literatura en Aragón*. Ed. Manuel Alvar et al. Zaragoza: Caja de Ahorros y Monte de Piedad de Zaragoza, 1984: 101–128.

——. "Poesía de justas y academias." *Fronteras de la poesía en el Barroco*. Barcelona: Crítica, 1990: 115–137.

——. "Literatura efímera: oralidad y escritura en los certámenes y academias." *Fronteras de la poesía en el Barroco*. Barcelona: Crítica, 1990: 138–163.

Étienvre, Jean-Pierre. "Visages et profils féminins dans les *academias* littéraires du XVIIe siècle." *Images de la femme en Espagne aux XVIe et XVIIe siècles*. Ed. Augustin Redondo. Paris: Publications de la Sorbonne, 1994: 351–364.

Ferri Coll, José María. "Academias literarias." *Diccionario filológico de literatura española. Siglo XVII*. Ed. Pablo Jauralde Pou, Delia Gavela, and Pedro C. Rojo Alique. Vol. 2. Madrid: Castalia, 2010: 697–706.

Fontanella, Francesc. *La poesía de Francesc Fontanella*. Ed. Maria-Mercè Miró. Barcelona: Curial, 1995.

Julio, Teresa. "Vejamen de Alfonso de Batres para la Academia de 1638 (Manuscrito inédito). Estudio y edición crítica." *Revista de Literatura* 75, 149 (2013): 279–306.

King, Willard F. *Prosa novelística y academias literarias en el siglo XVII*. Madrid: RAE, 1967.

Lacadena y Calero, Esther. "El discurso oral en las academias del Siglo de Oro." *Criticón* 41 (1988): 87–102.

Marín Pina, María Carmen. "Fuera del convento: las monjas en las justas poéticas aragonesas del siglo XVII." *Destiempos* [forthcoming].

——. "Los certámenes poéticos aragoneses del siglo XVII como espacio literario de sociabilidad femenina." *Bulletin Hispanique* 115, 1 (2013): 145–163.

Mas i Usó, Pasqual. *Academias valencianas del barroco. Descripción y diccionario de poetas*. Kassel: Reichenberger, 1999.

——. *Academias y justas literarias en la Valencia barroca: teoría y práctica de una convención*. Kassel: Reichenberger, 1996.

Molina Huete, Belén. "Nuevas flores poéticas de Pedro Espinosa y Cristobalina Fernández de Alarcón: un reencuentro con olvidados poemas de certamen." *Analecta Malacitana* [*AnMal Electrónica*] 26 (2009): 123–145.

Olivares, Julián, and Elizabeth S. Boyce. *Tras el espejo la musa escribe. Lírica femenina de los Siglos de Oro*. Madrid: Siglo XXI, 1993.

Osuna, Inmaculada. "Cristobalina Fernández de Alarcón y la poesía de circunstancias." *Studies in Women's Poetry of the Golden Age. Tras el espejo la musa escribe*. Ed. Julián Olivares. Woodbridge: Tamesis, 2009: 123–148.

——. "Las justas poéticas en el siglo XVI." *El canon poético en el siglo XVI. VIII Encuentro Internacional sobre Poesía del Siglo de Oro*. Ed. Begoña López Bueno. Sevilla: Universidad de Sevilla, 2008: 257–295.

———. "Las justas poéticas en la primera mitad del siglo XVII." *El canon poético en el siglo XVII. IX Encuentro Internacional sobre Poesía del Siglo de Oro.* Ed. Begoña López Bueno. Sevilla: Universidad de Sevilla, 2010: 323–365.

———. "Poesía de proyección ciudadana en tres autoras del siglo XVII: Cristobalina Fernández de Alarcón, María de Rada e Isabel de Tapia." *Península. Revista de Estudos Ibéricos* 2 (2005): 237–250.

Pérez Priego, Miguel Ángel. *Poesía femenina en los cancioneros.* Madrid: Castalia, 1990.

Pítima contra la ociosidad. National Library of Spain Ms. 9396.

Riquer, Martín de. "Don Martín de Agullana y el torneo poético de Gerona de 1622." *Homenaje a José Manuel Blecua.* Madrid: Gredos, 1983: 553–564.

Robbins, Jeremy. *Love Poetry of the Literary Academies in the Reigns of Philip IV and Charles II.* London: Tamesis, 1997.

Romero-Díaz, Nieves. "Aproximaciones a la poesía secular escrita por mujeres, 1650–1700. Una propuesta metodológica." *Calíope* 18, 1 (2012): 102–126.

Sánchez, José. *Academias literarias del Siglo de Oro español.* Madrid: Gredos, 1961.

Zuese, Alicia R. "Ana Caro and the Literary Academies of Seventeenth-Century Spain." *Women's Literacy in Early Modern Spain and the New World.* Ed. Anne J. Cruz and Rosilie Hernández. Farnham, UK; Burlington, VT: Ashgate, 2011: 191–208.

11
NOVELS AND NARRATIVES

Shifra Armon

Early modern Spanish women's narrative has coalesced into a distinct field of critical inquiry in the twenty-first century thanks to three developments. First, "gynocriticism" increased awareness that Spain's "herstory" remained to be uncovered and told; second, the history of the novel in Spain expanded its scope to embrace popular genres that had been either denigrated or overlooked, such as the chivalric romance and the courtly novel; and, third, New Historicism, by admitting fiction into the ranks of allowable historical documentation, created the possibility of reading women's cultural history through the optic of women's literary production. As a result, what began in the 1980s as a modest interest in women's narrative activity in Spain has grown into a significant body of publications seeking to insert the voices of Renaissance and Baroque women writers into the literary history of Spain, the history of the European novel, and the history of gender.

Gynocriticism

Gynocriticism, or women-centered criticism, responds to the centuries of literary criticism that privileged a masculine paradigm of moral and aesthetic judgment. In *Feminist Criticism in the Wilderness* (1981), Elaine Showalter recognized that female culture—much like class and race—exerts a creative force on literature that merited closer scrutiny. Instead of trying to fit women "between the lines" of the male tradition, Showalter and other North American feminists advocated the project of constructing "a female framework for the analysis of women's literature, to develop new models based on the study of female experience, rather than to adapt male models and theories" ("Toward a Feminist Poetics": 131). Beth Miller's essay collection, *Women in Hispanic Literature: Icons and Fallen Idols* (1983) marked a watershed moment in Spanish Golden Age gynocriticism. *Icons* aimed to "read or reevaluate aspects of Hispanic literature" from an inclusive women's studies perspective (25). Six years later, Alison Weber edited a special issue of the *Journal of Hispanic Philology* (1989) that registered growing interest in women's conventual writing as well as a groundswell of indignation at the patriarchal paradigm that Golden Age literature perpetuated.

Feminist scholars found, in Manuel Serrano y Sanz's *Apuntes para una biblioteca de escritoras españolas* (Notes for a Library of Spanish Women Writers), a rich bibliographic sourcebook of biographic documentation and literary excerpts written by hundreds of women writers in Spain, from 1401 to 1833. Serrano y Sanz's *Apuntes*, published in 1903 and 1905, have been augmented by the BIESES (Bibliografía de Escritoras Españolas [Bibliography of Spanish Women Writers]) research project, an online database that continues to expand and maintains live links to many digitized editions of women's works. Five female authors of secular prose fiction have emerged from this first wave of scholarship: Beatriz Bernal (c. 1504–1584), María de Zayas y Sotomayor (c. 1590–c. 1647), Leonor de Meneses, who wrote under the pseudonym of Laura Mauricia (c.1620–c. 1664), Mariana de Carvajal y Saavedra (c. 1620–c. 1664), and Ana Francisca Abarca de Bolea (1602–c. 1687). Beatriz Bernal is credited with being the first woman known to compose a chivalric romance. Zayas, Meneses, Carvajal, and Abarca de Bolea also wrote popular fiction; their works represent variants of the narrative sub-genre of the *novela cortesana* (courtly novel), also called the *novela corta romántica* (short romantic novella). Overall, these five writers published thirty-six narratives: a chivalric romance, four framing plots, thirty embedded novellas, and a short novel.

    The first female-authored work of prose fiction recovered by feminist scholars thanks to Serrano y Sanz's *Apuntes* was Beatriz Bernal's *Historia de los invictos y magnánimos caballeros don Cristalián de España, príncipe de Trapisonda y del infante Lucescanio, su hermano, hijos del famosísimo emperador Lindedel de Trapisonda* (History of the Invincible and Generous Knights, don Cristalián of Spain, Prince of Trapisonda, and of his Royal Brother, Lucescanio, Sons of the Most Famous Emperor Lindedel of Trapisonda) (Valladolid, 1545). This romance of chivalry was published at the height of that genre's popularity. Bernal's narrative adheres to chivalric convention beginning with the "found manuscript" topos that purports to certify the authenticity of the text. *Cristalián* also features intertwined love plots embellished with mythological elements, giants, enchantments, and battle scenes.

    The second pair of recovered women's narratives was written by María de Zayas y Sotomayor. The most prolific and well-known of the four authors, Zayas penned two *novella* collections, the *Novelas amorosas y ejemplares* (Exemplary Tales of Love) (Zaragoza, 1637) and its continuation, the *Segunda parte del sarao y noches entretenidas* (Second Part of the Soirée and Entertaining Nights), also known as the *Desengaños amorosos* (Disenchantments of Love) (Zaragoza, 1647). Each novel gathers ten short stories interspersed with verse within a framing narrative after the manner of Boccaccio's *Decameron* (1353) or Marguerite of Navarre's *Heptaméron* (1558) that introduces the narrators and explains their motives for storytelling. In the *Novelas amorosas*, the pretext is a Christmas celebration convened to entertain a convalescing maiden named Lisis at her home. Narrative units in the *Novelas amorosas*, called *maravillas* (tales of wonder), are recited by both male and female guests at the soirée. Ten years later in historical time, but only one year later in story-time, Lisis and her new fiancé's betrothal celebration comprises the framing device for Zayas's *Segunda parte*, the *Desengaños amorosos* (1647). The third female Spanish novelist to be recovered became Portuguese by virtue of the Restoration of the Portuguese throne in 1640; Leonor de Meneses Noronha published her novella, *El desdeñado más firme* (Scorned but Steadfast) (1655) under the pseudonym of Laura Mauricia.[1] Neither the date nor place of publication can be reliably determined because the only known edition of the *Desdeñado* lacks this information. The volume's dedication page, dated Paris, 1655, gives the impression it may have been published around that date in Paris; however, this information has not been confirmed, and the novella may have been published in the Iberian Peninsula. Written in Spanish and set in Madrid, the *Desdeñado* eschews the frame-tale device favored by Zayas. Instead, Meneses's omniscient narrator weaves a four-part cloak-and-dagger intrigue in which two eligible and noble cousins of the same name (Lisis once again) live under the same roof. This situation generates most of the novel's decidedly theatrical plot complications. As suitors arrive to court the two cousins, mistaken identities, the motif of the *mujer esquiva* (disinterested or manly woman), and the conflict produced by an unwilling betrothal, result in an intricate, suspenseful, yet open-ended plot.

In 1663, Mariana de Carvajal returned to the narrative embedding technique favored by Zayas. Carvajal's *Navidades de Madrid y noches entretenidas* (Christmastide in Madrid and Entertaining Nights) distributes storytelling across eight days, from the Feast of the Nativity, December 25, through January 1. As in Zayas's novellas, a mutually energizing relationship between diegetic units and their extradiegetic cornice also characterizes the *Navidades de Madrid*. Carvajal's framing narrative portrays a group of eight aristocratic men and women who gather each evening to regale one another with stories of courtship and matrimony. The hosts are two widows, primed to find spouses for their respective son and daughter. The group's nightly gatherings provide fertile ground for courtship; by New Year's, three couples among the guests announce their engagements. As a post-script, a second party is convened to celebrate these triple marriages. Instead of storytelling, guests at the second soirée recite burlesque fables in verse.

The fifth secular narrative penned by a woman is Ana Francisca Abarca de Bolea's *Vigilia y Octavario de San Juan Bautista* (Vigil and Octave for the Feast of St. John the Baptist) (Zaragoza, 1679). The *Vigilia* traces a narrative arc similar to that of Zayas's *Novelas amorosas* and Carvajal's *Navidades de Madrid*. Abarca de Bolea's narrators assemble on June 23, the night before (Vigil) the Nativity of St. John the Baptist, and they continue to meet for eight successive days (Octave) of devotion and merrymaking. The *Vigilia* replaces the urban setting favored by Zayas and Carvajal with a pastoral *mise-en-scène*. Abarca de Bolea's narrators purport to be herdsmen and shepherdesses who gather in a wilderness encampment near an abandoned hermitage, but their wealth, erudition, and courtliness belie the novel's rustic façade.

Vindication of commercial prose fiction

As Amy Kaminsky has noted, "women writers may be celebrated in their time only to be deprived of their place in literary history by the architects of official culture" (10). This certainly holds true for María de Zayas and Ana Abarca de Bolea. Sales of Zayas's books outpaced those of every other contemporary novelist except for Cervantes, Quevedo, and Alemán (Amezúa *Novelas amorosas*: xxxi). Over ten editions of Zayas's works appeared in Spain in the seventeenth century alone. (Vollendorf, "No Doubt": 105). Zayas earned the admiration of such illustrious peers as Lope de Vega, Juan Pérez de Montalbán, Ana Caro de Mallén y Soto, and Alonso de Castillo Solórzano (Greer and Rhodes: 8). She was even "roasted" by Francesc Fontanella, who lampooned her in verse at a poetry competition held in Barcelona in 1643 (Greer; Rhodes: 10). Although insulting, Fontanella's *Vejamen* (Vexamen) clearly counted on Zayas's name recognition to achieve its impact. In France, Molière, Scarron, Beaumarchais, Prévost, Marivaux, and others borrowed freely from Zayas's narratives in the seventeenth and eighteenth centuries, often without attribution (Paun de García; Yllera: 94–99). Zayas also left her stamp on Aphra Behn in England (Romero-Díaz, "Aphra").

Abarca de Bolea achieved fame in Aragonese literary circles. She corresponded with Aragonese bibliophile and patron of the arts, Vicencio Juan de Lastanosa, and her poetry merited Baltasar Gracián's encomium in "Discourse XXXI" of the *Agudeza y arte de ingenio* (1648). Royal Chronicler Juan Francisco Andrés de Uztarroz celebrated Abarca de Bolea in the preliminaries to a Carmelite treatise in 1651 (Campo Guiral, *Doña Ana*: 88, 89). Ustarroz's unfinished *Aganipe de los cisnes aragoneses*, a long panegyric poem comparable to Lope's *Laurel de Apolo* (Apollo's Laurel Crown), likewise pays tribute her hagiographic writings (Campo Guiral, *Doña Ana*: 89).

Despite their prominence during their lifetime, Zayas and Abarca de Bolea had to wait until the twentieth and twenty-first centuries to regain reknown (Marín Pina and Baranda Leturio).

Recuperating women's writings has depended, in part, on reappraising the genres that they cultivated, the chivalric romance and the romantic novel. The chivalric romance began to attract renewed critical interest in the twentieth century thanks to Maxime Chevalier, Harvey Sharrer, Daniel Eisenberg, and María Carmen Marín Pina, among others. In addition, the *Centro de Estudios Cervantinos* in Alcalá de Henares began re-editing dozens of sixteenth-century Spanish romances of chivalry, making them available to scholars and readers worldwide. In 2001, the *Centro* published Lucía Megías's anthology of chivalric romance, which includes excerpts from *Cristalián de España*. The following year, the Universidad Autónoma of Madrid devoted a special issue of its scholarly journal *Edad de Oro* to books of chivalry. Today, the University of Zaragoza's online database CLARISEL provides a central archive and clearing house for the study of the chivalric romance in Spain, with twenty-five entries related to Beatriz Bernal alone. This reappraisal has allowed Bernal's *Cristalián de España* increased exposure and critical attention.

If books of chivalry mark an initial phase in the history of commercial fiction made possible by the advent of the printing press, the short romantic novel or courtship novel favored by María de Zayas, Mariana de Carvajal, Ana Abarca de Bolea, and, to a lesser extent, Leonor de Meneses, follow closely behind. Writing in 1929, Agustín González de Amezúa established a tripartite schema for defining the *novela cortesana*: urban setting, aristocratic characters, and an "erotically motivated" plot (González de Amezúa, *Formación y elementos*: 11, 12). This latter dubious distinction gave courtly novels an unsavory tinge that other genres—chivalric, Byzantine and pastoral romance, not to mention lyrical poetry in general—managed to escape. However, González de Amezúa may be seen to overstate the immoral aspects of courtship plots, and to underplay women's agency in the process of selecting a spouse. Instead, it can be useful to call attention to female characters' active involvement in the courtship process by recasting this genre as the courtship novel (Armon, *Picking*: 13). Further disadvantaging the sub-genre of the *novela cortesana*, whose practitioners also included prominent male novelists, among them Castillo Solórzano (c.1584–c.1648), Pérez de Montalbán (1602–1638), and José de Camerino (1595–c. 1665), was its commercial appeal. María de Zayas humorously alluded to the financial stakes involved in the recreational book trade in a second prologue to the *Novelas amorosas*, "Prólogo a un desapasionado" (Prologue to a Dispassionate Reader). There, the prologuist pokes fun at bookstore patrons too miserly to purchase the volumes they browse on the sly in the shop (163–165). Although Evangelina Rodríguez Cuadros and Marta Haro Cortés credit the courtly novel with offering seventeenth-century readers an authentic literature of consumption for private reading (35), the *novela cortesana*'s commercial aspirations have also made it an object of contempt for later critics. As Judith Whitenack and Gwyn Campbell caution, "Until recently, critics had scarcely taken any interest in the genre, largely because—like the *libros de caballerías* from the sixteenth century—such stories had been viewed as popular fiction of scant literary value" (*Zayas*: viii).

Finally, Cervantes's fame has tended to eclipse the achievements of other novelists of his age, even those who drew inspiration from him (Cruz, "Paratexts"). In his Prologue to the *Novelas ejemplares* (1613), Cervantes had claimed to be the first to write autochthonous short stories in Spain (19). In his twelve-novella collection, Cervantes departed from the frame-tale format and reduced the poetic material intercalated within each tale. Although few seventeenth-century novelists after Cervantes followed in his footsteps, such critics as González de Amezúa, in *Cervantes: Creador de la novela*, deem Cervantes's anthology format superior to the Boccaccian model favored by Zayas, Carvajal, and Abarca de Bolea.

Attendant upon the problem of over-privileging the *Novelas ejemplares*, of course, is the inescapable shadow cast by Cervantes's great two-part novel, *Don Quixote* (1605, 1615). The novel's success tends to distort the on-the-ground reality of a period that produced over fifty collections of short stories between 1605 and 1685 (Whitenack and Campbell: *Zayas*: 255), many of which continued to rely on framing devices to unify their narrative material. Among those scholars who cleared a path for serious research in the field of the *novela cortesana*, three especially warrant mention: Caroline Bourland, whose *The Short Story in Spain in the Seventeenth Century* (1927) pays particular homage to Carvajal's *Navidades de Madrid*; Evangelina Rodríguez Cuadros, whose *Novela corta marginada del siglo XVII español* (The Marginalized Short Story in Seventeenth–Century Spain) (1979) was followed in 1987 by the *Novelas amorosas de diversos ingenios del siglo XVII* (Romantic novellas by Various Wits of the Seventeenth Century); and Begoña Ripoll, whose *La novela barroca. Catálogo biobibliográfica:1620–1700* (The Baroque Novella. Bio-Bibliographic Catalogue 1620–1700) (1991) registers Zayas, Meneses, and Carvajal among thirty-two authors of Baroque novellas.

It is also useful to acknowledge the hybridity of narrative fiction in the seventeenth century. Captivity, shipwreck, and enslavement motifs associated with the Greek or Byzantine romance complicate plot in the fourth novella of Mariana de Carvajal's *Navidades de Madrid*, "El esclavo de su esclavo" (His Slave's Slave). Abarca de Bolea's *Vigilia* enacts a semblance of the pastoral, and Zayas's novels portray many roguish or picaresque characters as well as hagiographic topoi of martyrdom. Read on its own terms rather than dismissed as pulp fiction or measured against Cervantes's *oeuvre*, the courtship novel comes into focus as a pliable and protean literary form accommodating to seventeenth-century women's (and men's) aspirations and concerns.

New historicism

Followers of the critical approach pioneered by Stephen Greenblatt, called New Historicism, recognize the generative power of literature, its capacity not only to imitate life, but also to produce and reproduce concepts of truth and authority. Both romances of chivalry and courtship novels weave cultural patterns, codes of conduct, gender constraints, and anxieties regarding social status into the fabric of their plots. Instead of imposing extraneous aesthetic criteria, New Historicists might ask how a given text positions itself with respect to significant issues of its time or how it participates in the circulation of symbols of authority. For Nieves Romero Díaz, for example, the novella after Cervantes provided a space for Spain's new urban elite to reimagine its identity, and for women in that society to articulate a new position for themselves as well. Barbara Mujica demonstrates the rewards of reading Meneses, Zayas, and Carvajal as witnesses to changes that undermined early modern women's power. For instance, the Royal Decree of Toro (1505) limited Spanish noblewomen's inheritance rights, placing increasing pressure on families to provide handsome dowries for their daughters. These financial concerns are reflected in Carvajal's short stories (Mujica xliii). Shifra Armon links Zayas, Meneses, and Carvajal's fiction to the royal succession crisis that plagued both Philip IV and his heir Carlos II from 1646 to 1700. Marriage within a dynastic context, Armon argues, assumes political dimensions that are played out in courtship plots (*Picking*: 143–190). Marina Scordilis Brownlee situates María de Zayas at a key moment in the history of subjectivity: "[Zayas] reveals a new understanding of sex, gender, and their implications for subjectivity in a wealth of responses to the patriarchy and to its traditional prescriptions for female behavior" (35). Evangelina Rodríguez Cuadros and Marta Haro Cortés discern in the conflicts that impel Baroque women's plots an interrogation of that sign called "woman": "un mito cultural cambiante, sometido a presiones económicas, políticas y, por supuesto, ideológicas" (a changing cultural myth subject to economic, political and, of course, ideological pressures) (112). Lisa Vollendorf seeks in Zayas's violent imagery answers to the enigmatic question of her proto-feminism: "In looking to her representations of violence in conjunction with the overt didacticism of the texts, we can decipher Zayas's innovative, body-based feminism out of the most striking aspects—acerbic cultural criticism and graphic depictions of violence—that appear in her fiction" ("No Doubt": 106). Margaret Greer and Elizabeth Rhodes read the reiterative call for improving women's education in Zayas's novels through the dark glass of contemporary moralists' opposition to female learning. Against Huarte de San Juan's assertion in the *Examen de ingenios* (1575) that women's humoral composition made them unfit students, Zayas insisted that women's cold and damp temperament actually made them more qualified than men for intellectual pursuits (*Exemplary*: 160). These examples hint at the ongoing value of approaching early modern Spanish women's narratives as cultural constructs that participate in the creation of social value rather than as closed aesthetic objects.

Women authors of prose fiction

Beatriz Bernal

Beatriz de Bernal was perhaps not the first woman to publish a book of chivalry in Spain, but she was the first to be identified as such. The popular belief that the anonymous author of the first two books of the Palmerín cycle, *Palmerín de Oliva* (1511) and *Primaleón* (1512) was female has lately fallen from favor (Marín Pina, "Ciclo"). The two *Palmerín*s were extremely popular; they underwent an estimated ten successive editions each (Kaminsky: 85). For her part, Bernal withheld her signature on the first edition of *Cristalián de España* in 1545. The frontispiece does, however, indicate that the narrative was "corrected and emended" by a "lady from Valladolid" (BIESES).

The *Cristalián* met with unusual success, undergoing three subsequent releases: two anonymous translations into Italian (Venice 1558 and 1609) and a posthumous second Spanish edition (Alcalá de Henares 1587), which revealed that Beatriz Bernal was its author. The licensure arrangement for this edition granted Beatriz's daughter, Juana Bernal de Gatos, the right to collect the profits from sales of her mother's book.

Bernal's four-part *Historia de los invictos y magnánimos caballeros don Cristalián de España, príncipe de Trapisonda y del infante Lucescanio, su hermano, hijos del famosísimo emperador Lindedel de Trapisonda* relates the feats of Cristalián, Lucescanio, and their father, Lindedel, with help not only from spells and enchantments but also wise-women and the valiant female warrior, Minerva. The novel is set in a region called Trapisonda, a common toponym in the Amadís cycle, also mentioned in *Don Quixote* (I.1) and a possible reference to the ancient Byzantine state of Trebizond.

Bernal grants female characters a wide range of roles, beginning with the narrative of transmission that explains how the female narrator discovered the manuscript lying in a coffin set across a mummified corpse's feet. Donatella Gagliardi speculates that the warrior princess Minerva functions as an alter ego for the author because, "like her creator, she ventured into men's private domains (weaponry / the arts) not due to any need but to natural inclination" ("Beatriz Bernal", n. p.). Marín Pina credits Bernal with creating a new kind of violent fantasy in her chivalric romance by crossing hagiographic motifs of bodily torture on the one hand, and motifs of magic on the other ("Suplicio"). Cruz detects in the suffering of the damsel figure in the *Cristalián* a possible precursor to parallel horror scenes in Zayas ("Violence"). José Enrique Ruiz Domènec situates Bernal's treatment of women in *Cristalián* within a historic trajectory stretching from Martorell to Cervantes. Jodi Growitz's critical edition of Beatriz Bernal's *Cristalián de España* was released in 2015. The online CLARISEL database provides extensive additional documentary and critical resources for future scholarship on Beatriz Bernal and her work.

María de Zayas y Sotomayor

María de Zayas succeeded in publishing her first collection of ten novellas, the *Novelas amorosas y ejemplares* (*Exemplary Tales of Love*) in 1637. Zayas had prepared an earlier version comprised of eight novellas in 1626 called the *Tratado honesto y entretenido Sarao* (A Decent Treatise and Entertaining Soirée), but the Castile Royal Council's ban on licensing novels and plays, lifted in 1634, delayed its publication (Cruz, "Paratexts": 60). The *Novelas amorosas* embeds ten *maravillas* (tales of wonder) narrated by different guests for the purpose of entertaining one another, and particularly Lisis, at a Christmas *sarao* (soirée). On the first night, Lisis' cousin and rival, Lisarda, recites "Aventurarse perdiendo" (Everything Ventured) and Matilda recounts "La burlada Aminta y venganza de amor" (Aminta Deceived and Honor's Revenge). On night two, don Álvaro narrates both "El castigo de la miseria" (The Miser's Reward) and "El prevenido engañado" (Forewarned but not Forearmed). Two women hold forth on night three, Nise and Filis, with "La fuerza del amor" (The Power of Love) and "El desengaño amando y premio de la virtud" (Disillusionment in Love and Virtue Rewarded), respectively. Don Miguel recites "Al fin se paga todo" (Just Desserts) and don Lope tells the story of "El imposible vencido" (Triumph over the Impossible) on night four. Finally, Lisis' fickle suitor, aptly named Don Juan, recounts "El juez de su causa" (Judge Thyself), followed by Lisis' mother Laura with "El jardín engañoso" (The Magic Garden) on night five. The geographic settings for the novellas vary, but Spanish and Italian cities predominate, which has led to speculation that Zayas accompanied her father to Italy, from 1610–1616.

The "exemplarity" that Zayas's *Novelas amorosas* promises to impart links her collection to Cervantes' *Novelas ejemplares* (*Exemplary Novels*) (1613). Both texts exemplify good writing, and call attention to the moral failings of their characters (Cruz, "Cervantes"). Stylistically, Zayas's writings reflect the Baroque predilection for ornament, complexity, digression, and allusion. Zayas's layered narrative moves between an omniscient narrator and multiple storytellers who speak among themselves, critique one another's performances, and recite poetry that, at times, slyly reveals the speaker's hidden sentiments. The novellas themselves revel in chiaroscuro changes of fortune that seldom reward virtue or punish evil. For example, "El prevenido engañado" centers on Fadrique, who espies his fiancée, Serafina, secretly giving birth to a child whom she immediately abandons. His faith in women shattered, Fadrique leaves Granada in search of an innocent wife. After numerous sexual misadventures with wily women, he returns to Granada to wed Serafina's foundling, Gracia, who had been raised in the seclusion of a convent. However, due to her inexperience and gullibility, Gracia falls prey to another man. Racy, suspenseful, hyperbolic, and entertaining, Fadrique's quest ends with the equivocal conclusion that educated women are preferable to simpletons because at least they know enough to dissimulate in order to uphold their honor.

Julián Olivares's complete critical edition of Zayas's first novel (2000) offers an indispensable scholarly apparatus and bibliography. H. Patsy Boyer published a complete translation, the *Enchantments of Love* (1990), whose novella titles are used above. Greer and Rhodes translated four novellas and their framing narrative (2000).

Ten years passed before Zayas's sequel came to light in Zaragoza under the title of *Segunda Parte del sarao y noches entretenidas* (Second Part of the Soirée and Entertaining Nights). González de Amezúa abbreviated the title to *Desengaños amorosos* (*Disenchantments of Love*) for his 1950 edition, a title that is widely accepted today. Like the First Part, the Second Part takes place over five days, in this case, during the Carnival season preceding Lent. This seasonal shift prefigures the penitential aftermath of the second *sarao*, which concludes with Lisis exhorting her male listeners to take heed and mend their ways: "Y a los caballeros, por despedida suplico muden de intención y lenguaje con las mujeres" (And to the gentlemen, by way of farewell, I implore you to amend the way you approach and speak to women) (509). The 1734 Barcelona edition added the ten descriptive titles by which the individual *desengaños* are commonly known today: "La esclava de su amante" (Slave to Her Own Lover), "La más infame venganza" (Most Infamous Revenge), "El verdugo de su esposa" (His Wife's Executioner), "Tarde llega el desengaño" (Too Late Undeceived), "Amar sólo por vencer" (Love for the Sake of Conquest), "Mal presagio casar lejos," (Marriage Abroad: Portent of Doom), "El traidor contra su sangre" (Traitor to His Own Blood), "La perseguida triunfante" (Triumph Over Persecution), and "Estragos que causa el vicio" (The Ravages of Vice) (Boyer's title translations). The D*esengaños* takes explicit aim at those men who criticize, entrap, seduce, and abuse women without remorse. At the same time, they also expose many institutional and legal obstacles facing early modern women. For example, at age eighteen, orphaned doña Inés of "La inocencia castigada" has little choice but to reside with her brother and his hateful wife because women required male "protection" under the law. Marriage offers the semblance of an alternative, but, as the narrator of "Inocencia" (Lisis' mother, Laura) warns proleptically, "se halló, por salir de un cautiverio, puesta en otro martirio" (attempting to escape captivity, she found herself caught in another martyrdom) (265).

Zayas's fiction continues to animate critical debate and attract new readings. Vollendorf argues that Zayas was a proto-feminist; El Saffar compared the distractions, deferrals, and amplifications of the *Novelas amorosas y ejemplares* to Zayas's conduct as a writing woman who disrupted conventional patriarchal assumptions (1995), while Yllera deems Zayas's feminism to be conservative (48–52). Brownlee discloses parallels between Zayas's paradoxical discourse and postmodern aesthetics (2000). Fernando Rodríguez Mansilla reads doña Inés's blindness in "La inocencia castigada" as a rebuke of the intensely visual poetics of neo-Platonic love (2014). Rhodes highlights the aesthetic of corporeal violence that marks Zayas's tales (82), while Armon notes that the *Desengaños*' male perpetrators often die cataclysmically as well ("Twisting": 224). It is a tribute to the consolidation of Zayas's corpus within the Spanish literary canon that the number of studies, translations, anthologies, dissertations, and monographs devoted to this enigmatic writer makes it impractical to cite them all.

Leonor de Meneses Noronha

There is something intriguing and off-kilter about Leonor de Meneses's courtship novel *El desdeñado más firme* (Scorned but Steadfast) (1655). The only known edition of the novel was dedicated in Paris in 1655 without the usual preliminary licenses, approbations, encomiastic poetry, etc. Meneses dedicated the work to another Portuguese noblewoman and possible relative, doña María Luisa de Meneses, Countess of Portalegre and Marquise of Gouveia. Both the author and the dedicatee numbered among fourteen ladies-in-waiting to Queen Luisa of Portugal at the newly restored court of Lisbon in 1641 (Armon *Picking*: 163). Leonor, whose first husband was Count of Serêm, and whose second husband was Count of Atouguia, nonetheless addresses María Luisa as "Vuestra Excelencia" (Your Excellency) and shows her great deference in the Dedication. Why did Leonor choose to dedicate her novel in Paris, and why does the volume not disclose the publisher or place of publication? What was the author's strategy in selecting María Luisa, as her dedicatee and protector? Furthermore, why did she write under the pseudonym "Laura Mauricia"?

The novel's courtship entanglements can scarcely be called romantic. Lisis of Toledo cares nothing for men. The courtship of her cousin Lisis of Madrid with her would-be suitor Jacinto, rather than advancing, loses momentum as the narrative progresses. First Lisis of Madrid's tyrannical, yet oddly ineffectual father, don Felipe, rejects Jacinto in favor of a marquis in line for a grandeeship, and then her cousin, Luis de Palomeque, mistaking Jacinto for a rival, fatally shoots him. César, the scorned but steadfast suitor of the novel's title, confuses Lisis of Madrid with Lisis of Toledo, and begins pursuing the wrong maiden. However, once he learns the truth, César continues to blunder. One night, he inadvertently ends up in Lisis of Toledo's chambers. Unfazed, Lisis demands César's dagger, stabs him with it, and throws his body out of the window and into the street where he is carried away by a passing friend. In a final plot complication, Felipe agrees to a man-to-man swap: instead of marrying his daughter to the marquis, he gives her to his nephew, Luis, and promises his niece, Lisis of Toledo, to the up-and-coming marquis. The two Lisis have no say in the decision. However, the novel closes before the engagements are finalized.

Compared to Zayas's rousing and polemical narrator, the *Desdeñado*'s omniscient narrator remains aloof, leaving the reader to decide for herself whether to interpret Meneses's novel as tragedy, melodrama, or slapstick. The suitors remain almost as two-dimensional and undifferentiated as the two Lisis, whom they alternately confuse, shuffle, and exchange like cards in a deck. Armon suggests that the novel's entropic courtship plot represents an allegorized political screed aimed at Philip IV. If the *Desdeñado* were intended to lambaste the Spanish king, Philip IV, doña Leonor would have been wise to seek the protection of a powerful patron, the safety of a pseudonym, and the freedom of expression afforded by a publishing venue far from home (*Picking*: 162–173). Whitenack and Campbell agree that Meneses's motive for using a pseudonym may have been to dodge Spanish censors (*Desdeñado*: 1–14). At the same time, members of literary academies of the period commonly adopted pseudonyms,[2] and Rodríguez and Haro point to a growing body of evidence indicating that women writers in Italy and Spain acquired a more public platform for disseminating their writing by taking part in literary academies (66–71). Indeed, Meneses, Zayas, Carvajal, and Abarca de Bolea all justify the intercalation of poetry in their novels by staging literary celebrations at which guests exchange occasional poetry reminiscent of such gatherings. For example, in "Discourse One" of the *Desdeñado más firme*, César's friends try to cure his melancholy by reciting verses composed in artificial academic style.

In light of the novel's lack of a prologue or framing device, the seeming randomness of its plot complications, and its open-ended finale, Whitenack and Campbell remark that *El desdeñado más firme* "goes beyond popular entertainment to the subversion of generic conventions" (*Zayas*: 249). For Mujica, the novel's juxtaposition of the rhetoric of courtly love with the dystopic and cynical reality played out in the four Discourses of Meneses's plot "expone la vacuidad del ideal neoplatónico, que en el siglo XVII se ha transformado en una especie de religión sin núcleo espiritual" (expose the emptiness of the neo-Platonic ideal, which, by the seventeenth century had become a kind of cult lacking a spiritual core) (*Women Writers*: 327). Whitenack and Campbell's critical edition of the *Desdeñado más firme* (1994) has spurred the novel's inclusion in subsequent anthologies, notably Rodríguez and Haro (1999), Whitenack and Campbell (2000), and Mujica (2004).

Mariana de Carvajal y Saavedra

Mariana de Carvajal y Saavedra's *Navidades de Madrid y noches entretenidas en ocho novelas* (Christmastide in Madrid and Entertaining Nights in Eight Novellas) was published in 1663. It was reissued in 1728 with the addition of two novellas, "Lisarda y Ricardo" (Lisarda and Ricardo) and "Riesgo del mar y de amar" (Perils at Sea and in Love), which Begoña Ripoll attributes to Juan Pérez de Montalbán and Matías Aguirre del Pozo, respectively (47). The 1663 dedication raises critical issues because the dedication was signed by the publisher rather than by the author, suggesting that Carvajal did not take part in the final stages of the publication process (Beltrán; Martín Gómez: 35–44). The eight novellas recited from Christmas to New Year's begin with "La Venus de Ferrara" (The Venus of Ferrara), followed by "La dicha de Doristea" (Doristea's Good Fortune), "El amante venturoso" (The Lucky Lover), "El esclavo de su esclavo" (His Slave's Slave), "Quién bien obra siempre acierta" (Kindness Always Pays), "Celos vengan desprecios" (Jealousy Avenges Disdain), "La industria vence desdenes" (Effort Vanquishes Scorn), and conclude with "Amar sin saber a quién" (Her Mystery Lover) (Armon's title translations).

Carvajal's writing style is less ornate than Zayas's, and her narrators generally refrain from inserting evaluative glosses on the actions that they recount. As in Zayas's novellas, poetic interludes adorn both the cornice and the individual narratives. Noteworthy is the change of poetic tone following the eighth novella, when a second reunion is convened to celebrate the frame tale's triple weddings. Within this amatory context, the intercalated verse takes a turn toward the ribald, after the manner of burlesque poet Salvador Jacinto Polo de Medina (1603–1676) (Zavala: 258). Isabel Colón Calderón has identified Aragonese poet José Navarro as the author of five of these risqué compositions. The mood of the frame-tale is one of courtly conviviality as the narrators engage in lively conversation, laugh at one another's quips and antics, exchange gifts and glances, and savor the delicacies that accompany each recitation. Carvajal's frame narrators and diegetic characters alike perform elaborate courtesy rituals that serve to measure one another's social worth (Armon, "Romance"). For example, in "La Venus de Ferrara" a field of eligible noblemen compete for the future Duchess of Ferrara's hand in marriage. Arrayed in finery, the suitors present cards inscribed with individualized slogans to signify their devotion to Venus. Venus, her mother Floripa, and a trusted advisor scrutinize each card for evidence of the suitor's strength of character. Although the Duke of Modena arrives incognito, his is the only motto that makes a favorable impression. Not only does the Duke's card deliver an appropriate message of love and respect, it also stands out as the best poetic composition of the lot.

Satisfaction for Carvajal's protagonists has more to do with conservation of lineage than with personal preference. Nonetheless, the most agreeable suitor in the *Navidades*'s eight courtship plots always turns out to be the most wellborn. In that sense, the plot is predictable: the best couple always end up together. The question that Carvajal's novellas pose is invariably how her male and female characters arrive at their matrimonial destination given the intervening obstacles. Among the difficulties that must be surmounted to obtain the suitor of choice, the *Navidades* presents wealthier rivals ("Industria"), captivity ("Venus," "Esclavo"), isolation ("Amar"), importuning suitors ("Dicha," "Celos"), and rigid protocol ("Amante"). Eligible maidens and widows exercise a surprising degree of liberty in both the frame-tale and the novellas. As noted above, for example, both Floripa and her daughter Venus in "La Venus de Ferrara" find ways to take the initiative in choosing their respective husbands. For this reason, Maria Grazia Profeti ranked the *Navidades* ahead of Zayas's fiction in terms of women's autonomy (244–245).

This is a point on which Noël Valis disagrees. For Valis, "Carvajal, unlike María de Zayas, is no dissenter" (252–253). Similarly, Caroline Bourland considered Carvajal a "naïve" writer whose acceptance of the status quo licensed her to portray local color, and domestic settings with a keen and knowledgeable eye ("Aspectos": 331). However, Louis Imperiale detects a "silent revolution" in Carvajal's non-combative novel that "presents an alternative vision of women to that found in patriarchal texts, since literary images can liberate the multiplicity of women's lives and characters in ways that the power-based language and assumptions of official records cannot, and would not do" (230). Maria Grazia Profeti, Evangelina Rodríguez Cuadros, and Marta Haro Cortés uncover a nascent bourgeois sensibility at work in Carvajal's narrative. "La industria vence desdenes," for example, depicts a noble family impoverished by gambling that renews itself when the heir, don Pedro, foregoes his inheritance and commodifies his artistic talent to ensure that his sister, doña Beatriz, attain a suitable match (103). For Moisés Martín Gómez, Carvajal's materialistic preoccupation responds to a new readership, that of a "nobleza de segunda fila con ciertos rasgos pseudo-burugeses" (a second-rate nobility with certain pseudo-bourgeois features) (56).

Three complete critical editions of the *Navidades* are available: Julio Jiménez's unpublished dissertation (1974); the editions by Antonella Prato (with an introduction by Maria Grazia Profeti [1988]); and Catherine Soriano (1993), respectively. Rodríguez and Haro anthologize three novellas (1999) and Whitenack and Campbell anthologize three. Martín Gómez provides a useful critical overview and bibliography of Carvajal criticism to 2003.

Ana Francisca Abarca de Bolea

By the time Francisca Bernarda Abarca y Vilanova arranged for the publication of her aunt, Ana Abarca de Bolea's novel, the *Vigilia y Octavario de San Juan Bautista* (Vigil and Octave of St. John the Baptist) in 1679, the Aragonese nun, poet, religious chronicler—and now novelist—was seventy-seven years of age. Numerous references in the novel's front matter indicate that doña Ana had written the *Vigilia* much earlier, but that it had remained hidden. The work was edited by Baltasar Vicente de Alhambra, a nobleman of Zaragoza, who dedicated the volume to the author's great-nephew, Bernardo de Bolea, third Marquis de Torres and Royal Equerry (Stable Master) to Philip IV.

Ostensibly a pastoral novel, the action in *Vigilia y Octavario* nonetheless attaches its bucolic *locus amoenus* to a precise geographic spot, the Sierras de Moncayo. The topographic exactitude contrasts with the idealized settings of much classical pastoral, and its religious, rather than pagan underpinnings further call into question the novel's pastoral pretenses. The Moncayo massif, or white-haired mountains, so named for their perennially snow-capped peaks that rise over the city of Zaragoza, as the *Vigilia*'s omniscient narrator explains, "dividía los fieles reinos de Aragón y Castilla" (separated the loyal realms of Aragon and Castile; 47). To its north lies the autonomous region and former kingdom of Navarra, from which doña Ana's father claimed direct descent. The transition of pastoral *mise-en-scène* to wilder settings is consistent with a Baroque aesthetic already visible in *Don Quixote*'s Sierra Morena (1605) and in Shakespeare's *As You Like It* (1623), whose shivering and malnourished shepherds nearly perish in a frozen and labyrinthine Forest of Arden.

Ana Francisca Abarca de Bolea populates her festive frame-tale with accomplished courtier-shepherds described as *ricos ganadores*, *mayorales*, and *rabadanes* (wealthy cattlemen, master-shepherds, and overseers). A group of simpler yet graceful shepherds accompanies them, providing picturesque folksongs and country dances. Completing the cast of characters in the frame-tale is the Prior of the Order of St. John who offers mass every day, and two Aragonese knights who compete in the bullfights held on Day Three: don Luis Abarca and don Juan de Castro. They return with another knight and a Church Canon on Day Five. Beyond these superficial distinctions, the characters generally do not individuate or develop unique personalities; rather, their voices resolve into a pleasing and intricate whole. Since it was common poetical practice to disguise contemporary court personalities in shepherd's garb, Willard King has speculated that the *Vigilia* functioned as a *roman à clef* abounding in thinly veiled historical figures (123). For example, Ana's father's name was Luis Abarca de Bolea, and the surname "Castro" appears in the author's genealogy. Campo Guiral conjectures that the Church Canon of Day Five might be linked to the author's good friend, Manuel de Salinas y Lizana, Canon of the Cathedral of Huesca (lxix n.114). She also discerns a possible connection between the shepherdess Anarda and the author (lxxi).

The *Vigilia* satisfies Baroque demands for *varietas* and *admiratio*, variety and wonder, by admixing pastoral, religious, historical, and courtly elements in an unexpected fashion that today might be considered postmodern. The Dominican friar, Francisco Sobrecasa, who certified that the *Vigilia* did not run afoul of Church dogma, praised the novel for having "una hermosa variedad, una dulce y erudita diversión, en que a un tiempo deleita, aprovecha y enseña, mezclando la sal de honesto donaire con la vianda provechosa de otras liciones" (an attractive variety, a sweet and erudite amusement that at once delights, profits and instructs, salting the nourishing substance of its lessons with honest wit) (15). Abarca de Bolea enhances the variety of her composition by including a wide range of poetic forms, a contest of wits in defense of the number seven, a joke session based largely on Latin–Spanish puns, and two novels, "Apólogo de la ventura en la desdicha" (Apology for Good Fortune Amid Bad) and "Novela del fin bueno en mal principio" (Novel of the Unforeseen Happy Ending). The framing narrative that describes the shepherds' ludic and devotional activities constitutes a further narrative element. The *Vigilia*'s combination of longer and shorter narratives recalls Lucas Gracián Dantisco's advice in his popular courtesy handbook, the *Galateo español* (c. 1583). Gracián Dantisco urged gentlemen to gain favor at court by cultivating not only the art of telling brief witty anecdotes, but also by adding quips and extended narratives to their *portmanteau* of courtly attainments.

The omniscient narrator of the novel explains that the eight days celebrating John the Baptist's birth provide the occasion for the novel's festive structure: "En éste, pues, si rústico, apacible albergue, celebraba la devoción de sus habitadores la fiesta de aquel divino Niño, precursor [. . .] Juan divino." (In this pleasant, if rustic, refuge the inhabitants used to celebrate their devotion to that divine Child, the Forerunner [. . .] the divine John). The holiday falls near the summer solstice, or "Midsummer's Night," a pre-Christian fertility festival charged with carnivalesque and sensual energies. Faint vestiges of Midsummer persist in the *Vigilia*: the shepherds, in addition to attending mass and reciting devotional poems, decorate the hermitage of St. John with flowers, play music, entertain one another with song, dance, and merry processions, and enjoy banquets, masquerades, games, and contests. They even decamp on day three to make a pilgrimage to the Sanctuary of the Virgin where they watch twin bullfights, one dignified by noble contestants, the other parodied by rubes. Two pair of characters who meet during the *Octavario* do become engaged, but, in defiance of both pastoral convention and the suggestive setting of St. John's Eve, Abarca de Bolea drains this development of romantic effect. In fact, the primary purpose of the double engagement seems to be merely to justify promising a continuation of the festivities at the marriage celebration.

Without doubt, Abarca de Bolea's two interpolated novels provide the most magical and erotic amusements of her Midsummer's Vigil. The first novel, "La ventura en la desdicha" (Good Fortune amid Bad), is recited by a shepherd named Mileno, host and organizer of the *Vigilia*, to round out night three's celebration. Magical elements—a gold ring that yields silk and fine linens, a purse that provides endless riches, a self-replenishing jewelry box, magical apples and figs—harmonize with John the Baptist's miraculous power in this exotic folktale. Lisardo is the impetuous protagonist who loses his family's magic objects one by one to a dissimulating woman named Florisbella. Lisardo's revenge on Florisbella for her cruel tricks, and the restitution of his family's fortunes, hinge on a magic apple and fig trees provided by St. John during Lisardo's penance in the wilderness. At the site of the magical trees, Lisardo founds a temple and a hospital dedicated to St. John. Nearby, a repentant Florisbella establishes a school for boys, a school for girls, and a convent of the same order. Looping and episodic, "La ventura" maintains a driving pace by charting Lisardo's dogged persistence in the face of Florisbella's humiliating swindles, a persistence that leads both characters, finally, to salvation.

The second narrative, "El fin bueno en mal principio," is recited in gratitude for the sonnet that preceded it. Much of the conflict in this romance stems from competition for inheritance rights between a noble Portuguese widow, Juana, and her marriageable son Fulgencio. Fulgencio and his friend Lisardo drift away from courting two virtuous women, Clara and Francisca, only to fall into the clutches of two evil women who subject the men to a series of sadistic deceptions. However, as promised in the novella's title, bad beginnings end well. The two friends finally realize their error and return to marry Clara and Francisca. As a sign of their repentance, they donate much of their wealth to the poor and to the Order of St. Bernard (Cistercians), to which the author belonged. "El fin bueno en mal principio" intercalates several remarkably profane occasional poems, including a *lira* that praises a lady with measles for acquiring the beauty of mottled marble (311–312) and a *seguidilla* that compares God to a sultan, nuns to his wives, and convents to a seraglios (329–330). Such poetry typified the *academias literarias* (literary academies) to which Abarca de Bolea is known to have contributed (Campo Guiral, *Vigilia*: xlv).

As a nun, doña Ana's life was well documented; in fact, we know more about her activities as abbess, writer, poet, and novelist than we do about Bernal, Zayas, Carvajal, or Meneses. Two indispensable resources for approaching the study of the *Vigilia* are María Ángeles Campo Guiral's exhaustive introduction to her critical edition of the novel (1994) and a second volume by the same author entitled *Doña Ana Francisca Abarca de Bolea*, which documents many aspects of the author's biography and her trajectory as a writer. Of "El fin bueno en mal principio," Willard King complained that the author cribbed the novella from *Aviso IV* (Warning IV) of Matías de los Reyes's *El curial del parnaso* (The Tribunal of Parnassus), published in 1624 and reissued in 1640 (122). After conducting a comparative analysis, Campo Guiral concludes that Abarca de Bolea borrowed certain plotting elements from Matías de los Reyes "parcialmente con un tratamiento escueto dentro de una novela de mayor complejidad argumental" (partially, with a cursory treatment, within a novel of greater narrative complexity) (xc). Whitenack and Campbell include both "La ventura en la desdicha" and "El fin bueno en mal principio." They note Abarca de Bolea's reworking of folk motifs and her defense of virtuous over evil women (*Zayas*: 356–358).

Directions for future scholarship

Beatriz Bernal, María de Zayas, Leonor de Meneses, Mariana de Carvajal, and Ana Abarca de Bolea operated within a complex matrix of literacy (Cruz and Hernández). Early modern women not only "read over men's shoulders" (Cruz, "Reading") and accepted book dedications (Baranda Leturio), but also, at times, succeeded in closing the communicative circuit by composing and publishing prose narratives of their own. Do these five authors complete the canon of early modern women novelists? It is not only hoped, but expected that future archival scholarship in Spain, Portugal, and their colonial territories will bring additional women's secular prose fiction to light. Paradoxically, convent archives promise to contribute to this search as well, for, as Marín Pina and Baranda Leturio recognize, religious women also composed works of theater, poetry, and fiction that seldom made it into print ("Universo": 21). Meanwhile, the mutually profitable tasks of recognizing female authors as cultural producers, on the one hand, and of reading women's prose fiction through the optic of early modern culture, on the other, are well underway. For example, the essays that Albers, Gumbrecht, and Felten have assembled link Zayas's writing to contemporaneous discourses of gender, medicine, authorship, and honor. However, more research on, and analysis of, the socio-historical context of women's literary production is needed. Our understanding of Ana Abarca de Bolea's interpolated novellas, for example, would benefit considerably if compared to the writings of María do Céu or other religious works. Similarly, new readings of the poems inserted in these novellas might be gleaned by studying them individually, and as part of the poetry produced within academic circles. Future scholarship will doubtless also build on existing comparative studies by Brink, Martínez Girón, Paun de García, and Romero-Díaz, who discern points of contact between Zayas and Madame de Sévigné, Madame de Lafayette, and Aphra Behn, as well as with other male authors. Finally, as Marín Pina and Baranda Leturio write with respect to the database BIESES, the digital humanities also promise to play an increasingly vital role in understanding and tracking women's literary activity in early modern Spain.

Notes

1. See the discussion on transnational women writers in Baranda Leturio in this volume.
2. On women's participation in literary academies, see Osuna Rodríguez in this volume.

Works cited

Abarca de Bolea, Ana Francisca. *Vigilia y Octavario de San Juan Baptista*. Ed. María Ángeles Campo Guiral. Huesca: Instituto de Estudios Altoaragoneses, 1994.

Albers, Irene, Uta Felten, and Hans U. Gumbrecht, eds. *Escenas de transgresión: María de Zayas en su contexto literario-cultural*. Madrid: Iberoamericana, 2009.

Antonio, Nicolás. *Bibliotheca hispana sive Hispanorvm*. Rome, 1672.

Armon, Shifra. *Picking Wedlock: Women and the Courtship Novel in Spain*. Lanham, MD: Rowman and Littlefield, 2002.

——. "The Romance of Courtesy: Mariana de Caravajal's *Navidades de Madrid*." *Revista Canadiense de Estudios Hispánicos* 19.2. (1995): 241–261.

——. "Twisting the Trope: Refiguring the Work of Wedlock in Baroque Spanish Women's Writing." *Perspectives on Early Modern Women in Iberia and the Americas: Studies in Law, Society, Art and Literature in Honor of Anne J. Cruz*. Ed. María Cristina Quintero and Adrienne Martín. Burlington, VT: Escribana Books, 2015: 220–234.

——. "Women and the *novela de cortejo*." *Zayas and Her Sisters 2*. Ed. Judith Whitenack and Gwyn Campbell. Binghamton, NY: Global Publications, 2001: 141–158.

Baranda Leturio, Nieves. "Women's Reading Habits: Book Dedications to Female Patrons in Early Modern Spain." *Women's Literacy in Spain and the New World*. Ed. Anne J. Cruz and Rosilie Hernández, Burlington, VT: Ashgate, 2011: 19–40.

Baranda Leturio, Nieves and María Carmen Marín Pina. "El universo de la escritura conventual femenina: Deslindes y perspectivas." *Letras en la celda: Cultura escrita de los conventos femeninos en la España moderna*. Ed. Nieves Baranda Leturio and María Carmen Marín Pina. Madrid: Iberoamericana, 2014: 11–48.

Beltrán, Pilar. "Problemas de edición en las *Navidades de Madrid y noches entretenidas* de Mariana de Caravajal." *Actas del Primer Congreso de Jóvenes Filólogos*. La Coruña: Universidad de La Coruña, 1998: 103–111.

Bernal, Beatriz. *Cristalián de España*. Ed. Jodi Growitz. Newark, DE: Juan de la Cuesta, 2015.

Bourland, Caroline. "Aspectos de la vida del hogar en el siglo XVII según las novelas de doña Mariana de Carvajal y Saavedra." *Homenaje ofrecido a Menéndez Pidal*. 3 vols. Madrid, Hernando, 1925. 2: 331–368.

——. *The Short Story in Spain in the Seventeenth Century*. NY: Lenox Hill, 1973.

Brink, Margot. "'No es trágico fin, sino el más felice que se pudo dar.' Renuncia y amor en las novelas de María de Zayas y Marie-Madeleine de Lafayette." *Escenas de transgresión: María de Zayas en su contexto literario-cultural*. Ed. Irene Albers, Irene, Uta Felten, and Hans U. Gumbrecht. Madrid: Iberoamericana, 2009: 225–239.

Brownlee, Marina S. *The Cultural Labyrinth of María de Zayas*. Philadelphia: U Pennsylvania P, 2000.

Campo Guiral, María Ángeles. *Doña Ana Francisca Abarca de Bolea*. Zaragoza: Gobierno de Aragón, 1993.

Carvajal y Saavedra, Mariana de. *Navidades de Madrid y noches entretenidas*. Ed. Catherine Soriano. Madrid: Comunidad de Madrid, 1993.

Cátedra, Pedro, and Anastasio Rojo. *Bibliotecas y lecturas de mujeres. Siglo XVI.* Salamanca: Instituto de Historia del Libro y de la Lectura, 2004.

Cervantes, Miguel de. *Novelas ejemplares.* Ed. Jorge García López. Barcelona: Crítica, 2001.

Chevalier, Maxime. *Lectura y lectores en la España de los siglos XVI y XVII.* Madrid: Turner, 1976.

CLARISEL: Bases de datos bibliográficos. Ed. Juan Manuel Cacho Blecua and María Jesús Lacarra. Zaragoza: The University of Zaragoza. http://clarisel.unizar.es/

Colón Calderón, Isabel. "Sobre un plagio de Mariana de Carvajal." *Dicenda: Cuadernos de Filología Hispánica* 18 (2000): 397–402.

Cruz, Anne J. "Cervantes, Zayas, and the Seven Deadly Sins." *Representing Women's Authority in the Early Modern World: Struggles, Strategies, and Morality.* Ed. Eavan O'Brien. Rome: Aracne, 2013: 59–91.

——. "Paratexts and Gender Ideology: On the Front Matter in the Novels by Cervantes and María de Zayas." *Paratesto: Rivista Internazionale* 11 (2014): 51–67.

——. "Reading over Men's Shoulders: Noblewomen's Literary Practices in Early Modern Spain." *Women's Literacy in Spain and the New World.* Ed. Anne J. Cruz and Rosilie Hernández, Burlington, VT: Ashgate, 2011: 41–58.

——. "Violence Repeated: Zayas, the Pleasure Principle, and Beyond." *Studi Ispanici* 40 (2015): 11–22.

Cruz, Anne J., and Rosilie Hernández, eds. *Women's Literacy in Spain and the New World.* Burlington, VT: Ashgate, 2011.

De Armas, Frederick A. *The Invisible Mistress: Aspects of Feminism and Fantasy in the Golden Age.* Charlottesville: Biblioteca Siglo de Oro, 1976.

Eisenberg, Daniel. *Castilian Romances of Chivalry in the Sixteenth Century: A Bibliography.* London: Grant & Cutler, 1979.

——. *Romances of Chivalry in the Spanish Golden Age.* Newark, DE: Juan de la Cuesta, 1982.

Eisenberg, Daniel, and María Carmen Marín Pina. *Bibliografía de los libros de caballerías castellanos,* Zaragoza: Prensas Universitarias de Zaragoza, 2000.

El Saffar, Ruth. "Ana/Lisis/Zayas: Reflections on Courtship and Literary Women in María de Zayas's *Novelas amorosas y ejemplares.*" *María De Zayas: The Dynamics of Discourse.* Ed. Amy Williamsen and Judith Whitenack. Cranbury, NJ: Associated UP, 1995: 192–216.

Gagliardi, Donatella. "Beatriz Bernal: Spanish Author, ca. 1504–ca. 1563." *The Women Writers' Networks Website:* October 2011.

——. "*Quid puellae cum armis?*" Una aproximación a doña Beatriz Bernal y a su Cristalián de España. Bellaterra: Universitat Autònoma de Barcelona, 2004.

——. *Urdiendo ficciones. Beatriz Bernal autora de caballerías en la España del XVI.* Zaragoza: Prensas Universitarias de Zaragoza, 2010.

González de Amezúa y Mayo, Agustín, ed. *Cervantes: Creador de la novela corta española: Introduccion a las Novelas ejemplares.* Madrid: Consejo Superior de Investigaciones Cientificas, 1956.

Gracián, Baltasar. *Agudeza y arte de ingenio.* Ed. Aurora Egido. Zaragoza: Institución Fernando el Católico, 2007.

Greenblatt, Stephen. *Renaissance Self-Fashioning: From More to Shakespeare.* Chicago: U Chicago P, 1980.

Greer, Margaret and Elizabeth Rhodes, eds. "Introduction." *Exemplary Tales of Love and Tales of Disillusion.* By María de Zayas. Ed. and trans. Margaret Greer and Elizabeth Rhodes. Chicago: U Chicago P, 2009.

Imperiale, Luis. "Women of the World and the World of Women in the Narrative of Mariana de Carvajal." *Women in the Discourse of Early Modern Spain.* Ed. Joan Cammarata. Gainesville: UP Florida, 1993: 213–234.

Jiménez, Julio. "Mariana de Carvajal: *Navidades de Madrid y noches entretenidas en ocho novelas.*" Unpublished Ph.D. dissertation. Northwestern University, 1974.

Kaminsky, Amy, ed. *Water Lilies: Flores del agua: An Anthology of Spanish Women Writers from the Fifteenth Through the Nineteenth Century.* Minneapolis: U Minnesota P, 1996.

King, Willard. *Prosa novelística y académica en el siglo XVII.* Madrid: Anejos de la RAE, 1963.

Lucía Megías, José Manuel., ed. *Libros de caballerías textos y contextos. Edad de Oro* 21 (2002).

Marín Pina, María Carmen. "El ciclo español de los *Palmerines.*" *Voz y letra: Revista de Literatura* 7.2 (1996): 3–28.

——. "Los motivos del suplicio en el *Cristalian de España* de Beatriz Bernal." *Revista de Poética Medieval* 26 (2012): 217–236.

Marín Pina, María Carmen and Nieves Baranda Leturio. "Bibliografía de escritoras españolas (Edad Media-Siglo XVIII): Una base de datos." *Actas del VII Congreso de la Asociación Internacional Siglo de Oro.* Ed. Anthony Close. Madrid: Iberoamericana, 2006: 425–435.

Martín Gómez, Moisés. *Mariana de Carvajal: "Industrias y desdenes": Un estudio de las "Navidades de Madrid."* Cádiz: Universidad de Cádiz, 2003.

Martínez Girón, María José. "Dos feministas *avant la lettre*: María de Zayas Sotomayor y Madame de Sévigné." *Océanide* (2010). http://oceanide.netne.net/articulos/art2-7.php

Meneses, Leonor. *El desdeñado más firme: Primera parte.* Ed. Judith Whitenack and Gwyn Campbell. Potomac, MD: Scripta Humanistica, 1994.

Miller, Beth K., ed. *Women in Hispanic Literature: Icons and Fallen Idols.* Berkeley: U California P, 1983.

Mujica, Barbara, ed. *Women Writers of Early Modern Spain: Sophia's Daughters.* New Haven: Yale UP, 2004.

Profeti, Maria Grazia. "Introduction." *Navidades de Madrid y noches entretenidas.* Ed. Antonella Prato. Milan: Franco Angeli, 1988.

Rhodes, Elizabeth. *Dressed to Kill: Death and Meaning in Zayas's* Desengaños. Toronto: U Toronto P, 2011.

Ripoll, Begoña. *La novela barroca: Catálogo biobibliográfico: 1620–1700.* Salamanca: Universidad de Salamanca, 1991.

Rodríguez Cuadros, Evangelina and María Haro Cortés, eds. *Entre la rueca y la pluma: Novela de mujeres en el Barroco.* Madrid: Biblioteca Nueva, 1999.

Rodríguez Cuadros, Evangelina, ed. *Novelas amorosas de diversos ingenios del siglo XVII.* Madrid: Castalia, 1987.

Rodríguez Mansilla, Fernando. "Génesis y poética narrativa del 'Desengaño quinto' (o 'La inocencia castigada') de María de Zayas." *Modern Language Notes* 129.2 (March 2014): 255–268.

Romero-Díaz, Nieves. "Aphra Behn y María de Zayas: En busca de una tradición (im)propia." *Hispanic Journal* 29.1 (2008): 23–36.

———. *Nueva nobleza, nueva novela: Reescribiendo la cultura urbana del Barroco.* Newark, DE: Juan de la Cuesta, 2002.

Ruiz Domènec, José Enrique. "Los placeres secretos de Beatriz Bernal." *El despertar de las mujeres. La mirada femenina en la Edad Media,* Ed. José Enrique Ruiz Domènec. Barcelona: Península, 1999, 322–332.

Serrano y Sanz, Manuel. *Apuntes para una biblioteca de escritoras españolas.* 2 vols. Madrid: Sucesores de Rivadeneyra, 1903.

Sharrer, Harvey. *A Critical Bibliography of Hispanic Arthurian Material.* London: Grant & Cutler, 1977.

Showalter, Elaine. "Feminist Criticism in the Wilderness." *Critical Inquiry* 8.2 (Winter, 1981): 179–205.

———. "Toward a Feminist Poetics." *The New Feminist Criticism: Essays on Women, Literature and Theory.* Ed. Elaine Showalter. London: Virago, 1986: 125–143.

Valis, Noël. "The Spanish Storyteller: Mariana de Caravajal." *Women Writers of the Seventeenth Century.* Ed. Katharina Wilson and Frank Warnke. Athens. GA: U Georgia P, 1989: 251–282.

Vollendorf, Lisa, ed. *Recovering Spain's Feminist Tradition.* New York: Modern Language Association of America, 2001.

———. "'No Doubt it will Amaze You': María de Zayas's Early Modern Feminism." *Recovering Spain's Feminist Tradition.* Ed. Lisa Vollendorf. New York: Modern Language Association of America, 2001: 103–120.

Weber, Alison, ed. *Feminist Topics.* Special Issue of *Journal of Hispanic Philology* 13. 3 (1989).

Whitenack, Judith, and Gwyn Campbell, eds. *Zayas and her Sisters: An Anthology of Novelas by Seventeenth-Century Spanish Women.* Asheville, NC: Pegasus, 2000.

———. *Zayas and Her Sisters 2.* Binghamton, NY: Global Publications, 2001.

Williamson, Amy. "Challenging the Code: Honor in María de Zayas." *María de Zayas: The Dynamics of Discourse.* Ed. Amy Williamsen and Judith Whitenack. Cranbury, NJ: Associated UP, 1995: 133–151.

Zavala, Iris Zapata. *Breve historia feminista de la literatura española (en lengua castellana): Desde la Edad Media hasta el siglo XVIII.* Barcelona: Anthropos, 1997.

Zayas, María de. *Desengaños amorosos: Parte segunda del sarao y entretenimiento honesto.* Ed. Agustín González de Amezúa y Mayo. Madrid: Aldus, 1950.

———. *The Disenchantments of Love.* Trans. H. Patsy Boyer. Albany: State U New York P, 1997.

Novels and narratives

——. *The Enchantments of Love: Amorous and Exemplary Novels*. Trans. H. Patsy Boyer. Berkeley: U California P, 1990.
——. *Novelas amorosas y ejemplares*. Ed. Agustín González de Amezúa y Mayo. Madrid: Aldus, 1948.
——. *Novelas amorosas y ejemplares*. Ed. Julián Olivares. Madrid: Cátedra, 2000.
——. *Parte segunda del sarao y entretenimiento honesto: Desengaños amorosos*. Ed. Alicia Yllera. Madrid: Cátedra, 1993.

12
WOMEN PLAYWRIGHTS

Amy R. Williamsen

> Solo en esto de poetas hay notable novedad
> por innumerables, tanto que quieren poetizar
> las mujeres, y se atreven a hacer comedias ya.
>
> (The only noteworthy news regarding poets—they've become so numerous that even women want to versify and they now dare to write plays.)
>
> Ana Caro, Valor, agravio y mujer

Over the past twenty years, our critical landscape has changed dramatically, especially in the field that was once best known as Golden Age theater. As a result of intensive scholarly and artistic engagement with the works of early modern female dramatists writing in Spanish, this area of study has begun to flourish. In archives, at conferences, in print, and on the stage, research and production have yielded new insights that serve as catalysts for further inquiry. Only a few decades after *La traición en la amistad* (Friendship Betrayed) was rescued from relative obscurity,[1] an article appeared in *Hispanic Review* proclaiming María de Zayas's *comedia* "a truly canonical play" (Bayliss: 1). Yet the crucial contributions of Zayas and others had been overlooked for centuries. In her 1992 study of Spanish *dramaturgas*, Urszula Asyzk underscores this critical oversight: "Female dramaturgy remains virtually unnoticed in the works of the most distinguished historians of literature and the theater, easily leading to the conclusion that in the entire history of Spanish dramatic literature, the plays written by women had minimal importance" (129).[2]

While much critical activity tends to center on a few major figures, in his fundamental study of the dramatic structure of the *comedia*[3] and minor dramatists, including a chapter devoted to Mexican playwright and poet Sor Juana Inés de la Cruz, Vern Williamsen argues convincingly that one can learn more from those operating in the margins. In fact, he finds that "the originality of the minor dramatists far surpasses that of the more commonly studied figures" (133), a statement that holds true for these talented women writers as well. Without question, women playwrights have been relegated to the critical margins as "minor" figures; nonetheless, as Lisa Vollendorf points out, their "plays challenge many fundamental assumptions scholars have made for years about Spanish literature" (272). They also call into question many critical commonplaces about European theatrical history, including the common identification of Aphra Behn as the first European professional woman playwright. In 1641, while Behn was still an infant, Ana Caro successfully claimed payment owed her for the dramatic works she penned as part of a celebration in Seville as recorded by José Sánchez-Arjona in 1887. The significance of these and other related archival documents, brought to light thanks to the meticulous research of Lola Luna, not only enhanced our understanding of Caro and her writing, they also helped spark renewed critical interest in early modern *dramaturgas* as a whole.

In 1994, a year after Luna published separate volumes of Ana Caro's two extant *comedias*, the *Asociación de Directores de Escena de España* (Association of Spanish Theater Directors) published the first anthology to focus on the theater of multiple early modern Spanish women playwrights, *Teatro de mujeres del barroco* (Baroque Women's Theater). Felicidad González Santamera and Fernando Doménech featured the *comedias* of María de Zayas and Leonor de la Cueva y Silva, and two of the *entreactos* (interludes) by Feliciana Enríquez de Guzmán. A few years later, Juan Antonio Hormigón and his team of researchers compiled *Autoras en la historia del Teatro Español (1500–1994)*, whose first volume includes a brief summary of works by women dramatists, both named and anonymous.[4] Nonetheless, many texts remained largely inaccessible to wider audiences until the 1997 publication of Teresa Scott Soufas's anthology, *Women's Acts*, which includes key play texts by the five women whose works I will consider in this brief overview dedicated to secular playwrights: Ángela de Azevedo, Ana Caro, Leonor de la Cueva y Silva, Feliciana Enríquez de Guzmán, and María de Zayas.[5] There are also two plays, accompanied by two minor pieces ("sainetillos"), by an anonymous "dama sevillana" (lady from Seville): *El ejemplo de virtudes* and *Santa Isabel, reina de Hungría* (The Model of Virtues and Saint Isabel, Queen of Hungary); and *La mayor desconfianza* and *Amar deidad a deidad* (The Greatest Distrust and Gods in Love). However, as interesting as these plays are, their versification and other textual/contextual elements seem to indicate that they belong to a later period, therefore lying outside the scope of the present study.[6] Admittedly, this temporal division serves as a scholarly convenience, akin to that created by the artificial division of the playwrights into two groups, secular and religious, determined solely by which side of convent walls they inhabited. As a deeper understanding of the material reality of women's lives in the early modern period is reached, it becomes clear that women, at different stages and for varying reasons, might transition from one realm to the other, even though the majority of those who professed would stay behind convent walls. Moreover, art, literature, and culture crossed back and forth over thresholds: *comedias* were performed within convent walls[7] and works composed in convents circulated outside in the secular world; secular plays often foregrounded religious concerns; conversely, convent theater often reflected worldly matters. Yet the very existence of the manuscripts penned by the *dama sevillana* raises several questions: How many other anonymous works may have been penned by women? Did this *dama sevillana* belong to the group of secular writers? How might her place be judged based exclusively on her extant texts? In order to appreciate fully the richness of these authors' legacies, further studies are needed that—recognizing the fluidity of psychological, spatial, social, and political borders—engage their works in dialogue with one another.[8]

Nonetheless, even when considered as a group unto themselves, the five authors addressed here are, as Ben Gunter suggests, "women to be reckoned with" in any consideration of early modern Spanish drama. Each poses challenges to artistic and societal conventions, often interrogating elements of what is now termed the intersectionality of identity: gender, race, class, ethnicity, religion, sexual orientation, among others.[9] Their works also serve to question textual, social, and political authority, particularly as exercised within a patriarchal framework.

As one might expect, many studies of female-authored *comedias* have focused on issues related to gender;[10] of these, several explore the complex dynamics of desire embedded in the texts. Some of these studies assert that women dramatists foreground relationships among women in ways that differ significantly from what one finds in male-authored texts. As Ferrer Valls affirms throughout a series of carefully constructed articles, these women-authored *comedias* "reveal an explicit intent on part of their authors to convert them into vehicles for expressing their opinions regarding certain current matters that affected women, contesting them or reinterpreting them from their own point of view" (14).[11] For instance, in Zayas's play, *La traición en la amistad* (*Friendship Betrayed*), which is generally accepted as having been written before 1632, Fenisa, a memorable character whom Margaret Boyle labels a "vixen," flouts societal expectations by pursuing countless lovers with apparent disregard for others' feelings. The remaining women rally together, demonstrating strength in friendship. Matt Wyszynski contends that Zayas's work counters the dominant belief of her time that friendship was a bond reserved for men. Others have argued that *La traición* rewards women who cooperate with each other while it discourages competition among them. Yet, in Monica Leoni's nuanced reading of the play, the text does not present an idealized sisterhood; rather, it depicts "politicized friendship" in which the women function as a coalition to achieve their mutual aims.[12] Boyle also considers the complex presentation of female community in this work, finding that the women's circle of friendship serves as another structure of containment. Although the character most often singled out for commentary by critics and contemporary audiences alike is Fenisa, deemed a female Don Juan,[13] there is a surprising lack of consensus regarding who serves as *the* lead character. Many claim Fenisa holds this role while some, like Mayhew, have argued that the other three women serve as a collective protagonist given the focus on female community. Others make the case for Marcia, who orchestrates the pairing of the couples in the end.[14] Yet, in a comparison of the percentage of lines assigned to any one character, it is the *gracioso* or "fool," León, who dominates the play (Williamsen, "From Page to Stage").[15] In this sense, Zayas's work may anticipate the popularity of the *comedia de figurón* (caricature plays), a subgenre that focuses on the foibles of a comic figure and peaks in popularity later.

No matter which character one identifies as the lead, it is clear that Zayas consciously plays with desire and its manifestations. From the play's very opening, when Marcia's description of Liseo inspires Fenisa's mimetic desire for yet another man, the play revolves around the (im)possibility of fulfilling one's desire (Stroud, "Demand"). In addition to Fenisa's relentless pursuit of any gentleman who crosses her path,[16] there are moments when same-sex attraction sparks between women, described by Soufas as a "brief erotic attraction." Susan Paun de García interprets these charged exchanges as evidence of loving friendship; however, the palpable presence of homoeroticism in the text remains undeniable (Delgado, "Lesbiagrafisis"). Vollendorf cogently argues that at the beginning of act two, when the abandoned Laura enters the scene, the interaction among the three women (Marcia, Belisa, and Laura) is highly eroticized, marked by both their language and their gestures. Unlike the homoerotic attractions that surface in other plays, especially in male-authored texts, as well as in Caro and Azevedo, none of the characters here appears cross-dressed, a fact that heightens the homoerotic impact of these scenes. In contrast, in Caro's *Valor, agravio y mujer* (*Courage, Betrayal, and a Woman Scorned*), Leonor seeks to avenge her dishonor by following her fickle suitor, Don Juan, to Flanders where she becomes entangled in complex amorous intrigues. In the process, Leonor dons male attire as do many wronged women in countless *comedias*. Yet, what sets her apart is that she vows that her being has changed as well: "his betrayal changed my being" (510). This statement anticipates current scientific insights; advances in cognitive science have demonstrated that experiences, especially traumatic ones, can trigger changes in hormones that affect the brain and the "sex" typing of the brain, lending credence to the early modern belief that such transformation could occur.[17] As Leonardo, s/he outshines the other suitors in her manliness, successfully competing for the love of the countess.

Whereas many contend that the destabilizing force of Leonor's cross-dressing and the homoerotic desire that it awakens yield to heteronormative order in the play's final scene, where she appears dressed as a woman, the asymmetrical closing allows for multiple interpretations. Vollendorf reads the exchange between Estela and Leonor as one that "shows women securing a sororal relationship with each other as a permanent substitute for their fleeting homoerotic bond" (286). Yet the ending consciously highlights the sexual economy behind marriage when Ribete accepts Flora's hand in marriage, stating "acepto / por los escudos" (I accept / for the gold coins) (vv. 2747–2748), thereby inviting parallels with the previous betrothal, in which the marriage match gains its value from extrinsic factors. Before Estela asks Fernando to marry her, a noteworthy inversion in itself, she begins by stating, "Quedemos hermanas, Leonor hermosa" (Let's become sisters, beautiful Leonor) (vv. 2732–2733). This wording assigns primacy to the relationship solidified with Leonor through Estela's marriage to her brother; moreover, the fact that she adds the laudatory epithet "beautiful" when addressing Leonor, including no such flattery when naming Fernando, further highlights the possibility that her desire for Leonardo/Leonor has not waned.

As this brief examination of cross-dressing in Caro's play reveals, even though a staple feature in many *comedias*, it often appears that women dramatists employ this stagecraft differently from their male counterparts.[18] In essence, cross-dressing can be considered an act of "passing." Sean McDaniel and Joyce Tolliver, in *Writing Counterfeit Subjects: The Representation of Passing in Spain*, suggest that "passing stories arise at times of anxiety about changes in the reliability of certain social categories for determining social meaning and individual identity." They demonstrate that "passing tales are powerful: not only is tension created by the imminent possibility that the pass will be exposed, but the examination of how passing acts are represented and received reveals the contours and power of the social categories that are transgressed." Although they focus mainly on narrative, the dynamic examined becomes even more complex in theatrical enactments of passing since the audience is, for the most part, aware that there is an act of deception unfolding, whereas the other characters may or may not be cognizant of the "pass." McDaniel and Tolliver's analysis further reveals that race is not the universal fundamental category determining social station and privilege; in cultures such as that of seventeenth-century Spain, religion as an identity category takes on a crucial role. Even in cases where the social category most obviously transgressed is that of class, the workings of gender and religious categories impinge repeatedly on those of class, and at times become inextricable from them. When changes of gender occur as passes in the *comedia*, attention immediately turns to myriad *mujeres vestidas de hombre*. Even more compelling in terms of what is learned about cultural construction of identity are the less frequent *hombres vestidos de mujer* (men dressed as women).[19] In Azevedo's *El muerto disimulado* (The Fake Dead Man or The Dead Impostor), Clarindo takes advantage of the fact that he is presumed dead. This nobleman dresses as a merchant woman named Clara, thus engaging in a double pass of gender and class. Though women, including his cross-dressed sister, note her incredible resemblance to the dead man, they accept Clara as a woman; yet they treat her as a fellow noblewoman despite her attempt to sell them wares. Given the complex dynamics that revolve around cross-dressing in this and other female-authored *comedias*, it is clear that these texts provide fertile territory for explorations of sexuality and desire, the boundaries of passing and the intersectionality of identity.

Even when the plays portray women as objects of desire, they do so in ways that pose challenges to established paradigms. For instance, two of Ángela de Azevedo's best-known works present women exploited by men who are subsequently championed by celestial intervention. In *La margarita del Tajo que dio nombre a Santarén* (The Pearl of the Tagus Who Gave Her Name to Santarem), Irene suffers as the object of three intersecting triangular relationships. In the opening scene, Britaldo, married to Rosimunda, fixates on Irene, a nun in a convent. His manservant, Etcétera, attempts to dissuade him, pointing out his folly in pursuing "una esposa del cielo" ("a bride of heaven"). Her unsavory confessor, Remigio, inflamed with jealousy sparked by Britaldo's wooing of Irene, gives her poison that provokes a false pregnancy. Dishonored, Irene is cast out from the convent. She wanders aimlessly, praying for salvation and understanding. In answer to her prayers, an angel appears to her while she sleeps, explaining why she appears to be pregnant and foretelling her martyrdom. She calls out in her dream for mercy, yet awakens too late to flee from Banán, who stabs her to death at Britaldo's behest. As angels accompany her flower-strewn corpse as it ascends to heaven, the men each confess their wrongdoing. The guilty men and long-suffering women announce that they will enter the monastic life: the men embarking upon a pilgrimage to the Holy Land to atone for their sins, the women seeking refuge in a convent. Etcétera declares "de no casar, no me pesa,/ quédese sin casamiento/ en buena hora la comedia" (not getting married doesn't bother me/ let the play end well without marriage) (4181–4183), highlighting how this ending breaks with theatrical and societal expectations, as *comedias* traditionally ended with the protagonists joined in matrimony.[20] In *Dicha y desdicha del juego y devoción de la Virgen* (Fortune and Misfortune in Gambling and Devotion to the Virgin),[21] impoverished siblings struggle to contract suitable marriages despite the fact that the only meaningful inheritance left to them by their parents when their father dies, destitute because of his gambling, is their mother's insistence that they honor the Virgin. Doña María's liminal status, marked by her biological sex, her socially constructed gender, and her lack of material resources, leads to her complete commodification. Her brother, Felisardo, misguidedly following the advice of an astrologer, attempts to gain his fortune by gambling in order to win the hand of the woman he loves, whose father has pledged her hand to a rich *indiano*, Don Fadrique. Although Felisardo has already beaten the odds, winning every hand and leaving Don Fadrique destitute, he cannot resist one final game in which he bets and loses his sister to his rival. He then renounces God in a deal with the devil, saved only by the intercession of the Virgin Mary, to whom he remains faithful. The Virgin Mary appears and wrests his soul from the devil himself, promising the repentant sinner that everything will be resolved as he wished. Simultaneously, as Fadrique enters to stake his claim on Doña María, the Virgin intercedes by having the dreaming maiden utter phrases that remind Don Fadrique of the solemn vow he had made to the Virgin when he pleaded for her rescue from drowning. Thus, even in the scene in which she voices the words that secure her future, Doña Maria lacks agency, serving only as a vessel for others. Nonetheless, rather than presenting the objectification of these women as an accepted aspect of worldly affairs, these texts resist it, presenting this as part of a larger struggle against evil in its many guises. Although the Virgin's explicitly gendered maternal power triumphs, these *comedias* ultimately convey a sobering vision in which divine intervention is required to protect women from the depravity of men.

Some female-authored *comedias* portray women as agents, relegating men to the status of objects. In Zayas's *Traición*, Fenisa seduces one man after another; in Caro, Estela in *Valor* and Rosaura in *El conde Partinuplés* ("The Count Partinuples," published in 1653) consider and discard suitors at their whim.[22] In these works, men seem to serve as interchangeable objects of desire. This is especially true in *El conde Partinuplés*, a highly regarded work that blends elements of the chivalric romance, including mythology and magic, with complex stagecraft as it follows the suitors' quests to accomplish feats in order to win the hand of Rosaura, the Empress of Constantinople, who must marry for the good of her subjects.[23] Leonor de la Cueva y Silva's *La firmeza en la ausencia* (Loyalty in Absence) emphasizes Armesinda's steadfastness in the face of the king's unwelcome advances—she never wavers in her devotion to her beloved Don Juan, even after hearing false reports that he perished while on a mission devised by the king to rid himself of his rival. She successfully employs her impressive command of legal language to fend off her royal suitor,[24] and in a delightful twist at the end of the play, the king finds himself reduced to a pawn in a political power play when he must marry, not in fulfillment of his own desire, but in order to secure peace for his people.

Not all instances of male objectification are equally serious; in fact, in several instances, the female dramatists employ sexual humor where men are the butt of the joke.[25] Lucía, Fenisa's servant in Zayas's *La traición*, shares her grandmother's folk wisdom about how women should treat lovers, wittily highlighting that if one man leaves, another will satisfy the need: "That is what my grandmother used to say—may she rest in peace—that lovers should exist in infinite number, just like garlic cloves in a mortar, so that when you are mincing them and one jumps out of the bowl, there will still be others left behind; and like the garlic cloves, if one of your lovers leaves or dies, you will never be left alone" (Larson: 121).[26] In a pointedly humorous scene in act three of Caro's *Valor*, Flora, the maidservant, drugs Tomillo and then frisks his inert body, commenting on all she finds along the way. The graphic belittling of male anatomy when she examines the suggestively shaped tobacco horn, "hombres-qué aquesto os dé gusto" (Men—to think that this could give you pleasure) (v. 2386),[27] represents a comic inversion of the traditional derision of the female body found in *comedias* (Williamsen,"Rewriting"). In addition to the laughter it provokes, this interlude is, as Leoni contends, "infused with a deeper, politically charged meaning" ("Silence": 205). Moreover, through emphasis on male objectification, these instances operate as inversions of male privilege.

In an even more serious vein, other instances of the extreme objectification of men remind one of feminist critic bell hooks's assertion that "patriarchy knows no gender."[28] Hooks speaks passionately about the need for feminist pedagogy and practice to come to terms with the violence inherent in oppressive patriarchal systems, especially the systemic injustice that class stratification engenders. These remarks, in turn, prove to be a powerful lens for the consideration of violence in early modern plays penned by women. In *comedias* by Ana Caro, Ángela de Azevedo, and others, women dramatists often reproduce the violence that characterizes works by their male counterparts.[29] In *La traición*, shortly before Don Juan, enraged by Fenisa's manipulations, restrains himself from killing Fenisa and resorts to slapping her across the face instead, Fenisa mimics male violence by backhanding the hapless León who has already been mistreated by his master, Liseo. Though most often played for laughs in accordance with the implicit stage directions (indications of action embedded in the text), when León bemoans his lost teeth, "ay, muelas de mis entrañas" (oh, molars of my soul) (v. 1410) and begs the audience for a cure, the moment prefigures the ending's violence, when Belisa and Fenisa will attack each other. In multiple instances, women characters excel at replicating violent behaviors accepted as masculine, often besting men in battles, whether of wit or weapons. In Azevedo's *El muerto*, the cross-dressed Lisarda also successfully intervenes in a duel, disarming Álvaro.[30] Leonor, in *Valor*, duels with Don Juan; intent at first on killing him, she wounds him, later coming to his aid when others attack. In addition to her transgressive cross-dressing, Leonor as Leonardo displays her skillful mastery of the male role by her successful deployment of violence and deception. In their depiction of women's perpetuation of patriarchal patterns of violence, these dramatists echo concerns expressed by women writing in prose. Critical insights into violence in the prose works of María de Zayas and others can also illuminate these dramatic texts.[31] Yet the visceral impact of staged violence can transcend that which remains limited on the written page; thus, we must not underestimate the latent power of these scenes only fully realized in performance.

Similarly, the female dramatists repeatedly display their artistic prowess through the skillful manipulation of generic conventions established by male dramatists. In a lively exchange with Caro's protagonist, Leonor, the *gracioso* Ribete protests against the limitations of his societal and theatrical roles: "I'm fed up with playwrights who depict all lackeys as starving frightened chickens. He who is born brave, why shouldn't he be so even if he is not noble? Can't a servant be twice as brave as the master?"[32] If one were to accept the playwright and critic Juana Escabias's contention—based on archival evidence she has found of a woman whom she identifies as Ana María Caro Mallén de Torres[33]—that the author who penned *Valor* may have begun life as a slave, this exchange and others that address the inequities in the social hierarchy take on even deeper meaning. Even if one remains unconvinced by this hypothesis regarding Caro's biography, there is no doubt that the dramatist flouts her incursion into the male-dominated sphere of playwriting by her criticism of social hierarchies, as evinced by the meta-theatrical aside that serves as an epigraph to this chapter.

Azevedo, Caro, and their contemporaries also indulge in self-reflexive word play: in *Dicha y desdicha*, master and servant engage in a poetry competition. In *Valor*, Ribete exclaims that the cross-dressed Leonor has wisely chosen the rhyme scheme with which she attempts to woo her rival, "What a difficult rhyme Leonor chose! She didn't too badly—give it to her hard in verse, since she can't be pointed in prose."[34] Conscious plays with the names of servants also abound: Tijera (Scissors—cuts); Papagayo (Parrot—repeats); Sombrero (Hat—shades); and, most highly reflexive of all, Etcétera, who is far from redundant repetition.

The subversion of generic conventions extends to the endings of the plays, which serve to question the "happily ever after" that supposedly reinscribes harmonious social order. As mentioned in the previous discussions of the endings of *Valor* and *Firmeza*, these works foreground the transactional nature of the marriage vows.[35] Leoni offers a cogent reading of the ways in which Flora's strategic silence at the end of *Valor* stands as protest against a system in which women had no voice ("Silence": 209–19). Moreover, women-authored endings are often asymmetrical, with attention drawn to the fact that not all players are paired off successfully at the end, as occurs in *La margarita, El muerto, Valor, El Conde*, and, most notably, *La traición*, in which the play closes with León hawking Fenisa: "My lords, as you can see, Fenisa is left alone without a single lover.[36] If one of you is interested, let me know and I will pass on her address" (Larson: 197).[37] In her study of marriage and subversion in *comedia* endings, Catherine Connor suggests, "Rather than simple subversion and restored order, a new order opens to new indeterminacies in life and in art" (40). This proves especially true in the problematic and problematizing *comedia* endings penned by women.

So far, the dramatists examined all chose to work within the paradigm of the three-act *comedia* as practiced by Lope de Vega and other male playwrights. The earliest female playwright whose works are extant, Feliciana Enríquez de Guzmán, stands apart. She championed a classical five-act structure in adherence with Aristotelian principles of unity, thereby openly challenging contemporary male authors. Her complex two-part work, *Tragicomedia de los jardines y campos sabeos* (Tragicomedy of the Sabaean Gardens and Fields) consists of two plays in verse, four *entreactos* (interludes) in prose, and is accompanied by fascinating paratextual materials including a *carta ejecutoria* (patent) and *licencias* (authorizations), the first set written in Portuguese. This intricate compilation has challenged scholars, eliciting several intriguing studies that attempt to elucidate the mythological and monstrous.[38] The play, richly informed by the tradition of chivalric novels, dramatizes the struggles of two royal couples who succeed in marrying happily only because of the intervention of mythological figures who triumph over villainous characters who would impede their happiness.[39] Enríquez de Guzmán's text is further complicated by the highly self-reflexive interweaving of elements from the dramatist's own relationship with her second husband, León Garavito. Bolaños's reading of her husband's wills, along with the careful consideration of other archival materials, has led to great insight into the playwright's life and artistry. Yet Enríquez de Guzmán herself stated that, in contrast to those who, following Lope's lead, sought popularity in the public theaters or acclaim from court productions, she wrote her works, *not* for presentation on stage, but to be read aloud in courts and *academias* ("A los lectores"). Ironically, however, she is now best known for her comic interludes that have been repeatedly performed in theater festivals on at least three continents,[40] especially *Las gracias mohosas* from the first part of the *Tragicomedia*, staged at Amherst College in English translation in 2013 as "The Moldy Graces" as part of Harley Erdman's production of *Suitors*, an adaptation of Caro's *El Conde Partinuplés*.[41] In a very politically incorrect, far-fetched parodic burlesque, six repugnant brothers come to woo three deformed sisters, vying for the honor of marrying them. In the asymmetrical ending par excellence, the dilemma is resolved by embracing polyandry, suggesting that all of them marry. While other *entremeses* (interludes) of the period also subvert gendered norms in courtship, notably Quevedo's two-part *El Marión*, in which three ladies woo the *doncello*, or male virgin, it is difficult to think of a more transgressive ending than one that ends up with two men for every woman.

The theatrical afterlife of Enríquez de Guzmán's interlude underscores that dramatists cannot determine the reception of their art, for "drama only comes into existence in the theater through the interaction of author, producer, actors and audience" (V. Williamsen: 134). Without question, our field will gain a great deal through further studies of production and performance. The women who dared to write in this period did so "fully aware of the battle she would have to wage to gain acceptance and respect" as a writer (Ferrer Valls: 30);[42] those who wrote for the stage faced these challenges on multiple fronts. Although we know that works by Caro, and probably Azevedo, were performed during their lifetimes, much remains to be learned about the performances of the plays during the early modern period. In addition to standard approaches, we may gain a great deal by closer investigations into the records of theatrical troupes themselves along the lines of Thornton Wilder's studies of Lope de Vega and Cervantes.[43] The growing number of contemporary performances[44] also merits close consideration, especially as multiple stagings emerge in different contexts, some that would certainly surprise their authors.[45]

As Vern Williamsen argues, "no literary genre is as receptive as is drama to changes [. . .] to the social, economic, and political developments that surround it. The minor writers are, at least theoretically, more responsive to those forces than canonical 'major' figures" (134). Precisely because of this responsive fluidity, there may be more to learn from research into the women playwrights or *dramaturgas* than from the study of their venerated male colleagues. By foregrounding the theoretical issues raised by the works of early modern women dramatists, critics may contribute to the elaboration of more inclusive theoretical paradigms.[46] Recent productions of these gynocentric texts have engendered great critical and scholarly interest— each production yields new insights into the (im)possibilities of performance. In turn, archival discoveries, including a last will and testament penned by Leonor Cueva y Silva in 1701 that asserts she was born in 1611 unearthed by Voros ("Al tribunal": 161), demonstrate how much there is still to learn about these writers and the material reality of their lives. At times, as in the case of Bolaños's work on Enríquez de Guzmán, researchers must look for threads interwoven throughout the often better-documented lives and histories of the writers' male relatives. Other patterns may lead scholars to look outside established boundaries, as does Hegstrom in archival and critical research on early modern women playwrights, both secular and religious, writing outside of Spain.[47] At every turn, critics must come to terms with the "underlying uncertainties of the unknown" (V. Williamsen, *The Minor Dramatists*: ii). Still, the prospects are exciting: if, in 2014, a researcher can announce his recovery and subsequent edition of a previously unknown text by Lope de Vega,[48] a playwright whose works have benefited from centuries of concentrated critical effort, what might yet be discovered about these women whose very act of writing for the stage defied societal and cultural expectations?

Notes

1 Although Manuel Serrano y Sanz included the text in *Apuntes para una biblioteca de escritoras*, the first modern stand-alone edition did not appear until 1983, published by Alessandra Melloni in Verona. The work was also included in Felicidad González Santamera and Fernando Doménech's *Teatro de mujeres del Barroco* (1994) but was not widely available in the United States until it appeared in Teresa Soufas, *Women's Acts: Plays by Women Dramatists of Spain's Golden Age* (1997), and later in the bilingual edition, *Friendship Betrayed*, translated by Catherine Larson and edited by Valerie Hegstrom in 1999. Entries on *La traición* are included in the Richard Tyler files, an archive of plot summaries that includes over 1800 plays, now housed at Eastern Central University's Linscheid Library.
2 "La dramaturgia femenina queda casi inadvertida en los trabajos de los más destacados historiadores de la literatura y el teatro, con lo cual fácilmente puede llegarse a la conclusión que en toda la historia de la literatura dramática española las piezas escritas por mujeres han tenido una importancia mínima" (45). English translation by Larson, "You Can't Always" (129).
3 The term *comedia* refers to the full-length secular plays of sixteenth- and seventeenth-century Spain. As David Pasto explains in his introduction for contemporary directors, they are "three-act dramas written in verse, which mix comic and serious elements in complex plots that often emphasize intrigue, disguises, music, and swordplay" ("*Comedia* in Translation." http://comedia.denison.edu/golden.html).
4 The collection encompasses many women, both secular and religious, including Ángela de Acevedo; Mariana Alcázar; Anónima ("Máscara conventual de 1692"); Anónima ("Una dama Sevillana"); Anónima ("Una devota musa"); Ana Caro Mallén de Soto; Isabel Correa; Leonor de la Cueva y Silva; Feliciana Enríquez de Guzmán; Juana Inés de la Cruz; Marcela de San Félix; María do Céu; and María de Zayas y Sotomayor, among others.
5 In addition, editions of plays by individual women playwrights have also appeared, including *Las comedias de Ana Caro* edited by María José Delgado (1998); Doménech's 1999 edition of two of Azevedo's plays ("La margarita del Tajo" and "El muerto disimulado"); Zayas's *La traición en la amistad / Friendship Betrayed* edited by Valerie Hegstrom and translated by Catherine Larson (1999); Zayas's *La traición* (2003); and Caro's *Valor, agravio y mujer* (2009), the latter two edited by Barbara López Mayhew.
6 Biblioteca Nacional de España, ms. 17430. See Soufas "Juegos con Santa Isabel" ("Plays with Santa Isabel").
7 See the chapter by Alarcón Román in this volume.
8 In her 1999 edition of Zayas's play, Hegstrom identifies over a dozen women playwrights who wrote in Spanish in seventeenth-century Europe (Spain, Portugal, and the Netherlands) and in Mexico. The arbitrary divisions imposed by critics must themselves be reconsidered. For example, Sor Juana Inés de la Cruz has traditionally been included in studies of Spanish Golden Age drama, achieving canonical status, as documented in "Charting Our Course." Yet, other women writers, like Isabel Correa in the Netherlands, who wrote in Spanish but lived beyond what is considered Spain today, have not been addressed (see Baranda Leturio's chapter in this volume for Correa as translator). Even within Spain's borders, we know of other dramatic works waiting to be recovered, such as the collection of *Doce comedias* that Mariana de Carvajal mentions in the prologue to her *Navidades de Madrid*.
9 For a helpful introduction to intersectionality, see Yuval-Davis, who builds upon the earlier work of Crenshaw, including "Demarginalizing" and "Mapping the Margins."
10 The body of scholarly work on these dramatists has expanded exponentially, encompassing a wide variety of approaches to the plays as well as to the playwrights' lives themselves. For examples, see Bolaños, Cecilla, Delgado, Doménech, Samson, Thacker, and Urban Baños. Technologically enhanced research tools, like the database found at www.bieses.net, are indispensable. In addition to literary studies, dramaturgical work carried out in conjunction with productions has also yielded valuable insights that may not be accessible through conventional research outlets; see Erdman, Mujica, and Pasto.
11 "ponen en manifiesto una voluntad explícita por parte de sus autoras de convertirlas en vehículos de expresión de sus opiniones sobre determinados temas de actualidad que afectaban a la mujer, contestándolos o reinterpretándolos desde su propia óptica" (14).
12 Leoni (62). Gorfkle analyzes female community as well, suggesting it serves as a source of moral instruction in which Belisa stands out as a positive model because of her steadfastness. See also Ferrer Valls.
13 See Hegstrom. Friedman labels Fenisa "a female Don Juan with unapologetic egotism and a voracious sexual appetite" ("Clothes Unmake the Woman"). Campbell considers Fenisa not as a "mujer varonil" (manly woman) but rather as an embodiment of "lo varonil" (the masculine). It is also noteworthy

that Lope de Vega's wily young lover in *La discreta enamorada* (In Love but Discreet) who flouts convention and manipulates her mother to marry the man of her choice, is named Fenisa.

14 Even in performance, the identification of the *dama principal* can be problematic, as the actors portraying Fenisa and Marcia may both consider themselves to hold the lead in the play.
15 For interesting discussions regarding *graciosos* in women-authored *comedias*, see Ferrer Valls, "Locuras y sinrazones," and Montauban, "Descuidóse la poeta."
16 Fenisa declares that she loves all men "solo por ser hombres" (just for being men) (l.2394) and that like heaven, "a todos doy lugar en mi pecho" (all of them find a place in my heart) (l.2340).
17 See Hines. For discussions on this topic in early modern Spain, see Velasco, *The Lieutenant Nun*, and Donnell, *Feminizing the Enemy*.
18 See Cortez, "El travestismo."
19 There are other instances of cross-dressed men in the *comedia*; however, many of these tend to involve servants, as in Lope's *La discreta enamorada* and Sor Juana's *Los empeños de una casa*. See Maroto Camino "Transvestism" for more on this topic in Azevedo, and Urban Baños "Juegos" for a study of the cross-dressed *galán* in Azevedo and Enríquez de Guzmán.
20 This metaliterary comment is typical of Azevedo's theater, as demonstrated by Ferrer Valls (2006). In fact, as we will discuss later, metatheatricality may well be a hallmark of women-authored *comedias* as the playwrights consciously manipulate theatrical conventions for their own purposes.
21 See Gascón.
22 Gil-Oslé concludes that Caro "retrata el proceso y criterios de elección del marido, por medio de un lenguaje altamente codificado en la cultura premoderna, en términos de interpelación femenina a la tradición androcéntrica, desde dentro del propio discurso cultural" (depicts the process and criteria for the selection of the husband through a highly codified language within premodern culture, in terms of a feminine interrogation of the androcentric tradition, from within the cultural discourse itself) (114).
23 See de Armas, Ellis, Finn, McVay, Pérez Romero, Quintero, Urban Baños, and Whitenack.
24 See Voros "Al tribunal."
25 See Williamsen "Lasting Laughter" for sexual humor in women's writing.
26 "Así decía mi aguela—qué Dios haya—/ que había de ser en números infinitos/ tantos como los ajos que puniendo/ muchos en un mortero,/ salte aquél que saltare que otros queda,/que si se va o se muere, nunca falte" (1508–1513).
27 In her edition, Soufas punctuates this line with an exclamation point while others have suggested that a question mark would more closely capture the sense of the original.
28 bell hooks' plenary address to the National Women's Studies Association, held in San Juan, Puerto Rico in November 2014, explicitly linked the prevalence of violence to patterns of patriarchal oppression; she convincingly argued, however, that women also perpetuate this violence. See Boyle for a reading of how the women's community in Zayas's play serves to reinforce established gender norms (62–76).
29 Ferrer Valls contends that like other women dramatists of the period, Azevedo employs established theatrical codes "pero que instrumentaliza para intervenir, desde su propia experiencia de género, en el discurso moral dominante acerca de la mujer" (but activates them to intervene, from her own gendered experience, in the dominant moral discourse about woman) ("Decir entre versos": 15).
30 See Múzquiz-Guerreiro on "Symbolic Inversion" in Azevedo's play.
31 See Bates, Friedman "Enemy Territory," Lauer, and Vollendorf "Reading the Body Imperiled."
32 "Estoy mal con enfadosos/ que introducen los graciosos/ muertos de hambre y gallinas./ El que ha nacido alentado,/ ¿no lo ha de ser si no es noble?/ ¿Qué no podrá serlo al doble/ del caballero el criado?" (529–535).
33 There are several assumptions by Escabias that are not adequately explained: she adds the name María, not usually associated with Ana Caro, and drops the second surname Soto, replacing it with Torres ("Ana María Caro Mallén de Torres"). She does satisfactorily explain the reference to the girl as "adulta" according to the standards of the period. Nonetheless, given the many disparities between the person named in the records and existing documentation on Ana Caro, it seems more likely that the documents Escabias discovered deal with another woman rather than the dramatist, especially since Caro was often referred to by her peers—including Zayas—as "la señora doña Ana Caro," titles that, given the social structure of the time, reflected status rather than mere formulaic courtesy.
34 "Qué difícil asonante / buscó Leonor! No hizo mal; / déle verso en agudo, / pues que no le puede dar / otros agudos en prosa" (1042–1045). Leonor's name itself is an *agudo*; in the passage that Ribete praises, she has chosen to rhyme words accented on the last syllable (agudos); significantly, ending on the stressed vowel "a," usually associated with the feminine when not accented. It was, of course,

Caro herself who chose the difficult rhyme scheme, highlighting once again her ability as a woman to engage in the male activity of writing a play in verse.

35 In *Dicha*, all couples end paired, however, the economic transaction is underscored when Tijera and Sombrero say that the "seis mil ducados" (six thousand ducats) in dowry their masters provide: "Suavice/ aqueso un yugo tan grande" (Softens such a heavy yoke) (Sombrero: 3719–3720); and "Tal cruz así se mitigue" (Such martyrdom is thus mitigated) (Tijera: 3721).
36 In many cases, it is also the women who decide who will marry whom as noted by Boglovits. This takes place in *El muerto* as well; moreover, in this instance, it is left up to the maidservants to decide which one of them will marry Papagayo.
37 "Señores míos, Fenisa / cual ven sin amantes queda./ Si alguno la quiere, avise/ para que su casa sepa." The divergent stagings of this ending, shaped by the blocking of the scene, reflect the possibility of multiple interpretations. In some, Fenisa remains center stage, highlighting her irrepressible freedom; in others, she is literally marginalized, cast outside the circle of couples.
38 See Ruíz and McVay on Enríquez de Guzmán. Ruíz (2010) in particular provides valuable political readings of the play.
39 For an in-depth consideration of Enríquez de Guzmán's relationship with the chivalric tradition, see Marín Piña.
40 See Hegstrom and Williamsen "Early Modern Dramaturgas" for a fledgling performance history of women dramatists, including details regarding Enríquez de Guzman's works. As Hegstrom explains, *Las gracias mohosas* became "a signature piece" for Juan Dolores Caballero, director of the Seville-based Compañía Teatro Velador (90).
41 See the recently published anthology of women playwrights by Romero-Díaz and Vollendorf, translations by Erdman.
42 "tomar plena conciencia de la batalla que se había de libar por ganar la aceptación y el respeto como poeta."
43 Wilder published some of his insights into Lope's *Peregrino* lists, gained from his readings of *repartos*, or casts. His unpublished notes, over a thousand pages, also include valuable information about actresses in the period.
44 Ben Gunter has worked tirelessly to increase appreciation of the *comedia* among theater professionals, organizing several sessions at American Society for Theatre Research and Association for Theatre in Higher Education, in the Orlando 2014 ATHE, including one that concentrated on women dramatists of sixteenth- and seventeenth-century Spain, in the hope that more of these women will find their way to the stage in translation. Already, archival videos of a handful of productions (Azevedo, Caro, Sor Juana, and Zayas) are available through www.ahct.org
45 As Ferrer Valls notes regarding the Brigham Young University performance of Azevedo's *El muerto disimulado*, "probablemente hubiera asombrado bastante a su autora" (probably would have considerably astonished its author; 215).
46 Time and time again, researchers have underscored that Spain is unique; the literary achievements of early modern female dramatists writing in Spanish certainly substantiate this difference; see Cohen "The Uniqueness" and Vollendorf "Desire Unbound."
47 In addition to our three collaborative projects, *Engendering the Early Modern Stage*, "Early Modern Dramaturgas: A Performance History," and "Gendered Matters: Engaging Early Modern *Dramaturgas* in the Classroom," Hegstrom has explored archives across Europe tracing the contributions of women writers.
48 García Reidy's discovery of Lope de Vega's manuscript, "Mujeres y criados," was front-page news across the globe. See the English version of the official press release from the Universitat Autònoma de Barcelona.

Works cited

Aszyk, Urszula. "Las mujeres dramaturgas en España: En busca de la identidad." *Estudios sobre escritoras hispánicas en honor de Georgina Sabat-Rivers*. Ed. Lou Charnon-Deutsch. Madrid: Castalia, 1992: 45–61.
Bates, Stephanie and Robert A. Lauer. "'Performativity' del género de Leonor/Leonardo y la creación de 'gender trouble' en *Valor, agravio y mujer* de Ana Caro." *Anagnórisis*, 1 (2010): 9–33.
Bayliss, Robert. "Feminism and María de Zayas's Exemplary Comedy: *La traición en la amistad*." *Hispanic Review* 76.1 (2008): 1–17.

Boglovits, Michael. "Engaños: el travestismo y la ruptura de las normas de género en dos obras del Siglo de Oro de España." Unpublished M. A. thesis. UNC Greensboro, 2015.

Bolaños Donoso, Piedad. *Doña Feliciana Enríquez de Guzmán. Crónica de un fracaso vital (1569–1644)*. Seville: Universidad de Sevilla, 2012.

———. "Doña Feliciana Enríquez de Guzmán y sus fuentes literarias: examen de la biblioteca de don Francisco de León Garavito." *Teatro de palabras: revista sobre teatro áureo, I* (2007): 1–28.

Boyle, Margaret E. *Unruly Women: Performance, Penitence and Punishment in Early Modern Spain*. Toronto: U Toronto P, 2014.

Campbell, Gwyn E. "(En)gendering Fenisa in Maria de Zayas's *La traicion en la amistad*." *Romance Languages Annual* 10 (1999): 482–487.

Caravajal, Mariana de. *Navidades de Madrid y noches entretenidas, en ocho novelas (1668)*. Ed. Catherine Soriano. Madrid: CEC, 1993.

Caro Mallén, Ana. *Valor, agravio y mujer*. Ed. Barbara D. López-Mayhew. Newark, DL: Cervantes, 2009.

Cecilla, María Angeles. "Dramaturgas del Siglo de Oro." *Las mujeres en la sociedad del Siglo de Oro: ficción teatral y realidad histórica: actas del II coloquio del Aula-Biblioteca "Mira de Amescua" celebrado en Granada-Úbeda del 7 al 9 de marzo de 1997, y cuatro estudios clásicos sobre el tema*. Ed. Juan Antonio Martínez Berbel and Roberto Castilla Pérez. Granada: Universidad de Granada, 1998: 185–195.

Cohen, William. "The Uniqueness of Spain." *Echoes and Inscritpions: Comparative Approaches to Early Modern Spanish Literatures*. Ed. Barbara Simerka and Christopher B. Weimer. Lewisburg, PA: Bucknell UP, 2000: 17–29.

Connor (Swietlicki), Catherine. "Marriage and Subversion in *Comedia* Endings: Problems in Art and Society." *Gender, Identity and Representation in Spain's Golden Age*. Ed. Anita K. Stoll and Dawn L. Smith. Lewisburg, PA: Bucknell UP, 2000: 23–46.

Cortez, Beatriz. "El travestismo de Rosaura en *La vida es sueño* y de Leonor en *Valor, agravio y mujer*: el surgimiento de la agencialidad femenina y la desnaturalización el binarismo del género. *Bulletin of the Comediantes* 50.2 (1998): 371–385.

Crenshaw, Kimberlé. "Mapping the Margins: Intersectionality, Identity Politics and Violence against Women of Color." Presented at World Conference Against Racism. http://socialdifference.columbia.edu/files/socialdiff/projects. Web. 2001

De Armas, Frederick. "Ana Caro Mallén de Soto." *Women Writers of Spain: An Annotated Bio-Bibliographical Guide*. Ed. Carolyn L. Galerstein. New York: Greenwood, 1986: 66–67.

———. "Dreams, Voices, Signatures: Deciphering Woman's Desires in Angela de Azevedo's *Dicha y desdicha del juego*." *Women in the Discourse of Early Modern Spain*. Ed. Joan F. Cammarata. Gainesville: UP Florida, 2003: 146–159.

———. *The Invisible Mistress: Aspects of Feminism and Fantasy in the Golden Age*. Biblioteca Siglo de Oro. Charlottesville, VA: Biblioteca Siglo de Oro, 1976.

Delgado, María José, ed. *Las comedias de Ana Caro: Valor, agravio y mujer y El conde Partinuplés*. New York: Peter Lang, 1998.

———. "Lesbiagrafisis: Exposición y expansión del deseo femenino en *La traición en la amistad* deMaría de Zayas y Sotomayor." *Romance Languages Annual* 1998; 10.2 (1998): 534–538.

Delgado, María José and Alain Saint Saens, eds. *Lesbianism and Homosexuality in Early Modern Spain: Literature and Theater in Context*. New Orleans: UP of the South, 1999.

Delgado, Maria M., and David Thatcher Gies. *A History of Theatre in Spain*. Cambridge: Cambridge UP, 2012.

Doménech Rico, Fernando. *La Margarita del Tajo que dio nombre a Santarén; El muerto disimulado*. Madrid: Asociación de Directores de Escena de España, 1999.

Donnell, Sidney. *Feminizing the Enemy: Imperial Spain, Transvestite Drama, and the Crisis of Masculinity*. Lewisburg, PA: Bucknell UP, 2003.

Ellis, Jonathan. "Royal Obligation and the 'Uncontrolled Female' in Ana Caro's *El conde Partinuplés*." *Bulletin of the Comediantes* 62.1 (2010): 15–30.

Erdman, Harley. "The Dramaturgy of Absence: Minding the Gaps in Tirso de Molina, Ana Caro and Feliciana Enríquez." *Remaking the Comedia: Spanish Classical Theater in Adaptation*. Ed. Harley Erdman and Susan Paun de García. London: Tamesis. 2015: 167–176.

Escabias, Juana. "Ana María Caro Mallén de Torres: Una esclava en los corrales de comedias del siglo XVII." *EPOS* 28 (2012): 177–193.

———. *Dramaturgas del Siglo de Oro: guía básica*. Madrid: Huerga y Fierro, 2013.

Ferrer, Joshua. "The Community of Women in María de Zayas y Sotomayor's *La traición en la amistad.*" Unpublished M.A. Thesis, Miami University of Ohio, 2004.

Ferrer Valls, Teresa. "Decir entre versos: Ángela de Acevedo y la escritura femenina en el Siglo de oro." *Ecos silenciados. La mujer en la literatura española. Siglos XII y XXVIII.* Ed. S. Gil-Albarellos and M. Rodríguez Pequeño. Segovia: Fundación Instituto Castellano y Leonés de la Lengua, 2006: 213–241.

———. "'Locura y sinrazones son las verdades': la figura del gracioso en las obras dramáticas escritas por mujeres." *La construcción de un personaje: el gracioso.* Ed. Luciano García Lorenzo. Madrid: Fundamentos, 2005: 297–316.

———. "Mujer y escritura dramática en el Siglo de oro: del acatamiento a la replica de la convención teatral." *La presencia de la mujer en el teatro barroco español.* Ed. Mercedes de los Reyes Peña. Seville: Junta de Andalucía, 1998: 11–32.

Finn, T. P. "Women's Kingdom: Female Monarchs by Two Women Dramatists of Seventeenth-Century Spain and France." *Bulletin of the Comediantes* 59.1 (2007): 131–148.

Friedman, Edward H. "'Clothes Unmake the Woman': The Idiosyncrasies of Cross-dressing in Ana Caro's *Valor, agravio y mujer.*" *Confluencia* 24.1 (Fall, 2008): 162–171.

———. "Enemy Territory: The Frontiers of Gender in María de Zayas's 'El traidor contra su sangre' and 'Mal presagio casar lejos.'" *"Ingeniosa Invención": Essays on Golden Age for Geoffrey L. Stagg in Honor of His Eighty-fifth Birthday.* Ed. Ellen M. Anderson and Amy R. Williamsen. Newark, DL: Juan de la Cuesta, 1999: 41–68.

Fuente, Macarena Baeza de la. "Dramaturgia femenina en el Barroco español: María de Zayas." *Apuntes: Teatro* 119–120 (2001): 192–198.

Gabriele, John B. "Engendering Narrative Equality in Angela de Azevedo's *El muerto disimulado.*" *Bulletin of the Comediantes* 60.1 (2008): 127–138.

García Reidy, Alejandro. "Mujeres y criados: una comedia recuperada de Lope de Vega." *Revista de Literatura* 75 (2013): 417–438.

Gascón, Christopher. "The Heretical and Herethical in Angela de Azevedo's *Dicha y desdicha del juego y devoción de la Virgen.*" *Bulletin of the Comediantes* 51 (1999): 65–81.

———. *The Woman Saint in Spanish Golden Age Drama.* Lewisburg, PA: Bucknell UP, 2006.

Gil-Oslé, Juan Pablo. "El examen de maridos en *El conde Partinuplés* de Ana Caro: la agencia femenina en el Juicio de Paris." *Bulletin of the Comediantes* 61.2 (2009): 103–119.

González Santamera, Felicidad, and Fernando Doménech, eds. *Teatro de mujeres del barroco.* Madrid: Asociación de Directores de Escena de España, 1996.

Gorfkle, Laura. "Female Communities, Female Friendships and Social Control in Maria de Zayas's *La traicion en la amistad:* A Historical Perspective." *Romance Languages Annual* 10 (1999): 615–620.

Hegstrom, Valerie. "The Fallacy of False Dichotomy in María de Zayas's *La traición en la Amistad.*" *Bulletin of the Comediantes* 46 (1994): 59–70.

———. *Engendering the Early Modern Stage: Women Playwrights in the Spanish "Empire."* New Orleans: UP of the South, 1999.

———. "Gendered Matters: Engaging Early Modern Dramaturgas in the Classroom." *Teaching Gender through Latin American, Latino, and Iberian Texts and Cultures.* Ed. Leila Gómez, Asunción Horno-Delgado, Mary K. Long, and Núria Silleras-Fernández. Boston: Sense Publishers, 2015: 81–98.

Hegstrom, Valerie and Amy Williamsen. "Early Modern Dramaturgas: A Contemporary Performance History." *Remaking the Comedia: Spanish Classical Theater in Adaptation.* Ed. Harley Erdman and Susan Paun de García. London: Tamesis, 2015: 83–92.

Hines, Melissa. *Brain Gender.* Oxford: Oxford UP, 2004.

hooks, bell. Keynote Address. NWSA. Puerto Rico. November 14, 2014. (Streaming video available online from nwsa.org).

Hormigón, Juan Antonio, Inmaculada Alvear, Carlos Rodríguez Alonso et al. *Autoras en historia del Teatro Español (1550–1994).* Vol. I. Madrid: Asociación de Directores de Escena de España, 1996.

Kaminsky, Amy Katz. *Water Lilies / Flores del agua: An Anthology of Spanish Women Writers from the Fifteenth through the Nineteenth Century.* Minneapolis: U of Minnesota P, 1996.

Larson, Catherine. "Gender, Reading, and Intertextuality: Don Juan's Legacy in María de Zayas's *La traición en la amistad.*" *INTI: Revista de Literatura Hispanica* 40.1 (1994–1995): 129–138.

———. "You Can't Always Get What You Want: Gender, Voice, and Identity in Women-Authored Comedias." *Gender, Identity and Representation in Spain's Golden Age.* Ed. Anita K. Stoll and Dawn L. Smith. Lewisburg, PA: Bucknell UP, 2000: 127–141.

Leoni, Monica. "María de Zayas's *La traición en la amistad*: Female Friendship Politicized?" *South Atlantic Review* 68.4 (2003): 62–84.

——. "Silence Is/As Golden . . . Age Device: Ana Caro's Eloquent Reticence in *Valor, agravio y mujer*." *Women in the Discourse of Early Modern Spain*. Ed. Joan F. Cammarata. Gainesville: UP Florida, 2003: 199–212.

——. "The Convenient Demonization of Fenisa and the Subsequent Creation of the 'Other.'" *Bulletin of the Comediantes* 59.1 (2007): 149–166.

López-Mayhew, Barbara D. "La protagonista tripartita en la comedia la *Traición en la amistad* de María de Zayas." Unpublished Conference Paper. El Paso: Association of Hispanic Classical Theater, 2003.

Luna, Lola. *Ana Caro, una escritora profesional del Siglo de Oro: Vida y obra*. Universidad de Sevilla, 1992.

——. "Ana Caro, una escritora 'de oficio' del Siglo de Oro." *Bulletin of Hispanic Studies* 72 (1995): 11–26.

Marín Pina, María Carmen. "Feliciana Enríquez de Guzmán, una dramaturga barroca seducida por los libro de caballerías." *Perspectives on Early Modern Women in Iberia and the Americas: Studies in Law, Society, Art and Literature in Honor of Anne J. Cruz*. Ed. Adrienne L. Martin and María Cristina Quintero. New York: Escribana Books, 2015: 596–614.

Maroto Camino, Mercedes. '"Ficción, afición y seducción': Ana Caro's *Valor, agravio y mujer*." *Bulletin of the Comediantes* 48 (1996): 37–50.

——. "María de Zayas and Ana Caro: The Space of Woman's Solidarity in the Spanish Golden Age." *Hispanic Review* 67 (1999): 1–16.

——. "Negotiating Woman: Ana Caro's *El conde Partinuplés* and Pedro Calderón de la Barca's *La vida es sueño*." *Tulsa Studies in Women's Literature*, 26.2 (2007): 199–216.

——. "Transvestism, Translation and Transgression: Ángela de Azevedo's *El muerto disimulado*." *Forum for Modern Language Studies* 37 (2001): 314–325.

McDaniel, Sean, and Joyce Tolliver. *Writing Counterfeit Subjects: The Representation of Passing in Spain* [forthcoming].

McKendrick, Melveena. "Women against Wedlock: The Reluctant Brides of Golden Age Drama." *Women in Hispanic Literature: Icons and Fallen Idols*. Ed. Beth Miller. Berkeley: U of California P, 1983: 115–146.

McVay, Ted. E. "The Use of Mythology in Feliciana Enríquez de Guzmán's *Tragicomedia de los jardines y campos sabeos*." *Engendering the Early Modern Stage: Women Playwrights in the Spanish Empire*. Ed. Amy R. Williamsen and Valerie Hegstrom. New Orleans: UP of the South, 1999: 139–150.

Melloni, Alessandra, ed. *La traición en la amistad*. Verona: Università degli studi di Verona, 1983.

Montauban, Jannine. "'Descuidóse la poeta; ustedes se lo perdonen': el gracioso en las comedias de Ana Caro." *Hispanic Research Journal* 12.1 (2011): 18–33.

Mujica, Bárbara. "María de Zayas' *Friendship Betrayed* à la Hollywood: Translation, Transculturation and Production." *The Comedia in English: Translation and Performance*. Ed. Susan Paun de García and Donald R. Larson. London: Tamesis, 2008: 240–254.

——. *Women Writers of Early Modern Spain: Sophia's Daughters*. Yale Language Series. New Haven: Yale UP, 2004.

Múzquiz-Guerreiro, Darlene. "Symbolic Inversions in Ángela de Azevedo's *El muerto disimulado*." *Bulletin of the Comediantes* 57.1 (2005): 147–163.

Ordóñez, Elizabeth J. "Woman and Her Text in the Works of María de Zayas and Ana Caro." *Revista de Estudios Hispánicos* 19.1 (1985): 3–15.

Pasto, David. "Comedia in Translation," 2016. http://comedia.denison.edu/golden.html

Paun de García, Susan. "*La traición en la amistad* de María de Zayas." *Anales de literatura española* 6 (1988): 377–390.

Pérez Romero, Antonio. "'Si me buscas me hallarás': Mujer buscada, hallada y admirada en *El conde Partinuplés* de Ana Caro." *eHumanista, Journal of Medieval and Early Modern Iberian Studies* 17 (2011): 334–348.

Quintero, María Cristina. *Gendering the Crown in the Spanish Baroque Comedia*. Burlington, VT; Farnham UK: Ashgate, 2012.

Rhodes, Elizabeth. "Redressing Ana Caro's *Valor, agravio y mujer*." *Hispanic Review* 73.3 (2005): 309–328.

Romero-Díaz, Nieves and Lisa Vollendorf, ed. Trans. Harley Erdman. *Women Playwrights of Early Modern Spain*. Phoenix, AZ: Iter Press; Arizona Center for Medieval and Renaissance Studies, 2016.

Ruíz, María Reina. "Cervantes, Góngora y Feliciana Enríquez de Guzmán: voces discordantes de la monarquía cómica." *Cuatrocientos años del Arte nuevo de hacer comedias de Lope de Vega. Actas selectas del XIV Congreso de la Asociación Internacional de Teatro Español y Novohispano de los Siglos de Oro: Olmedo, 20 al 23 de julio de 2009*. Ed. Germán Vega García-Luengos and Héctor Urzáiz Tortajada. Valladolid: Universidad de Valladolid, 2010: 929–936.

———. *Monstruos, mujer y teatro en el Barroco: Feliciana Enríquez de Guzmán, primera dramaturga española.* New York: Peter Lang, 2005.
Samson, Alexander. "Distinct Drama? Female Dramatists in Golden Age Spain." *A Companion to Spanish Women's Studies.* Ed. Xon de Ros and Geraldine Hazbun. Woodridge: Boydell & Brewer, 2011: 152–172.
Sánchez-Arjona, José. *El teatro en Sevilla en los siglos XVI y XVII.* Madrid: n.p., 1887: 241–250.
Soufas, Teresa S. "Ana Caro's Re-evaluation of the *Mujer varonil* and her Theatrics in *Valor, agravio y mujer.*" *The Perception of Women in Spanish Theater of the Golden Age.* Ed. Anita K. Stoll and Dawn L. Smith. Lewisburg, PA: Bucknell UP, 1991: 85–106.
———. *Dramas of Distinction: A Study of Plays by Golden Age Women.* Lexington: UP of Kentucky, 1997.
———. "María de Zayas's (Un)Conventional Play, *La traición en la amistad.*" *The Golden Age* Comedia: *Text, Theory, and Performance.* Ed. Charles Ganelin and Howard Mancing. West Lafayette, IN: Purdue UP, 1994: 148–164.
———. "Repetitive Patterns: The Unmarried Woman in Ana Caro's *El conde Partinuplés.*" *Engendering the Early Modern Stage: Women Playwrights in the Spanish Empire.* Ed. Amy R. Williamsen and Valerie Hegstrom. New Orleans: UP of the South, 1999: 93–106.
———. "Unanswering the Question: A Course on Spanish Golden Age Plays by Women." *Approaches to Teaching Early Modern Spanish Drama.* Ed. Laura R. Bass and Margaret R. Greer. New York: MLA, 2006: 92–98.
Soufas, Teresa S., ed. *Women's Acts: Plays by Women Dramatists of Spain's Golden Age.* Lexington: UP of Kentucky, 1997.
Soufas, Teresa S., et al. "Juegos con Santa Isabel: drama de la pluma de una adolescente desconocida." *Literatura y feminismo en España (s. XV–XXI).* Ed. Lisa Vollendorf. Barcelona: Icaria, 2005: 127–139.
Stroud, Matthew D. "Love, Friendship, and Deceit in *La traición en la amistad,* by María de Zayas." *Neophilologus* 69 (1985): 539–547.
———. "The Demand for Love and the Mediation of Desire in *La traición en la amistad.*" *María de Zayas: The Dynamics of Discourse.* Ed. Amy R. Williamsen and Judith A. Whitenack. Cranbury, NJ: Associated UP, 1995: 155–169.
Thacker, Jonathan. *A Companion to Golden Age Literature.* London: Tamesis, 2007: 88–91.
Universitat Autònoma de Barcelona, Press Release. "Unknown Comedia by Lope de Vega Discovered." Web 22 January 2014.
Urban Baños, Alba. "Dramaturgas seglares en la España del Siglo de Oro." Doctoral Thesis Barcelona: Universidad de Barcelona, 2014.
———. "Juegos de identidad en comedias de autoría femenina: galanes con disfraz mujeril." *Máscaras y juegos de identidad en el teatro español del Siglo de Oro.* Ed. María Luisa Lobato. Madrid: Visor, 2011: 543–556.
Velasco, Sherry. *Male Deliveries: Reproduction, Effeminacy, and Pregnant Men in Early Modern Spain.* Nashville: Vanderbilt UP, 2006.
Vollendorf, Lisa. "Desire Unbound: Women's Theater of Spain's Golden Age." *Women in the Discourse of Early Modern Spain.* Ed. Joan F. Cammarata. Gainesville: UP of Florida, 2003: 272–291.
———. "Reading the Body Imperiled: Violence against Women in María de Zayas." *Hispania* 78.2 (1995): 272–282.
———. "'Te causará admiración': el feminismo moderno de María de Zayas. *Literatura y feminismo en España (s. XV–XXI).* Ed. Lisa Vollendorf. Madrid: Icaria, 2005: 107–124.
———. "Women Onstage: Ángela de Azevedo, María de Zayas, and Ana Caro." *The Lives of Women: A New History of Inquisitional Spain.* Nashville: Vanderbilt UP, 2005: 74–89.
Voros, Sharon. "'Al tribunal de amor apelo': Leonor de la Cueva and the Language of Law." *Women's Voices and the Politics of the Spanish Empire.* Ed. Jennifer L. Eich, Jeanne Gillespie, and Lucia G. Harrison. New Orleans: UP of the South, 2008: 159–176.
———. "Fashioning Feminine Wit in María de Zayas, Ana Caro, and Leonor de la Cueva." *Gender, Identity and Representation in Spain's Golden Age.* Ed. Anita K. Stoll and Dawn L. Smith. Lewisburg, PA: Bucknell UP, 2000: 156–177.
Walthus, Rina and Helen Wilcox, eds. *Heroines of the Golden StAge: Women and Drama in Spain and England 1500–1700.* Kassel: Edition Reichenberger, 2008.
Weimer, Christopher B. "Ana Caro's *El conde Partinuplés* and Calderón's *La vida es sueño*: Protofeminism and Heuristic Imitation." *Bulletin of the Comediantes* 52.1 (2000): 123–146.
Whitenack, Judith A. "Ana Caro's Partinuplés and the Chivalric Tradition." *Engendering the Early Modern Stage: Women Playwrights in the Spanish Empire.* Ed. Amy R. Williamsen and Valerie Hegstrom. New Orleans: UP of the South, 1999: 51–74.

Wilder, Thornton. "New Aids toward Dating the Early Plays of Lope de Vega." *Varia variorum. Festgabe für Karl Reinhardt*. Münster-Colonia: Böhlau Verlag, 1952: 194–200.

——. "Lope, Pinedo, Some Child-Actors, and a Lion." *Romance Philology* 7 (1953): 19–25.

Williamsen, Amy R. "Charting Our Course: Gender, the Canon and Early Modern Theater." *Engendering the Early Modern Stage: Women Playwrights in the Spanish Empire*. Ed. Amy R. Williamsen and Valerie Hegstrom. New Orleans: UP of the South, 1999: 2–16.

——. "From Page to Stage: Readers, Spectators, Expectations and Interpretations of María de Zayas' *La traición en la amistad*." *Heroines of the Golden Stage: Women and Drama in Spain and England 1500–1700*. Ed. Rina Walthaus and Helen Wilcox. Kassel: Edition Reichenberger, 2008: 167–188.

——. "Lasting Laughter: Comic Challenges Posed by Zayas and Castellanos." *Echoes and Inscriptions: Comparative Approaches to Early Modern Spanish Literatures*. Ed. Barbara Simerka and Christopher B. Weimer. Lewisburg, PA: Bucknell UP, 2000: 46–58.

——. "Rewriting in the Margins: Caro's *Valor, agravio y mujer* as Challenge to Dominant Discourse." *Bulletin of the Comediantes* 44 (1992): 21–30.

Williamsen, Vern G. *The Minor Dramatists of 17th-Century Spain*. Boston: Twayne, 1982.

Wyszynski, Matthew A. "Friendship in María de Zayas's *La traición en la amistad*." *Bulletin of the Comediantes* 50.1 (1998): 21–33.

Yuval-Davis, Nira. "Intersectionality and Feminist Politics." *European Journal of Women's Studies* 13.3 (2006): 193–209.

Zayas, María de. *La traición en la amistad. Friendship Betrayed*. Ed. Valerie Hegstrom, Trans. Catherine Larson. Lewisburg, PA: Bucknell UP, 1999.

SECTION IV

Women in the public sphere

13
PUBLIC POETRY

María Carmen Marín Pina

The leap by early modern Spanish women writers from the private to the public sphere implies an important step in their social consolidation. The desire to be heard, to become visible, to make their literary abilities known, meant leaving their strict family circle and seeking the appropriate channels through which to appear in public. Poetry competitions, introductions to other authors' books, poetry anthologies, and separate publications in pamphlets and in books were the means employed by female poets, lay as well as religious, to enter the cultural marketplace. Thanks to the printing press, their poetry, both cultured and, to a lesser extent, popular, assumed the value of public and published poetry, as it becomes materially evident and visible to all. In the seventeenth century, women with poetic aspirations answered the call of poetic jousts, in which they competed with male writers.[1] Their poems were read aloud before the audience in public sessions, and winners had the chance to publish their verses, together with those by other poets, thus achieving local fame. The most fortunate ones, though scarce in number, attended literary academies and participated as spectators or clandestine poets in the literary activities programmed by these male associations.

Most of the women who went public were occasional poets, but others had a more sustained production and looked for alternative opportunities to become known. Ángela Sánchez, Alfonsa González de Salazar, Ana de Leiva, María de Rada, Ana de Agudo y Vallejo, and María Nieto de Aragón, among others, composed laudatory verses for works written by authors of their group, in which they praised, endorsed, and somehow sold others' literary creations.[2] They thus entered the world of marketing, with books as literary products, setting in gear the contacts established with other authors within their circle of friends, at the same time that they exhibited their poetic value. Unlike women poets dedicated to more personal religious poetry, or whose poems dealt mainly with family matters—and who, therefore, did not depend on the printing press to the same extent—, those who opted for the abovementioned channels cultivated occasional and civic poetry, not at all personal or intimate (Osuna, "Poesía"), but one adjusted to a particular event or lauded work, that required above all great skill in the basics of poetry writing. The most fortunate poets, such as Cristobalina Fernández de Alarcón, saw their poems published in well-known anthologies, such as the second part of *Flores de ilustres poetas* (Flowers by Illustrious Poets) (Osuna, "Cristobalina"). In these cases, they always appear in public backed by others, whether in a contest or included in someone's work that seems to authorize them. It was far more difficult to take the initiative themselves and appear in public with their own poetry under their own name.

María de Zayas, Leonor de Meneses, and Ana Francisca Abarca de Bolea, following the custom of seventeenth-century prose fiction, took advantage of their novels and inserted many related poems within their plot narratives. Their poetry, which otherwise might never have been published, was therefore made known to the public. One such case is that of Ana Francisca Abarca de Bolea, whose *Vigilia y Octavario de San Juan Baptista* (Vigil and Octave of Saint John the Baptist) (1679), a miscellaneous work with a pastoral plot, contains 109 poems on a wide variety of themes (Campo Guiral, CIII), a veritable songbook with pieces composed at different times that could have been published separately as a poetry book. However, publishing their poetry as a separate book was not easy: Valentina Pinelo apparently attempted to do so, as we read in the prologue to her *Vida de Santa Ana* (Life of Saint Anne) (1601) that she had already prepared a songbook for publication, yet there is no trace of such a book. The same determination guided Marcia Belisarda (pseudonym of Sister María de Santa Isabel), who was never published, although she left a manuscript with more than 100 compositions. A few examples of published poetry books do exist: in Portugal, the pastoral poem *Soledades de Buçaco* (Solitudes of Buçaco) by Bernarda Ferreira de Lacerda was printed in 1634, and in Spain, at the beginning of the eighteenth century, Teresa Guerra's *Obras poéticas* (Poetic Works) a poetry book of over 100 pages was published and announced in 1725 in *La Gaceta de Madrid* (Cruz).

Women's poetry pamphlets

For authors with a limited production of poetry, the pamphlet was the best means of presenting their work individually and immediately to the public. The pamphlet is, in general, "a booklet of a few pages, used to disseminate literary and historical texts among the mainly popular reading masses."[3] These leaflets focused on literary and/or current events; they were written in prose or verse and in popular or cultured style, priced economically, and aimed at the general public. In the case of poetry, which still circulated in manuscript despite the printing press's success, pamphlets promoted published poetry and helped standardize typography as its main means of dissemination. Authors were aware of the path opened by these lesser publications and took advantage of it, adjusting their poems to the pamphlet's requirements or even writing poems specifically for them. Given their print configuration and their contents, poetic pamphlets constitute an editorial genre in which various agents involved in the literary field actively interact in the creation and the circulation of the poetic work. Female writers became an active part in the machinery. Despite their lesser status, however, these texts were regulated and required a printing license to be circulated. Philip IV, in 1627, banned the printing of "anything without a license, no matter how small,"[4] a ban that was in place until 1680. Female writers therefore had to follow the necessary legal procedures to introduce their work into circulation; this meant personally applying for the license, or contacting a promoter (editor, printer, bookseller, or patron) interested in the work to apply for it. In order to reach this point, they created their network relations and sustained themselves through them.

The corpus of poetic pamphlets written by women in the seventeenth and first half of the eighteenth centuries contains no more than thirty pieces.[5] Their fragile binding, the paper's deterioration, and the scarce interest for collecting these booklets have ensured their destruction and only a few have survived. This modest collection must be rebound and given its value to reinstate the sense and function with which the poems were imbued during their time, and to appreciate the authorial image they projected of their female writers. From the cast of authors who signed the poetic pamphlets in the seventeenth and early eighteenth century—Beatriz de Aguilar, Ana Caro, María Nieto de Aragón, Salvadora Colodro, Eugenia Buesso, Mariana Bautista, and Luisa María Domonte—, only Ana Caro is relatively known, as her poetic and dramatic works have begun to be included in literary histories. Editions of her pamphlets have served as a base to discover the thematic and stylistic richness of this kind of poetry, as well as its functionality. Pamphlets by María Nieto and Eugenia Buesso have also been analyzed and contextualized in their historical moment. In the search for these humble pamphlets, new texts have been found from the early eighteenth century, one by Luisa María Domonte and several by Lucas del Olmo's daughter and sister (without mention of any name), and the latter not registered in Serrano y Sanz's bibliography. Except for Ana Caro, the pamphlets' signatories are fledgling authors who had published no other work save for the pamphlets and a circumstantial poem in others' books or in poetic jousts, and their rarely having left their local surroundings surely contributed to their oblivion. The poetry in these pamphlets entails very diverse subject matter, whose contamination does not easily allow any attempt at classification. Given this, we propose an approach to this corpus mainly taking account of its content, which ranges from accounts or relations of festivities to brief plays, with different kinds of celebratory and religious poetry.

Pamphlets of festive *relaciones* in verse

Of the various themes accounted for within the corpus as a whole, the most cultivated genre is the *relación* (narration of events). *Relaciones* are "brief texts with a specific historical theme that are meant to be conveyed through the publishing process."[6] Ana Caro, Eugenia Buesso, and Luisa María Domonte composed *relaciones* that celebrated historical events. Driven by the desire to inform the general public, they became "chroniclers" of the present in verse. In order to do so, they followed the course of events, kept abreast of national and local news, and themselves became informed in order to inform, since often they did not witness what they narrated, but relied on documentaries, memorial sources, chronicles, and accounts in prose. Despite their historical value, *relaciones* in verse are not mere chronicles; they are, above all, literary texts with a strong authorial intervention.

The act of writing a festive *relación* generally requires a mandate, usually from civil or religious authorities, that commits a local writer to compose a work and provide an account of a festive commemoration, in turn intended to celebrate a historical milestone (García Bernal). Qualified female poets are also engaged for these tasks, and become part of this productive cycle, in which everything takes place for the sake of profitability and economy (real and symbolic), of the exchange of goods. Female writers of festive *relaciones*, both civic and religious, interpret and formalize the historical event, and participate in its legitimization through their account, for which they are rewarded in one way or another. Presumably at the behest of the Franciscan convent of Seville, Ana Caro composed in octaves the *Relación en que se da cuenta de las grandiosas fiestas que en el convento de nuestro padre san Francisco de la ciudad de Sevilla se han hecho a los santos mártires del Japón* (Account of the grand celebrations held in the convent of our father Saint Francis in the city of Seville in honor of the holy martyrs of Japan) (Seville, Pedro Gómez, 1628). The pamphlet narrates the poetic account of celebrations organized to honor the beatification of these new Christians who were cruelly murdered in Nagasaki in 1597. The engraving with the emblem of the Franciscans on the cover links the author, the work and the convent, which was interested in disseminating news of the event and of the celebration of the beatification, which in turn helped to promote the order. In addition to the Franciscans, the celebration's commissioners were a group of noblemen from Guipuzcoa and Viscaya; among them, the then-assistant of Seville, Lorenzo de Cárdenas y Valda, and Juan de Elossidieta, to whom the author dedicates the *relación* and who assumed the financing. The poetic project was conditioned both before and after by religious and noble interests, which were adopted by the author and taken into consideration when composing the poem, for which she was no doubt remunerated.

The Seville parish of San José ordered the *Relación de la grandiosa fiesta y octava que en la iglesia parroquial del glorioso arcángel san Miguel de la ciudad de Sevilla hizo don García Sarmiento de Sotomayor, conde de Salvatierra* (Account of the grand celebration and octave held in the parochial church of the glorious archangel Saint Michael of the city of Seville by Don García Sarmiento de Sotomayor, Count of Salvatierra), also written by Ana Caro and published in Seville by Andrés Grande, in 1635. In the *relación*, she narrates in silva meters[7] the celebrations for the reparation of the sad events of Tillemont in Flanders, where the troops of M. de Chatillon looted, assaulted, and destroyed the churches (López Estrada, "Costumbres"; Luna). As counterclaim and in response to these hostilities typical of heretics, celebrations were organized throughout Spain, such as the one in this parish of Seville, in this case financed by García Sarmiento de Sotomayor, count of Salvatierra and assistant in Seville. Although her poem does not spare any praise for this royal governor, Ana Caro chose to dedicate it to his mother, Leonor de Luna Enríquez, governess at court of Prince Baltasar Carlos. Thus, the author seeks a double patronage: in Seville, where her fame is already spreading, and at court, from a significant court lady to whom she offers her services. Little by little, Ana Caro created an important network of relationships that allowed her to reach the highest echelons of power through her poems.

From Seville, Ana Caro traveled to Madrid in 1637, the year when she published a new *relación*, the *Contexto de las reales fiestas que se hicieron en el palacio del Buen Retiro. A la coronación de rey de Romanos y entrada en Madrid de la señora princesa de Cariñán, en tres discursos* (Context of the royal celebrations held in the Buen Retiro palace. In honor of the coronation of the king of the Romans and entry in Madrid of the lady Princess of Cariñán, in three discourses) (Caro; Luna; Voros). Her stay at court coincided with the celebrations organized at the Buen Retiro by the Count-Duke of Olivares to solemnize the entry of the Princess of Cariñán and the appointment of Philip IV's brother-in-law as King of the Romans. According to her dedication of the second discourse to Olivares (Caro: fol. 16r.), whom she praises effusively, Ana Caro apparently attended the celebrations, wrote the *relación* seen by the favorite, sent it to Seville ("I wrote to Seville"[8]), without aiming to publish it, and then, perhaps at the request of the city of Madrid, submitted it to the printing press with new additions. In its definitive form, the *relación*, published in quarto, comprises three discourses,[9] that is, three poems in different meters (octava real,[10] silva and romance, respectively), with different dedicatees: Agustina Spínola y Eraso, wife of Carlos Strata, Philip's Genoese banker; Olivares himself; and the city of Madrid, which paid from its coffers the sum of 1,100 reales for her poem. In the second discourse, she describes the celebrations in detail, including the mottoes (verses) and inventions (images in cartouches and cards) carried by the participating groups and so popular at the time. However, she does not mention the theatrical program, perhaps because she did not attend (Voros: 126). At court, Ana Caro's fame grew during these years, and she made important personal and literary connections beyond the Seville circle that accompanied the Count-Duke to Madrid (Baranda, "Words for Sale"). In a 1638 satire by the literary academy of the Buen Retiro, itself an imitation of the burlesque academy's festivities of 1637 (Julio, Academia) gingerly mentioned by Ana Caro in her relación (Caro: fol. 34v), the poet Alfonso de Batres targets her with his taunts. Repeating the topic of the female sex's mismatch between beauty and wisdom, developed as a topic at the 1637 academy, he states that Ana Caro is as ugly as a woman scholar, and as dirty as a poet:

> Here was a woman complaining, in not so very bad dirges, who from afar seemed to me as beautiful as two thousand women scholars, and from a closer distance, she seemed

as clean as a similar number of poets. It must be Doña Ana Caro, who among so many men and with very little urge to marry, complained how bored she was.[11]

All jokes such as this one aside, typical of this kind of satirical and festive poetry, although in this case with its misogynist trace, the name of Ana Caro was already being heard in 1638 in the literary circles of the court, thanks to the poetry of these pamphlets and to others commented below.

In contrast to Caro's, the fame of the Aragonese poet, Eugenia Buesso, another verse chronicler whose writings were dedicated to public service, did not transcend her surroundings. We have little to no information about her social and literary ties, although her two *relaciones* celebrating the appointment of Don Juan José of Austria as viceroy and vicar general of the Kingdom of Aragón may well have been promoted by the city itself. The *Relación de la entrada en la imperial ciudad de Zaragoça de su alteza sereníssima el señor don Juan* (Account of the entry in the imperial city of Zaragoza of His Serene Highness Don Juan) (1669) is completed with the *Relacion de la corrida de toros que la imperial ciudad de Zaragoza hizo en obsequio de su alteza* (Account of the bullfight held by the imperial city of Zaragoza as a gift to His Highness). These *relaciones*, like other similar ones, could have also been deployed by the impatient viceroy in his political campaigns, since the admiration shown by his subjects and sung in these poems is immense (Marín, "Eugenia"). By means of this pamphlet, Buesso chooses sides and publically places herself in Don Juan's political camp against the interests of the influential Jesuit, Juan Everardo Nithard, by then discredited, and those of the queen, Mariana of Austria. There is no extant version of her *Relación de las fiestas que en la Imperial Ciudad de Zaragoza se han hecho por la canonización de San Pedro Alcántara y Santa María Magdalena de Pazzi* (Zaragoza, Juan de Ibar, 1669) (Account of the celebrations held in the Imperial City of Zaragoza for the canonization of Saint Pedro de Alcántara and Saint Mariá Magdalena de Pazzi). However, if added to the others above, this lost festive-religious *relación* in hendecasyllabic lines, as described by Latassa, confirms Buesso as a professional author of *relaciones*.

Luisa María Domonte Ortiz de Zúñiga appears to write and publish under the auspices of the Society of Jesus. This writer from Seville, daughter of the Marquises of Villamarín, nun of the Augustinian convent of Santa María de la Paz, and sister of two Jesuit priests, heralded the Jesuit Order and in her own way, was its benefactor; she is an example of the aristocratic spiritual daughters sought by Saint Ignatius of Loyola for the society (Marín, "Pliegos": 244; Martínez de la Escalera). In 1730, the author's *relación* titled *Expressa a un padre jesuita los reales obsequios que el hispalense emporio consagró a sus reyes, en el feliz alumbramiento de la reina* (Describes to a Jesuit the royal gifts that Seville devoted to its kings at the time of the queen's happy delivery), published in a pamphlet without imprint, narrated the city's celebrations over the birth of María Antonia Fernandina, daughter of Philip V and Isabel de Farnesio, which took place in Seville and was also celebrated by the Society of Jesus, in view of the monarch's good relationship with the society. The Jesuits could also have requested the *relaciones* dated 1731, 1749, and 1760–1761, as all deal with very specific celebrations held by the order in Seville, such as the dedication of the Church of Saint Louis as a novitiate house, the celebration of the feast of Saint Ignatius, and that of the Immaculate Conception's patronage of Spain, which addressed the subject of the Virgin's immaculism. In her pamphlets known to date, Domonte Ortíz de Zúñiga never expressly reveals her identity, signing with the initials D.L.M.D.O.Z. only a few times, a quasi-anonymity common at the time in order to safeguard decorum, although no one around her questioned her authorship. Interestingly, Luisa María Domonte's compositions never mention her situation as a nun or her connection with the abovementioned Augustinian convent.

If we consider the pamphlet form's inherently humble beginnings, Ana Caro's are the most stylistically elegant and the closest in appearance to a traditional book. In addition to the dedications in prose, separated as paratexts, the front pages of the *Relación* of 1635 on the events in Flanders include a series of laudatory poems by unknown and occasional poets who praise Caro and her works. Although the author's network of literary contacts remained very local, these poems authorize her status as poet. Diego de Ortega Haro, for example, is glad that "for such a celebration / it was fitting to have such a chronicler."[12] By contrast, Eugenia Buesso and Luisa María Domonte included the dedications in their titles, rejecting the kind of paratexts that brought prestige to the work and its author.

All of these female versed chroniclers are very familiar with the genre of the festive *relación*. At the core and central stage of the poem is the historical event that inspires and gives it life. Its recreation, however, is soon dimmed and what becomes important is the poetic description, which assumes a panegyrical tone rather than a historical narration. Civic and religious celebrations have their own manner of narrating a spectacle and its staging, whose tempos are respected by the authors in order to faithfully represent the ceremony as it took place, albeit magnified by means of verbal art. Moreover, none of the authors ignores the dominant discourse of these kinds of poems, and all deploy specific elements from demonstrative and epideictic genres, since the ultimate aim of their verses is to exalt and praise those involved in the celebration, a rhetorical strategy that similarly redounds to their personal benefit. They lavish praise on the cities (*laudes urbis*), on their dignitaries, and on the event's attendees, listing them in detail by their first and last names. The celebration's mainly visual nature, in which ritual, gestures, images, and spaces have such overriding significance, likewise requires a descriptive discourse, the rhetoric of ecphrasis. Ana Caro, Eugenia Buesso, and Luisa María Domonte describe in detail the interior of churches, the altars, images, and ornaments, as well as the acts that make up the celebration, in order to emulate paintings, and thus visually recreate the festive event (Ledda). Everything surrounding the celebration is magnified by the voice of these female writers who, nonetheless, take refuge in the humility *topos*, also deployed by male writers in their public discourses, as they present themselves as ignorant, rude, uneducated, or simplistic little worms, whose works emanate from their "unsharpened pens" as "blots" or "crude discourses." This is a purely rhetorical stance, however, since theirs is a highly cultured style. Apart from their literary value, their *relaciones*, like those of male poets (Voros: 110), become instruments of political propaganda, yet the authors' own voice and social conscience can be heard beyond their poetry's forced subservience (Marín, "Eugenia"; Voros).

Among the poetic *relaciones* celebrating *toros y cañas* (bullfights and jousts with cane spears) archived in the Hispanic Society of America in New York, is a poetic pamphlet by Antonio Pérez Gómez titled *A la lanzada de a caballo en la fiesta de los completorios de nuestra señora de los Remedios. Por doña Mariana Bautista. Canción* (On spear throwing from a horse at the feast of the complines of our Lady of Los Remedios. By Doña Mariana Bautista. Song) (Bautista). Although not primarily a *relación*, it is related to the genre because of its contents, since the song recounts a knightly joust that presumably took place during a festive ceremony. Similarly to Eugenia Buesso, this unknown poet by the name of Mariana Bautista recounts one of the many bullfighting celebrations that enlivened civic and religious festivities throughout the Iberian Peninsula, in this case, in honor of the Virgin of Los Remedios. The pamphlet's sparse information omits the site of the celebration, and given the Marian devotion's popularity in Spain, it is difficult to locate where the festivity was held, although being filed with seventeenth-century Madrid themes would assign it to that city (Sánchez Alonso: 855). The author humorously presents a bullfight on horseback featuring a short knight named Ongo who, at the moment of impressing his lady, is deathly frightened and attempts to elude the bull. As in other burlesque situations, the author compares the protagonist and his lackey to Don Quixote and Sancho, as both were famous as laughable characters in celebrations, and the match is settled comically with the pants-less knight tossed up in the air (López Estrada, "Fiestas": 317). This pamphlet, with no imprint, exemplifies a type of uninhibited, festive public discourse that female writers did not hesitate to use.[13]

Celebratory poetry in pamphlets

Along with *relaciones* that narrated celebrations, poets also wrote about historical or specific events in poetic form that circulated in pamphlets. In 1633, Ana Caro published the *Grandiosa vitoria que alcançó de los moros de Tetuán Jorge de Mendoça y Piçaña* (Grand victory over the Moors of Tetouan by Jorge de Mendoça y Piçaña), a historical ballad in the style of fifteenth-century ballads on the victory of the general and governor of Ceuta, the Portuguese Jorge de Mendonça Pessanha ("Piçaña" in Ana Caro's poem), against the Moors of Tetouan, whose cattle he raided. The ballad could well have been ordered by the governor himself for promotional purposes, to make known his achievements as a knight who, in the author's view, was "an honor to Portugal / and excellence of Castille"[14] (vv. 539–540) (López Estrada, "La frontera": 345). In little more than five hundred lines, Ana Caro's poem, well documented and with careful attention to detail, evinces her skill at hyperbolically eulogizing a minor skirmish that took place at a border region.

María Nieto de Aragón, from Madrid, was more ambitious; a precocious poet, barely fourteen years old, in 1645 she published in Madrid *Lágrimas a la muerte de la augusta reina nuestra señora doña Isabel de Borbón* (Tears on the Death of the August Queen, our Lady Doña Isabel de Borbón), a ten-page pamphlet that, as with those by Ana Caro, resembles a book of poetry. To give authority to her text, the author includes her personal correspondence with Francisco López de Zárate and Manuel Faria y Sousa as social-literary paratexts, as preliminary pieces with a social purpose connected to the author's personal environment. Adding a *décima*[15] by Pedro Rosete Niño that praises her and her work ensures that she is in good company as she enters the public arena. Her dedication seeks the support of Catalina Manuel de Ribera y Pinto, wife of an influential Portuguese merchant in Philip IV's court, whose circle includes the young poet and her family. The pamphlet in quarto gathers a series of poems (sonnets, songs, a *décima*, and a *romance*), thoughtfully organized and all belonging to the genre of the funeral eulogy, or public funereal poetry (Marín Pina, "Pliegos"). Her verses form part of the many lamentations expressing affection for the queen written by the poets at the time of her death, and as in the case of Leonor de la Cueva y Silva, they served not only to eulogize Isabel de Borbón, but also to dignify their authors as poets (Romero-Díaz).

María Nieto remained attentive to events as they occurred, and years later, she celebrated the nuptials of Philip IV and Mariana of Austria in her *Epitalamio a las felicísimas bodas del rey nuestro señor* (Epithalamium for the Most Joyous Nuptials of the King our Lord) (1649), a pamphlet published without imprint, but dated 1649 given its topic. Less carefully organized and structured than the previous one, the pamphlet has as its only paratext a brief dedication to Doña Violante de Ribera y Pinto, who belonged to the same Portuguese family as above, whose social status had declined. The author's affection for the dedicatee and her family expressed at the front of the royal epithalamium responds to the desire, not so much to seek a personal patronage, as to obtain royal support for the *Judeo-converso* family in political and economic distress (Romero-Díaz: 21). The poem is a wedding song, a genre sought by the aristocracy and the higher nobility as a symbol of distinguished social status. With fourteen stanzas plus a final seven-line envoi in cultured, Gongorist style, the panegyric lends itself to the praise and flattering of monarchs, with the genre's usual rhetoric (Deveny: 30). The poem received favorable reviews and the author herself distributed copies among her protectors and acquaintances (Marín Pina, "Pliegos": 260). The Aragon chronicler Andrés de Uztarroz became Nieto's mentor, and her personal correspondence with him, as well as with Rodrigo Méndez Silva, reveal her formation as poet, her concern for style, her poetic projects, and her determination to make herself known in certain circles and make a name for herself. Her pamphlets partly helped to meet these expectations, since this poetry, deemed minor for its unassuming qualities, but of great significance due to its theme and style, would not have circulated otherwise solely under her name. Apart from specific poems composed for books written by others, these pamphlets reinforced young María Nieto's rising poetic career, and had she not left Spain after her marriage, she would undoubtedly have become renowned as a poet.

Luisa María Domonte also cultivated the epithalamium in the *Métrica expressión que hace en obsequio de las plausibles bodas de la señora doña Ana Virués y Caballero con su primo el señor D. Joseph Domonte* (A Declaration in Verse Given as a Gift for the Praiseworthy Nuptials of Doña Ana Virués y Caballero with her Cousin Don Joseph Domonte), a cultured poem composed in octaves to celebrate her brother, José Domonte's wedding. Published anonymously without imprint, the pamphlet was not intended for the public, like that of María Nieto, but must be understood as a sign of fraternal affection strictly within the family. The author gifts the couple with public compliments and praise, yet also takes advantage of the occasion for some self-admiration by copying, at the end of the pamphlet, the décima of an admirer who nearly reveals her identity and praises her discretion. Two other pamphlets with this kind of celebratory or commemorative poetry were composed by Domonte in honor of the first mass sung by her two Jesuit brothers. The first was for Francisco, *Al padre Francisco Domonte, de la Compañía de Jesús, da la enhorabuena de haber celebrado la primera missa y explica su crecido júbilo como parte tan interessada en función tan plausible, s.l.:s.n.:lost* (To Father Francisco Domonte, of the Society of Jesus, She Congratulates Him for Having Celebrated his First Mass and Explains Her Joy as an Interested Party in Such a Praiseworthy Act); the second, for Diego, *Expressión métrica que hace en elogio de la primera missa que en la casa professa de la Compañía de Jesús celebró el padre Diego Domonte, de la misma compañía*, Seville, 1732 (A Declaration in Verse Praising the First Mass Celebrated in the House of the Society of Jesus by Father Diego Domonte, of the Same Society). These poems, similar to those composed when novices took the veil (Baranda, "Cantos"), were valued as gifts and as an homage by the recipients, her brothers in this case, but they also had a propagandistic function for the Jesuit order. In the hendecasyllabic ballad addressed to Father Diego Domonte, along with her praise of her "dear brother,"[16] the author exalts the Society's treasures, "from a Xavier, the most sublime eloquence, / the most ardent zeal of an Ignatius."[17] Although both were published anonymously, Domonte's identity and gender are revealed through her style and by the reiteration of lines from her other compositions.

Pamphlets on religious poetry

The literary features and tone of the religious poetry disseminated through pamphlets are different from other kinds of poetry. One of the earliest poetic pamphlets that circulated under a woman's name is the *Romances compuestos por la madre Beatriz de Aguilar, en agradecimiento de algunas mercedes señaladas que Dios le hizo* (Córdoba, 1610) (Ballads composed by Mother Beatriz de Aguilar, in gratitude for some significant graces given her by God). Of noble descent and a native of Granada, Beatriz de Aguilar was a lay sister who, by mandate from her confessors, wrote down the graces she received from God. Her second confessor, the Jesuit Agustín de Quirós, posthumously published the four ballads, which narrate the soul's mystical encounter with God, in response to the public demand for her poetry after it circulated in manuscript. Although her poetry was expected to be published with the narrative of her life, as was customary in these cases, the pamphlet was published first in order to preserve the poetry as faithfully as possible through print, and perhaps to advertise future publications. A spiritual daughter of the Jesuits, Beatriz de Aguilar was educated and guided by the Society even as a young girl, and a female writer by mandate. Therefore, as her confessor notes in the pamphlet's prologue, she does not consider herself a poet, but takes these intimate verses as "little absurdities,"[18] "so the eyes must not focus on the poetry but on the substance they contain."[19] Beatriz de Aguilar and her work are a symbolic "creation" of the Jesuits, an example of those lay sisters "who are usually part of the Society of Jesus,"[20] and mentioned by the friar Ángel Manrique in the *Life* (*Vida*) of the Carmelite nun, Ana de Jesús (Martínez de la Escalera: 369). This is endorsed by the Jesuit order's seal on the pamphlet's cover, the xylographic engraving with the monogram IHS, symbol of the *Societas Jesu*, with the sunbeams, the cross, and the three nails from the Passion. The pamphlet form could certainly have become the alternative method by which to make known the religious poetry written by nuns and lay sisters; however, but the practice was not generalized and, consequently, many nuns' poetic production remains at best, scattered and dispersed in their biographies and autobiographies or, at worst, has been lost.

The pamphlet belonging to Salvadora Colodro includes a penitential ballad, *Afectos de un pecador arrepentido, hablando con un santo crucifijo a la hora de la muerte* (Emotions of a repentant sinner, speaking with a holy crucifix at the time of death) that appeared in Granada in 1663. The poem belongs to the genre of "the repentant sinner at the time of death," probably based on the popular *Avisos para la muerte* (Portents of Death) (Madrid, 1634) by Luis Ramírez de Arellano, and on Ignatian poems (Osuna, "Los avisos": 69). The poet adopts the stance of a contrite sinner at the moment of death, and in first person, gives a general confession in apparent dialogue with the crucified Christ (Cerdán: 533; Marín Pina, "Pliegos": 244), such as the one in the engraving on the pamphlet's cover.[21] The female author's imitation of this kind of poetry would explain the masculine poetic voice (a sinner, a devout) that she does not bother to change to the feminine gender.

The religious poetry published over half a century later by Lucas del Olmo Alfonso's daughter and sister, poets from Cádiz, has no relation with this mystical and penitential poetry. Although some of their pamphlets extend beyond the timeframe of this chapter, they deserve our attention because their authors were related by kinship to Lucas del Olmo Alfonso, who was the most prolific author of eighteenth-century religious ballads. As such, their poetry evinces a popular devotional style very different from the ones commented above. Lucas del Olmo's daughter, in one of her three extant pamphlets of religious poetry,[22] the *Romance de la santísima Cruz* (Ballad of the Holy Cross) (Valencia, 1758), portrays herself as a literate woman who crafts poetry almost spontaneously: "I was born daughter to the language / that I appreciate and profess / and by studying skills / I achieved felicitous occupations."[23] Her versifying ability is manifested in three popular ballads on the purity of the Virgin Mary, the Holy Trinity and the invention of the Cross, all intended to increase religious devotion. An identical objective guides Lucas del Olmo Alfonso's sister, the author of the *Verdadera relación y curioso romance en que se declara la vida y muerte del bienaventurado san Alejo* (True account and discreet ballad that declares the life and death of blessed saint Alexius) (Madrid, 1764), one of the many hagiographic ballads that circulated in the eighteenth century to instruct the public with exemplary lives, such as this one on an austere saint.

Theatrical and literary pamphlets

Through the pamphlet form, female writers were free to practice the most commercially successful literary genres of their time: plays and the *romancero* (ballad collection). In 1639, Ana Caro, a renowned poet in and outside Seville for her *relaciones* of celebrations and other celebratory verses, made public her interest in theater by composing the *Loa sacramental que se representó en el carro de Antonio de Prado, en las fiestas del Corpus de Sevilla, este año de 1639* (Seville, by Juan Gómez de Blas) (Sacramental play staged on Antonio de Prado's cart for the Corpus celebrations of Seville in 1639). This brief piece began the staging of the *auto sacramental* [24] on the merchant, Antonio de Prado's cart, contracted by the Seville chapter to celebrate the feast day of Corpus Christi. Prado, as producer, requested the services of Ana Caro and paid for the *loa*. Again, the author commercializes her writing, capitalizing on it now in a new venue, the theater, in which she would also succeed. She had long been interested in the theater, however, as her two plays, *Valor, agravio y mujer* (*Courage, Betrayal, and a Woman Scorned*) and *El conde Partinuplés* (*The Count Partinuplés*), were apparently written between 1609 and 1621, although they were published much later. With the *loa* printed in pamphlet form and under her name, a rare practice in minor works, Ana Caro officially declared herself a playwright, and a successful one at that, since for the following Corpus Christi celebrations she was contracted to write other *autos sacramentales* for which she was paid, but are now lost (López Estrada, "Una loa"; Luna: 149–151). In the *loa*, she addresses the religious theme corresponding to this kind of theatrical piece through an accomplished monologue delivered by a single actor who plays four roles (Portuguese, French, Morisco, and Guinean) and recites four *canciones* in four different languages. The pamphlet revealed a new facet of this professional poet to the general public, one who knew how to navigate easily in the complicated business world of the stage.[25]

Many of the themes that are treated in the theater and in short novels also appear in the *romancero*, and female authors echo them in their works as well. Lucas del Olmo Alfonso's daughter published the *Nuevo y curioso romance en que se da cuenta y declara la prodigiosa historia y cautiverio del bizarro don Luis de Borja* (New and discreet ballad that recounts and declares the prodigious history and captivity of the singular Don Luis de Borja), a poetic pamphlet that was repeatedly published undated in various Spanish cities throughout the eighteenth century. The ballad shows the author's ease in composing a fictional history in octosyllabic lines, with an agile rhythm and happy ending about Don Luis de Borja, a dauntless and spirited knight. In pagan lands, he wins the love of Zulema, the King of Algiers' daughter, who converts to Christianity at his pleading, and after her baptism marries him in Spain. Knightly jousts, maritime adventures, love, and religion comprise this Spanish ballad, one of the few written by women.

Conclusion

The repertoire of poetic pamphlets written by women that we have analyzed is characterized by the variety of genres and themes (*relaciones* of civic and religious celebrations, celebratory poetry on several subjects, religious poetry, theatrical and literary poetry) and by their metric diversity. Seen as a whole, it reveals their authors' disparity of interests, their ability and versatility to adapt to the demands of promoters, patrons, editors, and the reading public, who in one way or another are always present in the gestation of their works. In order to understand this process, it is essential that we know more about the publishing background of these pamphlets and research the different steps involved in their production. Although progress has been made in unearthing biographical information on Ana Caro, Beatriz de Aguilar, María Nieto, and Luisa María Domonte, it is necessary to continue to research their lives and to investigate the identities of Eugenia Buesso, Salvadora Colodro, Mariana Bautista, and Lucas del Olmo Alfonso's daughter and sister, who remain unknown. This information will allow us to trace the network of personal relationships that could have influenced or determined their activity and interests as female writers. Their works also require thorough literary analysis and attention to their appropriation of possible sources, and to their genre and style, which are often disregarded. And the women authors we have mentioned were not the only ones who celebrated contemporary historical events; there were others who exhibited their own style, in prose or verse. Comparing their works to those by male authors on the same subject or in the same genre will help in better appreciating women's poetic production. Contrasting the *relación* of the *Contexto de las reales fiestas* (1637) (Context of the royal celebration) by Ana Caro to that by Andrés Sánchez de Espejo (1637); comparing the pamphlet by Eugenia Buesso on the bullfight celebration in 1669 with that by José Tafalla Negrete on the same celebration (1670); or the poem by Salvadora Colodro with similar titles published by the same Granada printing presses will help us understand the process of poetic production by both genders. All the poets' creations must be appreciated against the poetic panorama of the time and in comparison to other authors.

Women's poems would almost never have been published if not for the possibility of publishing them in pamphlets. At the times when these women authors' pamphlets were published, none had written sufficiently so as to compose an entire book of poetry. Pamphlets, however, could potentially be made into booklets of two, four, ten, and up to sixteen pages. Individually, women's poems would probably have remained hidden in their personal files,[26] at best shared among the circle of their acquaintances by means of handwritten copies, without ever reaching the wide and diverse public of the pamphlet. Thanks to their pamphlets, therefore, all of these female authors became well known by the broader public and participated in the cultural networks of the Baroque and late Baroque. Their verses were their public voices, and through them they actively took part in society. Their poetry allowed them to become involved in contemporary local and national history, to rewrite it, and give their opinion, and take sides. They transformed current events into laudatory and panegyric poetry that contributed to the political propaganda of the monarchy and nobility; they defended the interests of different religious orders, collaborated in pastoral work, and stimulated entertainment. Through the publication of pamphlets, which widely disseminated literature of limited extension, these poets became visible and benefited socially and at times economically, as their poetic voice resounded in the public sphere.

Notes

1 For poetic jousts, see Osuna in this volume. For an updated bibliography on the authors mentioned in this chapter, see the database BIESES (www.bieses.net).
2 The poems can be consulted in the BIESES database under the entry "Preliminares."
3 "En general, un cuaderno de pocas hojas destinado a propagar textos literarios e históricos entre la gran masa lectora, principalmente popular" (Rodríguez-Moñino: 11).
4 "Cosa alguna sin licencia por menuda que sea" (qtd. by García de Enterría: 72; Reyes Gómez: 327).
5 The BIESES database includes abundant information on all of them.
6 "Textos breves de tema histórico concreto con una intencionalidad de transmisión por medio del proceso editorial" (Infantes, "¿Qué es una *relación*?": 208).
7 Poem consisting of hendecasyllabic and heptasyllabic lines.
8 "Escriví a Sevilla" (fol. 16r).
9 Caro's title may have been influenced by Andrés Sánchez de Espejo's prose account, *Relación ajustada en lo posible a la verdad y repartida en dos discursos. El primero, de la entrada de Madame María de Borbón, Princesa de Cariñán. El segundo, de las fiestas que se celebraron en el Real Palacio del Buen Retiro a la elección de Rey de Romanos*, Madrid, 1637 (Account adjusted as closely as possible to the truth and divided into two discourses. The first, on the entry of Madame María de Borbón, Princess of Carignan. The second, on the celebrations held at the Royal Palace of the Buen Retiro on the election of the King of Romans).

10 Poem consisting of eight hendecasyllable lines.
11 "Hacia aquí se quejaba una mujer y no en muy malas endechas, que desde lejos me pareció hermosa como dos mil entendidas, y desde más cerca aseada como otros tantos poetas. Doña Ana Caro será, que entre muchísimos hombres y entre poquísima gana de casarse, se quejaba de su hastío" (Julio, "Vejamen": 295). Batres's negative opinion is similar to the one on María de Zayas, Caro's friend, issued years later in 1643 by Francesc Fontanella also in a satire, in this case in the academy of Santo Tomás de Aquino in Barcelona, in which he describes Zayas as hardly attractive and more male than female.
12 "Que en tal fiesta fue razón, / que huviese tal coronista" (López Estrada "Costumbres": 119, vv.29–30).
13 A more satirical poetic pamphlet is one from the eighteenth century, anonymous and *sine notis*, titled *Sátira nueva, curiosa, donde se declaran las excusas que hazen los señores hombres cuando entra la Cuaresma para no comer pescado, o a lo menos para no ayunar. Compuesta por una Dama incógnita, en despique de la que se cantó contra las señoras mujeres. Como lo verá el curioso por esta nueva y graciosa Satirilla* (New and intriguing satire declaring the excuses men use during Lent for not eating fish, or at least for not fasting. Composed by an unknown Lady, in revenge for the one sung against ladies. As the curious will see in this new and amusing small satire).
14 "Es honor de Portugal / y de Castilla excelencia."
15 Poem of ten octosyllabic lines.
16 "Hermano caro."
17 "de un Xavier la eloquencia más sublime, / el zelo más ardiente de un Ignacio."
18 "Disparaticos."
19 "assí que no se deven poner los ojos en la poesía sino en la substancia que contienen" (Aguilar: h. 2v).
20 "De las que suele tener la Compañía de Jesús" (ibid.).
21 Inmaculada Osuna suggests that Colodro may have formado part of a collective, since in 1663 the same Granada press published several pamphlets on the same theme, with a small engraving on the front.
22 See the detailed description in the database BIESES. The extant testimonies are probably not the first editions. Some of these ballads have a long trajectory and were reedited in the nineteenth and twentieth centuries, although without female attribution.
23 "Hija nací de las letras, / que las estimo y profeso / y estudiando facultades / logré felices empleos."
24 Theatrical plays that celebrated the mystery of the Eucharist by combining the human, supernatural, and allegorical.
25 For women's roles other than playwrights in early modern Spanish theater, see Sanz Ayán.
26 As in the case of Catalina Clara Ramírez de Guzmán, whose manuscripts include the *Relación en coplas de pie quebrado de las fiestas que celebró Llerena al nacimiento de el príncipe nuestro señor don Felipe Próspero* (Account in mixed-line stanzas of the festivals in Llerena on the birth of the prince our lord Don Felipe Próspero). The "pie quebrado" is a stanza of octosyllabic lines interspersed with tetrasyllabic lines.

Works cited

Aguilar Pinal, Francisco. *Bibliografía de autores españoles del siglo XVIII*. Tomo IX. Anónimos I. Madrid: CSIC, 1999.
——. *Romancero popular del siglo XVIII*. Madrid: CSIC, 1972.
Baranda, Nieves. "Cantos al sacro epitalamio o sea pliegos poéticos para las tomas de velo. Deslindes preliminares." *Bulletin Hispanique*, 113.1 (2011): 269–296.
——. "Words for Sale: Early Modern Spanish Women's Literary Economy." *Mightier than the Spoon is the Pen: Economic Imperatives for Women's Writing in Europe before 1800*. Ed. Amsterdam: Rodopi, 2015 [forthcoming].
Bautista, Mariana. *A la lanzada de a caballo en la fiesta de los completorios de nuestra señora de los Remedios. Por doña Mariana Bautista. Canción.* [s.l.; s.n.], Relaciones poéticas sobre las fiestas de toros y cañas. Tomo V. Biblioteca de The Hispanic Society of America, III. (Siglos XVII y XVIII). Ed. Antonio Pérez Gómez. Cieza: ". . . la fonte que mana y corre. . .", 1973.
Bermúdez de Pedraza, Francisco. *Historia eclesiástica, principios y progresos de la ciudad y religión católica de Granada, corona de su poderoso reino y excelencias de su corona*. Granada: Francisco Sánchez, 1652.
BIESES. *Bibliografía de escritoras españolas*. www.bieses.net/
Brown, Kenneth. "María de Zayas y Sotomayor: escribiendo poesía en Barcelona en la época de la guerra." *Dicenda. Cuadernos de Filología Hispánica*, 11 (1993): 355–360.

Campo Guiral, María Ángeles, ed. *Ana Francisca Abarca de Bolea. "Vigilia y Octavario de San Juan Baptista."* Huesca: Instituto de Estudios Altoaragoneses, 1993.

Caro de Mallén, Ana. *Contexto de las Reales Fiestas que se hizieron en el Palacio del Buen Retiro a la Coronación de Rey de Romanos, y entrada en Madrid de la Señora Princesa de Cariñán, en tres discursos, por Ana Caro de Mallén,* ed. facsímil de Antonio Pérez Gómez. Valencia: Taller de Tipografía Moderna, 1951.

Cerdán, Francis. "Los afectos del pecador arrepentido a la hora de la muerte. Tensión anímica y expresión poética en el siglo XVII." *Muerte, religiosidad y cultura popular. Siglos XIII–XVIII.* Ed. Eliseo Serrano Martín. Zaragoza: Institución "Fernando el Católico," 1994: 531–550.

Cruz, Anne J. "Teresa Guerra, poeta entre el Barroco y la Ilustración." *Bulletin Hispanique,* 113/1 (2011): 297–312.

Deveny, Thomas. "Poets and Patrons: Literary Adulation in the Epithalamium of the Spanish Golden Age." *South Atlantic Modern Language Association,* 53.4 (1988): 21–37.

Entrambasaguas y Peña, Joaquín. *Poesías de Doña Catalina Clara Ramírez de Guzmán.* Badajoz: Imprenta de Antonio Arqueros, 1930.

García Bernal, José Jaime. *El fasto público en la España de los Austrias.* Seville: Universidad de Sevilla, Secretariado de Publicaciones, 2006.

García de Enterría, María Cruz. *Sociedad y poesía de cordel en el Barroco.* Madrid: Taurus, 1973.

Infantes, Víctor. "Los pliegos sueltos poéticos: constitución tipográfica y contenido literario (1482–1600)." *El libro antiguo español: actas del primer coloquio internacional (Madrid, 18–20 de diciembre de 1986).* Ed. María Luisa López Vidriero and Pedro M. Cátedra. Salamanca: Universidad de Salamanca; Madrid: Biblioteca Nacional, Sociedad Española de Historia del Libro, 1993: 237–248.

——."¿Qué es una *relación*? (Divagaciones varias sobre una sola divagación)." *Las Relaciones de sucesos en España (1500–1750). Actas del primer coloquio internacional (Alcalá de Henares, 8, 9 y 10 de junio de 1995).* Ed. María Cruz García de Enterría *et al.* Alcalá de Henares: Servicio de Publicaciones de la Universidad de Alcalá and Publications de la Sorbonne, 1996: 203–216.

Julio, Teresa. *Academia burlesca que se hizo en el Buen Retiro a la majestad de Filipo Cuarto el Grande. Año de 1637.* Madrid: Iberoamericana, 2007.

——. "Vejamen de Alfonso de Batres para la Academia de 1638 (Manuscrito inédito). Estudio y edición crítica." *Revista de Literatura,* 149 (2013): 279–306.

Latassa y Ortín, Félix. *Bibliotecas Antigua y Nueva de escritores aragoneses de Latassa, aumentadas y refundidas en forma de Diccionario Bibliográfico-Biográfico por don Miguel Gómez Uriel.* I. Zaragoza: Imprenta de Calisto Ariño, 1884.

Ledda, Giuseppina. "Recrear la manifestación festiva 'Para que la vea quien no la vio y quien la vio la vea por segunda vez'. Cultura y comunicación visuales a través de las relaciones de fiestas públicas." *Géneros editoriales y relaciones de sucesos en la Edad Moderna.* Ed. Pedro M. Cátedra and María Eugenia Díaz Tena. Salamanca: SEMYR, 2013: 231–248.

López Estrada, Francisco. "Una loa del Santísimo Sacramento de Ana Caro de Mallén, en cuatro lenguas." *Revista de dialectología y tradiciones populares,* XXXII (1976): 263–274.

——. "La *relación* de las fiestas por los mártires del Japón, de doña Ana Caro de Mallén (Sevilla), 1628." *Libro-homenaje a Antonio Pérez Gómez.* Vol. 2. Cieza: ". . .la fonte que mana y corre. . .", 1978: 51–68.

——. "Fiestas y literatura en los Siglos de Oro: la Edad Media como asunto festivo (El caso del *Quijote*)." *Bulletin Hispanique,* 84.3–4 (1982): 291–327.

——. "Costumbres sevillanas: el poema sobre la fiesta y octava celebradas con motivo de los sucesos de Flandes en la iglesia de san Miguel (1635), por Ana Caro Mallén." *Archivo Hispalense: Revista histórica, literaria y artística,* 203 (1983): 109–150.

——. "La frontera allende el mar: el romance por la victoria de Tetuán (1633) de Ana Caro de Mallén." *Homenaje a José Manuel Blecua ofrecido por sus discípulos, colegas y amigos.* Madrid: Gredos, 1983: 337–346.

Luna, Lola. "Ana Caro, una escritora de oficio." *Leyendo como una mujer la imagen de la mujer.* Prólogo, Iris M. Zavala. Barcelona: Anthropos; Seville: Instituto Andaluz de la Mujer, Junta de Andalucía, 1996: 138–157.

Marín Pina, María Carmen. "Eugenia Buesso, cronista en verso de la entrada de Juan José de Austria en Zaragoza (1669): un texto recuperado." *destiempos.com,* 19 (2009): 60–81.

——. "Pliegos sueltos poéticos femeninos en el camino del verso al libro de poesía. La singularidad de María Nieto." *Bulletin Hispanique,* 113.1 (2011): 239–267.

Martínez de la Escalera, José. "Mujeres jesuíticas y mujeres jesuitas." *A Companhia de Jesus na Península Ibérica nos sécs. XVI e XVII: Espiritualidade e cultura. Actas do coloquio internacional, maio 2004.* Vol. 1. Porto: Instituto de Cultura Portuguesa da Faculdade de Letras da Universidade do Porto, Centro Inter-Universitário de História da Espiritualidade da Universidade do Porto, 2004: 369–383.

Osuna Rodríguez, Inmaculada. "Poesía de proyección ciudadana en tres autoras del siglo XVII: Cristobalina Fernández de Alarcón, María de Rada e Isabel de Tapia." *Península: Revista de Estudos Ibéricos*, 2 (2005): 237–250.

———. "Cristobalina Fernández de Alarcón y la poesía de circunstancias." *Studies on Women's Poetry of the Golden Age. Tras el espejo la musa escribe*. Ed. Julián Olivares. Woodbridge: Tamesis, 2009: 123–148.

———. "*Los Avisos para la muerte de Luis Ramírez de Arellano*." *Revista Via Spiritus. Pregação e Espaços Penitenciais*, 16 (2009): 45–82.

Pizarro Gómez, Francisco Javier. "Artes y espectáculo en las fiestas reales del Retiro de 1637." *Norba-Arte*, VII (1987): 113–139.

R. de la Flor, Fernando. "Economía simbólica de la *relación* de conmemoración fúnebre en el antiguo régimen: gasto, derroche y dilapidación del bien cultural." *La fiesta. Actas del II Seminario de Relaciones de Sucesos (A Coruña, 13–15 de julio de 1998)*. Ed. Sagrario López Poza and Nieves Pena Sueiro. Ferrol: Sociedad de Cultura Valle Inclán, Colección SIELAE, 1999: 121–132.

Reyes Gómez, Fermín de los. "Los impresos menores en la legislación de imprenta (siglos XVI–XVIII), *La fiesta. Actas del II Seminario de Relaciones de sucesos (A Coruña, 13–15 de julio de 1998)*. Ed. Sagrario López Poza and Nieves Pena Sueiro. Ferrol: Sociedad de Cultura Valle Inclán, Colección SIELAE, 1999: 325–338.

Rodríguez-Moñino, Antonio. *Diccionario bibliográfico de pliegos sueltos poéticos (siglo XVI)*. Madrid: Castalia, 1970.

Romero-Díaz, Nieves. "Poesía femenil en la exequias por Isabel de Borbón: los casos de Leonor de la Cueva y Silva y María Nieto de Aragón." *Calíope. Journal of the Society for Renaissance and Baroque Hispanic Poetry*, 16.2 (2010): 9–43.

Sánchez Alonso, María Cristina. *Impresos de los siglos XVI y XVII de temática madrileña*. Madrid: CSIC, 1981.

Sanz Ayán, Carmen. "More than Faded Beauties: Women Theater Managers of Early Modern Spain." *Early Modern Women: An Interdisciplinary Journal*, 10.1 (Fall 2015): 114–121.

Serrano y Sanz, Manuel. *Apuntes para una biblioteca de escritoras españolas desde el año 1401 al 1833*. Madrid: Sucesores de Rivadeneyra, 1903; Atlas (BAE, 270–271), 1974.

Voros, Sharon D. "*Relaciones de fiestas*. Ana Caro's Accounts of Public Spectacles." *Women in the Discourse of Early Modern Spain*. Ed. Joan F. Cammarata. Florida: UP Florida, 2003: 108–132.

14
SPAIN'S WOMEN HUMANISTS

Emilie L. Bergmann

The names of three Spanish women humanists, Beatriz Galindo, Francisca de Lebrija, and Teresa de Cartagena, are inscribed on the Heritage Floor of feminist artist Judy Chicago's *Dinner Party* (1974–1979) at the Brooklyn Museum in New York. The irony is that, of these three, the writings of only one have survived: Teresa de Cartagena's *Arboleda de los enfermos* (Grove of the Infirm) and *Admiración operum Dey* (Wonder at the Work of God). An iconic figure of female erudition throughout Spanish intellectual history, Beatriz Galindo, "La Latina," was praised by her contemporaries for teaching Queen Isabel I and her children, including the devout, well-read, and ill-fated Catherine of Aragon.[1] The queen actively supported humanistic letters at court, engaging the humanists Lucio Marineo Siculo and Pietro Martire d'Anghiera as tutors for the young courtiers. Isabel's patronage of the University of Salamanca was instrumental in the reforms instituted by Antonio de Nebrija.[2] Although Galindo's name is associated with two scholarly commentaries on Aristotle and on other classical works, no copies have survived to support the praise of contemporaries, which remains the basis of her reputation for erudition and pedagogy.[3] Centuries of repetition established the commonplace that two women lectured on rhetoric at universities: Francisca de Lebrija, daughter of Spain's first lexicographer Antonio de Nebrija, at the Universidad Complutense, and Lucía de Medrano at the University of Salamanca.[4] As with the accomplishments of many early modern women, until the late twentieth century, praise was reiterated with scant documentation.

This essay surveys the rediscoveries and reevaluations of humanist women's writing from fifteenth- to seventeenth-century Spain on topics from which women have traditionally been excluded: the natural and social sciences, and theology, considered in the early modern period the common source or "mother" of all branches of knowledge. In his survey of changing views of the Renaissance in Spain from the early modern period to the mid-twentieth century, Ottavio di Camillo summarizes the differences and shared characteristics with other European Renaissances as they have been perceived by Spanish intellectual historians. Whatever differences may be found between the history of humanism in Spain and that of Italy or Northern Europe, the participation of Spanish women in the new approach to knowledge, as in other areas of the continent, is undeniable. Women's education in general was intended only to serve the limited purpose of reading devotional literature in the vernacular, although family commitments to erudition, an exceptional tutor, or an irresistible desire for knowledge allowed a few to extend their education to Latin, the gateway to the legacy of classical and humanistic letters. Cruz points out, however, that Latin "did not play so great a role in Spanish humanism" and thus may not have been as significant an obstacle to women's participation in intellectual and civic life as elsewhere in Europe.[5]

The two most important defenses of women's right to study and participate in the learned culture of their time were authored by women whose family background marginalized them while providing necessary resources for their advanced education: Teresa de Cartagena, a fifteenth-century deaf nun of Jewish descent, and Sor Juana Inés de la Cruz, an illegitimate nun in seventeenth-century New Spain whose grandfather's library nurtured her erudition. Teresa defended women's intellectual ability in *Admiracion Operum Dey* in response to doubts regarding her authorship of a theological treatise, *Arboleda de los enfermos*, on the spiritual benefits as well as the social stigma of her deafness. In *Admiracion*, she inverted the traditional gendered valuation of civic and martial strength over nurturing in the domestic sphere, and emphasized the interdependence of masculine and feminine, while impugning the faith of those unable to accept God's ability to endow her with intelligence and eloquence. Nearly two and a half centuries later, Sor Juana employed traditional rhetorical structure, irony, and displays of erudition to defend her dedication to the poetry, scientific investigation, and philosophical ingenuity that had won acclaim from high-ranking readers in Spain as well as at the Novohispanic viceregal court.

As universities functioned as pipelines for the exclusively masculine careers of priests and *letrados* (court officials trained in the law), women writers throughout Europe protested their curtailed educational possibilities. A powerful and much-cited argument is put forward by Filis, the narrator of the fifth novella, *Tarde llega el desengaño* (Disillusion Arrives Too Late) of María de Zayas's *Desengaños amorosos* (1647). She challenges the moral concerns that men cited to justify their opposition to women's learning; these concerns merely disguised their fear that well-educated women would surpass them and usurp their authority.[6] Less often cited is Filis's reference to the political acumen of "her highness the Infanta Isabel Clara Eugenia de Austria; since the Catholic king Philip II was so wise that he was called 'The Prudent,' he never made a move without consulting her: that's how much he valued her judgment."[7] In 1664, María de Guevara, Countess of Escalante, echoed Zayas's protest: "Since men made the laws, all are written in their favor, requiring women to be satisfied with the arms of the distaff and the pincushion. For by my faith, if women made use of letters, they would surpass men, which is just what men fear; they do not want women to be Amazons but rather to have their hands tied, making it unbecoming for a woman to leave her corner."[8] It was not only in poetry, theater, or fiction that women's ability was recognized; noble and royal women were significant actors in matters of state, and recent scholarship on their writings on the topic finds evidence of their intensive study of classical and Spanish sources.[9]

This overview of scholarship on women humanists centers on six learned women in Spain, Portugal, and colonial New Spain (Mexico), whose literary careers have been the focus of significant scholarly research: Teresa de Cartagena, Luisa Sigea, Oliva Sabuco, Luisa de Padilla, María de Guevara, and Sor Juana Inés de la Cruz. Male writers challenged the authenticity of three of these writers' authorship during their lifetimes, illustrating two key strategies addressed by Joanna Russ in *How to Suppress Women's Writing*: "She didn't write it" or "She wrote it, but she shouldn't have."[10] The reception of their work exemplifies the marginal status of women in the early modern world of letters: Teresa de Cartagena was accused of plagiarism and wrote her second treatise in defense of her authorship and women's ability to study and write erudite treatises. Luisa de Padilla, Countess of Aranda, concealed the authorship of her first three treatises on political reform.[11] In the first, she used the fiction of the "found manuscript," specifically, the text's posthumous discovery by the priest who published it. Oliva Sabuco's authorship was accepted by intellectual historians until the discovery, in 1903, of her father's testament, in which he claimed to have written the book published under her name,[12] while María de Guevara's contribution to seventeenth-century politics and ethics remained unpublished and neglected by scholars for three centuries. Beyond the Iberian Peninsula, when Sor Juana Inés de la Cruz was criticized by an ecclesiastical superior for daring to write a brilliant theological argument, she famously defended her scholarly pursuits in the *Respuesta a sor Filotea* (Letter to Sister Philothea).

Teresa de Cartagena, considered the first Spanish feminist writer, wrote two significant treatises: the first, *Arboleda de los enfermos* (Grove of the Infirm), written after 1450, argued for the dignity of persons with disabilities; the second, *Admiración operum Dey* (Wonder at the Works of God), defended her authorship against accusations she could not have written the erudite *Arboleda*. A member of the politically and intellectually powerful Santa María/Cartagena family in Burgos, she was the granddaughter of the chief rabbi of Burgos, Salomon Ha-Levi, who converted to Christianity, took the name Pablo de Santa María around 1390, and became bishop of Burgos in 1412. Estimations of Teresa's birth date range between 1420 and 1435, and the place and date of her death are unknown.[13] Two documents found in 2001 supply information about her transfer in 1449 from the Franciscan convent of Santa Clara to Las Huelgas, belonging to the Cistercian order, which had an unusual degree of autonomy and held a neutral position with regard to *conversos* (Jewish converts to Christianity and their descendants, including Teresa's family). Teresa's transfer coincided with the worst of the pogroms in Toledo and the subsequent introduction of the discriminatory statutes of *limpieza de sangre* (purity of blood) against *conversos*.[14]

While Cartagena's writings reflect her triple marginalization—as a woman, a *conversa*, and a deaf person—they are also evidence of her exceptional education in her family's libraries, and for "a few years at the University of Salamanca."[15] Her defense of her authorship as a woman in *Admiracion operum Dey* drew the attention of feminist readers in the 1970s; however, the *Arboleda de los enfermos* is important as the only extant woman-authored consolatory treatise, or *consolatio*, a philosophical genre much cultivated in the fifteenth century.[16] In it, she displays the subtlety of her interpretation of sacred texts and commentaries. Cartagena begins by describing her pain from illness, in addition to the deafness that brought her to "an island called [. . .] 'The Scorn of Mankind and Outcast of the People.'"[17] Cartagena explains that, after a long struggle, she was able to value her condition: "And I would have willingly endured this suffering from birth, so that no words that may have offended or deserved God could ever enter the cloister of my ears."[18] She constructs a spiritual plan based on her experience: "all the blessings of this world are food reserved for the healthy; so let us leave what we cannot have and get accustomed to our own diet."[19] While Kim charts Cartagena's representation of the body in pain in terms of medieval concepts of the body and theological views of suffering,[20] Encarnación Juárez reads Cartagena's *Arboleda* through the lens of recent autobiographical writings on disability by Lennard Davis, Susan Wendell, and Nancy Mairs. Juárez proposes that silence ironically allowed Cartagena to develop "a new voice because of her deafness":[21] "Although the texts she reads are written by men, her separation from the spoken word and from the authority of intermediary males (preachers, confessors) places her in a very privileged situation. Silence lets her hear God's voice with 'the ear of my understanding,' and in this act she gains authority and greater freedom of interpretation."[22] Alan Deyermond regarded Cartagena's work as a rare medieval example of "a writer's reflections on the creative process, an indication of how it feels to be a writer."[23]

In response to the challenges of "some prudent men and also discreet women" who were astonished ("se maravillan") at the erudition of the *Arboleda*, Teresa defended her authorship in *Admiración operum Dey*.[24] She cites Saint Augustine on the topic of miracles, affirming her faith that God's power can endow "a person afflicted with so many misfortunes" with unusual intellectual ability, and implicitly questioning that of her detractors who refuse to believe this to be possible.[25] She concedes the difference between men and women, but presents an inversion of the traditional image of woman as a vine embracing a supporting tree trunk. Instead, she compares woman to the vital pith that supplies nutrients to plants and trees, while man is the protective outer bark.[26] Ronald Surtz notes Teresa's clever use of a botanical image familiar to medieval readers, in which "the essential part, the *meollo*, corresponds to the female element, while the superficial interpretation, the *corteza*, corresponds to the male," suggesting an encoded meaning, "a hidden *meollo* of female superiority."[27] *Admiración* was dedicated to Juana de Mendoza, member of a powerful noble family, *camarera mayor* (chambermaid) to the Infanta Isabel, the oldest child of the Catholic Monarchs, and wife of the noble, writer, and political figure Gómez Manrique.

While late medieval modes of argument shape the learned nun Teresa de Cartagena's treatises, the polyglot Neo-Latin writer, Luisa Sigea (ca. 1522–1560), was celebrated as a distinguished humanist, a *puella docta* whose Latin works were praised in Italy, France, and Germany. Ironically, while one of her works, the poem, *Syntra*, has been available in print since the early sixteenth century, the name of this quintessential Renaissance woman faded from public recognition and her works have yet to be translated in full.[28] Baranda Leturio points out that her name became synonymous with "learned woman" in Spain, and "she even managed to do what most women could not: earn her living through this professional erudition which made her conscious of her own value and of her similarity to the male scholars whom she considered her peers."[29] More biographical data are available for Luisa Sigea than for most of the learned women of her time. Born in Tarancón, Luisa and her sister Ángela were taught by her university-educated humanist father, Diego Sigeo, who served as tutor for the children of Juan de Padilla, a leader of the *Comuneros* revolt. Diego left Spain in 1522 with Padilla's widow, María Pacheco, known for her knowledge of Latin, Greek, and mathematics. In 1530 he began serving the Duke of Bragança in Portugal.[30]

Sigea's erudition in ancient and modern languages and her musical training were preparation for a life at court or in a convent. A letter written by Sigea to Pope Paul III displayed her knowledge of Latin, Greek, Hebrew, Arabic, and Aramaic, and had the desired effect of securing a position at the court of the Infanta Doña María of Portugal. There, she joined other educated women including her sister Ángela Sigea, Paula de Vicente, and Joana Vaz, but when Sigea returned to Spain after her marriage in 1552, she was unable to find a position at the royal court or in aristocratic households.[31] Baranda Leturio suggests that the Portuguese court provided an opportunity that was not available to the numerous learned women among the Spanish aristocracy: "In sixteenth-century Spain there were noblewomen with an extensive classical education and interest in literature or erudition, but their courts did not encourage the expression of women's knowledge."[32] Sigea is known for two works: the panegyric *Syntra* (1566), which praises the rustic beauty of the forest of Sintra, across the Duero from Lisbon; and the Ciceronian dialogue *Duarum virginum colloquium de vita aulica et privata* (1552) (Dialogue between two maidens on courtly and private life), in which Blesilla, from Siena, home of the ascetic St. Catherine, defends a life of contemplation and austerity, against the Roman-born Flaminia's argument that the court, despite its corruption and its pleasures, is not inimical to a virtuous life. Manuel Serrano y Sanz published these works in Latin with a partial Spanish translation of *Syntra*, as well as Sigea's letters, in his bio-bibliographical *Apuntes para una biblioteca de escritoras españolas, desde el año 1401 al 1833* (Notes toward a library of Spanish women writers, from 1401 to 1833).[33] Seventy years later, Odette Sauvage published a study, edition, and French translation of *Duarum virginum colloquium* and co-edited a bilingual French-Latin edition of Sigea's letters. María Regla Prieto Corbalán provides a bilingual edition of Sigea's Latin letters, and Susanne Thiemann has published studies of her work.[34]

Among writings attributed to Spanish women, the authorship of the medical treatise published in 1587 under the name of Oliva Sabuco de Nantes, *Nueva filosofía de la naturaleza del hombre, no conocida ni alcanzada de los grandes filósofos antiguos* (New Philosophy of Human Nature), has provoked impassioned scholarly polemic. The debate, however, should not overshadow the text's brilliant uniqueness among early modern medical writing in breaking with the medical theory of its time. While other humanist writers on medical theory aimed for "a more faithful and authentic Galenic doctrine, based on the philological reading and restoration of the ancient Greek texts," *Nueva filosofía* rejected the Aristotelian and Galenic models of the body, as well as those of Averroes and Avicenna.[35] The sections of *Nueva filosofía* are arranged in increasing order of sophistication on the part of their intended readerships, ending with *Vera Medicina*, the last and most erudite section, written in Latin. In her annotated translation with detailed scholarly introduction, Gianna Pomata, a historian of medicine, aims to show the "radical novelty" of Sabuco's "new medicine."[36] Pomata argues that while *Vera Medicina* falls short of being a "forerunner of the experimental method," the "medical heresy" of this treatise is its recognition that the brain, rather than the heart or the liver, controls the body. This theory attributes the source of the body's nutrition to the brain's "white juice" or chyle, rather than blood, and views the emotions, rather than imbalances of the humors, as the primary cause of disease.[37] According to Pomata, in Sabuco's view of correspondences between microcosm and macrocosm, the traditional hierarchy of sun and moon is inverted, as the brain gives moisture and growth to the body with its white chyle, or milk, derived from the moon:

> mother and wet nurse, with her milk, chyle of the world, which is water.[. . .] Sabuco has a fascinating notion of 'environment' (*ambiente, ambiens*) as formed by the 'moon milk' surrounding and feeding all forms of life. [. . .] In other words, we are nursed by the moon milk by drinking and breathing.[38]

The idea that the moon has primacy over the sun, and humidity over heat, is "the most 'heretical' aspect of Sabuco's theory," in Pomata's account, which situates this theory among "Galenist feminists of the late sixteenth century" and medical arguments in the *Querelle des femmes* challenging the Aristotelian concept of women's inferiority. Pomata traces references to Oliva's theories among English physicians, including Robert Harvey: "The revolutionary attack on Galenism launched under a woman's name had lasting consequences on European intellectual history."[39]

Oliva Sabuco de Nantes's reputation as an extraordinarily learned woman and a pioneer in medical theory stood for three centuries. In 1903, the town clerk of her home town, Alcaraz, José Marco Hidalgo, published three documents from the town's archives in which Oliva's father, Miguel Sabuco, claimed authorship of *Nueva filosofía*. Most controversial among them is Miguel's last will and testament, signed in 1588, in which he wrote:

> I declare that I composed a book entitled *Nueva filosofía* or norm, and another book that will be printed, in all of which I gave and give as author the said Luisa de Oliva my daughter, only to give her the name and the honor, and I reserve for myself the fruit and profit that may result from the said books, and I bid the said daughter of mine, Luisa de Oliva, not to meddle with the said privilege, under penalty of my curse, in consideration of what has been said, beyond which I have made an attestation to the effect that I am the author and she is not. Which attestation is in a legal document executed before the notary Villarreal.[40]

The first volume of Serrano y Sanz's *Apuntes* appeared in 1903, the same year as Marco Hidalgo's discovery; the second, which includes the entry on Sabuco, in 1905. The bibliographer begins his entry by noting the uniqueness of this challenge to authorship, and claiming that Oliva has lost her cultural prestige; the alleged deception reduces her moral reputation.[41] Nevertheless, inclusion in the *Apuntes* signals implicit acceptance of her authorship, with a five-page entry on *Nueva filosofía*. This is the problem that confronts scholars interested in this medical treatise.

Because early modern female authorship was so frequently challenged, it is important to survey, if briefly, the current state of the question. The Biblioteca Nacional in Madrid, the U.S. National Library of Medicine, and Palau y Dulcet's authoritative *Manual del librero hispano-americano* (Manual of the Hispano-American bookseller; 1948–1977; updated in 1990) attribute authorship to Miguel Sabuco, although the Library of Congress catalogues *Nueva filosofía* under both names, with Miguel's as lead author, while Oliva is listed as the sole author of *Libro de conocimiento de sí mismo* (Knowledge of One's Self), which constitutes the first treatise, or chapter, of *Nueva filosofía*. Dámaris Otero-Torres and María-Milagros Rivera Garretas argued for reinstatement of Oliva Sabuco's authorship and reputation as a learned woman on the grounds that misogyny was the irrational basis for scholarly acceptance of Miguel Sabuco's claims.[42] In an article published in 2003, appealing to library cataloguers to restore the original attribution, and in their 2007 edition and translation, *New Philosophy of Human Nature*, philosophers Mary Ellen Waithe and María Elena Vintró presented arguments based on early modern Spanish publication protocols including strict requirements for obtaining licenses to print books. They also cite new archival information about Oliva and her husband, Acacio de Bueso, refuting the rumor that they left Alcaraz in disgrace after Miguel's usurpation of authorship.[43]

In an essay he considered important enough to publish twice (in 2000 and in 2009), José Pascual Buxó argues that Oliva was the "true author of the book, or at least, of some of its parts."[44] He notes that Oliva's prologue clearly anticipates doubts regarding her scientific knowledge and her authorship, as well as accusations of "atrevimiento" or "osadía" (literally, boldness or daring, but with particularly negative connotations for a woman). Buxó describes the intellectual life of Alcaraz, in particular the informal meetings of a group of scholars including Oliva's teacher, the humanist Pedro Simón Abril, and imagines a complex, collaborative process that included Miguel Sabuco, along with other local savants. The license to publish *Nueva filosofía* was issued under Oliva's name; thus her father, prevented from publishing it himself in Spain, sent his son Alonso to Portugal, where, in fact, it appeared many years later, in 1622, but also under Oliva's name: Miguel Sabuco was unable to wrest from her the privilege granted by the king "for all the days of her life."[45] That he reneged on his initially generous attribution bears witness to one of many obstacles to the recognition of women's role in Spanish humanism. Buxó concludes that her father was motivated by sheer greed and family discord following his second marriage.[46]

Pomata's contribution to the question of authorship draws upon her discovery of a significant mention of Oliva in Cristóbal de Acosta's *Tratado en loor de las mugeres* (Treatise in praise of women), published in Venice in 1592, but "probably written several years earlier."[47] Acosta describes "the book that this learned woman is writing on the new philosophy of the nature of man, and on the true medicine. In which you will find—those of you who will read it with attention and without prejudice—all the philosophy and medicine of the ancients and the moderns, renewed with great cleverness, wisdom, and many demonstrations."[48] Pomata finds that Waithe and Vintró provided valuable new perspectives through their archival research, and she agrees that "Oliva's authorship has been too easily discounted," but she finds their conclusions too speculative, and she is unconvinced by the feminist arguments of Rivera Garretas and Otero Torres; they are "just as unsatisfactory as the old solution in favor of Miguel, inspired as it was by a positivism strongly flavored with male chauvinism."[49] Much ink had already been spilled by 2014, when Baranda Leturio cited the uncommon assertiveness of the claim made in the prologue (the authorship of which is also debated) that this work by a woman is "superior in quality to those done by men, whether commoners or nobles," in addition to the uniqueness of its topic.[50] Baranda Leturio makes an important point: that the document granting permission to publish indicates that Oliva Sabuco appeared in person to obtain the necessary *privilegio* for publication in her own name, the earliest known instance of a Spanish woman writer having done so.[51] Despite this new evidence, Pomata uses the combined pronoun "she / he" (or "she or he") throughout her introductory essay, and concludes that "the mystery of the authorship of *Nueva filosofía* has not been solved yet."[52]

While Oliva Sabuco's authorship on the title page of a medical treatise was an anomaly that attracted scholarly attention in Spain, England, and Italy, women authored letters, *memoriales*, and treatises on matters of state, although they have remained obscure. Four volumes published between 1639 and 1644 on the reform of the nobility written by Luisa de Padilla, Countess of Aranda (ca. 1590–ca. 1646) have yet to be reprinted in modern editions. Nicolás Antonio lists three of her six prose works in *Bibliotheca Hispana Nova* and Serrano y Sanz published several letters and detailed tables of contents of all six books in his *Apuntes*, praising the Countess of Aranda's wealth of erudition, innovative thought, and ease and purity of style.[53] Carmen Peraita notes that this prolific writer was "known for her *ingenio* and indefatigable learning," and "Padilla's reputation as writer of moral philosophy was well established before her works appeared in print."[54] The countess's letters to the Aragonese chronicler Juan Francisco Andrés de Uztarroz and others are evidence of her interest in history and archaeology and her participation in the intellectual circles associated with the scholar and antiquarian Vincencio Juan de Lastanosa and Baltasar Gracián, who dedicated his *Agudeza y arte de ingenio* (1648) to the countess's husband, Antonio Jiménez de Urrea. Aurora Egido, Nieves Romero-Díaz, Rosilie Hernández, and Nieves Baranda Leturio have published significant scholarship on Padilla, bringing attention to the work of a woman writer who advocated a restoration of the prestige of Aragonese nobility through moral, social, and political reform and education in four major works: *Nobleza virtuosa* (1637), *Noble perfecto y segunda parte de la nobleza virtuosa* (1639), *Lágrimas de la nobleza* (1639), and *Idea de nobles y sus desempeños* (1644).

Egido analyzes the rhetorical structures, Neoplatonic concepts, and philosophical foundations of Padilla's *Idea de nobles* (1644), and integrates this work into the moral and political ideology of the first half of the seventeenth century.[55] Noting significant points of correspondence between the works of Gracián and those of the countess, Egido recognizes the vision of a "caballería a lo divino" (spiritual chivalry), a Counter-reformation ascetic and doctrinal reorientation of fundamental Italian humanist concepts, aimed at the moral and spiritual education of the nobility. she also cites Ignacio Atienza's critique of the paternalistic programs of social control advocated by Padilla and her intellectual circle. While Padilla recommended that the nobility provide schools for servants' children, she also detailed methods of surveillance to limit the influence of "restless souls, seeking novelty."[56] Egido imagines Padilla's biography of the Marqués de Santillana as a quixotic reframing of the medieval genre of the "mirror of princes," as a nostalgic Padilla censures her aristocratic contemporaries for their rejection of chivalric pursuits and their enjoyment of idleness and luxury in royal and noble courts.[57] Elizabeth Lehfeldt studies Padilla's political advocacy for reform among works that attributed the social, political, military, and economic decline of Spain to decadent masculinity and proposed measures to "restore a code of proper manhood."[58] Like Egido, Lehfeldt concludes that "these critics adopted a nostalgic posture and drew their inspiration largely from the Middle Ages"; thus, the moralists and arbitristas created an illusory ideal, failing to "forge a new paradigm of noble manhood."[59]

In her detailed account of the Aragonese writer's second published work, *Lágrimas de la nobleza* (1639), Hernández places Padilla's arguments for reform "well within the ideological project of many of the moralists, political reformers and *arbitristas* of the period."[60] *Lágrimas de la nobleza* indicts the nobility for its scandalous behavior, from blasphemy to adultery and poor childrearing practices; the list ends with their ill-treatment of vassals and servants. Hernández points out that by directly associating the nation's well-being and the empire's future stability with the way in which noblemen treat their wives, children, elders, and servants, Padilla "erases the boundaries between private and public practice." In addition, the countess challenges the arrogance based on entitlement by defining nobility as "a matter of virtue, and not of lineage."[61]

Hernández argues that "Padilla's defense of virility paradoxically substantiates her own position of authority [. . .] She is a devout Christian who has dedicated her own time to loftier and more 'masculine' occupations. [. . .] Her text is proof of her virile nobility."[62] Ironically, one of the devices Padilla used to frame *Nobleza virtuosa*, her first social, moral, and political treatise, was the traditional subgenre of the "mother's legacy" in which the author addressed her children in writing, anticipating the possibility that she might not survive their birth or infancy. In Padilla's case, however, motherhood appears to have been a literary fiction to justify her writing; since after her death, the conde claimed to have remarried reluctantly, only in order to produce an heir.[63] Padilla's *Nobleza virtuosa* (1637) was published under the name of fray Pedro Enrique Pastor, who claimed in the volume's preface to have discovered the manuscript among the posthumous papers of a nobleman, clearly intended for publication on condition that the "Autora's" name be concealed. The cleric presents the text to the Duke of Osuna as a "Cartilla para instruyr niños Nobles," or primer for the moral education of the heir to his title, modeled on the popular genre of the "mirror of princes." The most original writing in *Nobleza virtuosa*, however, is in the section advocating an active role for aristocratic women. Baranda Leturio notes the scarcity of bibliographic references in the margins of these pages, where a practical perspective dominates.[64] This practicality extends to the jewelry appropriate for unmarried and married women, and the exclusion of servants and children from the aristocratic woman's private space, which she specifies should be securely locked with a key, like the private study of a powerful prince or nobleman.[65]

The treatise on good government by María de Guevara, Countess of Escalante, is further proof that women could, and did, write authoritatively on political, military, and economic issues. Written in 1663, Guevara's work appeared in print in Serrano y Sanz's *Apuntes*[66] but was neglected until 1986, when María Isabel Barbeito Carneiro published parts of her study of early modern women writers. Guevara authored two important treatises on government that boldly argue for women's inclusion not only in matters of state, but in war. She refers to Amazons and powerful women rulers as historical models for men. Unlike Padilla's works, however, Guevara's remained virtually unknown, although two manuscripts were transcribed and published in Serrano y Sanz's *Apuntes*: Guevara's *Tratado y advertencias hechas por una mujer celosa del bien de su Rey y corrida de parte de España* (1663, Treatise and Warnings by a Woman, Concerned for the good of Her King, and Affronted on Behalf of Spain),[67] and a third-person narrative, *Relación de la Jornada que la Condesa de Escalante hizo a la ciudad de Vitoria a besar la mano a Su Majestad* (Report on the Journey that the Countess of Escalante Made to the City of Vitoria to Kiss Her Majesty's Hand), as well as the table of contents of Guevara's *Desengaños de la Corte y Mujeres Valerosas* (1664, Disenchantments of the Court and Valorous Women).[68] The bilingual edition by Nieves Romero-Díaz in the series "The Other Voice," *Warnings to the Kings and Advice on Restoring Spain*, includes a detailed analysis and provides the first English translation and the first annotated edition of Guevara's writings. Romero-Díaz's edition includes the *Tratado* and the *Desengaños* and, in two appendices, the document tracing the countess's noble lineage, *Memorial de la Casa de Escalante* (1654, Memorial of the House of Escalante); and the *Relación*.

Guevara's treatises reveal a remarkably authoritative assertion of women's place in all aspects of governing, grounded in her study of history. Regarding the breadth and depth of readings in Biblical, Classical, and Spanish texts on moral, political, and historical topics, clearly evident in the works of Luisa de Padilla and María de Guevara, Nieves Baranda Leturio observes that the former reshaped her sources to suit her purpose, while the latter, "a reader with her own ideas, weighed her readings against reality, and critiqued them without being overwhelmed by the weight of *auctoritas*."[69] The *Tratado* addresses Philip IV directly, and brings him into the conversation; while the *Desengaños* only mentions the future Carlos II in the dedication.[70] The *Tratado* addresses the topic of "Education of the Prince," a genre with medieval roots, but particularly popular in the seventeenth century, reflecting anxieties concerning the ability of Philip IV to govern as Spain began to lose battles in the Portuguese war of independence. Like Padilla, Guevara calls attention to the corruption and moral decay of the nobility and the neglect of their responsibilities toward their families and servants. Writing in the context of Spain's disastrous war against Portugal, Guevara emphasizes political status and foreign policy, that is, the importance of qualified military leaders and ministers to advise the king. Romero-Díaz notes that the countess borrows frequently from her humanist ancestor Antonio de Guevara's biography of Marcus Aurelius, *Relox de príncipes* (1529, Mirror of Princes), and she compares the countess's *Desengaños de la corte* to Antonio de Guevara's *Menosprecio de la corte y alabanza del aldea* (1539, Disparagement of the court and praise of the village). In addition to the contrast between the Renaissance ideal of country life and the baroque value of "prudence," or adapting to the circumstances, Romero-Díaz points out that María de Guevara drew upon her experience of rural life as an ideal setting for the nobility to fulfill their social and moral obligations, since she spent her life ably managing her estates, while her husbands were waging war or confined in enemy prisons.

The best-known early modern defense of women's right to intellectual pursuits is the *Respuesta a sor Filotea* (Answer to Sister Philothea) written by the Hieronymite nun Sor Juana Inés de la Cruz, born Juana de Asbaje in the Viceroyalty of New Spain (1648–1695). The *Respuesta* is the third in a series of polemical documents that began with the publication of Sor Juana's critique of a sermon preached forty years earlier by the Portuguese Jesuit Antonio de Vieira, on the topic of Christ's greatest *fineza*, or gift to humankind. In November 1690, Sor Juana's critique was published without her permission as *Carta Atenagórica* (Letter Worthy of Athena), together with a *Carta de sor Filotea* (Letter from Sister Philothea) admonishing Sor Juana to dedicate more time to religious pursuits instead of the secular literary activity that had brought her fame outside the cloister. Scholars generally agree that "Sor Filotea" was the feminine pseudonym of Manuel Fernández de Santa Cruz, the Bishop of Puebla, who had been an ally of Sor Juana. The *Carta Atenagórica* was republished later with Sor Juana's permission in Spain in 1692 as *Crisis sobre un sermón* (Opinion or Judgment About a Sermon) in her second volume of works. Sor Juana defended her intellectual life in the *Respuesta a sor Filotea*, dated March 1691 but not published until 1700, in *Fama y obras póstumas* (Fame and Posthumous Works).

Research continues on the political environment, the political enmities and alliances, in which the polemic unfolded following publication of the *Carta Atenagórica*. In 1980 Monsignor Aureliano Tapia Méndez discovered a surprisingly confrontational letter from Sor Juana to her confessor, known as the *Carta de Monterrey*, dated ten years before the *Atenagórica*. The Spanish original of Octavio Paz's *Sor Juana, o, las trampas de la fe* (Sor Juana, or, The Traps of Faith) was published in 1982, before the *Carta de Monterrey* had been fully accepted by scholars; however, Margaret Sayers Peden's 1988 translation includes the *Carta de Monterrey*. Paz's study still stands as the most comprehensive monograph on Sor Juana, as well as a great Mexican poet's response to a foremother whose work had not been adequately studied. Some new discoveries have challenged, while others confirm some of Paz's assumptions. Elías Trabulse's discovery of the *Carta de sor Serafina*, a highly codified letter of debated authorship in defense of Sor Juana, casts controversial new light on Sor Juana's relationships with her ecclesiastical superiors in the last years of her life.

While far more attention has been given to the *Respuesta*, in modern editions, studies, and translations into English, the *Carta Atenagórica* displays Sor Juana's theological expertise. One of her central points is the Portuguese Jesuit's audacious refutation of writings on the topic by the fathers and doctors of the church, St. Augustine, St. John Chrysostom, and St. Thomas Aquinas. In addition to these substantive issues of interpretation, she also addresses the flaws in the structure of Vieira's argument. Grady Wray's article, "Sacred Allusions," presents an accessible overview of the recondite arguments in Vieira's sermon and Sor Juana's *Carta*. His article, "Challenging Theological Authority," provides a far more detailed account of Sor Juana's defense of the saints' views, the polemic that ensued, and current debates regarding the *Atenagórica*'s challenge to New Spain's religious hierarchy as a whole and the Jesuits in particular. Although translations of the *Carta Atenagórica* are rare, Edith Grossman includes it with the *Respuesta* in *Sor Juana Inés de la Cruz: Selected Works*.

While the *Respuesta*'s eloquent arguments against the intellectual subordination of women and its picturesque childhood anecdotes attract scholars and students, a first encounter with the text is daunting in terms of the sheer erudition Sor Juana brings to her defense, the complex rhetorical structure of the sentences, the subtle irony, and the combination of conventions of the familiar letter and formal rhetorical argument. Electa Arenal and Amanda Powell's bilingual *The Answer/La Respuesta* illuminates a path through the labyrinth with a comprehensive introduction, indispensable annotations, and Powell's English translation. Rosa Perelmuter's analysis of the rhetorical structure of the *Respuesta* dispelled the misleading evaluations, in scholarship by both men and women, of its prose as plain ("llano"), natural, sincere, and simple: she reveals that "beneath its apparent lack of organization and perceived spontaneity lies a formal organization whose outstanding feature is precisely its ability to conceal itself."[71] From Sor Juana's references to silence and knowledge, not knowing what to say, and knowing but not saying, Josefina Ludmer developed a significant theory of "tricks of the weak." She views these references as recognition that saying and knowing "constitute opposing fields for a woman: whenever the two coexist, they occasion resistance and punishment," thus requiring the complex strategy of contradictions and ironies woven throughout the *Respuesta*.[72]

The *Respuesta* belongs, to a large extent, to forensic, or judicial, oratory, concerned with accusation and defense, and it adheres to the Ciceronian division into four parts: the exordium, or introduction; the narration, or statement of facts, which includes the *divisio*, a forecast of the main points; the proof, both affirmative and refuting contrary opinions; and the peroration or conclusion.[73] The formal structure, however, is clothed in the personal address and tone of a familiar letter, a literary form with precepts modeled on classical rhetoric, and, as would be expected in a familiar letter, the narrative section is the longest.[74]

The anecdotes illustrating the young Juana de Asbaje's passion for knowledge have been accepted as "archival data, of unquestionable authenticity": Sor Juana's refusal to eat cheese because it was said to dull the mind; her hair-cutting when her progress in Latin seemed too slow; begging her mother to dress her as a boy so she could attend the boys' school that prepared them for the university. Fred Luciani reads these episodes in terms of the rhetorical strategies of the *Respuesta*. He sees them as "self-fashioning," "strategic craftings of the self, employed as part of a larger persuasive design."[75] As Kathleen Myers points out, the narrative section adapts the conventions of spiritual biography, "the most acceptable form of self-expression available to a woman" of Sor Juana's place and time.[76] Thus, "the *Respuesta's* anecdotes are revealed as *topoi* that recall commonplaces of the genre: self-mortification, overcoming obstacles along the road to the realization of a vocation."[77] Sor Juana used the humanistic conventions of the familiar letter together with classical rhetoric and spiritual autobiography to construct not only a defense of her studies but those of women in general.

The *Respuesta* is such an elegant defense that it is disappointing to know that Sor Juana's last years were beset with opposition from her superiors. There were, however, pressures other than those of the clerics: famine resulting from torrential rains that destroyed crops, uprisings by the starving population, and epidemics. In 1692 she sold her books and musical and scientific instruments for charity and in the following years she reconfirmed her vows and renounced secular studies. With a few exceptions, she appeared to abandon both scholarly reading and writing.

Sor Juana's death at age forty-six has been used to cast her life as a tragedy in which a brilliant woman was silenced by ecclesiastical authorities, but recently discovered documents suggest that the silence was not absolute. Marie-Cécile Bénassy-Berling points out facts that are not sufficiently taken into account: the absence of any public act of renunciation of her intellectual activity, the retention of her fortune, and her continuing position as the convent's accountant, managing investments until the end of her life. Amid conflicting narratives, Bénassy-Berling and other scholars see adaptation rather than abject defeat.[78] Seductive as the enigma of silence may be, research continues to reveal the diverse voices of women who wrote, sometimes in defiance of masculine authority, on the natural sciences, political, social, and moral reform, and theology.

Although the majority of early modern Hispanic women authors, from Teresa de Cartagena to Sor Juana Inés de la Cruz, were women religious, and most, including Sor Juana, wrote devotional works, women also wrote on such secular topics as the physical sciences; politics, diplomacy, and courtly life; psychology; and philosophy of mind. Nicolás Antonio's bio-bibliographic *Bibliotheca Hispanae Nova* (Modern Spanish Writers) (1684) includes the authors of these works. In an appendix titled *Gynaeceum Hispanae Minervae* (Spanish Women's School of Wisdom), Antonio published brief entries on forty-nine women known for erudition but whose works were not available. Here he includes the much-repeated commonplaces about Beatriz Galindo, Francisca de Lebrija, and Lucía de Medrano.[79] In the early twentieth century, Manuel Serrano y Sanz included entire treatises, plays, poems, and fiction by women writers in the four-volume *Apuntes para una biblioteca de escritoras españolas, desde el año 1401 al 1833* (Notes toward a library of Spanish women writers, from 1401 to 1833) (1903–1905), abundant evidence of Spanish women's active participation in the lively intellectual debates of the early modern period.

Since the 1980s, male writers' praise of legendary women of letters, formerly thought to be all that remained of early modern women's intellectual activity, has been supplanted by accessible modern editions, creating an impressive, and growing, bibliography of texts and scholarly analyses that inscribe them unequivocally in the intellectual history of the period. In addition to Nieves Baranda Leturio's scholarly work, Elizabeth Teresa Howe's monographs on women's education and autobiographical writing, and Anne J. Cruz's studies of women's writing, as well as the essay collection *Women's Literacy in Early Modern Spain and the New World*, are indispensable resources for the study of early modern Spanish women's intellectual production. The BIESES website, an ongoing project, provides a rich source of digitized texts and information regarding manuscripts and printed texts by women found in archives beyond the National Library.[80]

Although scholars have addressed the works of the six writers discussed in this essay, much work remains to be done. Perhaps the most neglected among these are Luisa Sigea's Neo-Latin texts, which continue to await study by twenty-first-century scholars with a thorough preparation in Latin. Religious commentary and theological treatises by women, including Teresa de Cartagena's *Arboleda de los enfermos* and Sor Juana's *Carta Atenagórica*, have been relatively neglected, despite their significance in their time. As Sor Juana pointed out in the *Respuesta a sor Filotea*, theology was regarded as the source and culmination of all the arts and sciences, and it shaped the study of cosmology, which defined the place of human beings in the design of the universe. Sor María de Jesús de Ágreda was celebrated for her mysticism and correspondence with Philip IV; however, she also wrote a cosmological treatise, *Mapa de los orbes celestiales y elementales desde el cielo impíreo asta el centro de la tierra* (Map of the celestial and elemental spheres from the Empyrean heavens to the center of the earth), a reflection of the author's early interest in cosmology and geography, as well as a theological model of heaven.[81] Scholars have not resolved the differences among the numerous manuscripts of this work or its place in Ágreda's work. She is one of the two early modern women writers mentioned in Sor Juana's *Respuesta* (the other is Teresa de Jesús); Méndez Plancarte, Bénassy-Berling, and Merrim have noted the connection between another of Ágreda's works, *La mística ciudad de Dios* (Mystical City of God) with Sor Juana's *Ejercicios devotos para los nueve días antes de la purísima Encarnación del Hijo de Dios* (Devotional Exercises for the nine days preceding the Most Pure Incarnation of the Son of God), and Merrim invites scholars to explore this topic in greater depth.[82] Two other authors of theological works merit further attention: a verse commentary on the Psalms by the Cistercian nun, Constanza Osorio (1565–1637), *Huerto del celestial esposo* (Garden of the Celestial Husband), reproduced in Serrano y Sanz;[83] and commentaries published in French by an erudite Catalan nun, Juliana Morell (1594–1653).[84] In the process of researching the writing of secular women and women religious since the 1970s, scholars have been rewarded with fascinating evidence of women's participation in early modern Spanish intellectual life, and more opportunities for study of this field can be expected.

Notes

1 Antonio: vol. 2, 346b, 349b, 351a.
2 Howe: 43–44; Segura Graiño, "Sabias": 182–183; Surtz, "In Search": 48–70; Weissberger: 136–137; 263n2.
3 Howe: 188.
4 Antonio: vol. 2, 349b, 351a.
5 Cruz, "Introduction": 6; Ong: 113.
6 Zayas, *Exemplary*: 178. Zayas, *Parte segunda*: 228–229.
7 Zayas, *Exemplary*: 178. "la serenísima infanta doña Isabel Clara Eugenia de Austria, pues con ser el Católico rey don Felipe II de tanto saber que adquirió el nombre de Prudente, no hacía ni intentaba facción ninguna que no tomase consejo con ella: en tanto estimaba el entendimiento de su hija," Zayas, *Parte segunda*: 229.
8 Guevara: 72–73. "[los hombres] hicieron las leyes y todas fueron en su favor, queriendo que ellas se contenten con las armas de la rueca, y de almohadilla, pues a fe, que si usasen las mujeres de las Letras, que les sobrepujaran a los hombres, pero esto temen ellos, y no quieren que sean Amazonas, sino tenerles las manos atadas."
9 Baranda Leturio, *Cortejo*: 35–64; Nader: 15, 19.
10 Russ: 77.
11 The title pages of each of these volumes names the Augustinian Fray Pedro Henrique Pastor as having published them ("Dada a la estampa") but the author is not named. See Peraita for a detailed discussion of the question of authorial attribution.
12 Serrano y Sanz: 2.171.

13 Seidenspinner-Núñez and Kim, "Historicizing": 121–150.
14 Seidenspinner-Núñez and Kim: 127–128.
15 Cartagena, *Writings*: 80. "Los pocos años que yo estudié en el estudio de Salamanca"; Cartagena, *Arboleda*: 103.
16 Cartagena, *Writings*: 2.
17 Cartagena, *Writings*: 24. "[U]na ÿnsula que se llama 'Oprobrium hominum et abiecio plebis," *Arboleda*: 37. The island's name is derived from Psalm 21:7. *Writings*: 24n4.
18 *Writings*: 29. "E por mi voluntat, desde la cuna me fuera dada aquesta pasyón, porque no pudiera pasar las claustras de mis orejas palabra en qu' ofendido o no seruido a Dios aya." *Arboleda*: 44.
19 Cartegena, *Writings*: 46. "Todo el bien deste mundo es manjar de los sanos; pues dexemos lo ajeno y vsemos de nuestra dieta." *Arboleda*: 62.
20 Kim, *El saber femenino*.
21 Juarez: 136.
22 Juárez: 135, citing Cartagena, *Writings*: 29.
23 Deyermond: 25.
24 Cartagena, *Writings*: 87. "[A]lgunos de los prudentes varones e asy mesmo henbras discretas." *Admiracion*: 113.
25 Cartagena, *Writings*: 88. "[P]ersona que tantos males asientan." *Admiracion*: 113.
26 Cartagena, *Writing*: 88–90; *Arboleda*: 115–117.
27 Surtz: 29.
28 Baranda Leturio, "De investigación": n.p.
29 Baranda Leturio, "Luisa Sigea." www.womenwriters.nl/index.php/Luisa_Sigea
30 Baranda Leturio, "De investigación": n.p.
31 Baranda Leturio, *Cortejo*: 80.
32 Baranda Leturio, "Desterradas": 220–221. "En la España del quinientos hubo damas nobles con una gran cultura clásica e interés por las Letras o la erudición, pero en sus cortes no se observa intención de potenciar la expression del saber femenino." English translation mine.
33 Serrano y Sanz: 2. 394–471. This entry includes *Duarum virginum colloquium*: 419–471.
34 Baranda Leturio, "De investigación": n.p.
35 Pomata: 31.
36 Pomata: 33–34.
37 Pomata: 38–43.
38 Pomata: 49–60.
39 Pomata: 84.
40 Sabuco, *True Medicine*: 13 n32. "[A]claro que yo compuse un libro yntitulado nueua filo / sofia e una Norma y otro libro que se ymprimyran, / en los quales todos puse e pongo por autora a la dicha / Luisa de oliba mi hija: solo por darle El nombre e la honrra, / y Reservo El fruto y probecho que rretultare [sic] de los dichos / libros para my, y mando a la dicha my hija Luisa de oliua / no se entremeta en el dicho preuilegio, so pena de my maldiciòn / atento lo dicho demas que tengo fecha ynformacion de como yo soy / El autor y no Ella. La qual ynformación està en unas es / cripturas que pasà ante Villarreal escribano." Rodríguez: 203.
41 Serrano y Sanz: 2.171. "Ha quedado reducida a una mujer vulgar y aun pequeña moralmente."
42 Otero Torres: 9–27. Rivera Garretas, "Oliva Sabuco": 143–145.
43 Waithe and Vintró: 535–536.
44 Buxó: 584–585. "Verdadera autora del libro o, al menos, de algunas de sus partes." I cite the article published in 2009 in *Creatividad femenina*.
45 English translation mine. "En efecto, la licencia para la publicación del libro le fue concedida a doña Oliva, de ahí que su padre, ante la imposibilidad de imprimirlo en España por su propia cuenta, haya encomendado a su hijo Alonso hacerlo en Portugal, donde en efecto salió a la luz muchos años después, en 1622, pero también bajo el nombre de Oliva, a quien el Bachiller su padre no pudo arrebatar el privilegio que el Rey le había concedido 'por todos los días de vuestra vida'." Pascual Buxó: 584.
46 Pascual Buxó: 582.
47 Sabuco, *True Medicine*: 23.
48 Sabuco, *True Medicine*: 22–24. "El libro que esta sabia muger compone dela nueva filosofia y naturaleza del hombre, y dela verdadera medicina. En el qual vereis (vos y quien con consideracion y sin passion lo leyere) con mucha agudeza, prudencia y no menos demostraciones renovada toda la filosofia y medicine, de todos los antigos [sic] y modernos." citing Acosta: 106v–107r.

49 Sabuco, *True Medicine*: 17.
50 Baranda Leturio, "Razones": 45. "[M]ayor en calidad que cuantos han hecho los hombres, vasallos o señores (fol 1v)."
51 Baranda Leturio, "Razones": 45.
52 Sabuco, *True Medicine*: 22.
53 Serrano y Sanz: 2.97. English translation mine.
54 Peraita: 69.
55 Egido, "*Nobleza virtuosa*": 10.
56 Atienza, "Señor avisado": 155, 170; Egido, "La *Idea de nobles*": 66. "Ánimos inquietos, y deseosos de novedades," Padilla, *Nobleza virtuosa*: 119.
57 Egido, "La *Idea de nobles*": 64.
58 Lehfeldt: 464.
59 Lehfeldt: 491.
60 Hernández: 898.
61 Hernández: 902–903.
62 Hernández: 904.
63 Bergmann: 235–237, citing Serrano y Sanz: 2.98–99.
64 Baranda Leturio, *Cortejo*: 50.
65 Bergmann: 244–245; Padilla, *Nobleza virtuosa*: 247, 333.
66 Serrano y Sanz: 1.474–480. See also Barbeito Carneiro, *Escritoras* and *María de Guevara*.
67 Nieves Romero-Díaz translates "Corrida de parte de España" as "Affronted by Part of Spain," but a more accurate translation would be "Affronted on Behalf of Spain" or "on the Part of Spain."
68 Romero-Díaz's English title translates "Jornada" as "Day's Journey," but the three-day visit of the court in Vitoria, near some of Guevara's estates, afforded her ample opportunity to enjoy the respect of the highest dignitaries.
69 Baranda Leturio, *Cortejo*: 56. "Una lectora/oidora reflexiva, con ideas propias, que confronta el texto con la realidad y hace sus críticas sin dejarse abrumar por el peso de la *auctoritas*." Translation mine.
70 Guevara: 24.
71 Perelmuter, "*The Answer*": 186; "Estructura": 48. "Bajo la sencillez y naturalidad que todos notan, se oculta una elaboración cuyo máximo acierto consiste precisamente en no hacerse notar."
72 Ludmer, "Tricks": 87. "Saber y decir, demuestra Juana, constituyen campos enfrentados para una mujer; toda simultaneidad de estas dos acciones acarrea resistencia y castigo." "Tretas": 48.
73 Perelmuter, "*The Answer*": 187. "Estructura": 152.
74 Perelmuter, "*The Answer*: 192. "Estructura": 151–152.
75 Luciani: 80.
76 Myers: 460.
77 Luciani: 84.
78 Bénassy-Berling, "Actualidad": 284.
79 Antonio: 2.346b, 349b, 351a.
80 Marín Pina and Baranda Leturio, "Bibliografía": 425–436.
81 Serrano y Sanz: 1.595–598. Colahan's translation of selected chapters, titled, "Face of the Earth and Map of the Spheres," constitutes Chapter 3 of *Visions*: 47–91.
82 Bénassy-Berling, *Humanismo*: 117; Merrim: xii.
83 Serrano y Sanz: 2.90–94.
84 Serrano y Sanz: 2.63–66.

Works cited

Acosta, Cristóbal de. *Tratado en loor de las mujeres, y de la Castidad, Onestidad, Constancia, Silencio, y Iusticia: con otras muchas particularidades, y varias Historias*. Venice: Giacomo Cornetti, 1592.

Ágreda, Sor María de Jesús de. *Mapa de los orbes celestiales y elementales desde el cielo impíreo asta el centro de la tierra y lo principal que en ello se contiene y declaraciones de los misterios de la Iglesia militante y triumphante*. Madrid, Biblioteca Nacional, Ms 848.

Antonio, Nicolás, Rafael Casalbón, P. J. A. Pellicer, and Tomás A. Sánchez. *Bibliotheca Hispana Nova: Sive, Hispanorum Scriptorum Qui Ab Anno MD. Ad MDCLXXXIV. Floruere Notitia*. Madrid: J. de Ibarra, 1783.

Atienza, Ignacio. "El señor avisado: programas paternalistas y control social en la Castilla del siglo XVII." *Manuscrits* 9 (1999): 155–204.

———. "Mujer e ideología: una visión 'EMIC' del papel de la mujer aristócrata en el siglo XVII." *Revista Internacional de Sociología* 47.3 (1989): 317–336.

Baranda Leturio, Nieves. "De investigación y bibliografía. Con unas notas documentales sobre Luisa Sigea." *Lemir: Literatura Espanola Medieval y Renacimiento* 10 (2006): n. p.

———. "Luisa Sigea—Womenwriters." www.womenwriters.nl/index.php/Luisa_Sigea

———. *Cortejo a lo prohibido: lectoras y escritoras en la España Moderna*. Madrid: Editorial Arco/Libros, 2005.

———. "Desterradas del parnaso." *Bulletin Hispanique* 109.2 (2007): 421–447.

———. "Las razones del extraño autor: Mujeres escritoras y paratextos en la primera edad moderna española." *Paratesto: Rivista Internazionale* 11 (2014): 37–50.

Barbeito Carneiro, María Isabel. *Escritoras madrileñas del siglo XVII: estudio bibliográfico-crítico*. 2 vols. Madrid: Imprenta de la Universidad Complutense, 1986.

———. "María de Guevara." *Estudios sobre escritoras hispánicas en honor de Georgina Sabat-Rivers*. Ed. Lou Charnon-Deutsch. Madrid: Editorial Castalia, 1992: 62–78.

Bénassy-Berling, Marie-Cécile. "Actualidad del sorjuanismo (1994–1999)." *Colonial Latin American Review* 9.2 (2000): 277–292.

———. *Humanismo y religión en Sor Juana Inés de la Cruz*. Mexico City: Universidad Nacional Autónoma de México, 1983.

Bergmann, Emilie L. "The Fiction of a Maternal 'Arbitrista': Luisa de Padilla's Advice to Daughters." *Letras Femeninas* 35.1 (2009): 233–251.

Cartagena, Teresa de. *Arboleda de los enfermos*. BIESES.www.bieses.net/teresa-de-cartagena-arboleda-de-los-enfermos/

———. *Arboleda de los enfermos. Admiracion Operum Dey*. Ed. Lewis Joseph Hutton. *Anejos del Boletín de la Real Academia Española* 16 (1967).

———. *Arboleda de los enfermos. Admiracion Operum Dey*. MS II.h.24t, Escorial Library.

———. *The Writings of Teresa de Cartagena*. Ed. and trans. Dayle Seidenspinner-Núñez. Cambridge, UK: D.S. Brewer, 1998.

Colahan, Clark. *The Visions of Sor María de Ágreda: Writing Knowledge and Power*. Tucson: U of Arizona P, 1994.

Cruz, Anne J. "Art of the State: The Academias Literarias as Sites of Symbolic Economies in Golden Age Spain." *Caliope: Journal of the Society for Renaissance and Baroque Hispanic Poetry* 1.1–2 (1995): 75–95.

———. "Introduction." *Women's Literacy in Early Modern Spain and the New World*. Ed. Anne J. Cruz and Rosilie Hernández. Farnham, UK; Burlington, VT: Ashgate, 2011: 1–16.

Cruz, Anne J., and Rosilie Hernández, eds. *Women's Literacy in Early Modern Spain and the New World*. Farnham, UK; Burlington, VT: Ashgate, 2011.

Deyermond, Alan. "*El convento de dolencias*: The Works of Teresa de Cartagena." *Journal of Hispanic Philology* 1 (1976): 19–29.

Egido Martínez, Aurora Gloria. "La *Idea de Nobles* de la Condesa de Aranda y Baltasar Gracián." *El Conde de Aranda y su tiempo: Congreso internacional celebrado en Zaragoza, 1 al 5 de diciembre de 1998*. Ed. Eliseo Serrano Martin, Esteban Sarasa Sánchez, and José Antonio Ferrer Benimelli. 2 vols. Zaragoza: Institución Fernando el Católico, 2000: Vol. 2, 63–80.

———. "La *Nobleza virtuosa* de la condesa de Aranda, doña Luisa de Padilla, amiga de Gracián." *Archivo de Filología Aragonesa* 54 (1998): 9–41.

Guevara, María de. *Warnings to the Kings and Advice on Restoring Spain*. Ed. Nieves Romero-Díaz. Chicago: U Chicago P, 2007.

Hernández, Rosilie. "Luisa de Padilla's *Lágrimas de la nobleza*: Vice, Moral Authority and the Woman Writer." *Bulletin of Spanish Studies* 87.7 (2010): 898–914.

Howe, Elizabeth Teresa. *Education and Women in the Early Modern Hispanic World*. Aldershot, UK: Burlington, VT: Ashgate, 2008.

———. *Autobiographical Writing by Early Modern Hispanic Women*. Aldershot, UK; Burlington, VT: Ashgate, 2015.

Juana Inés de la Cruz: Selected Works. Trans. Edith Grossman. New York; London: W.W. Norton, 2014.

Juárez Almendros, Encarnación. "The Autobiography of the Aching Body in Teresa de Cartagena's *Arboleda de los enfermos*." *Disability Studies: Enabling the Humanities*. Ed. Sharon L. Snyder, Brenda Jo Brueggemann,

Rosemarie Garland-Thomson, and Michael Bérubé. New York: Modern Language Association of America, 2002: 131–143.

Kim, Yonsoo. *Between Desire and Passion: Teresa de Cartagena*. Leiden; Boston: Brill, 2012.

———. *El saber femenino y el sufrimiento corporal de la temprana edad moderna: Arboleda de los enfermos y Admiración Operum Dey de Teresa de Cartagena*. Córdoba: Universidad de Córdoba, 2008.

King, Willard F. *Prosa novelística y academias literarias en el siglo XVII. Anejos del Boletin de La Real Academia Española 10*. Madrid: Imprenta Silvero Aguirre Torre, 1963.

Lehfeldt, Elizabeth. "Ideal Men: Masculinity and Decline in Seventeenth-Century Spain." *Renaissance Quarterly* 61.2 (2008): 463–494.

———. "Tricks of the Weak." *Feminist Perspectives on Sor Juana Inés de la Cruz*. Detroit: Wayne State UP, 1991: 86–93.

Luciani, Frederick. *Literary Self-Fashioning in Sor Juana Inés de la Cruz*. Lewisburg, PA: Bucknell UP, 2004.

Ludmer, Josefina. "Las tretas del débil." *La sartén por el mango*. Río Piedras PR: Ediciones Huracán, 1984: 47–54.

Marco Hidalgo, Jose. "Dona Oliva Sabuco no fue escritora: estudios para la historia de la ciudad de Alcaraz." *Revista de Archivos, Bibliotecas y Museos* 7.9 (1903): 1–13.

Marín Pina, Maria del Carmen, and Baranda Leturio, Nieves. "Bibliografía de Escritoras Españolas (Edad Media—Siglo XVIII). Una Base de Datos." *Edad de Oro Cantabrigense. Actas Del VII Congreso Del AISO, 2007*. Madrid: Iberoamericana / Vervuert, 2006: 425–436.

Merrim, Stephanie. *Early Modern Women's Writing and Sor Juana Inés de La Cruz*. 1st ed. Nashville: Vanderbilt UP, 1999.

Myers, Kathleen. "Sor Juana's *Respuesta*: Rewriting the *vitae*." *Revista Canadiense de Estudios Hispánicos* 14.3 (1990): 459–471.

Nader, Helen, ed. *Power and Gender in Renaissance Spain: Eight Women of the Mendoza Family, 1450–1650*. Urbana: U Illinois P, 2004.

Ong, Walter J. *Orality and Literacy: The Technologizing of the Word*. London; New York: Methuen, 1982.

Otero Torres, Dámaris. "'Una humilde sierva osa hablar' o la ley del padre: Dislocaciones entre texto femenino y autoría masculina en 'La carta introductoria al Rey Nuestro Señor' de Oliva Sabuco de Nantes." *Taller de Letras* 26 (1998): 9–27.

Ottavio Di Camillo. "Interpretations of the Renaissance in Spanish Historical Thought." *Renaissance Quarterly* 48.2 (1995): 352–365.

Padilla, Luisa de, Condesa de Aranda. *Idea de nobles y sus desempeños*. Zaragoza: Hospital Real y General de Nuestra Señora de Gracia, 1644.

———. *Lágrimas de la nobleza*. Zaragoza: Pedro Lanaja, 1639.

———. *Noble perfecto y segunda parte de l nobleza virtuosa*. Zaragoza: Juan de Lanaja y Quartanet, 1639.

———. *Nobleza virtuosa*. Zaragoza: Juan de Lanaja y Quartanet, 1637.

Palau y Dulcet, Antonio, and Agustín Palau Baquero. *Manual del librero hispano-americano; bibliografía general española e hispano-americana desde la invención de la imprenta hasta nuestros tiempos, con el valor comercial de los impresos descritos*. Barcelona: A. Palau, 1948.

Pascual Buxó, Jose. "Oliva Sabuco de Nantes: sabiduria femenina y condena social." *La creatividad femenina en el mundo barroco hispánico*. Ed. Monika Bosse, Barbara Pothast, and Andre Stoll. 2 vols. Kassel: Reichenberger, 1999: Vol. 2, 575–595.

———. "Oliva Sabuco de Nantes: sabiduria femenina y condena social." *Destiempos: Revista de Curiosidad Cultural* 4.19 (2009): 93–110.

———. "Sabiduría y condena social: un caso de la España del siglo XVI." *Universidad de México* 593–594 (2000): 18–25.

Paz, Octavio. *Sor Juana Inés de la Cruz o las trampas de la fe*. Barcelona: Seix Barral, 1982.

———. *Sor Juana, or the Traps of Faith*. Trans. Margaret Sayers Peden. Cambridge, MA: Harvard UP, 1988.

Peraita, Carmen. "Circumventing Anonymity. Paratextual Strategies, and the Construction of Authorship in Luisa de Padilla." *Paratesto: Rivista Internazionale* 11 (2014): 69–79.

Perelmuter, Rosa. "The Answer to Sor Filotea: A Rhetorical Approach." *Approaches to Teaching the Works of Sor Juana Inés de la Cruz*. Ed. Emilie L. Bergmann and Stacey Schlau. New York: Modern Language Association, 2007: 186–192.

———. "La estructura retórica de la Respuesta a sor Filotea." *Hispanic Review*, 51.2 (1983): 147–158.

Pomata, Gianna, "Editor's Introduction." *Oliva Sabuco de Nantes y Barrera. The True Medicine*. Ed. and trans. Gianna Pomata. Toronto: Iter; Centre for Reformation and Renaissance Studies, 2010.
Rivera Garretas, María-Milagros. "Oliva Sabuco de Nantes Barrera." *Breve historia feminista de la literatura española (en lengua castellana) IV. La literatura escrita por mujer (de la Edad Media al X. XVIII)*. Ed. Iris M. Zavala. Madrid: Anthropos, 1997: 83–129.
Romero-Díaz, Nieves, ed. and trans. *María de Guevara: Warnings to the Kings and Advice on Restoring Spain: A Bilingual Edition*. Chicago: U Chicago P, 2007.
Russ, Joanna. *How to Suppress Women's Writing*. 1st ed. Austin: U Texas P, 1983.
Sabuco, Miguel. *New Philosophy of Human Nature: Neither Known to nor Attained by the Great Ancient Philosophers, Which Will Improve Human Life and Health*. Ed. D.A. Zorita, Mary Ellen Waithe, and María Elena Vintro. Champaign: U Illinois P, 2007.
Sabuco de Nantes y Barrera, Oliva. *The True Medicine*. Ed. and trans. Gianna Pomata. Toronto: Iter; Centre for Reformation and Renaissance Studies, 2010.
Segura Graiño, Cristina. "Las sabias mujeres de la corte de Isabel La Catolica." *Las sabias mujeres: educación, saber y autoría (siglos III–XVII)*. Ed. María Grana Cid, et al. Madrid: Asociación Cultural Al-Mudayna, 1988: 15–26.
Seidenspinner-Núñez, Dayle, and Kim, Yonsoo. "Historicizing Teresa: Reflections on New Documents Regarding Sor Teresa de Cartagena." *La Corónica*, 32.2 (2004), 121–50.
Serrano y Sanz, Manuel. *Apuntes para una biblioteca de escritoras españolas: desde el año 1401 al 1833*. Vols. 268, 269, 270, 271. Biblioteca de Autores Españoles. Madrid: Sucesores de Rivadeneyra, 1903–1905.
Sigea, Luisa. *Dialogue de deux jeunes filles sur la vie de cour et la bie de retraite (1552)*. Ed. Odette Sauvage. Paris: Presses Universitaires de France, 1970.
——. *Epistolario latino*. Trans. and ed. María Regla Prieto Corbalán. Madrid: Akal, 2007.
——. *Syntra*. Paris: Dionisii a Prato, 1566.
Surtz, Ronald. "In Search of Juana de Mendoza." *Power and Gender in Renaissance Spain: Eight Women of the Mendoza Family 1450–1650*. Ed. Helen Nader. Champaign: U Illinois P, 2004: 48–70.
——. *Writing Women in Late Medieval and Early Modern Spain: The Mothers of Saint Teresa of Avila*. Philadelphia: U Pennsylvania P, 1995.
Thiemann, Susanne. *Vom Glück Der Gelehrsamkeit: Luisa Sigea, Humanistin Im 16. Jahrhundert*. Göttingen: Wallstein, 2006.
——. "Weibliche Rede gegen männliche Ordnung? Zu Luisa Sigeas Duarum virginum colloquium de vita aulica et privata", *Varietas und Ordo. Zur Dialektik von Vielfalt und Einheit in Renaissance und Barock*. Ed. Marc Föcking and Bernhard Huss. Stuttgart: Franz Steiner, 2003: 59–73.
Waithe, Mary Ellen, and Vintro, Maria Elena. "Posthumously Plagiarizing Oliva Sabuco: An Appeal to Cataloging Librarians." *Cataloging and Classification Quarterly* 35.3–4 (2003): 525–540.
Weissberger, Barbara F. *Isabel Rules: Constructing Queenship, Wielding Power*. Minneapolis: U of Minnesota P, 2004. oskicat.berkeley.edu Library Catalog. Accessed June 15, 2015.
Wray, Grady. "*Challenging Theological Authority: The Carta Atenagórica / Crisis sobre un sermón and the Respuesta a Sor Filotea*." *Ashgate Research Companion to the Works of Sor Juana Inés de la Cruz*. Ed. Emilie L. Bergmann and Stacey Schlau. Farnham, UK; Burlington, VT: Ashgate [forthcoming].
——. "Sacred Allusions: Theology in Sor Juana's Work." *Approaches to Teaching the Works of Sor Juana Inés de la Cruz*. Ed. Emilie L. Bergmann and Stacey Schlau. New York: Modern Language Association, 2007: 66–76.
Zayas, María de. *Exemplary Tales of Love and Tales of Disillusion*. Trans. Margaret R. Greer and Elizabeth Rhodes. Chicago: U Chicago P, 2009.
——. *Parte segunda del sarao y entretenimiento honesto: Desengaños amorosos*. Ed. Alicia Yllera. Madrid: Cátedra, 1983.
Zuese, Alicia R. "Ana Caro and the Literary Academies of Seventeenth-Century Spain." *Women's Literacy in Early Modern Spain and the New World*. Ed. Anne J. Cruz and Rosilie Hernandez. Farnham, UK; Burlington, VT: Ashgate, 2011: 191–208.

15
WOMEN AND POWER

Nieves Romero-Díaz

In her classic *Women and Gender in Early Modern Europe* (1993), Merry Wiesner-Hanks decried the fact that, when studying early modern Europe, critics who addressed power hardly, if ever, referred to women, accepting a universal masculine experience as regards perspective and political action (288). Wiesner-Hanks alluded to two historiographical tendencies that could change that situation: on one hand, the revision and expansion of what it means to do political history; and, on the other, the analysis of aspects of women's lives from a political perspective, attending to the personal and domestic. Indeed, thanks largely to the growth of these two historiographical tendencies—in Europe for the past twenty years and in Spain for the past ten—there has been new interest in examining how women actively participated in the politics of their time, from queens to middle-class and marginal women. Because the category of gender was finally incorporated into historical analysis, the resulting work has managed to break from the monolithic and one-dimensional view of early modern history while redefining the meaning of the concept of power.

If such historical and political revision has been a mandate, it has also reconsidered the public/private space binomial, spaces that for early modernity are difficult to separate. As Magdalena Ortega states, it has been a true challenge not only to "integrate women in the historical discourse, but also to establish [and re-conceptualize] categories of analysis that allow us to evaluate the functions they carried out" (14).[1] That is, it has been necessary to broaden the definition of politics (Daybell, *Women and Politics*: 2), and to elide contemporary criteria of analysis when defining concepts so ideologically and sexually charged as power and authority or public and private spaces, among others. That does not mean admitting, as Barbara Harris explains, that women's political actions were the same as men's, nor that they participated in the same activities, because that would be falsifying the historical data ("Women": 260). On the contrary, in order to study women and their relation to power in early modern Spain, it is crucial to analyze and carefully (re-)examine the material means, the discursive strategies, the networks, and other socio-cultural alliances that women carried out to exercise political power. Only by doing this can we obtain a more complete vision of the early modern period.[2]

Along with this conceptual redefinition, it has also been essential to revise the literary history regarding the relationship between women and power in early modern Spain. Since the 1980s, most research from both sides of the Atlantic has focused on recovering texts authored by women. Figures like Teresa of Ávila (1515–1582) in Spain, and Sor Juana Inés de la Cruz (1648–1695) in Mexico have now been joined by numerous religious and secular poets, playwrights, and novelists, as the list of female authors of the time has been expanded.³ If the presence of female writers in literary history has been limited until recently, those who dedicated their pen to matters of a political nature have been far fewer. Yet recent research has demonstrated that, on the contrary, women did not have a marginal presence in contemporary politics, but were as actively involved as men. In fact, although the manner in which they addressed political issues did not correspond to a coherent theory of state and society (N. Baranda, "Beyond": 65), nor did they use genres clearly recognized as political, female writers who intervened in political matters were very much interested in issues of reason of state as well as international diplomacy. Certainly, a series of texts authored by women, of a more or less political nature, stands out, such as treatises of reason of state, memorials, and mirrors or manuals to educate the prince, such as the treatises by María de Guevara, Countess of Escalante, and the petition for a woman's prison by Magdalena de San Jerónimo. Also, we need to keep in mind another kind of text that some consider private, like letters, for example, the epistolary corpus by Luisa de Carvajal and by the nun Sor María de Jesús de Ágreda; and others, public, like encomiastic texts—for instance the biography about Philip III by Ana de Castro Egas, the poems by María Nieto de Aragón, and the reports and chronicles by Ana Caro de Mallén de Soto and Eugenia Bueso.

Aware of the challenge implied by writing and, even more so, by publishing, these women contributed, through their writings, to the debate about female authority, defending their position as authorial subjects, particularly as they were interfering in the field of politics, one not traditionally associated with their gender. These writers knew that they were attempting to influence political decisions; therefore, they understood that they were challenging the social and literary conventions of the time, hence their need to justify themselves. Indeed, these authors in one way or another all reminded their addressees that their writing was a daring and audacious act, particularly when published. Unlike the writings of other contemporary female authors, theirs dealt with matters supposedly inappropriate to their gender: "Who is a woman to meddle in this?" María de Guevara asked rhetorically while expressing her political and military opinions to King Philip IV; "giving lessons to superiors [. . .] does not belong to women," Sor María de Ágreda argued in her letters to King Philip IV. And Ana de Castro Egas was called "bold" and a "brave author" by the poets who praise her wisdom.

In many cases, these writers refer to their lack of authorization, despite the fact that their writings were legitimized by their institutional character, by responding to social interests, or principally, by their addressees, who were "royal figures on the occasion of their name days and other celebrations" (López Cordón, "Fortuna": 215).⁴ Social class, religious beliefs, social and cultural alliances and networks, or simply the duty to serve, praise, or defend their king and the Catholic monarchy, justified their participation in the politics of the time. Thus, Sor María de Ágreda, almost from the beginning of her correspondence with the Borja family, informs them that although her epistolary exchange with Philip IV is a daring act, she must obey him. María de Guevara is proud of her nobility and her lineage, which support her purpose, and she leans on her family and social networks and alliances, and, as in a *querelle*, authorizes herself as one of many women who throughout history have acted for the good of their country. Luisa de Carvajal is responsible to her king and her faith, which she defends at all costs against the English heretics. All of these women legitimate their boldness by stating their obligation to intervene for the good of the state and to defend it against its internal and international enemies in order to maintain the supremacy of the Spanish monarchy in some cases, and to restore it, in others. As Nieves Baranda explains ("Beyond"), the political recommendations, praises, and warnings contained in these women's writings are framed by proto-nationalist feelings.

Encomiastic writings had an intrinsically political character because, whether in prose or in verse, their main goal was to praise persons or events of civil and political life with a clearly propagandistic purpose. The number of women who participated in composing these texts could be considered relatively high in the first half of the seventeenth century, although their texts were not very long and varied little as to theme. Ana de Castro Egas and María Nieto de Aragón (ca. 1631–?) are the exception, both because of the type of composition and their topics and purpose. The only text known by Castro Egas is the *Eternidad del rey nuestro señor don Felipe III* (Eternity to the King our Lord Don Felipe III), published in 1629 and dedicated to Cardinal-Infante Ferdinand. The *Eternidad* is a panegyric in prose written to celebrate Philip III after his death in 1621. Some critics, like Anne J. Cruz, describe this text as an example of the biographical genre, albeit an "atypical biography" ("Challenging" and "Del Cuerpo"). Others, such as Carmen Peraita Huerta, distinguish it from the biography and other historical texts, comparing it the funerary eulogy (154). María Nieto de Aragón's works consist of two booklets in verse, one which mourns the death of Isabel of Borbón, *Lágrimas a la muerte de la augusta reina N. Señora Isabel de Borbón* (Tears for the death of the August Queen our Lady Isabel of Bourbon) (1645); the other celebrates the marriage between Philip IV and Mariana of Austria, *Epitalamio a las felicísimas bodas del Rey Nuestro Señor* (Epithalamium for the Most Joyous Wedding of the King our Lord) (1649). Both are dedicated to women of the *converso* Ribera-Pinto family, and addressed to King Philip IV. As Cruz explains, idealizing certain subjects by means of this kind of composition could be dangerous during the Spanish Baroque, when court factions were formed for and against the king's favorite ("Del cuerpo": 50).

It is for this reason that understanding these women's compositions as propaganda, a service of the monarchy or one of its factions, would be very reductionist. Definitely, the works by Castro Egas and Nieto de Aragón are celebratory and even vindicatory, of Philip III and the Lerma family in the case of the *Eternidad*, and of Isabel of Borbón, in the *Lágrimas*. Both texts, in fact, are published precisely at key moments of the anti-Olivarista reaction (the move against the power favorite, the count-duke of Olivares), and offer models of conduct to Philip IV (Cruz, "Challenging" and "Del cuerpo"; Romero-Díaz, "Poesía"). These authors' critique of Philip IV's politics, however, is quite subtle given that their already defunct models have been the object of a discursive "exaltation," and have been subjected to an excessive politization of their persona. Critical approaches by Cruz ("Gender," "Challenging" and "Del cuerpo"), Marín Pina ("Pliegos"), and Romero-Díaz ("Poesía") provide a fruitful analysis of those eulogies, comparing them with similar texts of the time and/or examining the biographical and female authors' sociocultural reality. The texts' popularity is noteworthy if we consider the way in which their contemporaries praised these women authors. Indeed, the works by these two women were very well received, as evidenced by the number of laudatory poems and letters of approval that are included in the printed texts, besides the personal relations that were formed after their publication, for example, the relationship between Nieto de Aragón and the Aragonese Francisco de Uztarroz (Marín Pina, "Juan Francisco" and "Pliegos"; Romero-Díaz, "Poesía"). Writing and publishing these encomia not only intend to immortalize and give fame to the protagonists of their texts—whether Philip III, Isabel of Borbón, Philip IV, or Mariana de Austria—the authors also manage, with their compositions, to immortalize themselves and reach eternal fame (Cruz, "Challenging" and "Del cuerpo"). Castro Egas's case, in this sense, is very explicit since the parallelism between the king's and the author's fame is stated throughout the more than forty poems that appear with the biography, as well as in Francisco de Quevedo's prologue and in the approvals. So why, despite such fame and recognition during the poets' lifetimes, have their works gone unnoticed by critics until very recently?

Among the corpus of texts dedicated to important people or events of the time, *relaciones de sucesos* (news pamphlets) should also be considered. Although a very popular form of literature and a preamble to modern journalism, *relaciones* did not receive much attention by scholars until well into the twentieth century and only recently has attention been paid to women's versions of the genre (Campo).[5] Ana Caro de Mallén, better known for her *comedias*, Catalina Clara Ramírez de Guzmán, a prolific poet from Extremadura, and Eugenia Bueso, a writer from Aragon, are the only known female authors of *relaciones* in the early modern period. Caro composed four *relaciones de sucesos*, one being the most politically explicit, the *Contexto de las reales fiestas que se hicieron en el Palacio del Buen Retiro a la Coronación de Rey de Romanos y entrada en Madrid de la Señora Princesa de Cariñán* (Context of the Royal Festivities Held at the Palace of the Buen Retiro for the Coronation of the King of Romans and the Entrance into Madrid of the Lady Princess of Cariñan) (1637).[6] Of the *relaciones* by Ramírez de Guzmán, there is only a manuscript copy, the *Relación en coplas de pie quebrado de las fiestas que celebró Llerena á el nacimiento de el Principe nuestro señor Don Phelipe prospero* (Chronicle in *coplas* of the Festivities celebrated in Llerena on the Birth of the Prince our Lord, Don Philip Próspero) (1657), which suggests the local character of her prose and her readers. Bueso composed two *relaciones* that we know of, both dated 1669, and both about Don Juan de Austria's visits to the city of Zaragoza: "Relación de la corrida de toros que la Imperial Ciudad de Zaragoza hizo en obsequio a su Alteza" (Chronicle of the Bullfight that the Imperial City of Zaragoza Held as a Gift to his Highness); and *Relación de la entrada en la Imperial Ciudad de Zaragoza de su Alteza Serenissima el Señor Don Juan* (Chronicle of His Most Serene Highness, the Lord Don Juan's Entrance into the Imperial City of Zaragoza).

All the *relaciones* refer to events intrinsically involved with Spanish politics in that, like the encomiastic texts, they relate national and international episodes (battles, deaths, and births) with propagandistic purposes (Luna; Marín Pina, "Eugenia"). Despite writing a genre of a public nature historically associated with male authors, these women are able to authorize themselves culturally by making use of the patronage networks of the period (Voros), and also by the fact that they are women (Villegas de la Torre). The female authors, "aware of the sociopolitical meaning of the *relación*, a genre at the service of power interests and utilized to create and form public opinion [. . .] find in their verses a means of establishing themselves politically and socially in the city as women and as writers" (Marín Pina, "Eugenia": 71–72).[7] Given the limited contribution (that is known to date) of women to the encomiastic genre and the *relaciones*, their texts must be read critically, keeping in mind the complex nature of the genre itself and its political and cultural function, as well as the social situation of the female authors, their networks of power, and their gendered perspective.

Despite their popularity in the sixteenth and seventeenth centuries, genres recognized as traditionally political (*arbitrios*, petitions, treatises, and mirrors) have been infrequently authored by women. The exception, however, may be petitions, as many women, even without having an authorial consciousness, write and address them to the monarch or to highly ranked figures requesting rewards or gifts for themselves or for members of their family, and according to the merits of their lineage or the deeds by their family members, past or present. María de Guevara, Countess of Escalante (c. 1620–1683) is introduced in the literary and political world through the publication of the *Memorial de la casa de Escalante y servicios de ella al rey Nuestro Señor* (Valladolid, 1654) (Petition for the House of Escalante and for its Services Rendered to the King, our Lord). In this petition, the countess reviews her family's noble branches, which tie her to the Asturian King Don Pelayo, the initiator of the Christian reconquest, and to the founders of the kingdom of Navarre. She also reminds the king of her properties as well as of the injustices that have put her in a difficult financial situation and forced her to appeal to the king for reparation. Like other women of her time, the absence of a husband (deceased or at war) positions her as head of her family, in charge of her household and her properties. María de Guevara deploys the petition from her noble house as a preamble to intervene years later in matters of state in more explicit and authorized form. Given the political, economic, and social crises that had occurred in Spain since the late sixteenth century, Guevara resolves to politically lead a society that needs to stay active in order to maintain and increase the prosperity of the monarchy. Authorized by her lineage and her connections within the court, Guevara represents herself as a mediator to reestablish order in the body of the state in crisis.

Her social and cultural competence, along with her personal experience as head of her family, bestow on her an identity that not only allows, but also compels her to act legitimately and to warn those who, in fact, are not carrying out their responsibilities. In the *Tratado y advertencias hechas por una mujer celosa del bien de su rey y corrida de parte de España* (1663) (Treatise and Warnings by a Woman, Concerned for the Good of her King and Affronted on the Part of Spain), addressed to Philip IV, and in *Desengaños de la corte y mujeres valerosas*(1664) (Disenchantments at the Court and Valorous Women), addressed to the future Carlos II, Guevara reminds the kings and also the noblemen (among them, her own husband) of the responsibilities they have to heal the infirm body of the state in such a way that it may be reestablished harmoniously. From a conservative perspective, her recommendations have a practical component and do not differ much from those found in the treatises and *arbitrios* (economic tracts) composed by men: for example, the importance of electing the right favorite and other counselors, the proposal of a military theory more effective in defending the empire and with regard to its soldiers' behavior and rewards, and the relevance of knowing history and having the right conduct models to imitate. The intervention of women in the restoration of the state is fundamental in Guevara's political discourse (Romero-Díaz, "Introduction"). Due to men's moral decline, which she often mentions in her texts, Guevara proposes women as models who can restore honor to her country, and among these models, she places herself as the leader, even as a substitute to the king himself. Guevara insists that women must participate actively in the politics of their time, fighting, advising their husbands and even ruling. The characteristics of these women's models correspond to those of the "*femme forte*" as they rely on the nobiliary privilege of women, as well as military merit, and "the abilities to govern or to cultivate literary writings (as indicators of their court function)" (Bolufer: 191); in sum, they are women with precisely those characteristics that are lacking in the men of Guevara's time.[8] The original, albeit conservative view of Guevara's political recommendations has remained silenced until the twentieth century. The bibliographer, Manuel Serrano y Sanz, rescued her from oblivion and made some of her writings available to scholars. However, save for the studies of Guevara's life and writings by Serrano y Sanz and María Isabel Barbeito ("María"), recognition of Guevara did not increase until the last ten years, thanks in part to the bilingual edition by Romero-Díaz (*Warnings*). Besides the introduction by Romero-Díaz to her edition, the works by Atienza; N. Baranda ("Lecturas" and "Beyond"); Barbeito ("María: *son politikon*"); Hernández ("Politics"); Langle de Paz; López Cordón ("De escritura"); Robles, and Romero-Díaz ("Discurso") have placed Guevara at the center of attention, by reclaiming the importance of a gendered perspective in the analysis of politics and literary genres in early modern Spain. As Langle de Paz states, Guevara's texts offer "a feminist and feminine vision of the world" from an "epistemological or creator 'I' who is the possessor of a knowledge which provides an alternative to the universalizing masculine 'I'" (472).[9]

As a petition to recover the social body of the country, there is also another treatise, addressed to Philip III, written by Mother Magdalena de San Jerónimo. It is the *Razón y forma de la galera y casa real* (1608) (Reason and Structure for the Galley and Royal House), in which she requests the king to help and support the construction of a jail in which to imprison women who lead an evil life. Magdalena de San Jerónimo was not a stranger to the court of Philip III. Her concern for these women had brought her to run the Pious House for repentant women in Valladolid since 1588, and there was a well-known relationship she and her family members (the Zamudio) had with the royal family and other members of the court. Magdalena de San Jerónimo herself, as Serrano y Sanz, Barbeito (*Cárceles*), and Boyle explain, had received favors from Philip II and Philip III, had accompanied the Archduchess Isabel Clara Eugenia to Brussels, perhaps in the capacity of governess to the archduchess's maids, and among her friends and epistolary correspondents were Luisa de Carvajal and the Carmelite nun Ana de Jesús. Her personal connections and her socio-political alliances, along with her personal experience, authorize her petition to the king. Magdalena de San Jerónimo is aware of the novelty of her request, not so much for the construction of a women's prison, but rather, as Lakarra explains, for the fact that the petition comes from a woman who demands punishment of a severity similar to that of men. The self-deprecating references that San Jerónimo makes about her work ("small treatise," "poor work") contrast with the level of severity in her request and the amount of detail in describing the institution-galley, in the end persuading the king to finance the foundation in Madrid.[10] The confinement and reform of sinful women not only would contribute to the healing of early modern Spanish society, but would also reinforce the image of a magnanimous king who worried about his country and worked for its benefit and the strengthening of his empire (Dopico Black). The gendered perspective introduced in this treatise, parallel to that of Guevara's texts, allows us to reformulate the monolithic vision of a solely male history of Spain and to acknowledge the commitment of both men and women to the success of their country's national and international politics.

The epistolary genre could be considered the one most employed by women in the early modern period. I do not refer to the poetic and literary epistle, so common during the Renaissance, but rather to personal letters, those that show us the family relations and the (inter)national networks that enabled women to intervene in, influence, and even change politics.[11] Most critics estimate that, in fact, women have dominated the epistolary genre (Torras Francés), preferring it over others, and making the most of it as a medium to express themselves, "becoming a form of mediation and acknowledgement of authority against the exclusions imposed by the patriarchal culture" (Castillo, *Entre*: 23).[12] Therefore, and despite the prescriptions of theologians and moralists to keep women confined to the home or the convent, women wrote letters to enter the public space, and, after the Counter-Reformation, letters were crucial for nuns to connect with the outside world (Campbell and Larsen: 11). The study of letters written by women has benefitted from the interest that the genre has generated in the last thirty years.[13] The main task of the last few years has been, and continues to be, the recovery of female letter collections from archives and libraries in order to edit and contextualize them historically, making them more accessible to scholars and general readers. Among others, worth mentioning is the correspondence between Ana de Dietrichstein and her mother Margarita de Cardona, the correspondence between the princess of Éboli and her son, the letters between the countess of Palamós and her daughter Estefanía de Requesens, and those by Luisa de Carvajal to a variety of religious and secular figures in Europe. From the convent we have the editions of letters by Saint Teresa of Ávila, Sor Ana de Jesús, Sor Mariana de San José, and Sor María de Ágreda.[14]

It was not until recently that women's letters were dismissed as solely related to personal, domestic, and religious matters (Tarbin and Broomhall: 8). However, it is precisely in these matters where women's political agency becomes evident, making it possible to continue to revise the notion of power by including in their analysis the dynamics of political and social interaction commonly associated with women. The collected essays by James Daybell, *Early Modern Women's Letter Writing, 1450–1700* (2001) and, especially, his monograph *Women Letter-Writers in Tudor England* (2006), are very valuable in understanding women's political activity through correspondence. As Daybell explains, through letters women could "persuade and influence; to maintain and extend kinship and patronage networks; to gather and disseminate news; to further the careers and marriages of children; to broker and dispense patronage; to acquire favor and intervene in suits normally viewed as a strictly male domain" (*Women*: 31). For Spain, two significant collections of political letters are those by Luisa de Carvajal, and by Sor María de Ágreda.[15]

Carvajal and Ágreda's addressees include figures from the royal family (among them, King Philip IV himself, with whom Ágreda exchanged more than six hundred letters); members of the court (some highly influential in the political decisions of the time, such as Rodrigo Calderón, favorite of the Duke of Lerma, Philip III's own favorite, and both correspondents of Luisa de Carvajal); important characters of the European aristocracy, religious and secular, and even popes, as well as family members and personal friends. The letters' contents range from information or details about daily events, to commentary, criticism, and recommendations, sometimes subtle, other times not-so-subtle, about political events on a national and international scale. In fact, the political opinions become intermingled with everyday matters (for example, the price of food in the London markets, or the illnesses of other nuns in the convent), blurring the lines so that the political elements become less evident, but not for that reason any less effective. In any case, and despite the presumably private nature of the letters, both women were aware of the inherent weakness in the process of circulation, distribution, and reading of letters at the time, thus the explicit mention made of the need to destroy and burn the missives once read, or the use of codes to conceal their contents, as we find in a large number of letters between Ágreda and Francisco and Fernando de Borja (C. Baranda, "La función"). Even those letters that apparently do not say much could have significant weight because of their very materiality, as they were evidence of the social networks and personal alliances between the correspondents (C. Baranda *Cartas* and "La función"; Sánchez Dueñas). The recovery, publication, and analysis of epistolary collections are fundamental, then, to understand the role of women in the political and cultural reality of their time and to more deeply comprehend the formation of feminine subjectivity and social self-representation.

Luisa de Carvajal and Mendoza (1566–1614) maintained active relations with members of the royal family and the nobility.[16] Her missionary (Jesuit) spirit and her willingness to become a martyr of the Catholic church took her to England in 1605, where she defended Catholicism against English heresy, provided assistance to persecuted Catholics, visited prisons, gathered and distributed relics from English Catholic martyrs, and even intended to found a convent of English women to pray and work for the Catholic faith in England. Because Carvajal never professed as a nun, her independence, leading role, and her free movements and decisions made her an uneasy case for both Spanish and English secular and religious authorities, despite the support she received from prominent members of those circles closest to power. However, the counterpoint to her transgression was her great devotion to the Spanish monarchy and its apostolic mission: she proclaimed herself a soldier of Christ for the Glory of God and the honor of Spain, just like she often repeats in her writings; in Cruz's words, "the freedom she attained as a 'disorderly' woman [. . .] could only be sustained through her absolute dependency on the Catholic Church and on the Duke of Lerma's protection" (Cruz, "Willing Desire": 189). In this sense, Carvajal counters the vision of a cloistered monastic life as proposed by the Counter-Reformation, since in her opinion, in that historical moment what the church really needed was a presence that was active, public, and determined to defend the Spanish Catholic empire. In her letters, particularly those to Magdalena de San Jerónimo in the Netherlands, and to Rodrigo Calderón in Spain, she clearly expresses her political activism, as specific in her criticism against the English heretics, as in her advice and recommendations to the Spanish authorities of the time. The studies by Colón, Adelaida and Antonio Cortijo, Cruz ("Luisa," "Willing," and "Relaciones"), Iglesias, Pando Canteli ("*Tentando*"), and above all, Levy-Navarro, are fundamental to a closer understanding of Carvajal's political mission during her stay in England. Among her activist and interventionist opinions is that of rejecting peace treaties between Spain and England, giving detailed information about the English attitudes and laws against Catholics, listing the required criteria for the position of ambassador, and warning about the consequences that certain marital arrangements could have for the royal family and the imperial position of Spain. Like Guevara in her treatises, Carvajal's letters make recommendations that, for the multinational politics of the time, could serve as mirrors of conduct for the prince. With her advice, she counsels on the best ways to run matters of state to benefit the king and his monarchy. And like Guevara, Carvajal recognizes the importance of female contacts in order to reach her goals, hence she finds support in other women who, throughout her life, will help her materially and spiritually in her work (Cruz, "Relaciones"; Pando Canteli, "Letters"), as is the case of the young women who accompany her in England and make up the unofficial order of soldier-maidens, "warriors for the true faith" (Levy-Navarro, 269).

Sor María de Ágreda (1602–1665) differs from Luisa de Carvajal in that the nun never left Ágreda (Soria); her correspondence nevertheless took her even beyond the Iberian Peninsula. Ágreda's addressees include Philip IV; Pope Alexander VI; Fernando and Francisco de Borja; María Teresa of Austria, Queen of France; religious women from other convents; and many Spanish noblemen and women. As a Conceptionist nun from a very young age, Sor María underwent a variety of mystical experiences, visions, raptures, and also bilocation, for which she gained national and international recognition, capturing the attention of the king himself, who decided to visit her in 1643 on his way to the Aragon front during the Catalan rebellion (C. Baranda, *Correspondencia*). This first visit was the start of a long correspondence that would last for twenty-two years, and included more than six hundred letters, which corroborates that the personal and spiritual relationship between them entered, on many occasions, into political terrain.[17] According to the historian Ricardo Fernández Gracia, the town of Ágreda would receive "immediate news of all that happened in the capital of Spain" and also in the rest of the country and even parts of Europe, and many noblemen and other curious people of the time came to the Conceptionist convent to inform or be informed, to ask for advice from the nun, or to use her to gain access to the king (103).[18] Without needing to leave the convent, Sor María de Ágreda was not only familiarized with the political and social events of the time, but from her direct knowledge of state matters, she advised the king, recommending that he become informed and that he act like a good prince for the good of the monarchy. In effect, the nun from Ágreda knew that it was essential to "be informed;" moreover, she was "aware that in her own way she was carrying out a 'job' in service to the common interest and to the monarchy" (C. Baranda, *Cartas*: 33).[19] Her advice could be compared to that of the *arbitristas* of her time in that it was important to reform social customs and to improve moral behavior. Her main goal at a political level, contrary to Carvajal, was not confrontational, since she preferred diplomatic alliances that helped to achieve peace in defending Christianity. Her influence spread by means of her correspondence, although as years went by and due to a change in the political vision of the monarchy, her recommendations would be charged with a strong "doctrinal content" (Martínez Millán: 41).[20]

The studies of María de Ágreda in general are perhaps the most fortunate in comparison with those of the other women writers mentioned in this essay. Her work, *Mística ciudad de Dios* (Mystical City of God), along with other works in prose, her bilocations, and above all, her correspondence with Philip IV have generated the interest of historians, scientists, and literary scholars, as well as followers and enthusiasts.[21] If we focus on the correspondence alone, from the critical edition of her letters by Francisco Silvela in 1885 to the most recent article by Rosilie Hernández in 2015, the editions of her work and secondary literature offer a very complete panorama of the personal and political relations between the nun and the king. Our knowledge of this relationship is due to the letters' conservation, so carefully regulated from the beginning by the king (Corteguera and Velasco). Probably the works by C. Baranda ("Correspondencia," *Correspondencia*, and "Función"), Fernández Gracia, Hernández ("Friends"), Manero Sorolla, Martínez Millán, Morte Acín ("Sor María"), Pérez Villanueva, and Sánchez de Toca offer the best analyses of their political content, and examine the relevant network of relations that surrounded the correspondents. For example, Martínez Millán has thoroughly studied the court environment that influenced the political relationship between the king and the nun from Ágreda, investigating the political stances taken by the court members, which affect in the end the view of the nun's ideological and political position. However, it is necessary to also study the networks between María de Ágreda and other members of the court, parallel to that of the nun and the king, in order to better comprehend the political discourse of this correspondence (Fernández Gracia and García Royo). Particularly worthy of mention is the correspondence of Ágreda and the noblemen, Fernando de Borja and his son, Francisco. Edited recently by C. Baranda (*Cartas*), this exchange of letters (1628–1664), equally as long as that of Ágreda's, provides "evidence enough that her letters to Philip IV were a political instrument, that they were part of a strategy of power struggles in which Sor María took an active role, by trying with determination and tenacity to influence the monarch; [these letters] allow us to see, more clearly than in those to Philip IV, that she was part of a dense network of members of the nobility and clergy that protected and supported her" (*Cartas*: 9).[22] Applying the analogy of medicine, so common among the *arbitristas*, the nun from Ágreda is explicit in her mission to cure the sick person (the king) but complains that her medicines (her advice, sometimes direct, other times through revelations, such as those received from the deceased queen, Isabel of Borbón and Prince Baltasar Carlos) have no effect. Her interventionist conscience is even more evident when at times, as in her involvement in the Aragonese conspiracy led by the Duke of Híjar against the king, Sor María begins to use in her correspondence with the Borja family a system of codes that conceals names and events.

The epistolary corpus by Sor María de Ágreda, however, is much more extensive. Many letters that she exchanged with members of the court have yet to be analyzed, like those with the president of the Council of Castile Juan Chumacero, among others, which are at the Conceptionist archive in Ágreda. Also letters that, because of their supposed informality or domesticity have gone unnoticed by Ágreda scholars, should be taken into account. I refer to a relatively large corpus of letters that Sor María exchanged with religious and secular women (from the court and the high nobility particularly) that in many cases have not been published yet. The gender analysis of these letters will help to draw Sor María's political networks in a more complete way, as there will be incorporated a gendered understanding of politics through alliances by, between, and for women (Frye and Robertson: 307). In this sense, it is worth referring to the recent works by Chicharro on the correspondence between Ágreda and the duchess of Alburquerque, and two by Romero-Díaz ("Autoridad" and "Del sarao"), one centered on the concept of feminine authority that the nun proposes to the queen of France, María Teresa de Austria, and the other, on the sociability networks that resulted from Ágreda's correspondence with women of the royal family, the aristocracy, and other nuns.

The task of recovering, publishing, and translating texts written by women, particularly those considered traditionally private such as letters, continues to be one of the most important goals for those interested in early modern Spanish women writers. Such recovery and publication will make those texts not just available to the reader, but will also help to rewrite our notion of the literary canon, to reconsider genres, revise matters of authorship and self-representation, rethink issues of distribution and reception of texts, analyze rhetorical feminine strategies, and understand the use of a specifically feminine language. The connection of these texts to the political sphere adds an extra facet to our analysis, as it compels us to reread genres not traditionally political from a perspective that is, indeed, political, and to reassess theoretical concepts such as power and authority from perspectives of history and gender. In this sense, it is necessary to carry out a more complex analysis of the sociability networks and thereby learn how women understood their political agency from an individual position and also as part of a community.[23] Although these networks are not exclusive to women, seeing as how they coexisted and were compatible with their husbands' networks and those of other male relatives (Daybell, *Women*: 9), it is essential to pay attention to and look into the way women took advantage of those connections that made them stronger and encouraged them to collaborate with each other emotionally and materially (Harris, *English*: 9). In which ways did women rely on each other at an emotional or material level in their political tasks? How were these communities formed through writing? At an intellectual level, who were their models of action? What did they read? Research about their female predecessors, both religious and secular, fictional and real, women of arms or women of letters, and their readings and libraries, will help us to better understand the authorizing strategies they used in the literary and political spheres. Moreover, transnational and comparative studies of political writings by women in other European countries will allow us to broaden the nationalist and short-sighted focus, particularly at a time when, as N. Baranda affirms, nations did not exist (at least not in the way they are currently conceived), and social and cultural networks and alliances were as global as they are today. In sum, the work has just begun and the study of early modern Spanish women writers and their relation to politics will continue to enforce the necessary redefinition of power as well as the revision of the literary canon and its genres, in order to acknowledge the active role women have always had as political subjects.

Notes

1 "integrar a las mujeres en el discurso histórico, sino también de establecer [y reconceptualizar] categorías de análisis que permitan la valoración de las funciones que tuvieron" (14).
2 Historiography has led the critical task of incorporating gender into historical analysis. See the summary of the most representative historical works related to women and political power in pre-modern Europe by Levine and Meyer.
3 The BIESES database is an excellent source of female writers and the great variety of genres in which they participated in early modernity, complementing the classic work by Serrano y Sanz.
4 "alguna persona real con motivo de onomástica o celebraciones" (López Cordón, "Fortuna": 215).
5 We should acknowledge the important task of recovering and studying these chronicles by Sagrario López Poza and her research group. See her web page, which includes a complete bibliography and database of *relaciones*.
6 Caro's three other *relaciones*, also of a propagandistic nature given their political and religious content, are: *Relación en que se da cuenta de las grandísimas fiestas que en el convento de N.P.S. Francisco de la ciudad de Sevilla se han hecho a los santos mártires del Japón* (Seville, 1628) (Chronicle that Tells of the Great Celebrations that the Convent of N.P.S Francisco in the City of Seville Held for the Martyr Saints of Japan); *Grandiosa Victoria que alcanzó de los Moros de Tetuán Jorge de Mendoza y Piçaña, general de Ceuta* (Seville, 1633) (Jorge de Mendoza and Piçaña, General of Ceuta's Magnificent Victory over the Moors of Tetuan); and *Relación de la grandiosa fiesta, y octava, que (en la Iglesia parroquial del Glorioso San Miguel de la Ciudad de Sevilla) hizo don García Sarmiento de Sotomayor [. . .] y su partido, por su Magestad* (Seville, 1635) (Chronicle of the Magnificent Celebration, and Octave that, in the Parish Church of the Glorious Saint Michael in the City of Seville, don García Sarmiento de Sotomayor [. . .] and his Party, held for his Majesty). See López Estrada ("Costumbres", "La relación") and Luna.
7 "consciente[s] del significado político-social del género de la *relación*, un género al servicio de los intereses del poder e instrumentalizado para crear y formar una opinión pública [. . .] encuentra[n] en sus versos un medio para afianzarse políticamente y socialmente en la ciudad como mujer[es] y como escritora[s]" (Marín Pina, "Eugenia": 71–72).

8   "las dotes para el gobierno o para el cultivo de las letras (como marcas de su función cortesana)" (Bolufer: 191).
9   "una visión feminista y femenina del mundo" from a "yo epistemológico o creador y poseedor de conocimiento alternativo al 'yo' masculino universalizante" (472).
10 See Boyle for homes for repentant women in general and their ties to early modern theater.
11 Among many general studies, see Doglio; Zarri, and more recently, Couchman and Crabb, and Campbell and Larsen. In this volume, see Vanessa de Cruz.
12 "pudi[endo] constituir una forma de mediación y reconocimiento de autoridad frente a las exclusiones operadas por la cultura patriarcal" (Castillo, *Entre*: 23).
13 Given the abundant material on this genre, I refer only to four essential contributions: Bouza; Castillo Gómez; Castillo Gómez and Sierra Blas; and Castillo Gómez and Saez Sánchez.
14 See Cruz Medina in this volume.
15 As Pando-Canteli explains, the epistolary connections between secular women and nuns, primarily Carmelites, in the Low Countries and France, are still a field to be explored, particularly regarding their socio-cultural alliances and political influences ("Expatriates").
16 The bibliography on Carvajal is substantial; see the BIESES database in general and, in particular, the works by Redworth, Rhodes, and more recently, McGrath and Redworth's edition and translation of Carvajal's letters, as well as the edition by Anne J. Cruz, which includes an extensive introduction, an updated bibliography, and an excellent selection of Carvajal's texts in English.
17 It was not unusual for kings and members of the nobility to ask advice from female visionaries and *beatas*; in fact, "consulting kings and politicians religious women was more frequent than one could imagine in other courts and European states, and among other Austrian monarchs" (Manero Sorolla: 119) (las consultas de los reyes y políticos a las religiosas era un hecho más frecuente de lo que en un principio pudiera imaginarse en otras cortes y estados europeos y entre otros monarcas de la casa de Austria). A notable case is that of Lucrecia de León and Philip II (Kagan).
18 "noticias puntuales de cuanto sucedía en la capital de España" (103).
19 "consciente de que en su propio ámbito realiza[ba] un 'trabajo' al servicio del interés común y de la monarquía" (C. Baranda, *Cartas*: 33).
20 "contenido doctrinal" (Martínez Millán: 41).
21 For a complete bibliography on Ágreda, see the BIESES database.
22 "suficientes pruebas de que sus cartas a Felipe IV son un instrumento político, formaban parte de una estrategia de luchas de poder en la que sor María tomó parte activa, persiguiendo con deliberación y empeño influir en el monarca; permiten entrever, con más claridad que las dirigidas a Felipe IV, que formó parte de una tupida red de miembros de la nobleza y del clero que le sirvió de protección y apoyo" (*Cartas*: 9).
23 Although studies of female communities in France and England have increased in the last few years, this has not been the case for Spain, with the exception of works on religious or court communities. See Martínez Millán and Marçal Lourenço, and Zarri and N. Baranda.

Works cited

Abad, Camilo María. *Una misionera española en la Inglaterra del siglo XVII, Doña Luisa de Carvajal y Mendoza*. Comillas: Universidad Pontificia, 1966.

Ágreda, Sor María. *Cartas de sor María de Jesús de Ágreda a Fernando de Borja y Francisco de Borja (1628–1664). Estudio y edición*. Introd. and ed., Consolación Baranda Leturio. Valladolid: Ediciones Universidad de Valladolid, 2013.

———. *Correspondencia con Felipe IV. Religión y razón de estado*. Introd. and ed., Consolación Baranda Leturio. Madrid: Castalia, 2001.

———. *Cartas de sor María de Jesús de Ágreda y de Felipe IV*. 2 vols. Ed. Carlos Seco Serrano. Madrid: Atlas, 1958.

———. *Cartas de la Venerable Madre sor María de Ágreda y del señor Rey Felipe IV*. 2 vols. Ed. Francisco Silvela. Madrid: Rivadeneyra, 1885.

———. *Cartas de la correspondencia entre sor María de Ágreda y Juan Chumacero*. Archivo Concepcionista de Ágreda, Caja 24, números 52–53.

Aguilar-Adan, Christine, and Anne Dubet. "Los arbitristas y la ampliación del espacio político." *La monarquía de Felipe III*. Vol. 3. Ed. José Martínez Millán. Madrid: Fundación Mapfre, 2008: 876–884.

Atienza Hernández, Ignacio. "Mujeres y cultura nobiliaria en el siglo de oro hispano: Doña María de Guevara, Condesa de Escalante." *Retrato de la mujer renacentista*. Coord. Amparo Serrano de Haro Soriano and Esther Alegre Carvajal. Madrid: UNED, 2012: 165–188.

Baranda, Nieves. "Beyond Political Boundaries: Religion as Nation in Early Modern Spain." *Women Telling Nations*. Ed. Amelia Sanz, Francesca Scott, and Suzan van Dijk. Amsterdam: Brill/Rodopi, 2014: 63–83.

——. "Lecturas de damas aristócratas en el siglo XVII." *Cortejo a lo prohibido. Lectoras y escritoras en la España moderna*. Madrid: Arco/Libros, 2005: 35–64.

Baranda, Consolación. "La función de la censura en la configuración de la religiosidad femenina del siglo XVII. Una propuesta." *Las razones del censor. Control ideológico y censura de libros en la primera Edad Moderna*. Ed. Cesc Esteve. Barcelona: Universitat Autònoma de Barcelona, 2013: 161–173.

——. "La correspondencia de María de Ágreda y su estilo literario." *La Madre Ágreda, una mujer del siglo XXI*. Dir. D. Gaspar Pablo. Soria: Universidad Internacional Alfonso VIII, 2000: 61–78.

Baranda, Consolación, ed. *Cartas de sor María de Jesús de Ágreda a Fernando de Borja y Francisco de Borja (1628–1664). Estudio y edición*. Valladolid: Ediciones Universidad de Valladolid, 2013.

——. *Correspondencia con Felipe IV. Religión y razón de estado*. Madrid: Castalia, 2001.

Barbeito Carneiro, María Isabel. "María de Guevara, *son politikon*." *Estudios sobre escritoras hispánicas en honor de Georgina Sabat-Rivers*. Ed. Lou Charnon-Deutsch. Madrid: Castalia, 1992: 62–78.

——. *Cárceles y mujeres en el siglo XVII*. Madrid: Castalia, 1991.

——. "María de Guevara." *Escritoras madrileñas del siglo XVII. Estudio bibliográfico-crítico*. Vol. 2. Madrid: Universidad Complutense de Madrid, 1986: 297–307.

BIESES. Bibliografía de autoras españolas. www.bieses.net/

Bolufer Peruga, Mónica. "Galería de 'mujeres ilustres' o el sinuoso camino de la excepción a la norma cotidiana (ss. XV–XVIII)." *Hispania* 60.1 (2000): 181–224.

Bouza Álvarez, Fernando. *Cultura epistolar en la alta Edad Moderna: Usos de la carta y de la correspondencia entre el manuscrito y el impreso*. Madrid: Universidad Complutense de Madrid, 2005.

Boyle, Margaret. *Unruly Women: Performance, Penitence, and Punishment in Early Modern Spain*. Toronto: U Toronto P, 2014.

Bueso, Eugenia. "Relación de la entrada en la Imperial Ciudad de Zaragoza de su Alteza Seteníssima el Señor Don Juan (1669)." Archivo Histórico Nacional. Estado, libro 921, fols. 282–283.

——. "Relación de la corrida de toros que la Imperial Ciudad de Zaragoza hizo en obsequio a su Alteza (1669)." *Colección de papeles relativos a Carlos II*. MSS. 18.443. Biblioteca Nacional de España.

Campbell, Julie, and Anne Larsen, eds. *Early Modern Women and Transnational Communities of Letters*. Burlington, VT: Ashgate, 2009.

Campo, Victoria. "La historia y la política a través de las relaciones en verso en pliegos sueltos del siglo XVII." *Les relaciones de sucesos (canards) en Espagne (1500–1750). Actes du premier Colloque International (Alcalá de Henares, 8, 9 et 10 juin 1995)*. Ed. María Cruz García de Enterría *et al*. Paris/Alcalá: Publications de la Sorbonne/Servicio de Publicaciones de la Universidad de Alcalá, 1996: 19–32.

Caro Baroja, Julio. "Una dama corajuda y arbitrista." *Vidas poco paralelas (con perdón de Plutarco)*. Madrid: Turner, 1981: 69–87.

Caro de Mallén, Ana. *Contexto de las reales fiestas que se hicieron en el Palacio del Buen Retiro a la Coronación de Rey de Romanos y entrada en Madrid de la Señora Princesa de Cariñan (1637)*. Ed. Antonio Pérez Gómez. Valencia: Tipografía Moderna, 1951.

Carvajal y Mendoza, Luisa. *Escritos Autobiográficos*. Ed. C. M. Abad. Barcelona: Juan de Flores, 1966.

——. *Epistolario y poesía*. Ed. Jesús González de Marañón and C. M. Abad. Madrid: Atlas, 1965.

Castillo Gómez, Antonio. *Entre la pluma y la pared. Una historia social de la escritura de los siglos de oro*. Madrid: Akal, 2006.

Castillo Gómez, Antonio, and Verónica Sierra Blas, ed. *Cartas-Lettres-Lettere. Discursos, prácticas y representaciones epistolares (siglos XIV–XX)*. Alcalá de Henares: UTE Universidad de Alcalá, 2014.

——. *Cinco siglos de cartas: Historia y prácticas epistolares en las épocas moderna y contemporánea*. Huelva: Servicio de Publicaciones Universidad de Huelva, 2014.

Castillo Gómez, Antonio and Carlos Sáez Sánchez, ed. *La correspondencia en la historia: modelos y prácticas de escritura epistolar*. Madrid: Calambur, 2002.

Castro Egas, Ana de. *Eternidad del Rey Don Felipe Tercero Nuestro Señor, el Piadoso. Discurso de su vida y santas costumbres. Al Serenísimo señor el Cardenal Infante su Hijo*. Madrid: Por la viuda de Alonso Martin, 1629.

Chicharro Crespo, Elena. "La correspondencia familiar en el ámbito conventual femenino: Cartas de María de Jesús de Ágreda a la Duquesa de Alburquerque." *CRESPO* 20 (2013): 191–213.

Colón, Isabel. "Linajes de mujeres y linajes nobiliarios: Rodrigo de Calderón, Bernardo de Sandoval y Rojas, el duque de Lerma y su entorno femenino en los textos de Luisa de Carvajal." *El duque de Lerma. Poder y literatura en el Siglo de Oro*. Ed. J. Matas Caballero, J. M. Micó, and J. Ponce Cárdenas. Madrid: Centro de Estudios Europa Hispánica, 2011: 317–340.

Corteguera, Luis and Sherry Velasco. "Authority in the Margin: Reexamining the Autograph Letters of Sor María de Ágreda and Philip IV of Spain." *Women's Voices and the Politics of the Spanish Empire: From Convent Cell to Imperial*. Ed. Jeanne L. Gillespie, Jennifer Eich, and Lucia Harrison. New Orleans: UP of the South, 2008: 235–262.

Cortijo, Adelaida and Antonio Cortijo Ocaña. "Entre Luisa de Carvajal y el conde de Gondomar: Nuevos textos sobre la persecución católica en Inglaterra (1612–1614)." *Voz y Letra. Revista de literatura* 13.2 (2002): 17–59.

Couchman, Jane and Anne Crabb, ed. *Women's Letters across Europe 1400–1700*. Burlington VT: Ashgate, 2005.

Cruz, Anne J, ed. and trans. *The Life and Writings of Luisa de Carvajal y Mendoza*. Toronto: Iter/Centre for Reformation and Renaissance Studies, 2014.

——. "Las relaciones entre las mujeres religiosas y sus patrocinadoras: Confluencias e influencias." *Letras en la celda. Cultura escrita de los conventos femeninos en la España moderna*. Ed. Nieves Baranda Leturio and María Carmen Marín Pina. Madrid: Iberoamericana/Vervuert, 2014: 134–146.

——. "Del cuerpo al corpus: La biografía como expresión literaria feminista en la Edad de Oro." *Mujeres en la literatura. Escritoras*. Ed. Lillian von der Walde and Mariel Reinoso. *Destiempos* 4.19 (2009): 41–59.

——. "Willing Desire: Luisa de Carvajal y Mendoza and Feminine Subjectivity." *Power and Gender in Renaissance Spain: Eight Women of the Mendoza Family, 1450–1650*. Ed. Helen Nader. Urbana and Chicago: U Illinois P, 2004: 177–193.

——. "Challenging Lives: Gender and Class as Categories in Early Modern Spanish Biographies." *Disciplines on the Line: Feminist Research on Spanish, Latin American and US Latina Women*. Ed. Anne J. Cruz, Rosilie Hernández, and Joyce Tolliver. Newark: Juan de la Cuesta, 2003: 103–123.

——. "Gender and Class as Challenges for Feminist Biographies in Early Modern Spain." *Laberinto Journal* (2002). www.laberintojournal.com/2002/cruz.htm. Accessed December 2, 2014.

——. "Luisa de Carvajal y Mendoza y su conexión jesuita." *La mujer y su representación en las literaturas hispánicas. Actas de XI Congreso de la Asociación Internacional de Hispanistas. Irvine 92*. Vol. 2. Coord. Juan Villegas. Irvine: U California P, 1994: 97–104.

Daybell, James. *Women Letter-Writers in Tudor England*. Oxford: Oxford UP, 2006.

Daybell, James, ed. *Women and Politics in Early Modern England*. Aldershot: Ashgate, 2004.

——. *Early Modern Women's Letter Writing, 1450–1700*. Basingstoke: Palgrave, 2001.

Doglio, Maria Luisa. *Lettera e donna. Scrittura epistolare al femminile tra Quattro e Cinquecento*. Rome: Bulzoni, 1993.

Dopico-Black, Georgina. "Public Bodies, Private Parts: The Virgins and Magdalens of Magdalena de San Jerónimo." *Journal of Spanish Cultural Studies* 2.1 (2001): 81–96.

Fernández Gracia, Ricardo. *Arte, devoción y política. La promoción de las artes en torno a sor María de Ágreda*. Soria: Diputación Provincial de Soria, 2002.

Fernández Santamaría, J. A. *Reason of State and Stagecraft in Spanish Political Thought, 1595–1640*. Lanham: UP of America, 1983.

——. *The State, War and Peace. Spanish Political Thought in the Renaissance, 1516–1559*. Cambridge: Cambridge UP, 1977.

Frye, Susan and Karen Robertson, eds. *Maids and Mistresses, Cousins and Queens*. Oxford: Oxford UP, 1999.

García Royo, Luis. *La aristocracia española y Sor María de Jesús de Ágreda*. Madrid: Espasa-Calpe, 1951.

Guevara, María de. *Warnings to the Kings and Advice on Restoring Spain*. Introd. and bilingual ed. Nieves Romero-Díaz. Chicago/London: U Chicago P, 2007.

——. *Desengaños de la corte y mujeres valerosas* (1664) R/4.496. Biblioteca Nacional de España.

——. *Tratado y advertencias hechas por una mujer celosa del bien de su Rey y corrida de parte de España* (1663). MSS. 12.270. Biblioteca Nacional de España.

——. *Memorial de la casa de Escalante y servicios de ella al Rey Nuestro Señor* (Valladolid, 1654). V-C 57–13. Biblioteca Nacional de España.

Harris, Barbara. *English Aristocratic Women, 1450–1550: Marriage and Family, Property and Careers*. Oxford: Oxford UP, 2003.

——. "Women and Politics in Early Tudor England." *Historical Journal* 33 (1990): 259–281.

Hernández, Rosilie. "Friends in High Places: The Correspondence of Felipe IV and María de Ágreda." *Perspectives on Early Modern Women in Iberia and the Americas*. Ed. Adrienne L. Martín and María Cristina Quintero. New York: Escribana Books, 2015: 422–442.

———. "The Politics of Exemplarity: Biblical Women and the Education of the Spanish Lady in Martín Carrillo, Sebastián de Herrera Barnuevo, and María de Guevara." *Women's Literacy in Early Modern Spain and the New World*. Ed. Anne J. Cruz and Rosilie Hernández. Burlington, VT: Ashgate, 2011: 225–241.

Iglesias, Miguel. "Luisa de Carvajal y Mendoza: Catolicismo y estrategia política en la Inglaterra jacobina." *Luisa de Carvajal en sus contextos*. Ed. María Luisa García-Verdugo Roncero. Madrid: Pliegos, 2008: 47–73.

Kagan, Richard. *Los sueños de Lucrecia: Política y profecía en la España del siglo XVI*. Trans. Francisco Carpio. Madrid: Nerea, 1991.

Lakarra, Eukene. "Magdalena de San Jerónimo: ¿muger contra mugeres?" *Actas del Primer Congreso Anglo-Hispano, Huelva, marzo 24–31, 1992. II. Literatura*. Ed. Alan Deyermond and Ralph Penny. Madrid: Castalia, 1993: 175–189.

Langle de Paz, Teresa. "En busca del paraíso ausente: 'mujer varonil' y 'autor femenil' en una utopía feminista inédita del siglo XVII español." *Hispania* 86.3 (2003): 463–473.

Levine, Carole, and Alicia Meyer. "Women and Political Power in Early Modern Europe." *Ashgate Research Companion to Women and Gender in Early Modern Europe*. Ed. Allyson Poska, Katherine McIver, and Jane Couchman. Burlington, VT: Ashgate, 2013: 341–357.

Levy-Navarro, Elena. "The Religious Warrior: Luisa de Carvajal y Mendoza's Correspondence with Rodrigo de Calderón." *Women's Letters across Europe 1400–1700*. Ed. Jane Couchman and Anne Crabb. Burlington, VT: Ashgate, 2005: 263–273.

López-Cordón, María Victoria. "La fortuna de escribir: escritoras de los siglos XVII y XVIII." *Historia de las mujeres en España y América Latina*. Vol. 2 *El mundo moderno*. Ed. Isabel Morant, M. Ortega, A. Lavrin, and P. Pérez Cantó. Madrid: Cátedra, 2005: 193–234.

———. "De escritura femenina y arbitrios políticos: La obra de doña María de Guevara." *Cuadernos de Historia Contemporánea* 1 (2007): 151–164.

López Estrada, Francisco. "Costumbres sevillanas: El poema sobre la Fiesta y Octava celebradas con motivo de los sucesos en Flandes en la Iglesia de San Miguel (1635) por Ana Caro Mallén." *Archivo Hispalense* 66.203 (1983): 109–150.

———. "La relación de fiestas por los Mártires del Japón, de Ana Caro de Mallén (Sevilla, 1628)." *Libro Homenaje a Antonio Pérez Gómez*. VVAA. Cieza: La Fonte que mana y corre, 1978: 51–69.

López Poza, Sagrario. *Boletín Informativo sobre las relaciones de sucesos españolas en la Edad Moderna*. www.bidiso.es/boresu/

Luna, Lola. "Ana Caro, una escritora de oficio." *Leyendo como una mujer la imagen de la mujer*. Seville: Anthropos, 1996: 138–157.

Manero Sorolla, María Pilar. "Sor María de Jesús de Ágreda y el providencialismo político de la casa de Austria." *La creatividad femenina en el mundo barroco hispánico. María de Zayas-Isabel Rebeca Correa-Sor Juana Inés de la Cruz*. Ed. Monika Bosse, Barbara Potthast, and André Stoll. Vol. 1. Kassel: Reichenberg, 1999: 105–125.

Maravall, José Antonio. *Teoría del estado en España en el siglo XVII*. Madrid: Centro de Estudios Constitucionales, 1997.

Marín Pina, María Carmen. "Pliegos sueltos poéticos femeninos en el camino del verso al libro de poesía: la singularidad de María Nieto." *Bulletin Hispanique* 113.1 (2011): 239–268.

———. "Eugenia Bueso, cronista en verso de la entrada de Juan José de Austria en Zaragoza (1669): Un texto recuperado." *Mujeres en la literatura. Escritoras*. Dossier edited by Lilllian von der Walde and Mariel Reinoso. *Destiempos* 4.19 (2009): 60–81.

———. "Juan Francisco Andrés de Uztarroz y el Parnaso femenino en Aragón." *Bulletin Hispanique* 109.2 (2007): 589–614.

Martínez Millán, José. "Política y religión en la corte: Felipe IV y María Jesús de Ágreda." *La corte en Europa: Política y Religión. Siglos XVI–XVIII*. Coord. J. Martínez Millán, M. Rivero Rodríguez, and G. Versteegen. Vol. 3. Madrid: Polifemo, 2012: 1377–1455.

Martínez Millán, José and Maria Paula Marçal Lourenço, coord. *Las relaciones discretas entre las monarquías hispana y portuguesa: las casa de las reinas (siglos XV–XIX)*. 3 Vols. Madrid: Polifemo, 2009.

McGrath, David and Glyn Redworth, trans. *The Letters of Luisa de Carvajal y Mendoza*. Ed. Glyn Redworth and Christopher J. Henstock. 2 Vols. Brookfield, VT: Pickering & Chatto, 2012.

Morte Acín, Ana. "Sor María de Ágreda y la vida cotidiana en Ágreda en el siglo XVII: una aproximación histórica." *Cuadernos de Historia Moderna* 39 (2014): 121–136.

———. *Misticismo y conspiración. Sor María de Ágreda en el reinado de Felipe IV.* Zaragoza: Institución de Fernando el Católico, Excma. Diputación de Zaragoza, 2010.

Nieto de Aragón, María. *Epitalamio por la bodas de Felipe IV y Mariana de Austria.* Np., nd. [ca. 1649].

———. *Lágrimas a la muerte de Isabel de Borbón.* Madrid: Diego Díaz de la Carrera, 1645.

Ortega, Margarita. Introducción. *Historia de las mujeres en España y América Latina.* Vol. 2. *El mundo moderno.* Ed. Isabel Morant, M. Ortega, A. Lavrin, and P. Pérez Cantó. Madrid: Cátedra, 2005: 13–23.

Pando-Canteli, María Jesús. "Letters, books and relics. Material and Spiritual Networks in the Life of Luisa de Carvajal y Mendoza (1564–1614)." *Devout Laywomen in the Early-Modern World.* Ed. Alison Weber. Oxford: Routledge, 2016: 294–311.

———. "*Tentando vados*: The Martyrdom Politics of Luisa de Carvajal y Mendoza." *Journal for Early Modern Cultural Studies* 10.1 (2010): 117–141.

———. "Expatriates. Women's Communities, Mobility and Cosmopolitanism in Early Modern Europe: English and Spanish Nuns in Flanders." *Women Telling Nations.* Ed. Amelia Sanz, Francesca Scott, and Suzan van Dijk. Amsterdam: Brill/Rodopi, 2014: 85–101.

Peraita Huerta, Carmen. "Apacible brevedad de los renglones, abreviada vida de monarcas: Ana de Castro Egas, Francisco de Quevedo y la escritura del panegírico regio." *La Perinola* 9 (2005): 151–170.

Pérez Villanueva, Joaquín. "Sor María de Ágreda y Felipe IV: Un epistolario de su tiempo." *Historia de la Iglesia de España.* Separata del vol. IV. Madrid: Biblioteca de Autores Cristianos, 1979: 359–417.

Ramírez de Guzmán, Catalina. *Relación en coplas de pie quebrado de las fiestas que celebró Llerena á el nacimiento de el Principe nuestro señor Don Phelipe prospero* (1657). MSS. 3884. Biblioteca Nacional de España.

Redworth, Glyn. *The She-Apostle. The Extraordinary Life and Death of Luisa de Carvajal.* Oxford: Oxford UP, 2008.

Rhodes, Elizabeth. *This Tight Embrace: Luisa de Carvajal y Mendoza (1566–1614).* Milwaukee: Marquette UP, 2000.

———. "Luisa de Carvajal's Counter-Reformation Journey to Self-hood (1566–1614)." *Renaissance Quarterly* 51.3 (1998): 887–911.

Robles, Tania. "María de Guevara: Consciencia histórica y política exterior." *Política y escritura de mujeres.* Ed. Elena Hernández Sandoica. Madrid: Abada Editores, 2012: 13–132.

Romero-Díaz, Nieves. "Del sarao zayesco a la carta agrediana. La sociabilidad cortesana femenina en la España de Felipe IV." *Sociabilidad y literatura en el Siglo de Oro.* Ed. Mechtild Albert. Madrid: Iberoamericana, 2013: 255–273.

———. "Poesía femenil en las exequias por Isabel de Borbón: Los casos de Leonor de la Cueva y Silva y María Nieto de Aragón." *Calíope: Journal of the Society for Renaissance and Baroque Poetry* 16.2 (2010): 9–43.

———. "El discurso reformista de Luisa de Padilla y María de Guevara ante las novedades y vicios de una sociedad en crisis." *Materia crítica: formas de ocio y de consumo en la cultura áurea.* Ed. Enrique García Santo-Tomás. Madrid: Iberoamericana, 2009: 59–75.

———. "Autoridad y genealogías femeninas alrededor de la Infanta María Teresa de Austria." *Letras Femeninas* 35.1 (2009): 311–337.

———. "Introduction." *Warnings to the Kings and Advice on Restoring Spain.* Chicago/London: U Chicago P, 2007: 1–41.

San Jerónimo, Magdalena de. "Razón y forma de la galera y casa real que el Rey, Nuestro Señor, manda hacer en estos reinos para castigo de las mujeres vagantes, y ladronas, alcahuetas, hechiceras, y otras semejantes" (1608). *Cárceles y mujeres en el siglo XVII.* Introd. and ed., María Isabel Barbeito Carneiro. Madrid: Castalia, 1991: 61–95.

Sánchez de Toca, Joaquín. *Felipe IV y sor María de Ágreda. Estudio crítico.* Barcelona: Minerva, 1887.

Sánchez Dueñas, Blas. "Otras autoras y géneros." *De la invisibilidad a la creación. Oralidad, concepción teórica y material preceptivo en la produccion literaria femenina hasta el siglo XVIII.* Seville: Renacimiento, 2008: 41–56.

Serrano y Sanz, Manuel. *Apuntes para una Biblioteca de Escritoras Españolas desde 1401 a 1833.* 4 vols. (1903). Madrid: Atlas, 1975.

Tarbin, Stephanie and Susan Broomhall, ed. *Women, Identities and Communities in Early Modern Europe.* Burlington VT: Ashgate, 2008.

Torras Francés, Meri. *Tomando cartas en el asunto. Las amistades peligrosas de las mujeres con el género epistolar.* Zaragoza: Prensas Universitarias de Zaragoza, 2001.

Villegas de la Torre, Esther María. "Transatlantic Interactions: Seventeenth Century Women Authors and Literary Self-Consciousness." *Identity, Nation, Discourse: Latin American Women Writers and Artists*. Ed. Claire Taylor. Newcastle: Cambridge Scholars, 2009: 104–121.

Voros, Sharon D. "*Relaciones de fiestas*: Ana Caro's Accounts of Public Spectacles." *Women in the Discourse of Early Modern Spain*. Ed. Joan F. Cammarata. Florida: UP Florida, 2003: 108–132.

Wiesner-Hanks, Merry. *Women and Gender in Early Modern Europe*. Cambridge: Cambridge UP, 1993.

Zarri, Gabriella, ed. *Per lettera. La scrittura epistolare femminile tra archivio e tipografia. Secoli XV–XVII*. Rome: Viella, 1999.

Zarri, Gabriella and Nieves Baranda Leturio, eds. *Memoria e comunità femminili: Spagna e Italia, secc. XV–XVII; Memoria y comunidades femeninas: España e Italia, siglos XV–XVII*. Florence/Madrid: Firenze UP/ UNED, 2011.

SECTION V

Private circles

16
DIDACTIC TREATISES

Rosilie Hernández

In this chapter, we will look at a number of compositional and thematic aspects of formally didactic texts written by women in early modern Spain. More precisely, we will look at texts that both in form and content are singularly meant to instruct, distinct from the broad category of didactic prose (*prosa didáctica*) that is associated with the Horatian *prodesse et delectare* topos that defined much of the literature of the early modern period.[1] The authors discussed, some in more detail than others, are Luisa Sigea de Velasco, Luisa de Padilla, María de Guevara, Ana de San Bartolomé, María de San José Salazar, Juana de la Encarnación, Francisca de Jesús Borja y Enríquez, and Feliciana de San José. Their texts, secular and religious, share important characteristics; yet each offers a unique voice and creative imagination that merits separate full-length studies. This essay proposes a conceptual framework for some areas of inquiry that are especially relevant to the study of women-authored didactic texts in the early modern Spanish context. It focuses on the site and conditions of production and the ways in which mastery and moral and spiritual superiority are asserted, as well as offering a general sense of the range of topics that appear in these texts.

The study of this kind of literature offers particular benefits because it identifies those early modern women writers who explicitly took it upon themselves to adopt the role of didact, one largely negated or curtailed strictly to the home and the rearing of children. Through the writing of these texts, women position themselves as legitimately capable of erudition, assume the agency expected in the authoring of a formally didactic text, and place themselves as worthy heirs to classical, scholastic, theological, and humanist traditions where the didactic genres first originated. Structured as systematic expositions of a topic or aspects of a discipline, the didactic genres venture into the philosophical, theological, scientific, and moral realms, going beyond and at times aiming to overrule that which nature seems to demonstrate and instinct calls forth.[2] Given these characteristics, early modern women writers who venture into the didactic genres challenge or altogether forgo at least two distinct, albeit connected cultural biases: that women are not intellectually suited for analysis and reasoning, and that they lack the capacity for the transmission of knowledge. Instead, through the didactic discourse women authors declare and demonstrate their superior competence in intellectual, moral, and/or spiritual matters. The task of presenting oneself as a master of a subject is thorny for women authors who must justify mastery while not overstepping prescriptions of modesty and obedience to their male superiors, whether this refers to a specific male confessor as is the case for nuns or in more general cultural terms as is the case for secular women; the rhetorical and discursive strategies employed to negotiate this contradiction, therefore, add a fascinating aspect to the study of their texts. Upon analysis what becomes evident is that, despite the hurdles that must be overcome, women didactic authors are able and willing to claim the expertise that grants them the right to teach and guide others. Moreover, although not always exclusively directed to female readers (this is particularly the case for secular authors), these texts assume that women have a need for and will be especially receptive to their themes and content, thus posting female readers as naturally and legitimately profiting from instruction.

The degree and types of access to informal and formal instructional experiences of Spanish early modern women have recently received considerable attention. Books such as Teresa Howe's *Education and Women in the Early Modern Hispanic World* and Anne J. Cruz and Rosilie Hernández's edited volume *Women's Literacy in Early Modern Spain and the New World* have done much to establish the coordinates for the study of women's education in sixteenth- and seventeenth-century Spain. As Cruz notes in her "Introduction," for most women, education was limited to the fundamentals of reading and the skills necessary for household management and devotional practices (3–4). Nieves Baranda Leturio confirms this point in her "Mujer y Escritura en el Siglo de Oro: Una relación inestable," by focusing on the strictures declared and anxieties manifested in conduct manuals and treatises that touched upon women's literacy. As documented by Baranda Leturio, the practice of reading for women was comprehended as purely utilitarian, applicable only to the basic competencies required by the household and to the edification of the soul ("Mujer y escritura": 63). Consequently, women's writing as a substantial practice was deemed suspicious because it exceeded the basic needs of familial and religious care: "[W]hile learning to read was defensible given the possibility it offered for acquiring knowledge of religious doctrine, learning to write seemingly had no spiritual ends and to the contrary opened the field for the expression of the profane, above all in the exchange of love letters" (Baranda Leturio, "Mujer y escritura": 64).[3] Despite these conditions, it is also evident that many women, either by individual choice or as a result of their specific family situation, were able to considerably expand their knowledge base (Cruz: 7). Frequently, women's writing attests through its citations and references to the many and varied resources to which their authors had been exposed.[4] Examining similar evidence, Howe focuses on the ways in which women-authored texts in turn function as important didactic tools for other women who avidly read and imitated these (both in content and in form) in their own living and writing practices.[5] The best-known and documented case of the transmission of knowledge from woman to text to other women is Teresa of Ávila, whose *Vida* (*The Book of Her Life*, 1562–1565), *Camino de perfección* (*Way to Perfection*, 1562–1564) and *Castillo interior* (*The Interior Castle*, 1577), despite their specificity as moral and religious treatises, became some of the most important sources— in form, rhetorical strategies, and content—for female readers and writers throughout the period. In sum, the general perceptions that emerge of women's education and literacy are the following: increasingly throughout the early modern period, women in Spain had concrete opportunities to learn to read and write in the vernacular and to a lesser extent in Latin; and those who wrote (whether for private and public consumption) demonstrate a broad array of knowledge and mastery of sources and forms, including classical and contemporary, as well as other women's writing.

As we then turn specifically to women-authored didactic literature, it is particularly useful to recall Linda Alcoff's theory of positionality, with its emphasis on the production and mediation of a particular woman's identity—how she positions herself—vis-à-vis the historical and socio-discursive context in which she exists at a particular moment in time:

> [T]he identity of a woman is the product of her own interpretation and reconstruction of her history, as mediated through the cultural discursive context to which she has access. [. . .] The concept of woman as positionality shows how women use their positional perspective as a place from which values are interpreted and constructed rather than as a locus of an already determined set of values.
>
> *"Cultural Feminism": 434*[6]

Alcoff's interest in the formation of female identity at the unstable intersection of historical conditions, dominant ideological structures, available discourses, and personal experience helps to nuance our study of women's cultural production by precluding essentialist interpretations of the categories of woman as oppressed and the patriarchal system as monolithic and unchanging. In the case of didactic texts, early modern women authors explicitly deploy arguments, perspectives, and opinions through which "values are interpreted and constructed." Navigating what Alcoff terms an "overabundance and inconsistency" (*Visible Identities*: 152) of content (variable and often contradictory categories, positions, and prescriptions within the ideological and social field) and shifting contexts, these works pay witness to women's fluid positional identities as writers, nuns, nobles, lay theologians, intellectuals, mystics, submissive servants of the Church, mothers, and wives; as well as to their personal histories, temperaments, sensibilities, and pathologies that together shape their *experience* of both content and context.

As demonstrated in the texts here examined, didactic literature is a prime site in which to investigate the strategies employed by women authors to filter, negotiate, and reconcile their "identity as positionality," rendered in the assumed voice of mastery and the transmission of adoptable and reproducible knowledge and values. Luisa Sigea's dedication of her *Duarum virginum colloquium de vita aulica et private* (Dialogue of Two Girls at Court and the Secluded Life, 1552) to María of Portugal, Duchess of Viseu, clearly establishes her authorial command, since she is one of the infanta's closest attendants. She is privy to court life, with access to the royal library, and names herself a "polyglossae nuncupatio" ("Dedicatio"). Calling upon her standing as a "grand lady of this Spanish kingdom" in her *Nobleza Virtuosa* (Virtuous Nobility: A1),[7] Luisa de Padilla, Countess of Aranda, offers her inherent nobility and possession of virtue as the foundational claim for her capacity to instruct. Also from the position of a noblewoman, in *Desengaños de la corte y mujeres valerosas* (Disenchantments at the Court and Valorous Women, 1664) María de Guevara launches into a critique of court life giving her reader the immediate impression that her personal experience makes her discourse incontestable. Those religious women who were also didactic authors similarly position themselves: their authorial positional identity as humble and yet knowledgeable, gifted, and chosen servants of God denies a facile contestation and facilitates the transmission of their personal vision for spiritual conventual life.

The rhetorical structure of these women-authored didactic texts follows immediately recognizable generic forms: exhortations, manuals, and dialogues. In this regard, because female didacts locate their texts in a literary tradition dominated from antiquity by men, they offer little innovation. An important difference, nonetheless, resides in that their texts uncharacteristically feature an array of female voices—with the dialogues being especially interesting in this respect—and are written for interpretative communities that include or are composed solely of women. For example, Sigea's *Colloquium*, María de San José Salazar's *Libro de Recreaciones* (Book for the Hour of Recreation, 1585), and Feliciana de San José's *Recreación espiritual compuesta en diálogos* (Book for Spiritual Recreation Composed in Dialogues, 1654) showcase a shared production of knowledge among numerous women, adapting the form to suit the female voice.[8] As Feliciana de San José explains in the first pages of her *Recreación*, "May God bless (o my dears) our Mother Prioress for having given us the license to talk to each other today; since I was improving so little in the virtue of kept silence, I desired to have your company for I believe it will be profitable in this regard" (2).[9] It is in this context of women speaking to and teaching each other that a number of capacities, perspectives, and sentiments can be expressed; or, as Alison Weber notes in regard to María de San José Salazar's *Recreaciones*, "The conversation among the three women (none of whom has the last word) demonstrates that women can be competent spiritual teachers to each other. Indeed, Maria implies, their shared experience, intimate knowledge of each other's character, and egalitarian relationship may allow them to succeed as spiritual guides where men might fail" (20).[10] The result is the expression of feminine voices in didactic forms that, even though contextualized within the expectations of classical and early modern traditions, are refashioned through coordinates identifiable with a female imaginary.

A consideration of these rhetorical forms quickly slips into an analysis of content and how specific concerns and ideological positions are expressed and filtered. Margarita Torremocha Hernández has pointed out, for example, how Padilla's *Lágrimas de la Nobleza* (Tears of the Nobility, 1639)—and I would extend this opinion to all six published manuals—holds as a primary area of concern the varied relationships between noblemen and women as father and daughter, husband and wife, and fellow parents.[11] In her chapter, "Concerning Valorous Women," Guevara also describes women in relation to the men whom they supported or otherwise upstaged—these range from the Virgin Mary to Antona García.[12] In the chapter that follows, "On Men's Discourtesy toward their Own Wives," Guevara extends this logic to the failure of men within the household:

> [T]he first thing that happens is he brings everything from Antón Martín home and then fills the house with children of his mistress (these are the profits that they give to their own wives), and he gambles away her dowry and her jewels, and if she speaks a single word, she will hear two thousand affronts; and if she defends him, it makes for a long journey. And at fault is her bad nature, while they are never blamed for anything. If they run into any sort of hardship, they return home like the prodigal son.
>
> 79, trans. Romero-Díaz[13]

And yet, for neither of these writers—nor for Sigea for that matter—is the discourse solely limited to the lessons imparted by corrupted male–female relationships within the domestic or private spheres. To the contrary, Padilla is equally interested in the management of state and its economic reform, including the importance of intellectual capacity within the political realm and the (mis)treatment of vassals in Aragon's feudal estates.[14] Guevara similarly widens the scope to include economic and social issues: "Houses are poorly governed and wealth is even more poorly managed, because the owners do not look after them, and so everyone is poor. [. . .] [T]hey have enough to give to buffoons and flatterers but not to the poor who, out of shame, are now perishing in their homes—although they were fine in the past" (69, trans. Romero-Díaz).[15] Sigea's *Colloquium*, written 100 years earlier, ascribed much of its condemnation of the court to similar deficiencies. As demonstrated by these examples, women-authored didactic treatises examine local and national matters, offering wide-ranging prescriptions through an ideological and discursive lens that also focuses on the affirmative notion of women as intellectually capable, morally virtuous, and spiritually worthy individuals and agents.

In the case of didactic texts written by nuns, Asunción Lavrin remarks on the category of "literature of devotional erudition" and the connection to the female author's faith: "When that faith was supported by the reading of key texts of Christian spirituality to explain itself and demanded the attention of readers not only through affectivity but also through exegetical analysis, we witness the devotional erudition to which I have refered" (66).[16] Lavrin's assessment is relevant

Didactic treatises

both in terms of authority and of content. Given that their goal is to teach fellow nuns how to better embark upon and maintain an enlightened conventual and spiritual life, the relationship of experience in the form of faith to exegetical/theological knowledge—and how together they are translated into the content—is pivotal to the analysis of these texts. When examined in detail, we find a variety of levels of intellectual and emotional engagement mixed in with scriptural and theological sources. On one end of the spectrum, Francisca de Jesús Borja y Enríquez's *De las exhortaciones que dejó escrita de su propia mano* (Exhortations that she wrote of her own hand, 1616) limits itself to generalized citations of the New Testament and Saint Claire's writings, such as "that the love that nuns posses is shown through good works" (24).[17] On the other, Juana de la Encarnación's *Dispertador del alma religiosa. Manual de ejercicios y dictámenes espirituales* (Manual of exercises and spiritual judgments, 1723) makes use of a battery of Scriptural sources for what is an equally extensive set of topics—mental prayer, how to withstand illness, flagellation, charity, conformity, the celebration of religious festivities, and so on—under the umbrella theme of how to reach religious perfection within the convent walls.[18] In between these poles, we have the dialogues of María de San José Salazar and Feliciana de San José, and Ana de San Bartolomé's *Conferencias espirituales* (Spiritual Lectures) and *Formación de novicias y ejercicios de piedad 1611–1624* (Formation of novices and exercises of piety 1611–1624), which include occasional citations—for the most part biblical and other religious sources such as hagiographies—integrated within the body of the text. The point is, however, that women didactic authors combine their intimate experience of divinity with the benefit tendered from learned sources in order to profitably navigate the instructional content their texts are meant to impart. Ana de San Bartolomé's thoughts on mortification serve as a perfect example:

> This virtue is so precious and praiseworthy that, wherever it is, the soul will always be in honest and holy perfection. For that which is true mortification is a total dying to all our natural desires and inclinations; while they live in us, we cannot consider ourselves true religious nor lovers of God, but rather we love ourselves and our whims, as is said of the children of Israel, who, having been freed from the captivity of the pharaoh and placed in the desert, cried for the onions of Egypt.
>
> Spiritual Lectures Pontoise July 1605, *trans. Donahue, 139*[19]

Tapping into her audience's knowledge of the exodus from Egypt, Ana de San Bartolomé demonstrates her mastery of both the Old Testament as a textual source and of the spiritual lessons procured through the divine word. The didactic aim is to warn against the disruptive and persistent capacity of the appetites, all this through the filter of her personal experience. There is perhaps no better way for woman didacts to assert the legitimacy of intent and the lessons they impart than through the appropriation of sacred sources imbricated with documentation of their lives.

Nevertheless, it is important to recognize the many conflicts and pressures that make challenging the construction of a uniform female didactic identity. As Juanita Feros Ruys points out regarding the analysis of medieval and early modern didactic literature:

> [W]e must be aware both of the efforts (successful and otherwise) made towards construction of a holistic didactic persona by an author, as well as competing intentions evident within these didactic authors. [. . .] [T]he implications are significant, because the creation of didactic meaning is thereby relocated, existing not now with the author, but rather with the reader/listener who is required to absorb, make sense of, and perhaps resolve, contradictory advice.
>
> *"Introduction": 6–7*

Following this logic, didactic literature displays more prominently than other genres authorial identities where formal requirements, the specificity of the social context, contesting ideologies, and the fragmented self perilously intersect. As indicated by Feros Ruys, the reader is thus tasked with reconciling often seemingly intractable incongruities in the positions adopted by the author. Early modern didactic texts, and we would argue most especially those written by women, function within and partake of contemporary technologies of power; these technologies discursively reproduce, perpetuate, and limit the possibility of actions in accordance with early modern patriarchal, aristocratic, and Catholic values. This is obviously a Foucauldian framing for power, its mechanisms, and discursive manifestations.[20] But, as Michel Foucault also noted, "Discourses are not once and for all subservient to power or raised up against it [. . .] [D]iscourse can be both an instrument and an effect of power, but also a hindrance, a stumbling-block, a point of resistance and a starting point for an opposing strategy" (*History of Sexuality*: 100–101). When we extend this logic to female-authored didactic texts, we find a way to simultaneously recognize the technologies of power in which these texts are inserted and the particular ways in which women authors position their distinct and disruptive didactic identities vis-à-vis those same technologies of power that their texts repeat and disseminate.

The sites of production for the texts here considered are fundamentally two: the family home or country estate (with its social connections to court culture and the city) and the convent. Upon examination, it becomes immediately evident that the imaginary coordinates and motivations are mainly conditioned by the physical and mental geographies of these sites. It is also clear that their experience—social, economic, psychological—of the site of production, and the knowledge that emerges from it, largely authorizes these women to write didactic texts; otherwise, these texts would have never been accepted by the male-dominated social and ideological structures that they inhabit. Padilla, Countess of Aranda, writes from her estate in Épila, Aragón, where she and her husband, Antonio Jiménez de Urrea, Count of Aranda, have retired and cultivate their intellectual and literary ambitions.[21] Guevara, thrice married, divides her time between Madrid, Valladolid, and her estates in an attempt to retain her social status and maintain close ties with the court of Philip IV.[22] One hundred years earlier, as Baranda Leturio reminds us, Sigea "does not include her own experience as part of the arguments, [but] we must not forget that this work was written shortly before she married and left the Portuguese court to go to Spain. Her life, her doubts as well as her reflections, become a part of this highly stylized literary work" (*Women Writers*, "Louisa Sigea"). All three give testimony to the murky dealings and sullied behavior of the nobility and locate their textual personas and created characters in an aristocratic milieu, which they dissect and to which they respond. The court, the public arena, and the home offer Sigea, Padilla, and Guevara locations from which to observe, gather relevant classical, Biblical and humanist sources, provide analysis, and draw teachable conclusions. These sites, understood as degraded by the lack of virtue displayed by much of the nobility, are precisely what feed their imagination, motivate their collection and scrutiny of sources, provoke an independent valorization of the circumstances in which they live, and frame their re-articulation of gendered and patriarchal values.

The convent is a parallel site whose physical and mental coordinates dictate a different type of didactic production. Unlike the family home or the court, the cloistered setting promotes a look inward, in terms of the self, the space, and the audience: "One should distinguish [. . .] a group of works destined for the instruction of communities [. . .]. Their aim is to modify conducts, convert words into action, and the target audience are the nuns in the convent among who the author occupies a position of authority, which allows for an immediate and even if restricted diffusion" (Baranda Leturio and Marín Pina, *Cortejo*: 34).[23] Didactic texts written by nuns illustrate and offer guidance on the heightening of the spiritual life and communion with the divine—

a process that is personal in nature but communally structured by and shared within the convent walls. The cloister serves as a stage for this process, facilitating the necessary ascetic locus and strict routines. The texts written by nuns thus primarily concern themselves with describing the proper physical, mental, and spiritual practices that lead to the purification of the soul, propitiously supported by the authors' immediate setting. As such, the convent is a space where the outside world is conceptually and physically abandoned and the didactic text is meant to shore up this separation and teach the higher values of a cloistered contemplative life. As presented by Juana de la Encarnación's *Manual de ejercicios*, after leaving the pernicious influence of parents and the known world behind (297), the novice's duty is to learn and avidly pursue a separate path as dictated by the religious order: "quick obedience, modesty, silence, and prayer, where God often talks to the heart. Being first in practicing all these exercises, and the saintly customs of our religious order" (298).[24] This pronouncement is followed by twenty-four chapters in which Juana de la Encarnación offers detailed directives on spiritual exercises and the cultivation of virtue within the cloister.

And yet, if the goal of religious didactic texts is to inculcate a withdrawal from the outside world and a renunciation of the self, their composition poses a contradiction; the intellectual work implied by the writing (and making public) of a didactic text may well qualify as a distraction for the writer from the inward-looking contemplative life promoted and taught in the text. In its composition, the female religious didact abandons the quiet and often solitary practice that informs her text in order to compile for and transmit knowledge to others, an authorial practice that puts her back in contact with a larger world outside of herself and (when the manuscript circulates or is published) of the convent walls she inhabits. In his essay "Technologies of the Self," Foucault asserts that the hermeneutics of the self implied by religious texts such as these is congruent with an effacement of the self; the I examines itself with the end goal of renouncing its will and self in the divine (249). I would argue that the opposite is palpable in Ana de San Bartolomé, María de San José Salazar, Juana de la Encarnación, Feliciana de San José, and Francisca de Jesús y Borja. Precisely in the act of composing the didactic text, the woman author who instructs her peers intentionally constructs on the page a knowledgeable, creative, and imitable self that cannot but take space—textually, intellectually, and psychologically. As Feliciana de San José proposes, the nuns will learn from her, "How to perfectly fulfill that which God desires" (I A),[25] a discursive act that places her at the center of the text as its constitutive subject and agent. Just as important, as María de San José and Feliciana de San José make clear through their fictionalized didactic dialogues, agency quickly proliferates among the nuns who form an interpretative community and share in their teacher's knowledge and desire to learn:

> For this reason, as their simple and unshowy words in fact show that they do know Scripture, I tried showing that mute tongues beget clear understanding such as all the Sisters possess, as they are greatly instructed in the things of God. With good reason are many learned men amazed at the wealth of these treasures, which I wanted to report not so that others might think I am one of the nuns who know something; rather, although I have achieved little, being the dullest and most ignorant of all, I confess that whatever I do know, I learned from these nuns.
>
> María de San José Salazar, trans. Powell: 34[26]

Secular and religious didactic texts written by women instruct the reader on the meaning of true virtue and the recognition and condemnation of vice. Seemingly universal concepts such as virtue, nobility, bravery, and justice are documented and related not as abstract categories but as lived experiences. The specific definition of these categories is therefore conditioned by their situatedness as early modern Spanish women; their perspectives and didactic positions are constructed in relation to and negotiation with the cultural contexts, power relations, and ideologies that frame their experience.[27] Secular women writers emphasize an education in worldly matters, even when Christian examples and the proper maintenance of a virtuous spiritual life remain a constant point of reference. For instance, Sigea's *Colloquium* portrays two young women, Blesilla and Flaminia, in a Socratic/humanist dialogue discussing, among other notions, the proper behavior of a prince, expectations of virtue and kindness, the comportment and appropriate dress of women at court, decorum, and the merits of silence. Sigea's characters are preoccupied with guiding one another to a happy life, one that is ultimately defined in the *Colloquium* as the attainment of a quiet and peaceful soul guided by God away from the court. Padilla's entire corpus is dedicated to the ideological relationship of virtue, nobility, and inherited titles. This is a topic that acquires a specific type of framing in *Lágrimas de la nobleza* where nobility is strictly defined as a matter of virtue, and not of lineage and where the etymological relationship of virtue to virility (*vir*) is questioned in the case of the many corrupt (and thus effeminate) noblemen that surround her.[28] For Padilla, therefore, the lesson to be learned from the countless examples she offers is that virtue, despite the Latin root of the word, is a signifier that has no intrinsic relationship to gender, so that virility and virtue are not inherently masculine. Guevara's *Desengaños* privileges instead the relationship between valor and virtue, and in so doing deploys the examples of historical and Biblical women whose actions reflect the physical and mental strength that serve as her source and inspiration.[29] Setting the tone with the Virgin Mary's example, Guevara favors above any other quality the display of valor (and thus of virility) in women. Queen Michal's strength and courage are made patent in her defense of David from her father, Saul; Abigail's, in her defense of her household from David's wrath; Judith's in her seduction and killing of Holofernes; and Mary Magdalene's in her brave, self-imposed exile to the desert.

Religious women, as should be expected, explicitly situate their didactic discourse in accordance with the parameters set by the Church, which oversees and sanctions their production. Notwithstanding these obvious strictures, their texts likewise reflect their intellectual dexterity, elevate the value of their female communities, and highlight their individual spiritual worth. Ana de San Bartolomé's *Conferencias espirituales* is a case in point. Although couched in a discourse of humility, holy fear, and the shunning of all vanity, she anchors and positions her and her fellow Carmelite nuns' spiritual potential in the God-like figure of the Virgin Mary:

> Let us take the Mother of God, our lady and patron, for our advocate. Let us call upon her in all our needs and desires for virtue and let us look to her as a perfect model of it, for from the moment she opened her eyes it was to look upon God, and she never took her eyes from this vision. *God was seen in her as in a mirror and infused his being in her in such a way that he made her like him; and one saint says that if there were no God he would have adored her as God.* May he be blessed who makes the things he beholds so like himself! Well, who better to obtain this vision for us than she who always had it perfectly? And who would have more compassion for our failings than she who has most knowledge of what we are? *Through this light of knowing she always had God*, and seeing that mankind didn't know him, she regretted greatly our loss and ignorance and blindness, for where there is no light all is darkness and shadow. Well, my dearest ones, we've come here to seek light and remedy for our wickedness, and for this we have approached the Virgin and taken her habit.
>
> *134, emphasis mine, trans. Donahue*[30]

Ana de San Bartolomé underlines Mary's nearness to God as a pure reflection of His image. Created in God's image and recognized by the saints as superior, Mary represents the sacred connection of all women to God and marks their path to the divine. Ana de San Bartolomé then assumes the image of Mary (she looks upon the mirror of Mary and transposes her own self onto the image of the Virgin) and claims for herself the Virgin's "light of knowing." It is at these discursive moments when secular and religious women didacts position their identities as worthy of the highest respect—as social observers, as intellectuals and exegetes, and as spiritual beings—yet they remain within the ideological context and structure of the Catholic church and early modern patriarchy inhabited by them.

Following a consideration of the site of production and situatedness, the issue of legitimacy and authority, and of which entity or set of conditions endorsed these women's incursion into the didactic genres, needs to be further deliberated.[31] As previously mentioned, female didacts subscribe to the genre's typical use of legitimizing sources that are either directly quoted in the body of the text or referenced in the margin; the scholarly breadth of sources and the extent of their application are expressly meant to demonstrate the woman author's intellectual capacity and shore up the claim of her authority. Of the women discussed in this chapter, Sigea is the most notable in this regard, as noted by Odette Sauvage in her edition and translation of the *Colloquium*: "[T]he Colloquium presents itself as a mosaic of citations; [. . .] No less than 472 passages borrowed from 'the greatest sages': 146 from pagan authors, 142 found in the Old Testament, 52 from the Gospel, and 130 from the Fathers of the Church" (49).[32] At the same time, it is also the case for all didactic authors, but especially women, that the assertion of their capacity to see and know what others do not is pivotal to their textual identity and positionality.[33] And yet, as Baranda Leturio correctly reminds us in *Cortejo a lo prohibido*, the citing of sources is practical in nature and does not take the place of the inclusion of these authors own independent theories, opinions, and proposals: "Their own ideas, when they expose that which is the fruit of their own thoughts and experience, mostly are exempt from the citing of *auctoritates* in the margins" (50).[34]

In this regard, the experiential claim is, therefore, fundamental. Sigea, Padilla, and Guevara fashion their textual voices as first-hand witnesses to the corruption and vice of the Spanish nobility. Religious women authors similarly anchor their knowledge and authority on their individual and communal devotional practices, as well as on the liturgical routines and festivities that constitute an important part of their habitual experience. Female didactic authors use both strategies, shoring up the lessons taught by experience and divine inspiration by citing classical, theological, and Biblical sources—directly in the text or on the margins. On the one hand, Padilla, citing Ovid as her source, claims to dress herself in the "feathers of wisdom" offered by "highly accredited writers" (*Lágrimas*; A3).[35] On the other, following St. Ambrose, she makes use of the "talents or inspiration" that God has bequeathed to her (*Lágrimas*: A4).[36] This is a stance Padilla takes further in *Elogios de la verdad* when she claims that, as Abraham, she will transcribe that which God relates: "that my tongue will be a pen, and I will write swiftly, and as in code, that with which you enlighten me" (A).[37] Guevara equally relies on classical sources when declaring the superior intelligence of women: "Marcus Aurelius in his writings speaks at length about women who have been valorous for their learning. He adds that if women were educated they would be sharper than men and that men should permit them a great deal and tolerate them, given that the Romans consider them wise and that the barbarians consider them slaves" (73, trans. Romero-Díaz).[38] Unlike Padilla, Guevara does not overtly credit divine inspiration, but she links her discourse to the sacred in so far as we must all appropriately respond to God's magnificence and grace: "We all have to give account closely to God for what each of us has received from His hand, for He only made us stewards in this life" (103, trans. Romero-Díaz).³⁹ Guevara's assertion, without a doubt plays out in two complementary ways: It affirms Guevara's deference to God's expectations—which authorize her text—and conversely marks those whom she accuses with the stigma of immorality and sin.

Given the nature of the lessons they wish to impart, religious women depend even more explicitly on the connection to the divine in their claim to authority. According to Ángela Muñoz Fernández, "From this contact with the divine came forth their words and in that communication, exempt from the mediation of a consecrated male superior, they sought the legitimization of their 'autoritas'" (296).⁴⁰ This is, of course, a source of distress for many within a male-dominated church hierarchy that could not readily accept women's intellectual and spiritual enlightenment; and, even less, a didactic capacity that seemed to contradict it. As Jerónimo de Sigüenza, María de Ajofrín's biographer, states, "the rule of the Apostle (Saint Paul) does not permit women to teach in the Church" ⁴¹ (cited in Muñoz Fernández: 296). The point to be stressed, therefore, by both the confessors who sanctioned these texts and women religious authors, is that the source of knowledge and the motivation for teaching come directly from God: the religious woman author is humbly relating and serving as an instrument of the divine message. The topos of *humilitas*, whereby God is recalled as the all-powerful paternal figure for whom the nun is an empty vehicle, may seem to undermine the nun's authority; a point that has been made by Lavrin.⁴² Nonetheless, we may also discern in this claim the opposite goal and effect. The nun author consciously positions her identity as coterminous with the sacred; her ability to correctly acknowledge and interpret the divine will (to differentiate the sacred from demonic influence or earthly temptation) is framed as a process that can only be related through the singularity of the author's experience and must, in turn, be taught to, practiced, and mastered by her intended interpretative community. Juana de la Encarnación makes this clear in her first "*dictamen*" (opinion), which is centered on her experience of the sacred and how to prepare oneself immediately upon entering the convent for an intimate communion with God: "Principally, characteristic of the Novitiate, is prompt obedience, modesty, silence and prayer, where God often talks to the heart. Being the first to practice all these exercises, and saintly customs [. . .]. So that in this manner the saintly fear of God becomes more and more ingrained, *for this is the beginning of the loftiest wisdom and religious perfection*" (298).⁴³ In sum, the use of sources (textual and divine) by female didactic authors signals specific meanings: women possess the required level of literacy and erudition, since the instructional capacity of the author is informed by a respected corpus of knowledge that she has been well capable of correctly analyzing, and that leads her to properly examine her own wider context, offer an evaluation, and transmit knowledge. Just as importantly, the targeted female reading audience is in turn invited to embark on a similar practice of scrutinizing the text and benefiting from the sources and analysis presented by the author.

Further considerations

Weber offers this conclusion regarding María de San José Salazar's feminism: "Maria's was instead an ecclesial feminism; it derived from her conviction, based on her own scriptural readings and experience as disciple of a reformer, that women had a legitimate role in serving the Christian community, and that this role was under attack. She keenly felt that women belonged to a subordinate group within the church and that they suffered wrongs as members of that church" (24). Taking into account the differences between religious and secular writers, a similar "feminist" argument could be made regarding the women didactic authors we have discussed in this chapter. In a context where the Church and the broader patriarchal society intrinsically shared the same values and prejudices, these women—secular and religious—adopt the position of didact, confirming their (and other women's) intellectual and spiritual worth and capacity. Despite and within the strictures set by the early modern ideological and social field they inhabited, and not without some contradiction (as discussed by Feros Ruys), women authors positioned themselves as expert exponents of erudition, worthy social values, and properly conceived religious practices. In doing so, they offer their readers a clear vision for the place of women as learned agents and legitimate didacts. Difficulties arise, nevertheless, in how we have here delimited the didactic genre as it relates to women's writing. Given the limited prospects for female authorship in the Spanish early modern context, the effect of strict categorization is not inconsequential since we run the risk of relegating a miscellanea of texts that often functioned as didactic tools for an audience that consciously sought to gain knowledge of a specific subject, practice, or belief. Mentioned previously, Teresa de Ávila's *Vida* and *Camino* are didactic insofar as they, through the recounted experiences of Teresa's life and mystical experiences, illustrate for the reader how to live a devout religious life.[44] Admittedly, Teresa's works are not formally instructional in the exact manner as the didactic manuals, treatises, and dialogues we have examined; however, an exemplary and instructional impetus motivates the discursive, ideological, and (conscious and unconscious) psychological choices, as made clear by the many instances in which she indicates in the prologues to her works the potential usefulness and intended edifying value of her writings for her fellow sisters. The prologue to the *Castillo interior* makes this point clearly:

> The man who ordered me to write this has suggested that the nuns in these convents of Our Lady of Mount Carmel could use a little assistance with certain questions they have about prayer. It seemed to him that women best understand the language spoken between women. He also thought that in light of their love for me, these nuns might pay special attention to what I have to say to them.
>
> *Trans. Starr: 31*[45]

Both in composition and reception, a consideration of didactic intentionality (rather than form or genre) may allow us to better contextualize and analyze a larger set of texts and our estimation of the women who wrote them.

As a result, therfore, we could also expand our consideration to other types of women's didactic writings not restricted to the formal categories generally associated with male authors, and which may have not well suited their personal needs, creative wills, or intellectual and social comfort zones. To be more precise, by choosing form over function we leave out types of writings—religious autobiographies and biographies, novels and poetry, personal correspondence, mystical writings, and so on—that clearly include didactic intentionality. We have already mentioned the case of Teresa de Ávila, but the exemplary literature of Valentina Pinelo, María de Ágreda, and María de Zayas could well be included; so might the didactic plays of Angela de Azevedo. Just as important, the epistolary genre plays a pivotal role in the transmission of knowledge and instructions to acquaintances and family members.[46] Sigea, for example, writes to Magdalena de Padilla, a Portuguese lady, instructing her on how to best practice a literary career while serving the court (113); in separate letters she instructs family members on the art of conversation (132), what books to read (132), and how best maintain an amatory relationship (136).[47] From a critical perspective, Baranda Leturio therefore broadens the scope of influence of letter writing by noting how, "For women, moreover, this implied surreptitiously overcoming certain hurdles that prevented them from participating in the public sphere: in the institutional context, since it offered them a means to deploy their power and negotiate; in the private sphere, since this communication exceeded the physical constraints imposed by the apparent rigidity of the honor code" ("Mujer y escritura": 79).[48] And, as Montserrat Pérez-Toribio demonstrates in her study of the letters sent by Hipólita de Rois i Liori to her daughter Estefanía and of Estefanía's own instructional letters to her son Luis, women's correspondence often "testifies to the intellectual and cultural transmission processes that took place" between mothers and their children (59).[49] I would add that an expressly didactic intentionality extends to letters exchanged with non-family members, as evinced in María de Ágreda's theological teachings imparted to Philip IV throughout their twenty-two-year correspondence. In the realm of the visual, we could consider examples such as the Chapel of Guadalupe in the Royal Discalced Convent in Madrid, for which Sor Ana Dorotea commissioned and designed a pictorial program meant to instruct the nuns and royal visitors about the lives and deeds of illustrious women of the Old Testament. Although the clearly demarcating the didactic form, function, and intentionality in women's writing may cause some difficulties, the methodological coordinates discussed here can well be modified and utilized when examining the instructional capacity of women-authored texts in general. What most matters is that the didactic intentionality of women's writing be fully acknowledged, seriously considered, and critically examined, thus validating this aspect as a core characteristic of and substantial motivating factor in their literary and cultural production.

Notes

1 Asunción Rallo Gruss addresses the issues around the function and formal limits of didactic prose in early modern Spain in her "Tópicos y recurrencias," 135.
2 This position functions as the guiding principle of *What Nature Does Not Teach: Didactic Literature in the Medieval and Early-Modern Periods*, edited by Juanita Feros Ruys.
3 All translations of primary and secondary texts are my own, except when expressly noted. "[M]ientras aprender a leer se defendía por la posibilidad que ofrecía de recibir doctrina religiosa, saber escribir no parecía tener ninguna finalidad espiritual y por el contrario abría un campo de expresión profana, sobre todo con los billetes amorosos" (Baranda Leturio, "Mujer y escritura": 64).
4 For a wonderful presentation of the variety of sources that make themselves present in women-authored secular texts and aristocratic library catalogs, see Baranda Leturio's "Lecturas de damas aristocráticas en el siglo XVII" in *Cortejo a lo prohibido*.
5 Howe explains: "It [. . .] demonstrates that these notable exemplary figures from the past, simultaneously admired and dismissed as exceptional by men, served as examples worthy of imitation by many of their female counterparts who eventually joined their ranks. More importantly, what becomes apparent is the embrace of their exemplarity by those women writers who first cite female examples from both their past and their present and then offer themselves as worthy exempla in their own right" (xi).
6 Alcoff adds, "Therefore, the concept of positionality includes two points: first, as already stated, that the concept of woman is a relational term identifiable only within a (constantly moving) context; but, second, that the position that women find themselves in can be actively utilized (rather than transcended) as a location for the construction of meaning, a place from where meaning is constructed, rather than simply the place where a meaning can be discovered (the meaning of femaleness)" ("Cultural Feminism": 434).
7 "gran señora de estos reinos de España" (*Nobleza Virtuosa*: A1).
8 Tracing the evolution of the female voice in dialogues from the classical period to the Renaissance, Ana Vián Herrero states that by the time of Erasmus of Rotterdam, women's voices achieve "literary citizenship" ["ciudadanía literaria"] in so far as they are represented following the same rhetorical codes that were used for male characters (519). She adds that by the time Sigea is writing, the possibilities for the representation of women's voices is notably more vast, with "illustrious women" ["mujeres ilustres"] that converse at the highest of levels on topics before preserved for men (526).
9 "Páguele Dios (o carísimas) a nuestra Madre Prioa el habernos dado licencia para hablarnos hoy; que como tan mal aprovechada en la virtud del silencio, lo deseaba por gozar de vuestra compañía y porque creo me ha de ser de provecho" (2).
10 Exactly the same assertion could be said concerning Feliciana de San José's *Recreación*.

Didactic treatises

11 See "'Lágrimas de la nobleza' o lágrimas por la nobleza. Luisa de Padilla, condesa de Aranda y su 'reformación de nobles.'"
12 Antona García was among the leaders of a conspiration against the count of Marialba in the city of Toro in 1496. Defender of the Catholic Kings against Juana la Beltraneja, Antona was condemned to death the same year and became a symbol of Catholic virtue and feminine valor.
13 "[L]o primero le lleva todo Antón Martín a casa, y luego se la llena de hijos de ganancia (que estas ganancias son las que dan a las mujeres propias) y juégale la dote, y las joyas, y si habla una palabra, oye dos mil desaires, y si lo defiende, hace una jornada larga, y tiene la culpa la mala condición de ella, que ellos nunca la tienen en nada; sucédeles un trabajo, y vuelven como el hijo pródigo a casa" (78). Anton Martín was the popular name for the San Juan de Dios Hospital founded by Anton Martín— a Hospitaller priest—in 1552 at Atocha in Madrid. The hospital specialized in treating patients with venereal and infectious diseases.
14 See Hernández, "Luisa de Padilla's *Lágrimas*."
15 "Las casas mal gobernadas, y las haciendas peores porque no las ven sus dueños, y así están todos pobres, y el que está rico no se lo envidio, porque o lo gana en puestos o en tratos, esto en todo género de gente, que no les falta para dar a bufones, y lisonjeros, y no a pobres vergonzantes que están en sus casas pereciendo, y se vieron en bien" (68).
16 "Literatura de erudición devocional"; "Cuando esa fe se apoyaba en un andiamaje de lecturas de textos claves de la espiritualidad cristiana para explicarse y demandaba la atención de los lectores no solamente a través de la afectividad sino a través del análisis de la exégesis, presenciamos la erudición devocional a la que me refiero" (66).
17 "que el amor que tienen las religiosas lo muestren con obras" (24).
18 We have to consider, nonetheless, the editorial role of Juana de la Encarnación's spiritual guide, Luis Ignacio Zevallos, who assembled and posthumously published her works and may have at that point added many of the citations found on the margins of the *Manual*. Nonetheless, it is Juana de la Encarnación's erudite references within the text that make possible the citations on the margin.
19 "Esta virtud es tan preciosa y loable, que adonde la hubiere, será siempre este alma en regla y santa perfección. Porque la mortificación que se puede decir que lo es de verdad, es un morir del todo a nuestros deseos naturales y inclinaciones; que mientras éstas viven en nosotras, no nos tengamos por religiosas verdaderas no amadoras de Dios, sino de nosotras mismas y que amamos nuestros antojos, como se cuenta de los hijos de Israel: que con haberlos librado del cautiverio de Faraón y tenerlos en el desierto, lloraban por las cebollas de Egipto" (Pontoise 1605: 601). In addition to the Pontoise lecture, Bartolomé wrote additional installments in Paris: 1606–1608; Antwerp: 1622–1624; and Antwerp: 1621–1623. All these can be found in Teresa de Jesús, *Conferencias espirituales*; see also Teresa de Jesús, *Formación de novicias*.
20 Foucault's propositions regarding technologies of power were first developed during the 1970s, most especially in *Discipline and Punish* (1975) and *The History of Sexuality, Volume I: An Introduction* (1976).
21 Luisa de Padilla's didactic works include Nobleza virtuosa (1637); Noble perfecto y segunda parte de la nobleza virtuosa (1639); Lágrimas de la nobleza y Tercera parte de la Nobleza virtuosa (1639); Elogios de la verdad e invectiva contra la mentira (1640); and Excelencias de castidad (1642). She is also supposed to have written an instruction manual for the upbringing of noble children, Cartilla de instruir niños nobles.
22 See Nieves Romero-Díaz's "Introduction" for more detailed information regarding Guevara's biography. Guevara wrote two major works, the *Tratado y advertencias de una mujer celosa del bien de su Rey corrida de parte de España* (1663) and *Desengaños de la corte, y mujeres valerosas* (1664).
23 "[S]e debe distinguir un [. . .] grupo de escritos destinados a la enseñanza comunitaria [. . .]. Su finalidad es modificar las conductas, convertir las palabras en actos, y sus destinatarios son las hermanas del convento entre quienes la autora ocupa una posición de autoridad, por eso tiene una difusión inmediata y restringida" (Baranda Leturio and Marín Pina, "El universo": 34).
24 "una prompta obediencia, modestia, silencio, y oración, donde Dios suele hablar al corazón. Siendo la primera en practicar todos los exercisios, y santas costumbres de la religiosa distribución" (298).
25 "Cómo cumplirán perfectamente lo que Dios quiere" (I A).
26 "por esta razón, viendo que se muestra en sus palabras simples y sin muestras que saben de la Escritura, quise con esto mostrar que las lenguas mudas engendran entendimientos claros, como todas los tienen, y tan enseñadas a las cosas de Dios. Y con razón muchos doctos se admiran de la riqueza de estos tesoros, de los cuales quise hacer reseña, no porque entienda ser yo de las que algo saben, mas, aunque como la más ruda e ignorante he alcanzado poco, mas confieso que tal cual es lo aprendí de ellas" (48).

In addition to the *Libro de Recreaciones* (Book for the Hour of Recreation) María de San José Salazar wrote three additional texts that should be considered formally didactic: *Consejos que da una Priora* (1590–1592), *Instrucción de Novicias* (1602), and *Avisos para el gobierno de las religiosas* (1606). For a discussion of these texts see Manero Sorolla.

27 In this context "situatedness" is defined as, "The dependence of meaning (and/or identity) on the specifics of particular sociohistorical, geographical, and cultural contexts, social and power relations, and philosophical and ideological frameworks, within which the multiple perspectives of social actors are dynamically constructed, negotiated, and contested" (Chandler).

28 See Hernández "Luisa de Padilla's *Lágrimas*."

29 See Hernández "The Politics of Exemplarity."

30 "Tomemos por abogada a la Madre de Dios, Señora y Patrona nuestra; llamémosla en todas nuestras necesidades y deseos de virtud, y mirémosla como a dechado perfecto de ella, que desde que abrió sus ojos fue para mirar a Dios y no los quitó jamás de esta vista. Y Dios se miraba en ella como un espejo e infundía en ella su ser, y de tal manera la hizo parecida a sí, que dice un santo, que si no hubiera Dios, la adorara por Dios. ¡Bendito sea, que tan parecido hace a sí las cosas que mira! Pues, ¿quién nos podrá alcanzar mejor esta vista que quien la tuvo siempre perfecta, y quién se compadecerá más de nuestras flaquezas que la que tiene más conocimiento de lo que somos? Por medio de esta luz que tuvo siempre de conocer a Dios, y ver que los hombres no le conocían y que sentía mucho nuestra pérdida y ignorancia y ceguedad, que adonde no hay luz todo es oscuro y tinieblas. Pues, mis carísimas, aquí habemos venido a buscar luz y remedio de nuestros males y para esto nos ha llegado a la Virgen y tomado su hábito; y si lo sabemos pedir con humildad, nos le alcanzará de virtudes de gracia, como la que está más en ella y parecida más a ella que ninguna otra criatura" (593–594).

31 This is a query that was already present in the moral epistles of Seneca, where the philosopher asserts the need to complement Nature by offering the lessons that are not evident to most people, thus framing the didactic discourse as an exhortation. See Feros Ruys's "Introduction" (1).

32 "Aussi le *Colloquium* se presente-t-il comme un mosaïque de citations; [. . .] pas moins de 472 passages empruntés "aux plus grands sages": 146 proviennent d'auteurs païens, 142 de l'Ancien Testament, 52 de l'Evangile, 130 des Pères de l'Eglise" (49). For further discussion on the use of sources by Sigea see Howe, especially 55.

33 Cuadra García et al. explain how, "Those who develop their own ideas acquire authority over those who come to know and follow doctrines therein enunciated. In the case of women the creation of a system of thought is wrought with grave difficulties since for them the necessary education was typically not available. Moreover, society does not consider that women can develop and defend a coherent system of thought; it is not necessary, it is not appropriate, and, even more, it can be dangerous" (35). ["Las personas que elaboran un pensamiento propio adquieren una autoridad sobre quienes conocen y siguen las doctrinas por ellas enunciadas. En el caso de las mujeres la creación de pensamiento ofrece graves dificultades, pues para ellas es imprescindible una instrucción que [. . .] no era la habitual [. . .]. Por otra parte, la sociedad no contempla que las mujeres elaboren y defiendan un pensamiento coherente; no es necesario, no es lo propio, y, además, puede ser peligroso" (35).]

34 "Sus propias ideas, cuando expone aquello que es fruto de su elucubración y experiencia, suelen llevar los márgenes casi limpios de *auctoritates*" (50).

35 "los muy acreditados Escritores" (*Lágrimas* A3).

36 "talentos o inspiraciones" (*Lágrimas* A4).

37 "que mi lengua será pluma, y escriviré con presteza, y como en cifra, aquello de que me dieredes luz" (A).

38 "Marco Aurelio dice en sus escritos mucho de las mujeres, que han sido valerosas por las letras; y añade que si se diesen a los estudios, fueran más agudas que los hombres, y que ellos deben sufrirles mucho, y tolerarlas, 15 y que los Romanos las tienen por sentencias, y los Bárbaros por esclavas" (72).

39 "Gran cuenta tenemos que dar a Dios, cada uno de lo que ha recibido de su mano, pues solo nos hizo mayordomos de por vida, y nos ha de tomar las cuentas en la otra" (102).

40 "De este contacto con la divinidad brotaba su palabra y en esa comunicación sin mediaciones interpuestas de varón consagrado buscaron la legitimación de su 'auctoritas'" (296).

41 "la regla del Apóstol (San Pablo), que no permite que las mujeres enseñen en la Iglesia" (cited in Muñoz Fernández: 296).

42 "They praised the writing of women as something coming directly from God, suggesting that the woman who wrote about religious subjects deserved respect for being a privileged vehicle, but, let's not forget, a vehicle after all" (67). ["Elogiaban los escritos de mujer como cosa venida directamente

de Dios, implicando que la mujer que escribía sobre asuntos religiosos merecía respeto por ser un vehículo privilegiado, pero, notemos, vehículo a fin de cuentas" (67).]
43 "Principalmente, como caracteríscos del Noviciado, de una prompta obediencia, modestia, silencio, y oración, donde Dios suele hablar al corazón. Siendo la primera en practicar todos los ejercicios, y santas costumbres [. . .]. Para que desta suerte se vaya arraigando más, y más, en el santo temor de Dios, *que es el principio de la mejor sabiduría, y religiosa perfección*" (298). Juana de la Encarnación cites as sources in the margin The Book of Hosea 2.14 and the Psalms 1.10.10 for this declaration.
44 It is for this reason that Rallo Gruss includes them in *La prosa didáctica en el siglo XVI*.
45 "Díjome quien me mandó escribir que como estas monjas de estos monasterios de nuestra Señora del Carmen tienen necesidad de quien algunas dudas de oración las declare, y que le parecía que mejor se entienden el lenguaje unas mujeres de otras, y con el amor que me tienen les haría más al caso lo que yo les dijese, tiene entendido por esta causa será de alguna importancia, si se acierta a decir alguna cosa" (345).
46 Even if not focusing on women's letters, Rallo Gruss includes as part of the didactic catalog written correspondence. See "Tópicos y recurrencias": 136.
47 See Sigea, *Epistolario*.
48 "Para las mujeres, además, suponía superar subrepticiamente ciertas barreras que les impedían participar en el ámbito público: en lo institucional, ya que les concedía un medio para ejercer el poder y negociar; en lo privado, puesto que la comunicación trascendía el encerramiento físico impuesto por el rígido código aparencial de la honra" ("Mujeres y escritura": 79).
49 See also Feros Ruys: "For parental authors in particular, this move [the authority given to experience] signifies the authorization of parenthood as a didactic locus, allowing parents to teach from their own personal knowledge, rather than simply replicating and transmitting traditional wisdom" (162).

Works cited

Alcoff, Linda. "Cultural Feminism versus Post-Structuralism: The Identity Crisis in Feminist Theory." *Signs* 13.3 (1988): 405–436.

———. *Visible Identities: Race, Gender, and the Self*. Oxford: Oxford UP, 2006.

Ana de San Bartolomé. *Autobiography and Other Writings*. Ed. and trans. Darcy Donahue. Chicago: U Chicago P, 2008.

Baranda Leturio, Nieves. *Cortejo a lo prohibido. Lectoras y escritoras en la España moderna*. Madrid: Arco, 2005.

———. "Mujer y Escritura en el Siglo de Oro: Una Relación Inestable." *Litterae: Cuadernos sobre Cultura Escrita* 3–4 (2003–2004): 61–83.

———. *Women Writers*. "Louisa Sigea, Spanish Writer, c. 1520–1560." www.womenwriters.nl/index.php/Luisa_Sigea

Baranda Leturio, Nieves, and Maria Carmen Marín Pina. "El universe de la escritura conventual femenina: Deslindes y perspectivas." *Letras en la celda: Cultura escrita de los conventos femeninos en la España moderna*. Eds. Nieves Baranda Leturio and Ma. Carmen Marín Pina. Madrid/Frankfurt: Iberoamericana/Vervuert, 2014: 11–45.

Borja y Enríquez, Francisca de Jesús. "De las exhortaciones que dejó escrita de su propia mano." *Escritoras Clarisas Españolas, Antología*. Ed. María Victoria Triviño. Madrid: Biblioteca de Autores Cristianos, 1992: 21–26.

Chandler, Daniel and Rod Munday. "Situatedness." *A Dictionary of Media and Communication*. Oxford: Oxford UP, 2011. www.oxfordreference.com.proxy.cc.uic.edu/view/10.1093/acref/9780199568758.001.0001/acref-9780199568758-e-2501

Cruz, Anne J. "Introduction." *Women's Literacy in Early Modern Spain and the New World*. Ed. Anne J. Cruz and Rosilie Hernández. Farnham, UK: Ashgate, 2011: 1–16.

Cuadra García, Cristina, María del Mar Graña Cid, Ángela Muñoz and Cristina Segura Graíño. "Notas a la educación de la mujeres en la Edad Media." In *Las sabias mujeres: educación, saber y autoría (siglos III–XVII)*. María del Mar Graña Cid, ed. Asociación Cultural Al-Mudayna, 1994: 33–50.

Feliciana de San José. *Recreación espiritual compuesta en diálogos*. Zaragoza: Domingo de la Payada, 1654.

Feros Ruys, Juanita, ed. *What Nature Does Not Teach: Didactic Literature in the Medieval and Early-modern Periods*. Turnhout: Brepols, 2008.

Foucault, Michel. *History of Sexuality*. Vol. 1. Trans. Robert Hurley. New York: Vintage, 1990.

———. *Technologies of The Self: A Seminar With Michel Foucault*. Ed. H. Luther Martin, Huck Gutman, and Patrick H. Hutton. Amherst: U Massachusetts P, 1988.

Guevara, María de. "Desengaños de la corte y mujeres valerosas." *Warnings to the Kings on Restoring Spain. A Bilingual Edition*. Ed. and trans. Nieves Romero-Díaz. Chicago: U Chicago P, 2007: 64–111.

Hernández, Rosilie. "Luisa de Padilla's *Lágrimas de la nobleza*: Vice, Moral Authority, and the Woman Writer." *Bulletin of Spanish Studies* 87:7 (2010): 897–914.

———. "The Politics of Exemplarity: Biblical Women and the Education of the Spanish Lady in Martín Carrillo, Sebastián de Herrera Barnuevo, and María de Guevara." *Women's Literacy in Early Modern Spain and the New World*. Ed. Anne J. Cruz and Rosilie Hernández. Farnham, UK: Ashgate, 2011: 225–241.

Howe, Elizabeth Teresa. *Education and Women in The Early Modern Hispanic World*. Aldershot, UK: Ashgate, 2008.

Juana de la Encarnación. *Dispertador del alma religiosas. Manual de ejercicios y dictámenes espirituales*. Madrid: Oficina Real de Nicolás Rodríguez Franco, 1723.

Lavrin, Asunción. "Erudición, devoción y creatividad tras las rejas conventuales." *Letras en la celda: Cultura escrita de los conventos femeninos en la España moderna*. Ed. Nieves Baranda Leturio and Maria Carmen Marín Pina. Madrid/Frankfurt: Iberoamericana/Vervuet, 2014: 65–88.

Manero Sorolla, María Pilar. "*Diálogos de carmelitas: Libro de Recreaciones de María de San José.*" *Actas del X Congreso de la Asociación Internacional de Hispanistas, Barcelona, 21–26 de agosto 1989*. Ed. Antonio Vilanova. Barcelona, PPU, 1989: 501–515.

María de San José (Salazar). *Avisos para el gobierno de las religiosas*. Ed. Juan Luis Astigarraga. Rome: Instituto Histórico Teresiano, 1977.

———. *Book for the Hour of Recreation*. Ed. Alison Weber; Trans. Amanda Powell. Chicago: U Chicago P, 2002.

Muñoz Fernández, Ángela. "La palabra, el cuerpo y la virtud. Urdimbres de la "auctoritas" en las primeras místicas y visionarias castellanas." *Las sabias mujeres: Educación, saber y autoría (Siglos III–XVII)*. Ed. María del Mar Grana Cid. Madrid: Al-Mudayna, 1994: 295–318.

Padilla, Luisa de. *Elogios de la verdad e invectiva contra la mentira*. Zaragoza: Juan de Lanaja, 1640.

———. *Excelencias de castidad*. Zaragoza: Juan de Lanaja, 1642.

———. *Lágrimas de la nobleza y Tercera parte de la Nobleza virtuosa*. Zaragoza: Juan de Lanaja, 1639.

———. *Noble perfecto y segunda parte de la nobleza virtuosa*. Zaragoza: Juan de Lanaja, 1639.

———. *Nobleza virtuosa*. Zaragoza: Juan de Lanaja, 1637.

Pérez Toribio, Montserrat. "From Mother to Daughter: Educational Lineage in the Correspondence between the Countess of Palamós and Estefania de Requesens." *Women's Literacy in Early Modern Spain and the New World*. Ed. Anne J. Cruz and Rosilie Hernández. Farnham, UK: Ashgate, 2011: 59–78.

Rallo Gruss, Asunción. *La prosa didáctica en el siglo XVI*. Madrid: Taurus, 1987.

———. "Tópicos y recurrencias en los resortes del didactismo: confluencia de diferentes géneros." *Criticón* 58 (1993): 135–154.

Romero-Díaz, Nieves. "Introduction." *Warnings to The Kings And Advice On Restoring Spain*. Chicago: U Chicago P, 2007: 32–76.

Sigea, Luisa. *Duarum virginum colloquium de vita aulica et private*. (Dialogue de Deux Jeunes Filles: Sur la Vie de Cour et la Vie de Retraite). Ed. and trans. Odette Sauvage. Paris: Presses Universitaires de France, 1970.

———. *Epistolario Latino*. Ed. and trans. María Prieto Corbalán. Madrid: Alkal, 2007.

Teresa de Jesús. *Obras completas*. Ed. Efrén de la Madre de Dios, O.C.D. and Otger Steggink, O.C. Madrid: Biblioteca de Autores Cristianos, 1962.

———. *Conferencias espirituales Pontoise 1605. Obras completas*. Ed. Julen Urkiza. Rome: Teresianum, 1981–1985.

———. *Formación de novicias y ejercicios de piedad. Obras completas*. Ed. Julen Urkiza. Rome: Teresianum, 1981–1985.

Teresa of Ávila. *The Interior Castle*. Trans. Mirabai Starr. New York: Riverhead, 2003.

Torremocha Hernández, Margarita. "'Lagrimas de la nobleza' o lágrimas por la nobleza. Luisa de Padilla, condesa de Aranda y su 'reformación de nobles.'" *Campo y campesinos en la España Moderna; culturas políticas en el mundo hispano, Vol. 2*. Ed. María José Pérez Álvarez and Alfredo Martín García. Madrid: Fundación Española de Historia Moderna, 2012: 2187–2198.

Vian Herrero, Ana. "La rebelión literaria de las cotorras mudas: Modelos de interlocutora femenina en la historia del diálogo." *Homenaje a Elena Catena*. Madrid: Castalia, 2001: 505–526.

Weber, Alison. "Introduction to María de San José Salazar." *Book for the Hour of Recreation*. Ed. Alison Weber. Trans. Amanda Powell. Chicago: U Chicago P, 2002: 1–26.

17
THE FAMILIAL LYRIC

Gwyn Fox

Although recent years have brought illuminating studies of women's literature in early modern Spain, few focus specifically on poetry to or about family. Similarly, the many available historical studies of family life in Spain do not venture into the field of women's literary production, perhaps the most direct path to an understanding of the inner lives of literate women. Yet this provides a valuable opportunity for new research, as lived experience can be glimpsed through verse intended mainly for domestic consumption, particularly that of accomplished and prolific poets like Catalina Clara Ramírez de Guzmán, Leonor de la Cueva y Silva, Sor María de Santa Isabel (who wrote as Marcia Belisarda), and Sor Violante do Céu, who will form the principal focus of this chapter.

The family in early modern Spain was the smallest element of social control exerted by the patriarchal establishment. Notions of the family stemmed from the Church fathers and from post-Tridentine doctrine, their strictures found in the works of such moralists as Juan Luis Vives (*Education of a Christian Woman*), Luis de León (*La Perfecta casada*), and Juan de Zabaleta (*El día de fiesta, por la mañana y por la tarde*). For secular women, family and home were the approved, indeed the only life-paths that Church, state, and moralists would countenance. As has often been noted, however, the multiplicity of moralist strictures and criticisms of women's behavior suggest that the realities of family life were very different from this supposed norm. María José de la Pascua Sánchez is just one historian who provides detailed discussions of the problems of family life, specifically focusing on women's recourse to ecclesiastical law in cases of abandonment ("Una aproximacíon") and in the enduring problems caused by family violence in the period in Cádiz ("Violencia y familia").

The traditional ending to the comedia in seventeenth-century Spain would see all problems and entanglements resolved through a satisfactory marriage, with lovers, honor, justice, and class all satisfied.[1] Although marriage without parental consent was legal after Trent, the requirement to marry before a priest and two witnesses made it difficult (Pérez Molina: 31). Nieves Romero-Díaz has noted contemporary criticism of the system in María de Zayas's critique of the commodification of women in *La burlada Aminta*, where Aminta becomes the focus of conquest for her wealth and nobility (119).[2] At the upper levels of society, however, there were distinct social benefits to be had through marriage. James Casey provides some fascinating examples of the machinations of the Spanish marriage market in early modern Granada, of attempts to contract suitable matches, prevent the dispersal of family fortunes, and create dynasties among the privileged (99–120).

Where women were able to secure socially advantageous marriages they also gained in prestige. Nevertheless, few indeed are the poems that actively extoll marriage or celebrate a specific event. One example of epithalamic verse is Ramírez de Guzmán's romance on the marriage of her youngest sister, Ana Rosalea (Borrachero Mendíbil and McLaughlan: 288).[3] It is hardly celebratory. Most of the romance focuses on the bride's beauty, engaging the conventional comparison of the bride and the sun.[4] Don García, the bridegroom, barely appears in the poem at all, except as the young man (garzón) whose hopes are realized in acquiring Anarda as his "sweet possession";[5] she becomes one more of her husband's assets and there is no suggestion that she also possesses him. It concludes in a conventional wish for a fruitful union, since children "eternalize your memory, / which is the greatest fortune."[6] Children not only perpetuated the family name, they provided patronage opportunities through military exploits or advantageous marriage. Ramírez de Guzmán wrote only one poem on marriage, though three of her siblings married, perhaps indicating her disdain for, or disapproval of the marriages finally settled upon by her family, assumptions in which she appears to have been correct.[7]

Perhaps the most negative view of marriage appears in the extraordinary, Boccaccesque novelas of María de Zayas, a wholly striking, even shocking view of courtship, honor, and the perils inherent in becoming the "possession" of a dominant and often cruel male. The novelas appeared in two collections, published ten years apart. While none of her poems specifically deals with family, her tales most assuredly do, and while space does not permit an extensive discussion of her work, it should be considered when studying the seventeenth-century family or the status of women.[8] In the first part of her collection, *The Enchantments of Love* (*Novelas amorosas y ejemplares*), the tales most often end in a happy marriage after many trials, but this is not the case in the second collection, *Disenchantments of Love* (*Desengaños amorosos*), where the disastrous relationships entered into by the various heroines end either in death or refuge in the convent.

It would be wrong, though, to assume that marriages, even those arranged for dynastic purposes, did not allow for the growth of genuine marital affection. Doña Mariana Barahona de Soto, for example, wrote an anguished sonnet, a sustained cry of despair, grief, and love on the sudden death of her husband, Luis Barahona de Soto, in 1595:[9] "Ah, dearest friend! Ah my pleasing husband! / Ah, bright sun that warms and lights my life!"[10] At the turn she reflects on his physical affection: "What sweet embraces, what tender glances."[11] In determining that she will never forget him she celebrates female constancy, always a matter for moralist criticism and suspicion. While this poem lies within the tradition of appropriate mourning verse of the period, it is also highly personal. Her husband was a well-known poet in Seville, but she does not extoll his excellence as a public man, published writer and poet; she remains in the close, physical and emotional realm of marital affection. Such poems remind us that not all wives resented their marriages and that not all husbands were unduly coercive. There is more work to be done here.

What was contained in the term "family" at a time when deaths due to famine, childbirth, disease, and war disrupted the family unit and where so many women entered convents, often unwillingly, through lack of dowry or perceived delinquency? The convent provided an alternative family, an enclosed, shared community of interest with similar hierarchical structures to those outside. Contemporary circulation of convent writing varied greatly, from published books, to correspondence with the wider community and convent visits, down to exchanges between the nuns and their confessors (Vollendorf, "Lives": 93–94).[12] Poetry, then, provided an outlet for expressions of familial devotion toward the sisterhood of the convent and the Holy Family, the perfect model for meditation and a surrogate for a family of one's own. Among the multiplicity of nuns' poetic offerings available to us, mostly on well-worn themes, are outstanding works by accomplished poets like Marcia Belisarda and Sor Violante do Céu, who reflected on the activities of both convent family and Holy Family.

Whatever the circumstances of marriage beyond the walls, poems celebrating the profession of nuns rejoice in this marriage to Christ. Marcia Belisarda provides a number of examples.[13] One romance announces: "that the supreme king pronounces his nuptials / with a daughter of the great Bernard,"[14] while a villancico to María de la Puebla opens with "Sweet bride of the lamb."[15] Petronila de la Palma's name is woven into humble, garden imagery, Eve's responsibility for the Fall and the redemption of female culpability through the Virgin Mary. As the newly planted palm metamorphoses into the bride of Christ, Marcia Belisarda advises: "[r]epay him, loyal bride, the fruits of your soul."[16] There appears to have been free communication between convents in Toledo, at least in the case of such an accomplished poet whose works would have been in demand, as she celebrates one profession in the Convent of San Torcuato (107) and another in the Convent of San Clemente (136).

Marcia Belisarda hints at convent contact with the community in her romance "To a great married lady whose husband detested her" (A una gran señora casada a quien aborrecía su marido [BNE ms. 7469], 33r). The poem is not burlesque, a form at which she was adept. Rather, it indicates that poets like Marcia Belisarda worked to emphasize the moral and intellectual worth of their subjects. The romance opens with the woman's discretion and beauty, moving quickly to a fine juxtaposition of right and wrong: "justly plaintive of your life with your unjust master."[17] As often in her burlesque verse, Marcia Belisarda criticizes masculine rationality: "He has an irrational soul, without doubt, not to aspire to a heaven borne in so many eyes."[18] Observing that her subject is admired by many who envy her husband, she makes her a heavenly goddess, fit only to be worshipped by them.

For a noblewoman, marriage and motherhood had other important connotations. For women of all classes, to raise sons to adulthood was the means to secure their own support in old age (Lerner: 122). Sons could bring wealth and power to the family through service to the king and the Church. As Vigil has observed in relation to the mother, however prescriptive her role may have been in the paintings of the period, she was otherwise almost invisible. The comedia gives the impression that either society has no mother or she appears in a frankly anti-maternal form (126). Anne Cruz describes the comedia as "the most egregious in its absence of maternal roles; when the mother appears on stage it is to fulfill an archetype, never to assume a 'real' subject position" ("The Search": 37).[19] Leonor de la Cueva appears not to have written poetry as wife, daughter, or mother, though she had two sons and writes on other male family members.[20] Poetic depictions of the maternal may have exposed mothers or daughters to a form of indecorous public view; Adrienne Martín discusses such difficulties for women attempting poetic self-portraits without betraying their modesty (114–115). The absence of such poetry may also show that it was not part of their poetic tradition, just as few men dedicated poems to their sons, except to commemorate a death.

In the frame tale of Zayas's *Novelas amorosas y ejemplares*, it is the mother, Laura, conveniently widowed, who takes charge of the proceedings; it is she who determines the form that the entertainment (*sarao*) will take, including directing the young men in their duties (the omniscient narrator notes that she alternates the tales of men with women so that the men will not complain of the women's pre-eminence).[21] At the end of the Disenchantments (*Desengaños*), Laura follows her daughter into the convent. Through the close mother and daughter relationship Zayas provides an alternative to the traditional, felicitous ending of the comedia—true happiness and freedom for women reside in the convent, with or without vows.

In spite of the paucity of poetry to mothers, Sor Violante do Céu, through the Holy Family, takes a positive view of motherhood, while Ramírez de Guzmán's near-ethnographic poetry does extend to her mother, although even in her abundant familial verse the mother is almost invisible, especially in comparison with the poems to her father and brothers, to whom she addressed more than twenty compositions, most lamenting their absence (Borrachero Mendíbil and McLaughlan, 35: 101–102). Teijeiro Fuentes, in anatomizing Ramírez de Guzmán's portrait verse feature by feature, discusses a number of her poetic blazons of her sisters (113–128).

In a poem where she rues the damage done to her mother's sight by constant needlework (Borrachero Mendíbil and McLaughlan: 207), the pictorial effect is evident; as her mother squints, her knitted brows appear to be in mutual dispute.[22] Ramírez de Guzmán regrets first the visual effect: "it is harsh to love your work so much, that you blind yourself, Silvia, for it";[23] then the personal lack of her mother's attention: "you treat me badly."[24] The poem reflects the wife of Luis de León's *La perfecta casada*: hard-working, self-sacrificing, and uncomplaining, busy with needlework and the household. It is written in playful tones, though Cruz observes that Ramírez de Guzmán reproaches her mother for her lack of affection in wordplay on the phrases "zurzir la badana" (sew fine leather) and "zurrar la badana" (maltreat through word or deed) ("La búsqueda de la madre": 59). Borrachero and McLaughlin see it differently: "We perceive playfulness in the wordplay zurzir-zurrar [. . .] it appears that the décima reflects a close relationship between mother and daughter," [25] an opinion with which I concur, as does Olivares, who sees it as "a humorous and sympathetic counterpoint to domestic confinement" (37). They wonder, in addition, whether the décima reflects with concern on the situation of women living in a home dominated by the male (102).

One of Ramírez de Guzmán's more surprising poems concerns a pregnancy, a subject invisible in poetry of this period: "On the pregnancy of a lady" (*A la preñez de una dama*). It is exceptional for its rare theme and more so for the physiological details of pregnancy and its informality (Borrachero Mendíbil and McLaughlan: 393–402). Martín has discussed this poem in some depth, noting Ramírez de Guzmán's portrayal of women's everyday life and observing that the "private sphere of motherhood and childbearing, which is totally marginalized in literature and on which relatively little scholarship has been written still, is here placed at the center of female domestic experience and writing" (104–106).

While the secular mother may be hard to find, there is no lack of praise for motherhood among the religious. The divine motherhood of Mary is accepted by all Christian churches, interpreted in patriarchal and conservative terms of virginity and submissiveness (Lerner: 127). Yet, as Shifra Armon has argued, the cultural archetypes provided to literate women in Counter-Reformation Spain taught more than mere silent obedience (26). Violante do Céu's *Parnaso lusitano* offers a number of views of a divine mother who is neither meek nor submissive in a sonnet sequence on the Mysteries, a number of which foreground Mary in a powerful familial role. Where Warner describes the Franciscan and Dominican view of Mary [as] leaving her "starry throne [. . .] to sit cross-legged on the bare earth like a peasant mother with her child" (Alone: 182), Violante sees a mother who subtly controls her destiny. In her sonnet on the Annunciation (Parnaso: 8), the Virgin controls the exchange with the angel through Mary's silence, as Christ, "obeying you in anticipation [. . .] will not descend without this glorious yes."[26] Divine obedience to a mortal mother emphasizes her moral worth, thus contesting the arguments devised to keep women in their position of powerlessness. The controlling father is not seen, either as God or man. Ironically, the power is wielded through silence, that which was most enjoined on women. In her acquiescence, Mary replaces the culpable figure of Eve and creates an entirely more favorable model of female agency as "the greeting of the angel—Ave—neatly reverse[s] the curse of Eve" (Warner, "Monuments": 60). Violante's versions of the Annunciation and Crucifixion owe nothing to scripture or to dogma; they seem to come from her own meditations, though she may have been influenced by Saint Francis de Sales or Cardinal Bellarmine (Ellington: 161).

In other sonnets from the sequence, Mary retains her prominence. In "On the birth of Christ our Lord" (*Del nacimiento de Cristo Nuestro Señor* [Parnaso: 9]), the Old Testament figure of Ruth is a model of loyalty and moral strength. Complex imagery links the Old Testament figure to the New and the humble birth, projecting long-held associations of the female body with the earth that nurtures the seed.[27] As both seedbed and gardener, Mary is firmly allied to the strong, peasant women who work in the fields and tend the plants, rather than to an impossible ideal of purity and parthenogenesis. Mary's foreknowledge of Christ's sacrifice is revealed in the second quartet: "water him well with those loving tears, since you know that you hold the sacred King, / chosen as the bread of souls."[28] The seed of the Old Testament will become the better bread of the New as the sonnet progresses and Violante moves away from simple, flawed humanity to the divine. Mary's divinity, linked to her role as loving mother, advances the value of domesticity as vitally important to family wellbeing. Also relevant here is Violante's celebration of Saint John's indissoluble linking with the Virgin by Christ from the cross (Parnaso: 27): "But how much more were you beloved, / (Oh John) [. . .] deservedly adopted son of the mother of God?"[29] She measures his merit not by his deeds, but by Christ's concern for his mother.

The Church used multiple images of the Holy Family to show how a Spanish family should comport itself. Alba Ibero has noted that the Church procured paintings in the Baroque period that had a didactic function, portraying the subjection of the mother to maternity (102–103). Particularly illustrative of this change are the paintings by Murillo of the Holy Family, where the Virgin is portrayed in her maternal role, passive, engaged in needlework while a young and virile Joseph busies himself with gaining the household income. While Violante often portrays the Virgin as strong and independent, she also uses such images as both examples of ideal maternity for her readers and representations of real and affectionate interest in the welfare of their children. On the fifth mystery, the loss of the child in Jerusalem (*Quinto Misterio: del Niño perdido* [Parnaso: 11]), Mary's tears are those of a worried mother for her missing boy: "the glory that you receive on finding him / equals the suffering of not seeing him."[30] Marcia Belisarda, too, prizes the mother–child relationship in a fine romance on this same subject, where Mary's actions are entirely domestic and maternal: "she recognizes the beautiful child, then joyously links her arms in his."[31] This is no worshipful acknowledgement of a divine figure. In Violante's "On the First Dolorous Mystery: The Prayer in the Garden" (*Al primer Misterio doloroso: a la Oración del Huerto* [Parnaso: 12]), she makes abundantly clear her view that Christ loved his mother as a devoted and human son. Christ's prayer is not about his ordeal but the suffering his crucifixion will cause his mother: "though it seems like human fear [. . .] it is more about love."[32] Violante repeats this mutual tenderness and devotion in "Christ Shouldering the Cross" (*de Cristo Señor Nuestro con la cruz al hombro* [Parnaso; 15]). Rather than use Christ stumbling under the weight of the cross as a metaphor for the burdens of human life and sin, she shows the strong and self-negating love of a son for his mother and in juxtaposing the fall with the Fall, shifts the burden of sin from Eve to Adam "The reason why he is fallen to earth (leave aside Adam's miserable sin), is [. . .] seeing himself deprived of your eyes."[33] The sight of his mother and awareness of their impending parting fills his eyes with tears.

Violante do Céu was an adult when she chose the convent, but it should not surprise us that relationships akin to maternity occurred in circumstances where professed nuns assumed care of and developed close bonds with new entrants to the convent, many of them very young, or foundlings who would ultimately profess and become part of the community (Casey: 107; Vollendorf: 9). Marcia Belisarda reveals this in: "To a Religious who cried desperately for the death of another who had reared her" (*A una Religiosa que lloraba sin medida la muerte de otra que la había criado* [BNE Ms 7469, 47v]): "Sing, you have wept enough / Sing, sing / you'll glorify the suffering / as much as its cause."[34]

Such poetry provides an interesting source for further exploration on familial relationships within the convent at a time when, as Silvia Evangelisti has noted: "[e]ntire female clans lived within the same walls: siblings, aunts and nieces, and even—though perhaps more rarely—mothers and daughters" (18). At the end of Zayas's *Disenchantments of Love* (*Desengaños amorosos*), after summarizing the terrible fates met by the various female protagonists of the tales, Lisis, the heroine, decides to enter a convent. Her mother Laura follows her, once she has ordered her affairs to enable their comfortable existence within the cloister, a reminder of widows' relative independence and therefore the suspicion that often fell upon them as uncontrolled women:

> The next day, Lisis, doña Isabel and doña Estefanía went off to the convent with great pleasure. Dona Isabel took the habit but Lisis remained secular.... Laura ... joined them so as not to be separated from her darling Lisis. Doña Isabel wrote the news to her mother and the moment she learned where her daughter was she likewise came to join them and donned the nun's habit.
>
> *"Disenchantments": 404*[35]

Hence, the convent becomes a convenient space for women of a certain class to exercise a degree of independence and live in peace and considerable comfort. While Zayas's view of marriage in the Desengaños is extremely dark, she values the mother–daughter relationship, while the convent is almost invariably the refuge of those who survive the depredations of their husbands and lovers.

While there may be little secular poetry addressed to or by the mother, women do write to and about their siblings, a subject almost devoid of strictures from the moralists. Through the verse of Cueva and Ramírez de Guzmán, a surprising closeness is revealed, given that it was the lot of boys to be sent away to be educated or to seek service in another household, while girls remained in the home. While Cueva poeticizes her brothers and other male relatives directly, Ramírez de Guzmán addresses all her siblings under pastoral names that barely conceal the subject's identity.

Communication between free brothers and enclosed or semi-enclosed sisters not only brought new ideas and interests into the home; brothers and fathers, in discharging their duties to the Crown, could also bring honor to the family. Perceptions of honor were paramount in securing social preferment and it was enhanced by displays of overt masculinity (*hombría*), principally in military prowess.[36] The importance of kinship networks in securing political patronage should not be underestimated in these works. When Cueva wrote in praise of her brother in the royal armies, she also recorded her own blood association, linking it with his prestige, as did Ramírez de Guzmán, writing to her brother Pedro, engaged in military campaigns and administration. A number of poems to her brothers, when they are far from, home express emotions from tenderness to sardonic amusement. The brothers' activities reflect the limited opportunities available to sons of the nobility; the older son followed the role of the father, and younger sons went into the Church or served the government.

Lorenzo was "one of those clerics of minor orders [. . .] more interested in love affairs than discipline" (Entrambasaguas: 21–22).[37] This opinion accords with two of Ramírez de Guzmán's poems to Lorenzo; one, a décima, "To a gallant who denied courting a pastrycook" (*A un galán que negaba el galanteo que hacía a una pastelera* [Borrachero Mendíbil and McLaughlan: 235]) trades humorously on the suspect content of pies. He is happy to flirt with a low-class baker, but not to acknowledge her otherwise, provoking the suggestion that the pastelera may have the last word "your cruel mistress / might put you in a pie / she has you so in shreds."[38]

Similarly, Ramírez de Guzmán laments Lorenzo's imprisonment, apparently effected by his religious superiors to punish his vanity in refusing to cut his abundant hair (Borrachero Mendíbil and McLaughlan: 374). It may have been the discipline that caused him to abandon the habit and emigrate, arriving in Guatemala in about 1650, where he married (Carrasco García: 109). Lorenzo was four years' Ramírez de Guzmán's junior and the poem expresses fond exasperation as she uses her reason in critiquing his failure to deploy this essentially masculine trait: "impelled by reason and by the pleadings of my love for you, I proposed to speak with you, though you may say I'm crying in the wilderness."[39] Their closeness is evident in a wordplay interlinking their relationship with her delight in exchanging verses, with his reading the opposite side of a sheet: "you know that the two of us know each other inside out."[40] It is noticeable also, that she compares her deployment of reason with his lack of this supposedly male characteristic.

She expresses this same closeness to her brother Pedro, an officer (*alférez*) of his father's military company. In 1680 he became lieutenant governor of Llerena, where he lived with Ramírez de Guzmán; he never married (Carrasco García: 111). Her loving ties with her brothers bear out Lawrence Stone's articulation of the close relationships between siblings of the opposite sex that characterized the early modern English family. He notes the lack of envy and bitterness often felt by a younger brother for the family heir (115). Ramírez de Guzmán, in poetically addressing a letter, describes Pedro as "the most valiant soldier [. . .] he who is my brother and my beloved" (Borrachero Mendíbil and McLaughlan: 221);[41] while this is lively and optimistic, a sonnet to him "To speak and clear my thoughts" (*Acertar a decir mi sentimiento* [Borrachero Mendíbil and McLaughlan: 181) is quieter. Her sadness at his absence on royal business is not overt; instead, the octet employs every possible manifestation of silence: "mutely [. . .] silence"[42] and at the end of the octet: "to speak silently what loving you I feel."[43] As in Violante do Céu's sonnet on the Annunciation, it is the power of silence, women's eloquent burden, which most clearly evokes the relationship. Through silence she expresses strong feelings of love and loss; from silence she moves to multiple protestations of love in the sestet that make the pain of absence bearable, emphasized by a reiterated crescendo: "to love you [. . .] care for you [. . .] adore you" (9–11).[44] She demonstrates a close sibling relationship, albeit set in the conventional frame of a Petrarchan love lyric.

Ramírez de Guzmán repeats her admiration in a romance in which Pedro leaves all others in his wake as a true Renaissance man, both Mars and Adonis, soldier and poet: "In you, arms and letters are like two brothers" (Borrachero Mendíbil and McLaughlan: 175).[45] It is notable the difference in tone between her poetry to Pedro and that to Lorenzo. In a décima to the latter she admonishes his attempts to get the better of "damas" in a business deal: "Lauro, he who deals with Ladies / needn't beat them down" (Borrachero Mendíbil and McLaughlan: 165).[46] The older brother garners much more respect than the younger, while there is also a marked difference between her verse to male kin and that to her mother and sisters, most of which is concerned with domestic matters, portraits, or birthdays.[47] While a number of portraits of her sisters adopt conventional form, she also enjoys lampooning the blazon, as in a portrait of her sister Ana: "Your throat is so transparent that we see the water in it when you drink" (Borrachero Mendíbil and McLaughlin: 191).[48]

Amanda Powell has noted that "[i]n praising another woman's beauty and virtue, lamenting absence from her, or rejoicing over her happiness, such poems maintain a perhaps affecting but unsurprising decorum" (55). In the case of Ramírez de Guzmán or Zayas, however, this may not always be so. Zayas, in the *Desengaños amorosos*, describes the disasters created by sisterly jealousy, as in "The Ravages of Vice (*Estragos que causa el vicio*) where Florentina plots the death of her sister to gain access to her husband. Similarly, in Laura's tale, which concludes the *Novelas amorosas y ejemplares*, the jealous Theodosia causes a fratricide.

When Cueva writes to her brother she incorporates affection and family pride; Antonio was an officer in Cardinal-Prince Ferdinand's army at the battle of Nördlingen in 1634. She addresses her octavas directly "To the Most Serene Prince-Cardinal Don Fernando of Austria" (*Al Serenísimo Infante Cardenal don Fernando de Austria* [BNE ms. 4127, 248v–250v]). In a related sonnet, "Congratulating my brother, Don Antonio, for this significant favor granted him by His Highness on the day he took the standard" (*Parabien a mi hermano don Antonio de esta MI [merced insigne?] que su Alteza le hizo el día que tomó el guión*). Cueva crowns her brother with laurels of congratulation, juxtaposing him and the king's brother in the opening lines: "Enjoy, privileged young gallant, / the notable favor of his Royal Highness" (BNE ms. 4127, 250–251r; 1–2),[49] and in the final tercet she describes him as her beloved brother.[50] In another, "To don Antonio de la Cueva y Silva, my brother, being highly favored by His Highness when he left for Flanders," (*A d. Antonio de la Cueva y Silva mi hermano estando muy favorecido de su alteza cuando partió a Flandes*) her love opens the poem: "May you enjoy fortunate and happy years / sweet, beloved brother" (BNE ms. 4127 269r, [1–2]).[51]

If brothers were accorded Petrarchan tropes of love, their absence from the home mourned, what of the father? As the fount of all power within the family, whatever form the family might take, the father at this time controlled everybody living in the household, including servants. The Church supported a stable family structure, but always enhanced the role of the father (King: 38). Even in mutually affective marriages, the father had absolute power to punish and to authorize marriage until the child reached the age of twenty-five years (Alcalá Zamora: 170). Nevertheless, according to Vigil, fathers were not always as distant and controlling as the moralists and the Church would have wished: "it was normally the fathers—not just the mother—who spoiled and gave in to their children" (132–134).[52] Certainly, given all the power that resided in a father's hands, secular poetry by Ramírez de Guzmán and Cueva and meditations by Violante do Céu show frank admiration and affection in verse that celebrates the father not as a distant figure of authority but as beloved and close.

Two sonnets written by Violante do Céu celebrate St Joseph's sanctity and power, but also his humanity as he fulfills the appropriate role as ideal head of the family. In the first she affirms that as the Christ child is obedient to his fate, he becomes Joseph's subject (*súbdito*), humbled before him in the hierarchy, while Joseph is both spouse and defender of the pregnant Mary: "And to defend his pure Mother / he made you his own Mother's husband, / and in you assured her good reputation" (Parnaso: 25).[53]

In the second sonnet, as the Holy Family flees Herod, she juxtaposes the Josephs of the Old and New Testament. Again, the new covenant of love is better than the old covenant of the law: "repository of another, better Bread" (Parnaso: 26).[54] Infused by the love of God, Joseph cares for his "sacred treasure"[55] in the center of the poem as Christ is cradled in an embrace. This protective Joseph becomes something of a Janus figure, caring for and protecting the child like a mother, guarding and managing his household as the ideal father. While these two representative poems from Violante's collection privilege the superiority of the father, they also show a bond of responsibility and love that extends beyond that accorded to revered divine figures.

Cueva's love for her dead father is clearly stated in the liras "On the death of my beloved father and lord" (*En la muerte de mi querido padre y señor*): "In such terrible pain / I can find neither rest, pleasure nor happiness / everything is distant to me / and I have only my wretchedness" (BNE ms. 4127 189–190, [7–10]).[56] This is entirely personal and domestic, unlike her sonnet "On the tomb of D. Francisco de la Cueva y Silva, my uncle" (*Al sepulcro de El Sr Don Francisco de la Cueva y Silva, mi tío* [Serrano y Sanz: 337]). This sonnet projects family honor in linking her name with his: "the great Silva and the distinguished Cueva" (14).[57] She resorts to elevated language and the ancients to praise him, but the poem is devoid of affection, suggesting that it was intended for a wider readership. Ana Agudo y Vallejo is another who writes such sonnets in praise of a father's works (Serrano y Sanz: 15). Encomiastic verse may therefore prove a useful source for further investigation.

Ramírez de Guzmán writes in completely different terms to and about her father. Her poems sympathize with her father coming from Madrid with painful gout (Borrachero Mendíbil and McLaughlan: 312). She uses wit to inveigle him into buying clothing, a form of tunic (*almilla*) in Madrid (Borrachero Mendíbil and McLaughlan: 150). In a décima, "The author pleading with her father to bring her a cloak, being in Madrid" (*Pidiendo la autora a su padre que la trujese un manto estando en Madrid* [Borrachero Mendíbil and McLaughlan: 306]), it seems that he fails to buy the desired item; this latter poem is read by Olivares as "an act of devaluation, a divestment of self-esteem. [. . .] a symbolic utterance of women's deprivation in general" ("Towards": 35–36). Borrachero and McLaughlan, while accepting this reading, find it difficult to detect deprivation or loss in the poem (306).[58] Certainly, it seems to me more a matter of getting her own way; Ramírez de Guzmán's burlesque and personal verse is lively and devoid of any sense of deprivation, and her poetry to and about her father shows little respect or fear, though perhaps less warmth than she shows to her mother. Adrienne Martín advocates a closer study of such verse as it relates to "women's everyday" (121).

While these poems give an insight into relationships between siblings, mothers, and children, in most the father remains a shadowy figure. In Violante do Céu's idealizing portraits of Joseph, he is a remarkably feminized individual; Ramírez de Guzmán's frankly affectionate poetry to her father demonstrates a relaxed and familiar relationship, and Cueva's sad liras point to genuine closeness and loss. Their more informal view of family life suggests that fathers were more actively involved in the emotional networks of family than moralizing treatises would suggest. Although the secular mother is seldom seen in familial verse, the celebration of Mary's divine motherhood provides the perfect model for the materfamilias, while siblings are teased, admired, and clearly valued. The family served as protector, source of religious fervor, social regulator, and means to social advancement. In an age before sentimentalism and romantic idealization, and before psychotherapeutic techniques and studies, it was affection and solidarity in the family that ensured physical and political survival in uncertain times.

Notes

1 For a more detailed discussion of marriage and its theatrical presentation in early modern Spain, see Carrión.
2 Of interest here is Anne Cruz's discussion of the unhappily married wife in "La bella malmaridada: Lessons for the Good Wife" in Cruz and Perry.
3 Ramírez de Guzmán's original manuscripts are in Spain's National Library, mss. 3884 and 3917.
4 "el es uno y que sus ojos son dos" (7–8).
5 "dulce posesión" (12).
6 "eternice su memoria / que es la fortuna mayor" (23–24).
7 Antonia Manuela notes in her testament of 1697: "Nunca tomado estado ni dejado hijos ni descendientes mis hermanos" (I never took that state, nor did my siblings leave descendants). Unmentioned is her brother Lorenzo's son, despite his loving relationship with Catalina Clara and an enduring correspondence between father and son (Borrachero Mendíbil and McLaughlin Mendíbil and McLaughlin, "Introducción, biográfica y crítica" (*Ramírez de Guzmán: Obra poética*: 17–39). Ana's husband was a lawyer who took her to Úbeda, leaving a trail of debt (Carrasco García: 113–114). Beatriz's marriage lasted two days, when her husband died (Gazul: 524).
8 See Armon, Marín Pina, and Williamsen in this volume. Boyer's introduction to her excellent translation of Zayas's *Novelas, The Enchantments of Love: Amorous and Exemplary Novels* neatly encapsulates

the structure of the collection of exemplary stories set within a frame tale which itself becomes an exemplary story (xi–xxx). See also Williamsen and Whitenack, Alcalde, Greer, and O'Brien.

9 Sourced from BIESES: Bibliografía de escritoras españolas/Bibliography of Spanish Women Writers: www.bieses.net. The original is in the library of the Archbishop's Palace, Seville, Códice 33–180f. 138 v.1.
10 "¡Ay, caro amigo! ¡Ay, mi agradable esposo! / ¡Ay, claro sol que dais lumbre a mi vida!" (1–2).
11 "¡Qué abrazos dulces, qué terneza de ojos!" (9).
12 For a detailed exploration of convent life and literature, see Arenal and Schlau, Vollendorf, and Lehfeldt ("Discipline"). On changes in attitude of nuns from confessional auto-denigration to personal expression in the seventeenth century see Baranda Leturio: 160–2; and the prologue to "Letras en la celda". Also, specifically on Marcia Belisardas works, Cerezo Soler.
13 See Evangelisti's discussion of the marriage celebrations of professions as part of a broad study of convent life in early modern Europe (13–39). Lehfeldt details the ceremonial ("Convents as Litigants": 646), and notes the change in the formalities after Trent ("Discipline": 1012).
14 "que el supremo Rey / sus desposorios celebra / con hija del gran Bernardo" (5–7). Unless otherwise stated all quotations of Marcia Belisarda's work are from BNE, Ms. 7469.
15 "Tierna esposa del cordero": 56r, 1.
16 "pagadle, esposa fiel, frutos del Alma" (8v, 10–11). For a more detailed reading of this sonnet see my *Subtle Subversions*: 169–172.
17 "justamente querellosa / vives de tu injusto dueño" (7–8).
18 "Alma irracional sin duda / tiene pues no aspira a un cielo / que tantos llevan en sus ojos" (13–14). Many of her works celebrate female rationality in comparison with male inconstancy. See BNE ms.7469, and a selection in Olivares and Boyce, *Tras el espejo la musa escribe*: 327–390.
19 See also McKendrick, Martín, and Bergmann.
20 Voros has uncovered Cueva's will and with it details of her family and her literary tastes.
21 "Y porque los caballeros no se quejasen de que las damas se les alzaban con la preeminencia, mezclando a los unos con los otros" (*Novelas*: 168).
22 "forman querella" (1).
23 "es rigor /amar tanto la labor / que ciegues, Silvia, por ella" (2–4).
24 "me zurzas la badana" (10).
25 "Nosotros [. . .] percibimos ludismo en el juego 'zurzir-zurrar' [. . .] nos parece que la décima refleja una relación de confianza entre la madre y la hija" (207, n10).
26 "obedeciendo anticipadamente, [. . .] no ha de bajar sin este *sí* glorioso" (7–8). I cite from the 1733 edition of Violante's verse, https://archive.org/details/parnasolusitano00conggoog
27 On the metaphors of the female body and its relation to the ploughing and seeding, see DuBois: 39–64.
28 "rociadle bien con este llanto amado / pues sabéis que le tiene el Rey sagrado / para pan de las almas escogido" (6–8).
29 "que fuistes tan amado, / si mereciste (O Juan) [. . .] de la Madre de Dios hijo adoptivo?" (13–14).
30 "Gloria, que os da despues de hallarle / es cual la misma pena de no verle" (10–11).
31 "Reconoce al bello niño / luego a sus brazos se enlaza / los de María gozosa" (BNE ms. 7469 54v [31–33]).
32 "Aunque temor de humano [. . .], / Más es temor de amante, que de humano" (3–4).
33 "La causa porque en tierra está caído / [Dejo del Adán el mísero pecado] / Es [. . .] verse de vuestros ojos dividido" (*Parnaso*: 5–8).
34 "Canta, basta que llore / [. . .] Canta canta / darás gloria a la pena / como a la causa (47v, 33–39).
35 "Lisis y doña Isabel, con doña Estefanía, se fueron a su convento con mucho gusto. Doña Isabel tomó el hábito, y Lisis se quedó seglar. [. . .] Laura [. . .] se fue con ellas por no apartarse de su amada Lisis, avisando a su madre de doña Isabel, que como supo dónde estaba su hija, se vino también con ella, tomando el hábito de religiosa" (*Desengaños*: 510).
36 For a discussion of *hombría* in early modern Spain, see Larson, Lehfeldt ("Ideal Men"), Cartagena Calderón, Romaniello and Lipp, Milligan, and Tylus generally provide a more nuanced view of *hombría* than that offered by Larson, finding a degree of anxiety regarding masculinity, linked to Spain's economic decline.
37 "uno de aquellos clérigos a medio ordenar que tanto abundaban [. . .] más amigos de amores que de disciplina."
38 "tu dueño crüel / no te eche en algún pastel, / pues te tiene tan picado" (8–10). Lorenzo is recorded as having a bastard son by a *pastelera* (Carrasco García: 113–114). Lorenzo arranged a marriage for the

woman, a servant of the house, and arranged the upbringing of his son, with whom he maintained a close relationship even after migrating to Guatemala. See Borrachero Mendíbil and McLaughlin (30–31) for more details on this matter.

39 "a instancias de la razón / y de mi amor a los ruegos, / propuse hablarte, aunque digas / que es dar voces en desierto" (5–8).
40 "sabes tú que los dos / nos entendemos a verso" (11–12).
41 "el más valiente soldado [. . .] el que es mi hermano y mi amante."
42 "mudamente [. . .] silencio."
43 "decir callando lo que amando siento."
44 "amaros [. . .] quereros [. . .] adoraros."
45 "Están como dos hermanos / armas y letras en ti."
46 "Lauro, quien con Damas trata / no ha de tener granjerías."
47 For detailed comment on this see Borrachero Mendíbil and McLaughlin (101–102). Also, Kaminsky: 383 and Teijeiro Fuentes: 113–139.
48 "Tienes la garganta / tan trasparente / que se ve en ella el agua / cuando la bebes."
49 "Goza joven gallardo la dichosa / Merced insigne de su Real alteza."
50 "querido hermano."
51 "Goza felices años dichosos, / querido y dulce hermano." Cueva not only writes to her brother, she looks beyond her immediate family in writing two highly adulatory poems to her nephew Juan de Peralta, son of her sister María Jacinta, on his prowess in the dangerous pastime of *toros y cañas*, which involved fighting wild bulls from horseback with lances (BNE ms. 4127, 268–269).
52 "era que los padres—no sólo la madre—mimaran y consintieran a sus niños."
53 "Y si en defensa de su Madre pura / esposo os hizo de su propia Madre, / y en vos su mismo crédito asegura."
54 "de otro mejor Pan depositario."
55 "sacro erario."
56 "En tan terrible pena / ni hallo descanso, gusto ni alegría; / de todo estoy ajena,/ y solo tengo la desdicha mía."
57 "El grande Silva y el insigne Cueva."
58 On familial verse, see Borrachero Mendíbil and McLaughlin: 101–104.

Works cited

Agudo y Vallejo, Ana. "A su tío, soneto." In Manuel Serrano y Sanz, *Apuntes para una biblioteca de escritoras españolas*. Madrid: Atlas, 1975: 15.
Alcalá Zamora, José. *La vida cotidiana en la España de Velázquez*. Madrid: Temas de Hoy, 1989.
Alcalde, Pilar. *Estrategías temáticas y narrativas en la novela feminizada de Maria de Zayas*. Newark, DE: Juan de la Cuesta, 2005.
Arenal, Electa and Stacey Schlau. *Untold Sisters: Hispanic Nuns in Their Own Works*. Albuquerque: U New Mexico P, 1989.
Armon, Shifra. *Picking Wedlock*. Lanham: Rowman Littlefield, 2002.
Baker, Edward. "Patronage: The Parody of an Institution in Don Quijote." *Culture and the State in Spain 1550–1850*. Ed. Tom Lewis and Francisco J. Sánchez. New York; London: Garland, 1999: 102–125.
Barahona de Soto, Mariana. *Códice 33–180 de la Biblioteca del Palacio Arzobispal de Sevilla*, f. 138 v. 1. BIESES: Bibliografía de Escritoras Españolas. www.bieses.net
Baranda Leturio, Nieves. *Cortejo a lo prohibido. Lectoras y escritoras en la España Moderna*. Madrid: Arco Libros, 2005.
Baranda Leturio, Nieves and María Carmen Marín Pina, eds. *Letras en la celda: cultura escrita de los conventos femeninos en la España moderna*. Madrid/Frankfurt: Iberoamericana/Vervuert, 2014.
Belisarda, María. Ms. 7469, Biblioteca Nacional, Madrid, Spain.
Bergmann, Emilie. "The Exclusion of the Feminine in the Cultural Discourse of the Golden Age: Juan Luís Vives and Luís de León." *Religion, Body and Gender in Early Modern Spain*. Ed. Alain Saint-Saëns. San Francisco: Mellen Research UP, 1991: 124–136.
Borrachero Mendíbil, Aránzazu and Karl McLaughlin, "Introducción, biográfica y crítica." *Catalina Clara Ramírez de Guzmán. Obra poética*. Ed. Aránzazu Borrachero Mendíbil and Karl McLaughlin. Mérida: Editora Regional de Extremadura, 2010: 17–39.

Boyer, H. Patsy. "Introduction." *María de Zayas, The Enchantments of Love: Amorous and Exemplary Novels.* Trans. H. Patsy Boyer, Berkeley; Los Angeles: U California P, 1990: xi–xxxv.

Carrasco García, Antonio. *La Plaza Mayor de Llerena y otros estudios.* Valdemoro: Tuero, 1985.

Carrión, María M. *Subject Stages: Marriage, Theatre, and the Law in Early Modern Spain.* U Toronto P, 2010.

Cartagena Calderón, José. *Masculinidades en obras: El drama de la hombría en la España imperial.* Newark, DE: Juan de la Cuesta, 2008.

Casey, James. *Family and Community in Early Modern Spain: The Citizens of Granada, 1570–1739.* Cambridge: Cambridge UP, 2007.

Cerezo Soler, Juan. "El libro de poesías de Marcia Belisarda. Notas al ejemplar autógrafo de la Biblioteca Nacional" Manuscrt.Cao, 13. www.edobne.com/manuscrtcao/wp-content/uploads/marcia-belisarda-web.pdf

Cruz, Anne J. "La búsqueda de la madre: psicoanálisis y feminismo en la literatura del Siglo de Oro." *Historia silenciada de la mujer. La mujer española desde la época medieval hasta la contemporánea.* Ed. Alain Saint-Saëns. Madrid: Editorial Complutense, 1996: 39–64.

——. *La bella malmaridada: Lessons for the Good Wife.* Ed. Mary Elizabeth Perry and Anne J. Cruz. Minneapolis: U of Minneapolis P, 1991: 145–170.

——. "Feminism, Psychoanalysis, and the Search for the M/other in Early Modern Spain." *Indiana Journal of Hispanic Literatures* 6–7 (Spring–Fall 1995): 31–54.

Cueva y Silva, Leonor, de la. "Soneto a Don Francisco de la Cueva y Silva, su padre." *Información en derecho divino y humano, por la puríssima Concepción de la Soberana Virgen Nuestra Señora.* Madrid: Juan Gonzalez, 1625.

Defourneaux, Marcelin. *Daily Life in Golden Age Spain,* Trans. Newton Branch. Stanford: Stanford UP, 1970: 133–134.

DuBois, Page. *Sowing the Body: Psychoanalysis and Ancient Representations of Women.* Chicago: U Chicago P, 1988.

Ellington, Donna Spivey. *From Sacred Body to Angelic Soul: Understanding Mary in Late Medieval and Early Modern Europe.* Washington, DC: Catholic U America P, 2001.

Entrambasaguas y Peña, Joaquín de. "Estudio preliminar." *Poesía de doña Catalina Clara Ramírez de Guzmán.* Ed. Joaquín Entrambasaguas y Peña. Badajoz: Centro de Estudios Extremeños, 1930: 5–41.

Evangelisti, Silvia. *Nuns: A History of Convent Life.* Oxford: Oxford UP, 2007.

Fox, Gwyn. *Subtle Subversions: Reading Golden Age Sonnets by Iberian Women.* Washington, DC: Catholic U America P, 2008.

Gazul, Arturo. "La familia Ramírez de Guzmán en Llerena." *Revista de Estudios Extremenos* 15.3 (1959): 499–577.

Greer, Margaret Rich. *María de Zayas Tells Baroque Tales of Love and the Cruelty of Men.* University Park, PA: Pennsylvania State UP, 2000.

Ibero, Alba. "Imágenes de maternidad en la pintura barroca." *Las mujeres en el Antiguo Régimen: Imagen y realidad.* Barcelona: Icaria, 1994.

Kaminsky, Amy, ed. *Water lilies/Flores de agua. An Anthology of Spanish Women Writers from the Fifteenth through the Nineteenth Century.* Minnesota: U Minnesota P, 1996.

King, Margaret L. *Women of the Renaissance.* Chicago; London: U Chicago P, 1991.

Larson. Donald R. *The Honor Plays of Lope de Vega.* Cambridge: Harvard UP, 1977.

Lehfeldt, Elizabeth A. *Religious Women in Golden Age Spain: The Permeable Cloister.* Aldershot, UK; Burlington, VT: Ashgate, 2005.

——. "Convents as Litigants: Dowry and Inheritance Disputes in Early Modern Spain." *Journal of Social History* 3.3 (Spring 2000): 645–664.

——. "Discipline Vocation and Patronage." *Sixteenth Century Journal* 30/4 (1999): 1009–1030.

——. "Ideal Men: Masculinity and Decline in Seventeenth-Century Spain." *Renaissance Quarterly* 61.2 (2008): 463–494.

León, Fray Luís de. *La perfecta casada.* Madrid: Libsa, 1998.

Lerner, Gerda. *The Creation of Feminist Consciousness: From the Middle Ages to Eighteen-Seventy.* Oxford: Oxford UP, 1993.

Martín, Adrienne. "Female Burlesque and the Everyday." *Studies on Women's Poetry of the Golden Age: Tras el espejo la musa escribe.* Ed. Julián Olivares. Woodbridge: Tamesis. 2009: 100–122.

McKendrick, Melveena. *Woman and Society in the Spanish Drama of the Golden Age: A study of the Mujer Varonil.* London, NY: Cambridge UP, 1974.

Milligan, Gerry and Jane Tylus, eds. *The Poetics of Masculinity in Early Modern Italy and Spain.* Toronto: Iter/Centre for Reformation and Renaissance Studies, 2010.

O'Brien, Eaven. *Women in the Prose of María de Zayas.* Woodbridge: Tamesis, 2010.

Olivares, Julián. "Vir Melancholicus/fémina tristis: Towards a Poetics of Women's Loss." *Studies on Women's Poetry of the Golden Age: Tras el espejo la musa escribe.* Ed. Julián Olivares. Woodbridge: Tamesis, 2009: 19–50.

Olivares, Julián and Elizabeth S. Boyce, eds. *Tras el espejo la musa escribe: Lírica femenina de los Siglos de Oro.* Madrid: Siglo XXI de España Editores, 1993.

Pascua Sánchez, María de la. "Una aproximación a la historia de la familia como espacio de afectos y desafectos: el mundo hispánico del setecientos." *Chronica Nova* 27(2000): 131–166.

———."Violencia y familia en la España del Antiguo Régimen." *Estudis: Revista de historia moderna* 28 (2002): 77–102.

Pérez Molina, Isabel. *Las mujeres en el Antiguo Régimen: imagen y realidad (s. XVI–XVIII).* Barcelona: Icaria, 1994.

Powell, Amanda. "¡ Oh qué diversas estamos, / dulce prenda, vos y yo!: Multiple Voicings in Love Poems to Women by Marcia Belisarda, Catalina Clara Ramírez de Guzmán, and Sor Violante del Cielo." *Studies on Women's Poetry of the Golden Age: Tras el espejo la musa escribe.* Ed. Julián Olivares. Woodbridge: Tamesis, 2009: 51–80.

Ramírez de Guzmán, Catalina Clara. *Obra poética.* Ed. Aránzazu Borrachera Mendíbil and Karl McLaughlin. Mérida: Editora Regional de Extremadura, 2010.

Romaniello, Matthew P. and Charles Lipp, eds. *Contested Spaces of Nobility in Early Modern Europe.* Farnham, UK; Burlington, VT: Ashgate, 2011.

Romero-Díaz, Nieves. *Nueva nobleza, nueva novela: reescribiendo la cultura urbana del barroco.* Newark, DE: Juan de la Cuesta, 2002.

Serrano y Sanz, Manuel. *Apuntes para una biblioteca de escritoras españolas.* Madrid: Atlas, 1975.

Stone, Lawrence. *The Family, Sex and Marriage in England 1500–1800.* London: Weidenfeld and Nicholson, 1977.

Teijeiro Fuentes, Carlos. "Catalina Clara Ramírez de Guzmán: La retratista de Llerena." *Revista de Estudios Extremeños* 68.1 (2012): 113–128.

Vigil, Mariló. *La vida de las mujeres en los siglos XVI y XVII.* Mexico, D.F.: Siglo Veintiuno Editores, 1986.

Violante do Céu. *Parnaso lusitano de divinos e humanos versos, compostos pela Madre Soror Violante do Ceo, Religiosa Dominica no Convento da Rosa de Lisboa, dedicado a Senhora Soror Violante do Ceo, Religiosa no convento de Santa Martha de Lisboa.* Primeyro tomo. Lisbon: Miguel Rodrigues, 1733.

———. *Parnaso lusitano de divinos e humanos versos, compostos pela Madre Soror Violante do Ceo, Religiosa Dominica no Convento da Rosa de Lisboa, dedicado a Senhora Soror Violante do Ceo, Religiosa no convento de Santa Martha de Lisboa.* https://archive.org/details/parnasolusitano00conggoog

Vives, Juan Luís. *The Education of a Christian Woman: A Sixteenth-Century Manual.* Ed. and trans. Charles Fantazzi., Chicago: U Chicago P, 2000.

Vollendorf, Lisa. *The Lives of Women.* Nashville: Vanderbilt UP, 2005.

Voros, Sharon D. "Leonor's Library: The Last Will and Testament of Leonor de la Cueva y Silva." *Hispanic Studies in Honor of Robert Fiore.* Ed. Chad Gasta and Julia Domínguez. Newark, DE: Juan de la Cuesta, 2009: 497–510.

Warner, Marina. *Alone of All Her Sex.* New York: Random House, 1983.

———. *Monuments and Maidens: The Allegory of the Female Form.* London: Picador, 1985.

Williamsen, Amy R. and Judith A. Whitenack, eds. *María de Zayas: The Dynamics of Discourse.* Cranbury, NJ: Associated UP, 1995.

Zabaleta, Juan de. *El día de fiesta por la mañana y por la tarde.* Ed. Cristóbal Cuevas García. Madrid: Castalia, 1983.

Zayas y Sotomayor, María de. *Desengaños amorosos.* Ed. Alicia Yllera. Madrid: Cátedra, 1993.

———. *The Disenchantments of Love: A Translation of the Desengaños amorosos.* Trans. H. Patsy Boyer. Albany: State U New York P, 1997.

———. *The Enchantments of Love: Amorous and Exemplary Novels.* Trans. H. Patsy Boyer. Berkeley; Los Angeles: U California P, 1990.

———. *Novelas amorosas y ejemplares.* Ed. Julián Olivares. Madrid: Cátedra, 2000.

18
PRIVATE CORRESPONDENCE

Vanessa de Cruz Medina

In 1637, Luisa María de Padilla, Countess of Aranda, stated in her treatise *Virtuous Nobility*, "with my experience in regard to letter writing and the reading of books, I disagree with the opinion of those who oppose the efforts of noblewomen even to learn to read and write. I think it far too rigid, since for a lady, this would be a great privation, both in order to read her husband's letters to her and to govern his house and even his estate in his absence, and she would deprive herself of the great spiritual benefit to be found in the reading of good books" (253).[1] Padilla thus inserted herself into the debates on women's education that took place in early modern Spain, defending the right of women of her same social status to correspond about family and business matters in her own hand. Hers was not the first voice at the time to make such a case against the humanists and moralists who, like Antonio de Espinosa, warned of the dangers brought about by women writing and reading letters.[2]

The voices against teaching women to write resonate the loudest against the epistolary activities of those early modern Spanish women who did not enter the convent. While most historians and literary scholars have focused on nuns, whose letters are not only abundant but also counted among their authors such luminaries as Teresa of Ávila—the correspondence of noble- and non-noblewomen dealing with personal and family matters, or even politics or the court, is still a little-explored field. Thus, in 2003, Nieves Baranda ("Mujeres y escritura" and *Cortejo*) pointed out that despite the studies and editions published at the time, it was impossible to have real critical knowledge of secular women's private correspondence due to the lack of an organized system of study. Although this correspondence has not received the same attention as in other countries,[3] there has been encouraging progress in the last two decades: new collections of letters have been found, deeper knowledge of letter writers has been gained, and the number of publications on the subject has increased significantly.

Private letters by women were first published solely as sources, responding to the interests of nineteenth-century Hispanists and the political histories of early modern Spain whose purposes were far removed from women's writing and epistolary correspondence. Only in literary histories concerned with establishing a canon of Spanish authors were women's letters published under their authors' names. However, due to the new areas of research that emerged during the last decades of the twentieth century, these letters have been re-edited and analyzed with very different purposes. Gender and social foci have become the two fundamental categories for the analysis of women's epistolary writing. These new lines of research have given rise to the history of written culture, a cultural history centered on the practices of reading and writing, and principally focused on material forms of writing in order to investigate writing competence and its modes of appropriation. The study by Diego Navarro Bonilla of the exchange of women's love notes found in Inquisition archives stands out among those applying this methodology. The love letter is one of the most-studied literary genres (Ynduraín), and it was precisely this type of romantic correspondence that was most feared by humanists and moralists such as Espinosa, since women of all social levels were depicted writing and receiving love letters in many early modern plays and novels.

The practices of epistolary writing and the various functions of noblewomen's letters in Golden Age Spain have been reconstructed by drawing from the history of written culture (Cruz Medina, "Cartas"). The sociocultural possibilities and conditions of women's epistolary writing at that time proved to be very similar to those of the rest of patriarchal Europe. Like their European counterparts, Spanish noblewomen were represented in the manuals printed in the vernacular that imparted the models of ideal feminine correspondence. While "letter books" written by women were published in France (Altman, Chartier) and Italy (Chamello), in England and Spain the models of feminine letter writing were compiled in book-length primers, guidebooks, formbooks, and manuals of familiar letters, all of them printed in the vernacular. Indeed, at the beginning of the seventeenth century, Gabriel Pérez del Barrio (1613) published a manual for secretaries in which he included a formbook dedicated to the correspondence of aristocratic women: "Collection of some familiar letters written by ladies to their queen, the *infantas*, and to other lady friends."[4] Moreover, Spanish legislation enacted by the kings established the appropriate forms of address that men and women should use according to their social level and made the masculine and feminine forms the same, with women receiving by law the same treatment as their male counterparts.[5]

Spanish women, mainly noblewomen, knew epistolary rhetoric perfectly and knew how to make superb use of different types of letter, depending on the recipient and the subject to be treated. In general, letters written by women were private, since women were not permitted to occupy public positions in the institutions that comprised the Spanish monarchy, with the exception of queens and *infantas*. Most female correspondence was composed of letters that were familiar in a double sense. On the one hand, as Pedro Martín Baños has shown, in early modern printed manuals, the term *carta familiar* (familiar letter) was synonymous with *carta cortesana* (courtly letter) ("Familiar"). That is, the term did not allude to family relationships or to intimate communication, but rather to the style required for letters of social obligation, formality, and business, recalling the precepts of the Ciceronian corpus. These are the private letters scholars have labeled *cartas de cortesía* (courtesy letters): condolences, Christmas greetings, and congratulations for births or marriages that were frequently exchanged among relatives, friends, and other members of court society. However, "familiar letters" are also those involving congratulations, petitions, requests, and recommendations of people and businesses that, for example, Spanish noblewomen sent to the Vatican between 1550 and 1700—of which a total of 344 written by 94 noblewomen to cardinals and Popes are extant (Cruz Medina, "Cartas").

On the other hand, scholars also deploy the term "familiar letter" as synonymous with "letter between relatives," which might or might not deal with private matters. These are, for example, the letters that Juana de Velasco, Duchess of Gandía sent to her husband advising him how to behave in order to be successful at court; the 108 affectionate letters that the Duke of Pastrana received from his mother, Catalina de Mendoza y Sandoval, Duchess of Infantado; and from his wife, María de Haro, between 1675 and 1681; and also the 129 letters exchanged by both male and female members of the noble houses of Mondéjar and Infantado during 1583 (Cruz Medina, "Cartas").

How did Spanish women carry out the practice of epistolary writing? As is well known, few women learned to write and those who knew how, often did not develop good writing skills: bad calligraphy was identified with women's writings, although also with the culture of the nobility. Noblewomen did not delegate all their correspondence to a secretary; they wrote in their own hand not only to communicate intimate, amorous, and secret matters, but for other occasions as well. Handwritten letters were required as a sign of deference between relatives, and as a symbol of consideration and obligatory courtesy toward rulers and social and power elites. Thus, even women who knew how to write frequently delegated the composition of their courtesy letters to their secretaries, although they signed the letters with their own hand. In fact, in early modern Spain there were many female "secretaries" charged with writing their mistresses' letters (Bouza, "Memorias") and, in many cases noblemen and noblewomen, especially married couples, shared the same secretaries who would be in charge of the correspondence of both their lords and ladies. Like their male counterparts, therefore, noblewomen delegated their correspondence to a secretary depending on the recipient, the matter, and the immediate purpose of their letters (Cruz Medina, "Cartas").

Noblewomen's correspondences

The letters written by Magdalena de Bobadilla in the 1560s and 1570s to Diego Hurtado de Mendoza and to Juan de Silva, Count of Portalegre, were the first published correspondence of a Spanish noblewoman. In 1901, the Hispanist Raymond Foulché-Delbosc published a modernized transcription of this correspondence in the journal *Revue Hispanique*, which he had founded a few years before. Magdalena de Bobadilla's letters—49 letters addressed to Hurtado de Mendoza and his eight replies, one letter to Juan de Silva and his two replies—were printed without annotations, context, or date, and have not been edited since. Although, during the twentieth century many studies used Magdalena's letters as a source for Diego Hurtado de Mendoza, the first study specifically on her letters did not appear until 1999, when Grace Coolidge utilized the transcriptions published by Foulché-Delbosc to discuss Magdalena of Bobadilla's agency ("Choosing" and *Guardianship*). Coolidge explains how this young lady-in-waiting to Princess Juana of Austria, orphaned at age fifteen, arranged and decided her marriage through her letters and in doing so, confronted Hurtado de Mendoza, a distant relative who had been appointed her guardian. Magdalena de Bobadilla also included news and opinions about Philip II's court in her letters, transcriptions that were examined by M.J. Rodríguez Salgado to investigate Queen Isabel de Valois's household. The collection by Foulché-Delbosc in *Revue Hispanique* does not include all the extant correspondence of this noblewoman, as there are 47 unpublished letters archived in Spain's National Library.[6]

The familiar letters written in Catalan by Estefanía de Requesens to her mother Hipólita Roís de Liori, Countess of Palamós, were published in Spain in 1942. However, this correspondence did not become known in a work on women writers or epistolary communication, but in the documentation that José M. March included in his study of Philip II's education. The letters of Estefanía de Requesens, sent from Madrid between 1533 and 1540, were considered historically relevant for the new information she offered about the court and the education of Charles V's son, and March placed them after the letters written by her husband, Juan de Zúñiga, Prince Philip's tutor, to the Countess of Palamós. The letters between mother and daughter contained not only news about the imperial family and the courtiers, political events and daily life in the palace, but also information about health and family matters such as the education of Estefania's sons—especially Luis, to whom she wrote instructions (Baranda, "Escritos"; "Los nobles")—in addition to the Countess of Palamós's business dealings and civil court cases.

Two other editions of Estefanía's correspondence have been published more recently. In 1987, Maite Guisado edited a collection containing a greater number of complete, unmutilated letters, since March had transcribed only the paragraphs that seemed most interesting to him and omitted the most intimate ones, such as those relating to maternity and birth. Guisado produced a philologically rigorous edition in which she brought to the fore the role of this noblewoman as letter writer and described the kind of intimate female correspondence typical of the early modern period. Eulalia de Ahumada's edition, published in 2003, included an analysis and formal description of Estefanía's letters. Ahumada also made important additions: letters sent by Hipólita Rois to her family members were published for the first time as well as business correspondence to her agent, Bernat Capeller, together with another 20 previously unedited letters from Estefanía to her mother. Among the most noteworthy researchers who have used these letters are Dominque Courcelle and, in particular, Montserrat Pérez-Toribio, who studied the educational aspects of this correspondence and has recently reconstructed how Hipólita Rois, the Countess of Palamós, managed her client networks and textile business through her letters ("From Mother," "A Public Household").

Other private letters of interest are those sent at the beginning of the seventeenth century by Luisa de Carvajal y Mendoza to her brother, Alonso; her cousins, Isabel de Velasco and Inés de Vargas; and to their husbands, the Marquis of Almazán and Rodrigo Calderón. Luisa de Carvajal, a noblewoman who belonged to the powerful Mendoza clan, renounced marriage and the convent, proclaiming herself a missionary and traveling to London with the intention of reconverting the Anglicans to Catholicism.[7] The letters she wrote to members of her family, together with those she sent to her nun friends, priests, and members of the nobility, have been edited along with her religious poetry by Jesús González Marañón and Camilo María Abad. We must also mention the studies by Elena Levy-Navarro, as well as by Christopher J. Henstock, of the 29 letters she wrote to Calderón, the powerful favorite of the Duke of Lerma. These letters show how Luisa wisely used her family connections so that her voice, opinions, and plans about the situation of Catholics in England and the Low Countries would be heard in the Spanish court, thereby gaining the protection of this important courtier of Philip III. The most recent edition of her letters, by Glyn Redworth and Christopher J. Henstock, represents the only complete correspondence of a Spanish noblewoman translated into English.

In the decade of the 1980s, two collections of private letters by noblewomen were partially published by Isabel Barbeito Carneiro (*Escritoras*): the familiar letters written by the sixth and seventh Countesses of Lemos, Catalina de Zúñiga y Sandoval and Catalina de Cerda y Sandoval, aunt and niece, kept in the Archivo de la Fundación de la Casa de Alba. Barbeito Carneiro included excerpts from the 28 familiar letters that Catalina de Zúñiga y Sandoval sent to her son Francisco, Count of Castro, between 1611 and 1620. Catalina de Zúñiga y Sandoval was the Duke of Lerma's sister, Queen Margarita of Austria's lady of the bedchamber and the owner of an impressive library ("La biblioteca"). Excerpts from the letters of Catalina de la Cerda y Sandoval, Lerma's daughter, to her husband, the seventh Count of Lemos, and to her brother-in-law, the Count of Castro, also appear in this collection. The paragraphs transcribed by Barbeito Carneiro reveal some of the matters that these countesses dealt with in their letters: their artistic patronage, their participation in client networks, and political and court business (192–202, 878–902). In spite of their interest, these familiar letters have not been completely edited and have only been used to reconstruct the history of this noble family: the biography of Catalina de la Cerda by M. Hermida Balado and Isabel Enciso's monograph on the seventh Count of Lemos, in which she analyzes the correspondence that Catalina maintained with her husband, are especially noteworthy among these studies.

Two other collections of private letters written by noblewomen drew the attention of scholars at the end of the twentieth century, although these have yet to be published. Araceli Guillaume-Alonso dedicated an essay to the familiar correspondence that Victoria de Toledo maintained with her father, Pedro de Toledo, Marquis of Villafranca. Victoria had to take charge of her siblings and manage the family home after her mother's death, given that her father, who was Captain General of the Naples fleet, was continually at sea. Victoria communicated with him by letter between 1594 and 1619, informing him and consulting him about family matters related to the house, the administration of properties, and the education of her siblings. According to Guillaume-Alonso, in addition to the 76 letters of Victoria de Toledo, those of her sister, María, are kept in the Archivo General de la Fundación Casa Medina Sidonia. Furthermore, Jamile T. Lawand published a study of the forgotten correspondence that Leonor de Castro, Countess of Rivadabia, maintained with her property administrator, which was brought to light by Manuel Serrano y Sanz (247). Written between 1575 and 1577 and archived in Spain's National Library, these numerous private letters, addressed to Martín Rodríguez, the Countess's groom in Valladolid, deal with administrative issues such as lawsuits and other legal matters, although they also contain some very emotional segments in her own hand.

The letters that Ana de Dietrichstein wrote to her mother between 1574 and 1583, kept in Brno (Czech Republic), have been edited recently (Cruz Medina, "Una dama"). Ana was the daughter of Adam of Dietrichstein, the Holy Roman Emperors, Maximillian II and Rudolph II's favorite, and Margarita de Cardona, a Spanish lady-in-waiting to Empress Maria of Austria. When Adam of Dietrichstein was appointed Imperial Ambassador he moved his whole family to Madrid, where they lived until 1573. Upon his return, he decided to leave his three daughters María, Ana, and Hipólita, to serve as ladies-in-waiting in the Spanish court. Ana de Dietrichstein, who at that time was fourteen, began to regularly send her mother privileged information, notices, and news about the inner workings of the Spanish Habsburg female households, as well as Philip II's political intentions and the Spanish court (Cruz Medina, "Y porque sale la reina"; "Ana de Dietrichstein"). Ana's familiar letters also fulfilled other functions: the correspondence served Margarita de Cardona to supervise the raising and education of her daughter, who constantly strove to demonstrate her achievements; at the same time, Ana became the agent and intermediary in charge of transmitting her mother's business, petitions, and wishes to the Spanish court (Cruz Medina, "La educación," "Manos que escriben," "In Service").

Letters by non-noblewomen

Depending on their writing competence, non-noble Spanish women either handwrote their own letters or delegated the task to professional scribes to communicate with their families and the power elite. In his *Cartas privadas de emigrantes a Indias* (Private Letters of Emigrants to the New World), Enrique Otte included the letters that women emigrants sent from America to their friends and relatives in the Iberian Peninsula.[8] The letters exchanged among women who lived in the West Indies, as well as the letters they received from Spain, were published by Rocío Sánchez Rubio and Isabel Testón Núnez. Both collections offer a new socio-cultural panorama of female epistolary writing. Beyond the court and elite culture—only ten percent of the writers mentioned by Otte belonged to the nobility—we find a significant number of non-noblewomen letter writers: aunts and nieces like Magdalena and Luisa del Castillo, daughters like Isabel Domínguez, and sisters like Inés de Cabañas (Otte: 383, 323, 387). Also, mothers like María de Acevedo and wives like María de Jesús, who wrote from Seville to her husband, a cattle rancher in Mexico, to let him know that she was aware he was trying to pass as a widower and marry another woman (Sánchez Rubio and Testón Núñez: 154–157, 231–233).

It must be emphasized that the letters' purpose conditions both the number of writers and their subject matter. Those published by Otte are known as *cartas de llamada*, that is, documents that the candidates for emigration gathered together in their applications to travel to America. In assessing the following statistics, we should keep in mind that most of the population that emigrated to the Indies was male: among the 529 senders of "letters of call" we find only 51 written by women; however, 242 letters were addressed to women, although their replies may not have been saved. Sánchez Rubio and Testón Núñez published letters presented before the Inquisition in Mexico as proof of different crimes, among which bigamy stands out. This explains why 58% of the 242 letters sent from the Old World in the sixteenth- and seventeenth centuries were written by women, while only 22.7% of those written on the American continent were by women. Both collections of letters have been used by Americanists interested in analyzing migration and daily life in the West Indies, by researchers of correspondence, and by those who study the uses of the Spanish language in the early modern period. However, only the analyses by Sánchez Díaz and by García Mouton focus on women letter writers, whose number has increased considerably thanks to the new letters published by Stangl.[9]

Future research

In general, we observe that Spanish women aristocrats were very familiar with the epistolary genre and that the patriarchal society of the Golden Age assumed it to be natural, appropriate, and even obligatory that noblewomen write letters (Cruz Medina, "Cartas"). Quantitatively, a significant number of writers and letter collections that contain references to other women writers and to letters that may or may not have been saved have been found in different archives and libraries. Similarly, some published letter collections by male authors indicate the existence of women's letters that have not yet been located. Thus, for example, the letters that Luisa Manrique de Lara, Countess of Paredes de la Nava, wrote to Philip IV have not yet appeared. Thanks to the publication of the king's letters to her, we know that the countess maintained a close epistolary relationship with the monarch while she was a lady-in-waiting at the palace and after she became a nun (Pérez Villanueva).

Were Luisa Manrique de Lara's letters expurgated or burned? Even if the burning of private letters was common among members of the early modern Spanish royalty and nobility (Bouza, "Guardar"), there still remains the work of searching for letters by women in the archives of the nobility—of more restricted and sometimes impossible access—as well as in state archives where the documentation of noble houses has been fragmented and expurgated to the extent that women's letters are often buried in volumes of papers labelled "without interest," "various," or "family matters." There are definitely more writers and letter collections to discover and study. For example, the letters written by Costanza de Acuña and those that she and her husband, the Count of Gondomar, received from other Spanish women have not yet been analyzed. Although Manuel Serrano y Sanz cited a uniform group of twenty-seven of Costanza de Acuña's letters, archived in Spain's National Library (10),[10] a greater number of missives came to light when Gondomar's private archive in the Library of the Royal Palace in Madrid was catalogued, since, as was common at the time, it included the countess's private archive.

The letter collection that best illustrates this fragmentation and scattering of Spanish women's letters is that of the celebrated Ana de Mendoza, Princess of Éboli. Few of Ana de Mendoza's letters were known until Helen Reed published an article on thirty-four unedited letters that the princess wrote to her son, Diego de Silva, Count of Salinas. Unlike the legend about her, the Princess of Éboli who emerged from this correspondence was a loving mother as well as head of her family, administrator of her estates, and a woman who used her great legal and political influence to deal with her adversities. The discovery of this familiar correspondence and her intimate relationship with her son, the Count of Salinas, led Trevor Dadson and Reed to continue searching for more of the princess's letters in Spanish, Italian, Portuguese, French, and British archives and libraries. Their years of research resulted in the publication of an impressive volume that includes 374 pieces of documentation (Dadson and Reed, *Epistolario e historia*) and a biography based on this documentation (Reed and Dadson, *La princesa*). The volume of letters and other documents written or signed by Ana de Mendoza includes 74 handwritten letters and private correspondence with Juan de Escobedo, revealing their close friendship.

There is a clear need to conscientiously search for letters written by women, not only in Spanish archives and libraries, but also in institutions in other countries. The Italian archives continue yielding excellent results: Alejandra Franganillo Álvarez, for example, has found in Florence a significant number of private letters written by Spanish noblewomen. She has analyzed the exchange of gifts and client relations or "networks of influence" established through correspondence by Spanish women and Christina di Lorena, Great Duchess of Tuscany. Standing out among these female letter writers is Leonor Pimentel, Countess of Benavente and lady-in-waiting to the queens Margarita of Austria and Isabel of Borbón, who reveals herself in her letters to be a political intermediary between the Great Duchess and the Spanish court.

The archives in the Czech Republic have also been especially valuable. Ana of Dietrichstein was not the only woman of her family who maintained a long correspondence with her relatives in Central Europe. Her sister Beatriz, Marchioness of Mondéjar and a lady-in-waiting to Queen Margarita of Austria, sent 340 folios of letters from Madrid to her brother, the powerful cardinal Francisco of Dietrichstein, Governor of Moravia and principal agent of the Counter Reformation in Central Europe. Between 1613 and 1631, Beatriz of Dietrichstein emerged as her brother's agent and political informer, writing from her rooms in the Madrid convent of Our Lady of Constantinople, where she lived as a widow. Her letters remain unedited, although they were the principal source of Bohumil Bad'ura's biography of her ("Markyza"; *Los países checos*). Similarly, the Prince of Lobkowicz's archive and library contain a great number of letters in Spanish exchanged between the descendants of María Manrique de Lara, a Spanish lady-in-waiting to the Empress Maria of Austria, and Vratislao de Pernstein, Grand Chancellor of Bohemia. Of this documentation, a collection of 175 intimate letters exchanged between Polixena of Pernstein and her second husband, Sdenco Adalbert Popel of Lobkowicz, have been studied, edited, and translated into Czech by Pavel Marek (*Svedectví*). This correspondence was written in Spanish to keep secret the news, notices, and political opinions exchanged between this married couple between 1619 and 1627.

Conclusion

Through their letter writing, Spanish noblewomen took care of the education of their children, arranged marriages, offered advice to their husbands, and managed the economy, business affairs, and legal issues of their households and properties. They informed what was happening at court and the palace, while at the same time demanding a great deal of information. They also created and maintained client networks of domestic as well as political, religious, and artistic patronage through the letters themselves or through gifts that often accompanied them. Whether cooperating with their husbands and relatives or on their own, noblewomen were able to accomplish all this without disrupting the social and cultural status quo, honor, reputation, and economic patrimony of their families, because the responsibilities of noblewomen within the family authorized them to act outside the domestic sphere. To date, there are still no editions and too few studies of non-noblewomen's correspondence to establish the uses and functions of their letters beyond those related to emigration to America. However, we expect to know more about these writers thanks to research projects such as the "P.S. Post Scriptum" led by Rita Marquilhas, whose main goal is to systematically search for, edit, and study private letters by women and men of various social levels in early modern Spain and Portugal.[11]

Notes

1. "con lo que he tocado de las correspondencias por cartas y lecturas de libros, declaro no seguir la opinión de algunos, que aún las mujeres nobles no quieren sepan leer y escribir. Paréceme rigurosísima y que sería una gran falta en una señora, así para las cartas de su marido, como para gobernar su casa y aún su estado en ausencia de él, y se privaría del gran provecho espiritual que se halla en la lectura de los buenos libros."
2. "resebir o embiar carta a quien no deven, como para abrir la de sus maridos, y saber otras escripturas o secretos que no es razón" (receive and send letters to those who should not be receiving them, as well as entice them to open their husband's letters, and learn about others' writings or secrets" (Espinosa: B5r, B6r).
3. See Bastl, Campbell and Larsen, Couchman and Crabb, Daybell (*Early Modern* and *Women Letter-Writers*), Doglio, Goldsmith and Winn, Hammerle and Saurer, Planté and Zarri.
4. "Formulario de algunas cartas familiares de señoras a su Reyna, a las Infantas y a señoras sus amigas."
5. For the *pragmática de las cortesías* (royal regulation of forms of address) published in 1586, see Martínez Millán and Lagomarsino. For the royal regulations published in 1586, 1594, 1600, 1611, 1636, and 1638, see Cruz Medina, "Cartas, mujeres y corte": 80–100.
6. The citation for Bobadilla's unpublished letters can be found in BIESES database, www.bieses.net
7. The extraordinary life, religiosity and writings of Luisa de Carvajal have been the object of numerous studies articles and monographs, most of which appear cited in several chapters in this volume; see Herpoel, Schlau, Sánchez, and Romero-Díaz.
8. For a partial version in English, see Lockhart and Otte. See Quispe-Agnoli's chapter in this volume on women's letters from the New World.
9. The letters may be accessed at: www. Boehlau-verlag.com/download/1630 79/978-3-412-20887-5_Bonus.pdf
10. Manuel Serrano y Sanz mistakenly identified Constanza de Acuña as the daughter, not the wife of the Count of Gondomar.
11. Some of these letters may now be consulted on the project website: http://ps.slul.ul.pt

Works cited

Ahumada Batlle, Eulàlia de, ed. *Epistolaris d'Hipòlita Roís de Liori i d'Estefania de Requesens (segle XVI)*. Valencia: Universidad de Valencia, 2003.

Altman, Janet Gurkin. "The Letter Book as a Literary Institution 1539–1789: Toward a Cultural History of Published Correspondences in France." Special Issue: "Men/Women of Letters." *Yale French Studies* 71 (1986): 17–62.

Bad'ura, Bohumil. "Markýza de Mondéjar." *Jižní Morava* 43 (2004): 81–108; 44 (2005): 59–82.

———. *Los Países Checos y España. Dos estudios de las relaciones checo-españolas*. Praga: Ibero-Americana Pragensia Supplementum 16/2006; Prague: Charles University of Prague, 2007.

Balado, M. Hermida, *La condesa de Lemos y la corte de Felipe III*. Madrid: Paraninfo Librería, 1949.

Baranda, Nieves. "Escritos para la educación de nobles en los siglos XVI y XVII." *Bulletin Hispanique* 97.1 (1995): 157–171.

———. "Los nobles toman cartas en la educación de sus vástagos." *Actas del IV Congreso Internacional de la Asociación Internacional Siglo de Oro (AISO)*. Ed. María Cruz García de Enterría and Alicia Cordón Mesa. Alcalá de Henares: Universidad de Alcalá de Henares, 1998: 215–223.

———. "Mujeres y escritura en el Siglo de Oro: una relación inestable." *Litterae. Cuadernos sobre Cultura escrita* 3–4 (2003–2004): 61–83.

———. *Cortejo a lo prohibido. Lectoras y escritoras en la España moderna*. Madrid: Arco/Libros, 2005.

Barbeito, Isabel. *Escritoras madrileñas del siglo XVII: Estudio bibliográfico-crítico*. Madrid: Universidad Complutense, 1986.

——. "La biblioteca de la VI Condesa de Lemos." *Varia Bibliographica: homenaje a José Simón Díaz*, Kassel: Reichenberg, 1987: 67–85.

Bastl, Beatrix, "Drei Wiener Projekte, Briefe adeliger Frauen: Beziehungen und Bezugssysteme." *Mitteilungen der Residenzen-Kommission der Akademie der Wissenschaften zu Göttingen* 6/1 (1996): 14–20. www.univie.ac.at/Geschichte/Frauenbriefe/index.html

Bouza, Fernando. "Guardar papeles y quemarlos en tiempos de Felipe II. La documentación de Juan de Zúñiga: un capítulo de la historia del fondo Altamira y II." *Reales Sitios. Revista del Patrimonio Nacional* 131 (1997): 18–33.

——. "Memorias de la lectura y escritura de las mujeres en el Siglo de Oro." *Historia de las mujeres en España y América Latina*. Ed. Isabel Morant, vol. 2. *El mundo moderno*. Ed. M. Ortega, A. Lavrin, and P. Pérez Cantó. Madrid: Cátedra, 2005: 169–191.

Campbell, Julie D. and Anne R. Larsen, eds. *Early Modern Women and Transnational Communities of Letters*. Aldershot, UK; Burlington, VT: Ashgate, 2009.

Chartier, Roger. "Des 'secretaires' pour le peuple? Les modéles épistolaires de l'Ancien Régime entre littérature de cour et livre de colportage." *La correspondance. Les usages de la lettre au XIXe siécle*. Ed. Roger Chartier. Paris: Fayard, 1991: 159–207.

Chemello, Adriana. "Il codice epistolare femminile. Lettere, 'Libri di lettere' e letterate nel Cinquecento." *Per lettera. La scrittura epistolare femminile tra archivio e tipografia. Secoli XV–XVII*. Ed. Gabriella Zarri. Rome: Viella, 1999: 3–42.

Coolidge, Grace E. "Choosing Her Own Buttons: The Guardianship of Magdalena de Bobadilla." *Power and Gender in Renaissance Spain. Eight Women of the Mendoza Family, 1450–1650*. Ed. Helen Nader. Urbana; Chicago: U Illinois P, 2004: 132–151.

——. *Guardianship, Gender, and the Nobility in Early Modern Spain*. Farnham, UK; Burlington, VT: Ashgate, 2011.

Couchman, Jane and Ann Crabb, eds. *Woman's Letters across Europe. 1400–1700. Form and Persuasion*. Aldershot, UK; Burlington, VT: Ashgate, 2005.

Courcelles, Dominique de. "Les lettres d'Estefania de Requesens, épouse de Juan de Zúñiga, à sa mere, la comtesse de Palamós (1533–1540): entre Catalogne et la Castille, l'affirmation d'un lignage à l'époque de Charles Quint." *Relations entre hommes et femmes en Espagne aux XVIe et XVIIE siècles*. Ed. Agustín Redondo. Paris: Publications de la Sorbonne; Presses de la Sorbonne Nouvelle, 1995: 67–78.

Cruz Medina, Vanessa de. "La educación de las meninas en la corte de Felipe II a través de las cartas de Ana de Dietrichstein a su madre, Margarita de Cardona." *Etnohistoria de la escuela. Actas del XII Coloquio Nacional de Historia de la Educación*. Burgos: Universidad de Burgos, 2003: 523–534.

——. "Manos que escriben cartas: Ana de Dietrichstein y el género epistolar en el s. XVI." *Litterae. Cuadernos sobre Cultura Escrita* 3–4 (2003–2004): 161–185.

——. " 'Y porque sale la Reyna a senar acabo, que es mi semana de serbir': la vida en palacio de la reina Ana y las infantas Isabel Clara Eugenia y Catalina Micaela en las cartas de Ana de Dietrichstein." *La reina Isabel y las reinas de España: realidad, modelos e imagen historiográfica*. Ed. María Victoria López Cordón and Gloria Franco Rubio. Madrid: Fundación Española de Historia Moderna, 2005: 427–445.

——."Ana de Dietrichstein y España." Suplementum: "Las relaciones checo-españolas." *Ibero-Americana Pragensia* 20 (2007): 103–117.

——. "Margarita de Cardona y sus hijas, damas entre la corte madrileña y Bohemia." *Las relaciones discretas entre las monarquías hispana y portuguesa: las Casas de las Reinas (siglos XV–XIX)*. Ed. José Martínez Millán and María Paula Marçal Lourenço. 3 vols. Madrid: Ediciones Polifemo, 2008. Vol. 2: 1267–1300.

——. "Cartas, mujeres y corte en el Siglo de Oro." Unpublished Ph.D. dissertation. Universidad Complutense de Madrid, 2010.

——. " 'In Service to my Lady, the Empress, as I have done every other day of my life': Margarita de Cardona, Baroness of Dietrichstein and Lady-in-Waiting of María of Austria." *The Politics of Female Households: Ladies-in-Waiting across Europe*. Ed. Nadine Akkerman and Birgit Houben. Leiden: Brill, 2014: 99–119.

Cruz Medina, Vanessa de, ed. *Una dama en la corte de Felipe II: cartas de Ana de Dietrichstein a su madre, Margarita de Cardona*. Prague: Charles University of Prague, forthcoming.

Dadson, Trevor J. and Helen H. Reed, eds. *Epistolario e historia documental de doña Ana de Mendoza y de la Cerda, princesa de Éboli*. Madrid: Iberoamericana-Vervuert, 2013.

Daybell, James. *Women Letter-Writers in Tudor England*. Oxford: Oxford UP, 2006.

Daybell, James, ed. *Early Modern Women's Letter Writing. 1450–1700*. New York: Palgrave-St. Martin's P, 2001.

Doglio, Maria Luisa. *Lettera e donna. Scrittura epistolare femminile tra Quatro e Cinquecento*. Rome: Bulzoni, 1993.

Enciso, Isabel. *Nobleza, Poder y mecenazgo en tiempos de Felipe III. Nápoles y el conde de Lemos*. Madrid: Actas, 2007.

Espinosa, Fray Antonio de. *Reglas de bien vivir muy provechosas (y aun necesarias) a la república christiana, con un desprecio del mundo y las lectiones de Job y otras obras*. Burgos: Juan de Junta, 1552.

Foulché-Delbosc, Raymond. "Correspondencia de doña Magdalena de Bobadilla." *Revue Hispanique* 8 (1901): 1–59.

Franganillo Álvarez, Alejandra. "La relación epistolar entre la Gran Duquesa Cristina de Lorena y algunas nobles españolas durante las décadas de 1590 y 1620." *Arenal. Revista de historia de las mujeres* 20/2 (2013): 369–394.

García Mouton, Pilar. "Las mujeres que escribieron cartas desde América (siglos XVI–XVII)." *Anuario de Lingüística Hispánica,* 12 (1996–1997): 319–326.

Goldsmith, E., and C. H. Winn. *Lettres de femmes. Textes inédits et oubliés du XVIe au XVIIIe siècles*. Paris: Champion, 2005.

González Marañón, Jesús, and Camilo María Abad, eds. *Doña Luisa de Carvajal y Mendoza, epistolario y poesías*. Vol. 179. Madrid: Biblioteca de Autores Españoles, 1965.

Guillaume-Alonso, Araceli. "Lettres à mon père. Aspects des rapports homme femme, a la fin du XVIe siécle, à travers la correspondance de Victoria de Toledo." *Relations entre hommes et femmes en Espagne aux XVIe et XVIIE siècles*. Ed. Agustín Redondo. Paris: Publications de la Sorbonne; Presses de la Sorbonne Nouvelle, 1995: 79–104.

Guisado, Maite, ed. *Cartes íntimes d'una dama catalana del s. XVI. Epistolari a la seva mare la comtessa de Palamós*. Barcelona: La Sal, 1987.

Hämmerle, Christa and Edith Saurer, eds. *Briefkulturen und ihr Geschlecht. Zur geschichte der privaten Korrespondenz vom 16. Jahrhundert bis heute*. Vienna: Böhlau, 2003.

Henstock, Christopher J. "Luisa de Carvajal: Text, Context, and (Self-) Identity." Unpublished Ph.D. dissertation. Manchester University, 2012.

Lagomarsino, David. "Furió Ceriol y la 'Pragmática de las Cortesías' en 1586." *Estudis: Revista de historia moderna* 8 (1979–80): 87–104.

Lawand, Jamile T. "Cartas de doña Leonor de Castro a su mayordomo: apuntes para un estudio de los asuntos cotidianos de una condesa." *Estudios de filología y retórica en homenaje a Luisa López Grigera*. Bilbao: Universidad de Deusto, 2000: 295–301.

Levy-Navarro, Elena. "The Religious Warrior: Luisa de Carvajal y Mendoza's Correspondence with Rodrigo de Calderón [sic]." *Woman's Letters across Europe. 1400–1700. Form and Persuasion*. Ed. J. Couchman and A. Crabb. Aldershot, UK; Burlington, VT: Ashgate, 2005: 263–273.

Lockhart, James and Enrique Otte. *Letters and People of the Spanish Indies. The Sixteenth Century*. Cambridge: Cambridge UP, 1976.

March, José M. *Niñez y juventud de Felipe II. Documentos inéditos sobre su educación civil, literaria y religiosa y su iniciación al gobierno (1527–1547)*. 2 vols. Madrid: Ministerio de Asuntos Exteriores, 1942.

Marek, Pavel, ed. *Svedectví o ztráte starého sveta. Manzelská korespondence Zdenka Vojtecha Popela z Lobkovic a Polyxeny Lobkovické z Pernstejna*. Ceské Bujovice: Documenta res gestas Bohemicas saeculorum 16–18 illustrantia, 2005.

Marquilhas, Rita. *P.S. Post Scriptum. Arquivo Digital de Escrita Quotidiana em Portugal e Espanha na Época Moderna*. European Research Council 7FP/ERC. Advanced Grant—GA 295562. http://ps.clul.ul.pt

Martín Baños, Pedro. "Familiar, retórica, cortesana: disfraces de la carta en los tratados epistolares renacentistas." *Cuadernos de Historia Moderna. Anejos: Cultura epistolar en la alta Edad Moderna. Usos de la carta y de la correspondencia entre el manuscrito y el impreso*, ed. Fernando Bouza, 4 (2005): 15–30.

Martínez Millán, José. "El control de las normas cortesanas y la elaboración de la pragmática de cortesías (1586)." *Edad de Oro* 18 (1999): 103–133.

Mitchell, Linda C. "Letter-writing Instruction Manuals in Seventeenth- and Eighteenth-Century England." *Letter-writing Manuals and Instruction from Antiquity to the Present: Historical and Bibliographic Studies*. Ed. C. Posted and L. C. Mitchell. Columbia: U South Carolina P, 2007: 178–199.

Navarro Bonilla, Diego. *Del corazón a la pluma: Archivos y papeles privados femeninos en la Edad Moderna*. Salamanca: Universidad de Salamanca, 2004.

Otte, Enrique. *Cartas privadas de emigrantes a Indias, 1540–1616*. México DF: Fondo de Cultura Económica, 1993.
Padilla, María Luisa de. *Nobleza Virtuosa*. Zaragoza: Juan de Lanaja, 1637.
Pérez del Barrio, Gabriel. *Dirección de secretarios de señores y las materias, cuidados y obligaciones que les tocan, con las virtudes de que se han de preciar, estilo y orden del despacho y expediente, manejo de papeles de ministros, formularios de cartas. . . y otras curiosidades*. Madrid: Alonso Martín de Balboa, 1613.
Pérez-Toribio, Montserrat. "From Mother to Daughter: Educational Lineage in the Correspondence between the Countess of Palamós and Estefaniá de Requesens." *Women's Literacy in Early Modern Spain and the New World*. Ed. Anne J. Cruz and Rosilie Hernández. Aldershot, UK; Burlington, VT: Ashgate, 2012: 59–78.
——. "A Public Household: Hipòlita Roís de Liori, Networking and (Text)Tiles Business in Sixteenth-Century Catalonia and Valencia." *Perspectives on Early Modern Women in Iberia and the Americas: Studies in Law, Society, Art and Literature in Honor of Anne J. Cruz*. Ed. Adrienne L. Martín and María Cristina Quintero. New York: Escribana Books, 2015: 131–149.
Pérez Villanueva, Joaquín. *Felipe IV y Luisa Enríquez Manrique de Lara, condesa de Paredes de la Nava. Un epistolario inédito*. Salamanca: Caja de Ahorros y Monte de Piedad de Salamanca, 1986.
Planté, Christine, ed. *L'épistolaire est-il un genre féminin?* Paris: Honoré Champion, 1998.
Redworth, Glyn and Christopher J. Henstock, eds. *The Letters of Luisa de Carvajal y Mendoza*. London: Pickering & Chatto, 2012.
Reed, Helen H. "Mother Love in the Renaissance: The Princess of Éboli's Letters to Her Favorite Son". *Power and Gender in Renaissance Spain. Eight Women of the Mendoza Family, 1450–1650*. Ed. Helen Nader. Urbana; Chicago: U Illinois P, 2004: 152–176.
Reed, Helen H. and Trevor J. Dadson. *La princesa de Éboli. Cautiva del rey. Vida de Ana de Mendoza y de la Cerda (1540–1592)*. Madrid: Centro de Estudios Europa Hispánica y Marcial Pons, 2015.
Rodríguez Salgado, M.J. "'Una perfecta princesa.' Casa y vida de la reina Isabel de Valois. Primera parte." *Cuadernos de Historia Moderna, Anejos II: Monarquía y Corte en la España Moderna*. Ed. Carlos Gómez. Centurión. 2003: 39–96.
Sánchez Díaz, M. Milagros. "La escritura de las legas en el siglo XVI: cartas." *La voz del silencio I. Fuentes directas para la historia de las mujeres (siglos VII–XVIII)*. Ed. Cristina Segura Graíño. Madrid: Asociación Cultural Al-Mudayna, 1992: 197–206.
Sánchez Rubio, Rocío and Isabel Testón Núñez. *El hilo que une. Las relaciones epistolares en el Viejo y Nuevo Mundo (siglos XVI–XVIII)*. Mérida: Universidad de Extremadura, 1999.
Serrano y Sanz, Manuel. *Apuntes para una biblioteca de escritoras españolas desde el año 1401 al 1833*. 2 vols. Madrid: Sucesores de Rivadeneyra, 1903; 1905.
Stangl, Werner. *Zwischen Authentizität und Fiktion: Die private Korrespondenz spanischer Emigranten aus Amerika, 1492–1824*. Köln/Weimar/Vienna: Böhlau, 2012.
Tanskanen, Sanna-Kaisa. "'Proper to their sex': Letter-writing Instruction and Epistolary Model Dialogues in Henry Care's *The Female Secretary*." *Instructional Writing in English: Studies in Honour of Risto Hiltunen*. Ed. M. Peikola, J. Skaffari and S-K Tanskanen. Amsterdam: John Benjamins, 2009: 125–139.
Ynduráin, Domingo. "Las cartas de amores." *Homenaje a Eugenio Asensio*. Ed. Luisa López Grigera and Agustín Redondo. Madrid: Gredos, 1988: 487–495.
Zarri, Gabriella, ed. *Per lettera. La scrittura epistolare femminile tra archivio e tipografia. Secoli XV–XVII*. Rome: Viella, 1999.

SECTION VI

Women travelers

19
FOUNDATION NARRATIVES

Darcy Donahue

The founding of a convent was a pivotal event in the lives of its members and the expansion of the order to which it belonged. Each new community was a link in the history of the order, and represented the continuation of its particular form of spirituality and goals. Writing the history of a convent's founding became an important way of reinforcing a sense of identity and purpose among its members, and communicating the progress of the order at large. Foundation narratives in general were intended to record the establishment or expansion of an order in a new site and serve as a form of religious historiography for each community. They form part of the larger body of convent chronicles which document the experiences of an individual cloister over time. "Convent chronicles in the vernacular ignore classical rules governing the composition of history and forge a collective past for their community on their own terms" (Lowe: 8). Although they vary significantly from writer to writer and convent to convent, foundation narratives also share certain characteristics. Experientially based and focusing on the collective rather than the individual, each account of a foundation bears witness to the commitment, purpose, and energy of the original members of a cloister.

In addition, these narratives often provide a minutely detailed account of the interaction between the religiously centered life of the cloister and secular society. A convent founding was a long and arduous process, involving negotiation of the property or convent site, economic patronage, and the support of the residents of the local community. Depending on the location of the convent, interaction between the founding nuns and local officials could range from mutual cooperation to open hostility, and the narratives reflect these differences. Furthermore, internal politics of a religious order are involved in many aspects of a convent's founding, including the selection of the original members, the prioress, and the spiritual director or convent confessor. Although the foundation accounts were generally mandated and approved by male superiors, they were also directed at present and future members of the convent/order as a form of community building and even recruitment. Nun readers would see their own material and spiritual lives corroborated in these accounts, and potential nuns would be persuaded by the representation of the community's holiness and shared values. Aware of this sisterhood of readers, the writers occasionally address them directly.

The narratives themselves take a variety of forms. Some, like Teresa of Ávila's *Libro de fundaciones* (Book of Foundations), which was the first of the foundation narratives, were written at the request of male prelates and may be considered official records. Most frequently written by the prioress of the new community, these narratives intertwine personal experience with the socio-political circumstances of the foundation sites, which vary greatly. Other accounts are embedded in formats such as letters or biographical texts in which the writers include foundations as significant events in their personal and professional lives or those of their co-founders. Although they are not recognized as official records, they may be the only documentation of a foundation. In some cases, the narrative was written during or shortly after the foundation, while in others many years elapsed between foundation and narrative. The foundation narratives are hybrid documents (autobiography, chronicle, communal history) that combine the individuality of the writers with their membership in the group experience of establishing a new religious community, or, in some cases, of re-establishing an existing community in a new locale.

With the exception of Teresa of Ávila, who founded both the Discalced Carmelite Order and sixteen of its convents in Spain, the writers in this section document foundations in other countries. During the sixteenth and seventeenth centuries many religious orders expanded beyond Spain. In the politically charged climate of the Counter-Reformation, religious orders assumed a significant role in maintaining or expanding Catholic influence throughout Europe, the New World, and to a lesser extent, Asia. As the Church moved to counter the advance of "heresies," these orders established convents in countries where Protestantism had gained substantial followings, or among the "pagan" indigenous populations of the New World. The purpose of these foundations was to recruit novices from among the native population and instruct them in the goals and practices of the order so that they would continue the order's expansion. In so doing, a cloister formed important relationships with both secular and religious authorities, as also occurred in the Spanish foundations. Each foreign foundation became a base for the dissemination of Catholic religious ideology and a link between Spain and the other country/culture. As Concepción Torres has observed, the mission of the Spanish nuns differed significantly from that of their male counterparts in the New World. "The Europe of the beginning of the seventeenth century cannot be compared with the first years of colonization. The Carmelite nuns arriving in territories where they are being installed don't have to civilize or colonize, but simply reaffirm through their presence the faith that has been interdicted by almost a century of religious strife. Their task will be to introduce the new Catholicism stemming from the Council of Trent and chase away the spirit of Protestantism. In some ways this task is more difficult than convincing the indigenous masses who have no point of reference."[1]

The success or failure of a community could hinge upon international relations as well as the local and internal politics described above. Heads of state occasionally became involved in foundation negotiations, and their support was vital to the continued existence of any imported community of Spanish nuns. Diplomacy, discretion, and leadership capacity as well as religious commitment were key factors in the foreign foundations. It was therefore necessary for order administrators to select the members of their extra-Spanish communities with particular care, although in some cases Church authorities in the selected country would indicate their preference for specific individuals who had acquired renown as saintly women.

The negotiation of convent communities outside Spain was complicated by linguistic, cultural, and religious difference. Even in countries like France and Italy whose languages and cultural traditions shared the same origins and were broadly similar to those of Spain, these differences could create significant obstacles to a successful foundation. In addition, the increasingly important and hostile French Protestant population was sizeable enough for France to be viewed as a "heretical" nation by many founding nuns. Depending on the location, a foundation could be subjected to surveillance and more overt forms of ill will by the local citizenry. Given the problems and even dangers involved in some foundations, it is not surprising that some nuns were reluctant to become part of these missions. Moreover, the journey from Spain to foundation site in travel conditions that were at best inconvenient and often dangerous created another drawback to participating in foreign foundations. Frequently women who had not lived in the same community prior to their foundation assignment were brought together to form the new convent, adding to the already enormous adjustment of life in a foreign culture. The distance between Spain and foundation, both geographic and cultural, became a source of nostalgia for some and discontent for others, while still others embraced the challenge of difference and the opportunity to serve God and Spain in a new cultural environment. The accounts of foreign foundations examined here reflect the experiences of collective displacement, relocation, and religious commitment from varied perspectives.

Teresa of Ávila's *Libro de fundaciones*

Like her other writings, Teresa of Avila's *Libro de fundaciones* became a model for women religious writers, whether or not they belonged to the Discalced Carmelite order she founded.[2] The book is a retrospective account of the sixteen Spanish foundations of Discalced Carmelite convents and the male community at Duruelo that were carried out between 1567 and 1582, the year of Teresa's death. Of its thirty-one chapters, twenty-four are dedicated to the convents, two describe the founding of the Duruelo monastery, and five are a kind of proto-manual for convent prioresses. Written during the last nine years of the saint's life, *Fundaciones* reflects the writer's increasing confidence in her role as foundress and is a memoir of the varied activities in which she engaged in that capacity. Furthermore, the book is a history of the Discalced Carmelite order, and of the lives, both individual and collective, of the members who carried it forward. Appropriately, it is the foundational text in what would become the ongoing chronicle of Carmelite reform. Part memoir, part propagandistic saga, part novella, it reflects, as always, the saint's keen awareness of the act of writing and potential audience response.

As Carol Slade has observed, with several successful foundations to her credit at the time she began writing in 1573, Teresa "portrays herself as founder, the one who conceives what Edward Said calls 'the beginning intention,' the 'created inclusiveness within which the work develops'" (110). In this role of founder and primary shaper of the reform, the saint foregrounds her own experiences as organizer, negotiator, and as Slade and Weber have both noted, operator par excellence, a crafty politician who will not be deterred from carrying out her divinely ordained project. In this function she encounters and deals with a broad range of adversaries and allies, including Church and lay bureaucrats, aristocratic patrons, irate landlords, members of the increasingly hostile mitigated or Calced Carmelites, and the meddling and pretentious Ana of Mendoza, Princess of Éboli, among others (Weber: 130–131). Even physical terrain becomes a crucial element in the often fiercely contested battle for spiritual and material space.

In her narrative of the politics of space and spirituality, Teresa is definitely center stage in overcoming the multitude of crises that beset the Discalced Carmelite foundations. The first person singular narrator predominates as the principal protagonist in these accounts, despite the many protestations of inadequacy and ineptitude that she intersperses throughout. Indeed, the textual persona who emerges in this narrator is an able administrator as well as a writer who wishes to placate possibly hostile readers by disavowing her own abilities.[3] Among the details of convent culture and political maneuvering, the narrator reveals her competence as motivator, mediator, and real estate appraiser. On one occasion, for example, she describes her final victory over the archbishop of Seville, Cristóbal de Rojas y Sandoval, who had resisted the foundation. "At last it pleased God that he should come to visit us, and I then told him of the trouble he was causing. Eventually he told me I could do just what I liked, and as I liked, and from that time forward he was helpful and kind to us on every possible occasion" (Peers: 129).[4] Although Teresa is always careful to attribute her ultimate success to divine assistance, on many occasions she expresses a strong sense of confidence in her own abilities. In discussing the endowment of the Alba de Tormes community, she states, "I have never lacked the courage and confidence to found religious houses without any endowment, on a basis of poverty: I have founded many such and I am certain that God will not fail them" (Peers: 103).[5] Similarly, the foundress expresses a sense of triumph and personal satisfaction at the conclusion of the troublesome Seville foundation. "My own joy, I can tell you was very great, especially when I saw that I was leaving the sisters in such a good house, so well situated, and that the convent was well known [. . .] What pleased me most of all was that I had shared their trials" (Peers: 134).[6]

However, the identity of St. Teresa as a convent foundress is not monolithic and frequently divides and subdivides into other, less self-focused personae.[7] At times the writer's narrated "I" assumes the voice of Mother Superior and counselor, directly addressing her spiritual daughters concerning the lived experiences of the convent community. At other times this same narrator becomes a historian/biographer, occupied with communicating the details of communal life and the individual lives of certain members of the convents she describes. While the narrating first person singular never entirely disappears, it does share its central position with other subjects, most frequently as part of the collective "we" of the group founding experience. In fact, the writer often shifts the focus from the narrating "I" to the communal first person plural. For example, in the case of the particularly problematic Toledo foundation, after relating in some detail the problems of finding adequate physical facilities for the convent, Teresa begins to describe the actual taking possession of the acquired property. In so doing, she juxtaposes the group activities with her own personal reactions: "We borrowed the articles which were necessary for having Mass said, and at dusk we went with one of the workmen to take possession of the house [. . .] I was full of misgivings. We spent all that night preparing the house" (Peers: 73).[8] Similarly, in describing the problems encountered at Medina del Campo, another arduous operation that required a surreptitious midnight occupation of the convent premises, the saint is careful to emphasize the moving process in collective terms before registering her own reactions: "We arrived at Medina del Campo at midnight on the eve of the festival of Our Lady in August. In order not to disturb anyone, we alighted at the monastery of St. Anne and went to the house on foot. Having reached the house, we entered the courtyard. The walls seemed to me in a very tumbledown condition[. . .] when I looked at the porch I saw that we should have to remove some of the earth from it; there were holes in the roof; and the walls were not plastered" (Peers: 11).[9]

Besides the predictable activities of foundation, Teresa, as both historian and propagandist, also includes many more heroic episodes, leading Slade to compare *Fundaciones* to the chronicles of exploration and conquest in the New World.[10] Writing of English nuns, Isobel Grundy states that in such narratives, "adventure is an exercise in gender solidarity,"[11] and this is certainly the case in this book. As she recounts the trip from the convent at Beas to the founding at Seville, St. Teresa is careful to emphasize the intense heat during the journey, addressing herself directly to her Discalced readership: "Though we did not travel during the siesta hours, I can assure you, sisters, that when the sun beat down on the carriages with all its might, getting into them was like entering purgatory. Sometimes by thinking of hell, and sometimes by remembering that we were doing and suffering something for God, the sisters bore the journey with great contentment and joy[. . .]so courageous were the six souls who were with me that I think I would have ventured into the country of the Turks in their company" (Peers: 124).[12]

The *Libro de fundaciones* has no real closure. The final foundation described is Burgos, certainly one of the most difficult, due at least in part to Teresa's poor health. As always, with the help of benefactors both human and divine, the problems are overcome. Teresa's description of the foundation concludes with an expression of confidence in its success that might well be applied to the reform as a whole: "Until now there has been no lack of persons to help us and Our Lord will not allow His brides to suffer if they serve Him as it is their duty to do" (Peers: 205).[13] As a postscript, Teresa returns to the Convento de San José in Ávila to describe its transferral to the jurisdiction of the reformed Carmelite order, bringing her narration full circle to the first Discalced convent. Each foundation described presents a unique set of problems, with some, such as Seville, Toledo, and Burgos occupying a good deal more space than the others. Yet despite the differences that may exist between the individual communities, the experience of founding is similar throughout, and so the narrative is essentially cyclical: "the present moment, constantly passing away and constantly renewed, is placed in sequential relation to a past of heroic action and a future of institutional continuity" (Grundy: 137).

Although *Fundaciones* was not published until 1610, it had circulated widely among Discalced convents in manuscript form. Following Teresa's death in 1582 and particularly her beatification in 1614, the written tradition continued as the order expanded throughout Europe and the New World. Women from varied socio-economic backgrounds chronicled the successes, failures, and even schisms of their order, often using *Fundaciones* as a main source. Moreover, many of the Discalced Carmelite writers had accompanied Teresa in the Spanish foundations. Ana de San Bartolomé and Ana de Jesús, whose narratives are included here, had been co-founders of numerous foundations with Teresa before moving to France.

The French Discalced Carmelites: Ana de San Bartolomé

The transferral of the Spanish woman-centered Carmelite reform to other cultures was a complex and challenging operation, involving political and cultural differences as well as differing forms of spirituality.[14] The negotiations for the French Discalced Carmelite foundations were long and complicated, and involved the politics of state as well as the Carmelite order. Begun in 1585, these discussions culminated in the arrival in Paris in 1604 of a group of six Spanish nuns with the purpose of initiating the Teresian Rule and Constitutions in a culture that they perceived as alien and heretical. Ana de San Bartolomé, a member of this group, documents her experiences in the French foundations. These narratives comprised several texts: autobiographies (1622, 1625), *Noticias sobre los orígenes del carmelo teresiano en Francia* (1608) (News about the Origins of the Teresian Carmel in France), and *Defensa de la herencia teresiana* (1619) (Defense of the Teresian Legacy), all of which provide an eye-witness account of the evolution of the order outside Spain. They also foreground her own struggle with French church authorities and occasionally with her compatriots in her role as foundress, prioress, and dissident.[15]

France had been of central concern to St. Teresa, who mentions it in *Camino de perfección* as a country greatly harmed by heretics (*Obras completas*: 197). Her awareness of the saint's desire to recover France for the Church was undoubtedly a decisive factor in Ana's own vision of the Discalced Carmelite undertaking. Although her narrative is at times a litany of personal trials and even persecutions, it is clear that she also recognizes the historical and political significance of her mission. In *Noticias sobre los orígenes del carmel teresiano en Francia* (News about the Origins of the Teresian Carmel in France), Ana alludes to the simultaneous founding of the Discalced convent at Ávila in 1562 and the start of the wars of religion between Catholics and Protestants in France.[16] For her this is not mere coincidence, but rather a sign that Teresa and her cohorts will save France from heretical perdition. The reconversion of France is, for Ana de San Bartolomé, the logical continuation of the Teresian reform in Spain. Her own situation is secondary in importance to the success of the order, but absolutely inseparable from it.

Cardinal Pierre Bérulle, the most ardent supporter of the Discalced Carmelites in France, had actively campaigned for Ana in a founding role and had actually traveled to Spain to accompany the initial group of nuns to France. A member of a group of French theologians who had imbibed the spirit of St. Teresa's works, and were actively engaged in reforming the French concept of the priesthood, Bérulle perceived the reformed Carmelites as the first step toward disseminating the Marian and Christocentric spirituality which he espoused.[17] At the outset a devotee of Ana, he gradually assumes an adversarial role in her writings. The French Cardinal revered Ana's close contact with St. Teresa and perceived her as essential to the success of the French foundations. Yet, as a highly regarded theologian and intellectual, and long accustomed to the obedience of those around him, Bérulle was not prepared for the forms of spirituality that the Spanish nuns would bring with them, nor for their reaction to the new cultural and spiritual environment. His attempts to exert control over the Discalced convents drew sharp reactions from Teresa's spiritual daughters in France, who viewed themselves as guardians of the reform.[18] While some of his most heavy-handed exercises of authority did not occur until after she left France for Belgium, Ana de San Bartolomé clashed with him repeatedly on matters of doctrine and governance, and this interaction figures significantly in her version of the French foundations. Never as triumphalist in tone as Teresa's *Libro de fundaciones*, her accounts are part of a larger corpus of writing in which she appears as Teresa's most faithful and beleaguered daughter.

Conflicts with Bérulle revolved around several issues—among others his reluctance to bring Spanish Discalced friars to France, and to found male monasteries in France in general. Ana also indicates that he and other superiors may have resented her close relationship with the French novices, whom they perceived as "in the palm of her hand" (*Autobiography and other writings*: 87). As Barbara Diefendorf observes, "The French superiors needed to secure and perpetuate their authority if they were to continue to move the order in the direction they thought it should take. The Spanish mothers, by contrast, hoped to replace the French superiors with Discalced Carmelites because that was how Teresa set up the order but also because they hoped to replace the French superiors with Discalced Carmelites" (110). In addition to these issues of governance there were personality and cultural differences that made communication between French superiors and Spanish nuns difficult. According to Ana, the French prelate turned her nuns against her, using cultural differences as the basis of his arguments. "I went to him one day and asked him, 'What's the matter with these sisters that they don't talk to me? He told me, 'It isn't necessary that they speak to you because they can get along without you. I've ordered it. They will do what I tell them; your spirit is not for them. It's against France and you're against us. I don't want you to be with them; your spirit is not good, it's the devil's spirit'."[19] As in previous descriptions, Ana represents herself as under attack, the victim of schemes and machinations which, it is clear, are not worthy of a man of God. Rather, they are the work of the devil, the father of all discord, who has influenced the thoughts and actions of her superiors.

The animosity between them was certainly aggravated by the fact that Bérulle was Ana's confessor, a source of constant frustration for her as she states in her autobiography: "I was angry on the inside with this Bérulle. And since I had no other confessor nor did he want to give me one although I asked him for it, this afflicted my heart, because I seemed to be in a state of sin."[20] Ana portrays Bérulle as imperious, devious, and fundamentally ignorant with regard to the realities of the Carmelite reform. She is quite outspoken in her condemnation of what she perceives as his willful persecution of her. Furthermore, her long experience as one of Teresa of Ávila's closest associates had empowered Ana to consider herself Bérulle's equal and even his superior with regard to knowledge of the reformed order. On a number of occasions, she depicts herself as openly confronting this prelate on his governance of the order, explicitly pitting her own experientially based knowledge against his learning. One particularly vivid encounter occurred while Ana was still weak from being bled for an illness. Although he was aware of her condition, Ana tells us, the cardinal refused to end his arguments: "I contradicted him and he said that he knew these matters as well as I. I told him that was not so; that he might know well from his reading, but not from experience as I did, about matters of the order. He told me that Spain was one thing and France was another."[21] It would not be an exaggeration to say that Ana presents these differences as a matter of life and death. When another nun suggested that her situation in Paris might kill her, she responded, "I hadn't done anything yet. Now that the situation presented itself, I would feel guilty to flee from the cross."[22]

It is impossible to know how much of Ana de San Bartolomé's colorful accounts of her life in the French foundations is true, and how much part of an effort to represent herself as the reform's staunchest defender. At the very least her narratives reveal an ongoing tension which resulted in her ultimate departure from France after having participated in the foundations at Paris, Pontoise, and Tours. Rather than foreground the collective experience, they reinvent her personal crusade to protect her vision of the Discalced Carmelite reform.

Ana de Jesús: the Discalced Carmelite Paris foundation

Ana de Jesús (Lobera), prioress at Paris,[23] also narrated her experiences as a member of the group of founding mothers in France in a letter from Paris, dated March 8, 1605, five months after her arrival there.[24] Although the letter is addressed only to "a religious in Spain" (*un religioso de España*), a copy in the archives of the Discalced Carmelite order in Antwerp indicates that the original was sent to Diego de Yepes, bishop of Tarazona and a benefactor of the Discalced Carmelites.[25] According to the letter, Yepes had written to Ana, requesting that she "tell him everything" about her situation in Paris.[26] The epistolary format conditions the style and to some extent the content. However, the letter shares many characteristics of the foundation genre: descriptions of travel conditions, the entrance into the foundation city and the convent site, and relations between the founders and the local population. For example, after referring to their hasty departure from Spain Ana describes the lengthy journey to Paris, and includes a commentary on the religious situation of France: "I can say that miraculously we arrived alive; without a doubt, of the 300 leagues on the road, we did 100 on foot with such great facility that the fatigue didn't last, nor did I feel it until we entered France and I saw how badly the Holiest Sacrament was treated."[27] Similarly, she shares with St. Teresa (*Camino de perfección*) the negative vision of the "heretics" whose land she has entered. Of the towns passed en route to Paris, she states "Almost everyone in these towns were heretics and you could see it in their faces, which are very like those of the damned."[28] Ana also notices that members of the reformed Benedictine and Capuchin orders whom they encounter call themselves "brothers" of the Discalced Carmelites and they "observe the Constitutions of our Holy Mother and they venerate her greatly," indicating that the order is highly regarded and not considered alien or a spiritual rival, as sometimes occurred in Spain (Manero Sorolla: 658).

Ana describes the entrance of the six Paris founders into the city as in secret because they wished to first visit the Cathedral of Saint-Denis, the site of the buried remains of St. Dionysius, before establishing themselves in their Paris convent.[29] Although she does not often engage in hyperbole, Ana finds that the relics at the Cathedral surpass her powers of description: "The relics cannot be described, all embedded in very precious stones." Comparing the French treasures to those of El Escorial in Spain, she finds the latter "is nothing."[30] The French propensity for grandeur does not always win her approval, however. Commenting on the convent building in Paris, she remarks that St. Teresa would have torn it down, "if secular people had not made it with piety and ignorance, because they've spent more than 60,000 ducats and it's still not finished."[31]

Although Ana had volunteered for the French mission, she refers to it as "exile" (destierro) in the opening line and there are moments in which she expresses a sense of nostalgia for Spain: "His Majesty has given me good health since I left Spain, to be able to move around here, although without much spirit, because it seems like I left both God and my spirit there (in Spain)."[32] This is not surprising, given her situation in Paris. Like Ana de San Bartolomé, Ana de Jesús had a problematic relationship with Cardinal Bérulle and, like her co-founder, she was inflexible in her adherence to the Teresian Constitutions, stating that she would return to Spain if they were not observed.[33] Moreover, Ana was adamant about not wishing to accept novices who had been Protestants, and had in fact wanted to reject as a novice the ex-Calvinist daughter of the French ambassador in Switzerland, a point of strong disagreement between her and Bérulle. In the letter she refers to this matter only indirectly.[34]

For the most part, however, Ana does not focus on her personal situation, but rather recounts in a concise and mostly objective style the activities of the Paris founders, mentioning, for example, a trip to Pontoise to install Ana de San Bartolomé as prioress. The founding of the convent at Pontoise is described as evidence of success of the French mission and this success is further emphasized in her description of the return to her Paris community: "They have a great love for us, and it's a miracle, because they have very little for people from Spain. They've been amazed to see the great friendship and solidarity between us and their French girls, and say that there aren't any daughters of the same father and mother in this kingdom who love each other this way."[35]

Although she never alludes directly to the problems with French superiors, perhaps because the letter format limits the elaboration of certain issues, Ana does refer to fundamental differences in the French and Spanish forms of religiosity and governance.[36] Commenting on the increasing quietist tendencies of French Catholicism, she mentions her efforts to have the novices observe and imitate Christ, rather than simply have an abstract concept of God, a form of spirituality that she does not understand. Never openly critical, Ana nevertheless creates the impression that French spirituality is often of appearances rather than substance: "Here in Paris, which is a whole world, there is a great show of Christianity. The frequency of sacraments is like that of the primitive Church and they're amazed we don't take communion more frequently."[37]

Like other foundation narratives, Ana's letter was mandated by a male superior but was directed to women readers as well. The letter-narrative closes with a request that the bishop show it to his spiritual daughters "our sisters" because she will not have time to write to them.[38] She also avails herself of the occasion to request books of published sermons and any writings of St. Teresa "our Holy Mother" that he might have. Finally, she mentions letters from Spain that she has not received, and specifies that that all correspondence be directed to the ambassador of Spain in France because the mails are unreliable. Ana signs as his "unworthy daughter and subject." Probably because of the letter format and its distinguished recipient, this narrative is informative and mostly positive, with few criticisms of the host culture and none of her companions, whom she does not identify by name with the exception of Ana de San Bartolomé. Like other such narratives, it focuses on the founding of religious community from the perspective of lived experience, and in this case the writing and the experience are simultaneous.

Catalina del Espíritu Santo: el Monasterio de Nuestra Señora de la Quietación

The geographic, linguistic, and cultural differences evident in Ana de San Bartolomé's and Ana de Jesús's narratives occasionally involve violent dislocation in other texts. In her *relación* of the founding of the Monasterio de Nuestra Señora de la Quietación in Lisbon, Catalina del Espíritu

Santo, a member of this Franciscan convent, describes the flight of a group of nuns who had been uprooted and literally chased by "heretics" from four different sites in Flanders until they arrived in the welcoming Catholic culture of Portugal where Philip II founded a convent for them. Dedicated to Sister Margarita de la Cruz, Philip II's niece, this narrative was written in 1627 and focuses on the persecution and exile from homeland of Franciscan friars and nuns from Flanders between the years 1566 and 1583.[39] It also reiterates the transnational bond of Catholicism across territorial and cultural borders.[40] In the dedication Catalina expresses her gratitude at having arrived in "such a peaceful and Catholic country as Portugal, where we can serve God and live according to our profession in peace and quiet."[41]

Catalina del Espíritu Santo includes some fairly graphic details of the physical as well as the psychological persecution suffered by the Low Country nuns. The daughter of Luis Carrillo, governor of the duchy of Brabant, and a member of the Poor Clares convent at Hoochstrat, she was the target of a possible kidnapping and ransom by an unnamed Spanish hidalgo and rebel who had aligned himself with the Protestant Prince of Orange, and so special care was taken to protect her. Although Catalina occasionally singles out a particular member, for the most part it is the group of refugee nuns representing the bravery and spiritual integrity of orthodox Catholicism who are at the center of this story. The narrative contains many descriptions of the suffering and martyrdom of members of the Franciscan order, both males and females, in Flanders and might easily be considered anti-Protestant propaganda as well as a chronicle of the founding of the Portuguese convent: "In this respect the work follows a Manichean rhetoric of good and evil with no shades of grey, as in popular propaganda leaflets" (Baranda: 73). Unlike the narratives of Teresa and Ana de San Bartolomé, there is no foregrounding of personal experience and much of the persecution Catalina describes was not actually witnessed by her. The narrative begins with a Prologue and ends with an Epilogue by her ex-confessor, Juan de las Llagas, both of which reiterate the anti-Protestant propaganda of the narrative they frame. According to Catalina's dedication to Margarita de la Cruz, Father de las Llagas had lent much support to the convent of refugee nuns and had encouraged Catalina to write the story of its founding.

In chapters 11 and 12 of her *relación*, Catalina describes the arrival in Portugal of nuns from Antwerp whose convent had been destroyed by Protestants and also another group of nuns from Brabant. There are details of their departure from Flanders and arrival, first in Santander, and then in Bilbao, where they were well received, but had to provide food for themselves and the priests who accompanied them. Previously they had attempted to seek shelter in Rouen, France, but the Franciscan order of Poor Clares there followed the Rule established by Sister Collette and therefore did not welcome the displaced and wandering nuns from Flanders.[42] However, the writer presents this group of fleeing nuns as resourceful. Upon learning that Philip II was in Lisbon, they prevailed upon his generosity and well-known religious fervor to help them on their way to Portugal. Despite the dangers of sailing on a ship that was small and loaded with heavy cargo, with the help of divine providence they reached Portugal and were met by a group of Capuchin monks who took them to their monastery where they were generously received. Catalina describes in the third person her own arrival in Lisbon in 1582 at the royal command of Philip II and mentions her role as an interpreter for the Flemish refugee nuns who did not know Portuguese.

Throughout this tale of arrivals and uprootings, Catalina emphasizes Philip II's generosity and compassion and that of members of the Spanish royal family Princess Margarita de la Cruz and Archduke Alberto, and even describes Philip as shedding tears at the plight of the long-suffering nuns. After all their wanderings, the refugee nuns had found peaceful sanctuary in Portugal. In one scene the Flemish nuns are invited to dine at the royal palace in Lisbon with

Philip, who speaks to each one personally with the help of an interpreter (probably Catalina), expressing sympathy for the distress they have undergone in their wanderings. In addition, he promises to help them and sustain them with donations, a promise that Catalina affirms has been kept to the present day (1627) through the generosity of the royal family. There is a description of the lavish procession accompanying the Flemish nuns to the Convento de Nuestra Senora de la Gloria in Lisbon where they stayed for four years. However, Catalina describes the site as very unhealthy ("muy enfermo") and they are moved to Alcántara, the site of the Convento de Nuestra Señora de la Quietación where they remained. This part of the narrative concludes with a list of the names of the professed Franciscan nuns and novices from Flanders who established the new community of exiled Poor Clares in Portugal. There is no description of the entrance into this new convent.

Catalina del Espíritu Santo ends her narrative with a "Petition and Charitable Plea" to the nuns at the Alcántara convent in which she identifies herself as the only remaining member of the original group of "wandering nuns" (*monjas peregrinas*). From this position of seniority, she exhorts the current residents of the convent to observe the vows of poverty, obedience, humble subjection to God's will, and disengagement from self that underlie monastic life. The inclusion of this "charitable plea" creates the impression that the 1627 community may be somewhat lax in its observance of monastic austerity, perhaps less committed to the sacrifices of cloistered life than the long-suffering founders.

The Spanish Capuchin foundation in Sardinia

On July 8, 1673, five Capuchin nuns from the Convento de la Concepción in Madrid arrived in Sássari, Sardinia to found the first Capuchin convent there. Although there is no official narrative of the foundation, two of the nuns—María Isabel Cándida (Carmona) and María Teresa (Morán)—wrote autobiographies at the request of Miguel Villa, their confessor in the new convent, and were the subjects of biographies by other co-founders and Sardinian novices.[43] There are also biographies of other co-founders, Mother María Josefa (Muñoz) and the abbess, Mother María Juana Francisca (Osorio) as well as a series of Cándida's letters and papers that she left written. Although the biographical writings contain many of the idealizing elements of hagiography, they also provide information about the motives and aspirations of the five women. All had come from the interior of Spain and may not have ever seen the sea, yet were moved by their fervent spirit and love" (*ferviente espíritu y amor*) to undertake a long sea journey to an unknown island that they believed to be a "land of barbarians" (*tierra de bárbaros*), where they would achieve the crown of martyrdom for their efforts. As Marina Romero Frías observes, the five women share certain characteristics: all were born in Spain, belonged to a privileged class, were educated in the fear of God, and felt the religious vocation from a very young age (Romero Frías: 1160–1161).

The idea for the Sardinian foundation arose in 1667. As a result of her religious fervor, Cándida had experienced an intuition that "my body will not rest here [in Madrid]."[44] Her words inspired the abbess Juana Francisca, who "was always anxious to make foundations and she imitated the holy mother Teresa de Jesús, who was her relative."[45] The abbess consulted with Cándida about the most appropriate nuns for this mission. Unlike other foundations these women were all from the same community, knew each other well, and formed a dedicated group. They enlisted the assistance of Don Manuel de Araújo, the Inquisitor of Sardinia and all were convinced that the foundation would take place successfully. Even before their departure from Spain, however, the trials and tribulations of establishing a new cloister in an alien context became evident to the aspiring founders.

As often occurred in establishing new religious communities, the residents of the selected foundation site were not disposed to accept the new convent and for two years the Spanish Capuchins received discouraging letters from Sássari. Political circumstances on the island contributed to the continuing delay of the foundation. The Marquis of Camarasa, the Spanish viceroy of the island, supported the foundation, but was assassinated as a result of his possible involvement in the murder of a political opponent, the Marquis of Láconi. In addition to political conflict, other conditions such as plague, counterfeiting, increasing banditry, and absenteeism of legal authorities made Sardinia an unpropitious site for a religious foundation.[46] Perhaps as a result of this discouraging situation, Cándida lost her confidence in the foundation and describes herself as unworthy of this daunting undertaking: "So I began to withdraw from dealing with them (the future co-founders). I found myself in a continuous torment, unable to tolerate myself."[47] Her narrative ends abruptly in 1669.

Teresa's autobiography also reflects the hardship of the seven-year delay between the ideation of the new cloister and its realization. Referring to the many obstacles that arose, she calls the situation a "camino de espinas" ("path of thorns"). Her narrative is, in general, more dramatic than Candida's with many references to visions, trances, and interior voices. After many imagined battles with the devil, who, in her view, tries to impede the foundation, Teresa experiences a post-communion vision in which the Lord reveals,

> Now there is a house (convent) and it was where in another time there had been one of nuns of his servant Benedict. With great contentment because of my certainty I told this to our Mother Abbess. And after a short time a letter came to Madrid that said the same thing about the house being in other times of Benedictine nuns from Pisa, with which we were all very content and it facilitated the licenses (for the foundation).[48]

After one of her visions, her confessor, Father Villa, was pleased and stated that "this must be written for the glory of God."[49]

Unlike the nun-autobiographers Cándida and Teresa, whose writing exhibits the topical humility frequently employed by women religious, their biographers, both Spanish and Sardinian, exalt their subjects' exemplary virtues. They cite specific instances and anecdotes in which Teresa, Cándida, and Juana Francisca exhibited generosity, humility, and piety among other traits, and they also praise their strength in the illnesses and penitence they suffered. Of Juana Francisca's capacities as abbess they state: "She had a particular gift and grace for governance, as all her daughters and subjects both in Madrid and Sardinia reveal, praising her great virtues and admirable prudence."[50] Although both the biographies and the autobiographies use the discourses of hagiography, all of these works testify to the excellence of the foundation/convent community itself as seen in the lives of its founders.

Despite the many impediments described in their narratives, after an adventurous journey by sea the group of five Spanish Capuchins arrived safely in Sássari where they were joyfully received by the authorities and the population in general. The joy was marred, however, by the death of the youngest member of the group, Inés (de León) shortly after they had arrived on the island.

Conclusion

The narratives examined here reveal many characteristics of foundation narratives in general. More specifically, each one reflects the conjunction of the personal and the political which marked the lives of its authors and the communities that they helped to establish. The separation of the cloister and the world outside its walls is a myth that all of these writers contradict.[51] In fact, the success of all of the foundations depends completely on the intersection of the secular and the religious communities. As is evident throughout these stories, the founding members of convents were constantly engaged in politics with both religious and secular authorities, and as in all politics, personalities and personal relationships come into play. In the case of Teresa de Ávila, Ana de San Bartolomé, and Ana de Jesús, their bond as founding members of the Discalced Carmelite order and its convents within and beyond Spain is apparent in the texts of all three. That is, there is a sense of the Holy Mother Teresa's commitment to her spiritual daughters in her writing, and her life and writing are present throughout the narratives of the other two. In all five cases the writers' lives are inseparably intertwined with the social and political circumstances of the time in which they write, a time which did not look kindly upon religious reform, particularly as carried out by women.

Catalina del Espíritu Santo expresses a similar bond with members of the Franciscan order, and specifically those who suffered the trauma of religious persecution. The intersection of religious and worldly matters is apparent in the physical conflict between Protestants and Catholics and the involvement of earthly authorities. Catalina's text, although it documents extreme circumstances, is similar to the others it in that it foregrounds the solidarity among members of a group who believe themselves to be favored by divine preference and who are pitted against more powerful opponents, in this case the Protestants of Flanders.

The five Capuchin nuns who founded in Sardinia experienced similar problems in the resistance they initially encountered to their convent and in the situation of political unrest that marked their foundation site. Like the other founders in this section, their commitment to the Sardinian community was fueled in part by their absolute faith in divine approval of their mission as well as their desire to expand their order.

All of the foundation stories involve elements of adventure and even heroism in the determination of their protagonists to surmount all odds. In some cases, the danger these women faced was real, as in the Low Countries. In other cases, the perception of other cultures as heretical and therefore less civilized than Spain augmented the fear of the unknown associated with the foreign missions, as in the case of Sardinia. Their final success rests upon the protagonists' perseverance and commitment to their mission as well as divine intervention/assistance. Like other foundation narratives, these five foreground the experience of community building within a specific social and cultural context. While some of them privilege the personal, they all testify to the collective experience of displacement, relocation, and continuation of a religious community based on shared values and experience.

Notes

1 "No se puede comparar la Europa de principios del siglo XVII con la América de los primeros años de la colonización. Las monjas carmelitas, a su llegada a los nuevos territorios donde se implantan no tienen que civilizar ni colonizar, simplemente reafirmar con su presencia una fe que que se ha visto puesta en entredicho por casi un siglo de luchas religiosas. Su labor será hacer presente el nuevo catolicismo surgido de Trento y ahuyentar el fantasma protestante;en algunos aspectos esta tarea será más difícil que convencer a las masas indígenas sin ningún tipo de referencias" (29–30).
2 There are several excellent studies of St. Teresa's identity as a writer by, among others, Carrera, García de la Concha, Rossi, Slade, and Weber.
3 See the classic study by Weber: 42–76.
4 "Ya fue Dios servido que nos fue a ver. Yo le dije el agravio que nos hacía. En fin, me dijo que fuse lo que quisiese, y como lo quisiese; y desde ahí adelante siempre nos hacía merced en todo lo que se

nos ofrecía y favor" (*Obras completes*: 591). With the exception of *Libro de fundaciones*, all English translations are the author's.

5 "Y para hacer muchos monesterios de pobreza sin renta, nunca me falta corazón y confianza, con certidumbre que no le ha Dios de faltar" (*Obras completes*: 574).
6 "De mí os sé decir que fue muy grande. (el consuelo). En especial me le dio ver que dejava a las hermanas en casa tan buena y en buen puesto, y conocido el monesterio. Y sobre todo me dio alegría haver gozado de los trabajos" (*Obras completes*: 593).
7 Both Slade (107–109) and Weber (23, 156–157) have noted the seeming schism in Teresa's self-representation in this work.
8 "Buscamos prestado aderezo para decir misa, y con un oficial nos fuimos a boca de noche para tomar la posesión [. . .]Y con harto miedo mío anduvimos toda la noche aliñándolo" (*Obras completes*: 569).
9 "Llegamos a Medina del Campo, víspera de nuestra Señora de Agosto, a las doce de la noche; apeámonos en el monesterio de Santa Ana por no hacer ruido, y a pie nos fuimos a la casa. Llegadas a la casa, entramos en un patio. Las paredes harto caídas me parecieron [. . .] Visto el portal, havía bien que quitar tierra de él, a teja varia, las paredes sin embarrar" (*Obras completes*: 526–527).
10 Slade (111–120) compares *Foundations* to the letters of Cortés to Charles V, basing the analogy on the mixture of evangelical and political motives in both writers.
11 Grundy's analysis of the situation of English nuns writing history (126–138) provides many analogies with Spanish nun-chroniclers.
12 "aunque no se caminava las siestas, yo os digo, hermanas, que como havía dado todo el sol a los carros, que era entrar en ellos como en un purgatorio. Unas veces con pensar en el infierno, otras pareciendo se hacia algo y padecía por Dios, ívan aquellas hermanas con gran contento y alegría. Porque seis que ívan conmigo eran tales almas que me parece me atreviera a ir con ellas a tierra de turcos" (*Obras completes*: 588).
13 "y hasta ahora no nos dejan de regalar algunas personas, ni dejará nuestro Señor padecer a sus esposas, si ellas le sirven como están obligadas" (*Obras completes*: 631).
14 See Sarah Owens' essay in this volume on the experiences of five Spanish Capuchin nuns in Argentina.
15 For an introduction to Ana de San Bartolomé's life and writings, see Urkiza, "Introducción" vol. 1. Also, Donahue: 6–25 and Howe: 118–141.
16 Ana refers to the period of military conflict and civil unrest between French Catholics and Protestants or Huguenots (1562–1598) often referred to as the French Wars of Religion.
17 On Bérulle and French spirituality, see Deville, chapter 3.
18 On the tension between Spanish Discalced Carmelite nuns and French superiors, see Diefendorf: 110–121.
19 "Yo fue a él otro día y díjele: 'qué tienen estas ermanas que no me ablan?' Dijo; 'No es menester que os ablen que ya bien pueden pasar sin vos. Yo se lo he mandado. [. . .] Ellas andarán por lo que yo las dijere, que vuestro espíritu no es para ellas, que es contrario a la Francia y andays contra nosotros. Yo no quiero que tratéis con ellas, vuestro espíritu no es bueno, que es espíritu del diablo" (Ana de San Bartolomé, *Defensa de la herencia teresiana*, Urkiza ed., I.410).
20 "Yo me enojava en mi ynterior con este Berul. Y como no tenía otro confessor ni me le quería dar, aunque lo pedía, esto me apretava el Corazon, que me parecía estava en pecado" (Ana de San Bartolomé, *Defensa de la herencia teresiana*, Urkiza, ed., I.411).
21 " Yo le dije que eso no, y él dijo que él sabía las cosas tan bien como yo. Yo le dije que eso no, que él sabría bien de sus letras, mas que no tenia esperiencia como yo de las cosas de Rrelisión y que no consentiría en ello Él me dijo que España fue una cosa y Francia otra" (Ana de San Bartolomé, *Autobiografía*, Urkiza, ed., I.348–349).
22 "Asta aora no avía hecho nada; aora que se me ofrece esta occasion, daráme escrúpulo vyr la cruz" (Ana de San Bartolomé, *Defensa de la herencia teresiana*, Urkiza, ed., I.412).
23 For Ana de Jesús's role in the Discalced Carmelite reform, see Moriones.
24 Unlike some of the other founding nuns, Ana de Jesús had volunteered for the French mission. Her situation within the Discalced Carmelite order was tenuous as a result of the reciprocal animosity between her and the Provincial General, Nicolás Doria. Her difficulties continued in France with Bérulle. See Manero Sorolla: 652.
25 Diego de Yepes (1530–1613), a member of the Hieronymite order, had been confessor to both Phillip II and St. Teresa prior to becoming bishop of Tarazona in 1599.
26 See Manero Sorolla: 648.

27 "y puedo decir milagrosamente llegamos vivas; de 300 leguas que havía de camino, sin duda anduvimos más de las 100 a pie, con tan gran facilidad, que nunca nos durava el cansancio, ni le sentí hasta que entramos en tierra de Francia y vi tan mal tratado el Santísimo Sacramento" (Manero Sorolla: 657).
28 "Casi todos los de estos pueblos eran hereges y veíaseles en los semblantes, que los tienen muy de condenados" (Manero Sorolla: 658).
29 St. Dionysius (Denis in French), according to legend, was a martyr and first bishop of Paris. Beheaded in 250, his remains are interred in the St. Denis Abbey.
30 "de reliquias no se puede dezir, engastadas en piedras preciosísimas [. . .] que es nonada lo del Escorial con lo que aquí hay" (Manero Sorolla: 660).
31 "si no la huvieren hecho seglares con piedad y ygnorancia, porque es cierto han gastado en ella más de 60,000 ducados y no está acavada" (Manero Sorolla: 660). St. Teresa's rejection of material comforts differed greatly from the French idea of convent life.
32 "Su Magestad me ha dado salud desde que salí de España para poder andar en ella, aunque tan sin spiritu, que parece dios y el alma se me quedaron allá" (Manero Sorolla: 664).
33 Despite the similarities of some of their experiences with Bérulle, the two Anas held very different opinions on matters of order governance. "Las disensiones entre las dos Anas se manifestarán a los pocos meses de la llegada a París" (Manero Sorolla: 663).
34 See Manero Sorolla: 662n.46.
35 "Es mucho el amor que nos han tomado, y es milagro, porque tienen poquísimo a los de España. Y assí se han espantado de ver tan gran amistad y conformidad entre nosotras y sus francesas. Affirman no ay hijas de un padre y madre en este reyno que assí se amen" (Manero Sorolla: 663).
36 As Manero Sorolla observes, Yepes would have been aware of some of these difficulties (653).
37 "Aquí en París, que es un mundo entero, grandes aparencias tienen de christiandad. La frecuencia de sacramentos parece lo de la primitive yglesia, y assí se espantan de que nosotras no comulguemos más."
38 Ana is referring to the nuns at the Discalced Carmelite convent in Tarazona, founded by Yepes in 1600.
39 Princess Margaret of Austria (1567–1633) was the daughter of the Emperor Maximilian II and his wife, María of Austria. She became a Poor Clare nun (Margarita de la Cruz) and entered the Convento de las Descalzas Reales in Madrid where she died at the age of sixty-six. She is buried in the convent.
40 Baranda attributes the forty-year gap between events described and writing to the renewal of hostilities between Catholics and Protestants in the Low Countries after 1621: "In a way, bringing the history to light must be considered part of the propaganda campaign that helped to create a favourable public opinion about war as resources and men were demanded to maintain it" (72–73).
41 "en tierra tan pacífica y católica como es Portugal, donde con descanso y quietud podemos servir a Dios y vivir conforme a nuestra profesión" (Catalina del Espíritu Santo: 1–2).
42 Sister Colette (1381–1447) was a reformer of the Poor Clare order of Franciscan nuns. She founded seventeen convents, often referred to as Colettine convents, throughout what are now France and Switzerland.
43 Relación que la Madre Sóror María Isabel Cándida escribe de su vida (An Account that Mother Sister María Isabel Cándida wrote of her life, Relación de la sobredicha sor María Theresa sobre su Vida, trasladada de lo que ella mesma en parte ditó a su Padre Confesor y en parte escribió de su puño (An Account of the Aforementioned Sister María Theresa about her life), taken in part from what she herself dictated to her Father Confessor and in part wrote with her own hand). See Romero Frías: 1161 for the titles of biographies.
44 "Al fin no descansará aquí mi cuerpo" (Romero Frías: 1171).
45 "anhelava siempre hazer fundaciones e imitaba a la santa madre Teresa de Jesús, al fin era su parienta" (Romero Frías: 1171).
46 For a discussion of the situation of the island, including the circumstances surrounding the two political assassinations, see Galiñanes and Romero Frías.
47 "Y así poco a poco me fui retirando de su trato. Me hallaba en un continuado tormento sin poderme sufrir a mí misma" (Romero Frías: 1176).
48 "ya había casa y que era donde en otro tiempo lo había sido de su siervo Benito. Yo, con el contento, por la seguridad que tenia, se lo dije a nuestra Madre Abadesa. Y de ahí a poco tiempo, vino una carta a Madrid [. . .] en que decía lo mismo que había casa donde en otros tiempos lo había sido de Monjas Benitas que llamaban de Pisa, conque quedamos todos muy contentos y fue parte para facilitar las licencias" (Romero Frías: 1179–1180).

49 "que se había de escribir esto para gloria de Dios" (Romero Frías: 117). Romero Frías suggests that Villa may have had aspirations to be spiritual director to another Teresa of Ávila (1162).
50 "tenia don y gracia particular para el gobierno,como lo confiesan todas sus hijas y súbditas así de Madrid como las de Cerdeña haciéndose lenguas de sus grandes virtudes y admirable prudencia" (Romero Frías: 1170).
51 See Lehfeldt: 175–216.

Works cited

Ana de Jesús. "Carta a un religioso de España. París 8 de marzo de 1605." Ed. Pilar Manero Sorolla. *Bulletin Hispanique* 95 (1993): 656–666.

———. *Escritos y documentos*. Ed. A. Fortes y R. Palmero. Burgos: Monte Carmelo, 1996.

Ana de San Bartolomé. *Obras completas de la Beata Ana de San Bartolomé*. Ed. Julián Urkiza, O.C.D. 2 vols. Rome: Teresianum, 1981.

———. *Autobiography and other writings*. Ed. and trans. Darcy Donahue. Chicago: U Chicago P, 2008.

Arenal, Electa, and Stacey Schlau, eds. *Untold Sisters: Hispanic Nuns in Their Own Works*. Trans. Amanda Powell. Albuquerque: U New Mexico P, 1989.

Baranda, Nieves. "Beyond Political Boundaries: Religion as Nation in Early Modern Spain." *Women Telling Nations*. Ed. Amanda Saez, Francesca Scott, and Susan van Dijk. Amsterdam and New York: Rodopi, 2014: 63–83.

Carrera, Elena. *Teresa of Avila's Autobiography. Authority, Power and Self in Mid-sixteenth Century Spain*. London: Modern Humanities Research Association and Maney, 2005.

Catalina del Espíritu Santo. *Relación de cómo se ha fundado en Alcántara de Portugal junto a Lisboa, el muy devoto monasterio de N.S. de la Quietación para monjas peregrinas venidas de la Provincia de Alemania Baxa, después de los hereges las aver perseguido y desterrado de tierras por quatro vezes. Prólogo y epílogo de fray Juan de las Llagas*. Lisbon: Pedro Craesbeeck, 1627.

Deville, Raymond. *The French School of Spirituality: an introduction and reader*. Trans. Agnes Cunningham. Pittsburgh: Duquesne UP, 1994.

Diefendorf, Barbara. *From Penitence to Charity. Pious Women and the Catholic Reformation in Paris*. Oxford: Oxford UP, 2006.

Galiñanes, Marta and Marina Romero Frías, "Relación de los Suzessos de Zerdeña desde el principio de las cortes que zelebró el Marqués de Camarassa hasta su muerte." *España y el mundo mediterráneo a través de las relaciones de sucesos (1500–1750)*. Ed. Pierre Civil, Francoise Cremoux, and Jacobo Sanz. Salamanca: Universidad de Salamanca, 2008: 191–202.

García de la Concha, Víctor. *El arte literario de Santa Teresa*. Barcelona: Icaria, 1984.

Grundy, Isobel. "Women's History? Writings by English Nuns." *Women, Writing, History, 1640–1740*. Ed. Isobel Grundy and Susan Wiseman. Athens, GA: U Georgia P, 1992.

Howe, Elizabeth Teresa. *Autobiographical Writing by Early Modern Hispanic Women*. Burlington, VT: Ashgate, 2015.

Lehfeldt, Elizabeth. *Religious Women in Golden Age Spain: The Permeable Cloister*. Burlington, VT: Ashgate, 2005.

Lowe, K.J.P. *Nuns' Chronicles and Convent Culture in Renaissance and Counter-Reformation Italy*. Cambridge: Cambridge UP, 2004.

Manero Sorolla, Pilar. "Ana de Jesús: Cronista de la fundación del primer Carmen Descalzo de París." *Bulletin Hispanique* 93 (1993): 647–672.

Moriones de la Visitación, Ildefonso. *Ana de Jesús y la herencia teresiana*. Rome: Edizioni del Teresianum, 1968.

Owens, Sarah, ed. and trans. *Journey of Five Capuchin Nuns (by Madre María Rosa)*. Toronto: Iter, Centre for Renaissance and Reformation Studies, 2009.

Peers, Allison, ed. and trans. *The Complete Works of St. Teresa of Jesus*. Vol. III. London: Sheed and Ward, 1973.

Romero Frías, Marina. "Emprendiesen obra tan ardua de tierras tan distantes. Historia de la fundación y de las fundadoras del convento de las capuchinas de Sássari (Cerdeña) sacado de los escritos de las mismas." *Las voces de las diosas, IX*. Ed. Milagro Martín Clavijo, Bartoletta Salvatore, et.al. Seville: ArCiBel: 1157–1184.

Rossi, Rosa. *Teresa de Ávila. Biografía de una escritora*. Barcelona: Icaria, 1984.

Slade, Carole. *Teresa of Ávila: Author of a Heroic Life*. Berkeley: U California P, 1995.

Teresa de Jesús. *Obras completas*. Ed. Efrén de la Madre de Dios, O.C.D. and Otger Steggink, O.C.D. Madrid: Biblioteca de Autores Cristianos, 1974.

Torres Sánchez, Concepción. *Conventualismo femenino y expansión contrarreformista en el siglo XVII: el Carmelo Descalzo español en Francia y Flandes (1600–1650)*. Florence: European University Institute, 1997.

Weber, Alison. *Teresa of Ávila and the Rhetoric of Femininity*. Princeton: Princeton UP, 1989.

Winston-Allen, Anne. *Convent Chronicles: Women Writing About Women and Reform in the Late Middle Ages*. University Park, PA: Pennsylvania State UP, 2004.

20

TRANSOCEANIC RELIGIOUS

Sarah E. Owens

Travel in the early modern world was not an easy task. While travelers on the Iberian Peninsula had the relative luxury of following royal roads, they still faced the threat of storms, flooding, and the ever-present bandits that roamed the countryside. Even traversing the short distance from Madrid to the small city of Plasencia involved a two-day trip by horse and carriage, whereas today it would take a few hours by car.[1] Once in the Americas, most routes were little more than uneven trails winding along rivers and crossing mountain passes. Travelers had to make their way through dense forests and vast swaths of lonely grasslands. Most journeys required participants to mount mules and, in some cases, carry themselves on their own two feet. Ocean voyages exposed sailors and passengers to perilous storms; warfare sank ships and took prisoners, while pirates and corsairs looted and pillaged sailing vessels. In the seventeenth century, the average ship voyage from Spain to New Spain (Mexico) could take four to six weeks, while the Manila Galleon—the transpacific crossing from Acapulco to Manila—averaged three to four months. Wind patterns, strong currents, and violent storms could add months onto any voyage.[2] Most travelers boarded one of the mercantile ships that comprised the Fleet of Indies. These convoys of ships, especially the route between Spain and Mexico, plied together for protection against enemy attacks. The yearly Manila galleons, on the other hand usually consisted of only one or two ships.

Despite these obstacles, small groups of early modern religious women left the relative comfort of their cloistered convents to establish new nunneries all over the Iberian empire. The strict reforms of the Council of Trent (1545–1563) dictated that all Catholic convents should be cloistered, but there were several exceptions to those decrees forced by warfare, infectious diseases, and natural disasters such as the threat of earthquakes.[3] Another reason to venture outside the relative comfort and safety of religious communities was the foundation of new convents. To that end, many religious orders wanted to expand their communities into Spain's global empire: first to Mexico, the Caribbean, and Central America, and then down South America to Peru, Chile, Argentina, and as far afield as the Philippines and China. Male religious orders, mainly the Franciscans, Dominicans, Augustinians, and later the Jesuits, had already established a strong presence in the New World. Their early missionary enterprise, focused on converting native peoples, came on the heels of the conquistadors' often-violent conquest of new territories. As the missionary enterprise began to gain traction, these same friars saw a need for female convents, in the beginning as a place for the unmarried daughters of the original conquistadors, and later as a place to cultivate potential saints to bolster their individual orders.

This chapter provides a broad panoramic view of the religious women who voyaged from Spain to the Americas while at the same time putting pen to paper. By no means is it meant to be exhaustive, especially because, as the field is still relatively new, there might be other women who may later be added to this list. The study sets out to shed light on literary nuns from three religious orders: Franciscans, Capuchins, and Bridgettines. These were not the only monastic orders that traveled to the Americas. Indeed, some *beatas* or third order religious women ventured across the Atlantic. For example, in 1530, Mexico City's first bishop, Juan de Zumárraga,[4] requested the help of beatas from Spain to teach young indigenous girls at a school in Texcoco, Mexico. Other Spanish beatas traveled to Mexico to teach at indigenous schools, but this endeavor was short lived since all these schools were closed by 1540 (Holler: 1–2). Finding references to these women, let alone their writings, is not always easy, but one way to uncover the transatlantic travels is to wade through the thousands of pages of passenger lists at the Archive of Indies in Seville, Spain. This is a difficult task because ship's manifests are often incomplete and do not always list women's names, especially when traveling in groups or as family units. Despite this, there is a reference, for instance, to Doña Leonor Pantoja, a Dominican nun who traveled with nine other nuns (all mentioned by name) to the island of Hispaniola in 1560 (Romera: 83).[5] At least one other order sent nuns from Spain to the Americas. In 1754, thirteen nuns, mostly from the Basque region of Spain, journeyed to Mexico to set up a community called the Order of Mary (known as *La Enseñanza*).[6] Other common orders such as the Carmelites opted not to send Spanish nuns across the Atlantic. Instead they used local women of Spanish descent to establish their convents in the Americas. Because of logistical and financial reasons, it was thought to be easier for nuns to travel by land than it was to bring them on long ship voyages from Spain. Some overland journeys could also be long and arduous. For instance, three nuns from a convent in Chuquisaca (modern-day Sucre, Bolivia) traveled by foot and mule a distance of over one thousand miles, across the Andes, to found the first Carmelite convent in Santiago, Chile in 1690 (*El arca*: 40–41).

The three orders studied in this essay already had a firm tradition of travel. The Italian Saint Clare of Assisi founded the first, the Franciscan order of Poor Clares in the thirteenth century. Convents of Franciscan nuns in Italy spread to France and Spain, and eventually as far afield as the Philippines (1621) and Macao, China (1634). Undoubtedly it was one of the most important orders in sixteenth- and seventeenth-century Spain. The second order discussed here, the Capuchins, was founded in the first half of the sixteenth century by a Spanish woman from Cataluña, María Lorenza Llonc, in Naples, Italy. She based her order on the strict First Rule of Saint Clare. Soon thereafter, Capuchins fanned out to the rest of Western Europe and later from Spain to Mexico (1665), Peru (1713), and Guatemala (1725). Of these three, the Bridgettine Order was the smallest in Spain.[7] It is unique because it began in Scandinavia in the fourteenth century, and then spread all over Eastern Europe, including Poland, Estonia, and Ukraine. In Western Europe, Bridgettine nunneries were set up in England, the Netherlands, Germany, Italy, Portugal, and Spain. After establishing five convents in Spain during the seventeenth century, the order expanded into Mexico in 1744.

The hierarchical structure of religious communities was already set in place before the groups of nuns left Spain. Some orders were stricter than others: The discalced orders, commonly called barefoot nuns, embraced a life of poverty and tried to live from the alms given by benefactors and the local community. The more common calced or shod orders required dowries and often had wealthy patrons who gave large sums of money to the community. They also allowed servants and slaves to cook, clean, and care for the sick. Regardless, a strong abbess would have been chosen to guide the nuns from shore to shore. To some extent, every religious community functioned like a small business; the chain of command, led by a mother abbess but supported by other key offices such as vicaress (a type of vice-abbess), provisioner, treasurer, and turn-keeper enabled a convent to pay its bills, feed and clothe its inhabitants, and interact with the local community. Known as choir or black-veiled nuns, these women not only came from wealthy, noble, and "Old Christian" families, but they were also chosen as teachers and role models for postulants. They also needed to have a basic knowledge of reading, writing, and elementary Latin (Lavrin: 310–311). Poor Spanish women who did not have the money to pay the dowry required by some orders, professed as white-veiled nuns, a secondary status that required them to perform chores and barred them from holding office. Mestiza, black, mulatta, and indigenous women also lived in convents, but they were relegated to the categories of servants and slaves (Arenal and Schlau: 296–297). In short, race and class hierarchies were firmly entrenched in convents in Spain and later this structure was transferred to monastic life in the New World.

The impetus for the establishment of new convents was varied and many of the factors were inextricably entwined. In some cases, as mentioned earlier, local friars wanted to expand their own order by bringing over nuns from Spain. Wealthy local patrons also played a large role in sponsoring new foundations. Pious widows and members of landed families would provide the initial donation of land and capital to start up a new convent. Oftentimes, beatas and other religious wrote countless letters to the Crown citing the need for a permanent convent. These petitions could last decades and in some cases they never came to fruition, as was the case with the Colegio de Santa Potenciana in the Philippines (R. Cruz: 129). Permission from the king, sponsorship from ecclesiastical authorities, conducts of safe passage, in addition to monetary donations to finance the trip, all had to be secured before nuns could leave their cloistered communities.

Convents either selected their candidates through a vote, or the future abbess in consultation with ecclesiastical authorities appointed them. No one was forced to accept these positions. Knowing very well the risks involved in transoceanic travel, and the fact that they would be leaving behind friends and family, these brave women voluntarily left their home communities. Some nuns saw it as an honor and a duty. Others saw it as a possibility to become part of the missionary machinery that allowed many of their male counterparts to preach the gospel to indigenous heathens, and in extreme cases, to become martyrs. In general, the small groups of nuns that left the Iberian Peninsula were young; on the one hand they needed to be in good health so that they could survive the hardships of the journey, and, on the other, they were expected to live a long time so that they could govern the new convent and impart their knowledge of prayer cycles, penance, and other daily routines to new recruits. But several exceptions did exist, as we shall see with Sor Jerónima de la Asunción (1556–1630), who was sixty-four years old when she left for the Philippines.

Founding nuns did not travel alone. Friars and male servants would accompany the women as their escorts. Not only did they protect the women during the journey but they also played other important roles: they bought the supplies for the sea voyages, arranged lodging along the route, and served as mediators between the nuns and local populations. Whenever possible the women tried to keep themselves "cloistered" during their journeys. In addition to maintaining their daily prayers, saying confession and taking communion, they closed carriage curtains and wore their veils in public. It was not always possible to completely separate the nuns from men. Travel by mule caravan and sleeping under the open sky inevitably exposed the women to fellow travelers and indigenous peoples.

Nuns boarded the Spanish ships with other sailors, soldiers, male religious, dignitaries, colonizers, servants, and slaves. Generally religious orders were given cabins in the ship's stern. Friars and servants guarded the door to the cabin, but the nuns would receive visits from the captain, noblemen, and other dignitaries. Ecclesiastical authorities often prohibited fasting during journeys so that the women could keep up their stamina. To prevent fires, Spanish galleons designated communal cookstoves for cooking. One of the servants would be in charge of heating up food and bringing it back to the cabin. Nuns, like other passengers, carried with them their own rations, purchased by their escorts. They brought live chickens for fresh meat, but also dined on dried fish and meats, cheese, "hard tack" (*bizcocho*), garbanzos, rice, olives, and wine. It must be said that many travelers, not just nuns, suffered from extreme seasickness and ate very little. In addition to the lack of fresh fruits and vegetables, which caused scurvy, many travelers disembarked from these journeys weak and malnourished (Pérez-Mallaína: 129–134). The ordained friars, who served as confessors to the women, provided solace in these times of great hardship and often later received permanent appointments as vicars of the new foundations.

Whether the nuns had to bury one of their own sisters at sea, or they celebrated mass on a mountaintop in the Andes, much of what we know about these women comes from their own writings. Indeed, a fascinating consequence of these new foundations was the nuns' interest in documenting the history of their communities. Typically known as convent chronicles or foundation narratives, such texts were at times written under a confessor's mandate, but nuns also encouraged each other to write these narratives. Such works served numerous purposes and cannot always be easily classified as standard chronicles. According to Alison Weber, they could "celebrate the convent, commemorate the lives of beloved sisters, advance a political agenda, praise patrons, or recruit novices" (36). Furthermore, these texts reminded the nuns, young and old alike, of the incredible obstacles that the women faced on the trade routes and waterways of the Iberian empire. It is not always easy to ascertain the exact authorship of the chronicles. Oftentimes, nuns collaborated on the manuscripts, each writing a different section, spanning periods of time that could last decades, even centuries. We need to be careful when applying contemporary notions of authorship to these writings, especially because the concept of plagiarism did not exist in the early modern world. Many authors would "borrow" or quote large sections from another text, often without acknowledging their sources. This was most common with male clerics who used nuns' manuscripts to publish their own works.[8]

In addition to convent chronicles, some of the traveling nuns composed spiritual autobiographies, biographies of exemplary female religious, and, in some cases, lengthy mystical texts. These texts incorporate formulaic structures (hagiographical elements) and discursive strategies (such as the humility topos) common to monastic writing (Myers: vii–viii). For the most part these writings circulated in manuscript form within communities, and in some rare instances they reached the printed page before the twentieth century.[9] Nuns themselves often acted as scribes so that copies could be sent back to the original communities. Even today, small archives held within convents (those that have survived wars, natural disasters, and confiscation of church property) are a good place to search for these texts. Some women wrote letters to their families and spiritual sisters in Spain. Nuns' missives captured their candid reactions to the new elements they encountered, like the different kinds of foodstuffs, and the emotions they experienced, such as the nostalgic longings for their loved ones left behind in the homeland.

The Franciscans

One friar in particular, José de Santa María, played a crucial role in the educational instruction of Sor Ana de Cristo (1565–1634), a Spanish nun who traveled with Sor Jerónima to the Philippines and became her first biographer. Sor Jerónima de la Asunción led a small cohort of nuns to establish the first Franciscan convent in Manila, Philippines, in 1621. We know Sor

Jerónima through her portrait, now in the Prado Museum, painted by the famous Spanish artist Diego de Velázquez when the nuns stopped in Seville on their way to the Spanish coast. The portrait, which portrays the stern abbess clutching a crucifix, captures her intractable desire to found a convent under the strict First Rule of Saint Clare.[10] The entire fifteen-month journey, from 1620 to 1621, required the nuns to travel from Toledo to the port of Cádiz, Spain; sail across the Atlantic to Veracruz; traverse Mexico by mule, and then navigate the Pacific Ocean to their final destination, Manila, in the Philippines. Not all of the women made it to the Philippines: a white-veiled nun died, probably from dysentery, sometime after setting sail from Acapulco.

At the time of their departure, Sor Ana tells us that she knew how to read, but had never learned how to write, a typical situation for many girls in early modern Europe, since reading and writing were taught as two separate skills.[11] During the journey and later in Manila, Fray José taught Sor Ana how to put pen to paper. Between the years 1623 and 1629, she composed a lengthy biography of Sor Jerónima.[12] The 450-folio text has never been published in its entirety.[13] Sor Ana's manuscript offers the present-day reader fascinating details of their travel saga from Toledo to Manila. Her text, however, cannot be labeled a conventional biography. Instead, it is a hybrid text that combines Sor Ana's own voice in the first person and transcriptions from Sor Jerónima's writings (all of which have been lost except for a few letters). The last section of the manuscript contains a compilation of other letters relating to the new convent in Manila and several short biographies of the first nuns to take their vows in the new convent. Despite Sor Ana's lack of formal literary training, and her statement that she had learned to write only later in life (she departed for Manila at age 55), she obviously hailed from a strong auditory culture within her convent; that is, nuns spent a lot of time listening to sermons, Bible passages (often in Latin), books on the lives of saints, and other devotional texts.[14] Sor Ana also possessed a basic knowledge of Latin, signs of which she dispersed throughout her writing. Her manuscript provides important insight into the religious female role models that inspired her to take up the task of biographer. The lives and writings of Saint Teresa of Ávila (1515–1582) and Mother Juana de la Cruz (1481–1534) (author of the *Conorte*), for example, played a formidable role in shaping her narrative of Sor Jerónima. Furthermore, future novices, although divided by two oceans from mainland Spain, would have the opportunity to learn from her writing about their venerable foremothers (Owens, "Monjas españolas": 379–392).

For the modern-day reader, the seven chapters (approximately 40 folios) that Sor Ana devotes to their global passage is the most riveting part of her text. Her description of the shrine of Our Lady of Guadalupe and the miracle that took place on the hill of Tepeyac in Mexico is, to the best of our knowledge, the earliest depiction of this site written by a nun (Owens, "Crossing"):

> The next day's journey in New Spain was to a chapel that they call Our Lady of Guadalupe; we spent the night there. It is a paradise and the image is one of much devotion. It was manifested when Mexico was won and dust was being thrown in the eyes of the enemies. She appeared to an Indian in that place where [the chapel] is now, that is, between two boulders and she told him to have a church built for her. A little fresh water sprang from the ground where her feet had touched. We saw it when we passed by the spot and it is boiling as if over a very large fire. We were given a jug and it tasted salty. Also, some lay women (beatas) who were taking care of the chapel, told us that the Virgin herself asked the Indian for his cloak made of cloth which measured from head to toe. Her image was imprinted on it and then she gave it back to the Indian, telling him to put it in that location where it makes many

miracles. There are more than forty silver lamps [in the chapel] and there are rooms for people who go there to pray novenas.

ff. 89–89v

Sor Ana also puts into sharp relief the women's contacts with indigenous peoples from the Caribbean, Mexico, and the Philippines. Wherever the women set foot, local people came out in droves to see the Spanish nuns. While in Mexico, they stopped at several *doctrinas* (parishes of recently converted indigenous), where local inhabitants adorned the nuns with garlands and crowns of flowers. The nuns, dressed in dark robes and their faces covered with veils, made a stark impression on the Amerindians. According to Sor Ana, rumors spread rapidly that the nuns were Spanish priests, while others believed that they were the priests' wives from Castile. Deeply woven in the fabric of this account is a gendered view offered to the modern reader of these remote outposts of Spain's global empire. The nuns' attitudes towards the local indigenous populations of Mexico and the Philippines provide a barometer with which to measure the imperial enterprise of transporting Catholicism to the Americas.

Some of the other nuns who traveled with Sor Jerónima and Sor Ana to the Philippines also put pen to paper. However, like the writings of many early modern religious women, to this day their works have not been published. One of the nuns, Sor María Magdalena de la Cruz (1575–1653), in addition to enduring all the hardships associated with their initial journey to the Philippines, later became one of the founders of the first Franciscan convent in the Portuguese colony of Macao. This was made possible in part because the Habsburg monarchs jointly ruled both empires between 1580 and 1640 (although Spain and Portugal officially remained separate) and they shared a strong Roman Catholic identity.[15] The Portuguese Franciscan order in Macao and Goa also wanted to replicate the type of community established by Sor Jerónima. Portuguese patrons and donors made repeated requests for the convent, including the captain of the fleet between Macao and Manila, Don António Fialho Ferreira (Sánchez Fuertes: 71). After years of negotiation with Franciscan friars and officials in Manila, in 1633 six nuns and one novice set sail across the South China Sea. The nuns stayed in Macao until 1644 when, due to power struggles between Franciscans and Jesuits (and within the convent itself), magnified by political tensions between Spain and Portugal, three of the Spanish nuns were expelled off the island of Macao (Penalva: 105). Upon expulsion, Sor María Magdalena's storied life reads more like an adventure novel than that of a cloistered nun. On their return trip to Manila, due to fierce winds, the ships had to take refuge off the coast of Cochinchina (Vietnam)—where it appears the whole crew was captured and sentenced to death. Although the circumstances are somewhat murky, the nuns were eventually pardoned and made it safely back to the Philippines.[16] While in Asia, Sor María Magdalena wrote a three-volume mystical treaty called *Floresta Franciscana* and penned her own autobiography (now lost). She also served as convent scribe for at least one other nun: Sor Juana de San Antonio.

Sor Juana de San Antonio (1595?–1661) was one of the original founding nuns that traveled with Sor Jerónima to the Philippines. One of the youngest of the expedition, she left Toledo in her early twenties and took her vows of profession during their stopover in Seville. A few years after arriving in the Philippines, Sor Juana dictated her spiritual autobiography, titled *Noticias de la verdad* (1629), to Sor María Magdalena. This lengthy four-volume set contains very little autobiographical material, but mainly describes Sor Juana's spiritual visions. Despite the fact that she held the position of abbess on several occasions, during the latter days of her life the Inquisition accused Sor Juana of heresy and ordered her to travel to Mexico to face trial. Extremely elderly and frail, even having lost the use of her legs, Sor Juana instead died while imprisoned in Manila ("Proceso").

The Capuchins

The Capuchins sent three separate expeditions to the Americas (Toledo to Mexico, 1665; Madrid to Lima, 1713; and Madrid to Guatemala, 1725) (Baranda Leturio, "Fundación": 173). In 1665, a cohort of six nuns left their convent in Toledo, Spain, to travel to Mexico City, where they established the first Capuchin convent in the New World. Although the women did not write a standard chronicle of their new convent, San Felipe de Jesús, five of the six nuns (one was probably illiterate) wrote hundreds of letters back to their sisters in Toledo and to their confessor, Don Francisco de Villarreal. Instead, Villarreal who accompanied the women from Toledo to Cádiz, took it upon himself to write the history of the foundation. His work, titled *La Thebayda en poblado. El convento de la Concepción capuchina en la Imperial ciudad* was published later in Madrid in 1686. In 1987, a Spanish scholar discovered the nuns' letters stored in a small chest in the attic of the original convent in Toledo.[17] The nuns wrote 488 folios of correspondence between 1655 and 1693. In some of their letters, they affectionately refer to themselves as "the navigators" (*las navegantas*). Like the Franciscan nuns who traveled from Toledo via Mexico and then on to the Philippines, the Capuchins from Toledo took a similar route to Mexico City, also stopping at the shrine of Our Lady of Guadalupe.

The topics of these letters are quite different from the more typical travel chronicles studied in this essay. "The navigators" wrote much more personal letters, never intended for publication or scrutiny by the watchful eye of the Holy Office. Homesickness and cultural shock permeate the letters. At times, the nuns include acerbic criticisms of their surroundings. For example, while waiting in Cádiz for a ship to take them across the Atlantic Ocean, the nuns spent over a month in a Conceptionist convent. Far from praising them, the nuns from Toledo criticize their hosts for withholding food and treating them with cold reserve. At one point, they can only rely on the servant class to provide them sustenance: "A black woman who is very devoted to us has come to our aid, bringing us rolls in her skirt pocket" (41). The topic of food is one that recurs frequently in these Capuchin letters. The women miss their familiar garbanzos and fish stews, and complain bitterly about the spicy cuisine of Mexico that causes upset stomachs. In reference to a blotchy rash that appeared to be shingles, one of the nuns writes: "I said that it was because of the stews; they put lots of pepper and tomato in everything" (82). As modern-day readers, we can learn much about the cultural milieu that the Spaniards encountered in their new community. Chocolate, for example, a widely consumed beverage by pre-Hispanic cultures in Mexico, also became very popular in New Spanish convents. The Spanish nuns viewed the ubiquitous drink with skepticism, depicting the "criollas" (Spanish women born in the Americas) as very lazy, "and when at home always drinking chocolate and *atoles*" (440).

In 1710, a half a century later, another group of Capuchin nuns embarked on a three-year odyssey from their nunnery in Madrid to Lima, Peru. These nuns knew about their Capuchin predecessors who had traveled to Mexico, and who inspired them to leave for Peru. Yet it was a much more difficult undertaking, since they would have to sail down the east coast of South America to Buenos Aires, trek across the Andes to Chile, and then embark on another ship to Peru. Their saga included a stint as prisoners of Dutch corsairs and the death of one of the nuns due to a devastating illness. We know much about their journey since the abbess of the future convent in Lima, Madre María Rosa (1660–1716), wrote a convent chronicle later edited in 1722 by one of her co-founders, Sor Josefa Victoria.[18] Madre María Rosa titled her 414-folio manuscript *Account of the Journey of Five Capuchin Nuns who Traveled from Their Convent in Madrid to Found the Convent of Jesus, Mary, and Joseph in Lima*. There are two extant copies of the manuscript, one in the original convent in Lima, and another at the National Library in Spain.[19] Like many convent chronicles, the text was never intended for publication. Indeed, it did not see print for the first time until the twentieth century.[20] However, María Rosas's prose is well organized and polished. It was obviously meant for consumption by the nuns in Lima and back in Madrid.

Generally, the seventeen chapters follow a clear linear narration. After discussing the precedents for the new foundation, Madre María Rosa describes their travels beginning in 1710 and ending in 1713. Couched between repeated descriptions of prayer cycles and Eucharistic piety, María Rosa livens her prose with portrayals of sites like the Giralda in Seville and observations of sharks and other sea life during their maritime voyage. One of the major obstacles that the nuns faced during their travels was the War of Spanish Succession (1701–1714).[21] Shortly after departing from the port of Cádiz, their Spanish fleet was easily overtaken by Dutch corsairs. The author's patchwork account of events highlights the global fabric of the early modern world and how the once powerful Spanish empire was beginning to wane. It also speaks to the complex interplay between the nuns and the different types of people and situations that they encountered along the route. Madre María Rosa describes the Dutch as brutish thugs that drank beer and beat the Spaniards. Yet, she also acknowledges that she and her sisters remained well cared for by one of the captains who secretly admitted to being a Catholic. After a time as "prisoners" in Lisbon for five weeks—where the Portuguese nuns showered them with gifts and attention—the five Capuchins eventually returned to Spain. Because the Dutch corsairs had stolen all of their documents, the women needed to wait another year and a half in Seville while their father confessor re-secured their travel permits to Peru.

Despite surviving the war and the long sea voyage from Spain to Argentina, death loomed large on these journeys. One of the tragedies that befell the Capuchin nuns still resonates today: breast cancer. Cited by early modern physicians as a common ailment in convents, this chronicle provides tantalizing clues to the treatment of (or lack thereof) and reaction to this implacable foe (Owens, "The Cloister": 323–324). Shortly after disembarking at the port of Buenos Aires, one of the five nuns, Sor María Estefanía, died of a "zaratán" (breast tumor). It had grown so large that the women had trouble removing her habit. The grief-stricken nuns had done their best to comfort their sister, providing her with medicinal cordials and praying for her at her bedside. Madre María Rosa best describes their pain at her passing when she writes: "Our grief and that of our father confessor was beyond words since we had witnessed her leave the cloister only later to die in a foreign land" (64).

Another unique part of Madre María Rosa's account provides a snapshot of the difficult trail from Buenos Aires to Santiago. The rough terrain of the Pampas, vast grasslands between Buenos Aires and Mendoza at the foothills of the Andes, required the women to ride in ox-driven carts and sleep under the open sky. The trip over the mountains was even more difficult because they had to mount mules, and according to the abbess, the nuns had never even ridden a horse before, much less a mule. Madre María Rosa provides a moment of comic relief, however, when she pokes fun at herself: "I had the additional problem of being quite fat, causing the mules to tire easily" (163).

The Bridgettines

The last group of female religious writers to cross the Atlantic to be discussed in this essay was the Bridgettines. These nuns hailed from the Basque country in northern Spain. Their home convent in Vitoria chose six nuns to travel to Mexico City and set up the first Bridgettine nunnery in the Americas in 1744. Like the Capuchins who traveled to Peru, these women also documented their foundation. The narrative, "Chronicle of the Convent of Nuestra Señora de las Nieves Santa Brígida de México" is a perfect example of shared authorship common in female monastic writing.[22] According to Anne Sofie Sivfert, six nuns wrote different sections: the first five between the years 1738 and 1782, and the last by an abbess between 1944 and 1952.[23] The only extant manuscript is divided into 31 chapters with 245 written pages and is located in the Bridgettine convent in Tláhuac, Mexico ("Advertencia": 23–27).[24]

The part of the chronicle that interests us most relates to the nuns' travels from Vitoria to Mexico City. This section is relatively short, covering only three chapters, but this may be attributed to the fact that it was not written by one of the original founders, but instead by the *criolla* nun Sor Isabel Antonia de Señor San Miguel (1715–1782).[25] Nonetheless, the author of this section obviously had access to first-hand accounts from the Basque nuns. She refers to them as "our mothers" (*nuestras madres*) and "their Reverences" (*las Reverendas*) as she weaves together fascinating details of the paths and waterways of their route to Mexico.

Sor Isabel Antonia uses the first person singular and plural to elucidate the hardships that the founders faced in their desire to leave the Iberian Peninsula. The first month of their journey went smoothly. They made several stops, one of which was a visit to the shrine of the Virgin of Atocha in Madrid. Things changed drastically, however, when they reached the coast as war broke out between Spain and England:[26] "And even though the nuns were consoled, being told that the war would soon be over, it did not happen this way and every day felt like a year" (57).[27] Actually, the days turned into months and then into years. All told, the group had to wait four years in Cádiz at the same Discalced Conceptionist Convent as the Capuchins from Toledo had done earlier, before it was deemed safe again for them to board a Spanish vessel.

Sor Isabel Antonia has no qualms about describing the dismal condition of the Spanish fleet. Her criticisms of the ships that were not equipped to fight the Royal British Navy, and then her acerbic depiction of their thirteen-day stay on the island of Puerto Rico, are reminiscent of the Mexican polymath Carlos de Sigüenza y Góngora's work, *Los infortunios de Alonso Ramírez*. In that account, the main character laments the poverty of his native Puerto Rico and the lack of employment in Mexico. After trying to increase his fortune by joining a poorly equipped Spanish vessel, he finds himself and his crewmembers quickly enslaved by a British ship.

Although it is doubtful that Sor Isabel Antonia would have read Sigüenza y Góngora's narrative,[28] she too sheds light on the large fissures starting to erode the Spanish empire. She paints a picture of San Juan as drought-stricken and plagued by death. The nuns took lodgings on the upper floors of the bishop's residence, vacant and in bad repair since the post had not been filled: "The bottom floor was packed with people and some of them were sick. The house was [constructed] in such a way that some of floorboards did not match and you could see the floors below. From the large cracks and holes rose the stench of black vomit causing Their Reverences to suffer the whole night because it was intolerable" (61).

After finally disembarking at the port of Veracruz, the Bridgettines made their way to the capital of New Spain. Like their predecessors, they also stopped at the shrine of Our Lady of Guadalupe. Theirs is yet another account that we can add to the historiography of women who described the shrine. Sor Isabel Antonia makes patent the growing cult of Guadalupe in the mid-eighteenth century when the nuns entered the chapel to see the miraculous image. She writes that they were joined by "a multitude of people from all walks of life, conditions, and ranks" (66). Her text reminds us that nuns, like other early modern travellers, commonly stopped at local chapels, churches, and shrines. Furthermore, local authorities often treated travelling nuns like dignitaries and wanted to show off their sacred sites.[29]

Conclusion

As was common in all new foundations, the difficulties of the long journey did not instantly disappear when the nuns reached their final destinations. Rather, they faced new challenges and difficulties in starting up a convent. The nuns' writings studied in this essay document these obstacles. The Bridgettines, for example, had to spend another whole year in the Conceptionist convent of Regina Coeli in Mexico City while they waited to take possession of their new home. Sor Jerónima in the Philippines fought bitterly with local authorities to transform her convent into a strict version of the order of Poor Clares. Although not in the purview of this study, these sections of the documents provide a privileged view of the Spanish nuns as they competed with rival communities by vying for postulants, courting convent donors, and finding enough funds to finance their mission.

The writings of the Spanish nuns who left their convents on the Iberian Peninsula and sailed on ships across the Atlantic and Pacific oceans are a testament to the bravery exhibited by these remarkable women. Although at times their pages are filled with windy rhetoric endorsed by the Catholic Church, these chronicles, biographies, and letters form a corpus of writing that can teach us much about the worldview of nuns outside the cloister. Among many things, we can learn about life for women on Spanish ships, encounters with native peoples, treatment of slaves and servants, and reactions to exotic new foods and customs. Indeed, there are many avenues of research that may be pursued in these documents. Historians, literary scholars, and anthropologists will find nuggets of information about early modern women on a global stage. There is a wonderful opportunity for specialists in the digital humanities to map out the trajectories of different cohorts of nuns. Interactive databases might list the convents, homes of high-ranking officials, rustic inns, and approximate camping sites where the women spent the night. They could feature the monuments and shrines they visited (like the Giralda in Seville or the shrine of Guadalupe in Mexico), and highlight the rivers, mountains, and oceans they crossed. These new areas of research have the potential to shed light on forgotten women's texts that have yet to be discovered in convent archives. The field is still wide open for more comparative studies between the accounts of these intrepid Spanish nuns and those of other Catholic European nuns who also travelled to distant shores.

Notes

1 This example comes from a group of Capuchin nuns that traveled from Madrid to Plasencia (1636) to set up a new convent (Sáenz de Lezcano: 9–10).
2 The return voyage from Manila to Acapulco would average around six months (Schurz: 262–264).
3 See Lehfeldt for a discussion of the impact of Trent's enclosure decree on convents (175–215).
4 Thanks to Zumárraga the first female convent, "Nuestra Señora de la Concepción" was founded in Mexico City in 1540. He did not bring over nuns from Spain to establish the community. Instead, the first postulants were pious Spanish women already living in the capital.
5 Ida Altman's archival research has also uncovered references to Spanish nuns traveling to Hispaniola to set up the first convent of Saint Clare in Santo Domingo in the 1550s (79n.56).
6 The second generation of *La Enseñanza* nuns wrote a chronicle thirty years after its foundation (*Relación histórica*). See also Lavrin (326).
7 It is formally known as the Order of the Most Holy Savior and originally was founded in Sweden in 1384 by the daughter of Saint Bridget.
8 Ginés de Quesada and Bartolomé Letona both used large sections of Sor Ana de Cristo's manuscript to publish their biographies of Sor Jerónima de la Asunción.
9 See for example, *Relación histórica*. See Baranda Leturio for a discussion on the divulgation of printed conventual texts (*Cortejo*: 158–160).
10 For an analysis of Sor Jerónima and Velázquez's portrait see Tiffany (49–76).
11 See Anne Cruz for definition of literacy (1). See also, A. Cruz's essay in this collection.
12 Sor Ana never gave a title to her manuscript, so I am opting for the same title used in the official *Positio* (papers for the process of beatification), *Historia de Nuestra Santa Madre Jerónima de la Asunción* (*Congregatio*: 648).

13 The *Positio* includes a partial Spanish transcription of the manuscript (*Congregatio*).
14 According to Stephen Haliczer, some early modern Spanish convents incorporated reading aloud into their daily routines. For example, one nun would read aloud a book about a saint while the other nuns sewed (39).
15 For more information on the dual Habsburg monarchy and their overseas policies, see Carla Rahn Phillips (71–75).
16 Their chaplain and escort, Fray Antonio de Santa María wrote a colorful account of their imprisonment for the nuns back in Macao. For a transcription, see Elsa Penalva (151–168). The original is located in the Archivum Romanum Societatis Iesu, Jap-Sin 68.
17 All quotes come from part I. of Emilia Alba González's dissertation; the translations into English are mine. The same author later published her dissertation as a book (*Fundación*). See also Owens, "Food."
18 I have been unable to find her years of birth or death. She took her vows of profession in Madrid in 1702 (Torradeflot Cornet: 165).
19 The quotes for this essay come from the English version of Madre María Rosa's chronicle. See Owens, *Journey*.
20 See Vargas Ugarte (259–381).
21 Fighting broke out all over Europe when Carlos II, the last Habsburg king of Spain, died without an heir.
22 See Donahue for shared authorship among nuns (116–117).
23 Sifvert wrote her doctoral dissertation on the chronicle including a partial transcription of the manuscript.
24 Due to the *Leyes de Reforma* (reform laws) under Benito Juarez, the nuns were forced to leave their first convent in the 1860s, never to return (Sifvert, "Advertencia": 25).
25 Sifvert postulates the Sor Isabel Antonia dictated her section of the chronicle to Sor Benita Francisca, another nun who also authored a section of the manuscript ("Advertencia": 26).
26 The war between Great Britain and Spain, known as the *Guerra del Asiento* in Spanish or The War of Jenkins' Ear in English, lasted between 1738 and 1748, but severe fighting had died down by 1742.
27 All quotes from the manuscript come from Sifvert's edition with Muriel. Translations are mine.
28 Sigüenza y Góngora did write about nuns, and there exists the possibility that Isabel Antonia might have been familiar with his chronicle of the Mexican Conceptionist convent of Jesús María, originally published in 1684 (*Paraíso*).
29 According to Stafford Poole, "By the 1570's Guadalupe had become the principal point of entrance into Mexico City, and it was customary for important figures, such as arriving viceroys and archbishops, to tarry there while being met by reception committees from the city" (50).

Works cited

Alba González, Emilia. *Fundación del Convento de San Felipe de Jesús de Clarisas Capuchinas en Nueva España*. D.F., Mexico: Ediciones Dabar, 2002.

———. "Presencia de América en Toledo: Aportación cultural y social." Unpublished diss. Universidad Complutense de Madrid, 1998. http://dialnet.unirioja.es 4 Feb. 2015.

Altman, Ida. "Spanish Women in the Caribbean (1493–1540)." *Women of the Iberian Atlantic*. Ed. Sarah E. Owens and Jane E. Mangan. Baton Rouge: Louisiana State UP, 2012: 128–147.

Ana de Cristo, Sor. *Historia de Nuestra Santa Madre Jerónima de la Asunción*. Ms. Archivo del Monasterio de Santa Isabel, Toledo. 1623–1629.

Arenal, Electa and Stacey Schlau, eds. *Untold Sisters: Hispanic Nuns in Their Own Works*. Albuquerque: U New Mexico P, 1989.

Baranda Leturio, Nieves. *Cortejo a lo prohibido. Lectoras y escritoras en la España Moderna*. Madrid: Arco, 2005.

———. "Fundación y memoria en las capuchinas españolas de la Edad Moderna." In *Memoria e Comunita Femminili: Spagna e Italia, secc. XV–XVII. Memoria y comunidades femeninas: España e Italia, siglos XV–XVII*. Ed. Gabriella Zarri and Nieves Baranda Leturio. Florence/Madrid: Firenze University Press/UNED, 2011: 169–185.

Congregatio Causis Sanctorum. Manilen, Beatificationis et Canonizationis Ven. Servae Dei Sororis Hieronymae ab Assumptione (in saec. H. Yañez), Fundatricis et primae Abbatissae Monasterii Monialium Excalceatarum S. Clarae Ordinis S. Francisci. . . Positio super Vita et Virtutibus. Rome, 1991.

Crónica del Convento de Nuestra Señora de las Nieves Santa Brígida de México. Eds. Josefina Muriel and Anne Sofie Sifvert. D.F., Mexico: Universidad Nacional Autónoma de México, 2001.

Cruz, Anne. J. "Introduction." *Women's Literacy in Early Modern Spain and the New World*. Ed. Anne. J. Cruz and Rosilie Hernández. Burlington, VT; Farnham, UK: Ashgate, 2011: 1–16.

Cruz, Reginald D. "Servir a Dios en Recogimiento: Religious Life as Woman's Space in the Archdiocese of Manila (1590–1700)." Unpublished diss. University of the Philippines, 2009.

Donahue, Darcy. "Wondrous Words: Miraculous Literacy and Real Literacy in the Convents of Early Modern Spain." *Women's Literacy in Early Modern Spain and the New World*. Ed. Anne J. Cruz and Rosilie Hernández. Burlington, VT; Farnham, UK: Ashgate, 2011: 106–122.

El arca de las tres llaves. Crónica del monasterio de carmelitas descalzas de San José. Santiago: Cochrane, 1989.

Haliczer, Stephen. *Female Mystics in the Golden Age of Spain*. Oxford: Oxford UP, 2002.

Holler, Jacqueline. *Escogidas plantas: Nuns and Beatas in Mexico City, 1531–1601*. (2002). gutenberg-e.org 16 May 2017.

Juana de San Antonio, Sor. *Noticias de la verdad*. 4 vols. Ms. Archivo del Monasterio de Santa Isabel, Toledo. 1629.

Lavrin, Asunción. *Brides of Christ: Conventual Life in Colonial Mexico*. Stanford: Stanford UP, 2008.

Lehfeldt, Elizabeth A. *Religious Women in Golden Age Spain. The Permeable Cloister*. Burlington, VT; Farnham, UK: Ashgate, 2005.

Letona, Bartholomé de. *Perfecta religiosa*. Puebla: Por la viuda de Juan de Borja, 1662.

María Magdalena de la Cruz, Sor. *Floresta franciscana de ilustraciones celestiales cogida al hilo de la oración en la aurora de María . . .*, 3 vols. Ms. Madrid, Archivo Franciscano Ibero-oriental (AFIO), 387/1, 387/2, 387/3. 1640–1647.

María Rosa, Madre. *Fundación del Monasterio de Capuchinas de Jesús, María y José de Lima*. Ms. 9509. Biblioteca Nacional, Madrid. 1722.

Myers, Kathleen Ann. *Neither Saints nor Sinners: Writing the Lives of Women in Spanish America*. Oxford: Oxford UP, 2003.

Owens, Sarah E. "Crossing Mexico (1620–1621): Franciscan Nuns and their Journey to the Philippines." *The Americas* 72.4 (October 2015): 583–606.

——. Editor's Introduction. *Journey of Five Capuchin Nuns*. By Madre María Rosa. Ed. and trans. Sarah E. Owens. "The Other Voice in Early Modern Europe" (OVIEME). Toronto: CRRS & ITER, 2009: 1–42.

——. "Food, Fasting and Itinerant Nuns." *Food and Foodways* 19.4 (2011): 274–293.

——. "Monjas españolas en Filipinas: La formación de lectura y escritura de sor Ana de Cristo." In *Las letras en la celda. Cultura escrita de los conventos femeninos en la España Moderna*. Ed. Nieves Baranda Leturio and María Carmen Marín Pina. Madrid: Iberoamericana /Vervuert, 2014: 379–392.

——. "The Cloister as Therapeutic Space: Breast Cancer Narratives in the Early Modern World." *Literature and Medicine*. 30.2 (Fall 2012): 295–314.

——. *Nuns Navigating the Spanish Empire*. Albuquerque: U New Mexico P, 2017.

Penalva, Elsa. *Mulheres em Macau. Donas Honradas, Mulheres Libres e Escravas (Séculos XVI e XVII)*. Lisbon: Centro de História de Além-Mar/Centro Científico e Cultural de Macau, 2011.

Pérez-Mallaína, Pablo E. *Spain's Men of the Sea. Daily Life on the Indies Fleets in the Sixteenth Century*. Trans. Carla Rahn Phillips. Baltimore, MD: Johns Hopkins UP, 1998.

Poole, Stafford. *Our Lady of Guadalupe. The Origins and Sources of a Mexican National Symbol, 1531–1797*. Tucson: U Arizona P, 1997.

"Proceso y causa criminal contra la madre sor Juana de San Antonio, religiosa de Santa Clara en las islas Filipinas." Archivo General de la Nación, Inquisición 603, No. 3. D.F., Mexico. 1668.

Quesada, Ginés de. *Exemplo de todas las virtudes, y vida milagrosa de la venerable madre Gerónima de la Assumpción, Abadesa, y Fundadora del Real Convento de la Concepción de la Virgen Nuestra Señora, de Monjas Descalzas de nuestra Madre Santa Clara de la Ciudad de Manila*. México: por la viuda de Miguel de la Rivera, 1713. Madrid: Antonio de Marín, 1717.

Rahn Phillips, Carla. "The Organization of Oceanic Empires. The Iberian World in the Habsburg Period." In *Seascapes: Maritime Histories, Littoral Cultures, and Transoceanic Exchanges*. Ed. Jerry H. Bentley, Renate Bridenthal, and Kären Wigen. Honolulu: U Hawaii P, 2007: 71–86.

Relación histórica de la fundación de este convento de Nuestra Señora del Pilar, Compañía de María llamado vulgarmente La Enseñanza en esta ciudad de Mexico y compendio de la vida y virtudes de N.M.R.M. María Ignacia de Azlor y Echeverz, su fundadora y patrona. Mexico: Felipe Zúñiga de Ontiveros, 1793.

Romera Iruela, Luis and María del Carmen Galbis Díez. *Catálogo de pasajeros a Indias durante los siglos XVI, XVII y XVIII.* Vol. IV (1560–1566). Seville: Ministerio de Cultura, 1980.

Sáenz de Lezcano, Juan Joseph. *Monte de la Myrra, y collado del incienso, trasladados, por la imitación al seráfico Monasterio de Señora Santa Ana de las Madres Capuchinas de la Nobilísima Ciudad de Plasencia.* Madrid: Miguel Gómez, 1718.

Sánchez Fuertes, Cayetano, OFM. "Los monasterios de Santa Clara de Manila y Macao." *Archivum Franciscanum Historicum* 105 (2012): 51–140.

——."Crónica de las monjas Brígidas de la Ciudad de México." Unpublished PhD dissertation. University of Stockholm, 1992.

Schurz, William Lytle. *The Manila Galleon.* New York: E.P. Dutton, 1959.

Sifvert, Anne Sofie. "Advertencia." In *Crónica del Convento de Nuestra Señora de las Nieves Santa Brígida de México.* Ed. Josefina Muriel and Anne Sofie Sifvert. Mexico City: Universidad Nacional Autónoma de México, 2001: 23–29.

Sigüenza y Góngora, Carlos de. *Infortunios de Alonso Ramírez.* Ed. Asima F. X. Saad Maura. Doral, FL: Stockcero, 2011.

——. *Paraíso Occidental.* D.F., Mexico: Consejo Nacional para la Cultura y las Artes, 1995.

Tiffany, Tanya J. *Diego Velázquez's Early Painting and the Culture of Seventeenth-Century Seville.* University Park: Penn State UP, 2012.

Torradeflot Cornet, Ignacio, ed. *Crónicas de la orden de las monjas capuchinas en España fundada por la venerable madre sor Angela Margarita Serafina. Parte Segunda.* Manresa: Imprenta Católica, 1909.

Vargas Ugarte, Rubén ed. *Relaciones de viajes (Siglo XVI, XVII y XVIII).* Lima: Biblioteca Histórica Peruana, 1947: 259–381.

Villarreal, Francisco de. *La Thebayda en poblado, el convento de la concepción capuchina, en la imperial Toledo, su fundación, y progresos, y las vidas de sus anacoretas religiosas que con su santidad le han ilustrado.* Madrid: Antonio Román, 1686.

Weber, Alison. "Literature by Women Religious in Early Modern Catholic Europe and the New World." *The Ashgate Research Companion to Women and Gender in Early Modern Europe.* Ed. Allyson M. Poska, Jane Couchman, and Katherine A. McIver. Farnham, UK: Ashgate, 2013: 33–51.

21
SECULAR WOMEN WRITERS IN THE NEW WORLD

Rocío Quispe-Agnoli

In 1536, the Spanish expedition led by Pedro de Mendoza arrived on South America's Atlantic coast and established the first foundation of Buenos Aires at the Río de La Plata (River Plate).[1] Isabel de Guevara was one of the travelers on this expedition. In 1541, Guevara married Pedro de Esquivel and took part in the Spanish foundation of Asunción, the capital city of present-day Paraguay.[2] In 1555, Governor Domingo Martínez de Irala distributed labor grants among the colonizers of Asunción, but Guevara and Esquivel were excluded from the distribution. A year later, Guevara wrote a brief account to Princess Juana de Austria, regent of Spain, in which she complained of this injustice, specifying her efforts and contributions to the conquest and population of Buenos Aires and Asunción, as well as the merits of other women who followed their husbands to the New World, and requested compensation to repair this omission.

Guevara's petition was not an isolated case in early colonial Spanish America. A few years before, in 1543, Inés Muñoz had written a similar account to the king of Spain requesting the restitution of the Indians who worked on her labor grants. Muñoz was the wife of Francisco Martín de Alcántara, half brother of conquistador Francisco Pizarro. She had arrived in the New World in the early 1530s and participated in the distribution of labor grants after the foundation of the cities of Jauja and Lima. Years later, when she was a widow and guardian of the children whom Pizarro fathered with women of the Inca elite, one of her labor grants was taken away by Spanish Governor, Cristóbal Vaca de Castro. This act motivated the writing of her letter to the king. Similarly, to Guevara, Muñoz described her services to the Spanish Crown during the conquest of Peru and her rescue of Pizarro's children, requesting the devolution of the Indians who had been assigned to her service as part of her *encomienda*, or labor grant. From these examples, one can gather that the textual production by women in the Spanish American colonies seems to have started with legal petitions, journals, and personal letters written or dictated by Spanish women travelers who sought the recognition of their services. These documents, which circulated in public venues, still remain understudied for the most part.[3]

Muñoz's and Guevara's letters provide early examples of women's use of writing in Spanish America. These texts complied with the royal command of *hacer relación* (making account) of what European travelers saw and experienced in the New World, and laid the foundation of narratives and representations of Spanish America.[4] Recent studies of women's letters from both sides of the Atlantic not only challenge the apparent absence of women writers in the Spanish American colonies,[5] but they also shed light on women's experiences in the New World, and their self-representation in their writings.

Until recently, the letters and documents of sixteenth- and seventeenth-century Spanish and Creole women such as Inés Muñoz, María de Escobar, and Jordana Mejia in Peru, and Isabel de Guevara, Isabel de Becerra y Mendoza, and María de los Cobos in Rio de la Plata have remained unmentioned in colonial literary studies based on Spanish American archives, yet all these women were travelers, as well as wives and daughters of Spanish conquistadors. In the second half of the sixteenth century, Muñoz, Escobar, and Mejía received and administered *encomiendas* (labor grants), while Guevara, Becerra y Mendoza, and de los Cobos participated in the colonization of Argentina and Paraguay, and, in the first decades of the seventeeth century, petitioned the rewards of their services and those of their fathers and husbands. With their writings, these women contributed to the textual description of events in the Spanish American colonies. They joined secular women writers like poets María de Estrada, Clarinda, and Amarilis, who wrote outside the convent walls, along with others that will be discussed in this chapter.[6]

The exclusion of secular women writers like the sixteenth- and seventeenth-century Spanish women travelers above mentioned could be understood in an area of studies in which petitions, accounts and letters of Indies, and private letters, have not been considered part of a literary tradition. By contrast, the apparent absence of Creole women poets, like Clarinda and Amarilis, could be explained by the fact that their identity remains anonymous. As Raquel Chang-Rodríguez explains, the majority of twentieth-century literary studies did not pay attention to the innovations of these women poets or to the American and transatlantic dialogic context that framed their poetry (*Discurso*: 13). The relatively few studies on the works of secular women writers like those mentioned here—and the ensuing academic recognition of feminine discourses that were produced beyond the limits of the control of the Church—are in part due to criteria used by colonial archivists to classify and file texts written by women. The difficulties in cataloguing such texts may be understood by the fact that women's letters made reference to public matters. Although one can appreciate women's opinions on these matters, such opinions usually appeared fragmented or intertwined with male voices and opinions in the same text (Quispe-Agnoli, "Taking Possession": 258–259). Furthermore, as Daybell points out in his study on women's letters in sixteenth- and seventeenth-century England, the epistolary genre that women practiced was very complex and multidimensional, since letters transmitted a great variety of contents that were of interest to the women of this period (181–184).

New directions of research on colonial women's gender roles in the periphery and margins, and discursive practices that expand the notion of "literary text" (Adorno: 177), indicate that the textual corpus of colonial women's writings continues to increase. This emergent group of texts reveals patterns of rhetorical strategies and recurrent themes such as feminine weakness and the rhetoric of modesty,[7] motherhood and family, daily life and domesticity, comments on public matters, sponsorship, fiduciary transactions, petitions and recommendations of relatives or servants, among others (Daybell: 182). The discursive analysis of these textual patterns gives us access to vital and affective experiences of Spanish and Spanish American women from the sixteenth to the eighteenth centuries (Baranda Leturio: 127–131; Vollendorf: 82). For example, Guevara and Muñoz used the legal discourse of the accounts of Indies with a very pragmatic objective: to receive compensation and to correct an injustice. Although the quill of a notary mediated their petitions, one can read in their texts women's voices that selected a combination of topics related to the femenine experience. Such topics were evinced in the legal discourses of their respective petitions and, in the case of Muñoz, in a significant number of notarial documents (Quispe-Agnoli, "Taking Possession": 277–278).

Approximately one hundred years after Muñoz's and Guevara's accounts, Creole writers such as María de Estrada Medinilla in New Spain and those known by the pseudonyms "Clarinda" and "Amarilis" in Peru again utilized the themes of motherhood, domesticity, feminine weakness, and the pride of an emergent Creole nation in their poetic creations. Their poetry was published and circulated in literary circles, joining the petitions and personal letters produced by women of different social groups in Spanish America. In these groups, we find Spanish American Creole women writers, as well as aristocratic Spanish women travelers like María Luisa Manrique de Lara and Gelvira de Toledo, vicereines of New Spain. These examples illustrate the need to examine the corpus of women's writings beyond those that were mediated by ecclesiastical discourses in the New World and were produced in colonial convents. The textual production discussed in this chapter, therefore, is that written solely by secular women in colonial Spanish America.[8] Their writings are distinguished by their preference for some genres such as personal letters, letters or accounts of Indies, and poems.

Letters and petitions initiated by women served legal interests and were produced by means of a notary or attorney. He would provide a structure according to a juridic rhetoric controlled by the institutional tenets of the viceroyal government. Many petitions and other texts produced for legal purposes, as well as poetic texts, were published only after they received ecclesiastical, social, and scholarly approval by censors. In sharp contrast with the public nature of these texts, one can observe the ambivalent character of personal letters. In this chapter, the term "personal letter" refers to texts that could have been written originally as private correspondence. The private nature of personal letters in the sixteenth and seventeenth centuries did not necessarily correlate to what we understand as "private correspondence" today.[9] Personal letters that were for private communication were not exposed, in principle, to public scrutiny. However, it was possible for these letters to circulate among several readers.[10] Some letters were intended to keep their strictly private and intimate character, as happened with the epistles of the vicereines commented on below. In other cases, personal letters were used for public purposes, such as *cartas de llamada* (recruitment letters) that were kept as part of official documentation. Recruitment letters were written in the Indies by Spanish colonists to invite relatives to come to the New World. They are documents that moved between the public and private spheres (Stangl: 2010).[11]

The women authors whose works are commented on here chose to express themselves by means of the usual themes and rhetorical strategies, and of genres such as the accounts of Indies (Añón; Silva). The study of these elements helps us understand the formation of scholarly communities in which these women participated, their contribution to the cultural production of Spanish and Spanish American letters, and their potential impact on the women writers who followed them.[12]

Letters from the Indies

Spanish and Spanish American Creole women expressed their experiences, ideas, and concerns in personal letters that either circulated privately, or publicly if they were used as legal resources/devices. These texts were written to a specific addressee and constituted a place to comment on familiar and affective themes and, if necessary, public matters. Examples of these are the letters compiled and studied from various perspectives (Fernández Alcaide; García Mouton; Otte; Sánchez Rubio and Testón Núñez; Silva; Vergara Quiroz), and the most recent editions of personal letters of two vicereines of New Spain (Calvo and Colombí; Dodge and Hendricks). We can add to these letters an extensive production of documents written with legal and fiduciary interests (accounts, petitions, wills, dowries, proofs of nobility, proofs of services, witness depositions). These letters were mediated by male agents (notaries, attorneys, secretaries) but were requested, written and/or dictated by Spanish and Creole women since the mid-sixteenth century, as we have seen in the cases of Muñoz and Guevara. It is important to remember that the written expression of these women authors by means of personal letters was heavily regulated by the ways in which they were intended to circulate, especially if they were defending individual and family interests.

In this regard, Yamile Silva has discovered a significant number of letters of Indies written by Spanish women in Río de la Plata during the first years of the seventeenth century. One can find among them, letters from María de los Cobos, Isabel Becerra Mendoza, and Mariana Osorio de Narváez. For instance, in 1621, de los Cobos produced a legal petition for restitution while using a subtle submissive tone that made reference to her husband's hardships and the ensuing material and symbolic losses. Years later, in 1608, Isabel de Becerra Mendoza included in her petition an account about the foundation of Santa Fe and Buenos Aires. Finally, in 1623, Mariana Osorio de Narváez requested the Crown's recognition of her father's services; according to her, he had fought as a hero against the tyrant rebels Gonzalo Pizarro and Hernández Girón. Yolanda Gamboa's recent study on early Spanish women travelers in Florida and their relationship to the "lettered city" provides evidence of a female textual agency manifested in their petitions that contributed to the formation of sixteenth- and seventeenth-century colonial feminine identity (160–161). The letters and accounts of these women share common features with those by Muñoz and Guevara in their use of feminine themes and concerns within the discursive frame of petitions. These women expressed their awareness of their participation in the history of the conquest and colonization of the New World, and represented themselves as crucial subjects in these historical processes. The main goal of their texts was to persuade the reader, who could have been the king or other members of Spanish administration, of the sufferings they had endured while loyally serving the Crown and thus, their deserved reward. In their documents, Spanish women travelers frequently referred to two themes also addressed by seventeenth-century Creole women poets: their weak feminine condition and false modesty to appeal the empathy of their reader, and the celebration of the American land with its infinite wealth, which enhanced the grandeur of the place from where they were writing.

Celebrating Spanish America as a place of abundance where these women travelers settled gave place to an incipient travel literature about the New World, full of natural and moral history as well as marvelous beliefs. Initiated by Christopher Columbus's "Carta a Luis de Santángel" (Letter to Luis de Santángel) in 1493, this travel literature about unknown places that seemed to be devoid of history, aimed to uncover the places in which European men, women, and their descendants observed the strange and supernatural customs of people unfamiliar with Christian beliefs. As these experiences were incomprehensible to Europeans, they justified the expansion of Christianity (Le Goff). Travelers, therefore, constituted a bridge between their societies and the foreign territories they visited; by narrating their experiences, they acted as mediators between cultures. It is in this experience of mediation that one can read the stories and accounts of Spanish women travelers.

Personal letters of aristocratic women in the Indies

In contrast to the public legal documents produced by Spanish women with the mediation of secretaries, notaries, and attorneys, there is another set of writings by women travelers in Spanish America that deserves attention. These are the private letters of secular women who had access to an education, writing tools, and the time and space in which to write. It is possible, also, that these women had the opportunity to participate in literary circles and in female reading communities.

Two recent editions allow to read the private letters of two vicereines of New Spain, María Luisa Manrique de Lara, Countess of Paredes, and Gelvira de Toledo, Countess of Galve.[13] The Mexican poet, Sor Juana Inés de la Cruz, dedicated several occasional poems to them, calling them "Lysi" and "Elvira" respectively. Manrique de Lara is well known for her patronage of the literary endeavors of Sor Juana Inés de la Cruz, as well as for her sponsorship of her works's publication. Hortensia Calvo and Beatriz Colombí have edited four texts written by Manrique de Lara: two letters written in Mexico and addressed to her cousin, María de Guadalupe de Lencastre, Duchess of Aveiro, and to her father, Vespasiano Gonzaga; and two poems dedicated to the works of Sor Juana Inés. Meredith Dodge and Rick Hendricks have transcribed and translated 27 letters written by the Countess of Galve,[14] most of which were addressed to her brother-in-law, don Gregorio de Silva y Mendoza, Marquis of Cenete and Duke of Infantado. The private nature of these texts reveals the personal experiences of these women in the viceregal court of New Spain. Even though the letters of the Countess of Galve are brief when compared with those written by Manrique de Lara, one observes common themes and rhetorical elements such as the expression of personal affections, complaints of the absence of news from Spain, matters of the viceregal court, the solitude that these women experienced in New Spain, recommendations of relatives and friends, and comments about the ladies and servants within their respective entourages.

Gelvira de Toledo's letters can be organized in two groups: the first one includes thirteen letters written in Madrid, possibly between 1687 and 1688, and addressed to her brother-in-law, Gregorio de Silva y Mendoza; the second is composed of fourteen letters sent to different people in Mexico City and dated between 1689 and 1696. Gelvira's letters, written before her trip to New Spain, show her great fondness for her brother-in-law, and her complaints when she does not receive news from him (Dodge and Hendricks: 187–208). In one of the last missives to him written in Madrid, she announces the appointment of her husband, Gaspar, as viceroy of New Spain. Between July 1689 and June 1696 the new vicereine of Mexico wrote several letters to her brother, Antonio de Toledo, in addition to her brother-in-law and his wife. Her affection for them is expressed in these letters with decorous distance and accompanied by comments on domestic and public matters, such as recommendations of servants, information about the fulfillment of favors and services, and fiduciary transactions. The vicereine's longest letter was written in May 1693 to her sister-in-law, Duchess of Infantado and wife of don Gregorio. In this missive, Gelvira announced sending a sum of money to Spain while describing an inventory of crystal pieces in great detail, their prices and the earnings after their sale (220–226). The countess also referred to other material goods from Mexico and China that were much valued in Spain (a painting of Our Lady of Guadalupe, chocolate, and fans). This information subtly suggests the aristocratic women's appreciation for the exotic and religious wealth of Mexico and its strategic location between Spain and Asia. In this textual exchange, that includes the offering of luxurious items for the home and personal use, one can appreciate the role of cultural transference among women. The letters also reveal that the Spanish aristocracy did not scorn labor and financial management, but paid attention to commercial goods and earnings.[15]

Among the topics dealing with women's daily lives, the vicereine wrote briefly about her illnesses (migraines, fever), her isolation in Mexico, and the "desazón en estas tierras" (uneasiness in these lands) caused by Indian rebellions (214). In contrast with the fondness she displayed towards her brother-in-law in her letters from Madrid, on the occasion of his death, the vicereine expressed her sympathy in a formal tone in her 1693 and 1694 letters (227–228). Daybell has pointed out the unsafe nature of correspondence that was exposed to various means of circulation, as they could be read by several others before reaching their intended addressee. The countess's awareness of this danger is obvious in her transatlantic letters. Her last letter, dated June 1696, states her moderated joy at soon returning to Spain after spending nine years in the New World. As vicereine, she applies the language of favor and reciprocity (Daybell: 187) when expressing her concern for the future of her ladies-in-waiting and female servants, especially those she would leave in Mexico. The change in an affectionate tone between the letters written in Spain and those written in Mexico may be explained if we look at the situations in which they were produced. Those written in Mexico may respond to the distance between the countess and Gregorio, the loss of privacy when sending her letters from Mexico to Spain, and the necessity to take on viceregal tasks with the ensuing care for her personal reputation.

The letters written by María Luisa Manrique de Lara also speak of affection, absence and distance, motherhood and matters of the viceregal court, solitude and concern for the people of her entourage, and recommendations for her relatives and protégés. Nevertheless, the letters of these vicereines are different in length, diversity of themes and details, and personal reflection. For example, María Luisa expressed her emotions towards her addressees as well as to the people close to her (her son, her brother in Spain, the members of the viceregal court). She also spoke fondly about the people of New Spain, from sor Juana Inés de la Cruz to the Indians of Mexico. Her 1682 letter to María de Guadalupe de Lencastre speaks fondly of her cousin and goes back and forth between public and private matters. Among the public letters, the vicereine comments on European political affairs and several personages at Queen Mariana of Austria's court. The vicereine also stressed the Christian character of some Mexican Indians in contrast with the vices of others, commented on Indian rebellions, noted the "insulsísima" (extremely dull) quality of life in the New World and mentioned expeditions sent to California and China.

With regard to New Spain, María Luisa offered a general report of its state, and like Gelvira, thought its location was ideal from which to continue to carry out explorations and colonization of other territories, and maintain the commercial route to Asia. In contrast to the details about Mexico offered by the letters of the Countess of Paredes, Gelvira's Mexican letters made minimal references to the New World, except for those about a "tumulto de indios" (revolt of Indians), and the Chinese fans and chocolate that the countess offered to send to her sister-in-law. In addition, although the Countess of Galve wrote about daily events, she made no reference to her 1688 transatlantic journey, her stay in New Spain, or her relationship with sor Juana Inés de la Cruz and other intelectuals or other noted persons of Mexico. A comparison between the topics addressed in the letters of these two vicereines, in addition to the participation of the Countess of Paredes in communities of learned women in Spain, Portugal, and Mexico, displays a difference in the intellectual profile of both, and points out the highly educated level attained by Sor Juana Inés's viceregal sponsor.

From a private and intimate point of view, María Luisa's letters offer other differences with those of Gelvira. The Countess of Paredes shared her concerns about "malestares" (discomforts) related to her pregnancies and the difficulties of motherhood. These topics also allowed her to comment on matters of the Spanish royal court like the expected birth of Carlos II's sucesor. The countess also spoke of her solitude in a place where she felt isolated and the remedy provided by the friendship of a "rara mujer" (unusual woman) whom she was sure her relative, the Duchess of Aveiro, would be pleased to meet (Calvo and Colombí: 177). She was referring to Sor Juana Inés de la Cruz, whose precocious intelligence, wrote the vicereine, "pasmaba a todos los que la oían, porque el ingenio es grande" (178)[16] (astonished everyone who heard her, because of her great intelligence). María Luisa's description of the Hieronymite nun highlights her "autodidactismo" (self-taught background), her humble origin, and her extraordinary intelligence.

Five years after this missive, the vicereine wrote to her father claiming not having received any news from him and updating him on her life. María Luisa informs him of how she feels toward several people. On the one hand, she speaks proudly of her son "Chepito," while on the other, she comments on the mutual distrust between her and her husband and the new viceregal couple of New Spain, the Counts of Galve. She also expresses her frustration over her delayed return trip to Spain and, similarly to Gelvira, she expresses concern about the women who serve her, especially those who have passed away or who will stay in Mexico after her departure. In the same letter, she calls attention to an "indiecito mudo" (a mute young Indian, 172) informally adopted by her and described as very smart, despite his incapacity and lack of development.[17] María Luisa extends her description of him to all the Indians of Mexico, whom the vicereine referred to as virtuous people.

The letters of the Countess of Paredes reveal not only her intimate world but also her intellectual and artistic interests. Towards the end of her letter to her cousin, who was very keen on painting, María Luisa claimed not having received a portrait that was painted by María de Guadalupe and was supposed to be sent to the vicereine. Calvo and Colombí explain that offering portraits as gifts among women was an expression of affection. In like manner, the vicereine took with her a portrait of Sor Juana Inés when she returned to Spain (68) and, a few years later, she would write poems to honor the Mexican poet. Calvo and Colombí attribute to the vicereine an anonymous acrostic ten-line stanza, published in the section of dedications to Sor Juana Inés's *Fama y obras póstumas* (Fame and Posthumous Works, 1700). This poem is titled "de una gran Señora muy discreta, y apasionada de la poetisa" (206) (from a very discreet Lady, passionate for the woman poet). A second poem by the Countess of Paredes was discovered in 1968 in the manuscript of *Enigmas ofrecidos a La Casa del Placer* (Enigmas Offered to the House of Pleasure).[18] In this ballad, the Countess of Paredes addresses sor Juana as her friend and describes *Enigmas* as a confirmation of her talent and extraordinary artistic talent. She also mentions the readers among whom Sor Juana's work circulated: a community of aristocratic and learned women of Spain and Portugal, who would enjoy Sor Juana's poetry without the Church's censorship in the New World: "Felizmente los ofreces/ en el más sagrado templo/ donde es corto sacrificio/ el más noble entendimiento" (Happily you offer them/ in the most sacred temple/ where the noble intelligence/ is small sacrifice) (Calvo and Colombí: 208). The ballad ends with a note of affected modesty, a rhetorical device frequently used by early modern women writers, as mentioned before.

Secular Creole poetry

Literary contests offered an opportunity for women in the New World to submit their poetic creations and have them published if their texts were awarded or selected for publication.[19] The Mexican historian, Josefina Muriel, who has studied these events in the New World since they began in the sixteenth century, highlights their importance in the development of women's poetry (141–142). In the case of Mexico, Muriel has commented on the works of religious and secular women who participated in literary contests from the seventeenth to the early nineteenth centuries. She makes reference to the works of several women who participated in these contests, like the nuns Teresa Magdalena de Cristo and Sor Juana Teresa de San Antonio, and the secular aristocrats Francisca García de Villalobo, Juana de Góngora, and Ana María González (269–312). One of these women authors is María Guerrero, daughter of Antonio Guerrero, a Creole intellectual who ran a school in his own house. María learned Latin and Spanish grammar in her father's school and, in 1720, when she was ten years old, recited two poems to honor Sor Juana Inés de la Cruz's works at a public event in Mexico City. In this way, the young poet joined other Spanish and Creole women who wrote poems to praise Sor Juana Inés, such as the Countess of Paredes, María Jacinta de Abogader y Mendoza, Francisca Echavarri, and Inés de Vargas (268–269).[20]

The secular women who practiced literary writing in the first half of the seventeenth century paved the way for the poetic creation of authors like Sor Juana Inés and other writers of the later seventeenth and eighteenth centuries. María de Estrada Medinilla was one of these poets. During the first half of the seventeenth century, she published at least two of her works after participating in literary contexts in Mexico City. The first was a 400-line poem titled *Relación escrita por doña María de Estrada Medinilla a una religiosa prima suya, de la feliz entrada en México día de S. Agustín, a 28. de Agosto de mil y seiscientos y quarenta años. Del Excellentissimo Señor Don Diego López Pacheco, Cabrera, y Bobadilla, Marqués de Villena, Virrey y Governador, y capitán General desta Nueva España* (Account written by doña María de Estrada Medinilla, to her cousin a nun, on the joyful entrance into Mexico of His Excellency, Señor Don Diego López Pacheco Cabrera y Bobadilla, Marquis of Villena, Viceroy and Governor, and general captain of New Spain, on the day of Saint Augustine, August 28 of one thousand six hundred and forty years). Estrada's text was published in the collection of poems compiled by Cristóbal Gutiérrez de Medina, *Viaje de Tierra y más feliz por mar y tierra que hizo el Excmo. Sr. Marqués de Villena* (Journey by land and more joyful travel by land and sea taken by His Most Excellent Lord, Marquis of Villena, 1640). A collection of encomiastic texts for public readership, it probably had its own frontispiece and other features of an autonomous printing and circulated in an independent manner. Two other poems have been attributed to Estrada: the first is a *glosa* (poem in *décimas* or ten-line stanzas) that won third place in a literary contest and was then published in the *Certamen poético que celebró la docta y lúcida Escuela de Estudiantes de la Real Universidad de México a la Inmaculada Concepción* (Poetic contest celebrated by the learned and splendid School of Students of the Royal University of Mexico in honor of the Immaculate Conception, 1654). The other poem was published by the town council of Mexico City with the title *Descripción en octavas reales de las fiestas de toros y cañas y alcancías* (Muriel: 136–141)[21] (Description in royal octaves of the feast of bullfights and tournaments).

As a poet inspired by Spanish poetic tradition, María de Estrada joins other upper-class Creole women whose poetry circulated in the New World. They not only shared European literary modes, but also rhetorical and thematic innovations. Clarinda and Amarilis are among these women writers. They published their works in consonance with those of other poets with whom they kept a transatlantic dialogue, while retaining their anonymity.[22] In 1608, Clarinda published "Discurso en loor de la poesía" (Discourse Lauding Poetry) as a prologue to the collection *Primera parte del Parnaso Antártico* (Part One of the Antarctic Parnassus), compiled by the Seville poet Diego Mejía de Fernangil. Although born in Spain, Mejía lived most of his life in Perú, and it is likely that the two poets knew each other.[23] In this 808-line poem, the author praises poetry from a philosophical perspective. Ten years later, Amarilis wrote a 335-line poem in *canzone* (Italian song) metrics, which she dedicated to Lope de Vega, titling it "Epístola a Belardo" (Epistle to Belardo), Lope's literary disguise. The renowned Spanish poet and playwright replied to Amarilis's literary letter, including in his response his original text of *La Filomena* (1621).

In contrast to women who wrote legal petitions in the sixteenth century, and the vicereines, among other noblewomen, who wrote personal letters, women in Spanish America who wrote and published poetry in the seventeenth century raise numerous questions. We need to inquire about the education these women received, their literary readings, the artistic and philosophical models they had in mind, and the American ideals with which they sympathized. In spite of their relative independence in the treatment of themes and motifs, the three women authors mentioned above submitted their creations to male scrutiny seeking their publication in a Spanish American market controlled by men. María de Estrada's participation in literary contests ruled by patriarchal institutions should be understood within this context, as well as Clarinda's and Amarilis's search for transatlantic dialogue with Spanish men who would sponsor their poetry's publication.

The works of these three women poets deployed devices to combat the silence in which seventeenth-century learned women were kept, especially in the New World where women with literary aspirations moved in a hostile environment (Sabat de Rivers: 161–162). Sabat de Rivers applied the term "mujer ilustrada" (learned woman) to refer to Spanish or Creole women who had acess to scholarly education, and the means and time to participate in literary exchanges and circles. They were women of the upper class and of wealthy families even if they did not belong to the nobility. Their work raises several questions. What European or Spanish American authors influenced the works of seventeenth-century Spanish American women writers, and what were their preferred themes? What rhetorical devices were employed to render their American version of poetry, and how were they able to publish their writings? Sabat de Rivers has reviewed the literary legacy of Spanish Golden Age literature and the context of influences in which these women poets wrote. According to the literary scholar, Spanish American women writers read representations of idealized women within the perfect world of the European bucolic tradition. They received an education that combined influences from Italian and Spanish Renaissance culture, governed by male views of idealized women and intended to control feminine behavior (111–112). These features also worked as restrictions and provoked reactions from poets such as Clarinda, Amarilis, and Estrada by means of literary creations. Sabat de Rivers has caracterized these creations as women's literary responses that had "una dialéctica doble y simultánea de agresión y subordinación" (113) (a double and simultaneous dialectic of aggression and subordination). Recent studies by Chang-Rodríguez on Clarinda and Amarilis ("La mirada femenina" and *Discurso*), and by Vettenrata on Estrada, confirm Sabat de Rivers' observations and assert these women's American and Creole situatedness. While their works imitated European poetic traditions, they also introduced changes in poetic language and subverted imperial expectations with their celebrations of Mexican and Peruvian-Antarctic magnificence. One can organize their innovations in three thematic areas: their reflections on poetry making and its relation to Spanish America; the (self)-representations of the learned woman and anxiety of authorship; and their intentionally ambiguous celebration of Spain by their Creole acknowledgment of America's grandeur.

Sabat de Rivers and Chang-Rodríguez have identified the reflection on poetry making as a theme that appears in the works of all three poets. In the "Epístola a Belardo," for example, we observe an emphasis on the senses by which the reader would "'oír' una poesía que entra por los ojos y de las emociones que levanta" (Sabat de Rivers: 145) ("listen" to poetry that enters through the eyes, and to the emotions provoked by this experience). Such poetry followed the medieval tradition of the affects entering through the ears with the ensuing emotion leading both characters, Amarilis and Belardo, to intellectual love and the display of their literary competence (Chang-Rodríguez, *Discurso*: 64–67). Amarilis also deployed poetry as the medium with which to manifest her friendship and admiration of Lope de Vega, identifying herself with the Ovidian *Heroides* tradition, the lamentation by women of the departures or death of their lovers (Sabat de Rivers: 131). Her poetic expression thus introduced a change in the tradition of Horatian epistle that meant to express mutual admiration and friendship between men (Chang-Rodríguez, *Discurso*: 128). Neither did Amarilis follow the Petrarchan model of the silent and passive woman; rather, she subtly criticized his literary work and requested that he write about religious topics, specifically the exemplary life of Saint Dorotea. In this way, the poet emphasized her self-confidence and superior position when she disapproved of Lope de Vega's flirtations, inviting him to get closer to God by writing religious poetry.[24]

Clarinda's poetry shared Amarilis's notions of affect but also extended the theme to a universal level. For this author, poetry was the key to knowledge of the entire universe: "cifra de saber de todo el universo" (Sabat de Rivers: 154) (cipher to know all the universe). Not only did this anonymous Peruvian writer know Classic and European notions about poetry, but she also stated its divine character and raised poetry to universal standards. In this way, Clarinda praised and defended the poetry that was written in the Americas, especially in Lima, the capital of the viceroyalty of Peru. Given Lima's location in the southern hemisphere and its distance from Spain, the seventeenth-century Peruvian Creole poets refer to it as the center of the Antarctic zone. Clarinda related the poetry of the Antartactic zone with the one written in the south of Spain (Chang-Rodríguez, *Discurso*: 162). She also established a dialogue of mutual admiration with the Seville poet Mejía de Fernangil, due, among other reasons, to their identification with the south. According to Trinidad Barrera, the south of Spain (Seville) and the south of America (Antartic) became, in the texts of Mejía and Clarinda, the ideal zones to write poetry (8). This laudatory approach to the "south" can be related to the celebration of what being born in Spanish America was, as we see later.

By contrast, María de Estrada established a relationship between poetic language and Baroque architecture when she described the entrance into Mexico of Diego López Pacheco, Marquis of Villena and Viceroy of New Spain. Triumphal arcs were built for such occasions, balconies were adorned with tapestries, and ladies observed the spectacle from there, while poems and images were created to adorn the city (Muriel: 125, 135). Differently from Clarinda and Amarilis, Estrada had the intention to create a literary dialogue with her cousin, a nun who could not attend the event; the poet then became the nun's eyes and ears. Although Estrada's poem does not express admiration for a male addressee, it highly praises the gallant figure of the viceroy, whose attractiveness would inspire her to write her account and comment on the reaction of several women who admired the viceroy as she did.[25]

The three women poets' anxiety of authorship and their representations of women are clearly observed in their works. Sabat de Rivers has explained that, in general, the women writers of colonial Spanish America expected to be acknowledged for their intelligence and their right to an intellectual experience (161). To this end, one of the most frequent rhetorical devices was the catalog of learned women narrated by Clarinda, Estrada, and, later, by Sor Juana Inés de la Cruz. Clarinda deployed a list of famous women warriors, "mujeres varoniles" (virile women), goddesses, and women artists of the classical pagan tradition (Juno, Sibilas, Safo, Pola Argentaria) and of the Christian world (Virgin Mary, Eve, Judith), whose extraordinary actions inspired or mediated poetic creation. In Clarinda's "Discurso," renowned women are given authority to write poetry (Virgin Mary, Eve) without being punished or censored,[26] and constitute the ideal intermediaries to deliver sacred messages as occurred in ancient classic prophecies (Chang-Rodríguez, *Discurso*: 117). Clarinda then distances herself from the *topos* of feminine weakness and is in solidarity with the members of her sex, especially with Peruvian women, whose names she decides to keep anonymous like her own (Sabat de Rivers: 165). Clarinda also attributes to herself characteristics that belittle her poetic self such as lacking education: a "mujer indocta" (uneducated woman), establishing equivalences between her poetry making and the work of insects like the spider, the butterfly, and the ant. By means of these associations with women and her expressions of modesty, the poet points out woman's creative and artistic capacity, the challenge to social expectations of her time, and the admiration that the display of such capacity provokes (Chang-Rodríguez, *Discurso*: 34).[27] The rhetorical subversion of feminine weakness joined the list of past and present illustrious women who are cited in Clarinda's poetry. Her goal was to point out that women writers and poetry of the Antarctic zone were infinite sources of inspiration for poetry making in the seventeenth century.

Women's audacity also characterized the poetic self that Amarilis construes in her "Epistle." In addition to her own identification with Ovid's *Heroides* who lamented the absence of their beloved partners, the lyric subject confirmed her literary competence and femenine strength when these were displayed in her critique to Belardo/Lope de Vega. Chang-Rodríguez has indicated features of the poetic persona that Amarilis embraced: a beautiful single woman, member of a wealthy family, and inclined to the reading of poetry and religion (56). She presents herself as a Creole woman who descended from Spanish conquistadors and *encomenderos* (labor grant owners) who settled in America and gave origin to courageous Spanish Americans like herself. She situates her identity at the center of the poem, characterizing her poetic voice as different from that of others in the early modern period: feminine and Creole (lines 169–180 cited by Chang-Rodríguez, *Discurso*: 47). The poem, fruit of her creative activity, is similar to the products of her land, America, that save Spain in the same way women like Saint Dorotea (and herself) can assist in the salvation of the poet's soul. In this way, Chang-Rodríguez proposes, Amarilis subverted the hierarchy of the sexes in the seventeenth century and established a relation of enriching dependence between Spanish America and Spain.

Creole identity and Spanish American subjectivity

As mentioned previously, María de Estrada stated in New Spain that she was the medium through which her cousin, a cloistered nun, could be informed about the triumphal entrance of the king's representative in Mexico. In her poem, Estrada paid attention to women's actions that she had seen and heard during the parade and, at the same time, used modesty *topoi* to engage her reader's empathy. Self-confident, she subtly criticized the social customs of her time that impeded her from moving around independently (Sabat de Rivers: 167–168). The poetic self-representation that Estrada offers in her *Relación* is intimately linked to New Spain's subjectivity and Creole identity that celebrated the spectacular wealth of their birthplace, Mexico. This brings us to consider the third theme that the poetic creations of these women share: the celebration of their native Spanish American land and their Creole pride.

When Lope de Vega replied to the "Epístola" that the anonymous Peruvian poet sent him in 1619, he addressed its author as "Amarilis Indiana" (Amarilis from the Indies). With this name, the Spanish poet recognized her quality as a lover ("Amarilis" was the poetic name of Lope de Vega's mistress, Marta de Nevares) and her origins as a Spanish American Creole woman. Yet the lyrical subject that is at the center of Amarilis's text also gives an account of her heroic Spanish ancestors, creating a link between the glorious historic past of her conquistador grandparents and the American lineage that she represents:

> Bien pudiera, Belardo, si quisiera,
> en gracia de los cielos
> decir hazañas de mis dos abuelos
> que aqueste nuevo mundo conquistaron
> y esta ciudad también edificaron,
> do vasallos tuvieron,
> y por su rey su vida y sangre dieron. [. . .]
> De padres nobles dos hermanas fuimos,
> que nos dejaron con temprana muerte, [. . .]
> y así nos inclinamos
> a virtudes heroicas que heredamos.
>
> *Chang-Rodríguez: 183–185*

(Belardo could, if he would like / in heavens' grace, / tell my two grandfathers' great deeds / who conquered this new world / and built this city where they had vassals / and where they gave their blood for their king / [. . .] / We were sisters of noble fathers / who left us with their early deaths / [. . .] / and so we were inclined [to have] / the heroic / virtues that we inherited).

At this moment, the poet mentions the Peruvian nation and its grandeur that, in spite of (or because of) the unavoidable changes in its colonial history, created an ideal place of enunciation to save the soul of the Spanish poet to whom she writes. In this way, she offers her poetry as "fruto nuevo" (new fruit) from Peru, a southern paradise that is so close to heaven and gives so many gifts that would simbolically and spiritually nourish the empire (Chang-Rodríguez, *Discurso*: 64–65). Thus, the hierarchy of superior (Spain, man) over inferior positions (Spanish America, woman) is subverted in order to attain the success of the future poetry written in Spanish.

Clarinda's "Discurso" also expressed, like Amarilis's "Epistle," great admiration for the American places from where it was written. In the dialogue she has with Mejía de Fernangil, the Seville poet who published her text, the Peruvian writer acknowledges him as a master of poetry. In this acknowledgment, we find the implicit association between Spain's south and that of Spanish America. The colonial south constitutes a privileged and chosen space from where Spanish art and literature were nurtured (Chang-Rodríguez, *Discurso*: 23–28). The value of Creole Spanish America, and even more the Antarctic zone and its writers and artists, implied then that the imperial center had to honor the periphery and its Creole poets (Chang-Rodríguez, *Discurso*: 28–29). This new privileged place of enunciation focuses on Creole agency and is confirmed with the catalog of illustrious women in which Clarinda inserted the poetic production of Peruvian women. Her poetry would not only take place in the "Parnaso Antártico" (Antarctic Parnassus), but southern Spanish America also constituted a privileged intellectual space in the seventeenth century wherein Peruvian women poets stood out. In his answer to Clarinda, Mejía de Fernangil represented her as a heroic poet that deserved being heard. This recognition reinforced the woman writer's voice and authority and, by extension, her message about Antarctic poetry.

In New Spain, María de Estrada's poetry was framed within the tradition of writers like Juan de la Cueva and Bernardo de Balbuena who, in a similar fashion to Clarinda and Amarilis, took advantage of laudatory poetry to situate the viceregal periphery at the center of imperial intellectual attention. Similarly to Balbuena, Estrada praised her native land as Mexican grandeur equivalent to Rome and wealthier and more elegant than Flanders or Turkey, with extraordinary nobility, great artists, and an illustrious local elite (Muriel: 126–129). Creole pride and patriotic tone gave testimony to Mexican *criollismo* (Creole nature) as the necessary foundation for the success of the empire. The Creole woman writer appropriated the rhetorical elements and philosophical principles of the Spanish Baroque to offer a laudatory representation of Mexico and the descendants of Spaniards who were born there. The wisdom, diversity, exotism, and abundance of the American native land have become the sources of material and symbolic riches for the empire's subsistence (Muriel: 129). Vettenranta has proposed that Estrada took an additional step in her Creole nationalism that can be read in her *Relación*. This scholar states that Estrada offered a carnivalization of the viceregal spectacle and, by means of a process of hybridization process in her poem, vindicated New Spain's heterogeneity. The Mexican poet, therefore, provided a political critique of Spain from the colonial periphery (43–44). In this context, the representation of the learned Creole woman, poet, and intellectual in the works of Clarinda, Amarilis, and Estrada negotiated and subverted the central position of the European empire and called attention to the privileged space of Spanish America in the literary production and the development of the arts. Such Creole female negotiations are part of the veiled process of the Baroque of counter-conquest, as Lezama Lima famously proposed in his essay on the "American expression," according to which the Spanish conquistadors were in fact conquered by their American colonies (80).

Secular women writers of Spanish America: a pending area of study

The Spanish American Creole women discussed here constitute an example of the development of women's agency beyond the walls of ecclesiastic institutions. In some cases, their texts were published and celebrated in their times; others remain unread in the archives of the Spanish American colonial documents. Since the late twentieth century, however, the development of women's studies and gender relations has focused academic attention on these texts. This in turn allows for the research and analysis of women's official, private, and public expressions, like those that have been discussed above.

Indeed, a review of the literary production of these Spanish and Creole women confirms that theirs were not unique or isolated cases that occurred only in certain areas of Spanish America. Instead, women's literary experiences took shape beyond the circles controlled by patriarchal institutions at that time. This tradition constitutes a field that requires much study and includes such themes as the perception and expression of affect and emotions, the feminine experiences of daily activities beyond the convent, and the church, the commercial activities of women commoners as well as aristocrats, the circulation of ideas and visual images in the colonies, and the written expressions of public and personal themes that caught women's attention. The revelation of this tradition increases every year thanks to the industrious work of new studies in archives and repositories of documents; however, still more needs to be done to make visible the textual and literary production of secular women in colonial Spanish America.

Notes

1 The first foundation, by Pedro de Mendoza in 1536, was destroyed and abandoned. In 1580, Juan de Garay founded the city of Santa María del Buen Aire, which became the site of Buenos Aires, the current capital city of Argentina.
2 There is no agreement as to Guevara's arrival in America. According to one study, she was one of eight Spanish women on this expedition of approximately 1,500 people (Martin: 28). Another study, however, does not find evidence of her presence in this expedition, although the names of Carlos de Guevara and Isabel de Laserna are mentioned (Lopreto: 46). A most recent study notes that Guevara married Esquivel in Paraguay and that they were not together on the journey from Buenos Aires to Asunción (Tieffemberg: 289).
3 Despite what is generally believed, sixteenth-century women's textual production is abundant (Quispe-Agnoli "Taking Possession," "Domesticando la frontera"). Although we are not familiar with any journals of early Spanish women travelers that would be similar to the letters and accounts of Muñoz and Guevara, it is plausible to believe that this kind of document exits yet remains invisible in colonial archives. For the transcription of Muñoz's letter and her translation into English, see Quispe-Agnoli, "Taking Possession": 280–283.
4 The *carta de Indias* (letter or account of Indies) was a legal genre used to establish, sustain, or justify power. Its main goal was to petition the royal recognition of merits and services and obtain a material reward (in the form of labor-grants, money, fellowships for relatives) as well as symbolic awards (titles of nobility, social and economic privileges). For a detailed description of this genre and its variants, as well as the differences between *carta* (letter), *relación* (account), and *historia* (history) or *crónica* (chronicle), see Mignolo. For the role played by colonial legal, scientific, and ethnographic discourses and the origins of Latin American literary narrative, see González Echevarría.
5 Guevara's letter was unknown to contemporary literary scholars and historians until its publication by Peña and Tieffemberg. Scott has pointed out the absence of published texts by early colonial women (3), noting that although letters from Spanish and Spanish American women soliciting rewards have been found, these texts, differently from Guevara's, seemed not to be able to provide a complete story (7n.1).

6   Baranda Leturio offers a programmatic proposal of the literary history of Spanish women from the middle ages to the eighteenth century (123–176). More recently, Vollendorf has compiled two lists of Spanish and Creole women writers from the sixteenth to the eighteenth centuries whose texts have survived (85–91, 95–98). These lists include the names of women authors, their themes, and the editions of their works. The first list includes 55 Iberian writers, 23 of whom were not associated with a convent (85–91). The second list contains 37 Spanish American authors. From these only one (María de Estrada) was not a religious woman in the seventeenth century, and another (Beatriz de Echegaray) told her visionary experiences in the eighteenth century (95–98). With the exception of Estrada, Vollendorf did not include in the second list the writers who are being reviewed here.
7   The rhetoric of modesty was a frequent topic in early modern women's writings. Pender has studied expressions of tropes of modesty in sixteenth- and seventeenth-century women's writings of England and New England. She proposes "authorial alibis" to refer to women's denial of their own authorial agency in order to negotiate the patriarchal restriction over feminine authorship at that time (2–3). Weber has also analyzed language in the works of Teresa of Ávila and has identified a "rhetoric of femininity" that distinguished her writing from that produced by men. One of the rhetorical devices applied is that of false modesty, which in the works of Saint Teresa, opened a space of self-denial wherein to disguise her feminine agency. This rhetoric allowed early modern women to use the "mother tongue" and a language of domesticity with authority that set a model of writing for other religious women authors of Europe and Spanish America.
8   This chapter does not include texts produced by women associated with religious institutions (nuns, holy lay women, visionaries) that are examined elsewhere in this volume. Neither does it discuss the textual production of indigenous and African women or their descendants in Spanish America. Texts produced by women of native elites have been recently studied by Burns, Graubart, Guengerich, Mangan, and Quispe-Agnoli ("*Mulieris Litterarum*"). For the case of African and African-Spanish American women, see McKnight and Garofalo.
9   See Vanessa de Cruz Medina in this volume for a discussion of personal letters similar to my own.
10 In addition to Stangl's ideas on the flexible nature of privacy in recruitment letters (2010, 16), Daybell argues factors related to the modes of composition (who wrote and in what material and social circumstances), the use of secretaries as mediators of writing, the use of models previously established in epistolary manuals, and the process of sending the letters that could expose them to public readings. These factors imposed a sense of self-censorship in the writers of personal letters (Daybell: 183–184).
11 The collections edited by Otte in 1988, and by Sánchez Rubio and Testón Núñez in 1999, include letters that remained private as well as recruitment letters. For a thorough review on "private letters" written by Spanish travelers in the Indies and a detailed commentary about academic editions of personal letters, see Stangl (2013).
12 Campbell and Larsen have studied learned communities in modern Europe and have pointed out three possible comunities of women writers: continental epistolary communities, transcontinental textual communities, and transnational literary circles (11–19).
13 The first was married to Tomás de la Cerda, Marquis of La Laguna and Count of Paredes, viceroy of New Spain, 1680–1686; the second, to Gaspar de la Cerda Silva Sandoval y Mendoza, Count of Galve, viceroy of New Spain, 1688–1696. Sor Juana Inés de la Cruz dedicated several poems to each of them. While the Countess of Paredes gave much attention to the nun poet and sponsored her work, it seems that Gelvira was not interested in the works of the nun.
14 The letters of the Countess of Paredes have been recently identified in the *Fondo de correspondencia de Virreyes* in the Latin American Library of Tulane University, New Orleans, United (Calvo and Colombí: 17–19). Dodge and Hendricks indicate in their introduction to the letters of the Countess of Galve (published in 1993) that hers were located in the *Sección Osuna* of the Archivo Histórico Nacional in Madrid, *legajos* 89 and 239 (xi); the *Sección Osuna* is now archived in the Sección Nobleza Hospital Tavera, Toledo.
15 This example of the commercial interest and administrative ability of members of the aristocracy is not an isolated case. Dadson has examined the efforts of the count of Salinas to increase his possessions, maintain his accounting books, organize and administer his assets. Most recently, Dadson has studied the influence of women in the count's endeavors, such as Antonia de Ulloa, his mother-in-law, who taught him to govern and administer the possessions of the Salinas family ("The Count of Salinas").
16 English translations come from various sources and are cited appropriately. If no translation is available in print, translations into English are the author's.
17 "Tengo en casa un indiecito mudo de que mucho gusto es para alabar a Dios la viveza con que se sabe explicar con las acciones [. . .] A mí me confunde, te aseguro, y creo se me ha de quedar enano,

pues aunque es muchacho, tiene muy chico cuerpo para la edad. Es donosísimo y a ellos no les falta ladinez y entendimiento con gran disimulo. Y porque son recatadísimos y desconfiados, harto me holgara yo de tener mucha parte en el bien de sus almas" (172) (I have a little young Indian for whom it is a pleasure to thank God, for the liveliness with which he can explain himself with his gestures and actions [. . .]. I assure you that it confuses me, and I am afraid that he will remain a dwarf, even though he is already a youth, as his body is too small for his age. He is very amusing and witty, as it happens with other Indians, even if they do not seem to be smart. Since they [the Indians] are very shy and distrustful, I would very much like to play a role in the good of their souls).

18 Martínez López edited Sor Juana's *Enigmas*, which he discovered in the National Library of Lisbon. Written probably between 1692 and 1693, the Countess of Paredes sponsored its circulation in a literary circle of learned women in Portugal and Spain (Arenal and Powell: xi). In the introduction, Sor Juana included a *romance* (ballad) and a sonnet, followed by *endechas* (dirges) and ballads written by Portuguese nuns, and a ballad by the Countess of Paredes. Antonio Alatorre published a critical edition of *Enigmas* in 1994.
19 See the chapter on literary contests in the Iberian Peninsula by Osuna Rodríguez in this volume.
20 These poems were published in the 1714 edition of *Fama y obras póstumas*. It is important to note that when María Guerrero was seventeen years old, she composed a *loa* (laudatory poem) in Latin and in Spanish to praise King Philip V (Muriel: 269).
21 Muriel also mentions a sonnet composed by Estrada to celebrate the publication of Francisco Corchero Carreño's *Desagravios de Cristo* (Apologies to Christ) in 1649 (141). She notes, however, that this poem is known only from Alfonso Méndez Plancarte's 1940 study of New Spain poets (141).
22 Marcelino Menéndez y Pelayo named this poet "Clarinda" (Chang-Rodríguez: 15n.15). The second poet is known as "Amarilis," the name used by the poetic voice to identify herself in the poem.
23 Mejía Fernengil came to Spanish America in 1582. He worked as a book merchant in Mexico and arrived in Lima in 1590. He was a member of the Antarctic Academy in Lima (Lohmann Villena: 126).
24 "Y temo tus peligros y mis faltas. / Tabla tiene el naufragio, y escaparte/ puedes en ella de la eterna muerte / si del bien frágil al divino saltas" (Chang-Rodríguez *Discurso*: 181) (And I fear your dangers and my faults./ The wrecked ship has a plank, and on it / you may escape eternal death/ if you jump from the fragile to the divine good). In his reply "Epístola de Belardo a Amarilis" (Belardo's Epistle to Amarilis), Lope de Vega rejected her suggestion (Chang-Rodríguez, *Discurso*: 68). Vinatea Recoba published another edition of Amarilis's epistle that may be also consulted.
25 Departing from the importance that such parades had for the interests of the Spanish empire, Vettenranta analyzes in detail the poetic language used by Estrada to describe the handsome appearance of the new viceroy, a radiant sun whose brightness amazes the attendants (37–39).
26 Sabat de Rivers points out Clarinda's strategy of mentioning Eve as God's creation without making any reference to original sin or to her creation from Adam's rib (163).
27 Chang-Rodríguez speaks of an entomological rhetoric to explain the association between insects and the woman writer. For example, Arachne competed with Minerva and defied the gods when she wove a tapestry in which their sensual deceptions were depicted. She was punished by Minerva and turned into a spider. The butterfly symbolized the insect's daring to come closer to the light of fire in spite of the risks of being burnt. Lastly, the preventive, organized, and vigorous work of ants would always cause admiration (29–34). Baranda Leturio (personal communication) calls attention to these positive readings of insects' characteristics and their energetic work, which, in the works of other authors, have been interpreted negatively. In this way, for instance, the spider makes silk, yet it also rejects the bee's mode of production. This rejection could be read as the denial of classical and humanist imitation.

Works cited

Adorno, Rolena. "New Perspectives in Colonial Spanish American Literary Studies." *Journal of the Southwest* 32.2 (Summer 1990): 173–191.
Alatorre, Antonio, ed. *Sor Juana Inés de la Cruz. Enigmas ofrecidos a la casa del placer*. Mexico City: El Colegio de México, 1994.
Amarilis (anon.). "Amarilis a Belardo." *Lope de Vega. La Filomena con otras diversas rimas, prosas y versos*. Madrid: Viuda de Alonso Martín, 1621: 137–144.
Añón, Valeria. "Women 'Cronistas' in Colonial Latin America." *The Cambridge History of Latin American Women's Literature*. Ed. Ileana Rodríguez and Mónica Szurmuk. Cambridge: Cambridge UP, 2016: 66–80.

Arenal, Electa and Amanda Powell, eds. *The Answer/La Respuesta (Expanded Edition)*. New York: Feminist P, City U New York, 2009.
Baranda Leturio, Nieves. *Cortejo a lo prohibido: lectoras y escritoras en la España moderna*. Madrid: Arco Libros, 2005.
Barrera, Trinidad. "Introducción." *Diego Mexía. Primera parte del Parnaso Antártico de obras amatorias*. Rome: Bulzoni, 1990: 8–34.
Burns, Kathryn. *Into the Archive*. Durham, NC: Duke UP, 2010.
Calvo, Hortensia and Beatriz Colombí. *Cartas de Lysi*. Madrid: Iberoamericana Vervuert, 2015.
Campbell, Julie D. and Anne R. Larsen, eds. *Early Modern Women and Transnational Communities of Letters*. Farnham, UK; Burlington, VT: Ashgate, 2009.
Chang-Rodríguez, Raquel. "La mirada femenina y el orgullo novohispano." *Cuadernos Hispanoamericanos*. 655 (2008): 25–30.
Chang-Rodríguez, Raquel, ed. *Discurso en loor de la Poesía. Epístola a Belardo*. Lima: Fondo Editorial de la Pontificia Universidad Católica del Perú, 2009.
Clarinda. "Discurso en loor de la poesía." *Diego Mexía de Fernangil. Primera parte del Parnaso Antártico de obras amatorias*. Seville: Alonso Rodríguez Gamarra, 1608: 9–26.
Columbus, Christopher. "Carta a Luis de Santángel." *Cristóbal Colón. Textos y documentos completos*. Ed. Consuelo Varela. Madrid: Alianza Universidad, 1982: 139–145.
Cruz, Anne J. and Rosilie Hernández, eds. *Women's Literacy in Early Modern Spain and the New World*. Aldershot, UK; Burlington, VT: Ashgate, 2011.
Dadson, Trevor. *Diego de Silva y Mendoza. Poeta y político en la corte de Felipe III*. Granada: Ediciones de la Universidad de Granada, 2011.
——. "The Count of Salinas and the Women in his Life." *Perspectives on Early Modern Women in Iberia and the Americas*. Ed. Adrienne L. Martin and María Cristina Quintero. New York: Escribana Books, 2015: 52–71.
Daybell, James. "Letters." *The Cambridge Companion to Early Modern Women's Writing*. Ed. Laura Lunger Knoppers. Cambridge: Cambridge UP, 2009: 181–193.
Dodge, Meredith and Rick Hendricks. *Two Hearts, One Soul. The Correspondence of the Condesa de Galve, 1988–96*. Albuquerque: U New Mexico P, 1993.
Estrada Medinilla, María de. "Relación escrita a una religiosa prima suya." En Josefina Muriel, *Cultura femenina novohispana*. México D.F.: Universidad Nacional Autónoma de México, [1982] 2000: 125–140.
Fernández Alcaide, Marta. *Cartas de particulares en Indias del siglo XVI. Edición y estudio discursivo*. Madrid: Iberoamericana Vervuert, 2009.
Gamboa, Yolanda. "Female Agency and Daily Life in Early Colonial Florida's Ciudad Letrada." *Perspectives on Early Modern Women in Iberia and the Americas*. Ed. Adrienne L. Martin and María Cristina Quintero. New York: Escribana Books, 2015: 150–164.
García Mouton, Pilar. "Las mujeres que escribieron cartas desde América." *Anuario de lingüística hispánica* 12–13 (1985): 319–326.
González Echevarría, Roberto. *Myth and Archive: A Theory of Latin American Narrative*. Durham, NC: Duke UP, 1998.
Graubart, Karen. *With Our Labor and Sweat: Indigenous Women and the Formation of Colonial Society in Peru*. Stanford: Stanford UP, 2007.
Guengerich, Sara V. "Capac Women and the Politics of Marriage in Early Colonial Peru." *Colonial Latin American Review* 24.2 (2015): 147–167.
Guevara, Isabel de. "Carta a la princesa Juana." *Madres del Verbo/Mothers of the Word*. Ed. Nina M. Scott. Albuquerque: U New Mexico P, 1999: 9–11.
Howe, Elizabeth. *Education and Women in the Early Modern Hispanic World*. Aldershot, UK; Burlington, VT: Ashgate, 2008.
Le Goff, Jacques. *Lo maravilloso y cotidiano en el Occidente medieval*. Barcelona: Gedisa, 1986.
Lezama Lima, José. *La expresión americana*. México: Fondo de Cultura Económica, (1957) 1998.
Lohmann Villena, Guillermo. "Huellas renacentistas en la literatura peruana del siglo XVI." *La tradición clásica en el Perú virreinal*. Ed. Teodoro Hampe Martínez and Franklin Pease. Lima: Fondo Editorial de la Universidad Nacional Mayor de San Marcos, 1999: 115–128.
Lopreto, Gladys. "Isabel de Guevara: la primera feminista." *Todo es Historia*, 34 (1991): 43–49.
Mangan. Jane E. "Indigenous Women as Mothers in Conquest-Era Peru." *Women of the Iberian Atlantic*. Ed. Sarah Owens and Jane Mangan. Baton Rouge: Louisiana State UP, 2012: 82–100.

Martin, Luis. *Daughters of the Conquistadores. Women of the Viceroyalty of Perú*. Dallas: Southern Methodist UP, 1983.

Martínez López, Enrique. "Sor Juana Inés de la Cruz en Portugal: un desconocido homenaje y versos inéditos." *Revista de Literatura* 33 (1968): 53–84.

McKnight, Kathryn and Leo Garofalo, eds. *Afro-Latino Voices: Documentary Narratives from the Early Modern Iberian World*. Cambridge, MA: Hackett, 2009.

Méndez Plancarte, Alfonso, ed. *Poetas novohispanos: Segundo siglo (1621–1721)*. México: Universidad Nacional Autónoma de México, 1940.

Mignolo, Walter. "Cartas, crónicas y relaciones del descubrimiento y la conquista." *Historia de la literatura hispanoamericana. Tomo 1*. Ed. Luis Iñigo Madrigal. Madrid: Cátedra, 1982: 59–78.

Muñoz, Inés. "Carta de doña Inés Muñoz de Ribera pidiendo la devolución de unos Indios, 20 de Mayo de 1543." In Rocío Quispe-Agnoli, "Taking Possession of the New World." *Legacy* 28.2 (2011): 280–283.

Muriel, Josefina. *Cultura Femenina Novohispana*. México D.F.: Universidad Nacional Autónoma de México, [1982] 2000.

Otte, Enrique. *Cartas privadas de emigrantes a Indias, 1540–1616*. Seville: Consejería de Cultura, Junta de Andalucía y Escuela de Estudios Hispano Americanos de Sevilla, 1988.

Peña, Enrique A. *Fragmentos históricos sobre temas coloniales dejados por Enrique Peña*. Buenos Aires: Imprenta Angel Curoto, 1935.

Pender, Patricia. *Early Modern Women's Writing and the Rhetoric of Modesty*. New York: Palgrave Macmillan, 2012.

Quispe-Agnoli, Rocío. "Taking Possession of the New World: Powerful Female Agency in Early Colonial Accounts of Perú." *Legacy. A Journal of American Women Writers* 28.2 (2011): 257–289.

———. "Domesticando la frontera: mirada, voz y agencia textual de dos encomenderas en el Perú del siglo XVI." *Guaraguao* 15.36 (Primavera 2011): 69–87.

———. "*Mulieris Litterarum*: Oral, Visual, and Written Narratives of Indigenous Elite Women." *The Cambridge History of Latin American Women's Literature*. Ed. Ileana Rodríguez y Mónica Szurmuk. Cambridge: Cambridge UP, 2016: 38–51.

Relación escrita por doña María Estrada Medinilla a una religiosa prima suya de la feliz entrada en México, día de S. Agustín, a 28. de Agosto de mil y seiscientos y quarenta años. Del Excellentissimo Señor Don Diego López Pacheco, Cabrera, y Bobadilla, Marqués de Villena, Virrey y Governador, y capitán General desta Nueva España. México: Francisco Robledo, 1640.

Sabat de Rivers, Georgina. *Estudios de literatura hispanoamericana. Sor Juana Inés de la Cruz y otros poetas barrocos de la colonia*. Barcelona: Promociones y Publicaciones Universitarias, 1992.

Sánchez Rubio, Rocío and Isabel Testón Núñez, eds. *El hilo que une: las relaciones epistolares en el Viejo y en el Nuevo Mundo, siglos XVI–XVIII*. Cáceres: Universidad de Extremadura, 1999.

Scott, Nina M. *Mothers of the Word. Early Spanish American Women Writers*. Albuquerque: U New Mexico P, 1999.

Silva, Yamile. "Prácticas escriturales femeninas: espacialidad e identidad en la Colonia (Río de La Plata, siglos XVI–XVII)." Unpublished Ph.D. dissertation. University of Massachussetts, 2011.

Stangl, Werner. "Consideraciones metodológicas acerca de las cartas privadas de emigrantes españoles desde América, 1492–1824. El caso de las 'cartas de llamada.'" *Jahrbuch für Geschichte Lateinamerikas* 47 (2010): 11–35.

———. "Un cuarto de siglo con Cartas privadas de emigrantes a Indias. Prácticas y perspectivas de ediciones de cartas transatlánticas en el Imperio español." *Anuario de Estudios Americanos* 70.2 (2013): 703–736.

Tieffemberg, Silvia. "Isabel de Guevara o la construcción del yo femenino." *Filología* 24 (1989): 287–300.

Vergara Quiroz, Santiago. *Cartas de mujeres en Chile, 1630–1885: estudio, selección documental y notas*. Santiago de Chile: Editorial Andrés Bello, 1987.

Vettenranta, Erja. "Desvelando tramoyas: 'La relación feliz' de María de Estrada Medinilla en la fiesta barroca de la Nueva España." *Guaraguao* 15.36 (2011): 34–48.

Vinatea Recoba, Martina, ed. *Epístola de Amarilis a Belardo*. Madrid: Iberoamericana Vervuert, 2009.

Vollendorf, Lisa. "Transatlantic Ties: Women's Writings in Iberia and the Americas." *Women, Religion, and the Atlantic World (1600–1800)*. Ed. Daniella Kostroun and Lisa Vollendorf. Toronto: U Toronto P, 2009: 79–112.

Weber, Alison. *Teresa of Avila and the Rhetoric of Femininity*. Princeton, NJ: Princeton UP, 1990.

22

TRANSNATIONAL EXCHANGES

Nieves Baranda Leturio

In the mid-fifteenth century, the Iberian Peninsula was comprised of five kingdoms, with Castile the largest in terms of size and population. By the end of the sixteenth century, all were governed by the Spanish monarch, along with the vast colonies in America, part of the southern Italian peninsula (Sardinia, Naples, Sicily), the Netherlands, and other smaller lands and islands. Spain's global power was exerted from the Madrid court, whence diplomats, agents, merchants, emissaries, military, and religious left to rule an empire that controlled the western world. Toward the middle of the seventeenth century, however, Spain's territories began a lengthy process of separation that first affected sections of Europe: Portugal declared its independence in 1640, finally achieving it in 1668 after continued warfare, and in 1648, the United Provinces of the Netherlands were recognized as an independent state. Spain's Italian dominions would not separate until the mid-eighteenth century, while its American colonies achieved independence in the nineteenth century.

These extensive territories could not be considered a nation, as their languages, histories, and cultural identities differed. Their divergence, however, did not keep them from forming a state under the Spanish monarchy's patrimonial rule. While the Spanish monarchs imposed confessionalism through the Inquisition in strict adherence to Counter-Reformation ideology, the territories were unified solely by monarchical rule. To apply the modern term "transnationalism" to the early modern period, therefore, is anachronistic, as nations, such as we understand them today, did not exist at the time; according to Anthony D. Smith, nation is defined "as a named human population sharing an historic territory, common myths and historical memories, a mass, public culture, a common economy and common legal rights and duties for all members" (14). The term *nación* in early modern Spain referred to the union of individuals according to their place of birth (fr. Latin, *natio*), although a common language, also associated with shared origins, soon formed part of the means of identification. As Pedro Ruiz Pérez points out, "the modern conscience of [the Spanish] nation first took hold with the reclamation of the vernacular, its emulation of Latin, and its rivalry against other Romance languages" (506).[1] Following this premise, this chapter will limit the term "transnational" to its linguistic, rather than its political meaning, that is, as a process of transference between different cultures that speak different languages. Our focus will be on women's authorship in Spanish, either on works written in Spanish by women who traveled to territories where the language was not prevalent, or of women authors from those same territories whose writings were translated into Spanish.

Nieves Baranda Leturio

Spanish authors and Spanish translators

The first works by women writers translated into Spanish and read by the larger Spanish public were those of Angela of Foligno and Catherine of Siena, published in Toledo, 1510, and Alcalá de Henares, 1512, respectively. While they may not have been given credit as authors, since their reputation at the time was that of holy women, due to the authority conferred on them by divine communication, both women proved the exception to Saint Paul's dictum that women should remain silent in public and not preach in church (*mulier in ecclesia tacet, I Corinthians*: 14.34). Their works, *Libro de la bienaventurada sancta Angela de Fulgino* (Book of the Blessed Saint Angela of Foligno) were of import, as they were translated at a very early stage, when women's writings provoked strong feelings of rejection. This was corroborated by Teresa of Cartagena (1425–1478), who wrote her *Admiración operum dey* (*Admiration for the Work of God*) in response to the criticism and disparagement that, as a woman, she had received for writing the treatise *Arboleda de los enfermos* (Grove of the Infirm).[2] Despite such a widespread attitude, the translations of Angela of Foligno's and Catherine of Siena's works, promoted as they were by the church, permitted a female sainthood that was not opposed to their role as teachers of doctrinal sources to Catholics. Although the authors and their writings differ greatly, they are similar in that the works include texts that were either spoken aloud or dictated to a person who then wrote them down; this person or someone else (a male) then functioned as editor, collating texts into a book as an anthology. The editions include in the front matter a hagiography of the author that attempts to respond to the controversies over the author's sainthood and serves as the basis for the texts' authority and religious orthodoxy. At a time when publishing a book elevated it to canonical status, the texts' publication implicitly affirmed that women's writings could be legitimized under certain conditions.

There are no data available with which to demonstrate that the translations of either Angela of Foligno's or Catherine of Siena's works influenced other women's writings, although most probably they served as the model for the book by Sor María de Santo Domingo (c. 1485–1525), known as the Beata of Piedrahita. The similarities of her *Libro de la oración* (Book of Prayer) (c. 1518) with the two editions reveal that the prologue's author took them as his inspiration and direct model when organizing her book (Huerga: 200–204). It was very likely thought that the readers would recognize its antecedents, its holy genealogy implicitly legitimizing Sor María (Baranda, "Nombres"). The influence of the Italian saints themselves on the Iberian peninsula's spiritual development was early and significant.[3] Huerga (199) maintains that it was not Catherine of Siena's edited works, but her life history that circulated widely. It is important to note, however, that several *beatas*, or holy lay women, from Andalusia were compared to her, and that one had written a "book of revelations more lofty than that of Saint Catherine of Siena" (Huerga: 206), proving that there was already a strong awareness of the Italian saint's gift of language and her public teaching. In Angela of Foligno's case, there was a later translation by a thirteen-year-old girl, Francisca de los Ríos (c. 1606–?), *Vida de la bienaventurada Santa Angela de Fulgino [. . .] Ahora de nuevo traducida de Latín en lengua castellana* (Life of the Blessed Saint Angela of Foligno [. . .] Newly Translated from Latin to Castilian) (1618).[4] In contrast to England, where numerous women writers were also acknowledged for their translations (Uman), in Spain, women translators do not assume relevance until the eighteenth century (López Cordón). Some, no doubt, intended the same goals as their English counterparts: to be publicly recognized by carrying out a literary activity that was not considered creative or first-rate. It would be unthinkable for an adolescent, for instance, to publish without parental approval, so Francisca de los Ríos was probably encouraged in her work by her parents, who then financed the edition. The translation may well have brought the family a degree of fame, as they capitalized on the daughter's elite education and Saint Angela as a holy model for the girl, who would become a nun. It had a great impact, as it is mentioned by several authors, from the seventeenth through the eighteenth century, such as Juan Pérez de Montalbán and Joseph Antonio Álvarez de Baena, and was highly praised:

> In my judgment, the most faithful and fit translation is the one done by Doña Francisca de los Ríos at the tender age of thirteen [. . .] The appropriateness of the registers with which she explains its concepts, leaving out not one bit of the original work's context, is admirable [. . .] It is a wonder that everything argues for great capability and virtuous practice at such a tender age. I have seen other translations in the Tuscan language, but none has seemed to me as fit as this one.[5]
>
> *Cornejo: 422*

Like those mentioned above, the few translations by women that were published in early modern Spain dealt with religious and moral themes, for example, *Verdadera quietud y tranquilidad del alma* (The Soul's True Stillness and Tranquility), attributed to Isabel de Sforza; the letter by Elizabeth Saunders to Francis Inglefield; and the moral epistles of the Lord of Narveza, written by a man, but translated by Françoise de Passier. These are all heterogeneous, of varying dates in time, and each due to diverse circumstances. The first, *Verdadera quietud y tranquilidad del alma*, is the work of Ortensio Lando, who, with Isabel de Sforza's consent, appropriated her name in order to avoid the censorship his other works had received (Daenens). It was really an Italian text that circulated in other European countries and in Spain in two different translations, one by Juan Díaz de Cárdenas (1560), and the other by Nicolás Díaz (1571). The *Traslado de una carta de cierta monja inglesa llamada Isabel Sandera* (Translation of a Letter by the English Nun Isabel Sandera) is a real letter written by the Catholic nun, Elizabeth Saunders, who narrates her stay in English prisons and how she managed to escape to her convent in France. The wide acceptance that this translation had in Spain, with two editions in broadsheets and as an insert in Diego de Yepes's well-known *Historia particular de la persecución de Inglaterra, y de los martirios que en ella ha avido, desde el año del Señor, 1570* (A Particular History of the Persecution in England, and of the Martyrs Who Have Suffered There Since the Year of Our Lord, 1570) (Travisky), is due to the anti-Protestant propaganda machine that the Jesuits operated in Seville and Valladolid through their English colleges, or seminaries to form priests who would export Catholic doctrine to England. As to the *Cartas morales del señor de Narveza, traducidas de lengua francesa en la española por madama Francisca de Passier* (1605) (Moral Epistles of the Lord of Narveza, translated from the French Language into Spanish by Madame Francisca de Passier), this work's first publication could have been meant as an homage by the translator's husband for his young wife's untimely death. The interest aroused by the translation, however, led to a second translation (1610), corrected and expanded by Cesar Oudin, one of the most prolific Spanish translators and teachers in France at that time (Cioranescu: 126–129; Zuili).

In comparison with these moral and religious works, the book by Marie Mancini (1639–1715) is definitely anomalous. The author, who was Cardinal Mazarin's niece, wrote *La verdad en su luz o las verdaderas memorias de madama Maria Manchini, Condestablesa Colona* (Truth Illuminated, or the True Memoir of Madame Maria Manchini, Condestable Colonna) in 1677, which was translated into English in 1679. She had married Lorenzo Onofrio Colonna and lived in Rome, but fled due to marital problems. After traversing the greater part of Europe, she arrived in Madrid, where she wrote *La verdad*, her autobiographical apologia in response to a scandalous apocryphal memoir that had been published two years earlier.[6] Although she wrote her memoir in French, she had it translated into Spanish so both versions could come out simultaneously in France and Spain. Her decision to publish, therefore, introduced into Spanish culture a work never before seen, as it publicized the private life of an aristocrat, without eschewing even intimate details.[7]

Save for Mancini's work, male mediators usually were the ones who exploited both the translations of works by women authors, and the works translated by women. This in itself does not negate female agency, which was sometimes acknowledged by the Spanish literary establishment. Among the female poets mentioned in his *Auto del hijo pródigo* (Seville, 1604) (Play of the Prodigal Son), Lope de Vega includes Isabel de Sforza: "[she] was illustrious in letters and virtue, and the Phoenix of Milan" (Vega Carpio: 41). Likewise, Yepes selects Elizabeth Saunders's letter, which had been printed earlier in ephemeral form, for inclusion in his work, transforming the text and its female voice into an official part of Counter-Reformation historiography.

Translations from Spanish to other languages

The two Spanish women writers who qualify as international best sellers are both nuns: Teresa of Ávila (1515–1582) and Sor María de Jesús de Ágreda (1602–1665). Teresa's fame as a saint and the expansion to other European countries of the Discalced Carmelite order that she had founded propelled the translations of her works.[8] The dates of the first translations of Teresa's works in the following languages show their rapid extension: French, 1601; Italian, 1603; German, 1649; Portuguese, 1653; Polish, 1664–1665; English, 1671; Latin (published in Cologne), 1626–1627.[9] If we also consider other editions, translations, and publications of individual works, as well as biographies, summaries, and abridged works, Teresa of Ávila emerges as the Spanish woman writer par excellence and a cultural icon recognized throughout Europe. The translations of her works were very likely promoted for proselytizing purposes by her order, her nuns, and the Catholic Church, and supported in some instances by government forces, such as occurred in France (Pageaux). Although with far less cultural and religious weight than Teresa, María de Jesús de Ágreda's posthumous text, *Mística ciudad de Dios* (1670) (Mystical City of God) also circulated extensively. This life of the Virgin Mary, dictated by her to the nun, defended the Virgin's immaculate conception, a highly controversial theme for the church at the time. The Spanish Inquisition, followed by the Roman Inquisition, banned the book, and although it was later removed from the Spanish Index, the Roman Inquisition's ban was never resolved. The book was also condemned by the theologians at the University of the Sorbonne. The polemic over the work lasted over one hundred years after its first edition (Morte: 236–243). Despite these problems, it was first translated into French in 1695, into Italian in 1703, and into Polish in 1731. There have been translations into Polish as late as the twentieth century, and into the twenty-first in abbreviated editions (Partyka).

However, apart from these authors, whose editorial success was based mainly on their sanctified status, Spanish women authors had little or no recognizable transnational impact, as their translations were frequently published without identifying the author and even modifying the title. The romance of chivalry *Cristalián de España* (Cristalián of Spain) by Beatriz Bernal was translated into Italian among the rest of the Spanish novels of chivalry that circulated in Europe.[10] Following generic convention, the novels were presented as translations of ancient texts, so their real authors were often ignored or the novels were published anonymously, presenting their author instead as their translator. *Cristalián*'s princeps edition of 1545 did not identify Beatriz Bernal as its author, although two features revealed her gender: the front cover stated that the novel was "corrected and amended from its ancient origins by a lady from the noble and most loyal town of Valladolid;"[11] and the dedication to Philip II narrated an episode that explained how a woman who was visiting churches with some lady friends had found the work in an old tomb and transcribed it. Its Italian translation, *La famosa et degna historia degli invitti cavalieri don Cristaliano di Spagna et Lucescanio suo fratello* (The Famous and Honorable History of the Victorious Knights Don Cristalián of Spain and Luzescanio, His Brother)[12] was published anonymously, with no trace of any female authorship (Gagliardi), as its Italian editors had deliberately removed the allusion to a woman on the cover and substituted the original dedication with one not containing the explanation of the book's "discovery" or its transcription by a woman.

This same case also occurred with other women authors. A section of the work *El noble perfecto* (The Perfect Noble) by Luisa María de Padilla, Countess of Aranda, was partially translated into Italian (Nider: 2012); however, the "extract," *Esercizio della morte. Estratto dal Libro intitolato "Il nobile perfetto" del padre maestro Pietro Enrico Pastore Agostiniano, Tradotto dall'idioma Spagnuolo nell'Italiano* (Death's Practice. An Extract from the Book Titled "The Perfect Noble," by Father Pedro Enrique Pastor, Agustinian, Translated from the Spanish Language into Italian),[13] although attributed to Pedro Enrique Pastor, who appears as the author of the Spanish edition, was not written by him. The case of Francisca del Santísimo Sacramento (1561–1629) was even more complicated, as her writings suffered various appropriations and manipulation as they were disseminated transnationally. The biographer, Miguel Batista de Lanuza, utilized Francisca's *Visiones*, written in manuscript, to write her biography, which then became the source of Juan de Palafox y Mendoza's *Luz de vivos y escarmiento en los muertos* (Light of the Living and Lessons of the Dead), which was then translated into Italian as *Lume a'vivi dall esempio de'morti* (Light to the Living from the Example of the Dead) (Naples, 1673).[14] Paradoxically, the visions of the nun, which her convent of Discalced Carmelites kept archived as private writings, and that angered the convent when they saw them as part of the published biography, managed to travel as far as another country (Ostolaza Elizondo: 288). While the linguistic, ideological, and cultural transformation determined the renewed reading and reception of the original egotexts, it sustained the feminine experience as its authorial source, reaching the readership albeit through male mediation.

Among the secular women authors, there is no doubt that María de Zayas garnered the most fame, although her authorship was not always recognized or mentioned. This was due in great measure because more than translations as such, we must refer to the adaptations, transformations, and hipertextuality of her works. That her two collections of novels, *Novelas amorosas y exemplares* (Amorous and Exemplary Novels) (1637) and *Desengaños amorosos* (Disenchantments of Love) (1647),[15] were each composed of ten novels that could be seen as separate and independent entities, facilitated the process of dissemination, at times in one volume and at other times as individual pieces. Although the collections were not translated in complete volumes until their French version in 1680 by Claude Vanel,[16] the individual novels had been translated much earlier:[17]

- Paul Scarron, *Les Nouvelles tragicomiques* (Paris, Antoine de Sommaville, 1656). Includes, from Zayas: "La Précaution inutile" ("El prevenido engañado"[*Amorosas*, 4])[18] and "L' Adultère innocent" ("Al fin se paga todo" [*Amorosas*, 7]).
- Antoine de Le Méthel, Sieur d'Ouville, *Les nouvelles amoureuses et exemplaires composées en espagnol par cette merveille de son sexe, Doña Maria de Zayas y Sotomayor* (Paris, G. de Luynes, 1656): "La précaution inutile" ("El prevenido engañado" [*Amorosas* 4]), "S'aventurer en perdant" ("Aventurarse perdiendo" [*Amorosas* 1]), "La Belle invisible, ou la Constance esprouvée" ("La fuerza del amor" [*Amorosas* 5]), "L'amour se paye avec amour" ("El juez de su causa" [*Amorosas* 9]), "La vengeance d' Aminte affronté" ("La burlada Aminta" [*Amorosas* 2]), and "A la fin tout se paye" ("Al fin se paga todo" [*Amorosas* 7]).

- Paul Scarron, *Le roman comique* (Paris, G. de Luynes, 1657): "Le Juge de sa propre cause" ("El juez de su causa" [*Amorosas*, 9]).
- François Le Métel, abbé de Boisrobert, *Nouvelles héroïques et amoureuses* (Paris: Pierre Lamy, 1657): "L'inceste supposé" ("La perseguida triunfante" [*Desengaños* 9]).
- Molière, *L'école des femmes. Comédie* (Paris, G. de Luyne, 1663) ("El prevenido engañado" [*Amorosas* 4]).
- Denis Clerselier de Nanteuil, *La Fille vice-roi, comédie heroïque* (Hanovre, Schwendimann, 1672) ("El juez de su causa" [*Amorosas*, 9]).

Given the numbers of translations, Yllera affirms that María de Zayas was "one of the authors of seventeenth-century brief novels who achieved the highest prestige in France, after Cervantes" ("Temas": 317).[19] Her works are translated as part of the French novel's renewal, which finds the narratives in Spanish literature to be closer to reality and more verisimilar (Cioranescu: 439–483), and whose attraction to authors and readers lends them to be translated often (Merino García, *La novella*: 416). In general, translators appreciate the Spanish novels' themes, which they see as witty, as well as their structure and innovative plots. However, they frequently criticize the style, which they attempt to improve on and polish in the French versions. The novels' paratexts incorporate the opinion about Zayas's works and, in some cases, the process the original has gone through, a valuable testimony on their reception, in contrast to the the silence Spanish women writers usually encountered. In this regard, d'Ouville (Antoine Le Methel) is especially laudatory, perhaps because he is attempting, through his defense of Zayas, to attack Scarron, who also had translated and/or adapted her work without citing her:

> From many of the novels written in Spanish, by a woman who may be compared, not only for her invention, but also for her elocution, to the most celebrated writers of the century; I have chosen six for you that I believe are the most agreable and worthy of being translated into our language [. . .] For me, who knows her merit and sufficiency, who knows that her style owes nothing to that of the most consummate authors of her nation, and who also knows that the heavens have been no less stingy with its favors and illumination to the beautiful sex than to ours; I say boldly that it is a woman from whom I receive pleasure here, and wish to follow and imitate, and I dare repeat even more boldly, that if I could imitate her, you would judge by this book alone that there are hardly any men who surpass her.[20]

The defense does not mean that d'Ouville attempted an exact translation, but that he followed the original texts more closely than did Scarron, who used Zayas's novels as a framework over which to create his own work.[21] His function was that of a cultural intermediary who underscores Spanish taste, but simultaneously modifies the concept to adapt the novels to the tastes of a French reader (Merino García, *La novella*: 416). These versions then became the foundation for other works, and through Scarron's rereadings, some of Zayas's novels achieved a long life (Cobos Castro) and were even known in England.

Until recently, Zayas's influence on the early modern English novel was entirely unknown, as there were no direct translations and her authorship was never explicitly recognized.[22] However, Dolors Altaba-Artal (1999) established without a doubt that Aphra Behn (1640–1689), the first profesional English woman writer, imitated some of Zayas's novels in her own: *Love letters between a nobleman and his sister* ("Estragos que causa el vicio" [*Engaños*, 10] and "La más infame venganza" [*Engaños*, 2]); *The History of the Nun or The Fair Vow Breaker* (London, 1689) ("El imposible vencido" [*Amorosas* 8]); *The Nun; or the perjur'd beauty* ("El imposible vencido" [*Amorosas 8*] and "La más infame venganza" [E*ngaños*, 2]); *The unhappy Mistake; or, The Impious Vow Punish'd* ("El traidor contra su sangre" [*Engaños* 8], parts 1 and 2); *The Lucky Mistake: A New Novel* ("El traidor contra su sangre" [*Engaños* 8], part 1); *The Unfortunate Happy Lady: A True History* ("La burlada Aminta" [*Amorosas* 2]) and *The Unfortunate Bride; or, The Blind Lady a Beauty* ("El verdugo de su esposa" [*Desengaños* 3]). Behn knew Zayas indirectly through the French translations, although Altaba-Artal posits that Behn could have read Spanish and that some details suggest she was directly familiar with Zayas's work (19, 166). Apart from any familiarity, however, critics have called attention to the feminist resonances between the authors, despite their many differences due to the process of cultural transference (Altaba-Artal: 202–223; Romero-Díaz). Like Zayas, Behn defended the right of women to be educated, to work, and to express themselves in a man's world; she found in Zayas's novels a feminist perspective that she could incorporate into her own.[23] This may be the reason why Behn, as a woman, is more interested in the *Desengaños amorosos*' assertive feminist ideology than in the more traditional *Novelas amorosas*, in contrast to the French male adapters, who preferred the latter.

Zayas's transnational dissemination proves that she was not only a successful author in Spain, but also that her novels, translated into French and transcribed by Behn into English, formed an integral part of the process of renovation and creation of early modern fiction, a significant contribution that is not generally emphasized about her writings, even by gender studies.

Spanish among Portuguese women authors

The close relations between the royal families and elites of Portugal and Spain from the fifteenth century on contributed to the use of Spanish as the common literary language among early modern Portuguese authors (Martínez Aomoyna and Viera de Lemos; Buescu). For this reason, some of the most important women authors in Spanish were native-born Portuguese speakers who achieved transnational visibility in their own language. Their works emerged within a cultural context shared across the Iberian peninsula, as the literary genres, thematics, and *topoi* were essentially the same in both territories and recognizable to all the authors and readers. There are, however, local differences and in Portugal women seem to be elevated to the level of an author—in all aspects of the term—and integrate into the socio-literary networks. This may be seen in the early publication of their works, and in the visibility given to their relations with male writers, who seem to consider them belonging to the republic of letters, and request their poems for paratexts of works, citing them frequently. Bernarda Ferreira de Lacerda (1595–1644), Violante do Céu (1607–1693), and María do Céu (1658–1754) share these characteristics, as can be seen in the numerous works published during the lives of their authors. Lacerda was not mistaken when she asserted in the preliminary verses to the *Hespaña libertada* (Spain Liberated) that she wrote in Spanish because it was a language that "came easily to all" and because her work would have more circulation: "so it will be more vernacular and better known;" "wishing that many will see it" (I.7). [24]

Indeed, writing in Spanish allowed Portuguese authors—male and female—to inscribe themselves in two different cultural systems: a socio-literary network within their Portuguese environment, most always Lisbon, and other, geographically distant networks, rooted in Castile, primarily Madrid. Only after having gained fame in their own surroundings were their works acknowledged there when they arrived, written as by already well-known *women* writers. Once famous, they seemed to be accepted by those who mention them as part of the Spanish literary canon (or Parnassus, to use the contemporary term). Although in some cases, their use of Spanish was considered an alienating factor that weakened Portuguese culture, it should be noted that this use also permitted them to participate in the literary networks of both languages, and were not at all affected by Portugal's war of restoration (1640–1668). As an example, a group of Lisbon nuns asked Sor Juana Inés de la Cruz to compose literary *enigmas*, which she sent them from Mexico around 1692–1693. The Countess of Paredes, previously the vicereine of Mexico, took part in the festive literary game (Morujão, *Por trás da grade*: 234–239). Another collaboration is that of Maria do Céu and Teresa Moncada, Duchess of Medinaceli; the Spanish aristocrat received over eighty poems from the nun that she then had translated into Spanish and published in Madrid as *Las obras varias y admirables de Maria do Céu* (Marín Pina). A different case is that of Ángela de Azevedo, about whom we have no trustworthy biographical information, yet who may have written her plays—always in Spanish—in Lisbon to be represented there in the second half of the 1600s.[25]

For the Portuguese women writers of the seventeenth century, employing Spanish as their literary language did not signify losing their cultural identity, which remained explicit in their works. Lacerda's *Hespaña libertada* narrates, in royal octaves, part of the medieval history of the Iberian Peninsula's reconquest from the Moslems. The narrative interlaces historical sources from both countries, modifying Castilian tradition by inserting noteworthy Portuguese heroes and lineages, and thus renovating Luso-Hispanic historiography in light of the new political situation. Since the book was published in 1618, only one year before Philip III's visit to Lisbon, Lacerda could have had a pragmatic purpose in mind, that of promoting herself and her family lineage (Baranda, "Mujer escritura": 235–237). Lacerda's second book is a collection of ballads that describe the Buçaco mountain near Coimbra, where the Discalced Carmelites had founded a hermitage. The *Soledades de Buçaco* (The Solitudes of Buçaco) (1634) ends with a prose epilogue in which the author responds to a letter from a "Castilian gentleman" who asks her whether her description of Buçaco is an exaggeration; this then allows her to praise the site point by point.[26]

According to the preliminaries of Violante do Céu's *Rimas varias* (Various Poems) (1646), the author did not intervene in its publication, which was prepared by Fray Leonardo de São José and possibly financed by the Count of Vidigueira, a patron of the arts who belonged to a Parisian circle in favor of Portuguese restoration (Violante do Céu: 15–17). The book mainly contains love and courtly lyrics, written over the nun's lifetime, some dating to 1624, others very recently dedicated to King João IV, who assumed the throne in 1640 (Violante do Céu: 59, 65, 95). The dedications do not necessarily indicate any political activism on the nun's part, although she was beloved by those in favor of restoration, who included her as one of their poets, and she maintained close relations with the Portuguese royal family and aristocrats, for whom she wrote very frequently (Baranda, "Violante"). The title of *Parnaso lusitano* (Lusitanian Parnassus) (1732–1733), a posthumous collection of her works, demonstrates that she was acknowledged as a *national* poet, despite the fact that all her life she wrote also in Spanish, as some poetic genres, such as the *villancico* and the *romance* required.

Other later women authors also continued the tradition of writing in both Portuguese and Spanish, their works circulating across the Iberian Peninsula and the colonies. Ángela de Azevedo's three plays deal with themes that allude directly to Portugal, whose action takes place in Lisbon, Oporto, and Santarém, and in some way appeal to the public's Portuguese identity. Longer works by women authors clearly reveal their bilingualism, with Spanish sharply declining in use and limited to specific genres, such as theater or for poetry, the *romances*, as mentioned above. By the first half of the eighteenth century, however, the countries had begun to lose their close cultural connection, and Portuguese works circulated in Spain only in Spanish versions or translations. Two nuns from the Mosteiro da Esperança, Lisbon's aristocratic convent, were well known in Portugal: Maria do Céu (1658–1753)[27] and Maria Magdalena Eufemia da Glória (1672–1759). María do Céu's book, *Las obras varias y admirables* (Various Admirable Works), appeared in Madrid in 1744, when she was already famous in Portugal for her abundant publications (Morujão, *Contributo*). The translator, however, stresses that she was unkown in Castile, and in the prologue, reveals his misgivings about "admirable," which he believes is too exaggerated a title: "too many flowers for a nun and too many pearls for one in sackcloth."[28] He admits that he first thought that the author may have been substituted, "I suspected, also, if a man might not have a hand in it, attempting to publish it under a woman's name for its novelty."[29] Its publication in Madrid was not due to its wide circulation in Castile, but to the Duchess of Medinaceli's patronage; she probably commissioned the publication to Fernando de Settién and surely financed the edition (Marín Pina).

Had María do Céu published her works in Lisbon and under a Portuguese title, the poems and plays in Spanish that she included therein would have gone unnoticed by a Spanish readership, even if they were written in that language.[30] The same occurred with Leonarda Gil da Gama, the pseudonym of Maria Magdalena Eufemia da Glória. Her allegorical work, the *Brados del desengano* (Cries of Disillusionment), combines Portuguese prose with a number of Spanish poems, with no apparent impact in Spain, while her biography, *Vida de santa Rosa de Lima* (Life of Saint Rose of Lima),[31] translated into Spanish, was published in the Philippines.[32] After 1700, the only literary works in Portugal written in Spanish are those pertaining to poetic and theatrical genres. The bilingualism that had previously served to promote Portuguese women authors in Spanish court literary circles no longer induces the transnational circulation of their works.

The Sephardic tradition

Throughout the seventeenth century, Iberian literature constituted an important literary tradition in the Netherlands, thanks to the Sephardic communities, whose main center was Amsterdam. The over 400 books published in Portuguese and Spanish also included some by women (Boer, "Más allá": 67). The most well known, Isabel Rebeca Correa, translated Guarini's *Il pastor fido* into Spanish, while other women authors composed poems in Spanish, preserved in preliminaries or anthologies: Isabel Henríquez (Díaz Esteban), Sarah de Fonseca, Manuela Nuñes de Almeida, Beatriz de Fonseca, Bienvenida Cohen Belmonte, Branca Roiz, Branca Rodrígues, and Felisinda Fenisia (Brown "La poetisa"). Such efforts probably followed the cultural life of the city marked by its literary academies (Rebollo Liebermann), since they demonstrated that "the cultured and intelligent Jewish woman—at times a poet, othertimes a patron—was seen favorably in that society."[33] The women's small poetic output, however, is unique in that its themes are either panegyrical or familial, some unknown within the Spanish tradition; for example, praise to a young boy, to newlyweds, and the defense of a sister criticized at synagogue: "Versos que fêz Branca Roiz a minha Irmã Rachel Curiel no tempo que não íamos a Snoga por causa dos pleitos" (Poem by Branca Roiz to my Sister Rachel Curiel When We Missed Synagogue Because of the Arguments) (Brown, "La poetisa": 456).

Isabel Rebeca Correa compiled a songbook of her own poems (López Estrada 13), but we are familiar with only one poem and her translation of *Il pastor fido*, published in 1694 in Amsterdam, although some editions give Antwerp to promote its circulation outside religious borders (Boer, *La literatura*: 52–56). This work, authentically transnational, extends beyond any political and religious identity: Correa was of Portuguese origin, she wrote in Spanish, lived in the Jewish sector of Amsterdam, and dedicated her book to Manuel de Belmonte, the Spanish monarch's regent and a patron of the arts, who presided over the Academy of the Sitibundos and the Academy of the Floridos (Israel: 382–382, 384). Ignoring the many frontiers she crossed, Correa defends as her only identity that of her gender, highlighted in her prologue, in which she debates with her reader how she justifies her work: "It seems that you are saying (kind reader), that, as a woman who presumes to be prudent, I respond like a bragging chatterbox."[34] In her defense, she lists women from classical antiquity and her own judgment about her strength and her studies, with which she reaches the conclusion that her translation is better than any other. She vindicates her work as her own on the front cover ("translated [. . .] and illustrated with reflections by Isabel Correa")[35] and in the text, which carries out a "recontextualization of the concepts of pastoral love, desire, and female agency in the bower from a woman's point of view" (Hernández-Pecoraro: 129).

The Sephardic women writers in Amsterdam appropriate Spanish literary tradition by deploying the Spanish language when translating their genres, acting with great freedom in adapting it in a very personal manner to their own cultural idiosyncracies and their gendered perspective.

Future research

Other than those already mentioned above, there is still a wide field open to the study of women writers from a transnational and translinguistic perspective. The crossing of cultural borders may be interpreted from two points of view: as submission to a colonizing language, or as resistance against the inherent codes of the adopted language. If the translations of María de Zayas assume a feminine perspective, the women authors from Portugal and Amsterdam who adopt the Spanish language actually reconfigure the literary system, since they function from the periphery as a point of resistance, while at the same time they propose new models for women writers at the center. The Spanish translations of women writers are in need of study, as well as their role as models for peninsular women writers and in the public imaginary, where some became indicators of prestige. More studies of translations by women writers should be carried out. The analysis of Isabel Rebeca Correa's translation, *El pastor fido*, alerts us to the need of detailed comparisons to determine how translation became a means of resistant readings and of gendered voices, even when prologues and titles insist on faithful translations countering such dangers. The relationship between Zayas and Aphra Behn suggests more comparative studies of the uses by women writers of fiction in general, along with the methods they employed to publicly propose a feminine agenda, and what that agenda was. Similarly, there is still more research needed on Portuguese women authors who wrote in Spanish, as new investigations may offer new writings and new countries to study. The search for translations of the great mystical writers in other languages is no less interesting, and the numbers of works, their editions, with what purpose were they promoted, when and how they were incorporated into the target culture, and what reactions they aroused, are questions whose answers still need to be discovered.

Notes

1 "la moderna conciencia de nación se abrió camino y se asentó sobre la reivindicación de la lengua vulgar, la emulación respecto al latín y la rivalidad frente a los otros romances."
2 There are abundant studies on Teresa of Cartagena; see BIESES for general studies; for a synthesis of her life and works, see Surtz (21–40) and Cortés Timoner. For a modern English translation, see Seidenspinner-Núñez.
3 By contrast, Saint Gertrude of Helfta, also widely quoted and read to great acclaim, was not translated until the early seventeenth century (Carvalho: 304).
4 Although there is no modern edition, the book's paratexts may be accessed in BIESES: www.bieses/ net/tabla_paratextos/
5 "en mi juicio la más fiel y ajustada traducción es la que hizo doña Francisca de los Ríos en la tierna edad de treze años. [. . .] Es admirable la propiedad de las vozes con que, sin faltar un ápice al contexto de su original, explica sus conceptos; de todo se arguye gran capacidad y buena práctica de virtudes

que en edad tan tierna es admiración. Otras traducciones he visto hechas en lengua toscana, pero ninguna me ha parecido tan ajustada como esta."
6   *Les Mémoires de M. L. P. M. M. Colonne, G. connétable du royaume de Naples* (Cologne: P. Marteau, 1676). The French version of her authentic memoir was titled *Vérité dans son jour, ou les Véritables mémoires de M. Manchini, connétable Colonne* (c. 1678); see Mancini (Memoirs) for a recent English translation.
7   There were no comparable female autobiographies until those written in the nineteenth century by Gertrudis Gómez de Avellanada and Juana de la Vega, Countess of Espoz y Mina.
8   This chapter does not address writings of nuns who traveled outside Spain. For those, see Donahue, and Owens in this volume.
9   For a complete and well-organized bibliography of Teresa's works, see Palau (v. 19; 451–502). There are also nineteenth-century Arabic translations of both Teresa of Ávila and María de Ágreda (Río Sánchez).
10 See Armon's chapter in this volume.
11 "Corregida y enmendada de los antiguos originales por una señora natural de la noble y más leal villa de Valladolid."
12 The Italian editions were printed in Venice by Michele Tramessino, 1558; and by Lucio Spineda, 1609.
13 Printed in Torino by Giorgio Battista Valetta, 1738.
14 Printed in Naples by Giancinto Passaro, 1673; see Álvarez Santaló.
15 See Armon's chapter, which explains the use of *Desengaños* as the title.
16 Translated in five volumes as *Nouvelles de Dona Maria de Zayas. Traduites de l'espagnol* (Paris: G. Quinet, 1680).
17 Yllera (317–328) and Losada Goya (516–528) offer a general review of attributions and translations. The titles in this list follow only the first edition in chronological order. See also Yllera "Las dos" and Paun de García for translations of Zaya's "El castigo de la miseria."
18 See Merino García ("La recepción").
19 "uno de los autores de novelas breves del siglo XVII que mayor prestigio alcanzó en Francia, después de Cervantes."
20 "Entre plusieurs Nouuelles composées en Espagnol, par une Dame qui se peut égaler, non seulement pour l'invention, mais pour l'élocution encore aux plus celebres Escriuains du siecle; ie vous en ay choisy six qui m'ont paru les plus agreables, & les plus dignes d'estre traduittes en nostre langue. [. . .] Pour moy qui connoist son merite & sa suffisance, qui sçay que son stile ne doit rien à celuy des Autheurs les plus acheuez de sa Nation, & qui sçay d'ailleurs que le Ciel n'a pas esté plus auare de ses faueurs et de ses lumieres à ce beau sexe qu'au nostre; Ie dy hardiment que c'est une Femme que ie prends icy plaisir, & de suiure, & d'imiter, & i'ose dire encore auec plus de hardiesse, que si ie la sçauois bien imiter, vous iugeriez par ce seul ouurage qu'il n'y a guere d'hommes qui la surpassent." "Advis au lecteur," *Les nouuelles amoureuses* (qtd. in Marino García, "la recepción": 180–181).
21 Scarron harshly criticizes Zayas's literary style: "It is an affront for all those of María of Zayas's gender who know how to write well for this Spaniard to have been placed so highly above them, as she writes in an extravagant style with no good sense whatsoever ("il fait tort aussi à toutes les personnes du sexe de Maria de Zayas, qui sçavent bien ecrire, d'avoir mis cent picques au dessus d'elles cette Espagnole, qui écrit tout d'un style extravagant et rien de bon sens") (qtd. in Merino García, *La novella*: 292). Yet by adapting the most novels from Zayas, he demonstrates how much he appreciated them.
22 There are translations into English of some novels by Scarron that reversed Zayas's: Scarron's novels Viz. *The judge in his ovvn cause. The rival-brothers. The invisible mistress. The chastisement of avarice. Rendred into English by John Davies of Kidwelly* (London, 1667).
23 For an excellent extended study of the two novelists' similarities, see Altaba-Artal.
24 "para ser más vulgar y conocida," "desseando que de muchos vista sea."
25 The scarce biographical information we do have is from the unreliable *Bibliotheca Lusitana* by Diogo Barbosa Machado (1759). Recently, Urban Baños has documented that Azevedo was in Lisbon in 1682, which matches with her plays' dates, since theater in Spanish continued in Portugal well into the 1800s. Although the three editions of Azevedo's plays lack information, they may have been published in Seville. See Williamsen's chapter in this volume.
26 For the poem, see BIESES: www.bieses.net. María D. Martos is preparing an edition of the work.
27 Maria do Céu's secular name was Maria Deça y Tavora; occasionally, she used the pseudonym Marina Clemencia. For her most complete biography, see Hatherly (xiv–xxi).

28 "muchas flores para una religiosa y demasiadas perlas para quien está vestida de sayal" (h. 9v).
29 "Receleme también si andaría por medio la mano de algún hombre que para brindar con la novedad al buen despacho se valiese del nombre de mujer" (h. 10v).
30 This would be the case with the plays in her *Triunfo do rosário* (1740).
31 For the poems, see the BIESES databank.
32 Published by Tomás Adriano in Manila, 1755, translation by Esteban de Roxas y Melo. Although the author's name appears on the front cover, the preliminaries do not mention her and the translator refers to the author as male, rather than female.
33 "la mujer judía culta, inteligente –unas veces poetisa, otras mecenas—era vista favorablemente en esa sociedad" (Brown "La poetisa": 445).
34 "me parece que me dices (benévolo lector) que como mujer que pica en discreta, soy jactanciosa con punta de bachillera que respondo." BIESES, Sección de 'Autoras desde el umbral": www.bieses.net/wp-content/uploads/2015/09/correa_1649.pdf
35 "traducido [. . .] e ilustrado con reflexiones por Isabel Correa."

Works cited

Altaba-Artal, Dolores. *Aphra Behn's English Feminism. Wit and Satire*. Selinsgrove: Susquehanna UP; London: Associated UP, 1999.
Álvarez Santaló, León Carlos. "El libro de devoción como modelado y modelador de la conducta social: el 'Luz a los vivos' de Palafox (1668)." *Trocadero* 1 (1989): 7–25.
Ángela de Foligno, *Libro de la bienaventurada sancta Angela de Fulgino, en el qual se nos muestra la verdadera carrera para seguir las pisadas de nuestro redemptor y maestro Jesu christo. . .* Toledo: Sucesor de Hagembach, 1510.
Baranda, Nieves. "Mujer, escritura y fama: la *Hespaña libertada* (1618) de doña Bernarda Ferreira de Lacerda." *Península. Revista de Estudos Ibéricos* 0 (2003): 225–239.
———."Violante do Céu y los avatares políticos de la Restauração." *Iberoamericana. América Latina-España-Portugal* 28 (2007): 137–150.
———. "Beyond Political Boundaries: Religion as Nation in Early Modern Spain." *Women Telling Nations*. Ed. Amelia Sanz, Francesca Scott, and Suzan van Dijk. Amsterdam; New York: Rodopi, 2014: 63–84.
———. "Nombres aniquilados: publicaciones femeninas y lectores." *Criticón* 125 (2015): 65–77.
Batista de Lanuza, Miguel. *Vida de la sierva de Dios Francisca del Santísimo Sacramento*. Zaragoza: José Lanaja y Lamarca, 1659.
Boer, Harm den. "Más allá de hispanidad y judaísmo. Hacia una caracterización de la literatura hispano-portuguesa de los sefardíes de Amsterdam." *Los judaizantes en Europa y la literatura castellana del Siglo de Oro*. Ed. Fernando Díaz Esteban. Madrid: Letrúmero, 1994: 65–75.
———. *La literatura sefardí de Amsterdam*, Alcalá de Henares: Universidad de Alcalá, 1996.
Brown, Kenneth. "La poetisa es la luna que con las de Apolo viene: nuevos datos sobre textos de varias poetisas sefardíes de los siglos XVII y XVIII." *La creatividad femenina en el mundo barroco hispánico*. Ed. Monika Bosse, Barbara Potthast, and André Stoll. Kassel: Reichenber, 1999. Vol. 2: 439–480.
Buescu, Ana Isabel. "Aspectos do bilinguismo Portugês-Castelhano na época moderna". *Hispania: Revista Española de Historia* 64, 216 (2004): 13–38.
Cartagena, Teresa de. *Arboleda de los enfermos. Admiración operum Dey*. Ed. Lewis Joseph Hutton. Madrid: RAE, 1967.
Carvalho, José Adriano. *Gertrudes de Helfta e Espanha: contribuição para estudo da história da espiritualidade peninsular nos séculos XVI e XVII*. Porto: Instituto Nacional de Investigação Científica, 1981.
Catalina de Siena, *Obra de las epístolas y oraciones de la bienaventurada virgen sancta Catherina de Sena de la orden de los predicadores*. Alcalá de Henares: Arnao Guillén de Brocar, 1512.
Cioranescu, Alejandro. *Le masque et le visage. Du baroque espagnol au classicisme français*. Geneva: Librairie Droz, 1983.
Cobos Castro, Esperanza. "Ductilidad y contingencias de la transtextualidad. Reflexiones en torno a *Al fin se paga todo* (María de Zayas), *L'adultère innocent* (Scarron) y *Le philtre* (Stendhal)." *Estudios de investigación franco-española* 1 (1988): 67–99.
Cornejo, Damián. *Chrónica seráphica. . .Parte tercera*, Madrid: Juan García Infanzón, 1686.
Cortés Timoner, María del Mar. *Teresa de Cartagena, la primera escritora mística en lengua castellana*. Málaga: Publicaciones Universidad de Málaga, 2004.

Daenens, Francine. "Le traduzioni del trattato *Della vera tranquillità dell'animo* (1544). L'irriconoscibile Ortensio Lando." *Bibliothèque d'Humanisme et Renaissance* 56.3 (1994): 665–694.

Davies, John, ed. and trans. *Scarron's novels Viz. The judge in his ovvn cause. The rival-brothers. The invisible mistress. The chastisement of avarice*. London: Printed for Thomas Dring, 1665.

Díaz Esteban, Fernando. "La poetisa entre los literatos. El ejemplo de Isabel Enríquez entre los judaizantes del siglo XVII." *La creatividad femenina en el mundo barroco hispánico. María de Zayas– Isabel Rebeca Correa– Sor Juana Inés de la Cruz*. Ed. Monika Bosse, Barbara Potthast, and André Stoll. Kassel: Reichenberger, 1999. Vol. 2: 419–437.

Gagliardi, Donatella. "Ediciones e impresores del *Don Cristalián de España* (con una nota sobre la difusión de los libros de caballerías en Italia)." *Atti della Accademia Nazionale dei Lincei*, serie IX, vol. XV, fasc. 4 (2004): 695–734.

Hatherly, Ana, ed. *Maria do Céu. A Preciosa, ediçao actualizada do códice 3773 da Biblioteca Nacional*. Lisbon: Instituto Nacional de Investigação Científica, 1990.

Hernández-Pecoraro, Rosilie. "Isabel Correa's Transformative Translation of Guarini's *Il Pastor Fido*." *Disciplines on the Line: Feminist Research on Spanish, Latin American, and U.S. Latina Women*. Ed. Anne J. Cruz, Rosilie Hernández-Pecoraro, and Joyce Tolliver. Newark: Juan de La Cuesta, 2003: 125–144.

Huerga, Álvaro. "Santa Catalina de Siena, precursora de Santa Teresa." *Cuadernos de Investigación Histórica* 10 (1986): 197–214.

Israel, Jonathan I. "Gregorio Leti (1631–1701) and the Dutch Sephardi Elite at the Close of the Seventeenth Century." *Conflicts of Empires: Spain, the Low Countries and the Struggle for World Supremacy (1585–1713)*. London and Rio Grande: The Hambledon Press, 1997: 375–390.

Juana Inés de la Cruz. *Enigmas ofrecidos a la casa del placer*. Ed. Antonio Alatorre. Mexico: El Colegio de México, 1994.

Lacerda, Bernarda Ferreira de. *Hespaña libertada. Parte primera*. Ed. Yolanda Beteta Martín. Madrid: Almudayna, 2011.

———. *Soledades de Buçaco*. Lisbon: Mathias Rodrigues, 1634.

López Estrada, Francisco. "Una voz de la Holanda hispánica sefardí: Isabel Rebeca Correa." *La creatividad femenina en el mundo barroco hispánico. María de Zayas– Isabel Rebeca Correa– Sor Juana Inés de la Cruz*. Ed. Monika Bosse, Barbara Potthast, and André Stoll. Kassel: Reichenberger, 1999: 395–417.

López-Cordón Cortezo, María Victoria. "Traducciones y traductoras en la España de finales del siglo XVIII." *Entre la marginación y el desarrollo. Mujeres y hombres en la Historia. Homenaje a M. Carmen García-Nieto*. Ed. Cristina Segura and Gloria Nielfa. Madrid: Ediciones del Orto, 1996: 89–112.

Losada Goya, José Manuel. *Bibliographie critique de la littérature espagnole en France au XVIIe siècle. Présence et influence*. Geneva: Droz, 1999.

Mancini, María. *La verdad en su luz o Las verdaderas memorias de madama Maria Manchini, Condestablesa Colona*. Zaragoza: [s.n.], 1677.

Mancini, Marie and Hortense Mancini. *Memoirs*. Ed. and trad. Sarah Nelson. Chicago: U Chicago P, 2007.

María de Jesús de Ágreda. *Mística ciudad de Dios*. Madrid: Bernardo de Villadiego, 1670.

María de Santo Domingo. *Libro de la oración*. Zaragoza, s.n. [Jorge Coci], s.a. [h. 1518].

Maria do Céu. *Obras varias y admirables*. Ed. and trad. Fernando de Setién Calderón de la Barca. 2 vols. Madrid: Antonio Marín, 1744.

Marín Pina, María Carmen. "De Portugal a Castilla no hay distancia: relaciones literarias entre sor María do Céu y la duquesa de Medinaceli" *Mulheres em rede/ Mujeres en red. Convergências lusófonas*. Berlin: Lit Verlag, forthcoming.

Martínez Almoyna, Julio and A. Viera de Lemos. *La lengua española en la literatura portuguesa*. Madrid: Imnasa 1968.

Merino García, María Manuela. "La recepción de la novela corta española en Francia: Sorel y Scarron." *Transitions: Journal of Franco-Iberian Studies*, 1 (2005): 6–19.

———. *La novela corta en el siglo XVII: Scarron y sus modelos españoles*. Tesis doctoral. Jaén: Servicio de Publicaciones de la Universidad, 2003.

Morte Acín, Ana. *Misticismo y conspiración. Sor María de Ágreda en el reinado de Felipe IV*. Zaragoza: Institución Fernando el Católico, 2010.

Morujão, Isabel. *Contributo para uma bibliografía cronológica da literatura monástica feminina portuguesa dos séculos XVII e XVIII (impressos)*. Lisbon: Universidade Católica Portuguesa, 1995.

———. *Por trás da grade: poesia conventual feminina em Portugal (sécs. XVI–XVIII)*. Lisbon: Imprensa Nacional-Casa da Moeda, 2013.

Narveza, Antoine de. *Cartas morales del señor de Narveza, traducidas de lengua francesa en la española por madama Francisca de Passier*. Tonon: Marcos de la Rua, 1605.
Nider, Valentina. "Texto y contexto de dos traducciones olvidadas: la *Carta a Antonio de Mendoza* de Quevedo y la *Instrucción al Exercicio de la muerte* de Luisa de Padilla, Condesa de Aranda." *Il prisma di Proteo. Riscritture, ricodificazioni, traduzione fra Italia e Spagna (sec. XVI–XVIII)*. Ed. Valentina Nider. Trento: Università degli Studi di Trento, 2012: 481–504.
Ostolaza Elizondo, Isabel. "La cadena de transmisión textual. El modelo de inspiración de la obra palafoxiana *Luz de vivos y escarmiento en los muertos*." *Lemir* 15 (2011): 285–304.
Pageaux, Daniel-Henri. "Traducción y recepción de Santa Teresa en Francia." *Traducción y adaptación cultural. España-Francia*. Ed. Francisco Lafarga Maduell and María Luisa Donaire Fernández. Oviedo: Universidad, 1991: 167–174.
Palafox y Mendoza, Juan de. *Luz de vivos y escarmiento en los muertos*. Madrid: María de Quiñones, 1661.
Palau y Dulcet, Antonio. *Manual del librero hispanoamericano. Bibliografía general española e hispanoamericana desde la invención de la imprenta hasta nuestros tiempos con el valor comercial de los impresos. Tomo XIX*. Barcelona: Librería Palau, 1967.
Partyka, Joanna. "*Iluminatrix plurimorum per exempla lucidissima vitae suae*: el conocimiento de la vida y la obra de sor María de Ágreda, Mística ciudad de Dios en los conventos femeninos polacos." *Letras en la celda. Cultura escrita de los conventos femeninos en la España moderna*. Ed. Nieves Baranda and María Carmen Marín Pina. Madrid: Iberoamericana, 2014: 393–403.
Paun de García, Susan. "Transnational Transformations of María de Zayas's 'El castigo de la miseria' in France and England." *Beyond Spain's Borders: Women Players in Early Modern National Theaters*. Ed. Anne J. Cruz and María Cristina Quintero. New York: Routledge 2016: 33–48.
Rebollo Lieberman, Julia. "Academias literarias y de estudios religiosos en Amsterdam en el siglo XVII." *Los judaizantes en Europa y la literatura castellana del Siglo de Oro*. Ed. Fernando Díaz Esteban. Madrid: Letrúmero, 1994: 247–260.
Río Sánchez, Francisco del. "Místicas españolas del Siglo de Oro en el Imperio Otomano: siete manuscritos árabes hallados en Alepo (Siria)." *Hipogrifo: Revista de Literatura y Cultura del Siglo de Oro*, 3.1 (2015): 187–201.
Ríos, Francisca de los. *Vida de la bienaventurada Santa Angela de Fulgino. En la qual se nos muestra el verdadero camino por donde podemos seguir los pasos de Nuestro Redentor. Escrita por la mesma santa (dictándosela el Espíritu Santo) para verdadera consolación de las almas devotas, y para provecho de todos. Ahora de nuevo traducida de Latín en lengua castellana*. Madrid: Juan de la Cuesta, 1618.
Romero-Díaz, Nieves. "Aphra Behn y María de Zayas: en busca de una tradición (im)propia." *Hispanic Journal* 29, 1 (2008): 23–35.
Ruiz Pérez, Pedro. "'Vengamos a los vulgares': clásicos y nacionales (1492–1648)." *Literatura y nación. La emergencia de las literaturas nacionales*. Ed. Leonardo Romero Tobar. Zaragoza: Prensas Universitarias de Zaragoza, 2008: 491–525.
Saunders, Elizabeth. *Traslado de una carta de cierta monja inglesa llamada Isabel Sandera, hermana del doctor Nicolás Sandero, escrita en Ruan, ciudad de Francia, a Francisco Englefild, caballero inglés residente en Madrid, en que da cuenta de las persecuciones y trabajos que ha pasado por nuestra santa fe en Inglaterra y de la maravillosa providencia que Dios nuestro Señor usó en conservarla y librarla dellos*. Seville: Clemente Hidalgo, s.a [h. 1598].
Seidenspinner-Núñez, Dayle. *The Writings of Teresa of Cartagena*. London: D.S. Brewer, 1998.
Sforza, Isabel de. *Obra utilíssima de la verdadera quietud y tranquilidad del alma [. . .] traduzida de lengua toscana en castellana, por el capitán Juan Díaz de Cárdenas*. Valencia: Pedro de Huete, 1560.
——. *Libro de la verdadera quietud y tranquillidad del ánima [. . .] Traduzido de lengua Toscana en nuestra Castellana por Nicolas Diaz, etc*. Salamanca: Juan Bautista de Terranova, 1571.
Smith, Anthony D. *National Identity*. London: Penguin, 1991.
Surtz, Ronald E. *Writing Women in Late Medieval and Early Modern Spain. The Mothers of Saint Theresa of Avila*. Philadelphia: U Pennsylvania P, 1995.
Travitsky, Betty S. "The Puzzling Letters of Sister Elizabeth Saunders." *Textual Conversations in the Renaissance: Ethics, Authors, Technologies*. Ed. Zachary Lesser and Benedict S. Robinson. Aldershot, UK: Ashgate, 2006: 131–145.
Uman, Deborah. *Women as Translators in Early Modern England*. Delaware: U Delaware P, 2012.
Urban Baños, Alba. "La empresa más lucida y más hermosa de Portugal: clave histórica para la datación de *El muerto disimulado* de Ángela de Acevedo." *Tiempo e historia en el teatro del Siglo de Oro*. Ed. Isabelle Rouane Soupault and Philippe Meunier. Toulouse: Presses Universitaires de Provence, 2015. n.p.

Vega Carpio, Félix Lope de. *Obras escogidas. III. Teatro*. Ed. Federico Carlos Sainz de Robles. Madrid: Aguilar, 1974.

Violante do Céu. *Parnaso lusitano de divinos e humanos versos*. 2 vols. Lisbon: Miguel Rodrigues, 1732–1733.

——. *Rimas varias*. Ed. Margarida Vieira Mendes. Lisbon: Editorial Presença, 1993.

Yepes, Diego de. *Historia particular de la persecución de Inglaterra, y de los martirios que en ella ha avido, desde el año del Señor, 1570*. Madrid: Luis Sánchez, 1599.

Yllera, Alicia. "Temas de María de Zayas en la literatura francesa." *Estudis en Memoria del profesor Manuel Sanchis Guarner*. Ed. Emili Casanova. Valencia: Universidad de Valencia, 1984: 317–324.

——. "Las dos versiones del 'Castigo de la miseria' de María de Zayas." *Actas del XIII Congreso de la Asociación Internacional de Hispanistas. Madrid, 6–11 de julio de 1998*. Ed. Florencio Sevilla and Carlos Alvar. Madrid: Castalia, 2000: 827–836.

Zuili, Marc. "César Oudin y la difusión del español en Francia en el siglo XVII". *La cultura del otro: español en Francia, francés en España; La culture de l'autre: espagnol en France, français en Espagne*. Ed. Manuel Bruña Cuevas *et al*. Seville: Universidad de Sevilla, 2006: 278–289.

INDEX

Abarca de Bolea, Ana Francisca 5, 30, 80, 81, 117, 170, 171, 172, 181; academy 160–61, 164; poetry in 206; *Vigilia y octavario de san Juan Baptista* 161, 171, 173, 179–81
academies 3, 5, 153; fictional 156; women's participation in 154–56; *see also* jousts, tournaments
Acuña, Costanza (Gondomar, Countess of) 290
Ágreda, María de Jesús de 6, 8, 65, 265, 266, 350; correspondence 88, 91, 93, 230, 238, 242, 244, 245; *Mapa de los orbes celestiales y elementales* 230; *Mística ciudad de Dios* 65, 93, 97, 230, 244; 350; political 96, 243, 244–45; translations of 350
Aguilar, Beatriz de 126; pamphlets by 206, 212–13, 214
Ahumada, Leonor de, Sor 67
Alarcón Román, María Carmen 4, 5, 104–05, 106, 119
Amarilis 8, 330, 336, 337, 338, 339–40
America *see* New World
Ana de Cristo, Sor 318–20
Ana de Jesús (Lobera), Sor 8, 69, 76, 78, 88, 93, 98, 310; in Paris 303–06; correspondence 242; poetry 116; *Vida* 213
Ana de la Trinidad, Sor 116, 123–24
Ana de San Agustín, Sor 66
Ana de San Bartolomé, Sor 7, 8, 76, 87, 88, 261; autobiography 69; correspondence 89, 90; in France 303–05, 306, 307, 310; poetry 116; treatises 255, 259, 262–63
Ana de San Jerónimo, Sor 115
Ángela de Foligno 8, 68, 348–49
Aranda, Countess of *see* Padilla, Luisa de
arbitrios 240, 241
Arenal, Electa 103, 104, 107, 109, 116, 125, 228; *Untold Sisters: Hispanic Nuns in Their Own Works* 69, 118, 121, 317; *see also* Schlau

Armon, Shifra 5, 173, 176, 177
Astorch, María Ángela 66
authorship 149, 265; anxiety of 124, 135, 138, 149; questioned 6; 220, 245; male 7; *see also* Cartagena, Sabuco
auto sacramental 105, 109, 214
autobiography 2; by command 4–5, 64, 69, 75; favors, 64; by nuns 4, 8, 63, 65, 66, 317; spiritual content 64, 69
Azevedo, Ángela de 6, 9, 188, 189, 192, 194, 265, 354; *Dicha y desdicha del juego y devoción de la Virgen* 191, 193; *La margarita del Tajo* 190; *El muerto disimulado* 190, 192

Barahona de Soto, Mariana 272
Baranda Leturio, Consolación 91, 97
Baranda Leturio, Nieves 4, 8, 33, 35, 117, 158, 225, 229, 241, 256, 285; *Letras en la celda: cultura escrita de los conventos femeninos en la España moderna* 119, *see also* Marín Pina
Barbeito Carneiro, María Isabel 1, 88, 103, 117, 241, 242, 288
Bautista, Mariana 206, 210–11, 214
Beatriz de la Concepción, Sor 89, 92, 97, 98
Becerra y Mendoza, Isabel de 330, 332
Behn, Aphra 171, 182, 187, 352, 353, 356
Benavente, Countess of (Leonor Pimentel) 291
Bergmann, Emilie L. 6, 10n6, 31
Bernal, Beatriz 170, 172, 174, 181; *Cristalián de España* 170, 172, 174, 350
BIESES [*Bibliografía de Escritoras Españolas*] 10, 104, 117, 124, 126, 170, 174, 182, 229
bilingualism 9, 354
biography 8, 21, 67, 75, 78, 79, 80, 181, 193, 225, 227, 239, 288, 291; New World 319, 355; spiritual 229; *see also Vida*, chronicle, hagiography, foundational narrative

Bobadilla, Magdalena de 7, 19, 287
Boccaccio 43, 48; *Corbaccio* 42, 45; *Decameron* 34, 170; *De claris mulieribus* 43, 50
Boyce, Elizabeth *see* Olivares, Julián
Bridget of Sweden 68; *see also* Bridgettine order
Bridgettine order 8; in New World 316, 322–23, 324
Bueso (Buesso), Eugenia 6, 206, 207, 209, 210, 214, 215, 238, 240

cancioneros 5, 46, 54, 121, 125–26; *Cancionero general* 46; convent *cancioneros* 115–16; poets 41
Cantar de los cantares 139–40
Capuchin order 8, 66, 78, 79, 88, 98; in France 305; in New World 316, 321–22, 323; in Sardinia 126, 308–09, 310
Cardona, Margarita de (Baroness Dietrichstein) 242, 289
Carmelite order *see* Discalced Carmelite
Caro de Mallén y Soto, Ana 5, 6, 146, 147, 156, 157, 158, 162, 163, 171, 187; biography 193, 196n33; *comedias* 187–88, 189, 214; *El conde Partinuplés* 191, 194, 214; pamphlets 206, 214; *relación* 206, 207–11, 215, 238, 240, 246n6; *Loa sacramental que se representó en las fiestas del Corpus Sevilla* 214; *Valor, agravio y mujer* 189, 190, 191, 192, 214; *vejamen* 157, 208–09
Carrión, monja de *see* Luisa de la Ascensión, Sor
Cartagena, Teresa de 6, 41, 50–51, 54, 219, 220, 229; *Admiraçión operum Dei* 50, 219, 220–22, 348; *Arboleda de los enfermos* 50–51, 219, 220–22, 230, 348; authorship 50, 221
Carvajal, Mariana de 5, 164, 170, 171, 172, 177, 181; *Navidades de Madrid* 171, 173, 177–79
Carvajal y Mendoza, Luisa de 5, 6, 69, 96, 238; correspondence 6, 238, 242, 243, 288; poetry 116, 117, 118, 122–23, 139, 140
Castro Egas, Ana de 238, 239
Catalina de Cristo, Sor *Vida* 78–79, 80
Catalina de Jesús y San Francisco 67
Catalina del Espíritu Santo, Sor 8, 310; Lisbon, foundation in 306–08
Catalina Micaela, *Infanta* 32
Catherine [Catalina] of Siena 8, 65, 68, 88, 222, 348
Cecilia del Nacimiento (Morillas), Sor 5, 103, 106; poetry 116, 117, 118, 121–22
Cervantes, Miguel de 5; *La Galatea* 34, 35, 172, 174; *see also Don Quixote*
chronicle 4, 8, 9, 81, 240; conventual 75–78, 79; 299, 302, 307, 318, 321–22, 324; *see also relación*, biography, hagiography, foundation narratives
Clarinda 8, 330, 331, 336–38, 340
CLARISEL (University of Zaragoza database) 172, 174

class (social) 1, 2, 6, 9, 15–17, 22, 27, 28, 29, 70, 119, 155, 169, 188, 192, 276, 301, 321, 337, 378; gender vs. 3, 17, 190, 237, 238
Cobos, María de los 330, 331
Colodro, Salvadora 206, 213, 214, 215
comedia see theater
convent, education in 3, 4, 28, 87; foundation 8, 78, 79, 299, 300, in Sardinia 308–09, 310; life in 21; schools 28–29; theater in 33, 106–09; writing 4, 63–69; *see also* chronicles, foundation documents
Convento de las Descalzas Reales (Royal Discalced Convent, Madrid) 18, 93, 266
Coolidge, Grace E. 3, 31, 287
Correa, Isabel Rebeca 9, 355–56
correspondence 2; conventual 4, 87–89, 92–95; elite women's 7, 285–89; emigrants 289; future studies on 35, 245; to New World 7; personal 92–94, 242; types of letters 94–97
Council of Trent 65, 95, 106, 315
Counter Reformation 65, 225, 243, 274, 291, 347
Creole poetry 335–36; identity 339–41
Cruz, Anne J. 3, 118, 122–23, 174
Cruz Medina, Vanessa de 7
Cueva, Leonor de la 7, 136, 137–38, 141, 188, 194; *La firmeza en la ausencia* 191; poetry, familial 271, 276, 277–79

dama sevillana 188
Deyermond, Alan 221
Dietrichstein, Ana de 242, 289, 291
Dietrichstein, Baroness *see* Cardona, Margarita de
Dietrichstein, Beatriz de 291
Discalced Carmelite order 28, 65, 69, 76, 87, 93, 106, 115, 300, 301, 310; 350 French Discalced, foundation of 76, 303–05; in Lisbon 77, 89; in Paris 305–06; *see also* Convento de Descalzas Reales
Don Quixote 172, 174, 179, 211
Donahue, Darcy 8

Éboli, Princess of (Ana de Mendoza y de la Cerda) 20, 34, 242, 301; letters to her son 290–91
education 255; *colegios de doncellas* 29, university 219–20; in convents 3–4, 28; for royals 30–31; schools 3, 28
ego-document *see* autobiography
elite women 22 *see also* class (social)
emigrants 7, 289–90
Enríquez de Guzmán, Feliciana 188; *Tragicomedia de los jardines y campos sabeos* 193–94
epistolary writing *see* correspondence
Escalante, Countess of *see* Guevara, María de
Escobar, Marina de *Vida maravillosa de* 69
Estrada Medinilla, María de 8, 330, 331, 336–38, 339, 340
Eucharist 116; poetry on 118
Eufrasia de San José, Sor 79

family 7, 271; convent as 92, 272; familial poetry 273–76; fathers 278, 279; mother-daughter relations 31, 35, 273
Feliciana de San José, Sor 255, 259, 261; *Recreación spiritual compuesta en diálogos* 257–58
female rulers 18–19
feminism 1, 42, 176, 257, 26; second wave 1; *see also* Zayas
Fernández de Alarcón, Cristobalina 5, 6, 117, 136, 128, 145, 160, 162
Ferreira de Lacerda, Fernanda 136, 146; *Soledades de Buçaco* 206
Fonseca, Beatriz de 9
foundation narrative 299; 317; *see also* chronicle, nuns
Fox, Gwyn 7, 143
Francisca de Jesús (Borja y Enríquez), Sor 255, 259, 261
Francisca de Santa Teresa, Sor 104–05, 106, 108, 119
Francisca del Santísimo Sacramento, Sor 351
Franciscan order 8; in New World 316, 318–20
Francomano, Emily 3

Galindo, Beatriz 30, 31, 32, 33, 219, 229
Galve, Countess of (Gelvira de Toledo) 8; correspondence 331, 333–35
Gandía, Duchess of (Juana de Velasco) correspondence 286
GEMELA (Grupo de Estudios sobre la Mujer en España y las Américas, pre-1800) 104, 110n10
gender, as category 237; *see also* elite women, theater, voice
Góngora, Luis de 28, 161, 162
Gregoria Francisca de Santa Teresa, Sor 5, 103, 107; poetry 116, 117, 123, 126
Grisel y Mirabella 51, 52, 53; *see also* querella de mujeres
Guerra, Teresa 206
Guevara, Isabel de 329, 330, 331, 332
Guevara, María de (Countess of Escalante) 6, 7, 22, 34, 220, 221, 226–27, 238, 240, 241, 242, 244, 255, 257, 258, 260, 262, 263, 264
Guimerá, Countess of (Isabel Inés de Eril) 155
gynocriticism 5, 169

hagiography 75, 79–80, 81, 117, 308, 309, 348; *see also* biography, chronicle, *Vida*
Hegstrom, Valerie 104, 108
Hernández, Rosilie 7, 225, 256
Henríquez, Isabel 9, 355
Hipólita de Jesús (Rocaberti) 89

Immaculate Conception, Virgin of the 119, 209, 350
Infantado, Duchess of (Catalina de Mendoza y Sandoval) familiar letters 286, 333

Inquisition, letters 286, 290; Mexican 7, 320; Roman 350; Spanish 33, 67, 347, 350
Isabel Antonia de Señor San Miguel, Sor 323; *see also* Bridgettine order, chronicle
Isabel de Borbón, Queen 32, 211, 239, 291
Isabel I of Castile 31, 33, 41, 42, 44, 50, 51, 52, 219
Isabel Clara Eugenia, Archduchess of the Netherlands 18, 28, 32, 220, 242
Isabel de Jesús: autobiography 68; poetry 117
Isabel de la Cruz, Sor 78
Isabel de Santo Domingo 97

Jerónima de la Asunción, Sor 8, 65, 139, 317, 318; biography 317, 318–20; canonization 65; portrait by Velázquez 319
jousts 3, 5, 32, 145, 205, 207, 210, 214
Juan de la Cruz, San (John of the Cross) 116, 118, 121, 122, 124, 126
Juana de Austria (of Portugal) 32, 287, 329
Juana de la Cruz, Madre 65, 69; *Libro del conorte* 64, 319
Juana de la Encarnación, Sor 255, 259, 261, 264
Juana de San Antonio, Sor 320
Juana Inés de la Cruz, Sor 6, 8, 54, 220, 229, 237; *Carta Atenagórica* 227, 228, 230; *Ejercicios devotos para los nueve días* 230; *Enigmas* 354; poetry 117, 124, 333–36, 338; theater 104, 187; *Respuesta a sor Filotea* 221, 227–29, 230
Judeo-conversas 27, 29, 33
Juliana de la Purificación, Sor 4, 78–79

Laura Mauricia *see* Meneses, Leonor de
Lavrin, Asunción 76, 94, 258, 264
Lebrija [Nebrija], Francisca 10n6, 219, 229
Lemos, Countess of (Catalina de Zúñiga y Sandoval) 7, 288
Lemos, Countess of (Catalina de la Cerda y Sandoval) 7, 288
letters, from Indies 331–32; types of 94–97; *see also* correspondence
literacy 1, 3, 4, 27, 28, 29, 30, 31, 69, 156, 181, 256, 264; rates 32–33; *see also* education
literature, 2, 4, 17; discursive strategies 6; oral 28, 33; secular 5, 6; *see also querella*
Luis de León 77–78; *La perfecta casada* 271, 274
Luisa de la Ascensión, Sor: correspondence 88, 98; poetry 117, 139–40
Luna, Álvaro de 44; *Libro de las virtuosas y claras mugeres* 46, 48–49

Magdalena de San Jerónimo 238, 241, 242, 243; *Razón y forma de la galera y casa real* 241
Mancini, Marie 349, 350
Manrique de Lara, Luisa (Countess of Paredes and Marquise of La Laguna) 8, 116, 290, 331; correspondence of 333–35

Manrique de Lara, María 291
Manuela de la Santísima Trinidad, Sor 78, 79, 126
Marcela de San Félix, Sor 103, 104–105, 106; poetry 116, 117, 118, 119, 120, 125, 139, 143
Marcia Belisarda (María de Santa Isabel, Sor) 7, 117, 136, 138, 143, 145, 146, 148, 206; familial poetry 271, 272, 275; on professing 273
Marcos Sánchez, Mercedes 4
Marguerite de Navarre 170
María de la Antigua, Sor 67, 68; poetry 116, 117, 118, 126
María de la Visitación, Sor 67
María de San Alberto (Morillas), Sor 5, 103, 106, 108, 117, 118, 119, 122
María de San José (Salazar), Sor 7, 77, 255, 259, 261, 264; correspondence 89, 94; *Fundación de los Descalzos y Descalzas* 77; *Libro de recreaciones* 77–78, 257, 258, 259; poetry 116, 123, 125
María de Santa Isabel, Sor *see* Marcia Belisarda
María de Santo Domingo, Sor *Libro de la oración* 348
María do Céu, Sor 181, 353, 354, 355
María Magdalena de la Cruz, Sor 320
María Magdalena Eufemia da Glória, Sor 354, 355
María Rosa, Madre 321–22; *see also* Capuchins 321–22
María Teresa de Austria 32, 97, 245
Mariana de Austria 18, 32, 97, 211, 239, 334
Mariana de Jesús (Baquero), Sor 66
Mariana de San José, Sor 18, 66, 90; on business 95–96; correspondence 88, 89, 91, 93, 242; personal 98
Marín Pina, María Carmen 6, 69, 75, 172, 174, 181, 182
marriage 6, 7, 17 19, 271; in *comedia* 192, 271–72; dowries for 4, 20–21; mystical 65, 273; noble 20–21; royal 18; urban elite 22–23; *see also* Zayas
Martínez de Toledo, Alfonso *Arcipreste de Talavera Corbacho* 45–46
Martos Pérez, María Dolores 5
Mauricia del Sacramento, Sor 70
Medrano, Lucía de 219, 229
Mendoza y de la Cerda, Ana de *see* Éboli, Princess of
Mendoza, Mencía de (Countess of Haro) 19
Mendoza, Mencía de (Marquise of Cenete) 34
Meneses, Leonor de 5, 171, 177, 181, 206; *El desdeñado más firme* 170, 176–77
middle class *see* class (social)
misogyny, in *querelle des femmes* 43
Montemayor, Jorge de *Los siete libros de la Diana* 34, 35
Morell, Juliana 30, 230

moriscas 27, 29, 30, 35
Mujica, Barbara 94, 120, 173, 177; *Women Writers of Early Modern Spain* 118

Nalle, Sara 29, 32–33
Narváez, Hipólita de 136, 143–44
networks, female 7, 160, 163, 203, 237, 238; convents 87, 95, 96, 97–98; kinship 7, 19, 215, 242, 279; literary 41, 210, 353; patronage 208, 240, 243, 245, 246, 288, 291
New World 7; autobiographies 69; Capuchins in 321–22; colonization of 8, 315, 331, 332; convent foundations 300, 303; letters from 289–90; Manila galleons 315; Mexico 8, 316; petitions 329–30; women in 8, 315, 317, 329–30, 334, 335; *see also* Creole poetry
Nieto de Aragón, María 206, 207, 211, 214, 238, 239; *Epitalamio a las felicísimas bodas del rey* 211, 239; *Lágrimas a la muerte de la augusta reina Isabel de Borbón* 211, 238, 239
nobility 1, 3, 15, 16, 18, 19–21, 31, 44, 153, 155, 159, 226–27, 260–61, 263; correspondence 287–89, 290
novellas 5, 170, 171, 172, 173, 175, 177, 178, 181; *see also* Zayas, María de and Carvajal, Mariana de
novels of chivalry 5, 33, 34, 170–72, 174, 193, 350; *a lo divino* 225
nuns 2; education of 3–4, 29, 33; foundations by 308–09, 310; writings by 4–5, 63–68 75; *see also* autobiographies, convents; Bridgettine, Capuchin, Discalced Carmelite, Franciscan, hagiographies, Trinitarian order

Olivares, Julián 116, 136, 175, 274; *Tras el espejo la musa escribe* 117, 118, 122 124, 141, 143, 149
Olmo Alfonso, Lucas del, daughter and sister of 207, 213, 214–15
Ortiz de Zúñiga, Luisa María Domonte 145, 206, 207, 209, 210, 212, 214
Osorio, Constanza 119, 230
Osorio de Narváez, Mariana 332
Osuna Rodríguez, Inmaculada 3, 5, 119
Ovid 48, 52; *Art of Love* 34; *Heroides* 337, 338; *Metamorphoses* 34, 53
Owens, Sarah E. 8

Padilla, Luisa de (Countess of Aranda) 6, 7, 9, 220, 227, 255, 260, 262, 263; authorship 220, 225, 351; *Lágrimas de la nobleza* 226, 258, 262; *Nobleza virtuosa* 31, 226, 257, 285; translation of 351
Palamós, Countess of (Hipòlita de Roís I Liori) 20, 37, 242, 266, 287–88
Paredes, Countess of *see* Manrique de Lara, Luisa
Paz, Catalina de 159
Pérez de Montalbán, Juan 162, 163, 171, 172, 177, 349

Petrarchism, in poetry 116, 122, 135, 137, 138, 141, 142, 143, 144, 145–46, 148, 277, 278, 337
Philip II 18, 22, 30, 32, 35, 162, 220, 242, 287, 289, 307, 308, 350
Philip III 18, 95, 159, 238, 239, 241, 242, 243, 354
Philip IV 6, 18, 32, 65, 88, 91, 95, 96, 161, 164, 173, 177, 179, 206, 208, 211, 227, 230, 238, 239, 241, 243, 244, 245, 260, 266, 290
Philip V 209
Pimentel, Leonor *see* Benavente, Countess of
Pinelo, Valentina 80–81, 265; *Las alabanzas de Santa Ana* 81; poetry in 206
Pizan, Christine de 53; *La cité des dames* 42
playwrights 5, 6, 103, 104, 187–94; nuns 106–09; *see also* theater
poetry 2, 5–6; ascetical-mystical 7, 109, 115–17; *cancionero* 53; courtly love in 53, 137, 139, 141, 143; familial 5, 7, 271; motherhood 273; in New World 8; occasional 144, 157; pamphlets 206, 213; private 7; professing, nuns 273; public 5, 205
Portuguese authors 353; *see also* translation
Poutrin, Isabelle 4, 68
printing press 5, 6, 145–46, 205, 206, 208, 215
prose, didactic 255; fiction 5, 6, 34, 41, 170, 171–74, 206; narrative 5, 116, 120, 122, 126, 148; style 78, 228; women authors of 174–81, 192, 206, 215

Querella de las mujeres (querelle des femmes) 3–4, 41, 42, 44, 50–54, 223, 238; fiction, in 51–54; misogyny in 3, 52; *see also* feminism
Quispe-Agnoli, Rocío 8

Ramírez de Guzmán, Catalina Clara 7, 136, 142–43, 240; familial 271, 273–74, 276–77, 279; poetry, epithalamic 272
relación 6; festive 207–11, 214; New World 329; *suceso*, de 239–40
Requesens, Estefanía de 7, 242, 266, 287–88
Rodríguez del Padrón, Juan *Triunfo de las donas* 46–47, 51
Rojas, Fernando de *La Celestina* 34, 35
Romero, Bernarda 5, 160
Romero-Díaz, Nieves 6, 241

Sabat-Rivers, Georgina 103, 104, 107, 125, 148, 337, 338
Sabuco de Nantes, Oliva 6, 35, 220; *Nueva filosofía de la naturaleza del hombre,* authorship of 223–25
Sallent, Mariana 80
San Pedro, Diego de *Cárcel de amor* 51–52, 53
Sánchez Hernández, María Leticia 4
Sandoval, María de 119
Schlau, Stacey L. 4, 5, 54, 69, 103, 109, 118, 121; *see also* Arenal

Sephardic tradition 9, 355–56
Serrano y Sanz, Manuel 1, 63, 103, 115, 116, 117, 118, 169, 170, 207, 222, 224, 225, 226, 229, 230, 241, 242, 290
Sigea, Luisa 6, 7, 30, 138–39, 220, 222, 230, 255, 257, 258, 260, 262, 263, 265
subjectivity 70, 135–36, 139, 140, 141, 173, 243; Spanish-American 339–41; *see also* Creole

Teixidor, Eularia 126
Teresa of Ávila 2, 4, 5, 8, 9, 21, 29, 33, 66, 67, 68, 75, 76, 77, 78, 80, 237, 300, 310, 319; *Camino de perfección* 256, 265, 303, 305; *Castillo interior* 256, 265; correspondence 87, 88, 90–94, 97, 242, 285; *Libro de fundaciones* (*Book of Foundations*) 8, 76, 299, 301–03, 304; poetry 115, 116, 117, 119–21, 125, 126; tournament for 159, 161; translations of works 350; *Vida* (*Book of Her Life*) 63, 64, 65, 76, 256, 265
theater: in convents 4, 103–09; cross-dressing in 190; gender 188; secular 6; women-authored endings 193; *see also comedia*, playwrights
Toledo, Gelvira de *see* Galve, Countess of
Toledo, Victoria de 289
Torrellas, Pere *Maldezir de mugeres* 45–47, 52–53
tournaments, 5, 153–56; Granada 160; Madrid 159; women in 158–62
translation: by Portuguese into Spanish 9; 353–55; by Sephardic Jews into Spanish 9, 355–56; of Spanish texts 8, 51, 119, 120, 175, 223, 224, 226, 227, 228, 348–49, 350–53
travel 315; conditions 300–01, 305; transnational 7–8; 315–16; *see also* Bridgettine order, Capuchin order, foundation narrative, Franciscan order, New World
treatises, didactic 7, 255–57, 260; humanist 6; religious 261, 263
Trinitarian order 105–08, 119

Uztarroz, Juan Francisco Andrés de 161, 171, 212, 225, 239

Valera, Diego de *Defensa de las virtuosas mugeres* 46, 47–48, 52
Vega, Isabel de 136, 137, 144
Vega, Lope de 103, 109, 125, 162, 163, 171, 193, 194, 336, 337, 339; *Auto del hijo pródigo* 350; *La dama boba* 156; *Novelas a Marcia Leonarda* 148
Vida 4; *see also* biography, chronicle, hagiography
Villena, Isabel de 80
Violante do Céu 7, 9, 116, 117, 124, 136, 139, 142, 144–45, 147, 354; familial poetry 271; fathers 278; motherhood 273, 274–75, 277
Vives, Juan Luis 27; *Education of a Christian Woman* 32, 271
voice, 5, 7, 21, 106; authorial awareness in 146–47, 210, 340; didactic treatises 257–58, 263; female gendered in poetry 5, 116, 118,

135–37, 139–40, 143–44, 146; male 137; neutral 138; *querella* 45, 54; subjectivity 140–41

Weber, Alison 118, 122, 169, 258, 264, 318, 318
Williamsen, Amy R. 6

Zarri, Gabriella 95; María de 5, 6, 9, 29, 54
Zayas, María de 5, 6, 141–42, 162, 163, 170, 173, 175–76; academia 157, 164; authorship 173, 351–52; in *El castigo en la miseria* 144; *Desengaños amorosos* 170, 174, 175, 220, 276, 277; in *La esclava de su amante* 148; exemplarity, 175, 265; feminism 29, 54, 174, 176, 178, 353; marriage 272, 276; *Novelas amorosas* 170, 172, 273; poetry in narrative 206; *La traición en la amistad* 187, 188, 189, 191, 192; translation of 9, 351–53, 356; *vejamen* 157, 158, 171